Kilimanjaro

THE TREKKING GUIDE TO AFRICA'S HIGHEST MOUNTAIN

also includes MOUNT MERU & guides to Arusha, Moshi, Marangu, Nairobi & Dar es Salaam

HENRY STEDMAN

TRAILBLAZER PUBLICATIONS

Contents

INTRODUCTION 7

When to go 16 An ideal planning schedule 21

Route options table 22

PART 1: PLANNING YOUR TRIP

With a group or on your own? 25 Budgeting 28

Getting to Kilimanjaro 34 What to take 39

Fitness, inoculations and insurance 52

Ethical trekking: looking after the mountain, the people who work on it – and the whole planet 59

PART 2: BOOKING YOUR TRIP

The routes up Kilimanjaro 67 Who to book with 72

The Tanzanian operators 76 (Tanzanian operators table 84)

Other activities 107

PART 3: TANZANIA

Facts about the country 112

Practical information for the visitor 119

PART 4: KILIMANJARO

Geology & topography 130 Climate 136

The history of Kilimanjaro 139 Fauna and flora 163

The people who live around Kilimanjaro: the Chagga 177

The people who work on Kili: your mountain crew 184

PART 5: DAR ES SALAAM & NAIROBI

Dar es Salaam 188 Nairobi 196

PART 6: ARUSHA, MOSHI & MARANGU

Kilimanjaro International Airport 203

Arusha 205 Moshi 223 Marangu 238

PART 7: SAFE & MINIMUM IMPACT TREKKING

Safe trekking 242 Minimum impact trekking 255

PART 8: MT MERU TRAIL GUIDE & MAPS

Introduction 257 – Practicalities 258 – Momela Gate to Miriakamba Huts 261 – Miriakamba to Saddle Huts 264 – Saddle to Meru Summit & back to Miriakamba 265 – Miriakamba to Momela Gate 260

PART 9: KILIMANJARO TRAIL GUIDE & MAPS

Using this guide 270

The Marangu Route 273
Marangu Gate to Mandara Huts 276 – Mandara Huts to Horombo Huts 280 – Horombo Huts to Kibo Huts 285 – Kibo Huts to Gillman's Point and Uhuru Peak 288

The Machame Route 292
Machame Gate to Machame Huts 294 – Machame Huts to Shira Caves 298 – Shira Caves to Barranco Huts 300 – Barranco Huts to Barafu Huts 304 – Barafu Huts to Stella Point and Uhuru Peak 307

The Lemosho, Shira Plateau & Northern Circuit routes 312
Lemosho Route 314 (Lemosho Glades to Mti Mkubwa 315, Mti Mkubwa to Shira 1 316, Shira 1 to Shira 2/Huts 320, Shira 2/Huts to Lava Tower Camp/Barranco Huts 324, Western Breach Trail to Uhuru Peak 325, Lava Tower Camp to Arrow Glacier 326, Arrow Glacier to Uhuru Peak 328); **The Shira Plateau Route inc Northern Circuit** 329 (Preparation 330 – Morum Barrier to Shira 1 or Simba Cave 331 – Simba Cave to Moir Huts 332, Northern Circuit 334)

The Rongai Route 337
Preparation 339 – New Rongai Gate to Simba Camp 340 – Simba Camp to Third Cave Camp 340 – Third Cave Camp to School Hut 348 – School Hut to the Kibo Huts Junction and Uhuru Peak 350

Umbwe Route 351
Umbwe Gate to Umbwe Cave Campsite 352 – Umbwe Cave to Barranco Huts 355 – Barranco Huts to Lava Tower Campsite 358

The descent routes 359
Marangu Route 360 – Via Mawenzi Route 361 – Mweka Route 362

PART 10: THE SUMMIT – KILIMANJARO

What's at the top? 369

APPENDICES

A: A Swahili primer 374
B: GPS waypoints 375
C: Recommended maps, books, music & films 379
D: New ascent routes 386
E: Acknowledgements 389

INDEX 390

MAP KEY 373

Contents

IN THIS EDITION

For this sixth edition I have, of course, given *everything* a thorough update, including my guides to the cities and towns and my reviews of the trekking operators.

On the mountain, there is also the arrival of new VIP huts on Kili's Marangu Route, complete with showers and central heating. The biggest change, however, is yet to happen, with the arrival of a whole new trekking route up the mountain, and the revival of a second one, both of which are due to open in 2024. We have summarised both of these routes on pp386-8.

Off the mountain, life in the towns that directly serve the mountain – Arusha, Moshi and Marangu – continues as normal, as it does in the East Africa's two main cities, Dar and Nairobi. Cafés, restaurants, trekking companies, hostels, hotels, and souvenir shops come and go, and I've recorded these changes in the guide to each of these places. Perhaps the main change is that this book features, for the first time, a train service running between Dar, Moshi and Arusha. The train tracks have always been there, as have the stations, but this is the first time in over twenty years that there's been a train service that uses them! True, the service is very slow and doesn't seem to be that popular at the moment. In spite of these drawbacks I'm just really glad the rail service has been revived on this route.

Anyway, as always, I welcome all updates, criticisms, and suggestions from readers on any aspect of the book.

www.climbmountkilimanjaro.com – the website!

The website that was set up in 2007 to accompany this book is still going strong. It was designed both to introduce the Kili-curious to some basic but fairly comprehensive info on climbing the mountain, and to keep my readers informed of the latest news and developments on the mountain. So if I discover something major has changed since the publication of the book, this is where you can find out all about it: park-fee increases, rule changes in the national park, tragedies, triumphs… if it's happening on the mountain, this is where you'll hear about it first. This is also the place where I can go into greater depth than in this book. For example, want to know how older trekkers fare on Kili and what advice I have for them? OR younger trekkers? Or how easy is it for gay travellers in Tanzania? If I can't fit it in this book, it will go on the website instead!

If you need to get in touch with me the email address on the website – henry@climbmountkilimanjaro.com – is your best bet; and unless I'm out trekking, I usually respond within 24 hours.

INTRODUCTION

Kilimanjaro is a snow covered mountain 19,710 feet high, and is said to be the highest mountain in Africa. Its western summit is called the Masai 'Ngà'je Ngài', the House of God. Close to the western summit there is the dried and frozen carcass of a leopard. No one has explained what the leopard was seeking at that altitude.

Ernest Hemingway in the preamble to *The Snows of Kilimanjaro*

On 13 August, 2014, Karl Egloff of Switzerland stood at Umbwe Gate on the southern slopes of Africa's greatest mountain, Kilimanjaro. I can imagine the scene that day, for it's one that's repeated there most days of the year. There would be the noisy, excitable hubbub as porters, guides and rangers packed, weighed, re-packed and re-weighed all the equipment; the quiet murmur of anticipation from Karl's fellow trekkers as they stood on the threshold of the greatest walk of their lives; maybe there was even a troop of blue monkeys crashing through the canopy, or the scarlet flash of a turaco's underwing as it glided from tree to tree, surveying the commotion below.

Herr Egloff's main goal that day was no different from the ambitions of his fellow trekkers: he wanted to reach the summit. Unlike them, however, Karl planned to forego many of the features that make a walk up Kili so special. Not for him the joys of strolling lazily through the mountain's four main eco-zones, pausing frequently to admire the views or delight in the unique mountain flora. Nor did Egloff want to experience the blissful evenings spent scoffing popcorn, sharing stories and gazing at the stars with his fellow trekkers. Nor, for that matter, was he looking forward to savouring the wonderful *esprit de corps* that builds between a trekker and his or her crew as they progress, day by day, up the mountain slopes; a sense of camaraderie that grows with every step until, exhausted, they stand together at the highest point in Africa.

Karl Egloff ran to the summit in an incredible 4 hours and 56 minutes

It is these experiences that make climbing Kilimanjaro so unique and so special. Yet Karl had chosen to eschew all of them because, for reasons best known to himself, he had decided to *run* up the mountain. Which is exactly what he did, completing the entire route from gate to summit in an incredible 4 hours and 56 minutes – on an ascent trail that takes the average trekker anywhere from four to six days to complete. For an encore he then ran all the way back down to Mweka Gate, and in doing so set another record for the fastest ascent *and descent* of Kilimanjaro, completing the round trip in just 6 hours and 42 minutes.

A mountain for eccentrics

Barking mad though Karl's exploits may have been, in his defence it must be said that he isn't exactly alone in taking an unorthodox approach to tackling Kilimanjaro. Take the Spaniard, Josep Llamo, who, in 1974, drove up to the summit on a motorbike. Or what about Douglas Adams, author of *The Hitchhikers' Guide to the Galaxy*, who in 1994 reached the summit for charity while wearing an 8ft rubber rhinoceros costume. Not to mention the iceman, Wim Hof, who in 2016 led a party of 26 to the top in less than 36 hours, 11 of whom were wearing just shorts and boots, despite the summit temperatures regularly dropping to -20C. Then there's the Irish team that in 2017 carried a 25kg washing machine all the way to the summit; and who can forget the (possibly apocryphal) story of the man who walked *backwards* to the summit in order to get into the *Guinness Book of Records* – only to find out, on his return to the bottom, that he had been beaten by somebody who had done exactly the same thing just a few days previously. And as I write this, a woman from Limerick (what is it with the Irish?) has just broken her own record for the highest altitude harp performance by performing a medley of tunes at the summit.

Douglas Adams reached the summit wearing an 8ft rubber rhinoceros costume

And that's just the ascent; for coming back again we've had skiing, a method first practised by Walter Furtwangler way back in 1912; snowboarding, an activity pioneered on Kili by Stephen Koch in 1997; and even paragliding, first attempted by a British team back in January 2013.

Don't be fooled

Cyclists, skiers, bikers, boarders and backward walkers: it's no wonder, given the sheer number of people who have climbed Kili over the past century and the ways in which they've done so, that so many people believe climbing Kili is a doddle. And you'd be forgiven for thinking the same.

You'd be forgiven – but you'd also be wrong. Whilst these stories of successful expeditions tend to receive a lot of coverage, they also serve to obscure the tales of suffering and tragedy that are just as frequent. And the reason behind most of these unhappy, and occasionally tragic, experiences is, of course, altitude sickness,

Left: Strolling through the forest at the start of the **Umbwe Route**, the quietest of all the routes on Kilimanjaro.

brought about by a trekker climbing too fast and not allowing his or her body time to acclimatise to the rarified air. Because Karl Egloff didn't just set a record by climbing Kilimanjaro in under five hours; he also, unwittingly, set a bad example.

For once, statistics give a reasonably accurate impression of just how difficult climbing Kili can be. According to the park authorities, almost one in seven people who climb up Kilimanjaro fail to reach even the crater. They also admit to there being a couple of deaths per annum on Kilimanjaro – though independent observers put that figure nearer six or seven.

There's no doubt the joys of climbing Kili are manifold; unfortunately, so are the ways in which it can destroy you. Because the simple truth is that Kilimanjaro is a very big mountain and, like all big mountains, it's very adept at killing off the unprepared, the unwary or just the plain unlucky. The fact that the Maasai call the mountain the 'House of God' seems entirely appropriate, given the number of people who meet their Maker every year on Kili's slopes.

The Marangu Route This is the only route up Kili where you don't have to camp. The first stage (**above**) begins with a walk through the rainforest and ends at Mandara Huts (**below**).

At one stage we were taking a minute to complete thirty-five small paces. Altitude sickness had already hit the boys and two were weeping, pleading to pack up. All the instructors with the exception of Lubego and myself were in a bad way. They were becoming violently ill. It was becoming touch and go. The descent at one stage was like a battlefield. Men, including the porters, lying prone or bent up in agony. Tom and Swato though very ill themselves, rallied the troops and helped manhandle the three unconscious boys to a lower altitude.

From the logbook of **Geoffrey Salisbury**, who led a group of blind African climbers up Kilimanjaro, as recorded in *The Road to Kilimanjaro* (1997).

The high failure and mortality rates speak for themselves: despite appearances to the contrary, climbing Kilimanjaro is no simple matter.

Above: The Breakfast or Barranco Wall is the nearest that trekkers get to actual 'climbing' but don't worry, it's not difficult to scramble up and is actually a lot of fun.

'Mountain of greatness'

But whilst it isn't easy, it *is* achievable. After all, no technical skill is required to reach the summit of Africa's highest mountain beyond the ability to put one foot in front of the other; because, unless you go out of your way to find a particularly awkward route, there is no actual *climbing* involved at all – just lots and lots of walking. Thus, anyone above the age of 10 (the minimum legal age for climbing Kilimanjaro *can*, with the right attitude, a sensible approach to acclimatisation, a half-decent pair of calf muscles and lots of warm clothing, make it to the top. Even vertigo sufferers are not excluded, there being at most only one or two vertical drops on any of the regular trekking routes that will have you scrabbling in your rucksacks for the Imodium.

Simply put, Kilimanjaro is for everyone. Again, statistics can back this up: with the youngest successful summiteer aged just six and the oldest, the venerable American Anne Lorimor, aged 89, it's clear that Kili conquerors come in all shapes and sizes. Amongst their number there are a few who have managed to overcome enormous personal disabilities on their way to the summit. Virtually every year there is at least one group of blind trekkers who, incredibly, make it to the top by using the senses of touch and hearing alone. There's also Bern Goosen, who has managed to manoeuvre his wheelchair to the summit *twice*, in 2003 and 2007; Erica Davis of Carlsbad, who became the first woman to do so, in 2011; Spencer West, who lost his legs at the age of five due to a rare genetic disorder but in 2012 managed to ascend entirely on his hands; and Kyle Maynard, who on January 15, 2012, became the first quadruple amputee to climb Mount Kilimanjaro without assistance, by crawling to the summit in just 10 days.

It is this 'inclusivity' that undoubtedly goes some way to explaining Kilimanjaro's popularity, a popularity that has seen 467,190 people on the mountain over the last decade since 2013. That's an average of almost 47,000 per year, thereby confirming Kili's status as the most popular of the so-called 'Big Seven', the highest peaks on each of the seven continents. And remember, those figures include the COVID years, when hardly anybody climbed at all!

The sheer size of it must be another factor behind its appeal. This is the Roof of Africa, a massive massif 60km long by 80km wide with an altitude that reaches to a fraction under 6km above sea level. Writing in 1924, one of the pioneers of the coffee industry in Moshi, Charles Dundas, claimed that he once saw Kilimanjaro from a point over 120 miles away. This enormous monolith is big enough to have its own weather systems (note the plural) and, furthermore, to influence the climates of the countries that surround it.

No technical skill is required to reach the summit of Africa's highest mountain

The aspect presented by this prodigious mountain is one of unparalleled grandeur, sublimity, majesty, and glory. It is doubtful if there be another such sight in this wide world.
Charles New, the first European to reach the snow-line on Kilimanjaro, from his book *Life, Wanderings, and Labours in Eastern Africa* (1873).

But size, as they say, isn't everything, and by themselves these bald figures fail to fully explain the allure of Kilimanjaro. So, instead, I must look to attributes that cannot be measured by theodolites or yardsticks if I am to understand the appeal of Kilimanjaro.

In particular, there's its beauty. When viewed from the plains of Tanzania, Kilimanjaro conforms to our childhood notions of what a mountain should look like: high, wide and handsome, a vast triangle rising out of the flat earth, its sides sloping exponentially upwards to the satisfyingly symmetrical summit of Kibo; a summit that rises imperiously above a thick beard of clouds and is adorned with a glistening bonnet of snow. Kilimanjaro is not located in the crumpled mountain terrain of the Himalayas or the Andes. Where the mightiest mountain of them all, Everest, just edges above its neighbours – and looks less impressive because of it – Kilimanjaro stands proudly alone on the plains of Africa. The only thing in the neighbourhood that can even come close to looking it in the eye is Mt Meru, over 60km away to the south-west and a good 1329m/4360ft smaller.

The fact that Kilimanjaro is located smack bang in the heart of the sweltering East African plains, just a few degrees (330km/205 miles) south of the

Below: The giant groundsel 'forest' above Barranco Campsite.

Above: School Huts Campsite sits on the slopes of Kibo and affords great views across the Saddle back to Mawenzi.

equator, with lions, giraffes, and all the other celebrities of the safari world running around its base, only adds to its charisma.

Then there's the scenery on the mountain itself. So massive is Kilimanjaro that to climb it is to pass through **four seasons in four days**, from the sultry rainforests of the lower reaches through to the windswept heather and moorland of the upper slopes, the alpine desert of the Saddle and Shira Plateau and on to the arctic wastes of the summit. There may be about 124 higher mountains on the globe but there can't be many that are more beautiful, or more tantalising.

In sitting down to recount my experiences with the conquest of the "Ethiopian Mount Olympus" still fresh in my memory, I feel how inadequate are my powers of description to do justice to the grand and imposing aspects of Nature with which I shall have to deal.

Hans Meyer, the first man to climb Kilimanjaro, in his book *Across East African Glaciers – an Account of the First Ascent of Kilimanjaro* (1891)

Nor is it just tourists who are entranced by Kilimanjaro; the mountain looms large in the Tanzanian psyche too. Just look at their supermarket shelves. The nation's favourite lager is called Kilimanjaro. There's Kilimanjaro coffee (grown on the mountain's fertile southern slopes), Kilimanjaro tea (ditto), Kilimanjaro mineral water (bottled on its western side), Kilimanjaro honey, Kilimanjaro long-life milk and Kilimanjaro yoghurt. While on billboards lining the country's highways, Tanzanian models smoke their cigarettes in its shadow, Air Tanzania planes are usually depicted soaring above it and cheerful roly-poly housewives compare the whiteness of their laundry with the mountain's glistening snows.

It was perhaps no surprise, therefore, that when Tanganyikans won their independence from Britain in 1961, one of the first things they did was plant a torch on its summit; a torch that the first president, Julius Nyerere, declared would '... shine beyond our borders, giving hope where there was despair, love where there was hate, and dignity where before there was only humiliation.'

To the Tanzanians, Kilimanjaro is clearly much more than just a very large mountain separating them from their neighbour Kenya. It's a symbol of their freedom and a potent emblem of their country. And given the tribulations and hardships willingly suffered by thousands of trekkers on Kili each year – not to mention the money they spend for the privilege of doing so – the mountain obviously arouses some pretty strong emotions in non-Tanzanians as well.

Whatever the emotions provoked in you by this wonderful mountain, and however you plan to climb it, I wish you well. Because even if you choose to walk rather than run, and forego the pleasures of wearing a latex rhino outfit, climbing up Kilimanjaro will still be one of the hardest things you ever do. But it will also, without a doubt, be one of the most rewarding.

Climbing up Kilimanjaro will be one of the hardest things you ever do. But it will also, without a doubt, be one of the most rewarding

We were in an amiable frame of mind ourselves and, notwithstanding all the toil and trouble my self-appointed task had cost me, I don't think I would that night have changed places with anybody in the world. **Hans Meyer** on the evening after reaching the summit, as recorded in *Across East African Glaciers – an Account of the First Ascent of Kilimanjaro* (1891)

The experience of climbing Kilimanjaro affected me so powerfully that, for a long time afterward, if I caught myself saying 'I'm not a person who likes to do that activity, eat that food, listen to that music,' I would automatically go out and do what I imagined I didn't like. Generally I found I was wrong about myself – I liked what I thought I didn't like. And even if I didn't like the particular experience, I learned I liked having new experiences.
Michael Crichton, from *Travels* (1988), a collection of essays on his worldwide wanderings

Below: At 5149m (16,893ft), Mawenzi is Kilimanjaro's second peak.

Top left: Leaving Karanga Valley Campsite with Kibo looming behind. **Top right**: On the way to Barafu Campsite with Meru in the distance. The toughest job on the mountain is that of the porters. **Right**: Alfresco lunch at Pofu Camp on the Northern Circuit. **Bottom left and centre**: Mawenzi Tarn Hut Campsite is spectacularly situated in a cirque beneath the jagged teeth of Mawenzi. Porters rest awhile as their colleagues erect the tents. **Bottom right**: Preparing lunch at Karanga Campsite.

When to go

Please note, before I begin, that climate change is definitely affecting the weather patterns on Kili. So while the following information is still (just about) correct, it will be both interesting and, let's face it, depressing to see how the climate of Kili is affected over the coming decades. Already, the arrival of the rainy season is sometimes earlier than usual, sometimes later, and sometimes it doesn't happen at all. This has always been the case, of course, as weather is always notoriously hard to forecast. But it's even less predictable now. For the time being, however, the following advice about when to trek is still, just about, the most accurate...

Kilimanjaro has two main trekking seasons, with each one corresponding with the mountain's two dry seasons (an imprecise term, the weather being

Below: Marching through the everlastings to the east of the Saddle, Kibo in the background.

❑ STAR GAZING

Having decided when to go you may wish to refine your dates still further by timing your walk so that on the final push to the summit, which is usually conducted at night, you will be walking under the brightness of a **full moon**. The weather is said to be more stable at this time, too. That said, the mountain is also at its absolute busiest at this time, which is why, with Kilimanjaro Experts, I arrange my treks so they don't reach the summit *on* the full moon, but a day or so either side. That way, you can enjoy the light of the (almost) full moon but without the hordes.

Of course, the night sky is less spectacular when it's a full moon as fewer stars are visible to the naked eye. For this reason, stargazers may wish to try to coincide their trip at a time near the **new moon**, when the sky is at its darkest and the stars at their clearest. Or they may want to climb when there's a major astronomical happening; the views of the night sky from Kili are, after all, quite exceptional.

It's good to know that it isn't just the costs of climbing Kilimanjaro that are astronomical; the rewards can be too.

often inclement during these periods too). **The two trekking seasons are January to mid-March and June to October**. Of course you can walk in the rainy season but not only is there a higher chance of walking in the rain, your views of Kibo and Mawenzi are likely to be obscured by thick cloud – at least, until you rise above the clouds – and for a couple of days of the year you may even be struggling through thigh-high snow to the summit. Indeed, several agencies even suspend their operations in April and May. Curiously, however, Christmas and New Year, when the weather is far from perfect, are actually amongst the most popular times to go. (You can read peoples' experiences of climbing during the rainy season in the box on pp136-7.)

The two main trekking seasons are January to mid March and June to October

As to the relative merits of the two trekking seasons, the differences are small though significant. The **January to March** season tends to be colder and there is a much greater chance of snow on the path at this time. The days, however, are often clearer, with only the occasional brief shower. It is usually an exceptionally beautiful time to climb and is often a little quieter than the other peak season of **June to October**, which coincides with the main academic holidays in Europe and the West. In this latter season the clouds tend to hang around the tree-line after the heavy rains of March to May. Once above this altitude, however, the skies are blue and brilliant and the chance of precipitation is minimal (though still present).

Although the June to October season tends to be busier, this is not necessarily a disadvantage. If you are planning on travelling by yourself to Tanzania but wish, for the sake of companionship or simply to cut down on costs, to join up with other travellers for the trek, the high visitor numbers in the June to October peak season will give you the best chance of doing this. And even if you do crave solitude when you walk, it can still be found on the mountain during this peak season. The trails are long, so you can usually find large gaps between trekkers to allow you to walk in peace; a couple of the routes – Umbwe, for example, the Northern Circuit, and Rongai, are quieter than others; indeed Umbwe seldom has more than one or two groups on it at any one time. And besides, Kilimanjaro is

Above: Between Stella Point and the summit after a snowfall.
Below: Sliding on your backside back down to Barafu Camp can be the safest way to descend if there's snow around.
Right: The last few steps to the top for a photo by the signboard.
Bottom right: The Southern Icefield on the summit of Kibo.

MOUNT KILIMANJARO
CONGRATULATIONS
YOU ARE NOW AT
UHURU PEAK, TANZANIA 5895M (19341Ft.) AMSL
AFRICA'S HIGHEST POINT
WORLD'S HIGHEST FREE-STANDING MOUNTAIN
ONE OF WORLDS LARGEST VOLCANOES

just so huge that its presence will dwarf your fellow trekkers to the point where they become, if you wish them to be, quite unnoticeable.

For what it's worth, **my favourite times to be on Kilimanjaro are mid February to mid March**, when the crowds are fewer and the skies still clear; **and also late September through to mid October**, for much the same reasons. However, with climate change affecting the mountain, I do think that in the very near future (possibly for the next edition) I will need to revise my opinion and opt for January or June. Why? Well, I like Kilimanjaro to have some snow on it; it looks more beautiful when it's got a white hat on. But if you come at the end of the dry seasons, ie March or August-October, you're unlikely to see much in the way of snow, and the glaciers themselves are shrinking fast. But in June and, particularly, January, there may well be some snow around, and the glaciers should be at their biggest. (What's more, January is a great time to visit the Serengeti – but that's a whole different consideration.)

Other factors that you may want to consider when deciding the exact date of your trek is whether your final push to the summit will coincide with a full moon (see box p17); and whether to go mid-week, when the number of people starting their trek should be lower (as many people like to start at the weekend to minimise the amount of time they need to take off work). But having said all that, you may choose to climb on a particular day in order to be on the summit on your birthday/anniversary etc – and that, I think, is as good a reason as any.

DAR ES SALAAM

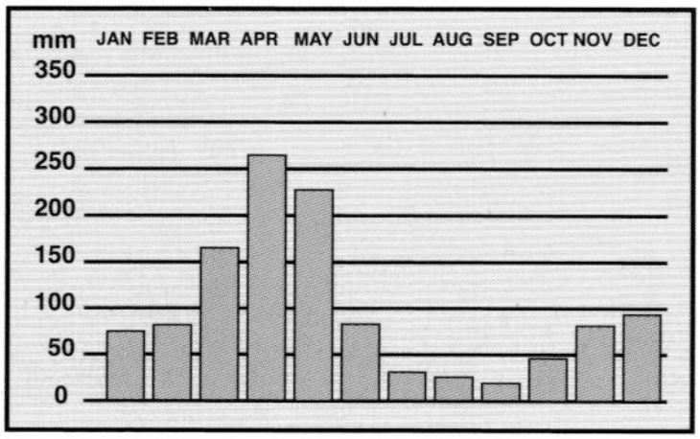

Average rainfall (mm)

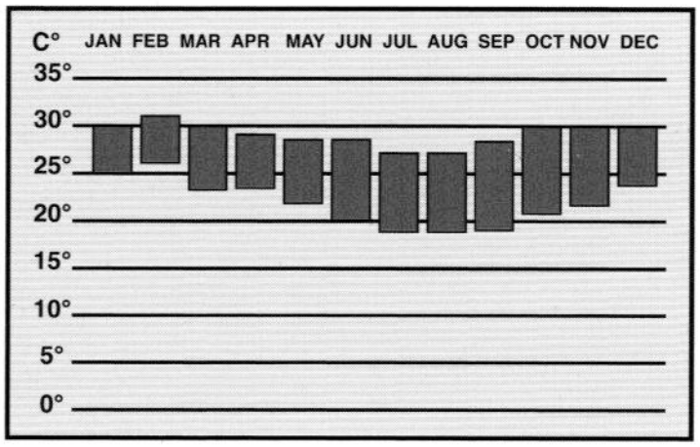

Average max/min temp (°C)

ARUSHA

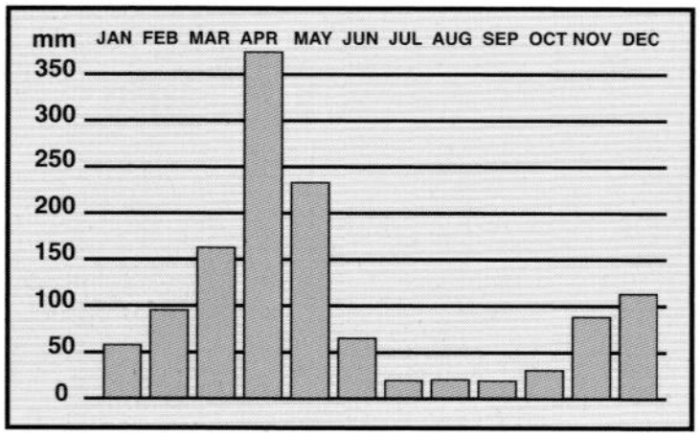

Average rainfall (mm)

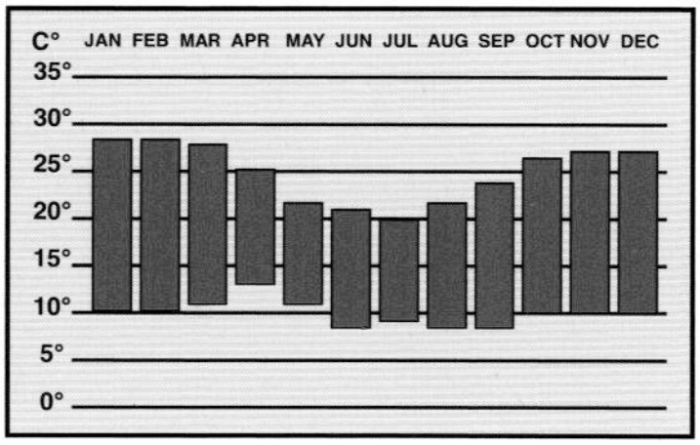

Average max/min temp (°C)

For statistics and graphs on the weather on Kilimanjaro, see pp136-9.

❑ AN IDEAL SCHEDULE FOR ORGANISING YOUR KILIMANJARO TREK

Note that this is just an *ideal* schedule. Most companies can arrange a trek at very short notice; sometimes in as little as 24 hours. But ideally, it's good to get the ball rolling a year in advance. It gives you a chance to get fit, buy some suitable clothing and equipment, arrange and book everything with your preferred operator, the flights should be cheaper – and the whole process will just be a lot less stressful.

12-9 months before you plan to start your trek

• **10. Decide whether you really want to** I'm positively evangelical about the benefits of climbing Kili, of course, but I realise that it isn't for everyone. Read the introduction and samples of people's experiences (pp271-2) and decide if it's really for you.

• **9. Choose when you want to go, which route you want to take, and who you are going to take with you** See pp16-20, p25, p67 and p136 to help you decide.

• **8. Book your trek** Choosing the company you climb with will have a significant bearing on the success of your trip, which is why I spend a lot of this book looking at your options; see p72-107.

• **7. Sort out your flights** Airlines publish their schedule about a year in advance, and I think it's better to get your flight sooner rather than later. In my experience, the cheapest fares I've got have been when I've booked early; and conversely, I've paid a fortune when I've left it late. Don't be caught out – cheaper flights may leave you waiting in an airport for 12 hours or more, so check the flight times closely. See pp34-7 for details of the airlines flying into Kilimanjaro Airport.

• **6. Work on your fitness** If you need to get fit for the climb, start as early as you can – anything you can do will help. But stop, or at least slow right down, a couple of months before your climb; at my own trekking company, I usually lose a couple of bookings per year through people injuring themselves just before the trek. See my advice on p52 for details on how fit you need to be and how to get in shape.

9-6 months before your trek

• **5. Sort out your vaccinations; maybe look at visas too?** Though this may seem a bit premature, remember that some vaccinations require two injections a few months apart. With Tanzanian visas, too, though they are valid from the date of issue and thus you'll need to wait until shortly before your trip to get one, you will need to make sure your passport still has a free page and more than six months left on it.

6-3 months before your trek

• **4. Work out what you need to buy and what you can rent for your climb** See p39 for details of what to pack, and what to pack it in. Your company should send you a packing list as well as a list of items you can rent from them.

3-0 months before your trek

• **3. Pay for your trek and work out your budget** Companies usually ask for payment about 60-30 days prior to the start of your trip. Work out your overall budget and set aside money for tips, meals when not on the mountain, souvenirs etc.

• **2. Purchase visas and insurance; pack; fly!** If you've done the groundwork, above, this phase will all be straightforward. But this is also when people get in a bit of a flap. Don't worry, this is perfectly normal; indeed, it's those climbers who don't write to me with questions that get me worried – makes me think they're not taking it seriously!

• **Walk!** By the time you actually get to Kili, in many ways you've done the hard bit. Your trekking company takes the reins, picks you up from the airport, takes you to your hotel, and from there to the mountain … everything is now largely out of your hands.

But you don't get a certificate for organising a trek up Kili; only for actual walking up it. So pick up your daypack, fill up your water bottles, put on your sunscreen, take a deep breath – and get ready for the adventure of a lifetime.

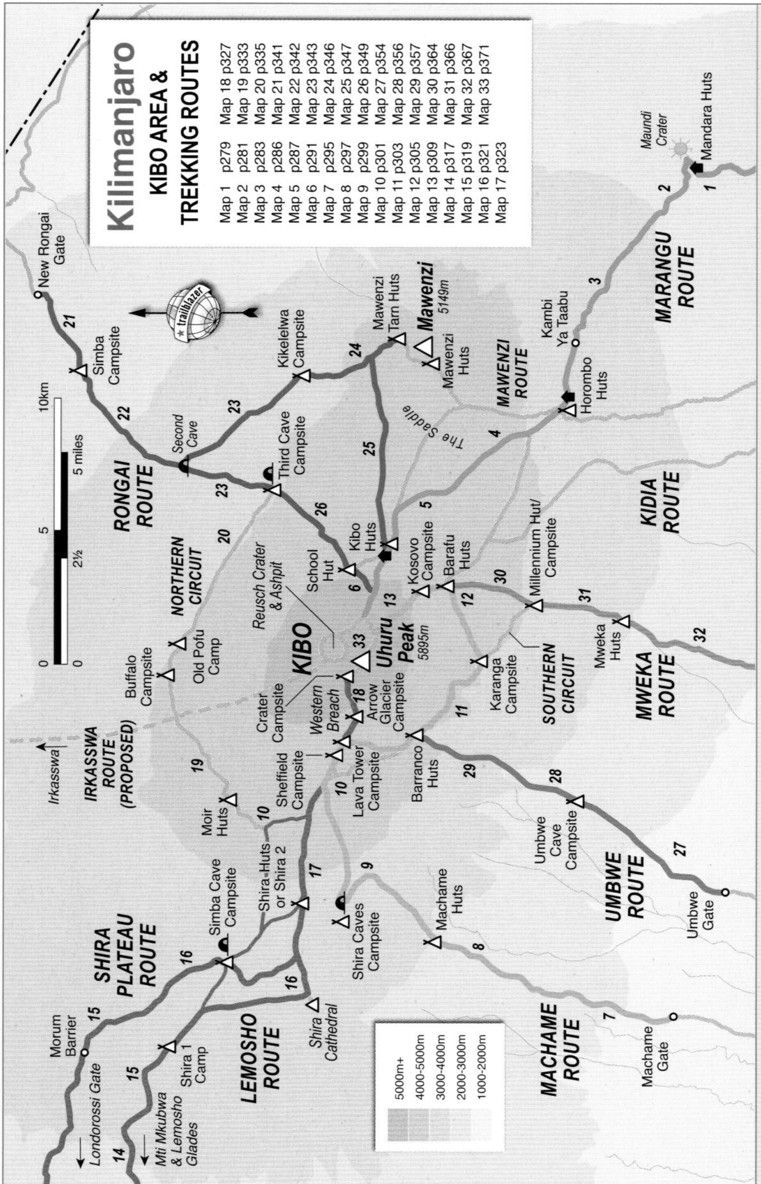
Kilimanjaro
KIBO AREA & TREKKING ROUTES
Map 1 p279
Map 2 p281
Map 3 p283
Map 4 p286
Map 5 p287
Map 6 p291
Map 7 p295
Map 8 p297
Map 9 p299
Map 10 p301
Map 11 p303
Map 12 p305
Map 13 p309
Map 14 p317
Map 15 p319
Map 16 p321
Map 17 p323
Map 18 p327
Map 19 p333
Map 20 p335
Map 21 p341
Map 22 p342
Map 23 p343
Map 24 p346
Map 25 p347
Map 26 p349
Map 27 p354
Map 28 p356
Map 29 p357
Map 30 p364
Map 31 p366
Map 32 p367
Map 33 p371
0 2½ 5 miles
0 5 10km
trailblazer
5000m+
4000-5000m
3000-4000m
2000-3000m
1000-2000m
New Rongai Gate
Simba Campsite
Second Cave
Third Cave Campsite
Kikelelwa Campsite
Mawenzi Tarn Huts
Mawenzi 5149m
Mawenzi Huts
MAWENZI ROUTE
The Saddle
Kambi Ya Taabu
Horombo Huts
Maundi Crater
Mandara Huts
MARANGU ROUTE
RONGAI ROUTE
NORTHERN CIRCUIT
Kibo Huts
School Hut
Reusch Crater & Ashpit
KIBO
Uhuru Peak 5895m
Kosovo Campsite
Barafu Huts
Millennium Hut/ Campsite
KIDIA ROUTE
Mweka Huts
MWEKA ROUTE
SOUTHERN CIRCUIT
Karanga Campsite
Buffalo Campsite
Old Pofu Camp
Crater Campsite
Western Breach
Arrow Glacier Campsite
Barranco Huts
Lava Tower Campsite
Sheffield Campsite
IRKASSWA ROUTE (PROPOSED)
Irkasswa
Moir Huts
Shira Huts or Shira 2
Simba Cave Campsite
SHIRA PLATEAU ROUTE
Shira Caves Campsite
Machame Huts
Umbwe Cave Campsite
UMBWE ROUTE
Umbwe Gate
Shira Cathedral
Morum Barrier
Londorossi Gate
Shira 1 Camp
LEMOSHO ROUTE
Mti Mkubwa & Lemosho Glades
MACHAME ROUTE
Machame Gate

KILIMANJARO ROUTE OPTIONS SUMMARY

Route	Duration	Total distance (ascent & descent)	Western Breach option?	Pros & Cons	See page
Machame	6-7 days	**60.76km** (40.16km ascent plus 20.6km descent on Mweka Route)	✔	PROS • Cheaper than most routes • Good success rate for a shorter route CONS • In peak season it's too crowded	**p273**
Marangu	5-7 days	**73.5km** (36.75km ascent plus 36.75km descent on the same route)	✖	PROS • Only route with huts (good if you don't want to camp) • Beautiful forest CONS • Can be busy • Lowest success rate for summiting • Climbers take the same route up and down so same scenery	**p292**
Lemosho & Shira Routes (including Northern Circuit)	6-9 days	**66.86km** (46.26km ascent + 20.6km descent on Mweka Route)	✔	PROS • Longer, so great acclimatisation and a high success rate • Beautiful CONS • More expensive than other routes • Getting more popular & crowded • Busy for the last few days (but not if on Northern Circuit)	**p312**
Rongai (including Mawenzi Tarn diversion)	6-7 days	**74.4km** (37.65km ascent plus 36.75km descent on Marangu route)	✖	PROS • One of the quieter routes • Wonderful views from Mawenzi Tarn • Good success rate • Descent is via lush Marangu Route CONS • Forest on this side of the mountain is sparse and takes only 20 minutes to walk through	**p337**
Umbwe	6-7 days	**48.31km** (27.71km ascent plus 20.6km descent on Mweka Route)	✔	PROS • Cheaper than most routes • Beautiful • Quietest route for first two days CONS • Steep for first two days • Very busy once you reach Barranco Camp	**p351**

Kidia (proposed new route; see p387) Irkasswa (proposed new route; see p388)

❑ The six golden rules for ascending Kilimanjaro safely and summiting successfully

- **Walk slowly** Emulate the deliberate, careful tread of an elderly, cautious elephant. Or a jaunty tortoise.
- **Drink plenty** Aim for at least three litres per day. Water, not beer.
- **Eat well** Don't worry, with all that exercise it's very unlikely you'll gain weight on your trek, so tuck in!
- **Take as long as you can** Six days minimum, seven better, eight best!
- **Climb up to high altitude before you arrive** If you've got a mountain in your back garden, now's the time to climb it. And if you haven't, why not tackle Meru (see p257), Kili's little brother?
- **Choose your trekking company carefully** To make the task simpler, check out my reviews of the trekking agencies beginning on p76.

Below: The view east from the summit of Mount Meru with Meru's Ash Cone in the foreground and both peaks of Kilimanjaro – Kibo and Mawenzi – visible in the background.

PLANNING YOUR TRIP 1

With a group or on your own?

INDEPENDENT TREKKING NOT AN OPTION

It's more than 30 years since the park authority made it compulsory for all trekkers to arrange their walk through a licensed agency. Furthermore, they insist that all trekkers must be accompanied throughout their walk by a guide supplied by the operator/agency. Even after these laws were introduced, for a while it was still feasible to sneak in without paying and many were the stories of trekkers who managed to climb Kilimanjaro independently, tales that were often embellished with episodes of encounters with wild animals and even wilder park rangers.

Fortunately, the authority has tightened up security and clamped down on non-payees, so these tedious tales are now few in number. **Don't try to climb Kilimanjaro without a guide or without paying the proper fees**. It's very unlikely you'll succeed and all you're doing is freeloading – indeed, stealing isn't too strong a word – from one of the poorest countries in the world. Yes, climbing Kilimanjaro is expensive. But the costs of maintaining a mountain that big are high. Besides, whatever price you pay, trust us, it's worth it.

SHOULD YOU CLIMB WITH FRIENDS . . . ?

So you have decided to climb Kilimanjaro, and have thus taken the first step on the path that leads from the comfort and safety of your favourite armchair to the untamed glory of the Roof of Africa. The second step on this path is to consider with whom you wish to go.

This may not be as straightforward as it sounds, because Kilimanjaro breaks friendships as easily as it breaks records. The tribulations suffered by those who dare to pit themselves against the mountain wear down the most even of temperaments and relationships are often the first to suffer. Idiosyncrasies in your friend's behaviour that you previously thought endearing now simply become irritating, while the most trivial of differences between you and your companion could lead to the termination of a friendship that, before you'd both ventured onto its slopes, you thought was as steadfast and enduring as the mountain itself. Different levels of stamina, different levels of desire to reach the top, different attitudes towards the porters and guides, even differences in your musical

tastes or the colour of your socks: on Kilimanjaro these things, for some reason, suddenly matter.

Then there's the farting. It is a well-known fact that the regular breaking of wind is a sure sign that you are acclimatising satisfactorily (for more about acclimatisation, see pp243-6); while the onset of a crushing headache, combined with loss of sleep and a consequent loss of humour, are classic symptoms

❑ ADVICE FOR ORGANISING A GROUP TREK

If you're planning on climbing Africa's highest mountain with a group of your friends or family, and have been nominated as the person who has to organise everything, you have my sympathies: you've got your work cut out.

So here are a few tips to help you organise a group trek – to make your job slightly less taxing:

- **1 Plan your trip far in advance** If you can, start to arrange your trek about a year in advance. It'll improve your chances of staying at the same hotel, travelling on the same flight, and will make the whole process less stressful.
- **2 Contemplate a private trek** It may cost you more, but will allow you to choose the start date, duration and route of your trek.
- **3 Remember you're in a strong bargaining position** After all, a group brings in more money for an operator, and for only a little more effort. Most companies automatically offer a cheaper per-person price for groups, ie the bigger the group, the lower the per person price. But if they don't, well, either negotiate so that they do, or go elsewhere.
- **4 Make sure your company is flexible** The larger the group, the more likely it is that the numbers of people in the group will change. Ideally, find a company that won't charge you a cancellation fee or keep the deposit if one of your party drops out – but will also still drop the price if someone else joins.
- **5 Set up a WhatsApp group (or similar)** This makes it easy for your fellow trekkers to ask questions and share information. It will also help to develop a strong *esprit de corps,* making everyone feel they are part of the team.
- **6 Tell your group to send in questions** Your group will only feel truly comfortable about the idea of climbing a very big mountain if they know exactly what it entails. So encourage them to send in their questions, either to you (so you can forward them to the trekking company) or directly to the company themselves.
- **7 Remember to distribute all documents you receive** If not, there's a chance you could be seen as the culprit should anything go wrong, as you won't have passed on all the information to your group.
- **8 Ask people to send in their medical conditions, personal details, and dietary requirements to the operator themselves** People may be too shy to share 'personal stuff' with other members of the group such as medical conditions or passport numbers. But your operator will need to know all this stuff – so ask your group to send in such details to your operator themselves.

In summary

The above rules make it all sound pretty straightforward. But trust me, it probably won't be. And you may not even receive much in the way of gratitude from your team for all the extra work you've had to do. But you can, at least, take some satisfaction from a job well done. Because without your endeavours, your group wouldn't have even got to Tanzania – let alone stand at the very highest point on the entire African continent.

suffered by those struggling to adapt to the rarified atmosphere. Problems occur, of course, when two friends acclimatise at different rates: ie, the prodigious and joyful flatulence of Friend A is simply not appreciated by Friend B, who has a bad headache, insomnia and an ill-temper. Put the two parties together in a remote, confined space, such as that provided by a two-man tent on the slopes of a cold and lonely mountain, and you have an explosive cocktail that can blow apart even the strongest of friendships.

It rained terrible all night, and we put most of the Wachaga porters in our tent. It was rather distressing to the olfactory nerves ... At 4am a leopard visited us but did not fancy our scent.
Peter MacQueen, *In Wildest Africa* (an account of an expedition of 1907, published in 1910)

Of course, the above is just one possible scenario. It may be that both of you adapt equally well/badly to the new conditions and can draw pleasure/comfort from each other accordingly. People from Northern Europe seem particularly good at making the best of the windy conditions: while researching the first edition of this book I encountered a party of four Germans holding a farting competition, and one particularly talented Dutch pair who even managed a quick game of Name that Tune. (It probably won't surprise you to know that all but one of the participants in these events was male.)

And there are plenty of advantages in going with a friend too, beyond mere companionship. For starters it's cheaper, because you'll probably be sharing rooms, which always cuts the cost, and if you are planning on booking your climb after you've arrived in Tanzania your bargaining position is so much stronger if there are two of you. Having a companion also cuts the workload, enabling, for example, one to run off and find a room while the other looks after the luggage. It also saves your being paired with someone you don't know when you book with an agency; someone who may snore or blow off more violently than your friend ever would. And, finally, if you *do* both make it to the top, it's good to know there will be somebody to testify to your achievements upon your return.

Climbing Kili with a companion has its problems, but there's no doubting the extra pleasure that can be gained as well. As the graffiti on the walls of the Kibo Huts tells us: '*What does not break us makes us stronger*'. If you are planning on travelling with a friend this, perhaps, should be your motto for the trek.

. . . OR ON YOUR OWN?

Those without friends, or at least without friends willing to climb a mountain with them, should not be too concerned. For one thing, you'll never truly be on your own, simply because the park authority forbids you from climbing without two guides (see p187) and you'll probably need at least one other crew member to act as porter/cook. Furthermore, planning to go on your own means you can arrange **the trek that you want**; you choose the trail to follow, the time to go and for how long; the pace of the walk, the number of rest-stops, when to go to bed – these are all your decisions and yours alone. You are the boss; you have nobody else's feelings to consider but your own.

If you want to join a group trek, for companionship or simply to make the expedition cheaper (a private trek for one person is always the most expensive

❑ **ADVICE FOR SOLO TRAVELLERS JOINING A PUBLIC TREK**

• **1 Choose your company carefully** This is perhaps the most important piece of advice, because companies' attitudes and policies towards solo trekkers vary widely. For example, some companies provide their **'solo trekkers' with their own tent, and make sure solo travellers get their own single room before and after the trek – and don't charge a single supplement either**. So make sure you know exactly what you're getting for your money.

• **2 Ask your company if there are some treks that are more suitable for you** For example, if you are a woman and prefer not to be the only one on the trek, ask your company what treks have women on them. (And if none do, ask if a female guide can work on the trek.)

• **3 Ask your company if you can contact the other trekkers beforehand** That way, the camaraderie can build before you even set foot on the mountain.

• **4 Choose a hotel that is more lively and sociable** The company with which you booked your trek should be able to recommend a suitable hotel. They may also be able to tell you where the other climbers on your trek are staying or which hotel has the best atmosphere. Because few people want to be stuck in a soulless, empty hotel in the middle of nowhere, with no-one but the receptionist for company.

• **5 Be more aware of any safety and security issues both on Kilimanjaro and in Tanzania** On the mountain there isn't much crime except, sad to say, the occasional theft from tents. But before and after your trek the likelihood of your being a victim of crime is that much greater. So make sure you read the safety advice about these towns, and also the Safety and security in Tanzania section on pp128-9. Please read – and keep yourself out of harm's way on your holiday.

option), that's not a problem. You can book your trek in your home country with a tour operator (they nearly always insist on a minimum number of participants before the trek goes ahead); or you can book with a company in Tanzania and ask to be put with other trekkers (which will often happen anyway, unless you specifically say otherwise).

Furthermore, even if it does transpire that you are walking alone, you can always meet other trekkers at the campsite in the evening if you so desire.

Trekking by yourself is fun and not the lonely experience many imagine; unless, of course, you enjoy the bliss of solitude and *want* to be alone. That's the beauty of walking solo: everything is up to you.

Budgeting

The most significant cost of your holiday, unless you opt for a few days at one of Tanzania's top-of-the-range safari lodges (US$8000-plus per night for a 4-person cottage is the most mind-boggling rate I've heard for a night's accommodation though there are probably other, even higher ones), is the walk itself. With the introduction of an 18% sales tax on park fees in July 2016, those already sky-high trek prices soared even further into the stratosphere. Set aside US$1200-plus for the *absolute cheapest* budget trek (though double this is more usual); more if you plan on taking more than the minimum – and thus not recommended – five days, or if you're ascending by the Lemosho/Shira or Rongai routes (which both have higher transport charges). You will also need to plan to spend more on your trek if you insist on walking without other trekkers. Once on the mountain, however, you won't need to pay for anything else throughout the trek (save, of course, for tips for the crew at the end – see pp32-3).

Away from the mountain and the other national parks, by far the most expensive place in Tanzania is Zanzibar. Elsewhere, you'll find transport, food and accommodation, the big three day-to-day expenses of the traveller's life, are pretty cheap in Tanzania and particularly in Moshi and Arusha – it's just unfortunate that Zanzibar and the national parks are pretty much all most visitors want to see of the country!

THE TREK: WHY IS IT ALL SO EXPENSIVE?

With little change from US$1300 for even the cheapest trek, it cannot be denied that climbing Kili is a relatively expensive walk, particularly when compared to other famous treks (prices for an all-inclusive trek on the Inca Trail, for example, start at around US$700); with no refund available to those who fail either, even if you are forced to give up after only a few minutes on the mountain, at first sight this trek can seem very bad value too – though to those who successfully reach the summit, of course, the sense of achievement and the enjoyment of the trek makes almost any amount seem worth it.

To give you an idea of where your money goes, the following is a breakdown of fees, wages and other outgoings incurred on the trek, while the box on p31 is an example of the expenses for an average trek. Don't forget that, in addition to the official costs outlined below, there is also the matter of **tips** (see pp32-5).

Park fees

- **Rescue fee** US$20
- **Conservation fee (formerly Park Entry fee)** US$70 per day
- **Hut fee (Marangu Route only)** US$60 per night
- **Camping fee (all routes except Marangu Route)** US$50 per night
- **Crew fees** US$3 per crew member per trip

All these fees are then subject to 18% VAT.

Take a look at these figures; already you can see just why the cost of climbing Kilimanjaro is so high. Even if you took the quickest (and thus not recommended) 5-day/4-night yomp up the Marangu Route, your park fees alone come to US$719.80 plus porter/guide entrance fees. See box p31 for how much a typical trek could cost.

Other costs

The following are the other major expenses involved in an expedition up Kilimanjaro. You don't pay for these items separately; they are all included in

❑ DISCOUNTS ON PARK FEES

Children over 10 years old are not only allowed on Kili but, thanks to the hefty discounts offered to under-16s, the park authority seems to be actively encouraging them to climb. (Children under 10 are still entitled to discounts, and under 5s are free, but you have to obtain permission from KINAPA, see box p165, before trying to climb.)

For example, where adults are forced to pay a whopping US$70 per day in Conservation fees, those **under 16 years old** are charged just US$20 per day. The story is similar with the Camping fees (US$10 per night for under 16s and free for under 5s as opposed to US$50 per night for adults) and the Marangu Route's Hut fees (US$20 per night for under 16s and free for under 5s compared to the US$60 adults' fee). Once all these fees have been subjected to the 18% VAT, this makes for a considerable reduction on the overall price. For example, on a 7-day Machame trek, once the VAT has been added to all fees, under 16s pay a colossal US$696.20 less. If you're travelling with someone under 16, make sure your company passes these discounts on *in full* – there is no reason why they shouldn't.

Nor is it just the under-16s who are entitled to a decent reduction in the park fees. Firstly, **those who hold a valid resident's permit for East Africa** are supposed to get a 50% reduction on the US$70 conservation fee compared to non-residents; you'll need to show either the resident's permit or the relevant stamp in your passport as proof. Diplomatic ID or a diplomatic passport are also accepted. **East African passport holders** do even better, with their Conservation fees set at just Ts10,000 per day (Ts2000 for those aged 5-16), while Camping fees are Ts10,000 per night (Ts5000 for those aged 5-16), and it's Ts5000 per night in the huts on the Marangu Route (Ts2500 for under 16s). This means that they enjoy discounts of at least US$100 per day when compared to the non-residents' fees.

Do make sure, however, if you're an East African passport holder, or a resident, or under 16, that you furnish your operator with the necessary proof well before your trek, in order that they can apply for these discounts. It will definitely be worth it!

the price the trek operator charges you. Note that, unlike park fees, with all of the following the more people in your group, the lower the per-person charge.

- **Wages**: If your company cares at all about its staff (and the only way to guarantee this is to check whether they are partners of KPAP or not; see pp84-5 & 87), they should be paying their porters about US$10 per day for the duration of the trek, the assistant guides and cooks US$15 per day, and the chief guide US$20 per day. Do note, however, that many porters working for non-KPAP companies are still being paid as little as Ts10,000 (less than US$4).
- **Food**: The price you pay for your trek needs to cover both your food and the food for your crew. Of course, the more people on the trek, the more the overall food bill – but the lower the cost per person too. If there's just two of you on the trek you can expect to pay around US$125 each, but if there are eight trekkers in the group the per person cost will be nearer US$80.
- **Transport to and from the mountain**: The exact cost of this depends where you're coming from (Arusha, Moshi or Marangu – or somewhere else) and which path you're taking, with Rongai and Lemosho more expensive as they're usually further away. But to give you an example, the cost of a transfer from

Arusha to Machame is about US$75 per vehicle, and the same for the return at trek's end.

- **Off-mountain costs** At the risk of sounding like I'm whinging, the costs for the company don't stop when the trek ends. Airport transfers and accommodation will probably also form part of your trek package, and maybe even a meal at the end of the trek at a nearby restaurant, all of which need to be paid for. And after you're safely ensconced back in your hotel, all the equipment will need to

❑ AN EXAMPLE: THE MACHAME TREK

A 7-day Machame trek (see p70) for two people, taking one guide, one assistant guide, one cook and ten porters would cost as follows:

Park fees		
Rescue fee (US$20 x 2 people)		US$40.00
Conservation fee (US$70 x 7 days x 2 people)		US$980.00
Camping fee (US$50 x 6 nights x 2 people)		US$600.00
Porter/guide entrance fees (US$3 x 13)		US$39.00
TOTAL	US$1659.00 + 18% VAT	**US$1957.62**
Wages		
Ten porters (assuming a wage of US$10 per day)		US$700.00
Assistant guide (assuming US$15 per day)		US$105.00
Cook (assuming US$15 per day)		US$105.00
Guide (assuming US$20 per day)		US$140.00
TOTAL		**US$1050.00**
Food		
Two people plus crew		**US$250.00**
Transport to and from the mountain		
Estimate US$75 each way per vehicle if coming from Arusha		**US$150.00**
GRAND TOTAL		**US$3407.62**
		(or US$1703.81 per person)

Obviously if there are more of you some costs, such as food, wages and transport, can be divided between the group, thus making it cheaper. Nevertheless, the above example gives you an idea of just how quickly costs add up. And note that this example doesn't cover the 'off-mountain costs' that I talk about above.

If you've found a company that is charging a lot less than US$1700 for your trek, you should ask yourself why. Is it because you are actually going to be part of a big group (ie 10 or more people), and thus the costs are split over a larger number of people? Or have you opted for a pared-down service on the mountain, employing fewer staff, in order to save on wages?

If the answer to both of these is no, and you can't see a good reason why your trek costs significantly less than US$1700, then the chances are the company simply isn't paying its staff enough. Which is why I recommend booking with a KPAP partner company – see pp84-5 & p87 for details of this. It's the only way you can guarantee that the company is paying a decent wage to its crew. But if it's too late, and you've already signed up with a company that's not a KPAP partner, one way you can compensate them for the poor wages they're probably receiving is to give each member of your crew a higher **tip** – a subject that I look into on pp32-3.

be cleaned, checked and, where necessary, repaired, and the oxygen tanks will also need to be refilled. Wages for office staff, bank charges, insurance, office rental and supplies, accountancy fees and the annual TALA licence fee (US$2000) that allows companies to operate in the first place all have to be covered too, as will various other company and director taxes. And not forgetting, of course, that the company will probably also want to make some sort of profit! So for all these reasons, the price you pay for your trek should be a fair bit more than the direct costs to the company of organising it.

TIPPING

Like a herd of elephants on the African plains, the subject of tipping is a bit of a grey area. What is certain is that, in addition to the cost of booking your trek, you will also need to shell out tips to your crew at the end. The gratuity system on Kilimanjaro follows the American style: that is to say, a tip is not so much a bonus to reward particularly attentive service or honest toil as a mandatory payment to subsidise the poor wages the porters and guides receive. In other words, **tipping is obligatory**.

To anybody born outside North America this compulsory payment of gratuities seems to go against the very spirit of tipping. Nevertheless, it is very hard to begrudge the guides and porters a decent return for their labours – and depriving your entourage of their much-needed gratuities is not the way to register your protest against this system.

How much should you bring for tips?

As to the size of the remuneration, there are no set figures or formulas, though I do urge you to let your conscience instruct you on this matter as much as your wallet. The following should help you, however, though they are mere guidelines; you may wish to alter them if you feel, for example, a certain porter is deserving of more than his normal share or if your trek was particularly difficult.

The simple version Most decent companies will now provide guidelines to their clients to help them negotiate the tricky topic of tipping. But just in case they don't, and to simplify matters, I suggest doing the following: **bring about US$400 for tips** in a mixture of large and small denomination notes to Tanzania (and more if you're going on safari too). This doesn't mean you will hand this entire amount over – most people give around US$250-350 – but it means you're pretty much covered for any eventuality. You can then discuss with your fellow trekkers and your guides how to divide up the total tips and who should get what. (Note there is one exception to this rule: if you're trekking in a private group for just one or two people, you should really bring nearer US$500-600.)

The more complex version Some of the most detailed advice I have found is provided by KPAP (Kilimanjaro Porters Assistance Project; see pp60-5), which suggests that a fair reward for a porter's work – ie the sum of wages and tips – should be Ts34,000, which is US$14 per day. Assuming they work on two treks every month, that will help them to maintain a decent standard of living. So what you pay depends to a large degree on what the company you are climbing with is already paying in wages to the porters. Once you've established that, you then just need to add enough to bring the total per diem rate to US$14 per day.

This means, of course, that if the company you're with *is* a KPAP partner and already paying their minimum wage of Ts20,000, you only need to bring a little more to bring it up to the Ts34,000 rate. If you're with a company that pays only Ts10,000 – yes unbelievably some still do – you'll have to pay Ts24,000 per day in tips. **In other words, a KPAP company may charge slightly more for their treks, but this is offset by the reduction in tips you are asked to pay**.

And don't forget inflation!

Finally, I am obliged to Hassan, a guide at Mauly Tours, who once accosted me halfway up the Breakfast Wall on the Machame Route to tell me to write, in bold, the following: **that the figures I quote opposite were correct for 2023.** If you're trekking in 2024 or later, ask your trekking agency, or KPAP, for the latest recommended tips, or add on another 5-10% to the above figures to allow for inflation; and thereafter, for every subsequent year, add 5-10% onto the figures. **What you mustn't do is use the figures in this book as an excuse for bringing a lower tip, as people have been known to do**.

How to hand over your tips

Having collected all the tip money together, the usual form is to hand out the individual shares to each porter and guide in turn. **Do not hand all your tips to the guide**; sadly, no matter how much respect and affection you have towards your guide, often he'll end up trousering most of it.

EXPENSES WHEN YOU'RE NOT ON THE MOUNTAIN

Accommodation

Basic tourist accommodation starts at around £6.50/US$8. You can get cheaper, non-tourist accommodation but this is often both sleazy and unhygienic and should be considered only as a last resort. I have not reviewed these cheap hotels in the book. At the other end of the spectrum, there are hotel rooms and luxury safari camps going for many thousands per night. Note that if you've booked your trek from home, you'll probably get at least a couple of nights' accommodation included in your package.

Food

Food can be dirt cheap if you stick to the street sellers who ply their wares at all hours of the day – though dirt is often what you get on the food itself too, with hygiene standards not always the highest. Still, even in a clean and decent tourist restaurant the bill should only be around Ts20,000-30,000 (£6.50-9/US$8-12.50) and in a local place it can be as little as a dollar or two. On the trek, meals will be included in the package.

Transport

Public transport is cheap in Tanzania, though it could be said you get what you pay for: dilapidated buses, potholed roads, inadequate seating and narcoleptic drivers do not a pleasant journey make, but this is the reality of public transport,

Tanzanian style. Then again, at approximately US$1-1.50 per hour for local buses and Coasters (the local minibuses that ply the route between Arusha and Moshi; see p122), it seems churlish to complain. That said, given the appalling number of accidents on Tanzanian roads (at one time it was said that road accidents were the third biggest killer in the country, with only AIDS and malaria killing more), if your budget can stretch a little further consider spending more on transport: extra safety and comfort are available on the luxury buses, and at only a slightly higher price.

Note that airport transfers and transfers to the mountain should be included in your trek package.

Getting to Kilimanjaro

One of the gladdest moments in life, methinks is the departure upon a distant journey into unknown lands. Shaking off with one mighty effort the fetters of habit, the leaden weight of routine, the cloak of many cares and the slavery of home, man feels once more happy... The blood flows with the fast circulation of childhood ... afresh dawns the morn of life.

Diary entry of **Richard Burton** (the explorer, not the actor), 2 December 1856

BY AIR

Tanzania has four major international airports: Dar es Salaam, Zanzibar, Mwanza and Kilimanjaro. The last one, as you may expect, is the most convenient for Kilimanjaro, standing only 43km away from the mountain town of Moshi and 50km from Arusha. There is a second airport that is reasonably convenient for Kili, Arusha Airport (three letter code ARK), which handles domestic flights only but has lots of connections to the national parks, Dar and Zanzibar. (The third airport near the mountain, Moshi, sees little activity.)

Information about flights to and from KIA (the acronym for Kilimanjaro International Airport, though the three-letter international airport code is JRO) and Arusha Airport now follows.

International flights to Kilimanjaro Airport

There are six intercontinental airlines flying into JRO, in addition to several domestic and regional carriers that I discuss later on. The six airlines flying in from outside Africa are:

- **Qatar Airways** (airline code QR; 💻 qatarairways.com) fly 10 times a week between Doha (DOH) and Kilimanjaro, arriving daily at JRO at 7.35am (QR1499) and three times a week at 4.25pm (QR1476). They are, I reckon, the most popular, and are particularly useful for those flying from Australasia (who've previously always been a little hard done by when it comes to getting to Kili). Each flight departs an hour after landing to head back to Doha.
- **Turkish Airlines** (TK; 💻 turkishairlines.com) fly four times weekly from Istanbul (Fri, Sun, Mon & Wed). The only problem is that they often arrive at Kili Airport in the middle of the night (around 2-3am) and depart again an hour

WHEN SHOULD YOU FLY IN AND OUT OF KILIMANJARO AIRPORT?

When should you fly into Kilimanjaro Airport?

It's a question I get asked an awful lot by people: how many days before the start of the trek should I arrive?

Well, **if you're flying in from somewhere else in Africa, or the Middle East**, I think it's OK to arrive just the day before the start of your hike.

Coming from places further afield, however, such as the **Americas**, **Australia**, or the **Far East**, ideally you should arrive at Kilimanjaro Airport at least 24 hours prior to the start of the trek. So if your trek starts on the 4th, for example, it would be idea to arrive on the 2nd. I realise that this will mean paying for an extra night's accommodation. But having this extra time before the trek gives you time to rest, relax and recover from your flight, as well as to prepare properly for the expedition ahead. It also gives your luggage another day to arrive, should it have been delayed (which it sometimes is). That said, I have to admit that many climbers completely ignore me, and arrive just the day before the trek; and to be fair to them, they don't seem to suffer unduly because of it.

That just leaves those **coming from Europe**. For you, I still think you should arrive at least 24 hours before the start of the trek; but if that is not practical you can arrive the day before and then set off onto the mountain the next day. It's not ideal – but is possible.

When should you fly out of Kilimanjaro Airport?

As for your **departure from Kilimanjaro Airport**, if you're really pushed for time you can actually fly out on the evening of the last day of the trek. All being well you should arrive at the exit gate on the mountain at about lunchtime, allowing you plenty of time to get to the airport and check in for your (evening) flight. However, you'll be dusty, grimy, sweaty and tired, and as such it's not the most pleasant experience. (If you need to take this option ask if your trekking company can sort out a shower for you at one of the hotels in Moshi before you head to JRO; it's better than trying to wash your armpits in a sink at the airport.)

But unless you're really pressed for time, spend at least one more night in a hotel, then either fly out or go on safari the next day. To me, that first night off the mountain is an essential part of the whole experience, for there is something magical about having that first shower, celebrating your climb with your friends, both old and new-found, and then sleeping in a proper bed, with real pillows and real sheets.

later (ie 3-4am). Thankfully, the trekking agencies and hotels are used to people arriving at this ungodly hour and you can still expect a transfer to your accommodation. Unfortunately, it does mean you have to pay for accommodation for that night, even though you'll only use the room for a few hours (ie from around 3am until check-out).

- **KLM** (KL; 💻 klm.com) usually fly daily in the high season to Tanzania, touching down in Kilimanjaro on their way (usually) to Dar or Entebbe. Flights leave Schiphol (Amsterdam) at around 10am, arriving the same day at Kili at 8.30pm (total travel time approximately 8½hrs). They then leave Kilimanjaro Airport an hour after landing. Note that they also fly into Zanzibar, allowing you to fly into JRO, and out of ZNZ – what is known as an 'open-jaw' ticket in the trade – which could be useful.

• **Edelweiss Air** (WK; 🖳 flyedelweiss.com) are a Swiss outfit flying every Tuesday morning and Friday night from Zurich, returning Tuesday night and Saturday morning.
• **Ethiopian Airlines** (ET; 🖳 ethiopianairlines.com) operate a pretty comprehensive pan-African network and are renowned for being one of the most reliable of African airlines and one of the cheapest too. They fly daily from Addis Ababa to Kilimanjaro. From London they have overnight flights to Addis Ababa daily that connect with the flight to Kilimanjaro. Connections with North America are more limited, with only Chicago (ORD), Washington Dulles Airport (IAD), New York (JFK & Newark, EWR) and Toronto (YYZ) served. But they are great if you want to explore both Africa (their network is one of the best on the continent) and Ethiopia itself (which I heartily recommend you do – it's a fascinating place!)
• **Kenya Airways** (KQ; 🖳 kenya-airways.com) have several flights daily to Kilimanjaro from Nairobi (usually with their subsidiary Precision Air). They also fly daily from London departing in the early evening from London to

❑ HOW OUR CLIMBERS GET TO KILIMANJARO

In my experience with Kilimanjaro Experts (see p96), I have noticed that climbers tend to use the same airlines depending on where they're coming from. Nothing surprising about this, of course, but I thought it might be useful for you to know what airlines are popular with what places:

• **From the US** Most of our climbers from the US find KLM a good option thanks to their partnership with Delta Airlines, which has an excellent US domestic network. (Indeed, some of our climbers think they're flying Delta all the way, and only realise they'll actually be on a KLM plane when they board it.) Qatar Airways also serve the major airports in the US (LA, New York, San Francisco, Chicago etc) and are getting more and more business.

• **From the UK** The slight majority of our climbers use KLM, again because they have a great network that links various local airports around the UK to Amsterdam's Schiphol Airport. By flying early in the morning from these airports to Amsterdam, you can connect with their flight to JRO and thus do the entire journey in one (long) day. That said, Qatar Airways are growing in popularity, their combination of reliability, super-swish planes and some keenly priced airfares leading many to overlook the fact that it's not the most direct service. We also get some passengers on Kenya Airways, though less so on Ethiopian and Turkish Airlines as they aren't as cheap as they used to be.

• **From Europe** KLM and Qatar are the dominant players here, with Kenya Airways and Ethiopian feeding off the scraps. We get a few climbers a year using the twice-a-week service with Edelweiss Air – I suppose it all depends if your itinerary coincides with their flights.

• **From Australia/Asia** I'm afraid the entire half of the globe is relatively poorly served compared to services from Europe and North America. Qatar Airways, Ethiopian Airlines and Kenya Airways are the only real options, with Qatar capturing the lion's share of business thanks to their extensive Australasian network.

• **From South Africa** Kenya Airways via Nairobi from Cape Town is really the only sensible option.

Nairobi, arriving at JRO around 9am. Again from the States services are limited, with only JFK served by direct flights. They do, however, have a service to Cape Town, thus providing the most direct connection to South Africa.

Flying between Kilimanjaro/Arusha and other airports in Tanzania and East Africa

Flying to and from Zanzibar Trekkers who are based in Arusha have an undoubted advantage here, for they can take flights from both Kili and Arusha Airports to and from Zanzibar (ZNZ). (For people in Moshi, Arusha Airport is well over two hours away and thus not very convenient.) **Precision Air** (💻 precisionairtz.com) are the most useful carrier here, with a couple of direct flights per day each way between Zanzibar and JRO, and around three from Arusha Airport (ARK) too. If none of their times is convenient, **Flightlink** (💻 www.flightlink.co.tz) operate three flights per day each way between Arusha and Zanzibar, while **Air Tanzania** (💻 www.airtanzania.co.tz) operate two flights each way between Kilimanjaro and Zanzibar, and there's one flight per day from Arusha Airport with both **Regional Air** (💻 regionaltanzania.com) and **Air Excel** (💻 airexcelonline.com). If you still can't find a suitable flight, it's worth approaching these companies for a charter flight instead, which may not cost too much more if you have enough people to fill all the seats.

Flying to and from the Serengeti and other national parks There are five main players serving the national parks of the Northern Circuit. Note that you can fly from Serengeti all the way to Zanzibar, which saves you having to return to Arusha again. Note, too, that there are several airstrips in Serengeti – make sure your tour operator knows which one is best for you.

The first and perhaps most established of these 'safari airlines' is **Coastal Aviation** (💻 coastal.co.tz). They're great if you're planning on flying to or from the Serengeti or the other national parks of Tanzania; flights to Dar via Moshi, Tanga and Pangani are also advertised. Their planes call in at both Arusha and Kili Airports (and even Moshi's little airstrip), and also fly to Zanzibar, Pemba, Mafia and other Tanzanian tourist hotspots.

Auric Air (💻 www.auricair.com) seem to operate in a similar way and serve the same 'niche' airports as Coastal – but with one big advantage: they have a luggage allowance of 20kg, compared to Coastal's 15kg.

Flightlink (💻 www.flightlink.co.tz) operate a daily service starting in Arusha and looping round the various airstrips of the Serengeti, as well as operating a daily direct service each way between Arusha and the main Serener airstrip in the Serengeti.

The fourth airline serving the safari airstrips is **Regional Air** (💻 regionaltanzania.com), with their 3.30pm service from JRO visiting Arusha, Manyara and several points in the Serengeti. Finally, there's **Air Excel** (💻 airexcelonline.com) who have a daily flight between Arusha (departing 8am) and various destinations in the Serengeti (Grumeti, Kleins, Seronera) as well as Lake Manyara, before finally arriving back at Arusha at 12.15pm. They also have an occasional flight from Dar and Zanzibar to Arusha.

Flights to and from other Tanzanian destinations Of the several small airlines buzzing around Tanzania, the most useful is undoubtedly **Precision Air** (🖳 precisionairtz.com). Owned by Kenya Airways, they are the most reliable and long-standing local airline and the one with the most extensive domestic network.

One of the many pet projects of former president John Magafuli was to oversee the restoration of the previously bankrupt national airline, **Air Tanzania** (🖳 www.airtanzania.co.tz). Their reputation isn't great, but their domestic network is growing and they connect Kili Airport with Mwanza and Dar, and from Dar you can then fly to several other destinations in Tanzania.

For a more extensive rundown of flights between Dar and Kili/Arusha airports, please see p195.

Flights between neighbouring countries and Kilimanjaro Airport

• **To Nairobi (Kenya)** **Precision Air** (🖳 precisionairtz.com). Owned by Kenya Airways, you'd expect this company to operate a frequent service to Nairobi and they don't disappoint, operating a couple of flights per day each way. Please see p202 for more details.

Safarilink (🖳 www.flysafarilink.com) operate a daily lunchtime flight from Nairobi's second airport, Wilson (WIL), to JRO, staying for just 15 minutes in Tanzania before returning home.

• **To Kigali (Rwanda)** **Rwandair** (🖳 rwandair.com) has three flights per week from Kili to Kigali, on Wed, Fri & Sun. Coming the other way, however, you have to fly via Dar, turning a 1½hr trip into a 4½hr trip.

• **To Entebbe (Uganda)** **Air Tanzania** (🖳 www.airtanzania.co.tz) fly directly between JRO & Entebbe (EBB) on Tue, Fri & Sun. **Uganda Airlines** (🖳 www.ugandairlines.com) fly from JRO on Thur, and to JRO from Entebbe on Tue & Sat.

OVERLAND TO TANZANIA

A big country lying at the heart of East Africa, Tanzania has borders with many countries including Burundi, Kenya, Malawi, Mozambique, Rwanda, Uganda and Zambia.

Several ferries ply their trade on Lake Tanganyika, including the *MV Mwongozo* between Kigoma in Tanzania and **Burundi**. There is also the venerable old *MV Liemba*, the last vessel of the German Imperial Navy that's still sailing anywhere in the world (and on which the subject of the Humphrey Bogart classic, *The African Queen*, is based). The ferry bounces along the eastern shores of Lake Tanganyika, calling in at Mpulungu in Zambia and Kigoma in Tanzania. If the ferries are out of action buses are another option.

The borders with **Rwanda** (at the Rusumo crossing), **Uganda** (most commonly crossed at Mutukula, north-west of Bukoba), **Mozambique** (over the Unity Bridge across the Ruvuma), **Malawi** (Songwe River Bridge) and **Kenya** (see p202 for details on the border crossing at Namanga) are all relatively straightforward and served by public buses.

Tanzania and **Zambia** are also linked by express train, running twice weekly between Dar es Salaam and Kapiri Mposhi via Mbeya.

What to take

CLOTHES

The best head-gear for all weathers is an English sun-helmet, such as are supplied by Messrs. Silver & Co., London; while a soft fez or smoking cap should be kept for wearing in the shade – one with flaps for drawing down over the ears on a cold night to be preferred.
Hans Meyer *Across East African Glaciers* (1891)

According to his book *Life, Wanderings, and Labours in Eastern Africa*, when Charles New attempted to climb Kili in 1861 he took 13 porters, all of whom were completely naked. New and his crew became the first to reach the mountain's snow-line, which is a rather creditable effort considering their lack of suitable apparel. Assuming your goal is to reach more than just snow, however, you will need to make sure you (and indeed your porters) are appropriately attired for the extreme conditions.

The fact that you will be paying porters to carry your rucksack does, to some degree, make packing simpler – allowing you to concentrate on warmth rather than weight. However, packing for warmth does not mean packing lots of big jumpers. The secret to staying warm is to **wear lots of layers**. Not only does this actually make you warmer than if you just had one single, thick layer – the air trapped between the layers heats up and acts as insulation – but it also means you can peel off the layers one by one when you get too warm and put them on again one by one when the temperature drops.

A suitable mountain wardrobe would include:

- **Walking boots** Mountaineering boots (ie ones with stiff soles that take a crampon) are unnecessary unless you're taking an unusual route or trekking in the low season when crampons may be required. If you're not, a decent pair of trekking boots will be fine. (If you're wondering about bringing trekking 'shoes' rather than boots, please see the box on p40.)

Just recently, I've noticed a proliferation of different categorisations of trekking footwear. Some readers have written to me asking whether they should be buying hiking boots or backpacking boots. Others have enquired whether they should be purchasing Category B, C or D boots. Suffice to say, the most important thing about boots is comfort, with enough toe room: on the ascent up Kibo you might be wearing an extra pair or two of socks, and on the descent your toes will be shoved into the front of the boots with every downhill step. Remember these points when trying on trekking boots in the shop. Make sure they are also sturdy, waterproof, durable and high enough to provide support for your ankles. Finally, ensure you break them in *before* you go to Tanzania, so that if they do give you blisters, you can recover before you set foot on the mountain.

If you insist on using these rather artificial and arbitrary categories invented by boot manufacturers and retail outlets, then, having read the definitions, I would advise **backpacking boots**, which are said to be more durable, over their lighter, flimsier hiking boots; or **type B or C** boots if you prefer that particular categorisation.

• **Socks** Ahhh, the joy of socks ... a couple of thick thermal pairs and some regular ones should be fine; you may stink but you'll be comfortable too, which is far more important. Some people walk in one thick and one thin pair of socks, changing the thin pair regularly.

• **Thermal underwear** The value of thermal underwear lies in the way it wicks, that is to say the way it draws moisture (ie your sweat) away from your body. A thermal vest and long-johns are sufficient.

• **Regular underwear** You won't need to wear thermals every day – indeed, many people save them just for the summit night. Most of the time your regular undies are fine. Women will probably feel the benefit of sports bras rather than regular ones – they're certainly more comfy, so I'm told.

• **Mid-layers/fleeces** Fleeces are light, pack down small, dry quickly and can be very, very warm. Take at least two: one thick 'polar' one and one of medium thickness and warmth. Make sure that you can wear the thinner one over all the T-shirts and shirts you'll be taking, and that you can wear your thick one over all of these – you'll probably need to on the night-walk up Kibo.

• **Trousers** Don't take jeans, which are heavy and difficult to dry. Instead, take a couple of pairs of trekking trousers, preferably one light and one heavy. I like the ones that zip off at the knee; they may not win any style awards, but essentially they're two items of leg-wear in one and you may appreciate the ability to

❑ ARE TRAIL RUNNERS OR TREKKING SHOES OK ON KILIMANJARO?

It's a question I'm getting asked more and more because people, clearly, love their trail runners. When I ask them why, the one word that is always included in their answer is 'comfort'. To be honest I've never worn a pair but they clearly must be the most comfortable footwear ever invented.

But are they really suitable for Kilimanjaro? My answer to this is, I'm afraid, a bit of a compromise. The thing is, I've led people up to the top in all kinds of footwear, including, most memorably, a pair of Oxford brogues worn by an Indian doctor. So yes, if you can climb to the summit in brogues, in theory you must also be able to get to the summit of Kili in trail runners or trekking shoes. And presumably, even in bare feet (though I notice that even famous extreme athlete and 'Iceman', Wim Hoff , wore boots – and little else – on his climb).

So it's difficult for me to issue a flat refusal to anyone who wants to wear them to the top. But I still don't recommend it. Because the runners' lack of ankle support, or warmth, limited waterproof qualities and lack of 'robustness' make me think that they're far from ideal.

So what I tell my climbers is that, if they genuinely do find their trail runners to be the last word in comfort, by all means bring them. But **bring boots too**, and look upon your trail runners as slippers, to be worn around the campsite after you've taken your boots off once all the trekking's over. Of course, you can try them on the trail, and if the weather and fortune is on your side, there's no reason why you can't wear them for most of the way up. But I fear for those who wear them for the night-time push to the summit, because they're just not warm enough, in my opinion; and for the descent, when twisted ankles are far more likely, I would pull on the boots instead.

wear them as shorts when walking through the sweaty forest. Note that some people bring salopettes and say they're great – but there are just as many reports from people who find them too bulky and thick, and just too sweaty when you're descending from the summit.

• **Sunhat** One reader wrote in to say that, because he wears glasses, a baseball cap or similar was much more useful than a regular sunhat as it kept the rain off his spectacles. This is a good idea but do make sure you have something to cover the back of your neck too. Whatever you choose, headgear is essential as it can be hot and dazzling on the mountain ...

• **Woolly/fleecy hat** ... but it can also be very cold. Brightly coloured bobble hats can be bought very cheaply in Moshi; or, better still, invest in one of those **balaclavas** which you can usually find on sale in Moshi, which look a bit like a miniature knitted pizza oven but which will protect your face from the biting summit wind.

• **Bandanna (aka 'buff')** This simple tube of cloth that you wear around your neck performs multiple roles on Kili, from keeping the dust out of your face when walking on the Saddle, to using as an ear-warmer on the final night, and mopping the sweat from your brow on those exhausting uphill climbs. Also useful for blocking out odours when using the public toilets at the campsites.

• **Gloves** Preferably fleecy; most people wear both a thicker outer glove and a thin thermal under-glove too.

• **Down jacket** Not necessary if you have enough fleeces and a lined waterproof jacket, but nevertheless wonderfully warm, light, compact – and expensive. Make sure it is large enough to go over all your clothes.

• **Rainwear** While you are more likely to be rained on during the walk in the forest, where it should still be warm, once you've got your clothes wet there will be little opportunity to dry them on the trek – and you will not want to attempt to climb freezing Kibo in wet clothes. A **waterproof jacket** is ideal, preferably made from Gore-Tex or a similar breathable material, hopefully with a warm or fleecy lining too, and big enough to go over all your clothes so you can wear it for the night-walk on Kibo. **Waterproof trousers** are a necessity too. Alternatively, one reader suggests a cheap waterproof **poncho** 'from a dollar store', preferably one that goes over your daypack as well as yourself.

• **Summer clothes** T-shirts and shorts are the most comfortable things to wear under the humid forest canopy. You are strongly recommended to take a shirt with a collar too, to stop the sun from burning the back of your neck (though a buff or sunhat with a wide brim will perform the same role).

OTHER EQUIPMENT

Any trekking operator worth its licence will provide a **tent**, as well as **cooking equipment**, **cutlery** and **crockery**. You will still need to pack a few other items, however, if you don't want to return from your trek as a sunburnt, snow-blinded, dehydrated wretch with hepatitis and hypothermia. Some of these items can be bought or rented in Moshi or Arusha. Your operator can arrange equipment rental, which is the most convenient way.

Note that the following lists concern the trek only; it does not include items necessary for other activities you may have planned on your holiday, such as binoculars for your safari or a bucket and spade for Zanzibar.

Before buying or renting all the following, check to see what your operator will supply as part of their trekking package. Many will provide mattresses and will purify all water for you, for example, which will save you a little.

Essentials

- **Sleeping bag** The warmest you've got. Four-season and even five-season – yes, such things do exist! – sleeping bags are obviously best but for many people a three-season bag (up to -10°C) is probably the most practical, offering a compromise between warmth and affordability; team this with a **thermal fleecy liner**, which is available in camping shops back at home for about £20-30/ US$30-45, to provide further insurance against the cold.
- **Sleeping mat** Essential unless you're following the standard Marangu Route as you'll be sleeping in huts. Trekking agencies sometimes supply these – check to see if yours does. In terms of what type to buy, again the warmest you can

❑ A PACKING LIST FOR WOMEN CLIMBERS

Clothing

The packing list I provide on pp39-41 is as relevant for women as for men. Though when it comes to underwear you'll probably want to wear a **bra**: the best option here is a **non-cotton sports bra** that wicks the sweat away from your skin. If nothing else, this will stop you from getting cold.

Other items

I've looked at various blogs written by women on Kilimanjaro and most of the items they suggest bringing have to do with hygiene and cosmetics. Do remember, however, that on Kili you'll probably get nothing but two hot bowls of water to wash with each day. And after the second day everybody reeks anyway. It's a situation that is mercifully ameliorated by the fact that you'll be wearing several layers most of the time, thus preventing body odours from escaping.

Other stuff to bring? Well, in my experience women tend to feel the cold on Kili more than men. If you fall into that category, some of those **hand warmers** may be a good idea. They're not just for your hands, either. You can put them in your boots before you put them on, in your gloves and even, so I'm told, in your bra. And remember to keep some aside for the summit nights – don't use them all on the first evening or you'll regret it.

Panty liners, min-pads, hand and vaginal wipes are all recommended too. If your period coincides with your climb, firstly, my sympathies: climbing Kilimanjaro is hard enough without all that going on too. Bring your usual sanitary stuff. One blogger recommends Diva Cups – whether they were sponsored for this I don't know (she also recommended coco-butter vaseline, which sounds rather specific). But you may want to investigate them anyway. Note, too, that the high altitude may trigger your period earlier than you expected.

Do remember to bring **paper bags or zip-lock bags** with you to collect your used sanitary products and toilet roll. (Tanzania has banned plastic bags (see p47) and you can no longer bring them into the country.)

afford. An inflatable one is not a good idea; there is always the possibility, however slim, of them developing a puncture, and besides you won't have the puff to inflate it at the higher camps.

• **Water bottles/Platypus Hoser/CamelBak system** On that final push up Kibo you'll need to carry three litres of water *at least*; many people take enough containers to carry four litres. It's certainly good to take a lot of water, though do remember you've got to carry it and four litres of water weighs four kilos.

Make sure your bottles are **thermally protected** or they will freeze on the summit. Regular water bottles are fine, though these days many trekkers prefer the **Platypus Hoser-style systems** (aka **CamelBak**), a soft, plastic bladder with a long tube from which you can drink as you walk along. I think they're great and they have several advantages over regular bottles, not the least of which being that they save you fiddling about with bottle tops and you can keep your hands in your pockets while you drink, which is great on the freezing night-time walk to the summit. But while they encourage you to drink regularly, which is good, they also discourage you from taking a break, which is bad. What's more,

In addition, the most useful item is what is marketed as a 'she-wee' (or shewee, or she-pee, or miss-piss). As the manufacturer says, this is a device that allows you to wee into a bottle. I'm a huge fan of a **pee bottle**, ie something to wee into when you're in your tent at night. It saves you having to get dressed and brave the freezing cold every time you need to go. And on Kili you'll want to pee a lot, particularly if you're acclimatising well, and even more so if you're taking Diamox, which is a diuretic.

So it's only fair that women can enjoy the same convenience and comfort as men. Which is where the she-wee comes in. It does, apparently, take a bit of practice to use a she-wee successfully, so try it in the shower at home before you head off to a big mountain in Tanzania. Online reviews are largely positive though two women on a previous trek I led offered contradictory opinions. The first said it had 'changed her life', which may be over-egging it a bit, but says a lot about her enthusiasm for the product. The second woman, however, was less enthusiastic, describing it as a 'bit dribbly'.

Make-up? Really?

Some women bring lipstick and mascara with them simply because, in their words, they'd feel naked without them. That's fair enough. If you're used to wearing **make-up** every day, and you'd feel uncomfortable without it, bring some. I'm a firm believer in trying, within reason, to make your trek as comfortable as possible for yourself. And if that means putting a bit of slap on in the morning, then so be it. But don't envisage stepping out of the tent in the morning like you've just stepped out of the salon. And by the end of the day you should expect some of your make-up to be covered in dust and grit. But if you want to do it, then do it.

As for your **hair**, well if it's long bring something to tie it back. There are dry shampoos that you can buy – but test them first to make sure they actually work. And if you want to avoid looking too filthy **trim your nails** short before you arrive. Everything gets grimy on Kili, including you, and dirt that can be difficult to shift gets under the fingernails; the alternative is to wear a very dark nail varnish. **Cutting your toenails**, too, has benefits. Not only will it avoid the build-up of toe-jam, but it will stop them hurting you when your feet thump into the front of your boots on the descent.

these bladders always freeze up on the way to the summit, especially the hose and mouthpiece. One way to delay this is to **blow back into the tube** after you have taken a drink to prevent water from collecting in the tube and freezing. (One reader suggested adding Dioralyte which apparently also helps to delay freezing, though this may in time permanently alter the flavour of any water you

❑ A KILIMANJARO WASHBAG

Hygiene is very, very important on Kilimanjaro. The last thing you want is a stomach bug due to the poor hygiene regime of one of your fellow trekkers or crew members – or, indeed, yourself. The trouble is, of course, that opportunities to wash are minimal on the mountain and water is limited the further up you go. Put the following in your washbag, however, and you should be able to maintain some sort of standards:

- **Anti-bacterial handwash** This stuff is very effective and though you won't find it on most kit lists, I think it's essential. Giving some to your cook before he prepares your meals is a good idea too!
- **Moist toilet tissues (Wet-wipes)** For mopping brows, mainly; use several at the end of the day and on most treks it's the closest thing you'll get to a shower on the mountain. Please dispose of properly – these things don't degrade.
- **Toothbrush and toothpaste** Ensure your dental checks are up to date; if there is one thing more painful than climbing to the summit of Kili, it's climbing to the summit of Kili with toothache.
- **Toilet paper** See box p254 for advice on how to dispose of used toilet paper.
- **Kula cloth** As I discuss elsewhere, there's a disappointingly large amount of toilet paper littering the trail-side. But how to prevent people using such a large amount of toilet paper, and then depositing it where they use it, is not an easy question to answer. So I'm indebted to Emily Winks for both bringing my attention to, and then reviewing, one potential solution: a 'kula cloth'. As Emily writes: 'I'm amazed so many folk who have paid huge amounts of money to visit such a unique place feel it's okay to litter it and leave plenty more behind than just footsteps. The Kula cloth is a tiny light fabric square which secures easily to the outside of your rucksack with poppers, allowing quick access when required as well as instant drying in the African breeze. Squat for your wee, pat yourself dry, fold and attach to your pack, and off you go. A quick wash at camp before hanging it out to dry and you're ready for the next day.'
- **Soap** Though you won't get through much of it on the mountain and your trekking operator should provide some for you.
- **Tampons/sanitary towels**
- **Contraceptives** For those with too much energy. But gentlemen be warned: if she says she has a headache on the mountain, the chances are she *really does have* a headache.

You should also bring a **towel**. The controversy here is over which sort to have. Many just bring one enormous beach towel because they plan to visit Zanzibar after the trek and don't see the point of packing two towels. At the other extreme there are the so-called 'travel towels', a sort of chamois-cloth affair sold in camping shops and airport lounges the world over. Some people swear by these but others usually end up swearing *at* them, finding that they have all the absorbency of your average brick. Nevertheless, I grudgingly admit that they do have their uses on Kilimanjaro, where opportunities (and desire) to wash anything other than face, hands and armpits are minimal. You can dry your towel by attaching it to the outside of your rucksack during the day.

❑ A KILIMANJARO MEDICAL KIT

According to Meyer, the Chagga treated their cuts and scars with the liberal application of cow dung. I advise, however, that you don't. Most agencies these days carry a pretty comprehensive medical kit, but if you're with a budget operator it might be an idea to bring at least the basics.

Your medical kit *could* include:

- **Antiseptic cream and plasters** For small cuts and grazes.
- **Bandages** Useful for twists and sprains as well as for larger flesh wounds.
- **Compeed/Second Skin** For blisters.
- **Elastic joint supports** For steeper gradients if you have knee/ankle problems.
- **Ice packs** One of my clients brought Koolpaks with him; these turn icy cold when squeezed and shaken and provide great relief for painful joints. Can be bought online, are very reasonable – and are ideal if you know that your knees or ankles will play up on the mountain.
- **Anti-malarials** You won't catch malaria on the mountain but if you're on a course of anti-malarials you should continue taking them. There is a belief among many guides that the popular anti-malarial drug Malarone interferes with the efficacy of Diamox, the anti-altitude sickness drug. Speak with your guide/doctor to get their opinion on this.
- **Aspirin/Paracetamol** Or other painkillers, though do read the discussion on Acute Mountain Sickness (AMS; see pp243-6) and the medical indications that come with the packet before scoffing these.
- **Imodium** Stops you going when you don't want to, which could come in handy.
- **Rehydrating powders** Such as Dioralyte. Usually prescribed to people suffering from diarrhoea but useful after a hot day's trekking as well.
- **Lip salve or chapstick/vaseline** See under *Highly desirables*, p47.
- **Throat pastilles** Useful, as the dry, dusty air causes many a sore throat.
- **Any medication you are on** Bring all your needles, pills, lotions, potions and pungent unguents.
- **Diamox** Diamox is the brand name for Acetazolamide, the drug that fights AMS – or at least the symptoms of it (see pp243-6) – and which many people use prophylactically on Kilimanjaro. See the box on pp248-9 to help you decide whether you want to bring a course of these with you.
- **Sterile needles** If you need an injection in Tanzania, insist that the doctor uses your new needles.

Carry everything in a **waterproof bag or case** and keep at least the emergency stuff in your daypack – where hopefully it will lie undisturbed for the trek's duration.

put in the bottle in the future.) So, if you are going to bring one of these, make sure it's fully insulated – and don't forget to take frequent breaks!

I think **the best combination is to bring both a 'CamelBak' and a regular bottle**. The bottle should keep insulated by wrapping in a towel or putting inside an old, thick sock inside your daypack, to be retrieved once your CamelBak has frozen. Another good tip is to **store the bottle upside-down in your daypack**; that way, if it, too, starts to freeze, it will do so from the bottom of the bottle, so you can still drink out of the top.

- **Water purifiers/filter** Essential only if your operator has stated they won't purify your water for you – though most now do. Of the two, **purifying tablets** such as iodine are more effective as they kill everything in the water, though they taste awful. A cordial will help to mask this taste and you can buy packets of powdered flavouring in the local supermarkets. **Filters** are less effective and more expensive, though the water they produce tastes much better.

There's a third option, the **Steripen**, which kills waterborne microbes by using ultraviolet light. The pen is simple to use: just turn it on, hold it in a litre of water for up to 90 seconds and ... that's it. I was on the mountain when I first saw one of these in action and promptly went and bought one of my own. My only quibble is that you can use it on only one litre of water at a time, so it can be awkward if you have, for example, a three-litre bottle.

- **Torch** A **head-torch**, if you have one and don't find it uncomfortable, is far more practical than a hand-held one, allowing you to keep both hands free; on the last night this advantage is pretty much essential, enabling you to keep your hands in your pockets for warmth. It's also pretty essential when going to the toilet after dark too, saving you from juggling toilet roll and torches while squatting and trying to maintain your balance.
- **Sunscreen** High factor (40-50) is essential. That sun is fierce at these altitudes!
- **Sunglasses** Essential for the summit where the light on Kibo can be really painful and damaging and cause snow-blindness.
- **Ice axe/crampons Ice axes** are really useful only if you are taking a highly unusual route on the mountain (ie none of the official ones) where you have to cross glaciers, or, possibly, if you're travelling out of season or in late December/early January when snow and ice are at their heaviest.

Crampons, too, would be useful on these occasions, though ask your operator first if they will be necessary before bringing them. Otherwise leave them, your snow boots, rope, karabiners and all that other mountaineering gear at home.

- **Glasses/contact lenses** For those who need them, of course. **Contact lenses** are fine but super-expensive ones should be avoided on the final assault to the summit as there's a risk that when the strong cold wind blows across the Saddle the lenses can dry, go brittle very quickly and fall out of your eye. I suggest affordable disposable lenses be worn but that spare **glasses** be carried, especially during the assault on the summit. Obviously you'll need to be extra careful to keep your hands super clean, dry and dust-free when putting in lenses.

Highly desirables

- **Trekking poles** If you've done some trekking before you'll know if you need trekking poles or not; if you haven't, assume you will. While people often use them for the entire trek, poles really come into their own on the descent where they minimise the strain on your knees as you trudge downhill.

For anyone over 40, I would say that trekking poles should really be in the 'Essentials' section of this chapter. Telescopic poles can be bought from trekking/camping outfitters in the West, or you can invest in a more local version – a Maasai 'walking stick' – from souvenir shops in Moshi or Arusha.

- **Boiled sweets/chocolate** For winning friends and influencing people. Good for energy levels too. And morale. If you can bring them from home so much the better; sweets sold in Tanzania may look similar to those at home but they seldom taste the same.

• **Chapstick/lip salve or vaseline** The wind on the summit will rip your sunburnt lips to shreds. Save yourself the agony by investing in a chapstick, available in strawberry and mint flavours from pharmacists in Moshi and Arusha.

• **She-wee** For details on the she-wee, see box p43. Men, by the way, usually make do with an empty water bottle – preferably one that they don't plan to drink out of again…

• **Camera and equipment** See box p48.

• **Mobile phone** You can get reception on much of the mountain now including, occasionally, on the summit. And there's **wi-fi** at the campsites on the Marangu Route too. What better place could there be from which to phone friends stuck behind their desks at work on a rainy day back home? The guides and porters know where reception is best at each campsite, so if you're having trouble making contact just ask one or simply follow them. I give general advice on the quality of phone reception at the start of the description for each trail. But a phone is no longer just a communication device, of course. It is also a camera, torch, GPS, iPod, radio and laptop. So for many people this will actually be an essential part of their equipment. That said, if you want a 'digital detox' from your phone, I struggle to think of a better time to do so.

Remember, too, that batteries last a lot longer if you keep the phone in airline mode. And if you're going to bring one of these it's a good idea to also bring…

• **Phone battery pack/power bank** Phones have a habit of dying on the mountain; it must be the cold. Revive them with a battery pack – they're portable and cheap and do the business.

❑ THE PLASTIC BAG BAN

In 2019, Tanzania did its bit in the global fight against single-use plastics by banning all shopping bags. Previously I had always recommended climbers to bring plastic bags, to keep stuff separate in one's rucksack that needs to be kept separate, and as an extra waterproof layer. Still, I have to say that I think the ban was a good move. Ribbons of plastic bag remnants decorating every acacia tree on the roadside used to be such an eyesore, and thanks to the ban and a simultaneous countrywide policy to clean up Tanzania, this sight is a rarity these days.

However, what I should warn you about, and it's something I had no idea about until I was packing for my last trip, was just how reliant, or addicted, to plastic bags we in the West have become. On my last trip, for example, I thought I'd got rid of all plastic bags in my luggage, but still found *four*: one contained a small hook that came with my new mosquito net; one was wrapped around an old bar of soap from a previous expedition; one contained a spare battery for my camera; and there was a doggy poo bag – unused – from when I use my rucksack on UK hikes.

So the advice is clear: before you even leave your house, check through your entire luggage to make sure a plastic bag hasn't successfully stowed itself away in your luggage in the hope of a better life hanging from a thorn tree in East Africa; it might save you an awful and expensive start to your holiday.

❑ CAMERAS AND CAMERA EQUIPMENT

It's important to prepare properly when it comes to taking a camera on Kilimanjaro. After all, it's likely that your camera will not have spent seven days in constant use before and almost certainly not in the dusty and/or humid conditions one finds on the mountain, with its extremes of temperature and weather.

The first thing to do is to make sure you have enough **memory cards**; I take an average of 400-600 shots each time I spend a week on Kilimanjaro. Indeed, sometimes I'm surprised I haven't ended up with camera-shaped tan lines on my face, such is the frequency with which I've found something worth photographing. But while those figures are probably a bit extreme, if you like taking photographs you could well match or even surpass these figures.

Bring at least one **spare set of batteries** and make sure all rechargeable batteries are fully charged before you set off on the mountain. More and more photographic equipment is becoming available for sale in Arusha and, to a lesser extent, Moshi, but I certainly wouldn't rely on them having the battery you require for your camera. And for goodness sake don't forget to bring the **charger**, so you can charge your batteries the night before you head off onto the mountain.

For those with an SLR, regarding **lenses**, I always take a couple of zooms: a wide-angle (around 18-135mm) and a telephoto. This latter is far less useful on Kilimanjaro, of course, as panoramic shots of the mountain and stunning wide-angle views are the order of the day; but occasionally it's nice to zoom in on a bird of prey or a particular part of the mountain. A telephoto zoom also comes into its own if you're going on safari after your trek (I suggest a 300mm lens minimum for this).

Other useful equipment includes: a **polarising filter** to bring out the rich colours of the sky, rocks and glaciers. A **tripod** is useful for those serious about their photography, in order to keep the camera steady and allow for maximum depth of field – though remember, you're the one who's going to have to carry it if you want to use it during the day (though you could ask your operator to provide a porter for this task); a bean-bag, or one of those bendy 'gorillas', would be a more portable alternative. One other essential investment is a **camera-cleaning kit**. Your camera goes through a lot of hardship on Kili, not least because of the different vegetation zones you pass through, from the humidity of the forest to the dusty desert of the Saddle. Either buy a ready-made kit from a camera shop or make one yourself by investing in a soft cloth, cotton buds, a blow brush and tweezers.

Many people with expensive SLR cameras also bring their smartphone; this is not a bad idea, as it doubles your chances of getting some photographic record of your journey.

Usefuls

- **Earplugs** Some porters have stereos and most have mobile phones, and they love advertising this fact by playing the former and speaking into the latter extremely loudly at campsites. A set of earplugs will reduce this disturbance.
- **Eye mask** Particularly useful on a full moon trek if the moon is really bright and shining through the canvas of your tent.
- **Gaiters** For every edition of this book I put these in the 'Useful' category; and every edition at least one trekker writes in to tell me that they should be in the 'Essentials' category. I've never worn them on Kili, though they are pretty vital if you don't have waterproof trousers and they are particularly useful on

the slopes of Kibo and the dusty Saddle to prevent small stones from entering one's boots. To be fair, many of the guides I have trekked with feel naked without them. So it's a matter of preference, really.

- **Sandals/flip-flops (shoes for the campsite)** Useful in the evenings at camp but make sure they are big enough to fit round a pair of thick socks.
- **Bootlaces/string**
- **Clothes pegs** Useful for attaching wet clothes to the back of rucksacks to allow them to dry in the sun while you walk; a reader wrote in to recommend **binder clips** (also known as bulldog or office clips) as a smaller, stronger alternative.
- **Penknife** Always useful, if only for opening beer bottles at the post-trek party.
- **Sewing kit** For repairs on the trail.
- **Insulating tape** Also for repairs, this time for shoes, rucksacks, tents etc, and as a last resort for mending holes in clothes if you have forgotten your sewing kit or are incapable of using it.
- **Watch** Preferably cheap and luminous for night-time walking.
- **Compass** Not essential, but useful when combined with ...
- **Map** See p379 for a list of my preferred maps; again not essential but will, in combination with a compass, help you to determine where you are on the mountain, and where you should be going.
- **GPS receiver** See box p50.
- **Whistle** It's difficult to get lost on Kilimanjaro but if you're taking an unusual route – on the northern side of the mountain, for example, or around Mawenzi – a whistle may be useful to help people find you. The international distress (emergency) signal is six blasts on a whistle.
- **Multi-plug adaptor** Not for Kili, obviously, where there's no power, though could be useful before and after the trek if you're staying in a room with only one socket and you have a camera/GPS/laptop/batteries to recharge.
- **Solar charger** Useful for charging smartphones, of course, and getting better, cheaper and lighter all the time. Prices are around £50-150, with BigBlue, Blavor and HiLuckey the biggest manufacturers.
- **Hand warmers** I've never used these myself, but, to judge by the number of them that I see discarded by the path, they are getting more and more popular. They're actually a very good idea, especially for putting inside your gloves on the way to the summit – but if you are going to use them, do dispose of them properly afterwards.

Luxuries

- **Hot water bottle** Several people have suggested this and a number of trekking companies now supply them as standard. Get your crew to fill it with hot water before bedtime and use the water in the morning for washing.
- **Pillow** One luxury I have never actually used on the mountain but would love is a pillow; not one of those inflatable travel ones but a proper, plump, goose-down number. Bulky and a pain to carry, of course – but so much nicer than resting one's weary head on a scrunched-up fleece at the end of the day.
- **Music** While some find the idea abhorrent, many trekkers bring their tunes on the trek, usually stored on their phone. There is nothing wrong with a little

mountainside music, of course, but do remember that while you may think you've found the perfect soundtrack for climbing up Kili, others may disagree: bring **headphones**, so as not to disturb.

- **Diary/reading material** A list of appropriate reading matter can be found on pp380-4. Note that more than one client has said that books and other forms of entertainment are essential to while away the hours in camp, whereas others say it's all unnecessary; it depends who you're climbing with, I suppose, and how well you're all getting along.
- **Champagne** For celebrating, of course, though don't try to take it up and open it at the summit – the combination of champagne and altitude sickness could lead to tragedy.

WHAT TO PACK IT IN

You'll need two bags: a **rucksack/duffle bag** and a smaller, lighter **daypack**. When choosing the former, a rucksack or duffle bag with a capacity of 70 litres is the minimum in my experience, with 80 litres-plus more practical for carrying all the equipment necessary for most climbs.

But while trekkers usually spend a long time finding the rucksack that's most comfortable for them, few bother to spend as long when choosing a daypack. However, on Kili it is the porters who traditionally carry your rucksack (usually on their heads, and often inside a rice sack or similar outer layer to protect it from getting wet or damaged), while you will carry your daypack. So

❑ GPS WAYPOINTS AND PHONE APPS

If you have a handheld GPS (Global Positioning System) receiver you will be able to take advantage of the waypoints marked on the maps and listed on pp375-8 of this book. Essentially a GPS calculates your position on the Earth using a number of satellites and the results should be accurate to a few metres. It is, of course, not essential that you use a GPS; your chances of getting lost on the mountain are very slim, given that you will be accompanied at every step by a guide who may have climbed on your route a hundred times or more.

If you do decide to use a GPS unit in conjunction with this book don't feel that you need to be ticking off every waypoint as you reach it; you'll soon get bored with that. But if you look at it occasionally – when you stop for lunch, for example – it will give you an idea both of where you are on the trail and also how far you have to go.

You have two ways of inputting the waypoints into your receiver. You can either manually key the nearest waypoint from the list in this book as and when the need arises. Or, much less laboriously and with less margin for keystroke error, download the complete list (but not the descriptions) for free from the publisher's website 💻 trailblazer-guides.com.

If you don't have a designated GPS receiver, you can still record your walk using your phone and one of the **apps** that are available. I find that these change regularly – none of the apps I recommended in the last edition, for example, is still available today. But for what it's worth, GPS Tracks seems great for recording a walk marking on waypoints and doing everything a regular GPS would do – though the 'pro' version (US$19.99) offers a lot more features. Surprisingly, the very popular Alltrails has a file for the Machame Route only, but presumably that will change over time.

❑ WHAT TO PUT IN YOUR DAYPACK

Normally you will not see your main backpack from the moment you hand it to the porter in the morning to at least lunchtime, and maybe not until the end of the day. It's therefore necessary to pack everything you may need during the day in the bag you carry with you. Some suggestions, in no particular order:

- sweets
- water (and perhaps water purifiers too)
- camera/batteries/film/memory card
- phone plus battery pack
- this book/maps
- sunhat/sunglasses and suncream
- buff/bandanna
- a light fleece as you reach the higher altitudes
- toilet paper and trowel
- bag for rubbish
- rainwear
- walking sticks/trekking poles knee supports
- medical kit, including chapstick
- packed lunch (supplied by your crew)
- your valuables (passport, money etc)

make sure you **choose your daypack with care** and that it is both comfortable and durable. It also needs to be big enough to hold everything you may need when walking. See box above for a possible list of these things.

A few more points. Firstly, it is not uncommon for bags to be delayed during your flight; indeed, at one point it was estimated that one in seven bags got lost or delayed in transit. (Though, to be fair, the statistics seem better now.) This is why it is imperative that you **wear or carry your boots on the plane**. Your daypack (which you should carry on as hand luggage) should also contain a waterproof coat and anything else you think you may need for your first day on the mountain (camera, medication etc). In other words, when you pack assume that you may be on the mountain by the time your main bag arrives in Tanzania. Sleeping bags and mats are probably too bulky to be carried as hand luggage on a flight so you'll have to discuss with your trekking operator/guide about renting this stuff from them, at least until your main pack arrives.

Once your main bag does arrive at its destination (and most delayed bags turn up within 24 hours of their scheduled arrival time), if your trekking company is half-decent they'll fetch it from JRO for you and will then give it to a porter to bring to you on Kili. Bearing this in mind, if you have brought some stuff in your main bag that you *don't* want to take on the mountain with you – a snorkel and fins for your post-Kili trip to Zanzibar, for example – pack this in a separate bag within the main bag. You can then give instructions to the operator on what you'd like removed from the bag and kept safely in their office, and what you want on the mountain. This 'non-Kili' stuff can then be removed by them easily without having to rummage through your entire luggage.

Once you're on the mountain **don't leave valuables in your rucksack**. Though porters are trustworthy on the whole, it's only fair that you do not put temptation in their path; and it saddens me to say that there have been a spate of thefts recently from bags and tents, particularly at Barranco Camp but elsewhere too.

Fitness, inoculations and insurance

FITNESS

I ascribe the almost perfect health I have always enjoyed in Africa to the fact that I have made every step of my journey on foot, the constant exercise keeping my bodily organs in good order. **Hans Meyer** *Across East African Glaciers* (1891)

There's no need to go overboard with fitness preparations for climbing Kili. The main reason why people fail to reach the summit is altitude sickness rather than lack of necessary strength or stamina. But the trek will obviously be more enjoyable for you the fitter you are, so anything you can do in the way of training can only help.

A fitness regime

Though I am tall, I always had secretly defined myself as a physically weak and somewhat sickly person. After climbing Kilimanjaro, I had to acknowledge that I was mentally and physically tough. I was forced to redefine myself. Climbing the mountain was the hardest thing I had ever done, physically, in my life, but I had done it.

Michael Crichton, *Travels* (1988)

When people ask us how fit you need to be to climb Kilimanjaro, I usually reply that you don't need to be especially fit, just *not unfit*. But while altitude sickness is the main reason why people fail to reach the summit – and this can strike you regardless of whether you are fit or not – there's no doubt that you *do* need to be in reasonable condition to tackle Kilimanjaro and will have a much more pleasant time on the mountain if you are fit and healthy. Note I'm not talking about being buff, beefy, ripped, sinewy, muscular, well developed, athletic, brawny, rugged, toned, or hunky. Just fit and healthy. That is all.

❑ HIGH-ALTITUDE HEALTH

Before you go, if you suffer from heart or lung problems (such as angina or asthma), high blood pressure or are pregnant, you must visit your doctor to get advice on the wisdom of climbing up Africa's highest mountain; many of the deaths on the mountain are due to pre-existing conditions that had previously gone undetected.

The illness you are most likely to suffer from is altitude sickness; indeed, it's a rare trekker on Kilimanjaro who doesn't suffer to some degree. Altitude sickness is caused by the body's inability to adapt quickly enough to the thinner mountain air present at high altitudes. It can be fatal if ignored or left untreated but is also preventable. For a run-down on the causes, symptoms and treatments of altitude sickness, read the section on pp242-52 carefully.

One more thing: if you're planning on relying on the wonder-drug Diamox (see pp248-9) on the mountain, try it before you go to make sure you have no severe adverse reaction to it.

For this reason, and to answer the many emails I get from people who want to undertake some sort of fitness regime before their trek, here is a typical daily exercise programme for Kilimanjaro. It should be started about four months (three minimum) before the climb. This should help to reduce body fat, improve aerobic fitness and also strengthen the muscles in the places where it really matters: your legs. Concentrate on aerobic exercises three times a week, alternating with leg-strengthening exercises for the other three days; then follow God's example and rest on the seventh day.

Note, too, that **for my climbers I usually recommend that they slow down their training a couple of months before the trek**. I've had more than one climber who's had to postpone their trek due to injury caused, more often than not, by them over-exerting themselves on the treadmill or exercise bike. So take it easy before the trek, and remember the reason why you're getting fit.

Aerobic exercise

Aerobic exercise is designed to improve oxygen consumption in the body. Thirty minutes to an hour of jogging, cycling, swimming, climbing stairs or even just brisk walking are all good aerobic exercises. Aim to exercise at 70% of your maximum heart rate for the best results.

Leg strengthening

Go to any gym and you'll come across plenty of contraptions designed to increase the strength of your calves, thighs, hamstrings and buttocks. These are fine though the usual warnings apply: always read the instructions carefully before using any machine and never be too ambitious and overload the machine with too much weight. Either course of action could lead to serious injury and the cancellation of your trek altogether.

If you don't have access to gym equipment, however, don't worry: there are exercises you can do without the need for machines. **Lunges**, where you take an exaggerated step forward with one leg, dropping your hips as low as possible while keeping your torso upright, are great for thighs, hamstrings and buttocks. A **reverse lunge**, which is the same as a regular lunge only you take a step *backwards*, until your forward thigh (ie the one you didn't take a step backwards with) is parallel to the floor, is also good, particularly for your hamstring. **Calf raises**, where you position yourself with the front half of your feet on a platform, then gently raise and lower yourself on your toes so your heel is alternately higher and lower than the toes, is also useful.

Take a hike!

While the above exercises certainly provide many benefits, I still maintain that nothing is better preparation for going for a long walk, than **going for a long walk**. A walk provides excellent aerobic exercise, is great for strengthening leg muscles and if the walk is long enough and involves plenty of uphills, can be great for improving stamina too. Wear the clothes you plan to take to Kilimanjaro – particularly your boots and socks – and the daypack that you hope to be carrying all the way to the top of Kibo, as well. Then find walks in your area or take a walking weekend or walking holiday. You never know, you may even enjoy it as well.

❑ ARE HIGH-ALTITUDE MASKS USEFUL WHEN TRAINING FOR KILI?

High-altitude masks, also known as workout masks, hypoxic masks and elevation masks, work by restricting the airflow to its user, thus limiting the amount of air (and thus oxygen) you take into you body when breathing. As such, they are supposed to mimic the sensation of being at high altitude. Some of the flashier ones even have an adjustable valve so you can feel what it's like to breathe at altitudes from 900m all the way to over 5000m. The idea is that by regularly using one during your training for Kili, they will improve lung function, endurance performance and mental strength. Which would be useful, right?

Unfortunately, the available evidence suggests that the beneficial effect they have is, at best, pretty marginal. As I discuss on p243, the body adapts to being at altitude, and the reduced amount of oxygen, by working harder. Unfortunately, this adaptation takes time and unless you're going to wear the mask all day and all night, you aren't really mimicking the *permanent* lack of oxygen your body is receiving. But even if you did, according to one study these masks do not "produce a low oxygen stimulus great enough to elicit the necessary physiological responses associated with high altitude"; in other words, none of the adaptations that your body normally makes at altitude seem to occur when wearing these masks; it appears your body is not fooled, and carries on functioning normally.

You will of course read lots of stuff on the internet about how these masks are essential for all Kili trekkers – some of it, sadly, from the trekking companies themselves. But the bottom line is that there seems little evidence that this is true; and that while they probably won't do you any harm, at least if they're used properly, these masks do little to train your body for the rigours of Kili.

Smoke

Finally, you could always take up **smoking**. I'd long heard the rumour that smokers have a better chance of reaching the summit, apparently due to the fact that their bodies are used to less oxygen because of the reduced functioning of their lungs; and certainly my experiences of taking smokers up the mountain bear this bizarre idea out. While those of my clients who've led a blameless, tobacco-free life frequently struggle with the altitude, long-term smokers tend to saunter up. Breathless, certainly, and often wheezing – but headache-free and happy.

Of course, I'm not seriously suggesting you take up smoking – but it is interesting, isn't it?

INOCULATIONS

Sort out your vaccinations a few months before you're due to fly. While you're doing it, do check to see what the latest **Covid** regulations are. Hopefully, you'll be chuckling to yourself on reading that instruction, because the days of Covid, lockdowns, face-masks and social-distancing are things of the past.

At the time of writing, there were no Covid regulations in either Tanzania or Kenya. Nevertheless, just nip onto one of the websites listed on pp56-7, for peace of mind if nothing else, to make sure they haven't reintroduced some new Covid rule.

Yellow fever: do you need the inoculation?

The only vaccine that is compulsory for entering Tanzania is yellow fever, and only if you're coming from a country where the disease is endemic (even if you were only transiting there, assuming you left the airport in that country and were there for more than 12 hours); see p120 for further details. In the UK the jab costs about £60-85 including a certificate (from what I understand it's about US$150 in the States though can climb to US$350) to prove you've been vaccinated.

The following inoculations are not compulsory, but are either recommended or at least worth considering:

• **Typhoid** This disease is caught from contaminated food and water. A single injection lasts for three years. Available on the NHS in the UK, but note that it is not 100% effective so you should still take precautions when eating food and drinking water. There is also a typhoid vaccine that is combined with one for...

• **Hepatitis A** This debilitating disease of the liver is spread by contaminated water, or even by using cutlery that has been washed in this water. The latest inoculation involves two injections; the first will protect you for a year, the second, taken six to twelve months later, will cover you for at least 25 years.

• **Polio** The polio vaccine used to be administered by sugar-lump, making it one of the more pleasant inoculations, though these days it's nearly always injected. The vaccine lasts for 10 years and there's a high chance you may already have been immunised for life if you had a course of inoculations during childhood – which if you're under 65 you probably will have done.

• **Tetanus** Tetanus vaccinations last for 10 years and are absolutely vital for visitors to Tanzania. The vaccination is usually given in combination with one for **diphtheria**. Once you've had five injections, you're covered for life. Once again, the chances you were immunised against this at childhood is high. If you need a booster, it should last for five years.

• **Meningococcal meningitis** This disease of the brain is often fatal though the vaccination, while not free, is safe and lasts for five years. Meningitis can

> **❑ HELP! MY DOCTOR WON'T GIVE ME A YELLOW FEVER JAB!**
>
> Those over 60 may find that health professionals are reluctant to administer the yellow fever vaccination, as it's widely considered dangerous for sexagenarians (and older) these days. This of course presents a problem to those who would otherwise need it; but there are two possible solutions:
>
> Firstly, if you've previously had the jab, and either have your old yellow fever certificate or can get hold of a copy, that should be sufficient – as the jab is considered to last a lifetime now, so it should still be accepted.
>
> Secondly, according to the website of the Tanzanian Embassy in Washington you can ask your doctor for a note explaining that you are too old to get the inoculation, which you can then brandish at the airport. Though I only found this on one website, from one embassy, I assume it applies to citizens of every country.

be caused by a number of infections so there are several different vaccines too – the relevant one for travellers is the MenACWY vaccine, also known as the quadrivalent meningococcal meningitis vaccine.

• **Rabies** If you're spending some time with animals or in the wilderness it's also worth considering having a course of **rabies** injections, consisting of three injections spread over one month, though it isn't pleasant and doesn't prevent you from contracting the disease – it just gives you more time to receive medical help if you do get bitten.

Malaria

Malaria is a problem in Tanzania, which is considered one of the highest risk countries in the world. While you are highly unlikely to contract malaria on Kilimanjaro, which is too high and cold for the anopheles mosquito (the species that carries malaria but which is rarely seen above 1200m – much lower than the altitude you start trekking from on Kili), it is rife in coastal areas and on Zanzibar. It's also present in Moshi and, despite an altitude above 1200m, in Arusha too.

When beginning a course of **anti-malarials**, it is very important to begin taking them before you go; that way the drug is established in your system by the time you set foot on Tanzanian soil and it will give you a chance to see if the drug is going to cause a reaction or allergy. Once started, complete the full course, which usually runs for several weeks after you return home.

Which anti-malarial you need depends on which parts of Africa you are visiting and your previous medical history. Your doctor will be able to advise on what drug is best for you. With Tanzania in the highest risk category, the chances are you will be recommended either Lariam/Mefloquine, or Malarone/Maloff. Stories of Lariam causing hallucinations, nightmares, blindness and even death have been doing the rounds in travellers' circles for years now but if you feel no adverse reaction – and millions don't – carry on taking it and don't worry. Malarone/Maloff are supposedly free of side effects but expensive.

Of course the best way to combat malaria is not to get bitten at all. A **repellent** with 30% Diethyltoluamide (DEET) worn in the evenings when the anopheles mosquito is active should be effective in preventing bites. Some use it during the day too, when the mosquitoes that carry yellow and dengue fevers are active. There's a new, all-natural repellent out that's apparently as effective as DEET called **PMD**. Effective for up to five hours, it's available in the UK under the brand name Incognito (💻 lessmosquito.com).

Alternatively, you could just keep covered up with long-sleeve shirts and long trousers, sleep under a **mosquito net** and with the air-con on high.

Further and up-to-date information

There are four websites that you should consult for the latest advice on vaccinations. In the UK the **NHS website** (💻 www.nhs.uk) is great, as is its sister website **Fit for Travel** (💻 fitfortravel.nhs.uk). Another UK-based website, **Travel Health Pro** (💻 travelhealthpro.org.uk), is good too; while for our

American friends the **US Center for Disease Control** (🖳 www.cdc.gov) provides a wealth of information.

INSURANCE

When buying insurance you must make clear to the insurer that you'll be trekking to the top of a very big mountain. If you are taking an unusual route and will be using ropes you need to tell them that too. Informing them that you're climbing Kili is usually enough to double the premium and may even exclude you from being covered altogether. But if you don't make this clear and pay the lower premium you'll probably find, should you try to make a claim, you aren't actually covered at all.

Remember to **read the small print** of any insurance policy before buying and shop around, too, for each insurance policy varies slightly from company to company. Details to consider include:

- How much is the deductible if you have to make a claim?
- Can the insurers pay for your hospital bills etc immediately, while you are still in Tanzania, or do you have to wait until you get home?
- How long do you have before making a claim and what evidence do you require (hospital bills, police reports etc)?

Remember the premium for the entire trip will probably double when you mention you are hiking above 4000-5000m, even though you will actually be above that altitude for only a few days. However, you will need to be covered for your entire trip: there are just as many nasty things that can happen – indeed, many more – when off the mountain than on it; theft becomes a much bigger issue too.

For **UK residents**, the following companies offer insurance that should cover your Kili trek:

- **Big Cat** (🖳 www.bigcattravelinsurance.com) Their Extreme Activity Pack seems to cover trekking over 4600m, which will be good for Kili and Meru.
- **British Mountaineering Council** (🖳 thebmc.co.uk/insurance) Their Alpine & Ski Policy is the one for Kilimanjaro.
- **Silver Surfers** (🖳 www.silversurfers.com/travel-insurance/) Insurance specialists for the over 60s, recommended by more than one climber.
- **True Traveller** (🖳 truetraveller.com) Their Adventure pack covers treks up to 4500m – but also includes Kilimanjaro.
- **World Nomads** (🖳 worldnomads.com) Their Standard and Explorer plans both cover you up to 6000m.

❑ HELICOPTER RESCUE

There is a helicopter-rescue service, **Kili Medair** (🖳 kilimedair.co.tz) on Kilimanjaro. It might be worth checking to see if your insurance covers this; if not, your trekking company may well offer some sort of helicopter rescue insurance instead which should cost only a few dollars. Helipads are marked on the maps.

❑ MY FAVOURITE PIECE OF ADVICE ON KILIMANJARO

'**WARNING** Due to the rise in the frequency and severity of human-leopard encounters, the Ministry of Tourism, Kilimanjaro Branch, Tanzania, is advising trekkers and anyone else that uses Kilimanjaro for recreational or work-related purposes to take extra precautions while on the mountain.

In particular, I advise that all trekkers wear little bells on their clothing. This will give advanced warning to any leopards that might be close by and thereby prevent you from taking them by surprise. I also advise anyone visiting Kilimanjaro to carry pepper spray with him or her in case of an encounter with a leopard.

Visitors should also be on the watch for any fresh leopard activity, and be able to tell the difference between leopard *cub* shit and big leopard shit:

Leopard cub shit is smaller and contains lots of berries and fur.

Big leopard shit has bells in it, and smells like pepper.

Enjoy your stay in Tanzania!'

This was sent to me by a friend via Facebook and caught me so much by surprise that I snorted tea out of my nose. Hope it had a similar effect on you. (In case you're wondering, it *is* a joke – and, what's more, leopard–human encounters are pretty much unheard of today.)

For **American trekkers** the following have been recommended by readers:

- **Global Rescue** (🖳 www.globalrescue.com) Insurance available for their members.
- **Redpoint** (🖳 redpointtravelprotection.com) Specialist rescue and evacuation insurance company.
- **Travel Guard** (🖳 travelguard.com) have an 'Adventure Sports Bundle' upgrade that covers trekkers on Kilimanjaro.
- **World Nomads** See UK listings, p57.

Ethical trekking: looking after the mountain, the people who work on it, and the whole planet

LOOKING AFTER THE MOUNTAIN

First the good news. I actually think Kilimanjaro, and indeed Tanzania in general, are a lot less blighted by litter than they used to be. The country has worked hard to clean up its act, banning plastic bags and organising clean-up projects throughout the country. And even on the simple drive between Moshi and Arusha, the benefits of these efforts are obvious. Sure, there's still litter around – but it's not as ubiquitous as it used to be. The Tanzanian people need to be congratulated on this: it's not like they don't have other problems to deal with, so to expend so much energy prettifying their country is admirable.

The mountain too, believe me, is a lot less messy than it used to be, even though there are a lot more people marching on it these days than when I first climbed it in 2001. Sure, there is still a lot of litter, and each time you see a piece it makes you despair a little more at humanity's disregard for its planet. But trekkers have, I think, tended to be at the forefront of trying to keep the natural world pristine, and when you think of what the average seaside resort looks like after a sunny bank holiday, I think the relatively small amount of litter on Kili bears out my opinion.

Below you'll see find a whole section on how you can do your bit to keep the mountain looking gorgeous. But while I'm not for one minute absolving trekkers of all blame for the litter on Kili (I have seen several climbers down the years whose attitude towards litter, and where it should be deposited, is shameful); but if there is still litter on Kili, and on the whole the climbers themselves aren't dropping it, then who is?

Well, the only other possible culprits are the trekking companies themselves, and their crews....

Leave No Trace (LNT)

It's all very well doing your best to keep the mountain looking as pristine as possible for the next visitor who follows in your footsteps – but how can you be sure that your company is being just as conscientious? The answer – perhaps – is to see if they have a relationship with the NGO **Leave No Trace** (💻 lnt.org). The non-profit Leave No Trace Center for Outdoor Ethics was formed in 1994 to promote minimum impact practices for anyone visiting the outdoors. At the heart of its work is education – teaching people about how to look after the countryside and the natural world in general. And their education programmes take in Kilimanjaro too, as with the collaboration they instruct a trekking company's mountain crews about conservation on the mountain. They also offer training courses to crew members (usually porters) so that they too can become LNT instructors, spreading the word and passing on their knowledge to others. Though the role of LNT instructor isn't paid, it should mean they get more work.

Having the Leave No Trace logo on their website means a company is an LNT partner and supports they work they do. Of course, carrying such a logo could be seen as little more than empty virtue signalling. But it does at least indicate that the company has thought about the problem of littering on the mountain and has made some sort of promise to adhere to the Leave No Trace principles.

LOOKING AFTER YOUR CREW

Nobody should underestimate the achievement of reaching the summit of Kilimanjaro. For five days or so you've dragged yourself up around 4000m of vertical height, through four different seasons, on terrain that may be as alien to you as the moon. Imagine then, trying to do the same trek while eating only one square meal a day, with nothing but a pair of second-hand plimsolls on your feet and tatty cast-offs for clothes; that your days on the mountain are spent carrying up to 30kg on your back or head, while your nights are spent sharing a draughty four-man tent with up to nine other people, often with no ground mats and inadequate sleeping bags. And that, should anything go wrong – which, given the conditions you're expected to work in, they very well might – there'll be no insurance to cover you.

Imagine, furthermore, climbing not out of a lifelong desire to be on Africa's highest mountain, but out of necessity; for if you don't submit yourself to these deprivations you won't be able to fund yourself through college or feed your children. Imagine, too, that your reward for putting up with such conditions is somewhere around Ts13,123 (US$5.50) per day (the average wage for porters with non-KPAP companies in 2022); and that, out of this, you have to pay for your transport to and from the mountain, your food whilst on the mountain (which is why you eat only once a day) and you may even have to bribe the guide in order to be allowed on Kili in the first place. No wonder you often end up relying on tips from tourists in order to take home any money from your labours – tips that, if you're unlucky, may end up in the pocket of that same guide you bribed in order to get a job in the first place.

Such is the lot for many porters on Kilimanjaro: a precarious existence that, at best, involves hardship and indignity, and at worst can lead to death, as happens to porters several times per year on the mountain. It is these kinds of conditions that various organisations are now trying to improve. Foremost amongst these – and the only one I trust – is KPAP.

The Kilimanjaro Porters Assistance Project (KPAP)

Registered at the beginning of 2003, KPAP (💻 kiliporters.org) is an initiative of the American-based International Mountain Explorers Connection (IMEC; see p64), which fights for porters' rights worldwide. In Tanzania their base is a small office (open roughly Mon-Sat 8am-4pm, and sometimes on Sunday too) on Boma Rd in Moshi, run by the capable and urbane Kelvin Salla.

According to their manifesto, the organisation's focus is on improving the working conditions of the porters on Kilimanjaro. They do this in several ways:

- Making available appropriate climbing gear for any porter or guide to borrow. KPAP has a couple of wardrobes full of good-quality trekking gear, much of it donated by climbers and clothing companies from North American and Europe and couriered over by trekkers. For a returnable deposit (which can be anything from a bicycle to a smart phone) the porter can borrow for free items of clothing such as fleeces, boots etc.
- Educating the climbers, travel industry and general public on proper porter treatment.
- Encouraging climbers and travel agents to select a climbing company with responsible practices towards their crew (KPAP partners).
- Assisting climbing companies with implementing procedures that ensure fair and ethical treatment of their porters.

The partnership scheme

KPAP tries to encourage the local climbing companies to improve the way they treat their crew via the **'Partner for Responsible Travel'** scheme. Established in 2006, the Partner Program was created to recognise and highlight those tour operators committed to fair treatment of the mountain crew.

Despite what several trekking companies may tell you, **there is no charge to become a KPAP partner.** Instead, in order to join the scheme companies have to conform to certain guidelines issued by KPAP. These include directives

❑ JAMBO BWANA – KILIMANJARO'S VERY OWN THEME TUNE

Jambo, Jambo Bwana,	(Hello, hello sir)
Habari gani,	(How are you?)
Msuri sana,	(I'm very well)
Wageni Wakaribishwa Kilimanjaro,	(Visitors are very welcome to Kilimanjaro)
Hakuna matata!	(No problem!)

Anybody who's spent more than a day or two on the mountain will undoubtedly have heard the guides and porters belting this song out. Indeed, it seems rare to arrive at a campsite these days and not hear it being sung by one expedition or another. By the end of the trek, it's highly likely you'll know all the lyrics and be singing along too.

The song was first recorded in 1982 by Them Mushrooms, a Kenyan ensemble formed in the early seventies who used to ply their trade at the luxury beach hotels in Mombasa. The song was written by the band's leader, Teddy Kalanda, though he borrowed heavily from traditional folk tunes around at the time. In the Mushrooms' version there was no mention of Kilimanjaro at all – instead the original song welcomed people to *Kenya yetu*, or 'our Kenya'.

The song proved to be a big hit, selling over 200,000 copies, and was subsequently covered by several other African bands including Mombasa Roots, Safari Sound Band, Khadja Nin and Adam Solomon. Worldwide fame, however, arrived when the German-Caribbean disco outfit Boney M released their version, *Jambo – Hakuna Matata* – though the lyrics were heavily doctored and only the first and last lines of the original survived.

on porters' wages (which KPAP have said has to be a minimum of Ts20,000 per day), a limit on the amount the porters are required to carry, the amount of food and water they receive on the mountain, what the sleeping conditions are like and how they are treated in the event of an accident or sickness. Several of these guidelines are already covered by KINAPA's (see p165) own rules. Unfortunately, some companies take advantage of the lack of enforcement. It is true that the bags are weighed at every gate to make sure the porter isn't over-burdened – but the practice of bribery is as widespread on the mountain as it is elsewhere in Tanzania; it doesn't take much for a guide to hand over a few thousand shillings to a warden to persuade him to record incorrectly what the scales are saying. Similarly, while KINAPA have set a minimum wage of US$10 per day for the porters, those companies (the majority) who want to pay their porters less than this just ignore it – which is why many porters end up with Ts10,000 (US$5) or less per day.

So it was left to KPAP to come up with a set of standards of their own and to devise a system to make sure they are followed properly. In order to be considered as a partner, the trekking operator not only has to adhere to KPAP's guidelines but also has to allow KPAP to monitor them, too, to make sure they stick to them. If the trekking operator manages to fulfil all these criteria the benefits, in terms of increased marketing opportunities and the extra demand that comes from being known as a Partner for Responsible Travel, are considerable.

There are several ways in which KPAP monitors their partner companies but the most effective way is the 'investigative porter' method, in which the partner company allows an undercover worker on *all* their climbs. This porter has been trained by KPAP to report back on the treatment meted out to the crew on each trek. This has proved to be a highly effective way of monitoring how well a partner company is treating their staff. If the company fails to meet the standards set by KPAP on the trek, they are advised on where they failed and how they can improve; if they continue to slip up, however, they will be forced to leave the Partnership scheme altogether.

I genuinely believe KPAP to be the *only* organisation that properly monitors what is happening on the mountain and, as such, their opinions should be relied upon to an even greater extent than more established campaign groups such as Tourism Concern. KPAP is a fantastic charity, working on a shoestring and fighting for the rights of porters, despite opposition and criticism.

KPAP's achievements

It's one thing to have set of noble aims, but quite another to actually achieve them, of course. Yet KPAP's methods seem to be working. According to their latest figures, where porters working for a non-KPAP company were paid on average Ts25,860 per day (in wages and tip) in 2022, a porter with a KPAP company can expect to earn an average daily amount of Ts36,074. That's almost a third more. And where porters who don't work for a KPAP partner company can expect two meals per day, porters with KPAP companies can expect three.

And so it goes on: by all other measures of welfare on the mountain – how much the porters are asked to carry, whether they sleep in a good tent with sufficient space for each person, whether the tipping procedure is transparent etc – the statistics show that a KPAP porter is simply treated better than his brethren who don't work with a partner company.

It is for this reason, perhaps, that the NGO has been recognised for its groundbreaking work, winning gold at both the WTM in London and the World Responsible Tourism Awards Africa 2022. No surprise, then, that they also took silver at the Meaningful Tourism Global Awards that same year for sustaining employees and communities during the pandemic. Theses prizes, though they were never the aim of KPAP, are richly deserved.

So how can you help?

The most straightforward way to help the campaign for the better treatment of porters is to **book your trek with a KPAP partner company**. This is a surefire way to ensure that your crew will be treated fairly by their employers. You may be persuaded by a company's website that drones on about how altruistic they are and how well they treat their porters. But if they aren't KPAP partners, you need to ask yourself: why not? Why aren't they prepared to subject themselves to the scrutiny of an independent body like KPAP? It's free, after all. What are they hiding? And having asked yourself why they aren't KPAP partners – you then need to ask them. They will doubtless come out with all sorts of excuses and a few may denigrate the work of KPAP and even slander them.

Several may try to hoodwink you and say that they are actually partners or are in the process of becoming one, when the reality is they aren't, and have no intention of doing so. For this reason it's **vital you visit the KPAP website** to find out the latest list of KPAP partners. You can also contact Kelvin Salla (💻 info@kiliporters.org) to ask about a specific company and see if their claims actually contain any truth.

What if, for some reason, you're not on a trek organised by a KPAP partner? While this list is extensive, if you can do any of the following it would be a help:

• **1 Make sure your porters are outfitted with appropriate clothing** Porters need adequate footwear, socks, waterproof jackets and trousers (pants), gloves, hats, etc. They are also required by the park authority to have a torch and sunglasses. Clothing can be borrowed for free at the KPAP office in Moshi; make sure your porters know this.

• **2 Fair wages should be paid to the porters** See p30 for the minimum wages KINAPA are proposing to introduce and enforce. Ask your porters how much they are paid and if it includes food. Showing that you care about such things will encourage all operators and guides to treat their porters fairly.

• **3 Make sure porters have proper food and water** If they are required to purchase their own food, wages should be increased accordingly.

• **4 Check the weights of porters' loads** Kilimanjaro National Park (KINAPA) has a maximum carrying weight per porter of 20kg. If you can, be there at the luggage weighing at the start of the trek to make sure no funny business is going on.

If additional porters need to be hired, do ensure that the tour company is paying each porter their full wage when you return.

• **5 Count the number of porters every day** Know the number of people in your crew. After all, you are paying for them. If there are any missing, ask where they are. If they've been sent down the mountain, ask why, and whether they will still receive both a fair wage and their share of the tips.

• **6 Make sure your porters are provided with proper shelter** Where no shelter is available (ie on all routes other than Marangu), porters need proper accommodation: that means their own tents and sleeping bags.

• **7 Ensure your porters are given the tips you intend for them** Give your tips to the guide and you run the risk that they won't pass on the full amount to your crew. Tipping directly to each individual crew member ensures they receive their fair share.

• **8 Ensure any sick or injured porters are properly cared for** Porters deserve the same standard of care as their clients. Sick or injured porters need to be sent back with someone who speaks their language and understands the problem.

• **9 Get to know your porters and thank them** Some porters speak English and will appreciate your making an effort to speak with them. The Swahili word *pole* (pronounced 'polay') – which translates as 'I'm sorry for you' – shows respect for porters after a hard day carrying your bags. *Ahsante* ('asantay') means 'Thank you'. Don't forget to share your sweets and snacks with any porter who happens to be passing – it's the easiest way to break the ice, even if they don't speak any English.

• **10 Report any instances of abuse or neglect** To both the trekking operator concerned and, more importantly, to KPAP.

• **11 Complete the post-climb survey** This is perhaps the most important and easiest thing you can do. Before heading off up the mountain, pick up a questionnaire from the KPAP office in Moshi, or the website, as this will remind you of what to look out for on the mountain. By providing KPAP with your feedback regarding the tour company's treatment of its staff, they will be able to share with the company any problem areas that need to be corrected.

12 Donate! Please visit 💻 kiliporters.org/support-our-work-donate.

Further details

Kilimanjaro Porters Assistance Project (KPAP) 💻 kiliporters.org; **Facebook**: 💻 www.facebook.com/kpaptz; **Instagram**: 💻 www.instagram.com/kilimanjaroporterstz/; **Twitter/X**: 💻 twitter.com/kpap_tz

• **International Mountain Explorers Connection** 💻 mountainexplorers.org IMEC is the umbrella organisation of which KPAP is a part.

LOOKING AFTER THE PLANET

You like travelling. You like visiting foreign destinations, tasting exotic food, engaging with different cultures, savouring unique environments and beautiful landscapes – and all that other lovely stuff that comes with going abroad. But in these times of global warming taking a multi-hour, multi-continent flight just to walk up a mountain for a week is not a particularly 'good look'; indeed, it can be seen as incredibly selfish. And I'm sure you would prefer it if, in indulging your passion for peregrinating, you weren't also simultaneously destroying the planet.

Which is where the whole concept of carbon offsetting comes in. Carbon offsetting is the process whereby you concede that by travelling you are inevitably generating more carbon that's pumped out into the atmosphere, but to compensate for this you partake in schemes that are designed to reduce the amount of carbon dioxide in the atmosphere. And when I say 'partake', I really mean 'donate money to', with the size of your donation a monetary equivalent of the amount of extra CO_2 your travelling emitted.

For example, you may decide to plant five trees in your back garden when you get home from your trip, and leave them to mature, thereby sucking carbon out of the atmosphere – which would, over time, more than balance the negative impact you had on the Earth's climate from your trek. But unfortunately, not all of us have the time or inclination to plant five trees, and even fewer of us have a garden big enough to plant them. Luckily, there are various organisations that, for a small fee, will do the offsetting for you. The most relevant, at least for visitors to the land of Kilimanjaro, is Carbon Tanzania (or CT, as I'll call them from now on; 💻 www.carbontanzania.com).

Carbon Tanzania

Set up a dozen years ago, Carbon Tanzania (CT) are actually based in England, but all the offsetting projects they work on are in East Africa, where they partner with the local villages in their conservation projects. CT provide the link between the local villagers who are preserving the land and the climbers who are interested in offsetting their trek so that it's carbon neutral.

So how does it work? The system, in its simplest form, works like this. The local villages have some land they are struggling to conserve, because they lack the necessary resources required to do so. CT step in to provide the resources and thereby enable this land to be preserved. At the end of the year, CT then call in third party 'carbon auditors', specialists who are able to quantify exactly the success of the project, and in particular, how much carbon, in tonnes, has been sequestered by this conserved land.

So, for example, Carbon Tanzania's Yaeda-Eyasi Landscape Project, which protects 110,500 ha of drylands forest, results in 172,000 tonnes of emission reductions. CT are then issued with 172,000 carbon credits, which they can then take to the market to sell (currently for US$15 per credit). Who to? Well, to climbers like you and me who want to offset the carbon emissions from their trek. The profits are then split between themselves and the village, with a minimum of 60% going to the villagers.

Thus, CT can be seen as acting as a bridge between the village and the climber, enabling both parties to benefit. The climber can have a guilt-free trek, because he is able to offset the carbon emissions from his trek, while the village earns money from their conservation efforts. What's more, this in turn provides an incentive to the village to continue to preserve their land because, by doing so, they will continue to earn money from it. And the more land they preserve, the more money they will earn, money which can then be spent on, for example, setting up a health centre in the area, or a primary school.

You talk about conserving the land, but I thought offsetting was more about planting trees and reforestation, rather than just conserving the ones we already have? It may surprise you to know that, because Tanzania still has about 46% forest cover (compared, say, to Kenya's 6%), so much of CT's work is actually about conserving what the country has. So, for the time being at least, the focus of the business (and it is, at the end of the day, a social enterprise, rather than an NGO) is on protecting the forests that exist, rather than reforestation.

Projects that CT were working on at the time of writing include the Yaeda Valley, home of Hadza hunter-gatherers (with whom some of you may be spending time on safari after your trek), and the Makame Savannah Project running south-east of Tarangire National Park.

So how much will it cost for me to have a carbon neutral trek? Trekking is a pretty low-carbon activity. CT have worked out that an average 7-day trek for two people, including one night in a hotel beforehand and airport transfers, would emit about a third of a tonne in carbon per person. Those emissions may come from the electricity you use in a hotel, or the transport you use to get to and from the mountain (they have assumed you are staying in Arusha). But there's little actual emissions once you're on the mountain.

CT sell a single carbon credit for US$15 per tonne. So if you want your trek to be carbon neutral, you need to **pay just US$5** to CT (ie the price of a third of a tonne), which they then take back to the village to share with them.

Note that if there are more than two of you in the group, the per person amount you would need to pay for a carbon neutral trek actually falls, as the emissions from the bus taking you to and from the mountain are shared between more of you.

Just US$5 to have a guilt-free trek? Great! Where do I sign up? Both African Environments and Kilimanjaro Experts have a formal relationship with Carbon Tanzania. If you sign up with them – probably all you need do is tick a box on your booking form – and a small sum will be added to your invoice to offset your trek. It's as simple as that. Of course, if you also want to offset your safari, that is a separate issue and a separate cost – but your company or CT should be able to provide an estimate of how much extra that would cost.

If you're not climbing with either company, but still want to be carbon neutral, you can buy carbon credits independently – just get in touch with Carbon Tanzania about this. Alternatively, at least one other company (take a bow, Tanzania Journeys) organise their own tree-planting program which should help to mitigate the emissions from your trip.

Do remember, too, that your flight is sure to be the biggest single carbon emitter for your trek – though hopefully your airline will also offer you the chance to offset your journey.

BOOKING YOUR TRIP 2

Welcome to the most boring chapter in the book. Boring but also, perhaps, the most necessary. For alongside your decisions on which friends should come with you and when to climb, which were covered in the previous chapter, your choice of route and trekking company will go a long way to determining whether your trek is a safe, successful and happy one… or an unmitigated disaster leading to the breakdown of relationships, divorce, subsequent financial ruin, loss of self-esteem and years of counselling.

So the following pages are devoted to briefly reviewing the routes and then looking in depth at the companies that operate treks up the mountain.

The routes up Kilimanjaro

This section is devoted to looking at the various paths leading to the summit of Africa's Highest Mountain (and back down from it too). Looking down at Kilimanjaro from above you should be able to count **eight paths** trailing like ribbons up the sides of the mountain. Six of these are **ascent-only paths** (ie you can only walk *up* the mountain on them; you are not allowed to come down on these trails); one, Mweka, is a descent-only path; and one, the Marangu Route, is both an ascent and descent trail.

It should be noted that KINAPA, the park authority, is planning to establish two other routes (Kidia and Irkwassa) up Kili, which I talk about on pp386-8.

The ascent routes [see colour map p22]

The ascent trails leading up to the foot of Kibo are (running anticlockwise, beginning with the westernmost trails): the **Shira Plateau Route**, **Lemosho Route**, **Machame Route**, **Umbwe Route**, **Marangu Route** (also a descent path) and, running from the north-eastern side, the **Rongai (Loitokitok) Route**.

Each of these eventually meets with a path circling the main Kibo cone, a path known as either the **Northern Circuit** or the **Southern Circuit** depending on which side of the mountain you are.

From the Northern and Southern Circuit paths, just three trails lead up to the Crater Rim and the summit itself: if open the **Western**

Breach Route (aka the **Arrow Glacier Route**), **Barafu Route** and the nameless third path which runs up from Kibo Huts to Gillman's Point, which I have always called the **Kibo Huts Route**. Which of these you take to the summit will depend upon which path you took to get this far: the Shira, Lemosho, Machame and Umbwe routes can use either the difficult Western Breach Route (closed at time of writing) or the easier, safer, more popular but longer Barafu Route, while the Marangu and Rongai trails use the Kibo Huts Route.

There now follows a *brief* introduction to each of the main *ascent* trails in the order in which they appear in the book. You'll see that for each trail I have written the *typical* number of days that it takes to complete each route. **Note these refer to the total time it takes from the gate to the summit and back down again to the designated exit gate. This descent is assumed to take a day and a half** whatever route you take; so, assuming you climbed to the summit during the night and arrived at the peak at dawn, you'll begin to descend from the summit soon after sunrise and, all being well, you'll reach the gate at around lunchtime the next day.

❑ WHICH ROUTE DO CLIMBERS TAKE?

Which route do they all take?

So which routes do all these climbers use? Based on the last available figures from KINAPA (the park authority) – I'm not sure how reliable they are, but they are the best I can get – the route choices are as below:

Machame: 20,339	**Rongai**: 4088	**Marangu**: 12,289
Umbwe: 589	**Shira/Lemosho**: 9927	

The thing that leaps out at you about these figures is that Machame is still, quite significantly, the most popular route, a position it has held since 2006/7 when it first knocked Marangu into second place. This won't surprise anybody who's trekked on this trail for the past few years – but will come as a blow to those many foreign agents who still try to hype the 'Whiskey Route' as a wild and untrammelled path. Remember, too, that the Marangu Route gets trekkers all year-round, because people on this route sleep in dormitories in huts rather than under canvas so it still gets trekkers during the rainy season, while the Machame Route is virtually deserted at that time; which means, of course, that during the rest of the year they must get many, many more people than the Marangu Route.

Other points to note? Well, it's interesting how much the Lemosho/Shira Route has grown in popularity to become the third busiest route (from 7807 in 2012). That may have something to do with this book, which has always sung its praises, as well as an increasing awareness amongst trekkers that a longer route is better for acclimatisation. I'm pleased it's doing so well – but there's a part of me, of course, that doesn't want it to get *too* popular – that just leads to overcrowding and a decrease in the magic that made it so special in the first place.

Finally, I do find it a little surprising to see how unpopular the Umbwe Route continues to be. It's a beautiful route and, being close to Moshi, a convenient one for the agencies to use. But its reputation as the 'hardest' route seems enough to deter most people from taking it.

Descending Kilimanjaro: the designated descents

In an attempt to control the number of people walking on each trail, and thus limit the amount of soil erosion on some of the more popular routes, KINAPA introduced regulations regarding the descent routes and which ones you are allowed to take. In general, the main rule is as follows: those ascending Kilimanjaro from the west, south-west or south (ie by taking the Machame, Umbwe, Lemosho, or Shira Plateau routes) must take as their descent route the **Mweka trail** (see pp362-8); whereas if you have climbed the mountain from the south-east or north (ie on the Marangu or Rongai/Loitokitok trails) you must descend by the **Marangu Route** (pp360-2).

Those trekkers who wish to **deviate from these rules** should first seek permission from KINAPA; begin making contact with them well in advance of your trek as the process can take a long time.

The Marangu Route (full description pp273-92; 5-6 days including descent) The oldest and once the most popular trail on the mountain, the Marangu Route also has the dubious honour of having the lowest success rate

HOW MANY CLIMBERS REACH THE TOP?

I was provided with one more table by KINAPA but whereas I am inclined to believe the other figures that they gave me, I am less inclined to trust these:

Point reached	Number of climbers	Percentage
Stella Point	1367	3.33%
Gillman's Point	12,784	31.14%
Uhuru Peak	26,685	65.00%
Unsuccessful	218	0.53%
TOTAL	**41,054**	**100%**

Why am I so sceptical about these figures? Well, firstly, they are incomplete: according to the above tables (taken from the last available figures), 47,232 people climbed Kilimanjaro, yet only 41,054 are recorded on this table. Secondly, their claim that only 0.53% fail to get even to the Crater Rim (ie either Stella or Gillman's) is, to be blunt, ludicrous. Thirdly, 31.14% got to Gillman's, yet only 3.33% got to Stella – even though they are at approximately the same altitude and more people access the Crater rim via Stella than via Gillman's. And lastly, at the risk of sounding cynical, if there's one set of statistics that KINAPA has an incentive to manipulate, it's the success rate – they want to make the mountain as appealing as possible, of course, and displaying a high rate of success for people attempting to get to the summit is one way of doing that.

Given that this table suggests only 41,054 people, rather than the full 47,232, I could, I suppose, assume that the 6178 people *not* recorded in this table (ie 47,232 less 41,054) *all* failed to reach the Crater Rim. This would give us a total of 218 + 6178 = 6396 who failed to get to either Gillman's or Stella, or approximately 13.5% of the total, which to us looks a lot more believable. But this is just guesswork on my part and as such is no more reliable than KINAPA's own figures on this matter.

for getting trekkers to the summit. This is presumably because it is the one route where you can pay to be on the mountain for just five days – where other routes require you to pay for a minimum of six. It is also the one that comes closest (though not very) to the trail Hans Meyer took in making the first successful assault on the summit (see pp154-7). Furthermore it is the only ascent trail where camping is not allowed, with trekkers sleeping in dormitory huts along the way. From Kibo Huts, trekkers climb up to the summit via Gillman's Point. The trail should take a minimum of five days and four nights to complete, though an extra night is usually taken after the second day to allow trekkers more time to acclimatise.

Though beautiful, the main disadvantage is that you descend on the same route as you ascended, so you essentially see the same scenery twice.

The Machame Route (full description pp292-311; 6-7 days including descent) The Machame Route has now overtaken Marangu as the most popular trail. Though widely regarded as more difficult than the Marangu Route, the success rate on this trail is higher, possibly because it is a day longer at six days and five nights (assuming you take the Barafu Route to the summit), which gives trekkers more time to acclimatise; most trekkers also take an extra acclimatisation day near the Karanga Valley, thereby making it seven days in total. You can also take the more difficult Western Breach Route (if open) though this shortens the trek by a day or two; it would thus be wise to build in acclimatisation days if taking this option.

The Lemosho, Shira Plateau & Northern Circuit routes (pp312-37; 6-8 days in total including descent) All these routes run from west to east across the centre of the Shira Plateau. The **Shira Plateau Route** is the original plateau trail though it seldom sees trekkers these days, with much of it now a 4WD track used mainly by emergency vehicles. Walkers embarking on this trail often begin their trek above the forest in the moorland zone at the Morum

❑ DAY TRIPS

If for some reason you cannot climb all the way to the top but nevertheless wish to experience the pleasure of walking on Africa's biggest and most beautiful mountain, it is possible to enter the park for one day only. There are some advantages in doing this. It's safer for one thing, for few will get beyond 3000m altitude in one day so altitude sickness shouldn't be an issue. With no camping or rescue fees, porters' wages or food to pay, it will work out much cheaper too: factor in US$70 per day entry fee, plus a wage for the compulsory guide, transport to and from the mountain and a packed lunch, and the whole package can cost as little as US$100.

Marangu Gate has a **3-hour nature loop** through the cloud forest, which is lovely and from which you can descend either via the trekkers' trail or the less scenic but faster porters' route. There are also some seldom-visited waterfalls in the area. The ambitious can attempt to reach the Mandara Huts (p278 & p280) and descend again in one day. Furthermore, just 15 minutes beyond the Huts – through a small patch of forest alive with monkeys – is Maundi Crater (p278), with excellent views of Kibo and Mawenzi to the north-west and the flat African plains stretching away to the east.

❑ FREE ADVICE

Remember that if this chapter is too long and dreary for you, simply get in touch with us via my website 💻 climbmountkilimanjaro.com, tell us what you're looking for from your trekking company and the budget you have for your trek and I'll do my best to advise you. I promise you that I will try to be as unbiased as possible, and won't treat our conversation as a chance to push you towards my own company Kilimanjaro Experts – even though, of course, I think everyone should be organising their trek with us! And best of all, I don't even charge for this advice!

Barrier. After traversing the plateau the trekker has several choices. Firstly, one can climb Kibo via the Western Breach/Arrow Glacier Route; follow this route and you can expect the trek to last a total of six days and five nights. Or you can take the longer and easier Barafu Route, which extends the trek by a day to around seven days, or eight days if extra overnight stops on the plateau and around the Karanga Valley are taken. Or there's another option, heading round the quieter northern slopes of Kibo on the Northern Circuit, ascending via School Huts and Gillman's Point to the summit, for a 7- to 8-day trek in total.

The **Lemosho Route** (aka the **Lemosho Glades Route**) improves on the Shira Plateau Route by starting below the Shira Ridge, thus providing trekkers with a walk in the forest at the trek's start, giving them more time to acclimatise and enabling them to enjoy, in my opinion, the best forest on the mountain. As with the Shira Plateau Route, you can ascend Kibo either by the Western Breach (if open), the Barafu Route or the Northern Circuit; allow six or seven days for the first one, or a recommended eight days for the last two options.

The Rongai Route (pp337-51; 6-7 days including descent) This is the only official trail to approach Kibo from the north. Indeed, the original trail began right against the Kenyan border, though recently it shifted eastwards and now starts at the Tanzanian town of **Loitokitok** after which the new trail has been named (though everybody still refers to it as the Rongai Route it is also sometimes called the **Nalemuru/Nalemoru Route**, after the nearby river).

For the final push to the summit, trekkers take the Kibo Huts Route, joining it either at the huts themselves or just below Hans Meyer Cave, after spending the penultimate night at School Huts. You're not allowed to take fewer than six days and five nights on this trail, though if you've taken the detour to camp beneath Mawenzi peak, you might take seven.

The Umbwe Route (pp351-9; 6-7 days including descent) The hardest and statistically the least popular trail (Shira probably comes a close second in the unpopularity stakes but its figures tend to be lumped together with those of Lemosho), the Umbwe Route is also, in my opinion, perhaps the most beautiful. The trek involves a tough vertical slog up Kili's southern slopes, in places using the tree roots as makeshift rungs on a ladder. Having reached the Southern Circuit, trekkers traditionally continue north-west to tackle Kibo from the west and the more difficult Arrow Glacier/Western Breach Route, though you can also head east round to Barafu and approach the summit from there. The entire walk takes a minimum of six days though seven days, while a long time for such a short trail, is much more sensible for acclimatisation purposes.

New ascent routes See pp386-8 for details of the planned revival of the Kidia Route and the introduction of a completely new trail, Irkwassa, in 2024.

Who should you book with?

A brief flick through these pages will lead you to realise that I have concentrated on Tanzanian companies rather than the overseas agents. The reason for this is obvious: **the Tanzanian companies are the ones that are actually going to take you up the mountain**.

When a company in the US, UK, Europe etc offers you a trek, all they are doing, usually, is acting as middlemen for a Tanzanian company who will be the ones who organise the hike. True, some of the more involved ones will have an influence on how the local operator runs its treks, and several agencies have actually set up companies so they can effectively control how their trek is organised. But more often than not no matter what the branding may say on the side of your tent or on the T-shirts that the porters wear, the people inside those T-shirts are not in the employment of the foreign agency through whom you may have booked your trek, but the ground operator that your agent uses to organise and run the expedition.

So, I hear you ask: why not cut out the middleman and book directly with the ground operator? Well, it's a good question and in most instances, yes, it's cheaper to book with the local operator. That said, there could be some advantages with booking instead through an agent in your home country. The drawbacks and advantages of both options are discussed now.

SHOULD YOU BOOK WITH A TANZANIAN OPERATOR – OR WITH AN AGENT FROM YOUR HOME COUNTRY?

The answer to this depends on what the foreign agencies are adding to the package provided by the local ground operator. In many cases they may be adding nothing at all, except perhaps the reassurance that comes from dealing with an agency that you may already know and one that is based in your home country. It may also be easier for you to get compensation from them should something go wrong, and their insurance is likely to be more comprehensive should something go *seriously* wrong on the mountain.

Occasionally, some agencies send a North American or European tour leader to work alongside the local guide on each trek, which some people are reassured by; I've mentioned a few of the agencies I know that do this in the box opposite. But even assuming they don't, your agency will hopefully have done its homework and checked out the ground operators thoroughly, and flown to Moshi or

Arusha to compare a few of them, thus providing you with peace of mind that the Tanzanian operator you'll be climbing with isn't totally terrible.

Another advantage, with UK and European agencies at least, is that they are required to provide a bond or to join an institution such as ABTA which means that, should they fall into financial trouble, their clients' money is safe and will be refunded; other countries may have similar schemes. What's more, the chances are that the language spoken by the agent in your country will be your language; and if that language is English, it will be superior to that of the Tanzanian operator, for whom English will be his or her third language (after Swahili and their tribal tongue). Your agent's response may also be more prompt; though the situation has improved, Tanzanians can sometimes be rather slack at replying to an enquiry.

And then there's the payment. It always feels a lot less, well, *scary*, sending payment to someone in your home country, rather than transferring thousands of dollars to some bloke in deepest, darkest Africa whom you've never even met. And if you pay by credit card, the banking system in Tanzania charges somewhere between 3% and 5% for this – which can easily amount to several

❑ ARE THERE ANY OVERSEAS AGENCIES THAT STAND OUT?

Most overseas agencies are pretty indistinguishable from one another. But there are one or two who stick out from the crowd because they offer something different. The following agents, for example, always **send one of their own representatives to 'lead' the group**.

As these individuals do not have the necessary licence to be in charge of the actual trek, they work alongside the local guide who, in the eyes of the park authority, will be the real leader of the trek. The Western representative will also be called something like 'tour leader' to distinguish them from the (local) head guide. These guides vary in quality and experience, of course, though most will have some sort of medical qualification, usually **Wilderness First Responder (WFR)**, and will probably have climbed Kili and several other mountains on numerous occasions before.

In the US, **Rainier (RMI)**, **Alpine Ascents** and **International Mountain Guides** all send a tour leader to accompany their treks, while in Europe look at **Earth's Edge** in Ireland, **Action Challenge** in the UK (who both include a doctor as well as a Western tour leader on their treks) and **Kauffman** of Switzerland.

One other agency that I have come to respect over the years is **African Travel Resource** (ATR). They have been around as long as I've been working on Kilimanjaro, and have always seemed more knowledgeable than most about the mountain (and the African continent as a whole, as their name would suggest), as well as honest and friendly. They also innovated, being one of the first to offer the **ALTOX oxygen system** (see p252) with their operator, The African Safari Trails (TAST). Now obviously ALTOX has its detractors and isn't universally adored, which is perhaps why it hasn't been adopted by every other agency and operator. But the fact they bothered to introduce it shows that they do think about the service they provide, and try to offer something different to their climb.

Finally, **Ultimate Kilimanjaro**, **Kandoo** and **Peak Planet** all deserve a mention too; they don't offer anything out of the ordinary but, given the sheer number of trekkers they bring each year, it would be perverse *not* to recognise them.

hundred dollars in total; pay by credit card with your agent at home and the charges, if they exist at all, are unlikely to be anything like as large.

Booking with a Tanzanian operator

Looking at the other side of the argument, **it will nearly always be cheaper to book directly with a Tanzanian operator**. By doing so, you'll be cutting out the middleman (ie the agency in your country) and removing any fee that they have added to the basic trek cost. **You'll also be dealing directly with those who are actually organising the trek**, and who have a lot of experience on the mountain – rather than somebody who has never climbed Kilimanjaro, indeed may never have been within 5000 miles of the mountain, and when answering your emails must resort to spouting something they were taught at a workshop when training for their job (a role for which they've probably been given the ludicrously inaccurate title of 'trekking expert', 'Kilimanjaro specialist' or some other such nonsense).

And while it may be true that the response of the foreign agent will usually be more prompt, you'll get a more precise reply from a Tanzanian agent who will probably know first-hand how difficult the third day on the Rongai Route is, for example, or how likely it is to rain in September on the Lemosho Route, or what kind of menu you can expect as a vegetarian. Furthermore, a few local agencies actually have a 'Westerner' as one of the owners or managers, and often they'll be the person who answers the emails – so their response to your enquiry may not be that tardy after all, and may be written in English that's every bit as good as yours.

Of course, you don't even need to wait until you arrive in Tanzania before booking with a local operator: pretty much every operator in Arusha and Moshi now has online-booking services and while it may seem a bit scary sending a four-figure sum to people in East Africa whom you've never met, most companies are used to receiving bookings this way and are trustworthy. What's more, if you go with an operator that's been recommended in this book or by friends, there's no reason why it should be any more risky than if you were booking with an agency in your home country; indeed, there's a slim chance that you might even end up joining a group who *did* book their tour abroad and paid more as a consequence.

Before you do commit to anything, however, do visit my website and drop me a line at henry@climbmountkilimanjaro.com to make sure that the company you're interested in is still running and still has a good reputation. Similarly, if you want to book with a KPAP-partner company, do check out the KPAP website (🖳 kiliporters.org) for the latest list and write to them to find out how well your company is treating its porters.

WHAT TO LOOK FOR IN YOUR TREK PACKAGE

So, having done all the necessary research, you've found a suitable operator offering the trek you want for the required duration at an acceptable price. Before you sign on any metaphorical dotted lines, however, you need to be absolutely sure that you know what you're paying for. In other words, **you need to sort out *exactly* what is and isn't included in the price of the trek**.

Don't just ask what you are getting for your money: ask what you *aren't* getting too – ie what you will need to pay out of your own pocket. Once you have this information you'll get a good idea of exactly how much extra you need to pay in addition to the basic cost of the trek.

The following should be included:

- All park fees (see p29) and forest fees for your group.
- Hire of porters, assistant guides and guides, their wages, park fees and food.
- Food and water for the entire trek. Get a breakdown of exactly how many meals per day you will be given: normally trekkers are served three main meals per day plus a snack – typically a hot drink with popcorn and biscuits – upon arrival at camp at the end of the day; see box p272 for more details on food on the trek.
- Transport to and from the park at the beginning and end of the hike.
- Hire of camping and cooking gear. If you have brought your own gear, you might be able to persuade the operator to reduce the cost of your trek, though it will be by only a small amount.
- Hire of any equipment – torches, trekking poles, spare water-bottles – that you don't want to bring with you from home. There will probably be a small surcharge for these; just make sure that whatever you agree is included in the contract.
- Any special dietary requirements or other needs, all of which should be stipulated in the contract.
- Any free night's accommodation at the beginning or end of your climb that the trekking company has agreed to cover.

In addition to the above, clients who are booking from abroad and have agreed that transfers from and to Kilimanjaro Airport are included should again make sure that's stipulated in the contract.

Please note: items that are rarely, if ever, included in the package include cigarettes, all drinks except water and hot drinks that accompany meals (and any other beverages that the crew give to you to help you get to the summit or celebrate once you get there) and the tips you dish out to your crew at the end. (There is only one company I know of that *includes* tips as part of their package – take a bow, Fair Travel Tanzania; see pp92-4.)

One final note: if you're already in Tanzania and dealing with the companies face to face, you still need to **make sure that *everything* the operator has promised they will provide, including everything listed above, is specified in a contract**. This is important because, as you are probably aware, a verbal contract is simply not worth the paper it isn't written on. The trekking companies all have standard contracts which should include most of the above but will not include specific things such as the hire of any equipment you need or any free nights' accommodation that you have managed to negotiate into the package. These will need to be written in as well.

The Tanzanian operators

As discussed on p74 these are the people who actually run the treks. They are often referred to as 'ground operators', particularly by the overseas agents and it's a term I will sometimes use here too. There are hundreds of local companies that offer climbs up Kilimanjaro. The vast majority are based in either Moshi or Arusha, though there are a few in Marangu and elsewhere. In all probability, and assuming you booked your trek before you arrived, you won't have any reason to visit the company's offices. But if you have decided to hold off booking your trek until you arrive in Tanzania (see box p78) you'll need to choose where to base yourself when shopping for your trek.

Of the several hundred companies that are licensed to operate on the mountain, I have reviewed 65. I didn't really have any set criteria when deciding which ones to review. These 65 may have earned the right to be included in this book because they are the biggest companies, or the most popular, or the most well-known, or the oldest, or the most ethically minded, or simply the ones readers have asked us about the most. In fact, if I did have any guidelines when it came to choosing which companies to include, it was that I thought they would be the 65 companies that people would most want to read about.

Writing about 65 may seem like overkill but do remember that **booking with the right operator is perhaps the single most important factor in determining the success or otherwise of your trek**. It is the local operator who supplies all the equipment, builds the menus and buys the food, employs the personnel – guides, cooks, porters etc – who are going to work on the trek, arranges the transport to and from the mountain for you and your crew, books your hotel for before and after the climb, organises and pays for the park fees… and so on, and so on. So take your time choosing your operator. Because unless you are a guide, porter, guidebook writer or just plain daft, climbing Kili will be a once-in-a-lifetime experience – and an expensive one too – so it's important that you get it right.

To save you wading through all 65 reviews, I have also created a table (see pp84-5 & p87) that provides you with an overview of these companies. I have organised them into price order, with the cheapest first. **The prices in the table (which are *per person* prices) are for a group of four people for an 8-day Lemosho trek**; if you have a bigger group or want fewer days on the mountain the per person price will be smaller; whereas if your group is smaller, or your trek longer, you can expect the per person price to be higher. The last column in the table shows you where you can read each company's review.

In addition I've scattered boxes across the following pages that hopefully help you to find the company that suits you best; if you want to carry your own luggage on the mountain, or want to go with an ethical company, you'll find boxes that will help you to narrow down your search.

ONLINE REVIEWS vs MY REVIEWS

Which are more reliable?

It's a fair question: Why have I gone to the trouble of reviewing these operators when the internet has thousands of reviews from clients on various websites, many of which will be more up-to-date than the ones printed here?

Well, I have two main answers to this. Firstly, as I mention on p67, I think that choosing the right operator is one of the most important decisions you'll make, so it would be remiss of me to not even attempt to offer you some guidance on this matter. And secondly, I felt compelled to write it because of late I have become rather sceptical about some of the reviews I'm seeing online.

Please don't misunderstand me. A genuine, detailed online review can be useful. The people who write these reviews have usually actually climbed with the company concerned, whereas I probably won't have done, so they have first-hand experience and a far better knowledge of what it's actually like to climb with them which is invaluable. This is the main limitation of my reviews: I haven't climbed with most of the companies I review.

The limitations of online reviews

There are several arguments, though, as to why I think an online review may be of limited help. For starters, in all probability it was the reviewer's first and only time on Kili, so he or she has nothing with which to compare it. At the risk of sounding like a braggart, I have now climbed the mountain more than thirty times – so I think I have.

Secondly, as a general rule, clients tend to be happier if they make the summit and think better about their company as a result; whereas those that don't make it tend to feel less enamoured of their company, and may even blame them for their 'failure' to reach Uhuru Peak, even if that company actually ran a better trek than the one where everyone got to the top. How? Well, as I've pointed out several times, getting to the summit is usually a matter of chance and depends to a large degree on whether you acclimatise to the rarified air or not.

The company you choose to take you up there can make only a marginal difference to your chances of getting to the summit. Where their expertise and professionalism do come to the fore, however, is when it comes to getting you off the mountain if you aren't acclimatising well. For it's only then that you'll truly be grateful that you chose a decent company, one with a decent medical kit and excellent evacuation procedures. Unfortunately, the person evacuated may not appreciate what their company has done and may be a bit grumpy that they failed to make the summit. As a result, they'll be less likely to review the company positively, even though in reality they may have saved his or her life. Whereas the person who went to the summit with the bad operator may write a glowing review, not realising that if the situation had been reversed and they, too, had needed to be evacuated, their company may have killed them through incompetence and ignorance.

Result: good company gets an average review, bad company gets a positive one.

(cont'd on p80)

❑ HOW TO MAKE YOUR TREK CHEAPER – AND HOW NOT TO

Kilimanjaro is an expensive mountain to climb. But there are several ways in which you can make it cheaper. I'm not talking about saving a four-figure sum – though with a bit of luck and effort and by following the guidelines listed here, you could save yourself a three-figure one:

• **Bring your friends** Simply put, the larger your group, the lower the per person price – so try to persuade your friends and family to come along too (first insisting, of course, that they all individually buy a copy of this book; and maybe even two each, just to be safe).

• **Join a group** If you're travelling by yourself or with just one or two friends, look to join a public trek; most of the big companies organise these and you *may* save yourself a fair bit of cash by opting to join an open group trek rather than booking a private one.

• **Decide what 'luxuries' you don't need** Don't require a private toilet on Kili? Or a mess tent? Or chairs? Then ask your company if they can leave them behind. It could save you a few dollars as you'll need fewer porters.

• **Book your trek in Tanzania** It is possible to just turn up at the airport, get a taxi to Moshi or Arusha (US$50), and begin negotiating with the companies there. Obviously you can do this only if you have the time to wander around Moshi or Arusha and haggle with the trekking companies, but I find that by dealing with them face-to-face you can save a little off the price of your trek.

• **Volunteer with a Tanzanian charity** Trekking companies in Moshi often offer a discount for volunteers who are based in the town.

• **Travel outside the high season** You won't save much with your trek by doing this but you may well save several hundred dollars by *flying* outside the busiest months. I've booked a return flight from Heathrow to Kilimanjaro with Kenyan Airways for just over £300 in March – but I've also paid over £1200 for a return flight in August (and that took 20 hours each way!). Many hotels in Tanzania also reduce their prices in the quieter months.

• **Choose your airline carefully** There's a wide variation in airfares and it pays to shop around. Some airlines, such as Ethiopian, charge less because the route they take is lengthy and inconvenient. Others, such as Turkish Airlines, charge less because they touch down at Kilimanjaro Airport at some godforsaken hour in the morning, which means you may have to pay for an extra night's accommodation – thus reducing any money you've saved by flying with them. But Kenyan Airways are usually both cheap and pretty direct, and I've always found their service to be good too; and to judge by their popularity, Qatar must also be cheap at the moment. If you fly with an airline such as Turkish, KLM, Qatar or Ethiopian, look to see if they'll include a free stopover at their hub cities (ie Istanbul, Amsterdam, Doha or Addis Ababa respectively). It won't save you any money, but it will at least make the airfare feel like better value, allowing you to enjoy two holidays in one!

• **Haggle** Again, this is easier if you are booking for a large group as your bargaining position is so much stronger (because the companies will be even more desperate for your custom). Don't be shy but don't be too aggressive either, as this just creates a bad feeling. And remember, if you're not with a KPAP partner (see pp60-5), any money you save may well come out of the wages of the mountain crew.

• **Be aware of any discounts on the park fees that you are due** Under 16 years old? East African citizen? Tanzanian resident? Then you're entitled to a significant discount on your park fees (see p29) and there's no reason why this discount shouldn't be passed onto you *in full* by your trekking company.

Unfortunately, many of them don't, so make sure you know what you're entitled to and don't accept anything less than the full discount. See p83 and table pp84-5 & p87 for which companies I found were passing on the 'child discount' in full.

• **Book your safari with the same company** Many trekking companies run first-rate safaris as well and offer a 'climbers' discount' if you book both with them.

• **Look at charity climbs** Some trekking agencies, particularly in the UK, specialise in offering 'charity climbs', where the price of a trek is lower if you manage to collect a certain amount in sponsorship for a charity. How do these companies manage to offer such a low price for their treks? Because some of the sponsorship money you collect goes not to the charity but to the trekking company who invoices them.

I personally think it's better to just arrange the trek yourself and then organise your charity fundraising separately. The whole process is more transparent this way and you can then climb with whatever trekking company you want. But while I'm not at all convinced by these charity climb companies, I suppose it is another way of lowering the price you pay.

But do be warned: many are the horror stories of people who signed up with these companies, couldn't raise the minimum required sponsorship – and ended up paying a lot of money for a pretty mediocre trek.

How not to save money

There are, of course, other ways in which you can make it cheaper but which I *don't* recommend. The following, I think, are not sensible ways of lowering your costs – because by reducing the amount you pay, you may also be reducing your chances of reaching the summit and/or your enjoyment of climbing Africa's highest mountain:

• **Don't carry your own luggage** There are companies that allow trekkers the opportunity of doing this and the trek is slightly cheaper as a result. If you want to do this purely for the extra challenge that's fine – but don't do it as a way of saving money. The saving is small – essentially it will be equivalent to the wages that would be paid to that porter, which is only US$10 per day even if he is paid the KINAPA minimum.

Furthermore, in my experience those that carry their own luggage on the mountain tend to succumb to altitude sickness more than those who don't. If you want the extra challenge of being more self-sufficient then, yes, carrying your own luggage is a good way to do that and there are companies that will allow you to

• **Don't take fewer days than you can afford** Sure, if your budget allows you to climb for only six days, then take a 6-day climb.

But don't opt for a 6-day climb if you can actually afford seven; and unless you absolutely have to, don't opt for a 5-day trek at all unless you've acclimatised somewhere else beforehand, as I think this is insufficient time for allowing your body to get used to the rarified air.

• **Don't base your choice of company purely on the prices they charge** Companies that charge more for their treks usually do so for a reason: because their equipment is better, their crew more knowledgeable and helpful, their food tastier and healthier, their portions bigger, and their all-round service superior. Sure, there are some that do over-charge, and some who are great value – and in this chapter I try to sift through to point out which companies fall into which category; so read the specifications of every company carefully to find out what they offer and why they charge what they do.

• **Don't scrimp on the tips you give to your crew** Come on, where's your dignity?

Trusting the review websites

But as well as casting doubt on the usefulness of the reviews, I'm also a little sceptical about how much one can rely on the review websites that host these reviews. My suspicions were initially raised when I noticed that the companies that rank highly on all these websites are rarely the ones that feature prominently on the mountain. In other words, if you were to believe these review websites *and nothing else*, the companies with the highest number of five-star reviews or which are at the top of their rankings should be the best operators on Kilimanjaro. The reality, alas, is that they are often anything but. In my experience many of these highly ranked and well-reviewed operators often: **a)** don't run that many treks, and I rarely see them on the mountain; **b)** seldom have a lengthy history or experience of climbing Kilimanjaro; **c)** are rarely members of KPAP; and **d)** are not, as far as I can tell, doing anything outstanding for their customers or crew. Indeed, often the first and only time I've heard of them is when they appear on these websites!

How can this be? Well, some websites charge the companies that advertise on them, and the companies have to pay more if they wish to feature more prominently. In other words, on some websites greater prominence is not given to the 'best' companies, but merely those that pay the most. But I also know it to be true that some operators are just better at publicising themselves online and using the web to their advantage. These operators (and their agents), if they know their clients have had a successful trek, will push them to write a review on one of the websites almost as soon as they come off the mountain.

In light of this, don't make the mistake of thinking that the company with the most 5-star ratings is automatically the best one; all it really means is that they are the best at getting their happy clients to write reviews. Similarly, those that feature at the top of search-engine rankings (Google etc) are there not because they run the best treks; it simply means they are the best at getting themselves to the top of the search engines.

I have also received a couple of emails from people who had had a pretty poor trek but were then offered significant bribes (amounting to several hundred dollars) *not* to write a bad review online. These people refused and decided instead to publicise as much as possible their whole sorry experience, which included writing to me. But does this mean that there are dozens of people who *did take* a bribe and as a consequence never wrote about their experience? I've also heard of at least one instance where a negative review mysteriously disappeared from a website. Neither the reviewer nor I have any idea why this would happen, but it does somewhat make a mockery of the whole system if only positive reviews are allowed, particularly if, as I suspect, complaints from a company about a negative review resulted in its removal.

Using multiple sources

Please understand, I am not saying that you should believe my reviews and nobody else's. After all, as mentioned earlier, I have not climbed with most of the operators I review, unlike nearly everyone who posts online reviews. Given the diktats of limited funds and tight publishing deadlines, I've done as much research as I can; in many cases I've seen the companies operate on the mountain, and I've asked KPAP and other bodies to find out what they know about the company. But I don't for one minute pretend that I am omniscient.

In summary, I think you should look on this chapter as just a useful tool, one of several in your toolbox that you should utilise when deciding on which company to choose; one that can then be supplemented by looking online or asking friends. And hopefully by doing so you'll end up with the company that's right for you; because that is what we all want.

HOW I RESEARCHED THIS SECTION

As with the previous editions I once again did as much of my research as possible anonymously. In other words, the companies I contacted thought I was just a regular punter and had no idea I was researching the next edition of the book.

Having first checked out each company's website, the next step was to email them in order to find out a bit more about the service they could provide and what they would charge for it. To do this I invented a fictional family of four (see below), set up an email address for them, and then sent a standard email to each trekking operator. My research didn't stop there, however. I also asked trekkers I met on Kilimanjaro or in Arusha/Moshi of their experiences; consulted all the letters and emails from climbers that I'd received, in which recommendations and complaints about operators often featured; and finally, I talked with KPAP (see box pp60-5) to find out how well or badly each company treated and paid their staff on the mountain.

Please bear in mind that **the reviews are my opinions only**. Remember, too, that things change very quickly in this part of the world, so some of the following will inevitably have altered by the time you begin your research. **For the latest advice and information please do not hesitate to get in touch via email (🖳 henry@climbmountkilimanjaro.com)** and I'll be happy to oblige; and if you have any advice, comments, praise or criticisms about any of the agencies, again, please contact me – I am always delighted to receive them.

How to read the table **[see pp84-5 & p87]**

In the table the **companies are listed in price order**, with the cheapest first. The price is for an 8-day Lemosho trek for 4 people, and was given to me by the companies in response to an anonymous email I sent to them in which we pretended to be a family of two adults and two children, with one child 17 years old and one aged 13. Sometimes, a company doesn't actually deal with the public directly but only through agents. When this is the case, I quote the price provided by one of the company's main agencies – and mark it as such with an asterisk. I note which agent I contacted in the notes below the table.

I also asked all the companies several other questions which form the basis of the other columns in the box:

• **Location** This is where their main office is located. **M** is for Moshi, **A** for Arusha; there are also a few companies that are based in Marangu, Usa River, Rongai, Nairobi and elsewhere; I have noted them too.

• **Airport transfers** If airport transfers are included in the price you'll see a tick in this column; if they aren't the price the company charges is noted.

• **Accommodation** This column displays the hotel where you'll be staying before and after the hike as part of the overall trek package. If no accommodation is included, this is denoted by an '**✘**'. With most/all companies, you can choose to pay a little more and stay in a better class of hotel if you are unhappy with the one in the package.

❑ WHY CAN'T I SEE MY TREKKING COMPANY IN THE TABLE?

It's a question I get asked a lot, and there are two main reasons why your operator may not feature in this review.

The first is, simply, that there are hundreds of companies operating on the mountain, many of them very small, and as a result it's impossible to keep tabs on all of them. Many of these companies will remain small for their entire existence and survive on just a few treks per year. For this reason they either fly completely under the radar or, if I have heard of them, I'll decide they are just too inconsequential to merit any space in this guide. Please understand: this is not necessarily a reason to dismiss them altogether; many of them organise great treks and, after all, we've all got to start somewhere.

The second reason, however, will perhaps be more surprising to many readers. Because the truth of the matter is, **many of the bigger companies that advertise treks on Kilimanjaro are actually just agents, not operators.** I've just typed 'Kilimanjaro' into Google and of the four companies that appear on the first page, three of them are agents; in other words, only one actually operates its own treks.

The simple fact is that some of the biggest and most visible names in the industry, that between them take several thousands of bookings every year, don't actually run their own treks. To name just three; Ultimate Kilimanjaro (who, from the last I heard, use TDMC to operate their treks), Kandoo (ditto) and Peak Planet (who I believe still use Gladys); these are all major names sending thousands of people onto the mountain each year. But all of them are agents using a local ground operator, and don't actually run the trek themselves.

Of course, just because they don't actually organise the treks themselves does not mean you shouldn't book with them. As I say on pp72-3, they may add something to the booking process, or provide something extra to the trek, that may make booking with them an attractive option. Moreover, just because they are an agent doesn't mean to say that they don't have any input into the way the trek is run. Many of the bigger companies will want some sort of say in the way their trek is organised, which guides lead the trek, what food is served etc. Furthermore, the fact that these agencies have chosen an operator to run their treks is pretty much a guarantee that the operator will be good; after all, they're hardly likely to leave their reputation, indeed their very existence, in the hands of a trek operator that isn't up to scratch, so they probably won't choose a trek operator purely on the fact that they're cheap. And in turn that operator will often make sure their best guides, cooks and equipment are employed on those treks that the agency have organised, because those treks are the very lifeblood of the operator, without which they simply wouldn't be able to survive.

Nevertheless, because, *in most cases*, it is not the agent who actually operates the trek, but the ground operator, and the agent *usually* has very little say in how the trek is run, so we haven't included them in this book.

• **Child discount** This column is worth paying attention to even if you don't have children. Because in many ways, it can be seen as a **measure of a company's honesty**. If a trekker is under 16, they are entitled to a significant discount off the park fees that, **for an 8-day Lemosho trek, amounts to US$802.40**. I admit that it is difficult to calculate this amount exactly, especially with the introduction of 18% VAT in 2016. Nevertheless, there is no reason why any company can't pass this discount on in full to the customer. So if the company offers only a discount of, for example, US$250, you know that they are making a profit of US$552.40 by not passing on this discount in full. Interestingly, some companies, perhaps desperate for the custom, or who couldn't work out the correct figure, actually offered considerably more than the park fee reduction as a discount! I have noted the amount each company offered as a discount in this column.
• **KPAP** This column shows which companies are partners of KPAP, the body that looks after the welfare of porters. If you care about the crew that is going to take you up the mountain pick a KPAP partner company; see pp84-5 & p87.
• **Oxygen** I asked each company if emergency oxygen is included as part of your trek (as I think it should be). A tick means it is included; if a company does not include it as part of their standard package, the amount they charge to have it included is noted in the box. A cross means it wasn't offered at all.
• **Western Breach** Many companies refuse to work on the Western Breach anymore because, they say, it is too dangerous because of rockfalls. In this column I show those companies that are still willing to take climbers on this route when it is open.

TREKKING OPERATORS IN TANZANIA

Africa VIP Travel (🖳 africaviptravel.com; **A**) Fairly small company with few treks, though their response to my email was considerate and comprehensive and showed a reassuring degree of knowledge. Also include some nice touches in their Kili package, including, uniquely, a pre-trek trip to Arusha National Park, a Gamow bag for Kili and *three* nights at lovely Ilboru Safari Lodge. Unfortunately, they are also the most expensive company in my list who *aren't* KPAP partners.
• **Summary** Rivals in this luxury price bracket are busier and better known so will doubtless get the majority of the market, and while their package is a strong one, their refusal to be KPAP partners is a definite black mark.

African Environments (🖳 africanenvironments.com; **A**) Established in 1987, African Environments (AE) are the only company with no Tanzanian ownership (they were founded before this became mandatory). They're a top-of-the-range operator with a history on Kili that's both lengthy and impressive. They were instrumental in pioneering the Lemosho Route, for example (though annoyingly they call it the Shira Route), and remain the No1 specialists on the Western Breach. Indeed, uniquely, they were the only company to push us towards the Western Breach ahead of all the other routes. I personally don't think there's anything wrong with that, but it is interesting given how just about every other company refused to offer us a Western Breach climb because I had a child in my party. They were also the first to equip *all* their expeditions with WFR-trained guides and Gamow hyperbaric bags. Continuing their trailblazing, they now offer their clients a night or two at their acclimatisation camp, Itikoni, on the slopes of Meru before their Shira/Western Breach climbs.

(cont'd on p86)

TANZANIAN TREKKING OPERATORS (UP TO $3000pp) – BY PRICE (ALL US$ PER PERSON)

Trekking Operator	Office Location	Airport transfers included	Usual accommodation	Lemosho Route	Child discount	KPAP	O2 provided	Western Breach	Info
Kessy Brothers	M	✔	Keys Hotel	$1745	$200		✔	✔	p95
Enosa	M	✔	Panama Garden Resort, Brubru	$1850	$750		✔	✔	p90
Kilimanjaro Heroes Adventures	A&M	✔	Keys Hotel	$1900	$190		✔	✔	p96
Tanzania Joy	M	✔	Parkview Inn	$1900	$1030		✔	✔	p105
Viva Africa	M	✔	Rafiki, Salinero Kilimanjaro	$1905 HOSTEL	$560		✔	✔	p107
Origin Trails	M	✔	Chanya Lodge	$1930	$630	✔	✔	✔	p101
Monkey Adventures	M	$50 p/v o/w	✘	$1950	$800		✔	✘	p100
African Spoonbill Tours	M	✔	Keys Hotel	$1990	$220		✔	✔	p86
Kisambi	M	✔	✘	$2040	$290		✔	✘	p97
Kili Worldborn Safaris	M	✔	Lindrin, Parkview, Chanya Lodge	$2050	$850	✔	✔	✔	p95
Maua Adventures	M	✔	Parkview Inn	$2190	$547		✔	✔	p99
Snowcap Tanzania Tours	Rongai & M	✔	Moshi Leopard/Snowcap (half board)	$2196	$460	✔	✔	✔	p103
Mega Adventures	M	$40 p/v o/w	✘	$2196	$1032		✔	✔	p100
Kilimanjaro Brothers	M	✔	Parkview Inn	$2200	$700 ($700)		✔	✔	p96
				$2700 (de luxe, with ALTOX Oxygen system)					
Nyange Adventures	M	✔	Bristol Cottages	$2247	$447	✔	✔	✔	p101
Kilimanjaro Vikings	M	✔	Parkview Inn	$2300	$400 (for both kids)		✔	✔	p96
Kwetu Tanzania	A	✔	Outpost Lodge	$2320	$1340		✔	✘	p97
Top Climbers	M	✔	Parkview Inn	$2350	$650		✔	✔	p106
Keys Hotel Tours	M	one-way only	Keys Hotel	$2353	$851		✔	✔	p95
Popote Africa	M	✔	Weru Weru/Parkview/Lindrin/ Kilimanjaro Wonders	$2355	$825		✔	✔	p101
Local Moshi Adventures	M	✔	We Travel/Climbers Corner	$2305	$505	✔	✔	✔	p97
			Keys/Panama/Parkview/Stella Maris	$2400					
Shah Tours	M	$80 o/w	Bristol Cottages	$2385	$680	✔	✔	✔	p102

Ahsante Tours	M	✔	Weru Weru	$2410	$723/860 (17-year-old US$210)		✔	✔	p86
Homeland	M	✔	Maisha Khalisi Cottages	$2450	$450		✔	✔	p94
Zara Tours	M	$20pp o/w	Springlands	$2451	$735.30		$12pd	✘	p107
African Scenic Safaris	M	✔	Chanya Lodge	$2465	$830	✔	✔	✘	p86
Sunny Safaris	A	✔	Venus Hotel	$2535	$470		US$70	✔	p104
Majestic Kilimanjaro	A	✔	Outpost Lodge	$2587	$798	✔	✔	✔	p98
Gladys Adventure	M	✔	Kilimanjaro Wonders/ Salinero Kilimanjaro	$2598	$792	✔	✔	✔	p94
Real Life Adventure Travel	M	✔	3 nights Parkview/ Salinero Kilimanjaro	$2650	$830 ($400)	✔	$50	✔	p102
Tanzania Climbing Outfitters	A	✔	Outpost Lodge	$2658	$1458		✔	✔	p104
African Safari Trails (TAST)	A	✘	✘	$2672	$802		✔	✘	p106
Climb Kili	A	✔	Summit Safari Lodge	$2675	$300		✔	✔	p88
African Zoom Adventure Tours	A	✔	Mount Meru Hotel	$2696	$948	✔	✔	✔	p86
Tanzania Journeys	M	✔	Chanya Lodge	$2700	$680	✔	✔	✔	p104
Easy Travel & Tours	A	✔	Arusha Planet Lodge	$2741	$700	✔	✔	✘	p89
Good Earth	A	✔	Airport Planet Lodge	$2790	$640	✔	✔	✔	p94
Big Expeditions	A	✔	Mount Meru Hotel	$2800	$300 ($100)	✔	✔	✔	p88
Marangu Hotel	Marangu	$85 o/w	✘	$2819	$799	✔	✔	✔	p99
Maasai Wanderings	A	✔	Rivertrees	$2840		✘	✔	✔	p97
Everlasting Tanzania Travels	A	✔	Ilboru Lodge	$2850	$350	✔	✔	✔	p91
Kilimanjaro Experts	Usa	✔	Outpost Lodge	$2879	$802.40	✔	✔	✔	p96
Kili Zone/Bush to Beach	A	✔	3 nights Kilimanjaro Wonders	$2895**	$680	✔	✔	✔	p95
Tanzania Experience	Usa	✔	Meru View Lodge	$2910	$630		✘	✘	p104
Altezza	M	✔	Aishi Machame/Brubru Lodge	$2915	$1024	✔	✔	✔	p88
Trek2Kili	M	✔	Kilimanjaro Wonders	$2970	$1782	✔	✔	✘	p106
Fair Travel Tanzania	A	✔	✘	$2995 inc tips	$600	✔	✔	✔	p92
Follow Alice	M	US$25pp	Lindrin Lodge	$2995	$780	✔	✔	✘	p93

For key see p87

(cont'd on p87)

(cont'd from p83) Prices are as steep as the mountain itself (US$8889pp *excluding* pre- and post-trek accommodation!) though thankfully some of that money filters down to their mountain staff, for they pay some of the best wages on Kili and they are KPAP partners. Child discount was rather meagre given the amount you're being charged for the trek, at US$531.

• **Summary** There's no doubting the excellence of their treks and their acclimatisation camp on Meru is a brilliant idea. Ludicrously expensive, of course, but if you're contemplating paying this amount for a trek, presumably, money's no object anyway.

African Scenic Safaris (**ASS**; 🖳 africanscenicsafaris.com; **M**) Operating from the highly regarded Hostel Hoff in Moshi, ASS have done pretty brisk business over the past few years thanks to a simple winning formula of keeping their prices fair (Lemosho Route US$2465pp for four people, with an impressive US$830 reduction for under 16s) and ethical standards incredibly high. They are KPAP partners and are certified by TravelLife (the highest sustainability certification available for tour operators) and actively work to strengthen their community with funding and support for local projects through their charity, Path to Africa. Their treks are well regarded with some extensive and effusive reviews from readers and online.

• **Summary** A likeable bunch doing good work for their clients, their crew and their community. Perfect for volunteers, who may well be staying at their hostel, but also for anyone looking for a reasonable trek that doesn't exploit the mountain crew.

African Spoonbill Tours (🖳 africanspoonbilltours.com; **M**) First, the good points: they are very long-standing and are always amongst the first to reply to my emails. The price is very reasonable, too, at US$1990, though the under-16 discount was a miserly US$220. Bad points? Well the 99% success rate claim seems far-fetched, their attack on KPAP in their reply to my email was, of course, unfair – and you can't offer such low prices and a high-spec trek (with oxygen, airport transfers and accommodation at Moshi's Keys Hotel) and still pay your porters a fair wage. You just can't. Reviews are also variable. US$290 is also a lot to ask for a private toilet for the trek.

• **Summary** Hard – actually, make that virtually impossible – to believe their claims; I think there are better and more trustworthy agencies in the same price bracket.

African Zoom Adventure Tours (🖳 africanzoom.com; **A**) Small company but one that's experienced, pleasant and polite. Don't do a huge amount of business but there's a lot to like: wholly Tanzanian-owned, KPAP partners, WFR-trained guides and very fair prices of US$2696pp, with the under-16 park fee discount given US$948 – more than the expected US$801.40. Only (slight) hesitation is that I can find very few reviews online – probably because the bulk of their business comes from agents. Surprisingly, the accommodation they included was the smart Mount Meru Hotel – though their website mentions Outpost, which we think is probably the more realistic option at this price.

• **Summary** Not easy to judge them, but they're certainly fairly priced and worth contacting for those seeking a trek with a KPAP partner in the mid-range.

Ahsante Tours (🖳 ahsantetours.com; **M**) No longer the rock-bottom cheapest but still a reliable operator, their extensive list of overseas agencies that work with them proving their dependability. They were the first company I ever climbed with back in 2001, though they've grown considerably since, with the plush Weru Weru River Lodge (see p234) part of their portfolio now too. They remain a fair-value option, with a good service, excellent guides and many happy customers. Price-wise they hover between budget and mid-range, with 8 days on Lemosho US$2410pp including two nights at lovely Weru Weru. The under-16 discount, which was originally a decent US$723, was then increased to an even more generous US$860 – and they even offered a

(cont'd from p85)

TANZANIAN TREKKING OPERATORS ($3000pp AND ABOVE) – BY PRICE (ALL US$ PER PERSON)

Trekking Operator	Office Location	Airport transfers included	Usual accommodation	Lemosho Route	Child discount	KPAP	O2 provided	Western Breach	Info
Pristine Trails	M	✔	Kilimanjaro Wonders	$3045	$970	✔	$90	✘	p101
Kibo Slopes	A & Nairobi	✔	Kibo Palace	$3059	$801	✔	✔	✔	p95
East African Voyage	A	✔	Arusha Planet Lodge (1 night, on public treks only)	$3085	$750	✔	✔	✘	p89
Team Kilimanjaro	A	✔	Outpost Lodge/Mvuli	$3169	$800		✔	✔	p105
Detasa	A	✔	3 nights Ilboru/African Tulip/Aishi	$3200	$800		✔	✔	p89
Tanzania Travel Company	A	✔	Arusha Planet Lodge	$3202	$980		✔	✔	p105
Climbing Kilimanjaro	A	✔	Mount Meru Hotel	$3250	✘		✔	✘	p89
Alika Africa	A	✔	Rivertrees	$3399	$802.40	✔	✔	✘	p88
Serengeti Pride Safaris	Usa	✔	Arusha Planet Lodge	$3399	$680	✔	✔	✔	p102
TDMC	M	✔	Bristol Cottages	$3200-3815*	✘	✔	✔	✘	p105
Eco-Africa Climbing	M	✔	Panama Garden Resort	$3550	$680	✔	✔	✔	p90
Summit Expeditions & Nomadic Experiences (SENE)	M	✔	Mbahe in Marangu/Chanya (3nights)	$3990	$1490	✔	✔	✘	p103
Africa VIP Travel	A	✔	3 nights Ilboru Safari Lodge	$4836	$2418		✔	✔	p83
Nature Discovery	A	$100 o/w	Rivertrees Country Inn	$5014/4378	$802	✔	✔	✔	p100
Summits Africa	A	✔	Ngare Sero Mountain Lodge	GB£4300/$5444	✘	✔	✔	✔	p103
Tusker Trail/Tembo Trails	M	✔	3 nights at Parkview Inn/Bristol Cottages	$6340	$954	✔	✔	✘	p106
African Environments	A	✔	✘	$8889 (Shira)	$531	✔	✔	✔	p83

Key p/v = per vehicle o/w = one-way pp = per person pd = per day

These quotes supplied by agents: *Kandoo/Ultimate (see p82) ** Bush 2 Beach ¶Africa Travel Resource † Embark § Aardvark Safaris

US$210 discount to my fictional 17-year-old too, which was a lovely surprise!
• **Summary** One of the better-value operators on the mountain, reliable and experienced – but no longer KPAP partners.

Alika Africa (💻 dumaexplorer.com; **A**) The husband-and-wife team behind one of my favourite operators, Duma Explorer, sadly went their separate ways a few years ago.

The new company that has emerged, Alika, are KPAP partners with a lot of experience, a strong commitment to sustainability, great reviews and guides that are WFR-trained. Indeed, Alika Africa has kept everything that was so good about the old Duma Explorer, and has also managed to shed those little niggles that I moaned about in the last edition (airport transfers and accommodation – at swish Rivertrees – are now included, where previously they were extra). They charge US$3399pp and even proffered the *exact* child discount of U$802.40. Reviews are great and justifiably so – because I think Alika, though not the cheapest or biggest, are great too. They also have an office in the USA.
• **Summary** Looking for a mid-range trek with a decent, ethically minded company? Alika are one of a handful of companies in this price range that I recommend without hesitation.

Altezza (💻 altezza.travel; **M**) By their own reckoning the busiest company on the mountain these days, having grown quickly and successfully by mining the previously untapped Russian market (though they are at pains to point out that their climbers now come from all over the world.) Their responses in English are fluent and informative, and their prices are sensible at US$2915pp (with under 16s given an unnecessarily generous but very welcome US$1024 discount). Their climbs are of a pretty high spec and praised frequently on the internet, with WFR-trained guides and accommodation at Aishi Machame, near Machame gate, and at their own hotel (Brubru Lodge, see p234) in Shanty Town all included.

• **Summary** Good and very fairly priced – and the decision to become a KPAP partner is the cherry on the top.

Big Expeditions (💻 bigexpeditions.net; **A**) Longstanding company and KPAP partner with surprisingly few reviews given their fine reputation and nearly two decades of existence. Responded promptly to my email and replies seemed sensible, including a stipulation that they only organise treks on the Western Breach for those with some sort of proof that they are 'professional summitters'.

Itineraries seem fairly standard but they do try to make themselves slightly different by hosting the best post-trek celebrations of any company at the end of each trek, with a buffet lunch set up on trestle tables at Mweka Gate and musicians, singers and a man in drag leading the dancing. Prices are neither outstandingly cheap nor extortionate at US$2800pp. My only complaint is that the child discount of US$300 was less than half of what I expected – though, weirdly, they did offer a US$100 discount off for my fictional 17-year-old too.
• **Summary** My hunch is that they grab most of their custom these days from foreign travel agents such as Alpine Ascents, whose clients have no idea they are actually climbing with Big Expeditions. But they are fairly priced KPAP partners – and a lovely welcome awaits their climbers at the end of the trek.

Climb Kili (💻 climbkili.com; **A**) Experienced outfitter with many reviews from happy clients and their own agents in both the UK and America. But I have to say I've never been won over by them in previous editions and remain unpersuaded in this one too. They make big claims on their website about being an ethical company, but when I asked why they aren't with KPAP, rather than provide an explanation they proceeded instead to knock the companies who are, stating that less than 10% of KPAP companies have more than one trek per year (which is nonsense). Such tactics are all very familiar – I've seen this from them in previous editions of the book too. Also claim to have more successful climbs than anyone else (there's no way they could know that, but I'd be very surprised if that's correct). Price-wise they charge US$2675pp, with child discount a miserly US$300, with accommodation at the obscure Summit Safari Lodge included. All their guides are WFR-trained and their treks are, by all accounts, pretty good. Note that only the Machame and Lemosho routes are advertised on their website. They also have offices in the USA and UK (also for the EU).

• **Summary** Popular and successful and they doubtless run good treks. But, as with previous editions, my correspondence with them always leaves me far from convinced.

Climbing Kilimanjaro (🖳 climbing-kilimanjaro.com; **A**) This is a mysterious operator. There's very little indication on the website as to who is behind this company – despite their being an 'About us' page on their website. I'm prepared to bet that there's some foreign input somewhere – at the risk of offending the locals, the website and their emails are too slick for there not to be. But, pretty much uniquely, there are no names or biographies of the owners or founders on the site, just the guides, and little other info save for the bald statement saying that they've been in business since 2009. Their response to my email was polite – though they very adroitly dodged my questions about being KPAP partners, which wasn't surprising. Price-wise they're US$3250pp, with, disappointingly, no child discount offered.

• **Summary** Their back-story and even identity are so opaque that I, personally, would have trouble putting my trust in them, let alone give them money. Their refusal to offer any child discount also suggests that they're not playing fair. It appears that I'm in the minority with my scepticism, however, for their comprehensive website, high ranking on Google and some positive reviews has helped them to get a healthy chunk of the market.

Detasa (aka Destination Tanzania Safaris; 🖳 detasa.com; **A**) A medium-sized operator founded by two brothers that specialise in Lemosho/Western Breach. The price of US$3200pp includes oxygen, hyperbaric chamber, airport transfers and *three* nights' accommodation at Ilboru Lodge/African Tulip. All but US$2 of the full child discount was proffered too. Certainly the specification for their treks seems fairly impressive – and I really like the fact that the owner guides around a third of the treks himself – though the price is, I think, too high and, perhaps for this reason, reviews online are few. They are also, surprisingly, anti-KPAP, which is a shame as being a KPAP partner could be just the thing they need to boost sales. Also have an office in the US.

• **Summary** Reviews are generally positive but at this price point I think you can get better.

East African Voyage (EAV; 🖳 eastafricanvoyage.com; **A**) Founded by a former guide and his wife, a Canadian human rights lawyer, EAV are a great little company that lacks for nothing except, perhaps, more customers. Surprisingly, given his heritage as a trip leader with African Environments, EAV don't climb on the Western Breach, considering it to be too dangerous. But they're still worth contacting: they're beloved by KPAP, their guides are WFR-trained, their kit is of a high quality, the reviews of their treks are pretty much always positive and their response to my enquiry was eloquent, thorough and informative. Prices are perhaps a little high at US$3085pp particularly given the quality of the other companies in this price range, and also because they don't include accommodation or airport transfers. Under-16 discount was not quite the full amount, at US$750.

• **Summary** Definitely worth enquiring with if you're after a solid mid-range company, though do perhaps try to bargain to make them better value.

Easy Travel & Tours (🖳 easytravel.co.tz; **A**) Long-established company, efficient and very busy, and more renowned for their safaris though they do seem to be concentrating more on Kili treks these days.

Response to my enquiry was quick, courteous and comprehensive, with several useful attachments on packing, fitness, etc. Prices are reasonable (US$2741pp), they're KPAP partners and, to be honest, I can find little reason not to recommend them (other than the price of a private toilet on the trek; at US$236, that's absurd!)

• **Summary** Doing a fair bit of Kili business now and I can see why; long established, loads of good reviews (including a few about Kili, though largely about safaris) and clearly very accomplished.

Eco-Africa Climbing (🖳 eco-africaclimbing.com; **M**) New company that, as the name makes clear, has decided to tack towards the ethical end of the market in an attempt to carve their own niche in the overcrowded Kili marketplace. Which means that, in addition to being KPAP partners they also profess an ethical approach to their treks, which is laudable. Such benevolence doesn't come cheap, however, and their quote of US$3550pp took me by surprise, especially as everything about their website suggested they were a very local company (which usually means cheaper). Still, reviews are good and it's hard to fault a company with seemingly such a strong moral compass.

• **Summary** Seems churlish to moan about the price when they're doing so much right.

Enosa (🖳 enosaexpeditions.com; **M**) Company that manages to secure a fair bit of business by offering treks at bargain-basement prices and combining that with some some good reviews on Tripadvisor and other sites. Their email to me was con-

❑ BEST ETHICAL COMPANIES

Many companies bang on for pages on their website about being an ethical company. Whether that's looking after the mountain, looking after their crews, looking after the local community, or looking after the planet as a whole, there are several NGOs that have been set up to enable operators to 'do their bit' for both humanity and the planet – and by aligning themselves with these NGOs, the companies are better able to demonstrate that they're doing their bit too.

The main concern on Kili is the welfare of the people who work on it and in particular the porters. Given my scepticism about other bodies that claim to oversee the welfare of porters (including the various porters' unions and the Kilimanjaro Association of Tour Operators, or KIATO), I believe KPAP's endorsement – and only KPAP's. And I think that you should too. So if you want to be sure that you're climbing with a company whose mountain crew are being treated fairly, make sure they are KPAP partners. There are three warnings that I need to give here:

• **Don't necessarily believe a company if it tells you that they are members of KPAP** During my research, about half a dozen companies lied to me and said they were KPAP partners but weren't. To find out if they truly are or not, visit the KPAP website (see p60); look for the partners' page and you'll find all current partners there.

• **Don't necessarily believe a company even if it has the KPAP logo on their website** Again, this is not a cast-iron guarantee that they are a KPAP partner, because they could have just stolen it, or not removed it when they stopped being a partner. Just visit the KPAP website to find out the most up-to-date list.

• **Don't necessarily believe this book!** The list of KPAP partners changes regularly as new companies are added and existing partners fall foul of KPAP's strict standards. So while this book is as up-to-date as possible when it goes to print, and is a good place to begin your search, the only surefire way to make sure your company is a KPAP partner is to look on KPAP's website.

cise but full of common sense, and included an eloquent and lengthy defence of why they weren't with KPAP, but how they treat their porters just as well as any KPAP partner. (Which, if true, makes you wonder why they don't just become a KPAP partner?). You can't argue with the price, however, at US$1850pp for 8 days on Lemosho, and I was impressed that almost the full discount for under 16s was offered within the first paragraph of their reply.

● **Summary** If they really do treat and pay their porters as well as they say, they need to become a KPAP partner pronto, and any doubts about their decency will vanish and I could recommend them wholeheartedly. But it must be very difficult, if you're operating at the cheap end of the market, to both pay your crew properly and still make a profit – so I'm sceptical that this operator is going be a partner anytime soon. Still, if you aren't too bothered about such considerations and just want a dirt-cheap trek, Enosa are worth approaching.

Everlasting Tanzania Travels (💻 everlastingtz.com; **A**) Wholly Tanzanian-owned company run by three ex-guides that has a lot going for it. They have a strong ethical outlook, are highly regarded by KPAP (with whom they are partners), and have a deserved reputation for taking massive groups on Kili – indeed, they took one of the largest groups ever to climb the mountain, with 117 out of the initial 120 making it to the top. Their emails are informed and informative, and they supply all trekkers with a 12-week training program, which many will find reassuring. The attention to detail doesn't stop once you're

Of course, being nice to your porters and crew is only one way of being ethical. Looking after the mountain, looking after the planet, and sponsoring initiatives in the local community are all ways that companies can 'do good'. There are several companies that I think stand out in this regard (and note, once again, I have not considered my own company, **Kilimanjaro Experts** – this is not about advertising us!):

Four companies that I believe stand out:

• **Fair Travel** (p92) Company that in many ways has set the standards in porter welfare and is still the only company brave enough to include the tips as part of the package, so you don't need to pay them separately (and the porters know exactly what they are earning from the trek).
• **Good Earth** (p94) Again a long-term KPAP supporter and one that also sponsors and supports local children's education as well as various local environmental projects.
• **Eco-Africa** (opposite) New-ish company but already a fervent KPAP partner and some of their guides are LNT (see pp59-60) instructors. Also donate some of their profit to a tree-planting project in Moshi.
• **African Scenic Safaris** (p86) KPAP partners and holders of a TravelLife certificate (the highest sustainability certification, apparently, available for tour operators). Also actively work on local projects through their charity, Path to Africa.

For budget travellers with a conscience

If you're gung-ho about personal safety and couldn't give a monkey's about how the porters are treated then, yes, it is still possible to get a trek for about US$1500pp on the Lemosho Route. But for those who have been blessed with some sort of social conscience, at the time of writing these were the cheapest members of KPAP. Do check with KPAP before booking, though, as the cheaper companies tend to be the ones that struggle to keep to KPAP's strict guidelines. The companies are: **Origin Trails** (see p101); **Kili Worldborn** (p95); and **Snowcap** (p103).

in Tanzania, either, for their treks are efficiently run and all climbs have a WFR trained guide working on them. Indeed, the only negative I can find is that the under-16 discount offered was a rather disappointing US$350, though otherwise their prices are fair at US$2850pp, a figure that includes Flying Doctor's Membership (to cover helicopter rescue) plus two nights *full board* at Arusha's pleasant Ilboru Lodge.

• **Summary** Undoubtedly very good, particularly with large groups.

Fair Travel Tanzania (🖳 fairtravel.com; **A**) For those who care about the welfare of porters, there are few better than this bunch. Fair Travel Tanzania are KPAP partners who describe themselves as a non-profit company, founded by a Swede who won a large amount of money on a TV game show and decided to invest it by setting up Fair Travel. What's refreshing is that they were the first to approach the question of porter welfare from a whole new angle by firstly determining what amount a porter needs each month to maintain a decent standard of living, then paying them a daily wage, assuming that they work on two treks each month, that will equal this amount. It's a model that KPAP themselves have since adopted. All of which means that the porters on a Fair Travel climb earn US$18

❑ ROUTE SPECIALISTS

Some companies have become associated with certain routes on the mountain. In a couple of instances this is because they actually pioneered the trail; in other cases it is just because they have concentrated on this route for one reason or another. Note that these companies all offer other routes in addition to the one they're associated with; and conversely, there are countless other companies that offer treks on these routes.

Just because they're specialists on one particular route doesn't mean it follows that they're particularly expensive: indeed, Snowcap, the pioneers of the Rongai Route, are amongst the cheapest companies on the mountain (and are KPAP partners too!).

Northern Circuit Several companies now use the Northern Circuit, attracted by its relative peace and serenity. **Nature Discovery/Thomson** incorporate the Northern Circuit in their Grand Traverse Trek and **Kilimanjaro Experts** use it a lot on the very popular Alternative Lemosho and Full Circuit Umbwe treks.

Rongai The father of the boss (at the time of writing) of **Snowcap** helped to establish and popularise the Rongai Route, built the School Hut/Outbound Hut on the slopes of Kibo, and they own lovely Snowcap Cottages – the only accommodation near Rongai Gate.

Marangu **Marangu Hotel** has been running treks on the oldest established route since the 1930s and continues to be the go-to company for this trail. Originally the treks started at the gates of their lovely hotel (as Michael Crichton writes in his account of his trek; see *Travels* p383) but these days, like everyone else, they bus their clients up to the gate.

Shira While most companies ignore the Shira Trail these days as it's largely a 4WD track, **Nature Discovery/Thomson** positively promote it, claiming – justifiably I suppose, given their success rates – that it is great for acclimatisation; though I still think it's a shame to drive past the lovely forest on Kili's western slopes!

Umbwe I love this route and have a soft-spot for the people that, in my opinion, do more on the Umbwe trail than most. **Summit Expeditions and Nomadic Experiences (SENE)** is run by Simon Mtuy, who took this route up to the summit when breaking per day (rising, so it is hoped, to US$20 in 2024) – a startling amount when you consider KPAP's own minimum daily wage is half that! It also means that their clients are not obliged to pay any gratuities for their crew and the porters don't need to rely on unreliable tips to survive.

I think this needs to be emphasised: ***on a Fair Travel Tanzania trek you are not obliged to pay any tips***. They are the only company to do this. So while their prices are US$2995pp, in order to compare them fairly with their competitors you need to subtract about US$300-400 – that sum being, approximately, the tips you'll be asked to pay with other companies. All of which is very laudable but what is their service like? Well, I love the transparent way they conduct their business, providing potential clients with a breakdown of how their prices are made up. I do have a few gripes: accommodation isn't included in the price, the child discount of US$600 was not perfect (but not derisory either), and they ignored my request for the Lemosho Route at first, preferring instead to push us onto overcrowded Machame. As for the quality of their treks, they make no claim towards luxury but they're pretty standard in that respect, their guides are very good, and the reviews (though few) are almost universally positive.

the world record for the fastest unassisted ascent of Kilimanjaro and who promotes Umbwe quite heavily. Tusker and my own Kilimanjaro Experts offer unconventional versions of the route that extend the Umbwe experience from 6 to 8 days.

Lemosho and the Western Breach Alongside the late Scott Fischer's Mountain Madness company, **African Environments (AE)** helped pioneer both the Lemosho route and the ascent to the summit via the tricky Western Breach.

One of AE's former employees, Lema Peter, has set up his own company, **Serengeti Pride Safaris**, that also specialises in this route and the Western Breach approach to the Crater – and at half the price! A third company, **Detasa**, also claim to specialise in this route.

Machame Such a popular trail, there are no real specialists; indeed, there are a few companies who specifically *avoid* this route now because it's so busy.

Kidia See pp386-7 and Summits Africa (pp103-4).

Companies that have invented their own routes

I like companies that design their own routes. I think it shows a company's confidence in what they're doing and comprehensive knowledge of the mountain and the paths. It also shows that they are striving to give their climbers the best experience possible. Whether it's avoiding the crowds and queues that form on a regular, 'official' route, taking in a particularly beautiful part of the mountain, or to allow their climbers to better acclimatise, there are many reasons for designing a new trail.

It should be pointed out that you are not allowed to actually blaze a completely new trail, so these new routes they've invented are actually formed from existing trails which they've then combined to form a new route to the summit.

Special mention must go to **Nature Discovery** and its Grand Traverse, which offers a grand sweep of the mountain from west to east, from Lemosho Gate to Rongai's Mawenzi Tarn and then onto the summit; **Tusker**'s Kili 360 which starts on the mountain's quietest trail before heading round the Northern Circuit to the summit; and my own company, **Kilimanjaro Experts**, which has a Full Circuit Umbwe trek and the very popular Alternative Lemosho Route.

• **Summary** Their transparency is staggering and the innovative and ethical way they approach their business is worthy of the highest praise. If the fair treatment of porters is high on your wish list you must send them an enquiry.

Follow Alice (💻 followalice.com) A large international operation offering holidays all over the globe. Normally I'd shy away from corporations that offer treks all over the world, because usually, in their efforts to specialise in multiple destinations, they end up specialising in none, and the Kili packages they offer are rather humdrum as a result. But to be fair to Follow Alice (the name is a reference to *Alice in Wonderland* following the rabbit down the hole – there's no real person called Alice behind the company) they are going about things the right way: setting up a local company to organise their treks and aligning themselves with NGOs such as KPAP and Leave No Trace. They also seem to have picked up some sensible advice on what makes a good Kili package and their treks are fair value at US$2995pp (though airport transfers are extra at US$25pp each way), including accommodation at Lindrin Lodge, and the under-16 discount was only US$22.40 shy of what it should have been.
• **Summary** With some companies you get the feeling that their best days are behind them and, with their outmoded practices and lack of ethical principles, that they rightly belong in the past. With Follow Alice and their adroit use of the internet, YouTube videos, ethical standpoint and smart marketing, the opposite applies – they feel like they are setting the template for future corporations looking to muscle in on the Kili market. I don't think they're the best, or even the best in their price range – but for a relatively new Kili company, it's an impressive start.

Gladys Adventure (💻 gladysadventure.com; **M**) If nothing else, this company has a great backstory. Gladys started off by trading with trekkers who had finished their trek, offering souvenirs in return for any bits of kit they no longer required.

From this, she was able to set up the first and best equipment rental agency in town. Then about a decade ago she moved into organising the treks themselves – which she turned out to be rather good at too. Sadly, the lady herself died a few years ago but the company she founded is still going strong and by all accounts continues to provide a great service on the mountain. I do, however, have a couple of misgivings. Firstly, their reply to my enquiry didn't directly address the questions I had set; it left me with the strong impression that they don't really have time for individual enquiries, presumably because they are kept busy organising the treks for their agents (they are used by Peak Planet, I believe, amongst others). Still, they're long-term KPAP partners, their price of US$2598pp for 8 days on Lemosho was very fair, their child discount was just US$10 shy of the true discount at US$792 and I've received good reviews from readers about their operation, with knowledgeable guides and a reassuring focus on the health and wellbeing of their clients.
• **Summary** KPAP partners, reliable and well-priced.

Good Earth (💻 goodearthtours.com; **A**) A very good option. Their website rightly boasts that they practise responsible tourism, providing scholarships, books, and supplies to local children, and financial support to various environmental groups as well as being longstanding KPAP partners. Price-wise they're solidly mid range, with the Lemosho price for my family of four quoted at US$2790pp including two nights at the lovely Arusha Planet Lodge (which they own) and airport transfers. Now with both Canadian and US offices, their treks are fine, the reviews are great and I like them an awful lot.
• **Summary** Regularly cited by KPAP for their exemplary treatment of porters, this lot are a good-hearted bunch with pretty much everything going for them.

Homeland (💻 homeland-adventures.business.site; **M**) One of the bigger success stories of the last few years, Homeland was set up by Muksin, the first Tanzanian to cycle to the top of Kili. A lot of business comes from their successful Mountain Bikes House in Moshi (see p227), though their climbers are actually put up in Maisha Khalisi Cottages, near their restaurant of the same name, to the north of Shanty Town. Treks are cheap (US$2450pp). Their reviews are largely positive but, it must be said, largely old too; that, and the fact they're not KPAP partners, makes me think that there are better options available at this price point.

• **Summary** I like their hostel and their restaurant but wonder if the focus of the business is on those now rather than their trekking operation.

Kessy Brothers (🖳 kessybrotherstours.co.tz; **M**) The brothers win the award for being the cheapest of all the operators I approached, with their 8-day Lemosho program a jaw-dropping US$1745pp. And your jaw will drop even lower when you realise this supposedly also includes two nights' accommodation at Moshi's Key's Hotel, oxygen, airport transfers and even, so they say, kit hire. They make no claim to being partners of KPAP – it would be staggering if they were – but weighed against this is the positive reviews they get online.

• **Summary** For a rock-bottom climb they're worth looking at given the wealth of positive reviews – assuming you can tuck your conscience away in your daypack and not care about how much they pay their porters.

Keys Hotel Tours (🖳 keys-hotel-tours.com; **M**) Still very busy Moshi operator that's been going for about 30 years. Offers a refreshingly honest appraisal of The routes up Kili (correctly describing Machame as overcrowded, for example, and talking about the acclimatisation problems on the Marangu Route). Hotel's nice too. No longer KPAP partners, but to be fair I understand they're paying a good wage these days. Price-wise they charge US$2353pp for Lemosho (note one-way airport transfer only is included with this price), with the under-16 discount a pleasantly surprising US$851.

• **Summary** Experienced, competent and busy. Struggle to endorse them because of their on-off relationship with KPAP, so any claims about their fair treatment of porters can't be independently verified – but their treks are unquestionably fair value.

Kibo Slopes (🖳 kiboslopes.com; **A & Nairobi**) Smart and professionally run company and the biggest of those operating out of Kenya. Offer Kilimanjaro treks using their own climbing outfit, Kibo Slopes Tanzania, based in Arusha. Prices are high at US$3059pp.

• **Summary** Not brilliant but they are KPAP partners and, if you have to book your trek with a Kenyan operator, they're the best option.

Kili Worldborn Safaris (KWS; 🖳 www.kili-worldborn-safaris.com; **M**) To be honest, this lot surprised me. Firstly, KWS offered incredible value with their quote for 8 days on Lemosho being just US$2050pp, with more than the full under-16 discount (US$850) offered too. Toilet, accommodation at Lindrin Lodge, emergency oxygen, Mountain Hardware tents, and airport transfers were all bundled into the package too. They've even recently become KPAP partners. Drawbacks? Well, for some reason, they want to charge US$780 per group if you have any dietary requirements – something that just about every other company will provide for free. Oh, and there's a *complete* lack of online reviews, which is just mystifying.

• **Summary** There's much to recommend KWS if you judge them purely on the specifications of their trek. But the lack of online reviews is puzzling, so ask them to provide you with contact details of someone who has climbed with them *recently*. If they can't do that, maybe look elsewhere. But if they can, and the person is positive about their experience with KWS, I think they're worth a punt – as long as you don't have any particular dietary requirements.

Kili Zone (🖳 kilizone.co.tz; **A**) They have their own website but if you want to elicit any kind of response from them you have to go via agents 💻 bush2beach.com (though it's actually the same people). Can't fault their experience, with most guides having completed at least 100 successful ascents of Kili. As they're a KPAP partner, too, so I can't fault the treatment of their staff, either. As for the treks themselves, as you'd expect they're very good and the price tag of US$2895pp seems justifiable, especially as it includes *three* nights at Kilimanjaro Wonders Hotel (thus making them the only company that I can think of which is based in one city but puts its climbers up in a different one). They are also one of the very few companies to offer the ALTOX Oxygen system (US$200pp). Don't seem to be getting too much work at the moment – and recent reviews are hard to come by – but that's the only concern I have.

• **Summary** A few more *recent* reviews about their climbs would be reassuring; nevertheless, a high-quality company.

Kilimanjaro Brothers (💻 kilimanjaro brothers.com; **M**) Moshi-based company who, if you were to believe everything on their website, would be amazing, and their reviews are largely positive too. On their site they make a big song-and-dance about taking the safety of their clients very seriously, with Gamow bags (see pp251-2), oxygen and pulse oximeters on every climb. Reviews are largely positive too. I also can't fault the value – US$2200 for an 8-day Lemosho climb, and though the email wasn't the clearest (nor the most enthusiastic), it appears they were offering a child discount of US$700 to both children, even though one was above 16 years old and thus shouldn't have been due any discount. They also, unexpectedly, offer climbers on their Deluxe package the use of the ALTOX personal oxygen system and supply climbers with someone to carry their daypack for the summit climb. Their refusal to engage with any of my questions about KPAP, however, tells its own story. They also have a US office.

• **Summary** One of a slew of companies that seem to do everything right, but I can't recommend wholeheartedly because of uncertainties about how they treat their porters. Becoming a KPAP partner would solve that, of course – but the way they ignored my questions on this subject suggest that's not going to happen anytime soon.

Kilimanjaro Experts (💻 kilimanjaroex perts.com; **Usa River**) Trekking company and KPAP partner run by the author of this book and a couple of colleagues. I won't write any more about us here because presumably you are reading this book for advice, not an advert. But do get in touch – because I think we're the best value on the mountain, of course!

• **Summary** Please don't hesitate to enquire (💻 henry@kilimanjaroexperts .com) to find out more about our service – we'd love to have you along!

Kilimanjaro Heroes Adventures (💻 kilimanjaroheroes.com; **M**) At first glance this company looks good, with a swish website, offices in both Moshi and Arusha and some incredibly cheap prices (US$1900pp) offered. Unfortunately, however, everything is not quite as rosy as it seems, for they're yet another operator happy to lie about being KPAP partners (indeed, according to statistics I have seen they pay some of the worst wages on the mountain). Also, the children's discount was a very paltry 10%, or US$190.

• **Summary** Good specifications for their trek, really cheap, and garner a lot of custom from the overseas volunteers working in Moshi; but poor wages paid, so I hear, and for all their chat on their website about being an ethical company, I'm not convinced.

Kilimanjaro Vikings (💻 kilivikings .com; **M**) Small but one of the slickest at the budget end of the market. Admits they aren't partners of KPAP – in fact, they say they're treating their porters better than KPAP guidelines! – but at least the price is good at US$2300pp. The child discount of US$200 is, alas, less than exemplary but, to be fair, they applied it to both of my (fake) children; though that still adds up to only half of what it should be (US$400 in total as opposed to US$800 for one person). But reviews of their service on the mountain are fairly numerous and pretty good.

• **Summary** Little bit mystified as to why Kilimanjaro Vikings are succeeding while a whole slew of very similar companies aren't, though they do seem to run fair if unexceptional treks.

Kisambi (💻 kisambitours.com; **M**) Small company garnering some exceptional reviews on TripAdvisor. The initial price they quoted us was a very reasonable US$2040pp, though do note that no accommodation is included and the under-16 discount was a pretty pathetic US$290. Looking at their reviews they seem to cater more for those looking for a safari or day trip rather than a Kili climb, though they do seem to know their stuff when it comes to the mountain, with an itinerary, tipping guidelines and packing list all attached to their email. Note, however, that they don't offer treks up the Western Breach.

• **Summary** Not outstanding but worth contacting if you're after a budget trek.

Kwetu Tanzania (💻 kwetutours.com; **A**) Straightforward and upfront, Kwetu profess an ethical outlook (their director, Dennis, who seems to run the whole operation, works with a California-based charity looking to improve health and education in East Africa). If nothing else, I admire the honesty of Dennis, who confessed that Kwetu was not a KPAP partner before he would even provide us with a quote. The most surprising aspect of their response, however, was the humungous US$1340 child discount – over US$500 more than the total discount in the park fees!

The price they asked for adults, US$2320pp, was fair, particularly as they boast that they 'operate a fair-traded policy where I employ only qualified local staff, pay them well above average rates with annual profit-share bonuses, and I do not compromise on park fees, equipment and services.' All of which sounds laudable, though without the independent scrutiny of a body such as KPAP these claims are, as always, difficult to verify.

• **Summary** Fairly priced and they seem decent and honest; worth writing to if it suits your budget, though do enquire further – and try to verify – about how much they pay their crew.

Local Moshi Adventures (💻 www.localmoshi.com; **M**) This bunch are a great addition to the Kili trekking scene. They are both KPAP and Leave No Trace partners with some excellent-value treks that, if their online reviews are to be believed, are highly regarded by their climbers. What I particularly like about them is their flexibility, with accommodation options ranging from the budget to the luxury, and daytime summits also readily suggested. They charge $2305pp for treks with hostel-type accommodation and $2400pp for hotel accommodation. The only negative I can see is that their under-16 discount was only US$505 – less than the expected US$802.40 – but otherwise, these people tick just about every box.

• **Summary** New and definitely worth contacting for budget trekkers with a social conscience.

Maasai Wanderings (💻 maasaiwanderings.com; **A**) Company established by an Australian woman and her Tanzanian husband that boasts repeatedly on their website about how 'ethical' they are, though I have to say they hardly covered themselves in glory when I contacted them. In my correspondence they claimed to be KPAP partners, though I could find no evidence of this; offered us *no* child discount; *and* refused to quote us for Lemosho too, pushing us instead towards the Marangu Route (even though it's an inferior trail in just about every way). Then to cap it all off, they quoted an eye-watering US$350 for a toilet on the trek. Given the price they did eventually quote for a Lemosho Route trek – US$2840pp – there are definitely more trustworthy operators around at this price.

• **Summary** Dishonest about their relationship with KPAP, declined to offer us any discount for the 13-year-old – even though they, of course, have to pay a lot less in park fees – and tried to push us to an inferior route rather than sticking with Lemosho. In summary: not my favourites.

Majestic Kilimanjaro (🖳 majestickilimanjaro.com; **A**) I must confess I have a soft spot for Majestic, having known their owner, Tumaini, since he was a guide with Team Kilimanjaro. Garnering good reviews from their clients, their treks are justly priced at US$2587pp and all but US$5 of the under-16 park fee discount was passed on to us too.

Their Australian backers (they have an office in Australia) take no income from the business and their half of the profits go to community projects in East Africa, which is very laudable.

• **Summary** Though seemingly concentrating more on safaris these days, KPAP partners Majestic continue to hoover up a reasonable share of the Kili market by offering fairly priced mid-range treks and an ethical outlook.

Marangu Hotel (🖳 maranguhotel.com; **Marangu**) No company can boast the pedigree and experience of Marangu Hotel, which has been sending climbers up Kilimanjaro since – wait for it – 1932! Always had a good reputation for treating

❑ CLIMBING WITHOUT PORTERS

Several companies on Kili offer a cheaper, stripped-back version of their treks. By reducing/eradicating the amount of non-essential equipment provided such as mess tents, tables and chairs, the size of the crew can be dramatically reduced because fewer porters are required, so the company is able to drop the price. Some companies will also offer you the chance to carry your own luggage. Indeed, in extreme cases, you can get away with no porters whatsoever, and just have two guides (the minimum number of mountain crew allowed these days).

These treks come under various names: Alpinist, lite, superlite, ironman/ironwoman. But while the concept of trekking without porters may seem a simple one, the reality of hiking up Africa's Highest Mountain with only minimal assistance is very much not. Because **these minimally supported treks are not be underestimated.** Remember, your body is already undergoing a considerable amount of strain just by being at high altitude. Carrying your own luggage – often about 25kg in total, once you've added food, camping and cooking equipment to your personal effects – only adds to the stress on your body.

There is also a *lot* of extra work involved after you've finished trekking too; jobs that you simply wouldn't have to do on a regular Kili trek, such as:

- Putting up your own tent at the end of each day's walking.
- Fetching water for drinking, cooking and cleaning.
- Preparing your own meals each day.
- Washing up the cutlery, crockery, pots and pans each day.
- Breaking camp each morning after breakfast, as well as packing everything, including litter, and make sure the campsite is spotless for those coming after you.

How will I know if I can climb without porters?

As I write on my website, **these hikes are for seasoned, experienced trekkers only**. You also need to be used to heavy physical stress and activity, and to have a lot of experience of being at high altitude. If you're not sure whether that description applies to you, then before booking a porter-free trek, try to carry 25kg on a multi-day trek in your home country. Then imagine carrying that at high altitude where the air is thin, oxygen is scarce and you may well already be suffering from the various symptoms of altitude sickness.

their porters well and clients are not only introduced to their crew at the start of the trek but are encouraged to mix more with them too, resulting in a camaraderie that is absent from treks with other agencies. At the end of the climb the hotel also throws a bit of a party for *everyone* to celebrate; little wonder they've been partners with KPAP since the organisation's inception. Trek-wise, the price quoted was US$2819pp, with virtually the full discount offered for under 16s. Surprisingly, on top of that you need to add on accommodation at their hotel (see p241), airport transfers (US$85 per vehicle each way to Marangu) and even oxygen (US$100) – though. Wonderfully, other rental equipment (sleeping bags, coats etc) are free. Reviews from readers and on the net are recent and enthusiastic.

● **Summary** I have always loved this hotel and by all accounts their treks are fine too. Worth enquiring with for any route and there's no better choice for those looking for a mid-range Marangu climb.

Maua Adventures (💻 mauaadventures.com; **M**) Moshi-based company operating out of Moshi's Shanty Town which, though not dwelling in the absolute bargain basement, gets a decent slice of business from

If you not only survive that experience, but enjoy it, and you are confident that you are still capable of carrying your own bag on Kili, that's excellent. But if it's a struggle in any way, don't even consider it.

Will a porter-free trek save me much money?

Given the paltry wages that porters are paid, deciding to go without them probably won't lead to as bigger drop in price as you were hoping for. So **do not attempt this sort of trek just because you want to save money.** That is a terrible idea. These pared-down treks are for those who like the idea of challenging themselves by carrying their own luggage, rather than for those who want to save every last penny.

That said, you will doubtless save three figures, and possibly four, by opting to reduce the size of your crew. The companies that offer these minimally supported treks are usually at the more expensive end of the budgetary scale, too, and some of the features of their regular, pricier treks – the stuff that made their prices so expensive in the first place – are often present on their cheaper treks too. For example, if a company has WFR-trained guides on their 'normal' treks, it's highly likely they'll also be present on their budget treks.

So which companies offer treks without porters?

Kilimanjaro Experts (p96) Our **Ironman series** is for those who want as little support as we are allowed to provide. In other words, just guides and some cooking and camping equipment. Food is dehydrated to save on weight. If that sounds too Spartan, we also offer **hybrid climbs** where you get to choose exactly the level of support you receive. So if you don't want a whole army of porters, but think that one or two may make life on the mountain a lot more pleasant, that's not a problem. And if, for example, you're happy to forego mess tents, tables and chairs, but would quite like a private toilet, or would really prefer fresh food to dehydrated, that's also not a problem; we'll tell you how many porters you'll need and how much extra it will cost.

Team Kilimanjaro (p105) TK run a **Lite series** of climbs where you agree to carry 12kg of their own luggage and forego the pleasures of a mess tent. They also offer the ascetic-style **Superlite**, where climbers have to provide and carry all their own food and equipment, make their own way to Arusha from the airport and book their own accommodation.

the hordes of volunteers who want to summit Africa's Highest Mountain before returning home at the end of their trip. Their relationship with KPAP, however, clearly remains awkward. In the last edition they claimed to be in the process of becoming a KPAP partner (though they weren't), but for this edition they've dropped the pretence and now argue that KPAP are there just to kill local companies. Which, of course, just isn't true. It's a shame, for if they could get over their animosity towards KPAP there is a lot to like: the price was fair (US$2190pp), the children's discount a slightly small but not disastrous US$547, and oxygen, airport transfers and accommodation at Parkview are all included, Reviews are generally OK too. They have an office in the USA.
• **Summary** They need to increase their prices, pay higher wages to their crews, then join KPAP; until they do, bring extra money for tips to supplement the meagre wages the company is clearly paying.

Mega Adventures (💻 megaadventures travel.com; **M**). Another budget outfit, this time operating out of Moshi's We Travel Hostel from where it dredges a fair bit of custom. It took us several attempts before they deigned to reply, but when they did the price of US$2196pp for four people for eight days on Lemosho was very good; and the fact they then offered over US$1000 as a discount for the under-16 was both laudable and amazing. True, airport transfers are excluded from their trek package but they only charge US$40 per vehicle for these (US$10 less than the normal rate); accommodation is also excluded though seeing as they are based at the We Travel Hostel, one of the nicest (and cheapest) budget options in town, it's no real hardship. But what are the treks actually like? Well, good, according to all the reviews I could find: climbs are basic but comfortable and with attentive staff.
• **Summary** Obviously the wages they pay to their porters will be lower than average – at these prices, they can't be anything but – but they seem pretty upfront and doing a good job. As always, however, bring greater tips if you choose them to compensate for the probably lower wage.

Monkey Adventures (💻 monkey.travel/en; **M** & **A**) Probably the most popular of the budget operators, its business model revolves around selling large quantities of no-frills treks cheaply. On the plus side, their prices are indeed cheap (US$1950pp, though no accommodation or airport transfers are included in this price), and their child discount was pretty much spot-on at US$800. They are also definitely proficient, and the reviews would suggest their treks are fine too. You have to admire their honesty: they said they weren't KPAP partners because they would have to put up their wages, which would in turn put up their prices. It's a dilemma that a lot of companies face, of course, but at least they are open about it. Uniquely, they also said they can organise a private 'KPAP-standard' trek for us where the crew is paid more. Weighed against all these positives is the fact that they aren't as local as they would like you to think – the 'About us' section of their website is very opaque and the contact numbers are all European/North American.
• **Summary** Cheap, reliable, but not KPAP partners, which I find disappointing.

Nature Discovery (💻 naturediscovery .com; **A**) Upmarket company – founded and still partly managed by Brits – that's been in operation for over 30 years. Working closely with the large safari operator Thomson, this lot are ahead of the pack when it comes to offering high-spec treks. Their safety record and procedures are certainly amongst the best, with every guide WFR-trained. A hyperbaric chamber/Gamow bag accompanies every trek too, as well as a 'medical porter' who stays with the clients at all times. I really like their optional 'add-ons', where for a supplement you can have your own heated lounge tent complete with inflatable furniture, coffee table and soft flooring, or a proper frame bed (with mattress), or hot showers, or solar charging kits. I also really like the look of their Grand Traverse Tour, an 8-day odyssey that starts on the Shira Plateau and heads east towards Mawenzi Tarn before looping back to School Hut; encompassing the northern/western, eastern and southern sides of the mountain, there is no trek that takes in more of Kili than this one. Group treks are also available. They are also KPAP partners, pay their staff very well (the only porters who are fully clad in Gore-Tex!). Of course, such a fine service doesn't come cheap, and it's US$5014pp for their most popular, 'Superior' standard treks, and even their 'lite' option is US$4378pp, with pre- and post-trek accommodation and airport transfers, and any of the add-ons listed above, extra. A precise US$802 child discount was offered too.

● **Summary** It's hard to find fault with these people and if money is no object then Nature Discovery are, to coin a phrase, probably the best a man (or woman) can get.

Nyange Adventures (💻 nyangeadventures.com; **M** & **A**) Impressive budget operator with a lot of clients and a KPAP partner too. Seldom misses a trick when it comes to attracting custom, from advertising group treks in cafés around town to paying the taxi drivers who drive people from the airport to promote their tours too. And once you've contacted them, you'll get emails on an almost weekly basis. Have seen some outstanding reviews for their treks and they're fairly priced at US$2247pp, with the under-16 discount US$447. They also have an office in the USA.

● **Summary** Amongst the slew of little companies operating in Moshi, Nyange stand out for maintaining their KPAP partner status for many years. Though that partnership isn't always 100% secure, for a budget trek with a conscience they're definitely worth contacting.

Origin Trails (💻 origintrails.co.tz; **M**) It's hard to find a reason *not* to like Origin. KPAP partners – the cheapest ones I could find – they are a small company but one that appears to be run with honesty, professionalism and courtesy. Origin Trails was set up by cheerful local Emanuel whose CV, including several years' work for Summits Africa, is impeccable. This experience has put him in good stead, enabling him to recruit some of his former WFR-trained guides as employees in his new venture (though do check this as a WFR-trained guide can't be guaranteed on every trek). Emanuel himself still leads some of the climbs too (indeed, he said he was off to the mountain as soon as he'd finished replying to my enquiry). Price-wise they're very good-value given the quality of their treks, what is supplied (including sleeping bags and a private toilet), with the 8-day Lemosho trek costing US$1930pp for four people and the under-16 discount US$630. Clients are usually housed in Moshi's Chanya Lodge (two free nights included); oxygen and airport transfers are also included. Few reviews as they operate few treks, but I expect them to be busier in the future.

● **Summary** One to watch and enquire with if your conscience is bigger than your budget; not a huge operation, but very good value.

Popote Africa (💻 popoteafrica.com; **M**) One of the more successful of the little companies in Moshi, largely because of successful exploitation of a review website. They're slick and good value, with prices US$2355pp, including *full board* nights at a couple of good-quality hotels in Moshi, Lindrin Lodge and Parkview Inn. The under-16 discount is an impressive US$825. Just wish they were KPAP partners too (and I don't buy their excuse that if they did become KPAP partners, they 'wouldn't be able to ensure the safety of our clients'); if they did, they'd tick just about every box.

● **Summary** Popular and good value and worth investigating for a cheaper trek; not members of KPAP so do interrogate them on their treatment of porters and bring more money for tips to make sure your crew doesn't go short.

Pristine Trails (💻 pristinetrails.com; **M**) Going for well over a decade now, this Moshi-based operation has been garnering good reviews throughout this time and I have been a fan for almost as long. There have a been a few changes since the last edition – one of the founders has moved over to the States, and the prices (US$3045pp) they charge for their treks are a lot more than they used to be, which has moved them out of the budget bracket and firmly into the mid-price range (and even beyond!). But apart from these concerns they do still fulfil most of the criteria I look for: an entirely Tanzanian-owned KPAP partner company (though an American woman helps take the bookings and writes excellent, comprehensive responses to all enquiries from potential customers) that provides professionally run treks by head guides who are all WFR trained. Airport transfers, oxygen, private toilet, pre- and post-trek accommodation at Kilimanjaro Wonders are all included and the under-16 discount was a more-than-it-should-have-been US$970 off the adult fee! Operate open groups too (which are about US$150pp cheaper than private treks) and, uniquely, also operate 100% risk-free refundable booking policy.

● **Summary** No longer outstanding value but still much to admire in most of what they do.

Real Life Adventure Travel (🖳 reallife adventuretravel.com; **M**) Wholly Tanzanian-owned KPAP companies are rather rare, so Real Life are to be treasured for this reason. Their response to my enquiry was prompt and polite. The price of US$2650pp was fair, the under-16 discount of US$830 even more so – and the US$400 discount offered to my fictional 17-year-old was a big and very pleasant shock (just to remind you, there shouldn't be a discount for 17-year-olds.) Nor did the surprises stop there, for they also include a chemical toilet – free – on each trek, and, uniquely, power banks to charge your phones while you're on the mountain; they also offer three free nights' accommodation rather than the standard two in their trek package – again, an unusual decision (only four other companies offer this) but a great one.

● **Summary** Few treks so difficult to judge and recommend without hesitation. But otherwise they tick all the boxes: knowledgeable, experienced, accomplished, and they seem to have thought long and hard about what their climbers would like. I'm really impressed – and I just hope they start to get the number of climbers they deserve.

Serengeti Pride Safaris (🖳 serengeti pridesafaris.com; **Usa River**) Small but likeable joint Tanzanian and American-owned company that has been going for almost a decade now. Email responses are eloquent, thorough and polite and they deserve praise on several fronts: for maintaining standards of safety (their expedition leaders are all WFR-trained and all treks are equipped with a Gamow bag, oxygen and oximeters); the treatment of their crew (they are solid KPAP partners); and the quality of their service (with pre- and post-trek accommodation at the plush Planet Lodge in Arusha and a decent set of online reviews from happy clients). Highly recommended in particular for those who want to climb the Western Breach and sleep in the crater – specialists on this route are hard to come by and the most well-known one, African Environments (see p83), is terrifically expensive; the co-owner of Serengeti Pride, however – who himself used to work as a guide with African Environments and runs his climbs along their lines – has set his prices (US$3399pp) at less than half of his former employers.

● **Summary** Well worth investigating, particularly for those looking to take the Western Breach Route to the summit.

Shah Tours (🖳 www.shah-tours.com; **M**) Family-run and in business for over 40 years, Shah are a reliable and reasonable choice. Wonderfully, after years of having no truck with KPAP, they've seen the error of their ways and are now active partners. Rates-wise, they're good value at US$2385pp (child discount US$680), a price that includes two nights at their Bristol Cottages. Their pricing system is slightly confusing, however, for as well as some hidden charges (private toilets are US$45 per day, for example, and airport transfers are an extra US$80 each way) there are also some extras that can be included, from self-inflatable mattresses to fruit platters served at the exit gates at trek's end.

● **Summary** Cheap-ish, reliable, and for the first time in 20 years, I have no hesitation in recommending them.

Snowcap Tanzania Tours (💻 snowcap.co.tz; **M & Rongai**) There are a couple of big reasons to contact Snowcap. Firstly, by my reckoning, they're one of the cheapest KPAP partners. Secondly, they are also the go-to company if you're interested in the Rongai Route, which they concentrate on more than any other company and which they've done more than any other to popularise. The father of the owner, at the time of writing, did so to help the employment prospects on this north-eastern corner of the mountain, and they also renovated the School Hut, the final hut on the standard Rongai ascent, and built the rather lovely Snowcap Cottages on the Kenyan border by the start of the trek (see p234). Small but very experienced, their treks are very good value (their Lemosho package is US$2196pp, which includes two nights half-board at the smart Snowcap Cottages), they have a good heart (the boss, Kenneth, is a genuinely good fellow) and the only negatives I could find was that their child discount was a meagre US$460, and reviews of them online are hard to find. They have an office in the USA.

● **Summary** If you are on a budget but still want to do the right thing by your mountain crew they've got to be worth considering. Also recommended for those on the Rongai Route, and especially if you're coming from Kenya and want to climb the mountain without schlepping all the way to Moshi or Arusha to arrange it.

Summit Expeditions and Nomadic Experience (aka **SENE**; 💻 nomadicexperience.com; **M**) Run by the irrepressible force of personality that is Simon Mtuy – an ultra-racer and the holder of the record for the fastest unaided ascent and descent of Kili (see p150) – SENE just do things slightly differently to everyone else when it comes to tackling Africa's highest mountain and for this they are to be highly praised. They tend to concentrate mainly on the Lemosho Route (which accounts for about 80% of their climbs) though also, refreshingly, run several climbs per year on little-used Umbwe Route. Not cheap – US$3990pp on Lemosho – though the child discount was a whopping US$1490. The price includes a stay at Simon's lovely farm at Mbahe, 15 minutes' west of Marangu Gate, a Moshi walking tour and a Mbahe village walking tour, which both provide a brief glimpse into the day-to-day lives of rural Tanzania. Furthermore, the treks themselves are by all accounts excellent, and I've received some truly glowing reports from delighted trekkers about them down the years. They've been partners of KPAP since the beginning, and they are also used by several Western agencies who appreciate SENE's ethical and ecologically minded approach to climbing.

● **Summary** I love these people. They're not cheap, but by any measure they're worth it.

Summits Africa (💻 summits-africa.com; **A**) One of the leading companies on the mountain, formed and still run by the son of one of the founders of Hoopoe Adventure, one of the biggest names in climbing and safaris in recent years. Very safety-conscious with WFR-trained guides, and ethically minded too, having been with KPAP since its inception. They run three levels of treks: Standard (lightweight mess tent, table and stools); Luxury (private toilet, sleeping bag and backed chairs rather than stools all included); and VIP (walk-in tents, cots). I have to say, providing stools, as they do on their standard treks, rather than chairs with backs just seems cruel — even the cheapest companies provide proper chairs as standard. Reluctant to take direct bookings, preferring instead that you use one of their agents such as Aardvark in the UK. Contacting Aardvark, they offered a 'Standard-spec' trek on Lemosho for eight days for £4300pp (equivalent to US$5444pp at the exchange rate at the time of writing) but, rather shamefully, no child discount. Whether this was the agent's fault or Summits' I've no idea – but there's no real excuse. (Also contacted A&K, another agent that uses Summits, and this time was quoted over US$8000pp – again, with no child discount.) They have also been one of the main driving forces behind the new Kidia Route (see below).

● **Summary** Not my favourite of the luxury operators because of some minor quibbles that, at this price point, simply shouldn't exist. But still very good indeed and their promotion of the VIP-only Kidia Route (see pp386-7) that should be opened in 2024 could give them a big advantage over other companies.

Sunny Safaris (sunnysafaris.com; **A**) Once one of the busier budget agencies but a little quieter now – possibly because their office on Middleton Rd sees far fewer budget travellers than in years gone by when this part of town was Backpacker Central. I mention them here purely because you may still see them recommended in some old publications but, to be honest, these days there are better, more highly regarded options at this price point (US$2535pp for eight days on Lemosho).

● **Summary** Few climbs these days and, if you are after a budget trek, they are neither the cheapest nor the best.

Tanzania Climbing Outfitters (**TCO**; kiliclimboutfitters.com; **A**) Once a fairly obscure Arusha-based company known as Kili Climbing Outfitters, TCO's email to us was concise and informative and initially I was quite impressed. Their treks are of a decent specification, with all guides WFR trained, oxygen is issued as standard and pre- and post-trek accommodation is offered at Outpost Lodge. Given this, their treks were, I thought, pretty good value at US$2658pp, with their under-16 discount a ludicrous US$1458 off the adult price. My only hesitation in recommending them is that in the last edition they said they were meeting with KPAP to discuss being partners – but KPAP denied any meeting ever took place. And according to TCO's email for this edition, they are *still* waiting to become a KPAP partner almost seven years later! Which, to be honest, I just don't believe.

● **Summary** Talk a good talk if their website is to be trusted. But that's the problem, really – because they've been less than truthful about their relationship with KPAP in the past, I'm inclined not to accept many of their other claims either.

Tanzania Experience (tanzania-experience.com; **Usa River**) Established and run with significant help from German backers, Tanzania Experience have been operating since 2007 and offer both scheduled departures and private climbs. Price-wise they're pretty average at US$2910pp, including accommodation at the quirky Meru View Lodge. Note, however, that oxygen is *not* issued on group climbs (they even said it wasn't necessary, which will probably raise a few eyebrows among their fellow companies). In terms of how they treat their porters, they're upfront about no longer being KPAP partners and by all accounts do treat their crew well – though I am a little sceptical about the claim in their email that they pay more than the KPAP minimum. Treks, too, receive a lot of praise in their reviews.

● **Summary** Offer reliably decent treks but no oxygen. Really?!

Tanzania Journeys (tanzaniajourneys.com; **M**) Formed in 2005, Tanzania Journeys boast a UK connection, are friendly and profess an ecological and humanitarian outlook. Indeed, they have recently committed to having a female guide working on *every* trek and run a tree-planting program to combat deforestation on Kili. In response to my email I found this KPAP partner to be honest, well-informed and fairly priced, with Lemosho eight days US$2700pp for their standard service including two nights B&B in Moshi's Chanya Lodge (see p234), helicopter rescue cover and transfers from either Kilimanjaro Airport or, unusually, Nairobi. WFR-trained guides, private toilets (US$150 per trek) and Gamow bags are also available. The discount in park fees for the under 16 was US$680, which is better than most but not perfect. Service on the mountain is, by all accounts, very good.

● **Summary** I like them and think they're

worth contacting for an ethically minded mid-range trek.

Tanzania Joy (🖳 tanzaniajoytours.com; **M**) Another central Moshi company that is so cheap at US$1900pp, with the child discount an equally stupifying US$1030. This is pretty much the only thing that lifts them above the ordinary, however. Not with KPAP but instead say they have set up an NGO that helps young children to access education. Good reviews overall so busy and popular; they also have an office in the USA.

• **Summary** Cheap and positive appraisals online but make sure you bring a lot of extra cash for tips, to compensate for the probable meagre wages.

Tanzania Travel Company (aka **TTC**; 🖳 tanzaniatravelcompany.com; **A**) Small company run by Tanzanian naturalist Sam Diah that offers, despite the name, safaris all over East Africa. Their Kili treks are rather secondary to their safaris, which are clearly Sam's passion. Claimed in their email to us to be KPAP partners, which they aren't, which is naughty. Also clearly care little for copyright infringement, with some of the text on their website taken from a previous edition of this book. They're not alone in doing that, but if you're copying something wholesale from another source it does suggest a lack of familiarity with the subject, which is a concern. Their price of US$3202pp for the 8-day Lemosho is too much, even when the very generous US$980 child discount is taken into account.

• **Summary** They're clearly trying – the website is pretty and slick – but I still can't find much to recommend their climbs. Sam should probably stick to safaris – and you should look elsewhere.

TDMC (**M**) You won't find these people at all on Google, nor find a website for them, nor even an office. But this company take more people to the summit than anyone else, I think. For this KPAP partner works with two of the biggest agencies on Kilimanjaro – and takes no individual bookings themselves. Having climbed with them I found, on the plus-side, the equipment supplied to be very good, the food great, but the guides disappointing – though this was a few years ago. The biggest disappointment, however, is the prices charged by their agencies. One quoted us US$3815pp with no child discount(!), while their other main agency charged for airport transfers, and offered a paltry US$60 per day child discount, despite charging over US$3200pp. Both, interestingly, deny being agents at all but strongly imply that they are the ground operators.

• **Summary** Given the bombast on a couple of their agents' websites you'd think that this bunch were the Holy Grail of trekking companies and they certainly do a lot of business. But given the prices charged you'd expect more; presumably the agencies are just as much at fault here as TDMC themselves – but it is nevertheless disappointing.

Team Kilimanjaro (🖳 teamkilimanjaro.com; **A**) There's no doubting the quality of this well-established company, though they do seem to be a shadow of their former selves since the boss took a bit of a hiatus to further his political ambitions. Their guides are, on the whole, very good, which has always been their biggest selling point, and the reviews seem to be still largely positive. There have always been question marks over the amount of wages they pay – and though I would love to be surprised, given the boss's intransigence I think we'll see hell freezing over before they join KPAP. Price-wise, they're firmly in the upper/mid-range bracket at US$3169pp, with all but US$2.40 of the full under-16 discount passed on to their clients. Note they also provide cheaper versions of their treks, including a Lite version (US$2693pp for eight days on Lemosho) with no pre- or post-trek accommodation, mess tents or airport transfers, and you have to carry around 12kg; and Superlite (US$2129pp), where you provide and carry all your own food and equipment too.

• **Summary** Nowhere near as big or as busy as their glory days, though one or two of their best guides remain, and everything is in place for them to come roaring back; though I do find myself wondering if their hearts are still in it. If you're contacting them, do as always enquire about their treatment and salary of porters; the explanation you'll get will doubtless be long and eloquent – but I'll leave it up to you whether you find it convincing too.

The African Safari Trails (**TAST**; 🖳 theafricansafaritrails.co.tz; **A**) TAST grew out of the wreckage of former climbers' favourite African Walking Company and its owner, Paulo Lazare, was once a guide there before progressing to become its manager. While their response to my email was remarkable largely for its brevity (20 lines in total, with no attachments), Paul and the gang have worked with some of the biggest agents in the business, including Exodus, World Expeditions and African Travel Resource (ATR). As such, The African Safari Trails are used to operating with the ALTOX oxygen system, as used by ATR on their treks (for US$335 extra). As for the actual quality of their service on the mountain, well their strategy of including neither pre- and post-trek accommodation nor airport transfers is certainly unique, but not in a good way. But plus points are several: they are KPAP and Leave No Trace partners, they calculated the under-16 discount almost *precisely*, their staff are experienced and private toilets are provided as standard on their treks. Online reviews are few, though presumably that's because most of their climbers have been sent by one of these big agents, and thus climbers have no idea they're on a TAST trek.

• **Summary** Any company that is used by the agent African Travel Resource (ATR) must be recommended in my opinion. And while most of their climbers are sent by agents such as ATR and Exodus, they were happy to arrange a trek for us too – and they're good value and worth considering for a solid mid-range trek.

Tusker Trail/Tembo Trails (🖳 tusker.com; **M**) The ground operator may be Tembo Trails but everybody knows them as **Tusker**, a very successful American company and KPAP partner that's been operating for over 40 years now (second only to Marangu Hotel, I believe). The quality of their treks is beyond reproach though prices are pretty wince-making at US$6340pp but a healthy US$954 child discount softens the blow a little. At that price you'd expect every aspect of the trek to be top notch, and to be fair Tusker do their best to justify the price, with oxygen, airport transfers, three or four nights' accommodation all included (though surprisingly at Moshi's Bristol Cottages or Parkview Inn, rather than the classier Kilimanjaro Wonders), as well as catering on Kili from a properly trained, qualified chef, private toilets, guides who receive amongst the best medical training, and first-rate gear, much of it specifically designed by Tusker themselves. I also like the enthusiasm they clearly demonstrate towards the mountain, with regular interesting and intelligent articles about Kili produced for those who subscribe to their website. They also run a 'Kili360' tour that begins on the Umbwe Route before heading round the northern side of Kibo, aiming for the summit via the Kibo Huts.

• **Summary** Still first-rate and always worth enquiring with if you have the financial wherewithal.

Top Climbers (🖳 topclimbersexpedition.com; **M**) Cheap and seemingly excellent value, with Lemosho price a budget US$2350pp, including a reasonable child's discount of US$650 and two nights at Parkview Inn. How can they do it, I asked? Well, sad to say that, despite their claims, I have seen reports that their treatment of porters is not exactly exemplary and certainly not as good as they boast. What can't be argued with is that they do get glowing reviews online.

• **Summary** If their treatment of porters is as good as they claim then they're great and I'll wholeheartedly recommend them. If not, and I don't believe they are, they're only for those who can leave their conscience at the hotel before climbing.

Trek2Kili (🖳 trek2kili.com; **M**) This company is great. Owned and founded in

2010 by easygoing former porter and guide, Azizi, this company has everything going for it: a good success rate, great online reviews for their treks and a desire, if their emails are anything to go by, to genuinely treat porters well; indeed, they applied to join KPAP before they'd even taken a booking. Treks are all led by WFR-trained guides and are justifiably in the mid-range at US$2970pp with two nights' accommodation at Kilimanjaro Wonders thrown in. Also offered us a staggering US$1782 discount for under 16s – significantly more than the US$802.40 reduction in park fees. Has open-group climbs too.

• **Summary** I'm really impressed by this lot. True, their prices are getting a little too high but in pretty much every other aspect this company is admirable.

Viva Africa Tours (🖳 vivaafricatours.com; **M**) Operating out of Rafiki Backpackers, Viva Africa Tours have been grabbing a fairly healthy slice of the budget market recently. Perhaps deservedly so, too, for their prices start at US$1905pp with two nights' accommodation at Rafiki Backpackers or Salinero Kilimanjaro thrown in. Online reviews suggest they're doing a good job though according to research the wage they pay their porters is disappointingly low.

• **Summary** Not bad but if you can afford to pay a little more to sign up with a company that pays a better wage, please do so.

Zara Tours (🖳 zaratours.com; **M**) Once the biggest and oldest operators on the mountain, Zara are no longer the trekking behemoth they once were. Originally founded in 1986, Zara has struggled to compete with the rise of several other large-scale operators, and the fact that they aren't KPAP partners has clearly reduced their appeal amongst tourists. But they do still get good reviews online. Prices: US$2451pp, child discount US$30% which equates to US$735.30. Airport transfers are US$20pp extra each way, oxygen is US$12 per day, but two nights at their own hotel, Springlands (see p234), are included.

• **Summary** Competent, cheap-ish and their Springlands Hotel is still pleasant – but I think there are now better options for the money. Personally, I think they should swallow their pride and join KPAP – it would be better for them and their crews in the long run.

Other activities

There are plenty of things you can do with Kili apart from just walking up it.

CYCLING UP KILIMANJARO

Cycling up Africa's highest mountain has been allowed for about half a dozen years now, and several hundred people have followed in the tyre tracks of the Crane brothers, who cycled up in the early '80s, and Muksin Mushi, the first Tanzanian to do so.

Where once it was frowned upon, KINAPA now positively encourage it, and have even opened up a track just for those on two wheels, and set a new itinerary for cyclists to follow too. This new route takes advantage of a 4WD track which starts at the tiny settlement of Kilema and ends near the Last Water Point on the Marangu Route. It's a track that was previously the sole preserve of emergency vehicles ferrying the sick off the mountain. KINAPA assume that cyclists will take two days to reach the end of this 4WD track and have established a simple campsite on the route.

As with many hikers on the Marangu trail, the following two nights are spent at Horombo, using the third day to acclimatise by cycling up to Mawenzi Huts and back. On the fourth day cyclists retrace this path, via the unusual Zebra Rocks, before continuing on to Kibo Huts for another two nights. On the fifth day of the adventure, cyclists carry their bicycle up to Hans Meyer Cave, where they store them, before walking back down to Kibo Huts.

Reaching the summit

Unlike the majority of trekkers, cyclists actually tackle the summit in the daytime. That final push begins on the morning of the sixth day. It involves a return to Hans Meyer Cave to fetch their bikes and carry them up to Gillman's Point. Even from Gillman's there's very little actual cycling to be had. The path, for the most part, is too narrow. So it is only on the final push from Stella to Uhuru that cyclists get back on the saddle.

After the summit, cyclists return down to Kibo Huts. From there they indulge in one of the longest downhill rides anywhere. It's a 30km plummet from Kibo Huts to Kilema, interrupted only by one last night at Horombo.

How much does it cost and how do I organise it?

KINAPA are asking for just an extra US$50 per person per day. This daily fee is in addition to the regular park fees (see p29) paid by those pedestrians who merely want to walk up to the summit. Companies such as Summit Expeditions and Nomadic Expeditions (SENE; p103) or Ahsante Tours (p86) offer this.

CYCLING *AROUND* KILIMANJARO

As the upper slopes of Kilimanjaro get ever busier, the desire to get a different perspective on the mountain – and to step away from the hordes! – grows ever stronger. Recognising this, several trekking agencies have added cycling trips to their roster. The composition of these cycling trips varies widely and may include itineraries to Tanga on the coast or even to the parks of the Northern Circuit, where you swap two wheels for four to enjoy a game drive.

For us, however, the **best cycling route is that which takes in Kilimanjaro's little-visited northern side**. For those interested in the culture of the people who call the mountain their home – a culture that, on this side of the mountain, remains largely untouched by the trespasses of the tourist – this trip has no equal.

It's in the small things that you notice just how little the outside world has infiltrated into this sunny corner of Africa. For example, the children here ask not for 'chocolate', 'school pen' or 'money' – requests that you'll hear pretty much everywhere else; instead, the kids here just want the chance to say 'Jambo' to the (in my case) sweating middle-aged *mzungu* wobbling past on his bike. It's very lovely and very, very refreshing.

Such an unexpected reception emphasises the fact that you are now in a different sort of Tanzania, one that has so far been left pretty much untouched by outsiders. Which is why I need to make the following request: don't spoil it. In particular, please do not give out gifts to locals you meet on the way. I know the children are cute and the locals look both friendly and, often, quite poor. But all it takes is one thoughtless act of 'kindness' by a visitor and suddenly that innocent interaction between tourist and local will be much harder to come by. Inevitably, one day, the Maasai and Chagga of northern Kilimanjaro will come to view the tourist in the same light as people in most other parts of Tanzania, and friendly greetings will be replaced by requests for material goods, or simply hard cash. I recognise that. But let's try not to accelerate that process.

I must also add a word of warning: cycling round the northern side of Kili can be tough. Admittedly, regular cyclists, the fit and the under-thirty may find it a breeze. Those, however, who have, ahem, lived a little, carry a paunch, and whose normal idea of an exercise regime is to walk the dog for an hour a day round the gentle hills of Sussex, may find themselves wobbling in the wake of the rest of the team. If that sounds like you, you can always extend the expedition by a day or two to allow yourself to cycle for shorter distances each day. After all, this is a trip that needs to be savoured and the peace and stillness that can be experienced round Kili's northern side is one that's best enjoyed without the perpetual screaming emanating from one's calf muscles.

So how long does it take? Well, from my experience of this 'Tour de Kili', **I was able to pedal from Marangu, on the south-eastern side of the mountain, to Simba Farm, on Kili's western flank, in 2½ days**. That's not going at a frenetic pace at all and for more experienced cyclists that's really quite slow going. But it does give you plenty of time to take in the scenery and visit the markets on the way.

On such a trip you'll quickly notice that each side of the mountain has its own character. On the eastern side, for example, the newly built road has made cycling much more straightforward but it also means that the traffic is greater. This is also, interestingly, the hardest side, particularly the long haul up to **Useri** – a climb that cyclists have dubbed, not inaccurately, Heartbreak Hill. It's a relentless climb, guaranteed to make you sweat and swear while uniformed schoolchildren shout cheerful insults that are addressed to you, though in all honesty are intended more for the amusement of their classmates. If you have begun your trip in Marangu and this first day reduces you to tears, don't despair: the cycling on subsequent days is more straightforward, the gradients less severe and what you see is more diverting too.

Approaching the north-eastern corner of the mountain, you'll pass through patches of forest, where turaco shout encouragement from the trees, huge blue butterflies flit between the members of your convoy, and the occasional colobus monkey will stop eating for a second to peer through the branches at the strange and colourful pedalling parade. And by the time you move around the northern side, and leave the tarmac behind at **Kamwanga**, a tranquillity settles on the landscape that is just lovely. Few are the cars that drive along this stretch and your fellow road-users will, on the whole, be pedestrians travelling to and from the local markets.

The lively village of **Kigielli** is a venue for one such market, where you can pick up a pair of Maasai sandals (the ones made out of old tyres) for about US$3-5. Thereafter, the scenery of neat, fertile farmland gives way to a dusty wilderness of acacia and savannah, where the tyres on your bike squelch through the dung of buffalo and elephant that occasionally cross the track. Maasai children sometimes appear out of the bushes at the side of the road, herding their precious cattle, but otherwise humanity seems a long way away.

Further on, the village of **Kitendeni** signals some sort of return to civilisation and the next village, **Lerangwa**, is big enough to require its own school. Many cycle groups camp for the night in the school grounds, much to the amusement of the pupils who arrive for lessons at 7am the next day.

By the time you reach the mountain's western side, the slopes of Kili have been divided up among several huge farms, including Mountainside Farm, where eland and antelope can still be seen roaming. (You can read about the experiences of the farmer, David Read, who established Mountainside, in his memoir *Another Load of Bull*, see p381.)

Their neighbours are **Simba Farm**, where rooms and hospitality await (see pp232-3). From here, it's another couple of hours down to the main Arusha–Moshi road and **Boma Ng'ombe**, a ride that's described (in reverse) in the introduction to the Lemosho and Shira Routes on p313.

Of course, there's nothing to stop you from completing an entire circumnavigation of Kili by cycling along the road via Moshi and all the way to Marangu – a distance of around 65km in total. But for many, the main highway between Arusha and Moshi is a poor substitute for what has gone before and they are happy to hang up their helmets and give their aching limbs some time off.

ENDURANCE EVENTS

How about entering the **Kilimanjaro Marathon** (💻 kilimanjaromarathon.com)? Taking place in late February or early March, the race is run over the standard 26 miles/42.2km and starts by heading out along the road to Dar before returning to Moshi via a climb to Mweka. As such, it doesn't actually enter into the national park at all – though given the levels of exhaustion suffered by your average marathon participant, it's probably just as well that they don't have to climb a mountain too.

A half-marathon, a 10km disabled wheelchair and handcycle race and a fun run are held at the same time, with prizes of Ts4 million each to the winners of the men's and women's full marathon (Ts2 million for the half-marathon, plus prizes for the various disabled categories). It's become one of the biggest events in Northern Tanzania's social calendar.

Still not exhausted? Then sign up to the annual **Kilimanjaro Trail Run** (💻 kilimanjarostagerun.com), an 8-day, 260km (approximately 160 miles) slog around the mountain. Led by Simon Mtuy – record holder for a speed ascent on Kili (see p160), founder of the highly regarded SENE trekking operator (see p103) and all-round good egg – the trail runs along dirt tracks and footpaths, taking you past breathtaking scenery – which is a bit unfortunate when you're spending most of your time running. Simon is at pains to point out that this is *not a race*, so the competitive aspect of the trip is reduced to a minimum, allowing a strong *esprit de corps* to develop amongst the participants instead. It's not cheap – the 2023 price was US$2515 per person for an 11-day package – but what an adventure!

TRAVEL BY CABLE CAR UP THE MOUNTAIN

Well, you can't go up Kilimanjaro on a cable car, *yet*. But it may not be too far away. The government, and the park authority, have given the green light to the project in their efforts to reinvigorate tourism in the country following the Covid pandemic. Strong enough to carry 15 six-person cars, the cable would run alongside the Machame Route, the mountain's most popular trail. The ride itself is set to last for about 20 minutes and would take passengers up to the Shira Plateau.

There is plenty of opposition to the plans. The trekking companies feel, justifiably, that a cable car that runs alongside the mountain's most popular trail will inevitably have a deleterious effect on business; and that in turn will have a negative impact on the livelihoods of the porters, guides, cooks etc who make their living from the mountain.

But the main objection is, of course, environmental. The park is, after all, a UNESCO World Heritage site – and erecting ugly concrete pillars on its face is always going to raise objections. At the time of writing KINAPA were trying to persuade UNESCO that a large cable car slung up the southern slopes of Kili would not be incompatible with their aims of ensuring the protection of the planet's natural and cultural heritage. Understandably, this is taking a while; however, if they overcome this hurdle it might just be that, by the time it comes to writing the next edition of the guide, I'll have to dedicate a chapter to Kili's very own cable car.

3 TANZANIA

'Strange country isn't it?'
'Yes. It seems so cruel one moment, then suddenly kind and very beautiful. Maybe there are parts God forgot about – he meant it all to be like this.'
Robert Taylor and **Anne Aubrey** discuss the land we now call Tanzania in the 1959 swashbuckling classic *Killers of Kilimanjaro*

Although this book concentrates specifically on Kilimanjaro, some background knowledge of the country in which it stands, Tanzania, is necessary. For the chances are that climbing Kilimanjaro forms only one part of your trip to Tanzania and, as such, you are going to need to know what this beautiful country is like and how to travel around it. With this in mind, the following chapter is divided into two parts. The first provides a background of the country by looking at the history, economy, culture etc. This should both increase your enjoyment of visiting Tanzania and serve to put Kilimanjaro in its national context. The second half deals with the more practical side of things, offering advice and tips to help the visitor.

Facts about the country

GEOGRAPHY

Tanzania occupies an area of 945,087 sq km – a little over twice the size of California – made up of 886,037 sq km of land (including the offshore islands of Pemba, Mafia and Zanzibar) and 59,050 sq km of water. This makes it the largest country in the geo-political region of East Africa. It is bounded to the north by Uganda and Kenya, to the west by the Democratic Republic of Congo (DRC), Burundi and Rwanda, to the south by Mozambique, Malawi and Zambia, and to the east by the Indian Ocean. The terrain in that 886,037 sq km of land includes a wide, lush coastal plain and a large and dusty central plateau flanked by the eastern and western branches of the **Great Rift Valley** (see box p131). There are highlands in both the north and south of the country and in the centre of the plateau are some volcanic peaks which again owe their existence to the Rift Valley. **Interestingly, over a quarter of the country is given over to national parks or nature reserves.**

Tanzania is also a land of extremes, housing Africa's largest national park, the **Nyerere National Park** (covering 30,000 sq km), and the **Serengeti**, the park with the greatest concentration of migratory game in the world. Its borders also encompass a share in the continent's largest lake, **Lake Victoria**, and part of **Lake Tanganyika**, the longest and, after Lake Baikal in Siberia, deepest freshwater lake in the world. The third largest lake in Africa, **Lake Malawi**, also forms one of Tanzania's borders. These lakes were formed when the Great Rift Valley, which runs through the heart of the country, opened up about 30 million years ago. As a direct result of the formation of this valley, Tanzania contains Africa's lowest point, the floor of Lake Tanganyika, some 350m below sea level. It is also, of course, the proud owner of Africa's highest.

Beautiful as this country undoubtedly is, it is also beset by enormous environmental problems, from deforestation to desertification, soil degradation, erosion and reef bombing. Significant damage has already occurred, and is still occurring, with added pressures on the land caused by the meteoric rise in tourism over the past couple of decades. For details of how you can minimise your impact on the environment of Kilimanjaro, see pp255-6.

CLIMATE

Tanzania's climate varies greatly; you'll be encountering just about all of the variations in the four or five days it takes you to walk to the top of Kilimanjaro. For more about this, see the Kilimanjaro climate section on pp136-9.

Away from the mountain, the narrow coastal strip tends to be the hottest, most humid and tropical part of the country, with the inland plateau being of sufficient elevation to offer some cooler temperatures and respite from the heat. On the coast the average temperature during the day is a sticky 27°C; luckily the sea breezes temper this heat and make it bearable. On the inland plateau you're looking at an average temperature of around 20-26.5°C during the cooler months of June to August, up to a roasting 30°C between December and March.

The **rainy seasons** extend from November to mid-December (the short rains), and from mid March to May (the long rains). On the coast the average annual rainfall is around 1400mm; inland it is a much drier 250mm, though in mountainous areas it can be a magnificent 2000mm; unsurprisingly, flooding can be a problem at this time.

HISTORY

[For a detailed history of Kilimanjaro, see pp139-63]

We, the people of Tanganyika, would like to light a candle and put it on the top of Mount Kilimanjaro, which would shine beyond our borders, giving hope where there was despair, love where there was hate, and dignity where before there was only humiliation.
Julius Nyerere in a speech to the Tanganyika Legislative Assembly in 1959. Following independence in 1961, an expedition was indeed launched to put a torch on Kili's summit.

The discovery of the 1,750,000-year-old remains of an early hominid, **Australopithecus (Zinjanthropus) boisei**, at Olduvai Gorge in the Ngorongoro Crater (near hominid footprints that could be as much as three-and-a-half million years old), suggest that Tanzania has one of the longest histories in the world. I am now going to cram these three and a half million years into the next three and a half pages – a task made considerably simpler by the fact that this history has, until the last 200 years or so, been unrecorded.

We know that **Khoisan speakers** (from southern Africa) moved into the area of modern Tanzania around 10,000 years ago, to be joined between 3000BC and 1000BC by Cushitic speakers from the Horn of Africa (Ethiopia and Eritrea), who brought with them more advanced agricultural techniques. Over the next few hundred years **Bantu speakers** from West Africa's Niger Delta and Nilotic peoples from the north and Sudan also migrated to the area we now know as Tanzania.

By 400BC merchants from Classical Greece knew about and traded with the coast of East Africa, which they called **Azania**. Some of them eventually settled here to take advantage of the trading opportunities, to be joined later by **traders from Persia** and, by the end of the first millennium AD as trade routes stretched into China, merchants from **India**. The majority of immigrants, however, proved to be the seafaring **traders from Arabia**, and soon the Swahili language and culture, an amalgamation of the cultures of Arabia and the Bantu speakers who had also settled on the coast, began to emerge there.

Portuguese, Arabs, Germans and British

Life on the coastal strip of what is now Tanzania continued, as far as we know, pleasantly enough for a number of centuries, a fairly idyllic existence that was rudely shattered by the arrival of the **Portuguese** following Vasco da Gama's legendary expedition at the end of the 15th century. As greedy as they were intrepid, they built the coastal village of Kilwa Kisiwani into a major trading port which, in typical Portuguese style, they later sacked. Understandably unpopular, the Portuguese nevertheless held on grimly and gamely to their East African possessions for almost 200 years until the end of the 17th century. That they managed to survive for so long is largely due to a lack of a united opposition, which didn't arrive until 1698 in the form of **Omani Arabs**, summoned to help by the long-suffering traders of Kilwa Kisiwani. Unlike the Portuguese, the Omani Arabs were keen to forge trading links with the interior. They pushed new routes across the plains to Lake Tanganyika, thereby facilitating the extraction of gold, **slaves** and ivory from deep within the continent. The Arabs grew inordinately wealthy from the fat of Africa's land to the extent that the Omani sultan decided to pull up his tent pegs from the desert sands of Arabia and relocate, establishing his new capital at Stonetown on Zanzibar.

While this was going on, the Europeans returned to Africa. Initially it was just a trickle of **missionaries** and **explorers**, hell-bent (if that's the right term) on making converts and mapping continents respectively. Indeed, one man who famously combined both vocations, Dr David Livingstone, spent a while in Tanzania searching for the source of the Nile, and it was at Ujiji, on the Tanzanian side of Lake Tanganyika, that Henry Morton Stanley is believed to have finally caught up with him and uttered those immortal words 'Dr Livingstone, I presume'.

With intrepid, independent Europeans now roaming all over the continent, it could only be a matter of time before one European country or another would come up with the idea of full-scale colonisation. By the late **1880s** Britain had already secured a dominant role on Zanzibar. But over on the mainland it was Germany who was making the most progress.

Or rather, one German, for it was **Carl Peters** who, acting independently of his government, established German influence on the mainland at this time, negotiating treaties with local chiefs in order to secure a charter for his **Deutsch-Ostafrikanische Gesellschaft** (DOAG, the German East Africa Company). A few years later and with his homeland's government now supporting his work, Peters' DOAG was formally given the task of administering the mainland. This left the British on Zanzibar fuming – and not a little scared – at the German's impertinence, and war was averted between the two superpowers only with the signing of an accord in 1890 in which Britain was formally allowed to establish a protectorate over her Zanzibar territories. One year and further negotiations later and the land we now know as Tanzania (Zanzibar excluded) officially came under direct German control as **German East Africa**.

The Germans brought a Western education, a rail network, and a higher level of healthcare with them to Africa. They also brought harsh taxes, suppression, humiliation and no small amount of unrest. They were eventually replaced as colonial overlords after World War One by the **British** following a League of Nations mandate. The territory was renamed Tanganyika at this time. After World War Two a near bankrupt Britain clung on to administrative control, though officially Tanganyika was now a 'trust territory' of the fledgling United Nations.

Independence

Life under the British was marginally better than under the Germans, with greater political freedom and an improved economy thanks to the cultivation of export crops; but it was only marginal and soon political groups were springing up all over the country with each campaigning for the same thing: independence. The most important of these was the Dar es Salaam-based Tanganyika Africa Association which, in 1953, elected teacher **Julius Nyerere** as its president. Pressure from Nyerere and his party (now known as TANU, or the Tanganyika African National Union) forced Britain to agree to the formation of an internal self-government. Indeed, so impressed was Britain with Nyerere that the only condition they placed on the establishment of this new regime of self-government was that he should be its first chief minister.

Such a vote of confidence by the British was well founded, for Nyerere seemed to have the necessary intelligence, courage and popularity to ensure a smooth transfer of power. The following extract is from Nyerere's radio broadcast in September 1960, following his accession to Chief Minister, as quoted in Ranford Pratt's *The Critical Phase in Tanzania 1945-68: Nyerere and the emergence of a socialist strategy*. It typifies his wisdom and good sense, and gives a decent indication, I think, of the calibre of the man:

I know the people of this country have already earned the admiration of millions of other people abroad through the way in which the struggle for freedom has been conducted. Militant nationalism has been combined with a smile and humour. Temptation to violence and lawlessness as a means of independence has been resisted. The people of Tanganyika became fervently nationalist without becoming racialists (sic). Colonialism was hated but the hatred did not spread to the people who represented colonialism. Bad laws were resented but there was no resort to lawlessness in order to remove them. This is maturity. I know this maturity has a firm foundation in our character as a people.

Now a mere formality, **independence** for Tanganyika was eventually declared on 9 December 1961, with Nyerere, just as Britain had hoped, as prime minister. Exactly one year later it was formally established as a **republic**, with Nyerere promoted to president.

On **Zanzibar**, meanwhile, things were going less smoothly. Whilst the Zanzibaris won their independence not long afterwards (December 1963), the two parties that formed the first government did not enjoy popular support but instead had been thrust into power by the departing British because of their pro-British leanings. With a tenure that was decidedly shaky, it came as no surprise when they were toppled in a revolution just a month later. In their place came the popular, radical Afro Shirazi Party (ASP).

Less than a year after independence, on 26 April 1964 the ASP leader, Abeid Karume, was signing an act of union with his mainland neighbours and the **United Republic of Tanganyika** was formed. In October of the same year the name was changed to the **United Republic of Tanzania**, the name being a neat combination of the two former territories. The two maintained separate governments, however, even after 1977 when ASP and TANU were combined by Nyerere to form **Chama Cha Mapinduzi** (Party of the Revolution), or **CCM**, the party which maintains political control of Tanzania to this day.

Modern history

From 1967 to the late 1980s Nyerere and his party followed a socialist course; the economy was nationalised, the tax regime was deliberately aimed at redistributing wealth and new villages were established in order to modernise the agricultural sector and give the rural poor greater access to social services. Unfortunately, the 20-year experiment was eventually deemed a flop, with the economy in seemingly perpetual decline. By 1992 things had got so desperate that the CCM took the unprecedented step of legalising opposition parties after pressure from Western donors for more democracy in the country.

Curiously, this move seems to have done little to achieve this. Three years after the legalisation of political opponents, the first democratic elections were held and the CCM, now under the leadership of **Benjamin Mkapa** following Nyerere's resignation in 1985, emerged once again as the major force in

Tanzanian politics. The elections in late 2000 confirmed their dominance with over 95% of parliamentary seats won by CCM candidates. While they undoubtedly remain Tanzania's most credible political party, the scale of the victory suggests that proper political debate is all but impossible; an assumption that the election of **Jakaya Kikwete** in 2005 and 2010 and, in 2015 and 2020, **John Magufuli,** both CCM candidates, did little to dispel.

On semi-autonomous **Zanzibar**, things, as usual, have been a little more explosive. Throughout the 1990s and into the 21st century the elections have consistently been marred by accusations of ballot rigging and intimidation of the opposition leaders. These 'voting irregularities' have often brought about a violent response from the people, such as in January 2001 when 27 protesters were shot dead in Pemba as they marched through the streets. Even as recently as 2015 the election was cancelled after the opposition CUF party was said to have prematurely announced their victory. When the vote was rerun the following March the CUF urged its followers to boycott it in protest at the way they had been denied victory the last time round. As a result, the CCM candidate, the incumbent President Ali Mohamed Shein, who first came to power in 2010, was returned with a jaw-dropping 91% of the votes cast. The president at the time of writing, Ali Hasan Mwinyi, is another CCM member and first came to power in 2020.

The future

In some ways Tanzania is a model African nation, garnering international acclaim for its fight against corruption and its efforts to reform itself peacefully, as exemplified by the move towards democracy in the 1990s. That said, given that the ruling CCM party was the only legally permitted party prior to the restoration of the multi-party system in 1992 and has won every election since, one must wonder at the quality of democracy practised in the country.

Samia Suluhu Hassan, the president at the time of writing, came to power following the (perhaps not unexpected) demise of Magufuli, who, having spent most of his time in office denying Covid, promptly went and died from it. (Though, officially at least, the authorities in Tanzania insist it was actually a long-standing heart issue that killed him.) The first woman president of Tanzania, and the second Zanzibari to hold the post, Samia has looked to steady the ship after her more energetic, charismatic but autocratic predecessor.

The outlook for the economy seems rosy: in 2010 Tanzania joined its neighbours in forging an East African Common Market. In 2012 huge gas reserves were discovered off the Tanzanian coast. The Chinese, too, have invested heavily in the country, as anybody who has witnessed the growth of Arusha over the last few years, with its gleaming new towers and tarmac roads, will testify.

It remains, however, a nation beset by problems. The usual African ailments – poverty, AIDS, and a lack of clean water, basic healthcare and decent education – are as prevalent in Tanzania as they are over much of the continent. Corruption remains rampant too; if you speak with many locals today they will tell you that, post-Magufuli, the bad old days of corruption are back again.

In addition to those pan-African ailments, however, Tanzania has other local problems to contend with, from a lack of credible opposition to the main autocratic CCM party to the secessionist grumblings of many on Zanzibar who were never happy with the union with the mainland – a dissatisfaction that six subsequent decades and more of turmoil have done little to dispel. The influx of refugees from neighbouring Burundi and Congo has also put added pressure on the country, particularly in the west around lakes Victoria and Tanganyika. It remains to be seen whether the moderate line Tanzania has taken throughout its independence will continue into the future; and whether this thoughtful, conservative (with a small 'c') attitude will be enough to help it to overcome the enormous difficulties it still faces.

ECONOMIC AND POPULATION STATISTICS

Tanzania is one of the world's poorest countries, in the bottom 10% of nations in terms of per capita income. Its per capita GDP stands at a modest US$1099 (2021 estimate) and just over 26.4% live below the poverty line. Nevertheless, these are significant improvements on the figures recorded in the first edition of this book back in 2001 when GDP per capita was US$264 and over 50% lived below the poverty line. Other statistics also suggest that Tanzanians are better off than they were in 2001. Infant mortality stands at a level of 34.1 per 1000 births in 2021 (down from 85 per 1000 in 2001), and life expectancy is now 66.41 (2020 figure), up from 49. Presumably some of this improvement can be put down to the decrease in HIV infection, with 4.6% of the population now estimated to be infected, down from 8.38% of the population in 2001 (though that 4.6% still represents over 1.7 million people).

It's early days yet but the economy is starting to show some positive signs too. Growth in real GDP, for example, hovers around the 4.9% mark. This figure is a bit surprising given that Tanzania is still largely an **agricultural** country. The style of agriculture is mainly traditional, the large collective farms introduced under Nyerere's socialist experiment having been rejected on the whole in favour of the age-old system whereby each farmer cultivates a small plot of land called a *shamba*. The most popular home-grown crops are cotton, rice, *sorghum* (a nutritious grain similar to millet), sugar, bananas and coconuts; *sisal* (a flowering plant whose leaves have fibres that can be used in matting, rope-making etc), coffee and tea are produced principally for the export market, while cloves and other spices are still grown on Zanzibar and the coast. Agriculture accounts for about 30% of Tanzania's GDP and employs three-quarters of the workforce.

Tanzania also has a solid **mining** base with oil, tin, iron, salt, coal, gypsum, phosphate, natural gas, nickel, diamonds and, of course, tanzanite all extracted in the country. Tourism is now a major contributor to the GDP too and is a vital source of much-needed foreign currency, particularly in the north and on Zanzibar.

THE PEOPLE

With around almost 66.5 million people split into more than a hundred ethnic groups, numerous local languages and dialects and three main religions, Tanzania is something of an ethnic and cultural hotchpotch. It is a credit to the country that they exist largely in harmony, without succumbing to the sort of ethnic hatred that has riven many other countries around these parts.

Native Africans make up 99% of the population; of these, the vast majority (estimated at 95%) are of Bantu origin, though even here there are over 130 tribes. The other 1% are of European, Arabian or Indian origin. Around Kilimanjaro it is the Chagga people, one of the more wealthy and powerful groups in Tanzania, who dominate.

A 2020 Pew survey – the latest figures I have – found the **religious division in Tanzania** to be 34.1% Muslim, 63.1% Christian, while 1.2% profess traditional indigenous beliefs, 1.5% are unaffiliated, and 0.1% are Hindu. This last group undoubtedly has a highly visible presence in Tanzania with some large, ostentatious Hindu temples in Dar, Arusha and Moshi.

The Chagga people around Kilimanjaro are largely Christian; you can read more about them, their culture and their beliefs on pp177-84.

Practical information for the visitor

DOCUMENTS AND VISAS

For the moment, while Kenya now requires travellers to get an eTA (see p120) online in advance, a visa can still be bought for Tanzania either online in advance or on arrival.

For Tanzania

For the latest on the visa situation for Tanzania, please visit 💻 immigration.go.tz. Visitors from pretty much every country pay US$50 for their visa; visitors from the United States, however, have to buy a multiple-entry visa, for which they must fork out US$100.

A visa is typically valid for 90 days from the **date of issue** (and not the day you arrive in Tanzania, though I have to say many officials don't seem to recognise this). There are two ways of purchasing it:

Buying your visa online The process for buying your Tanzanian '**eVisa**' used to be so infuriating that I used to recommend people buy their visa on arrival at the airport. The online system would ask you a huge ream of questions and if you paused momentarily to answer one – which most people did when it asked for their passport details – the system would freeze and applicants would have to start again.

These days, however, the online visa portal is much more efficient and most people are buying their Tanzanian visa by this method. You'll need scans of both a passport photo, and the personal information page of your passport. Just make sure you apply at least a week or two beforehand (10 days according to the website), to give your application enough time to be processed. Remember that your passport must have a minimum of six months left before it expires.

The official site is 💻 visa.immigration.go.tz. If you find yourself being charged more than you expected, in all probability you've ended up on the visa application page of an agent, who is charging a fee for their service.

Buying your visa on arrival in Tanzania Note that there is still an argument for buying it at the airport on arrival: you won't get scammed by an online agent, you don't require a photograph, the process takes minutes (rather than 10 days), and when I last tried it people who had bought their visa at the airport had their own dedicated passport desk – thereby avoiding the large queues that those who had bought theirs beforehand had to join. My only hesitation is that I think at some point in the future Tanzania will insist on everyone buying their visas beforehand – so do check online first to see what the latest rules are.

Everyone can buy their visa at the airport on arrival in Tanzania *except* for citizens of: Afghanistan, Abkhazia, Azerbaijan, Bangladesh, Chad, Djibouti, Equatorial Guinea, Eritrea, Ethiopia, Kazakhstan, Kyrgyzstan, Lebanon, Mali, Mauritania, Morocco, Niger, Nigeria, Palestine, Senegal, Somalia, Sierra Leone, Sri Lanka, Tajikistan, Turkmenistan and Uzbekistan.

You can pick up a visa at Dar es Salaam, Kilimanjaro and Zanzibar International Airports as well as at several land border crossings (including Namanga, the border crossing between Nairobi and Arusha).

Yellow-fever vaccination certificate It seems that once again it is compulsory for visitors to Tanzania to show evidence that they have been vaccinated against yellow fever if coming from a country where the disease is endemic, or if travelling via a country where yellow fever is present and if you stayed there for more than 12 hours.

Given that airport staff in Tanzania have in the past asked to see proof of inoculation whether you require the jab or not, you could argue that it's best to play it safe and get one anyway. The certificate can be picked up from your doctor after you have received the inoculation and is usually free, though the jab itself is not. **Please see my advice in the box p55 for those over 60 and others for whom getting the inoculation is not a good idea**.

Visas – now eTAs – for Kenya

In recent years the Kenyan government insisted that everyone must apply for their Kenyan visa before arriving at the airport or land border. It was a very time-consuming process as you had to scan and send various documents.

However, Kenya has announced that from January 2024 travellers need an **Electronic Travel Authorisation (eTA)**. This costs US$30 and you have to apply for it in advance online at 💻 www.etakenya.go.ke/en. There will be those who say that nothing has really changed except the name.

MONEY AND BANKS

Currency

The **Tanzanian shilling (Ts)** is the national currency. It's fairly stable but cannot be imported except by residents of Tanzania, Kenya and Uganda, and cannot be exported.

> **❑ EXCHANGE RATES**
>
> To get the latest exchange rates visit 🖳 www.xe.com/currencyconverter. At the time of writing they were:
>
> | | |
> |---|---|
> | UK£1 | Ts3224 |
> | €1 | Ts2750 |
> | US$1 | Ts2580 |
> | Can$1 | Ts1878 |
> | A$1 | Ts1673 |
> | NZ$1 | Ts1533 |
> | S Africa R1 | Ts136 |

Cash Foreign currency can be imported and exported without limit. **Dollars** and, to a lesser extent, **sterling** and **euros** are the best currencies to bring.

The question is: in what form should you take your money to Tanzania, ie: should you just bring cash? Or should you rely solely on your credit/debit cards and use the latter to get money out of cashpoints in Tanzania? I advocate bringing credit/debit cards, with a few hundred US dollars in cash as back-up in case you can't find an ATM that will take your card.

Dollars are also very useful for those occasions when the Tanzanian shilling is not accepted, such as when paying for upmarket hotel rooms and air tickets, both of which, officially at least, must be paid for in hard currency. The downside of cash is, of course, that it is also the riskiest way to carry money. How many dollars you bring, of course, depends on how much of your trip you've paid for in advance, how long you're staying, and what you hope to do while there.

You will need cash – probably dollars – for **tipping**. For a rough guide as to how much you should take, see pp32-3 – then add a few dollars, just in case.

One more thing: when it comes to bringing dollars, **make sure they are new notes** – notes printed before 2016 are seldom accepted and if they are, attract a lower exchange rate.

Credit/debit cards **Credit cards** are useful in major tourist hotels, restaurants, gift shops and airline offices and their usefulness is increasing.

Both **debit and credit cards** enable you to withdraw cash from an ATM; credit cards tend to be more expensive as you get charged interest from the moment that you withdraw money (unless you 'pre-load' your card so it is in credit and remains so even after you've withdrawn money).

Of course, you run the risk that the ATMs will reject your card or, worse, swallow it, leaving you stuck in Africa with no means of support. So bring some cash as well.

Banks, ATMs and moneychangers

Banking hours are typically 8.30am-4pm Monday to Friday and 8.30am-1pm on Saturday. However, these days many banks no longer change money and if they do the queues for a cashier can be long. As such, most people visit a moneychanger to swap their currencies.

Moneychangers are nowhere near as numerous as they used to be but I have pointed them out in the city/town guides.

As a general rule, you get a better rate for large denomination bills (US$50 and $100 bills) than small ones. Make sure your US dollar notes were printed after 2016 or you'll get a lousy rate for them – and they may well be rejected outright. Keep your **exchange receipts** so that when you leave the country you can change your spare shillings back into hard currency.

There are **ATMs** in every town in Tanzania and Kenya. Not only are they getting more numerous, they are also becoming more reliable and these days tales of cashpoints swallowing cards or giving out the wrong amount are rare. Alas, **Tanzanian ATMs have started charging for withdrawals**. The cost varies according to how much you want to take out and which bank's ATM you are using. The only banks I found that were still offering fee-free withdrawals were the **Kenyan Central Bank** (KCB) and **EcoBank** – though I should imagine there's a chance that they, too, will have started charging by the time you read this.

GETTING AROUND

Public transport in Tanzania is unreliable, uncomfortable, slow, and not recommended for those with either long legs or haemorrhoids. It is also dangerous. A little-known but highly pertinent fact about Tanzania's transport system is that 3% of total deaths in Tanzania are road-accident victims. Reckless driving is by far and away the biggest cause of most of these accidents, with poor maintenance of roads and vehicles also significant contributors.

That said, Tanzanian transport is cheap, convenient and, it must be said, cheerful: conversation usually flows pretty easily on a bus or dalla-dalla (providing you can make yourself heard above the noise of the stereo). And while some roads are little more than a necklace of potholes strung together with tyre tracks, the main roads between towns are splendid, well-maintained tarmac strips – with speed ramps to deter drivers from going too fast.

By bus

The most luxurious form of ground transport is provided by the **express bus** companies. A few of them, such as Kilimanjaro Express, deserve their reputation for safety and comfort; you may want to ask your hotel or a local which bus company is currently the most reliable. These express buses run to a fixed timetable and will leave without you if you're late. Buy your ticket in advance.

The cheaper alternative is the ordinary buses or **Coasters** – minibuses which leave when full. These are cheap but you definitely get what you pay for. As with all forms of local transport, ask your fellow passengers what the correct fare is before handing any money over to the 'conductor'; rip-offs are the rule rather than the exception on many journeys. In addition there are the indigenous **dalla-dallas**: minibuses (smaller than Coasters) plying routes around and between neighbouring towns. They're usually a tight squeeze as drivers pile in the customers to maximise their takings. If you're being pushed into one that looks full-to-bursting, simply refuse to enter; there'll be another along in a minute. In Kenya these minibuses are known as **matatus**.

Finally, there are the **shuttle buses** that convey passengers from Nairobi to Arusha/Moshi and back. Comfy and reasonably priced, they're by far the best way of crossing the border overland. See the relevant chapter for more details.

By car

You can **hire a car** in Dar es Salaam and from many of the bigger tour and trekking agencies in Moshi and Arusha – usually with driver included. Make sure you choose a vehicle that is suitable for your requirements. Don't, for example, be tempted to conduct your own off-road safari in a two-wheel drive.

You can **hitch** around the country, though payment will often be expected from a Western tourist; it is, of course, wiser not to hitch alone.

By train

One of President Magufuli's more positive decisions during his time as president was to improve and enlarge the passenger train service. As such, **there is now a train service between Dar and Arusha via Moshi**. It's slow, it's unreliable, it's regularly late, it's infrequent – and I can't think of a more charming or picturesque way to travel. I give details of the service in the relevant town and city guides on p195 (Dar es Salaam), pp221-2 (Arusha) and p238 (Moshi).

By air

Flying is an efficient way to cover the vast distances of Tanzania and there are several small chartered and scheduled airlines including Coastal Air, Precision Air, Air Excel, Flightlink, Auric Air and the national airline Air Tanzania. For details of airlines flying to Kilimanjaro, see pp34-7.

ACCOMMODATION

Tanzania's guesthouses and hotels can be split into three sorts: those that welcome tourists, those that accept them, and those that refuse them altogether. These last are usually the cheapest, double as brothels, have minimum security and advertising and can safely be ignored.

Room rates for the other two start at about US$10/15 per night for a single/double; dorms are a rarity (though where you can find them they start at about US$8/Ts20,000 per night). Bear in mind that many hotels still have two tariffs, one for locals and people living in Tanzania (commonly known as the '**residents' rate**') and a more expensive one for foreigners. If business is slow, it doesn't take much effort to persuade some of the smaller hotels to charge you the residents' rate, regardless of whether you live in Tanzania or not.

Take your time when choosing a hotel, particularly in the towns featured here where there are lots of options. **Standards** vary widely but you'll probably be surprised at how pleasant some of them can be, with mosquito nets and attached bathrooms and maybe even a telly.

In Nairobi, safety is a concern in some of the hotels, though the ones I have chosen to recommend in this book were fine. Accommodation on Zanzibar, incidentally, is generally much more expensive.

Note, too, that in Swahili *hotel* or *hoteli* sometimes means restaurant rather than accommodation (*mazate*).

For details of **accommodation on the mountain**, see pp271-2.

ELECTRICITY

Tanzania is powered by 250V, 50 cycles, AC network. Those bringing electrical items from home may wish to invest in a power breaker: Tanzania's electricity supply can be erratic on occasions and power surges could seriously impair the efficacy of your electrical instruments, if not melt them altogether. **Plugs and sockets vary in style, though by far the most common are the British three-square-pin** or, less common, European two-round-pin style.

TIME

Tanzania is **three hours ahead of GMT** and thus, ignoring any Daylight Savings Time, Tanzania is two hours ahead of Western Europe, three ahead of the UK, eight ahead of New York, eleven ahead of San Francisco, one ahead of Johannesburg, seven hours behind Sydney and nine behind Wellington.

A point of endless confusion for travellers, and with the potential to cause major problems for the uninitiated, is the concept known as **Swahili time**, used throughout much of East Africa where Swahili is the *lingua franca*. Swahili time begins at dawn, or more precisely at 6am. In other words, 6am is their hour

❑ HOLIDAYS AND FESTIVALS

The following are **public holidays** in Tanzania; note that some (eg Zanzibar's Revolutionary Day) are not held nationwide but are celebrated locally only.

1 Jan	New Year	**7 July**	Industrial Day
12 Jan	Zanzibar Revolutionary Day	**8 Aug**	Farmers' Day
April	Good Friday/Easter	**9 Dec**	Independence/Republic Days
26 April	Union Day (National Day)	**25 Dec**	Christmas Day
1 May	International Labour Day	**26 Dec**	Boxing Day

Islamic holy days

The dates of the following holidays are determined according to the Islamic lunar calendar and as such do not fall on the same date each year. Their **approximate dates** for the next few years are given. The extent to which these days are celebrated and whether these celebrations will impact on your holiday depends to a great extent on where you are in Tanzania; remember that around Kilimanjaro the people are largely Christian so the impact tends to be minimal, though some shops and businesses close.

- **Id al Fitr** (End of Ramadan – a two-day celebration) approx dates: 10 April 2024, 21 March 2025, 20 March 2026
- **Eid El-Hajj** (also known as Eid El-Adha or Eid Al-Kebir) approx dates: 16 June 2024, 6 June 2025, 27 May 2026

zero (and thus equivalent to our midnight); 7am in our time is actually one o'clock in Swahili time, and so on.

To add further confusion, this system for telling the time is not prevalent everywhere in Tanzania, with most offices, timetables etc using the standard style for telling the time. Whenever you're quoted a time it should be obvious which clock they are using but always double check.

BUSINESS HOURS

These are typically 8am-5pm Monday to Friday and 8am-1pm for some private traders on Saturdays. Some businesses take a lunch hour, usually 1-2pm.

POST AND TELECOMMUNICATIONS

Telephone

> The telephone country access code for Tanzania is ☎ 255.

If you're staying in Tanzania for more than a couple of weeks you'll probably find it a good idea to invest in a **Tanzanian SIM card** (Ts2000). The process of getting a SIM card is straightforward enough: simply visit the store of the network provider you wish to patronise (Vodacom, Airtel etc), and they'll guide you through the process; if you're unsure, ask a member of your trekking agency to accompany you to the store. You may have to show some ID, so bring along your passport/driving licence etc.

Topping up on credit is simple too – you'll find credit vendors on most street corners and hopefully they would have explained to you when you bought your SIM card what you need to do.

Buying a SIM in Tanzania can save you a small fortune in bills compared to using a mobile and SIM from your home country. That said, telephoning in Tanzania has always been a hit-and-miss affair and sometimes it's an illogical one too. Phone a Tanzanian landline from a Tanzanian mobile, for example, and you often still have to dial Tanzania's international dialling code (☎ +255). Furthermore, if you are having trouble ringing home, try tacking an extra '0' on to the front of the international dialling code: for example, if you wish to ring the UK but the phone continues to bar your call, dial ☎ 00044 rather than just ☎ 0044. But even if you follow these rules, there are still occasions when it's impossible to get any sort of connection.

Of course the best and cheapest way of ringing abroad is via **Skype, Zoom, WhatsApp** etc; most hotels now offer some sort of internet service and if the speed is fast enough it's possible to have a reasonably fluent conversation.

Internet access/wi-fi

Most restaurants and nearly all hotels now advertise wi-fi. If your hotel internet is sub-standard there'll doubtless be a café somewhere with a better connection.

If you didn't bring your own smartphone, laptop or iPad you'll probably have to resort to Tanzania's **internet service cafés** to get online. They're efficient and good value, charging about Ts1000 per hour. Some of the equipment is a little dated, as you'd probably expect, and the speed of the connection can be a little slow.

Post

Thanks to the presence of the English missionaries, matters have already advanced so far in Jagga that the Europeans stationed there get their letters and newspapers not more than a month old. **Hans Meyer** *Across East African Glaciers* (1891)

The postal system in Tanzania has improved since Meyer's day but not massively. Reasonably reliable and reliably sluggish, things do occasionally get 'lost in the post' but most gets through… eventually. You should allow about a week for postcards to reach their destinations from Dar, a day or two longer from regional post offices.

FOOD

The native foods do not offer much variety, though they do differ widely in different districts; but if the traveller is not too dainty and is prepared to make the best of what is to be had, it is wonderful what can be done. **Hans Meyer** *Across East African Glaciers* (1891)

Tanzanian food is, on the whole, unsubtle but tasty and filling. If there's one dish that could be described as quintessentially East African, it would be *nyama choma* – plain and simple grilled meat. If the restaurant is any good they'll add some sauces – often curry and usually fiery – to accompany your meat and the whole lot will usually come with rice, chips, plantains or the ubiquitous *ugali* (a stodgy cornmeal or cassava mush). Usually served in a single cricket-ball-sized lump that you can pick up with your fork in one go, ugali has the consistency of plasticine and gives the impression of being not so much cooked as congealed. A bit bland, it nevertheless performs a vital role as a plate-filler and acts as a soothing balm when eating some of the country's more thermogenic curries.

The food of Kilimanjaro's local tribe, the Chagga, is dominated by bananas, which you'll see growing all over the lower slopes of the mountain. Not only do they brew their own beer from them (see opposite) but the fruit (and its cousin the plantain) crop up in dishes such as *mchemsho*, a kind of banana and meat stew.

Aside from the Chaggas' bias for the banana, the indigenous cuisine of Tanzania caters mainly for carnivores, allowing the country's significant Indian minority to corner the market for vegetarian fare. Indian restaurants abound in Dar, Moshi, Arusha and Nairobi, catering mainly for the budget end of the market; that said, the cuisine at a top-notch Indian restaurant in Tanzania is amongst the best served outside Britain or India.

For details about food on the trail, see p272.

DRINKS

The usual world-brand **soft drinks** are on sale in Tanzania. Juices are widely available and pretty cheap, though be warned: a lot of upset stomachs are caused by insanitary juice stalls. Coconuts are far safer and are ubiquitous at the coast and on Zanzibar.

Beers include the tasty Serengeti (my favourite), Ndovu (a pretty close second), Safari and Kilimanjaro from Tanzania, Tusker from Kenya, and the potent Chagga home-brew *mbege*, or banana beer. You'll usually be offered this if you take a stroll around Marangu (or indeed any Chagga village), particularly if it's market day when the world (or at least the male half of it) seems to be intent on obliterating itself by imbibing vast quantities of the stuff from jerrycans.

THINGS TO BUY

***kíRìmíyà** – A Chagga term meaning a treat brought home by mother to kids upon completion of a successful day at market*

From **University of Oregon**'s *Word of the Week* website

Tanzania has the usual supply of weavings and woodcarvings, T-shirts, textiles and trinkets. Amongst the T-shirts are a number of variations on the 'I climbed Kili' motif. Witchcraft items, battle shields, Maasai beads and necklaces as well as bows and arrows are up for grabs in the high streets of Moshi and Arusha. Kilimanjaro **coffee** makes for a good and inexpensive present for the person who's been feeding your cat while you've been away; buy it in a wooden box or velvet bag in a souvenir store, or pick a

Freshly ground coffee makes a great souvenir.

❑ ABOUT BARGAINING

I promise this is the first and last time I will lecture you on how to behave. But I just have one simple message: **please don't bargain too hard**. I used to take a certain amount of pride in how cheaply I could obtain various goods and services when travelling and how tenaciously I would stick to my price until, out of sheer desperation (and probably to get rid of me as much as anything else) the vendor would relent and give me the price I demanded. Not asked, note, but demanded.

It is only recently, having now spent a fair bit of time here, that I am able to see the living conditions of many people in this country – and I realise how wrong my approach to bargaining has been. Sure, nobody wants to get ripped off and if you think you're being taken for a sucker it's important that you stand up for yourself. Furthermore, it is the culture to haggle in this country and you will be expected to engage in some sort of a discussion about how much you're willing to pay for something. But do it with a smile and treat the process as a bit of a game rather than a war to be fought to the death. Because if you've just spent 20 minutes haggling over some item in order to save yourself the equivalent of 40p, it's not just the price that will have been reduced – you'll probably find your dignity will have diminished too.

simple bag of it for a third of the price in a supermarket. Though not grown on the slopes of Kilimanjaro, the organic Africafé has been described by one enthusiastic reader as the best instant coffee in the world and makes an affordable souvenir.

Another popular souvenir is the *kanga*, the traditional Tanzanian woman's dress that usually has a message or motto running through the print, or the similar but smarter and message-less *kitenge*.

Also popular are those cloth **shoulder-bags**, dubbed 'volunteer bags' by locals as they are said to be popular with women working for charitable causes.

It depends on your taste, of course, but Zanzibar is widely reckoned to have a better selection and higher quality of souvenirs (though I think the shops of Arusha are catching up; check out Sanaa, for example, see p212). Some of the items in Zanzibar, particularly the carved door jambs and furniture, are lovely, though difficult to get home; furthermore, these people are extremely tough negotiators, know the true price of everything and bargains are few.

In the afternoon I bought some small capes made of hyrax skins, of a style formerly much in vogue, and two long spears of the most modern narrow-bladed pattern, which were quite works of art. **Hans Meyer** *Across East African Glaciers* (1891)

SECURITY

Tanzania is a pretty safe country, at least by the standards of its neighbours. That said, the standards of its neighbours are very, very low indeed – as anybody who has already been to Kenya's capital, known to many travellers as 'Nairobberi', will testify – so do take care. Violent crime is relatively rare during the day but not unknown, especially in Dar es Salaam and Arusha, while pickpockets are common throughout the country and reach epidemic proportions in busy areas such as markets and stations. The best (if somewhat contradictory) advice is:

- Keep a close eye on your things.
- Don't walk around after dark but take a taxi.
- Wear a moneybelt and don't flaunt your wealth.
- Be on your guard against scams and con merchants...

... but at the same time don't let a sense of paranoia ruin your holiday and remember that the vast majority of travellers in East Africa spend their time here suffering no great loss beyond the occasional and inevitable overcharging. If you are unfortunate enough to become the victim of a mugging, remember that it's your *money* they're after, so hand it over – you should be insured against such eventualities anyway. Report the crime as soon as possible to the police, who are generally quite helpful, particularly when the victim is a tourist. This will help to back up your claim from the insurers and may prevent further crimes against visitors in the future.

HEALTH

Diarrhoea is often symptomatic of nothing more than a change of diet rather than any malignant bacteria, so if you get a vicious dose of the runs and your sphincter feels like a cat flap in the Aswan Dam, don't panic and assume you've got food poisoning. That said, there are problems with hygiene in Tanzania, so it's wise to take certain precautions. Take heed of that old adage about patronising only places that are popular – so food doesn't have a chance to sit around for long – as well as that other one about eating only food that has been cooked, boiled or peeled.

Stick to **bottled**, **purified** or **filtered water** and avoid ice unless you're certain it has been made from treated water. Washing fruit, vegetables and your hands and ensuring food is thoroughly cooked can all prevent food poisoning. Shellfish, ice cream from street vendors and under-cooked meat should all be avoided like the plague, or you could end up feeling like you've got it. Slathering yourself in an **insect repellent** to prevent you from being eaten alive by the smaller members of Tanzania's animal kingdom is a good idea too.

We could go into a detailed examination here of all the dreadful diseases you could catch in Tanzania. But the truth is that for most of the worst ones you should have already had an inoculation or be taking some sort of prophylactic. Besides, it's unlikely that you'll suffer anything more in Tanzania than a dose of **the runs**, some **altitude sickness** or, if you're careless, a touch of **sunstroke**. If you've got the first, just rest up and take plenty of fluids until you recover; to protect against the last wear a high-factor sun lotion and a hat and again drink a lot of fluids. As for altitude sickness, which the majority of trekkers on Kili suffer from to some extent, as well as other ailments that you may contract on the trail, read the detailed discussion on pp243-55.

4

KILIMANJARO

Geology and topography

HOW KILIMANJARO WAS FORMED: THE GEOLOGY

Our geological work was especially delightful... Every rock seemed to differ from another, not only in form but in substance. In half-an-hour it was no uncommon thing for us to pick up specimens of as many as two-and-twenty different kinds. **Hans Meyer** *Across East African Glaciers* (1891)

Rising 4800m above the East African plains, 270km from the shores of the Indian Ocean and measuring up to 40km across, Kilimanjaro is a bizarre geological oddity, the tallest freestanding mountain in the world and one formed, shaped, eroded and scarred by the twin forces of fire and ice. It is actually a volcano, or rather three volcanoes, with the two main peaks, **Kibo** and **Mawenzi**, the summits of two of those volcanoes. The story of its creation goes like this:

About three-quarters of a million years ago (making Kilimanjaro a veritable youngster in geological terms) molten lava burst through the fractured surface of the **Great Rift Valley**, a giant fault in the earth's crust that runs through East Africa (see box opposite; actually, Kilimanjaro lies 50 miles from the East African Rift Valley along a splinter running off it, but that need not concern us here). The huge pressures behind this eruption pushed part of the Earth's crust skywards, creating the **Shira volcano**, the oldest of the volcanoes forming the Kilimanjaro massif. Shira eventually ceased erupting around 500,000 years ago, collapsing as it did so to form a huge *caldera* (the deep cauldron-like cavity on the summit of a volcano) many times the size of its original crater.

Soon after Shira's extinction, **Mawenzi** started to form following a further eruption within the Shira caldera. Though much eroded, Mawenzi has at least kept some of its volcanic shape to this day. Then, 460,000 years ago, an enormous eruption just west of Mawenzi caused the formation of **Kibo**. Continual subterranean pressure made Kibo erupt several times more, forcing the summit ever higher until reaching a maximum height of about 5900m. A further huge eruption from Kibo 100,000 years later led to the formation of Kilimanjaro's characteristic shiny black stone – which in reality is just solidified black lava, or **obsidian**. This spilled over from Kibo's crater into the Shira caldera and around to the base of the Mawenzi peak, forming the so-called Saddle. Later eruptions creat-

❑ THE GREAT RIFT VALLEY

According to the theory of plate tectonics, the Earth's exterior is made up of six enormous plates that 'float' across the surface of the planet. Occasionally they collide, causing much buckling and crumpling and the creation of huge mountain ranges such as the Himalayas. At other times, these plates deteriorate and break up because of the massive forces bubbling away in the earth's interior. When this happens, valleys are formed where the Earth fractures.

The Great Rift Valley, whose origins are in Mozambique but which extends right across East Africa to Jordan in the Middle East, is a classic example of a fracture in the Earth's surface caused by the movement of these plates. The same monstrous internal forces that two million years ago caused the disintegration of the tectonic plate and the formation of the Rift Valley are also responsible for the appearance of volcanoes along the valley, as these forces explode through the surface, pushing the Earth's crust skywards and forming – in the case of Kilimanjaro – one huge, 5895m-high geological pimple.

Of Africa's sixteen active volcanoes, all but three belong to the Rift Valley. Kili was just one of a number of volcanic eruptions to hit the valley; others included Ol Molog (to the north-west of Kilimanjaro), Kilema (to the south-east) plus, of course, the jaw-dropping Ngorongoro Crater.

By the way, don't be misled into thinking that these kinds of major tectonic shifts happened millions of years ago and have little relevance to the present day: the earthquake in Arusha in 2007 shows that this 'active rifting' is still occurring, and even minor movements can have major repercussions.

ed a series of distinctive mini-cones, or **parasitic craters**, that run in a chain south-east and north-west across the mountain, as well as the smaller **Reusch Crater** inside the main Kibo summit. The last volcanic activity of note, just over 200 years ago, left a symmetrical inverted cone of ash in the Reusch Crater, known as the **Ash Pit**, that can still be seen (see p373).

While eruptions are unheard of in recent times, Kibo is classified as being dormant rather than extinct, as anybody who visits the inner Reusch Crater can testify. A strong sulphur smell still rises from the crater, the earth is hot to touch, preventing ice from forming, while occasionally *fumaroles* (a small hole or opening through which sulphurous gases escape) emerge from the Ash Pit that lies at its heart. Indeed, according to the 2003 Nova documentary *Volcano Above the Clouds*, scientists say that Kibo is actually becoming more active again and that, using estimates based on the temperature of some of the fumaroles, magma lies only 400m below the surface and a cataclysmic landslide, similar in magnitude to the one that led to the formation of the Western Breach (see p133), could happen any day!

WHAT DOES IT LOOK LIKE TODAY? THE TOPOGRAPHY

And surely never monarch wore his royal robes more royally than this monarch of African mountains, Kilimanjaro. His foot rests on a carpet of velvety turf, and through the dark green forest the steps of his throne reach downward to the earth, where man stands awestruck before the glory of his majesty. Art may have colours rich enough to fix one moment of this dazzling splendour, but neither brush nor pen can portray the unceasing play of colour – the wondrous purples of the summit deepening as in the Alpine afterglow; the dull greens of the forest and the sepia shadows in the ravines and hollows, growing ever darker as evening steals on apace; and last, the gradual fading away of all, as the sun sets, and over everything spreads the grey cloud-curtain of the night. It is not a picture but a pageant – a king goes to his rest. **Hans Meyer** *Across East African Glaciers* (1891)

Kilimanjaro is not only the highest mountain in Africa, it's also one of the biggest volcanoes on the entire planet, covering an area of approximately 388,500 hectares. In this area are the three main summits or peaks – from west to east Shira, Kibo and Mawenzi – that betray its origins as the offspring of three huge volcanic eruptions:

The Shira Ridge and the Shira Plateau

The oldest and lowest peak, known as Shira, lies on the western edge of the massif. This is the least impressive of the three summits, being nothing more than a heavily eroded ridge, 3962m tall at its highest point, **Johnsell Point**. This ridge is, in fact, merely the south-western rim of the original Shira crater, the northern and eastern sides being covered by later material from Kibo (see below).

The Shira Ridge forms the western edge of the **Shira Plateau**. This large rocky plain, 6200ha in size, is one of Kilimanjaro's most intriguing features. It is believed to be the *caldera* (a collapsed crater) of the original volcano, that was subsequently 'filled in' by lava from later eruptions which then solidified and turned to rock.

Kibo peak and the Saddle

The Shira Plateau rises gently from west to east until it reaches the youngest and main summit, Kibo. This is the best-preserved crater on Kilimanjaro. Michael Crichton describes it as looking 'safe, matronly. More like a breast than a mountain.' I'm not sure I entirely agree with the comparison but I get his point: its gently voluptuous slopes do look 'safe' and welcoming, especially when compared to its spiky neighbour, Mawenzi (see opposite). If you study Kibo's southern lip you'll find that it is slightly higher than the rest of the rim; and the highest point on this southern lip is **Uhuru Peak** – at 5895m the highest point in Africa and the goal of just about every Kilimanjaro trekker.

Kibo is the only one of the three summits which is permanently covered in snow or ice, thanks to the large **glaciers** that cover some of its top. The fact that the summit is now around five metres shorter than it was 450,000 years ago (see pp134-6) can be ascribed to the simple progress of time and the insidious glacial erosion down the millennia. These glaciers, advancing and retreating across the summit, created a series of concentric rings like **terraces** near the top of this volcanic massif on the western side. The glaciers were also behind the formation of the valleys and canyons, eroding and smoothing the earth into gentle undulations all around Kibo. It's one of the reasons why Kibo's slopes are gentle, too, allowing trekkers as well as mountaineers to reach the summit (though this is less true on the drier northern side where the glaciers on the whole failed to reach, leaving the valleys sharper and more defined).

The **crater of Kibo**, measuring 1.9 by 2.7km, is not a perfect, unbroken circle. There are gaps in the circumference where the walls have been breached by lava flows; the most dramatic of these is the **Western Breach**, through which some climbers gain access to the summit each year. The crater has also subsided a little over time, leading to a landslide 100,000 years ago that created the **Barranco** on Kibo's southern side. Nevertheless, Kibo is the one peak that really does look like a volcanic crater; indeed, there are three concentric craters on Kibo. Within the inner **Reusch Crater** (1.3km in diameter) you can still see signs of volcanic activity, including fumaroles, the smell of sulphur and a third crater, the **Ash Pit**, measuring 130m deep by 140m wide. (For more on the Kibo summit, see pp369-71.)

To the east of Kibo lies the **Saddle**, at 3600 hectares the largest area of high-altitude tundra in tropical Africa. This really is a beautiful, eerie place — a dusty desert almost 5000m above sea level, featureless except for the occasional parasitic cone dotted here and there, including the **Triplets**, **Middle Red** and **West Lava Hill**, all running south-east from the south-eastern side of Kibo. (A *parasitic cone* is a mini cone on the slopes of a volcano caused by a later, minor eruption; amazingly, there are said to be some 250 parasitic cones on Kilimanjaro.)

Mawenzi peak and Lake Chala

Nothing could be more marked than the contrast between the external appearance of these two volcanoes – Kibo, with the unbroken, gradual slopes of the typical volcanic cone – Mawenzi with its bewildering display of many-coloured lavas and its fantastically carved outlines, the result of long ages of exposure, combined with the tendency of its component rocks to split vertically rather than horizontally. The hand of time has left its impress upon Kibo too, but the havoc it has wrought is not to be detected at a distance.

Hans Meyer *Across East African Glaciers* (1891)

Seen from Kibo, Mawenzi, the second summit, looks less like a crater than a single lump of jagged, craggy rock. This is merely because its western side also happens to be its highest and hides everything behind it. Walk around Mawenzi, however, and you'll realise that this peak is actually a horseshoe shape, with only the northern side of the crater having been eroded away. Its sides too steep to hold glaciers, there is no *permanent* snow or ice on Mawenzi, and the gradients are enough to dissuade all but the bravest and most technically accomplished climbers.

Mawenzi's highest point is **Hans Meyer Peak** at 5149m but so shattered is this summit, and so riven with gullies and fractures, that there are some other distinctive peaks including Purtscheller Peak (5120m) and South Peak (4958m). There are also two deep gorges, the Great Barranco and Lesser Barranco, scarring its north-eastern face.

Few people know this but Kilimanjaro does actually have a crater lake. **Lake Chala** (aka Jala) lies some 30km to the south-east, lying right across the Tanzanian and Kenyan border. Though only four square kilometres in size, at around 95 metres deep it's actually deeper than the lake with the largest surface area in Africa, Lake Victoria!

THE GLACIERS

It is now time to consider the discovery on which Mr Rebmann particularly prides himself, namely, that of perpetual snow. **WD Cooley** *Inner Africa Laid Open* (see box pp146-9)

At first glance, Kilimanjaro's glaciers look like nothing more than big smooth piles of slightly monotonous ice. On second glance they pretty much look like this too. Yet there's much more to Kili's glaciers than meets the eye, for these cathedrals of gleaming blue-white ice are dynamic repositories of climatic history – and they could also be providing us with a portent for impending natural disaster.

You would think that with the intensely strong equatorial sun, glaciers wouldn't exist at all on Kilimanjaro. In fact, it is the brilliant white colour of the ice that allows it to survive as it reflects most of the heat. The dull black lava rock on which the glacier rests, on the other hand, *does* absorb the heat; so while the glacier's surface is relatively unaffected by the sun's rays, the heat generated by the sun-baked rocks underneath leads to glacial melting.

As a result, the glaciers on Kilimanjaro are inherently unstable: the ice at the bottom of the glacier touching the rocks melts, the glaciers lose their 'grip' on the mountain and 'overhangs' occur where the ice at the base has melted away, leaving just the ice at the top to survive. As the process continues the ice fractures and breaks away, exposing more of the rock to the sun... and so the cycle begins again. The sun's effect on the glaciers is also responsible for the spectacular structures – the ice columns and pillars, towers and cathedrals – that are the most fascinating part of the upper slopes of Kibo.

You would have thought that, after 11,700 years of this melting process, (according to recent research, the current glaciers began to form in 9700BC) very little ice would remain on Kilimanjaro. The fact that there are still glaciers is due to the prolonged 'cold snaps', or ice ages, that have occurred down the centuries, allowing the glaciers to regroup and reappear on the mountain. According to estimates, there have been at least eight of these ice ages, the last a rather minor one in the 15th and 16th centuries, a time when London's River Thames frequently froze over and winters were severe. At these times the ice on Kilimanjaro would in places have reached right down to the treeline and both Mawenzi and Kibo would have been covered. At the other extreme, before 9700BC there have been periods when Kilimanjaro was completely free of ice, perhaps for up to 20,000 years.

The woes of Kilimanjaro – where have all the glaciers gone?

Of the 19 square kilometres ($7^1/_3$ sq miles) of glacial ice on Africa, only 2.2 square kilometres (just less than 1 square mile) can be found on Kilimanjaro. Unfortunately, both figures used to be much higher: Kili's famous white mantle has shrunk by a whopping 90% since the first survey of the summit, in 1912, and even since 1986 there has been a decline of 75%. At this rate, according to UNESCO report published at the end of 2022, Kili will be completely ice-free by 2050; though many experts actually feel it could be as early as 2040.

'We found that the summit of the ice fields [on Kilimanjaro] has lowered by at least 17 metres [almost 56 feet] since 1962. That's an average loss of about a half-metre (a foot and a half) in height each year.' said Professor Lonnie Thompson of Ohio State University back in 2002. This is a man who has spent over half his lifetime studying Kili's glaciers and is the foremost expert on the subject.

Since he made that statement, the situation has only got worse. The Uhlig Glacier, to the north-west of the Western Breach, has disappeared completely, while the famous Furtwangler Glacier, near Crater Camp, is vanishing fast and could disappear by 2030. Even the summit's mighty Northern Icefield, where the glaciers used to be over 40m tall (131¼ft), is not immune. Since the start of the 21st century it has lost about a third of its volume and has now split in two, exposing parts of the summit that haven't seen the sun for several thousand years.

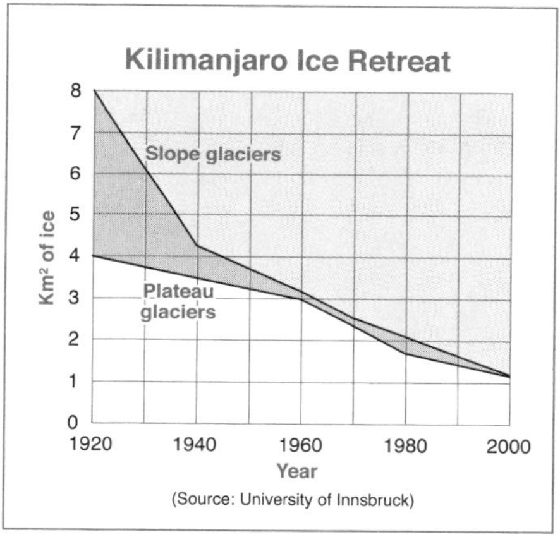

(Source: University of Innsbruck)

The big question, therefore, is not whether they are shrinking, but why – and should we be concerned? Certainly glacial retreats are nothing new: Hans Meyer, the first man to conquer Kilimanjaro, returned in 1898, nine years after his ascent, and was horrified by the extent to which the glaciers had shrunk. The ice on Kibo's slopes had retreated by 100m on all sides, while one of the notches he had used to gain access to the crater in 1889 – now called Hans Meyer Notch – was twice as wide, with the ice only half as thick. Nor are warnings of the complete disappearance of the glaciers anything new: in 1899 Meyer himself predicted that they would be gone within three decades and the top of Kili would be decorated with nothing but bare rock.

What concerns today's scientists, however, is that this current reduction in the size of Kili's ice-cap does seem to be more rapid and more extensive than previous shrinkages. The National Academy of Sciences revealed that the ice cover atop Kilimanjaro decreased steadily, at a rate of approximately 1% from the years 1912 until 1953. But from 1989 until 2007, the rate of decrease more than doubled to a perturbing 2.5%. Such a decline led NASA's Earth Observatory, which had been monitoring the decline in glaciers using satellite imagery, to conclude that '…it's no longer a question of whether the ice will disappear, but when.'

Of course, you don't need me to tell you that global warming is behind the glaciers' disappearance. And when Kilimanjaro does lose its icy top, the repercussions could be extremely serious, particularly for those villagers who live on the mountain slopes and for whom the glaciers are a source of water. It could also have a negative impact on tourism, the region's biggest industry and largest employer. After all, how much less attractive, indeed less magical, would Kili be without its glistening white summit?

For an excellent (and refreshingly readable) summary of the latest on Kilimanjaro's glaciers, do check out 💻 kiboice.blogspot.com, the website of the University of Massachusetts' Climate System Research Center.

Climate

The only predictable thing about the weather on Kilimanjaro is its unpredictability. That's always been true, of course, but is even more so today in this time of global warming and shifting weather patterns. So while I will provide here the same information that we've always given in this book about Kili's climate as it still, just about, holds true, I do find myself wondering if I'll need to rewrite this section in future editions.

The theory behind the weather patterns on Kilimanjaro is essentially very simple. Strong winds travel across the oceans, drawing moisture up as they go.

❑ TREKKING IN THE RAINY SEASON

For those who have absolutely no choice but to walk during the rainy season, don't get too downhearted. For one thing, it's not uncommon for the rains to fail altogether – devastating for the local farmers, of course, but good news for your average trekker. (I was on the mountain in late November once and didn't see a drop of rain the whole time I was there.) And even when there is rain, it doesn't necessarily make for a dreadful trek. I have had letters from several readers who positively recommend the experience. For example, take Jack Hollinghurst from the UK who wrote to me with the following:

'*...I do think that you don't give enough encouragement to walking in the rainy season. I was forced to walk at this time by holiday dates and thought it excellent. Due to the hugely reduced numbers of trekkers on the mountain me and my friend were given our own room at all of the huts (including Kibo, where it is about 12 beds to a room) and* [your] *advice about having dinner early at Horombo is irrelevant as there were about five other groups there at the most.*

...the walking is [also] *much more enjoyable when you have some peace and quiet... Maybe you should advise walkers to wear waterproof trousers at this time of year (although I didn't take any and was fine) but otherwise I wouldn't walk at any other time of year.*'

His sentiments were endorsed by Martin Fehr from Denmark, who wrote to me of his experience a few years later:

'*Don't be afraid to recommend climbing the mountain* [at the end of] *April. Our porters were so happy to have work in low season, we didn't get a lot of rain, and there were absolutely no climbers on the mountain besides us, which made our climb exceptionally great! Plus the top of the mountain was all covered in snow – a challenge, but soooo beautiful (and it was great to be able to "sleigh" down the mountain as well)*'.

Eventually they collide with a large object – such as a mountain like Kilimanjaro. The winds are pushed upwards as they hit the mountain slopes, and the fall in temperature and atmospheric pressure leads to precipitation or, as it's more commonly called, rain and snow.

In one year there are two rain-bearing seasonal winds buffeting Kilimanjaro. The south-east trade wind bringing rain from the Indian Ocean arrives between March and May. Because the mountain is the first main obstacle to the wind's progress, and by

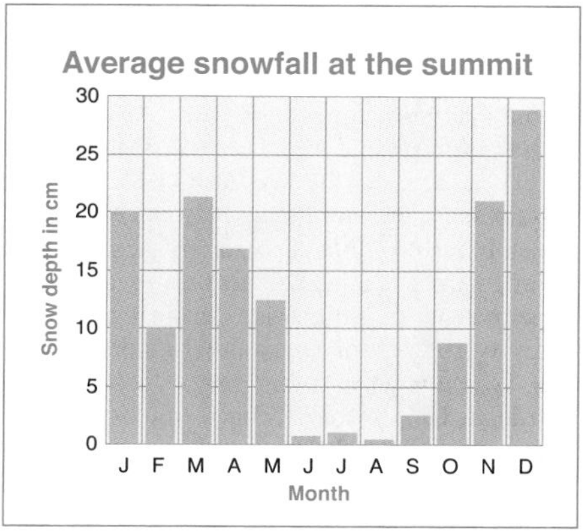

Adapted from DR Hardy's *Kilimanjaro snow* in: AM Waple & JH Lawrimore (eds.) *State of the Climate in 2002*, Bull. Am. Meteorol. Soc., 84, S48

However, Martin does go on to warn: *'Of course, by climbing the mountain during the low season you are very much at the mercy of the elements – and conditions can be quite extreme at this time.'*

Martin's experience – and his opinion of walking in the low season – seems similar to that of Tom Stoa, another reader and Kili conqueror who sticks up for the rainy season:

'I went in April despite the recommendations of you and everyone else to avoid April due to weather, simply because that is when I could go. No regrets. I chose the Marangu route, six days, because of the huts – I figured that despite the rain, we would be warm, dry and comfortable in the huts at least. And that was correct (and we were lucky, it mostly just rained at night). Being the off season, my son and I had a hut to ourselves each night, and the big dining hut was also nearly empty.

We made the summit just fine. My only regret was not having crampons for the big icy snowfield between Hans Meyer Cave and before Gillman's Point. We were gingerly kicking steps in the snow, or trying to step in the steps of others. Having some alpine climbing experience, I know that a slip would have resulted in a nasty, long slide with a crash onto the rocks below. I know that crampons are not customary on Kili, but for that route, on that day, they would have made all the difference between a very sketchy and slow slog, versus an "easy" and safe walk up.'

So there you have it. It would seem that if you have an adventurous spirit, would consider the Marangu Route (the only route on the mountain where you sleep in huts rather than under canvas), have crampons and/or ice axes, can put up with some pretty extreme conditions and are prepared for some possibly treacherous walking – the low season is a fine time to climb!

far the largest, a lot of rain falls on Kili at this time and for this reason the (late) March-to-May season is known as the **long rains**. This is the main wet season on Kilimanjaro. As the south-east trade winds run into the southern side of Kili, so the southern slopes tend to be damper and as a consequence more fertile, with the forest zone much broader than on the northern slopes.

Then there are the dry **'anti-trade' winds** from the north-east which carry no rain and hit the mountain between May and October. These anti-trade winds, which blow, usually very strongly, across the Saddle (the broad valley between Kilimanjaro's two peaks), also serve to keep the south-east trade winds off the upper reaches of Kilimanjaro, ensuring that the rain from the long monsoon season stays largely on the southern side below 3000m, with little falling above this. Which is why, at this time of year, the first day's walk for trekkers on the Marangu, Umbwe or Machame routes is usually conducted under a canopy of cloud, while from the second day onwards they enjoy unobscured sunshine.

A second seasonal rain-bearing wind, the north-east monsoon, having already lost much of its moisture after travelling overland for a longer period, brings a **short rainy season** between November and December. While the northern side receives most of the rain to fall in this season, it is far less than the rain brought by the south-east trade winds and as a result the northern side of Kili remains on the whole drier and more barren than the southern side. Once again, the rain falls mainly below 3000m.

This theory seems fine in principle but it does pose a tricky question: if the precipitation falls below 3000m, how did the snow and ice on the summit of Kibo get there in the first place? The answer, my friend, is blowing in the (anti-trade) wind: though these winds normally blow very strongly, as those who walk north across the Saddle will testify, they occasionally drop in force, allowing the south-east trade winds that run beneath them to climb up the southern slopes to the Saddle and on to the summit. Huge banks of clouds then develop and snow falls.

The temperature at the summit: bikinis – or brass monkeys?

It's a question many trekkers want to know the answer to: just how cold is it on the summit of Kilimanjaro? Well, there is an old mountaineer's saw that says that once you climb above 4000m, for every 150 metres you ascend the temperature drops by 1°C. Given that the average temperature at around 4000m is 0°C, by the time you reach the summit you would have ascended through about 13 lots of 150m. In other words, the temperature would be around -13°C. Pretty chilly you may think, but bearable. But this, of course, fails to take into consideration the wind-chill factor which can push that figure even further downwards, to around -30°C – though these extremes are rare, as you can see in the graph. This shows the average monthly air temperatures over the year at weather stations at 2340m, 3630m, 4570m and 5800m. It gives an idea of how much the temperature drops as you ascend through the various vegetation zones: montane rainforest (2340m/7677ft), heathland (3630m/11,909½ft), alpine desert (4570m/14,993½ft), and on an icefield at 5800m (19,029ft), just 95m/311½ft below Uhuru Peak. You can see that even in the warmest month the mean temperature doesn't rise above -5°C at the top; the mean temperature at the summit, by the way, is -7.1°C. I have also mapped mean precipitation (ie rain – or, at this altitude, snow) at this higher weather station.

It is beyond the scope of this book to go into Kili's climates and weather patterns in any further detail, so instead I'll just point you in the direction of the fascinating *General Characteristics of Air Temperature and Humidity Variability on Kilimanjaro, Tanzania* by WJ Duane, NC Pepin, ML Losleben and DR Hardy, from which much of the material in this section was taken. While for the latest on the readings from the weather stations and other news, do visit University of Massachusetts' blog at kiboice.blogspot.com.

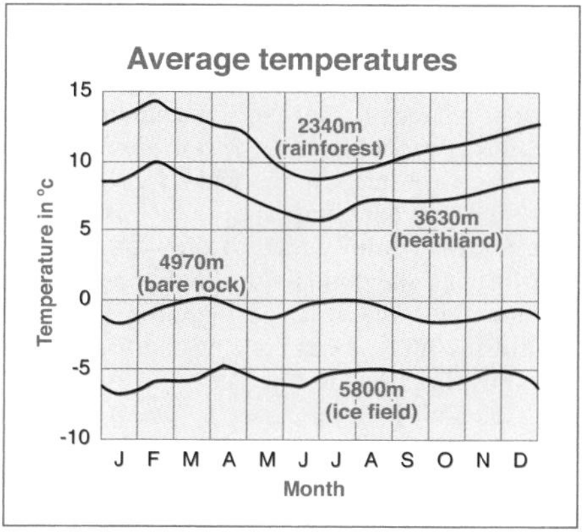

Temperature graph adapted from *General Characteristics of Air Temperature and Humidity Variability on Kilimanjaro, Tanzania* by WJ Duane, NC Pepin, ML Losleben and DR Hardy

The history of Kilimanjaro

EARLY HISTORY

Thanks to several primitive **stone bowls** found on the lower slopes of Kilimanjaro, we know that man has lived on or around the mountain since at least 1000BC. We also know that, over the last 500 years, the mountain has at various times acted as a navigational aid for traders travelling between the interior and the coast, a magnet for Victorian explorers, a political pawn to be traded between European superpowers who carved up East Africa, a battlefield for these same superpowers, and a potent symbol of independence for those who wished to rid themselves of these colonial interlopers. Unfortunately, little is known about the history of the mountain during the intervening 2500 years.

It's a fair bet that Kilimanjaro's first inhabitants, when they weren't fashioning bowls out of the local terrain, would have spent much of their time hunting and gathering the local flora and fauna, Kilimanjaro being a fecund source of both. Add to this its reputation as a reliable region both for fresh drinking water and materials – wood, stones, mud, vines etc – for building, and it seems reasonable to suppose that Kilimanjaro would have been a highly desirable location for primitive man and would have played a central role in the lives of those who chose to take up residence on its slopes.

Unfortunately, those looking to piece together a comprehensive history of the first inhabitants of Kilimanjaro rather have their work cut out. There are no documents recording the life and times of the people who once lived on the mountain; not much in the way of any oral history that has been passed down through the generations; and, stone bowls apart, little in the way of archaeological evidence from which to draw any inferences. So, while we can *assume* many things about the lives of Kilimanjaro's first inhabitants, we can be certain about nothing: and if Kilimanjaro did have a part to play in the pre-colonial history of the region, that history, and the mountain's significance within it, has, alas, now been lost to us.

And so it is to the notes of foreign travellers that we must turn in order to find the earliest accounts of Kilimanjaro. These descriptions are usually rather brief, often inaccurate and more often than not based on little more than hearsay and rumour rather than actual first-hand evidence.

❑ KILIMANJARO – THE NAME

The meaning of the name Kilíma Njáro, if it have any meaning, is unknown to the Swáhili... To be analysed, it must first be corrupted. This has been done by Mr Rebmann, who converts Kilíma Njáro into Kilíma dja-aro, which he tells us signifies, "Mountain of Greatness." This etymology... is wholly inadmissable for the following reasons: 1st. It is mere nonsense...

So said **WD Cooley** (see pp146-9), leading British geographer during the mid 19th century in his book *Inner Africa Laid Open*. Nonsense Rebmann's suggestion may have been but in the absence of better alternatives the translation is as valid as any other. For the fact of the matter is that despite extensive studies into the etymology of the name Kilimanjaro, nobody is sure where it comes from or exactly what it means.

When looking for the name's origin, it seems only sensible to begin such a search in one of the local Tanzanian dialects, and more specifically, in the language spoken by those who live in its shadow, namely the Chagga people. True, the name Kilimanjaro bears no resemblance to any word in the Chagga vocabulary; but if we divide it into two parts a few possibilities present themselves. One is that Kilima is derived from the Chagga term *kilelema*, meaning 'difficult or impossible', while *jaro* could come from the Chagga terms *njaare* ('bird') or *jyaro* ('caravan'). In other words, the name Kilimanjaro means something like 'That which is impossible for the bird', or 'That which defeats the caravan' – names which, if this interpretation is correct, are clear references to the sheer enormity of the mountain.

Whilst this is perhaps the most likely translation, it is not, in itself, particularly convincing, especially when one considers that while the Chagga language would seem the most logical source for the name, the Chagga people themselves do not actually have one single name for the mountain! Instead, they don't see Kilimanjaro as a single entity but as two distinct, separate peaks, namely Mawenzi and Kibo. (These two names, incidentally, are definitely Chagga in origin, coming from the Chagga terms *kimawenzi* – 'having a broken top or summit' – and *kipoo* – 'snow' – respectively.)

One of the first-ever descriptions of East Africa is provided by *Periplus of the Erythraean Sea*, written anonymously in AD45. *Periplus* – a contender for the title of the world's first-ever guidebook – is a manual for seafarers to the ports of Africa, Arabia and India and includes details of the sea routes to China. In it the author tells of a land called Azania, in which one could find a prosperous market town, Rhapta, where 'hatchets and daggers and awls ... a great quantity of ivory and rhinoceros horn and tortoise shell' were all traded. Yet interestingly, there is no mention of any snow-capped mountain lying nearby; indeed, reading *Periplus* one gets the impression that the author considered Rhapta to be just about the end of the world:

Beyond Opone [modern-day Ras Harun on the Somalian coast] *there are the small and great bluffs of Azania ... twenty-three days sail beyond there lies the very last market town of the continent of Azania, Rhapta ...*

Just over a hundred years later, however, **Ptolemy of Alexandria**, astronomer and the founder of scientific cartography, wrote of lands lying to the south of Rhapta where barbaric cannibals lived near a wide shallow bay and where,

Assuming Kilimanjaro isn't Chagga in origin, therefore, the most likely source for the name Kilimanjaro would seem to be Swahili, the majority language of the Tanzanians. Rebmann's good friend and fellow missionary, Johann Ludwig Krapf, wrote that Kilimanjaro could either be a Swahili word meaning 'Mountain of Greatness' – though he is noticeably silent when it comes to explaining how he arrived at such a translation – or a composite Swahili/Chagga name meaning 'Mountain of Caravans'; *jaro*, as I have previously explained, being the Chagga term for 'caravans'. Thus the name could be a reference to the many trading caravans that would stop at the mountain for water. The major flaw with both these theories, however, is that the Swahili term for mountain is not *kilima* but *mlima* – *kilima* is actually the Swahili word for 'hill'!

The third and least-likely dialect from which Kilimanjaro could have been derived is Maasai, the major tribe across the border in Kenya. But while the Maasai word for spring or water is *njore*, which could conceivably have been corrupted down the centuries to *njaro*, there is no relevant Maasai word similar to *kilima*. Furthermore, the Maasai call the mountain *Oldoinyo Oibor*, which means 'White Mountain', with Kibo known as the 'House of God', as Hemingway has already told us at the beginning of his – and this – book. Few experts, therefore, believe the name is Maasai in origin.

Other theories include the possibility that *njaro* means 'whiteness', referring to the snow cap that Kilimanjaro permanently wears, or that Njaro is the name of the evil spirit who lives on the mountain, causing discomfort and even death to those who climb it. Certainly the folklore of the Chagga people is rich in tales of evil spirits who dwell on the higher reaches of the mountain and Rebmann himself refers to 'Njaro, the guardian spirit of the mountain'; however, it must also be noted that the Chagga legends make no mention of any spirit going by that name.

So we are none the wiser. But really, it's not important: what the mountain means to the many thousands who walk up it every year is far more meaningful than any name we ascribe to it.

inland, one could find a '**great snow mountain**'. Mountains that wear a mantle of snow are pretty thin on the ground in Africa; indeed, there is only one real candidate – and that, of course, is Kilimanjaro.

How exactly Ptolemy came by his information is unknown, for he almost certainly never saw Kilimanjaro for himself. Nevertheless, based on hearsay though it may have been, this is the earliest surviving written mention of Africa's greatest mountain. It therefore seems logical to conclude that the outside world first became aware of Africa's tallest mountain in the years between the publication of *Periplus* in AD45, and that of Ptolemy's work, written sometime during the latter half of the 2nd century AD.

THE OUTSIDERS ARRIVE

Arabs, an anonymous Chinese writer and some Portuguese

Following Ptolemy's description, almost nothing more is written about Kilimanjaro for over a thousand years. The Arabs, arriving on the East African coast in the 6th century, must have heard something about it from the local people with whom they traded. Indeed, the mountain would have proved essential to the natives as they travelled from the interior to the markets on the East African shore: as one of the few unmissable landmarks in a largely featureless expanse of savannah and scrub, and with its abundant streams and springs, the mountain would have been both an invaluable aid for navigation and a reliable source of drinking water for the trading caravans. But whether the merchants from the Middle East actually ventured beyond their trading posts on the coast to see the mountain for themselves seems doubtful, and from their records of this time only one possible reference to Kilimanjaro has been uncovered, written by a 13th-century geographer, **Abu'l Fida**, who speaks of a mountain in the interior that was 'white in colour'.

The Chinese, who traded on the East African coast during the same period, also seemed either ignorant or uninterested in the land that lay beyond the coastline and in all their records from this time once again just one scant reference to Kili has been found, this time by an anonymous chronicler who states that the country to the west of Zanzibar 'reaches to a great mountain'.

After 1500 and the exploration and subsequent conquest of the African east coast by Vasco da Gama and those who followed in his wake, the Arabs were replaced as the major trading power in the region by the Portuguese. They proved to be slightly more curious about what lay beyond the coast than their predecessors, perhaps because their primary motive for being there was as much colonial as commercial. A vague but once again unmistakable reference to Kilimanjaro can be found in a book, *Suma de Geographia*, published in 1519, an account of a journey to Mombasa by the Spanish cartographer, astronomer and ship's pilot **Fernandes de Encisco**:

West of Mombasa is the Ethiopian Mount Olympus, which is very high, and further off are the Mountains of the Moon in which are the sources of the Nile.

Amazingly, in the 1400 years since Ptolemy this is only the third reference to

Kilimanjaro that has been found; with the return of the Arabs in 1699, it was also to be the last for another hundred years or so. Then, just as the 18th century was drawing to a close, the Europeans once more cast an avaricious eye towards East Africa.

THE 1800s: PIONEERS . . .

With British merchants firmly established on Zanzibar by the 1840s, frequent rumours of a vast mountain situated on the mainland just a few hundred miles from the coast began to reach their ears. British geographers were especially intrigued by these reports, particularly as it provided a possible solution to one of the oldest riddles of Africa: namely, the precise whereabouts of the source of the Nile. Encisco's 16th-century reference to the 'Mountains of the Moon in which are the sources of the Nile' (see opposite) is in fact a mere echo of the work of Ptolemy, writing 1400 years before Encisco, who also cites the Mountains of the Moon as the true origin of the Nile.

But while these Mountains of the Moon were, for more than a millennium, widely accepted in European academia as the place where the Nile rises, nobody had actually bothered to go and find out if this was so – nor, indeed, if these mountains actually existed.

Interest in the 'Dark Continent' was further aroused by the arrival in London in 1834 of one Khamis bin Uthman. Slave dealer, caravan leader and envoy of the then-ruler of East Africa, Seyyid Said, Uthman met many of Britain's leading dignitaries, including the prime minister, Lord Palmerston. He also met and talked at length with the leading African scholar, **William Desborough Cooley**. A decade after this meeting, Cooley wrote his lengthy essay *The Geography of N'yassi, or the Great Lake of Southern Africa Investigated,* in which he not only provides us with another reference to Kilimanjaro – only the fifth in 1700 years – but also becomes the first author to put a name to the mountain:

The most famous mountain of Eastern Africa is Kirimanjara, which we suppose, from a number of circumstances to be the highest ridge crossed on the road to Monomoezi.

Suddenly Africa, long viewed by the West almost exclusively in terms of the lucrative slave trade, became the centre of a flurry of academic interest and the quest to find the true origins of the Nile became something of a *cause célèbre* amongst scholars. Long-forgotten manuscripts and journals from Arab traders and Portuguese adventurers were dusted off and scrutinised for clues to the whereabouts of this most enigmatic river source.

Most scholars preferred to conduct their research from the comfort of their leather armchairs; there were others, however, who took a more active approach, and pioneering explorers such as Richard Burton and John Hanning Speke set off to find for themselves the source of the Nile, crossing the entire country we now know as Tanzania in 1857. This was also the age of Livingstone and Stanley, the former venturing deep into the heart of Africa in search of both knowledge and potential converts to Christianity, and the latter in search of the former.

. . . AND PREACHERS

David Livingstone preaching near Lake Tanganyika. (HG Adams, 1873)

Yet for all their brave endeavours, it was not these Victorian action men but one of the humble Christian missionaries who arrived in Africa at about the same time who became the first European to set eyes on Kilimanjaro. **Johannes Rebmann** was a young Swiss-German missionary who arrived in Mombasa in 1846 with an umbrella, a suitcase and a heart full of Christian zeal. His brief was to help **Dr Johann Ludwig Krapf**, a Doctor of Divinity from Tubingen, in his efforts to spread the Christian faith among East Africa's heathen. Krapf was something of a veteran in the missionary field, having previously worked for the London-based Church Missionary Society in Abyssinia. Following the closure of that mission, Krapf sailed down the East African coast to Zanzibar and from there to Mombasa, where he hoped to found a new mission and continue his evangelical work.

Instead, his life fell apart. His wife succumbed to malaria and died on 9 July 1844. His daughter, born just three days previously, died five days after her mother from the same disease, while Krapf too fell gravely ill with the same; and though he alone recovered, throughout the rest of his life he suffered from sporadic attacks that would lay him low for weeks at a time.

But though his body grew weak with malaria, his spirit remained strong, and, following the death of his wife, over the next six months Krapf both translated the New Testament into Swahili and devised a plan for spreading the gospel throughout the interior of Africa. Estimating that the continent could be crossed on foot from east to west in a matter of '900 hours' (37½ days), Krapf believed that establishing a chain of missions at intervals of one hundred hours right across the continent, each staffed by six 'messengers of peace', would be the best way to promulgate the Christian religion on the dark continent. Unfortunately for Krapf, Islam had got there first, which made his job rather tougher; indeed, in the six months following his arrival in Mombasa, the total number of successful conversions made by Krapf stood at a nice round figure: zero. Clearly, if the faith was to make any inroads in Africa, fresh impetus was required.

That impetus was provided by the arrival of Rebmann in 1846. Having recovered from the obligatory bout of malaria that all but wiped him out for his first month in Africa, Rebmann set about helping Krapf to establish a new mission at Rabai-mpia (New Rabai), just outside Mombasa. The station lay in the heart of Wanika territory, a tribe who from the first had proved resistant to conversion. Even the founding of a mission in their midst did little to persuade the Wanika to listen to their preaching: by 1859, 14 years after Krapf first arrived, just seven converts had been made.

It was clear early on that they would have little success in persuading the Wanika to convert. So almost from the start the proselytising pair began to look to pastures new to find potential members for their flock. In 1847 they founded a second mission station at Mt Kasigau, three days' walk from Rabai-mpia – the first in their proposed chain of such stations across the African continent – and later that same year they began to plan the establishment of the next link, at a place called **Jagga** (now spelt Chagga). Rebmann and Krapf had already heard a lot about Jagga from the caravan leaders who earned their money transporting goods between the interior and the markets on the eastern shore and who often called into Rabai-mpia on the way. A source of and market for slaves, Jagga was renowned locally for suffering from extremely cold temperatures at times, a reputation that led Krapf to deduce that Jagga was probably at a much higher altitude than the lands that surrounded it. This hypothesis was confirmed by renowned caravan leader Bwana Kheri, who spoke to Krapf of a great mountain called 'Kilimansharo' (this, incidentally, being the sixth definite reference to Kilimanjaro). From other sources, Krapf and Rebmann also learned that the mountain was protected by evil spirits (known in the Islamic faith as *djinns*) who had been responsible for many deaths, and that it was crowned with a strange white substance that resembled silver, but which the locals simply called 'cold'.

Following protracted negotiations, Bwana Kheri was eventually persuaded to take Rebmann to Chagga in 1848 (Krapf, being too ill to travel, remained in Rabai-mpia). The parting caused great distress to both parties, as detailed in Krapf's diary:

Here we are in the midst of African heathenism, among wilful liars and trickish men, who desire only our property... The only earthly friend whom I have, and whom he has, does at once disappear, each of us setting our face towards our respective destinations while our friends at home do not know where we are, whither we go and what we are doing.

Rebmann's journey and the discovery of snow

And so, armed with only his trusty umbrella – along a route where caravans typically travelled under armed escort – Rebmann, accompanied by Bwana Kheri and eight porters, set out for Chagga on 27 April 1848. A fortnight later, on the morning of 11 May, he came across the most marvellous sight:

At about ten o'clock, (I had no watch with me) I observed something remarkably white on the top of a high mountain, and first supposed that it was a very white cloud, in which supposition my guide also confirmed me, but having gone a few paces more I could no more rest satisfied with that explanation; and while I was asking my guide a second time whether that white thing was indeed a cloud and scarcely listening to his answer that ***yonder*** *was a cloud but what that white was he did not know, but supposed it was* ***coldness*** *– the most delightful recognition took place in my mind, of an old well-known European guest called* ***snow****. All the strange stories we had so often heard about the gold and silver mountain Kilimandjaro in Jagga, supposed to be inaccessible on account of evil spirits, which had killed a great many of those who had attempted to ascend it, were now at once rendered intelligible to me, as of course the extreme cold, to which poor Natives are perfect strangers, would soon chill and kill the half-naked visitors. I endeavoured to explain to my people the nature of that 'white thing' for which no name exists even in the language of Jagga itself...*

Johannes Rebmann from his account of his journey, published in Volume I of the *Church Missionary Intelligencer,* May 1849 *(cont'd on p148)*

❑ WD FAULTY? – THE GREAT SNOW DEBATE

The most relentless critic was a redoubtable person, for long years a terror to real explorers, Mr Desborough Cooley, a kind of geographical ogre, who used to sit in his study in England, shaping and planning out the map of Africa (basing his arrangements of rivers, lakes and mountains on ridiculous and fantastic linguistic coincidences and resemblances of his own imagination), and who rushed out and tore in pieces all unheeding explorers in the field who brought to light actual facts which upset his elaborate schemes. **HH Johnston** *The Kilima-njaro Expedition – A Record of Scientific Exploration in Eastern Equatorial Africa* (1886)

Though Rebmann's accounts of Kilimanjaro caused a minor sensation amongst the wider reading public when first published in the *Church Missionary Intelligencer* of May 1849, the response it elicited from academic circles back in Europe was initially as cool as the top of Kibo itself. Leading the sceptics was one **William Desborough (WD) Cooley**. Cooley was widely regarded in his day as one of Britain's leading geographers and something of an expert on Africa (though he never actually ventured near the continent throughout his entire life). Indeed, Cooley had already added to the stock of knowledge about the mountain way back in 1845, a full four years before Rebmann's essay was published, by providing the world with a description of Kilimanjaro that he had managed to construct from details furnished to him by the slave-dealer-cum-ambassador Khamis bin Uthman (see p143).

But if he is remembered at all today it is as the man who refused to believe that Kilimanjaro could be topped with snow, as this response to Rebmann's first account (see p145, pp148-9 & p150) makes clear:

I deny altogether the existence of snow on Mount Kilimanjaro. It rests entirely on the testimony of Mr Rebmann... and he ascertained it, not with his eyes, but by inference and in the visions of his imagination. *Athenaeum*, May 1849

Absurd as it seems now, Cooley's reputation in intellectual circles at that time was as high as Kili itself and such was the reverence with which his every pronouncement was received in the mid 19th century that it was his version of reality that was the more widely accepted: as far as people in Europe were concerned, if Cooley said Kilimanjaro did not have snow on it, it did not have snow on it.

A second report by Rebmann, following his trip to the Chagga lands in November 1848, did little to stem the scepticism, even though he went to great lengths to back up his earlier report:

... during the night, I felt the cold as severely as in Europe in November; and had I been obliged to remain in the open-air, I could not have fallen to sleep for a single moment: neither was this to be wondered at, for so near was I now to the snow-mountain Kilimandjaro (Kilima dja-aro, mountain of greatness), that even at night, by only the dim light of the moon, I could perfectly well distinguish it.

If Rebmann hoped to persuade his critics, however, he was sadly mistaken: if he was capable of making a mistake once, they countered, then surely he could be wrong a second and third time too. And so for much of the next two years Rebmann's account of his time on Kili was treated with equal parts suspicion and derision.

Indeed, it wasn't until 1850 and the publication of an account by Rebmann's friend and mentor, Dr Krapf, that doubts began to be cast on Cooley's ideas. In an edition of the *Church Missionary Intelligencer* in which he recounts his own experiences working in the Ukamba region immediately to the north of Kilimanjaro, Krapf baldly states that:

All the arguments which Mr Cooley has adduced against the existence of such a snow mountain, and against the accuracy of Rebmann's report, dwindle into nothing when one has the evidence of one's own eyes before one; so that they are scarcely worth refuting.

Suddenly it became that much harder to deny the existence of snow on Kili: after all, there were now two Europeans who had seen the mountain for themselves – and both of them had insisted that they'd seen snow there.

Yet Cooley remained adamant in his convictions and, thanks to the support of some pretty influential friends to back up his arguments, enjoyed popular public support. No less a figure than the President of the Royal Geographical Society, **Sir Roderick Murchison**, said that the idea of a snow-capped mountain under the equator was to *'a great degree incredulous'* (even though there are other snow-capped mountains in the Andes and Papua New Guinea that fall 'under the equator', and which were already known about by the mid 19th century).

Even those who *had* been to Africa for themselves had serious reservations about the missionaries' claims. The esteemed Irish explorer **Richard Burton**, for example, having listened to Krapf give a talk on Kilimanjaro in Cairo, declared that *'These stories reminded one of a de Lunatico'*; while **David Livingstone**, recently returned from his latest adventures in Africa, lent further weight to Cooley's arguments during an address to the Royal Geographical Society. In it, Livingstone related a story about some mountains in the Zambezi Valley which were described to him by locals as being of a *'glistening whiteness'*. Livingstone initially believed that these mountains must be covered by snow, until, having seen the mountains for himself, he realised that they were in fact composed of *'masses of white rock, somewhat like quartz'*.

As if to drum home the point of the tale, Sir Roderick Murchison later declared at the same meeting that Livingstone's account:

... may prove that the missionaries, who believed that they saw snowy mountains under the equator, have been deceived by the glittering aspect of rocks under a tropical sun.

The next broadside fired by either side occurred in 1852 and the publication of Cooley's grandly (but inaccurately) titled *Inner Africa Laid Open*. This, Cooley clearly hoped, was to be his masterpiece: the culmination of a lifetime's armchair studying, this was the opus that would secure his reputation during his lifetime and ensure his name lived on in perpetuity as one of the great intellectual heavyweights of the 19th century. As it transpired, the book did indeed serve to preserve Cooley's name for posterity – though presumably not in the way that he had hoped.

To read the book now, it is clear that Cooley hoped it would once and for all dismiss all this nonsense about snow on Kilimanjaro. Within the first few pages almost every part of Rebmann's account is called into question, with the claim of snow on Kilimanjaro being treated with particularly vehement derision:

... it is obvious that the discovery of snow rests much more on 'a delightful mental recognition' than on the evidence of the senses... But in his mind the wish was father to the thought, the 'delightful recognition' developed with amazing rapidity, and in a few minutes the cloudy object, or 'something white,' became a 'beautiful snow mountain', so near to the equator.

Later in the book Cooley forgets the conduct becoming of an English gentleman and the attacks on Rebmann border on the personal, starting with an attack on his eyesight:

(cont'd overleaf)

❑ WD FAULTY? – THE GREAT SNOW DEBATE *(cont'd from p147)*

Various and inconsistent reasons have been assigned for this failure [by Rebmann to see Kilimanjaro from a nearby hill], *but the only true explanation of it is contained in Mr Rebmann's confession that he is very short-sighted. He was unable to perceive, with the aid of a small telescope, Lake Ibe, three days distant to the south, which his followers could discern with the naked eye; nor could he even see the rhinoceroses in his path.*

... betraying weak powers of observation, strong fancy, an eager craving for wonders, and childish reasoning, could not fail to awaken mistrust by their intrinsic demerits, even if there were no testimony opposed to them.

To further back up his argument, Cooley was able to point out a number of inconsistencies between Rebmann's and Krapf's accounts, such as the postulation by Krapf that the mountain is 12,500ft (3810m) high – this after Rebmann had estimated the height to be closer to 20,000ft (6096m, a pretty good guess by the myopic Rebmann).

Cooley's desire to prove Rebmann wrong was fuelled by more than just a desire to crush a young upstart in a field in which he considered himself the ultimate authority. He was also frightened that the existence of snow on Kilimanjaro would provide support for his rivals' theories at the expense of his own. In the big debate that raged in academic circles in the mid 1800s on the exact location of the source of the Nile, Cooley was firmly of the opinion that the river started from a large lake in Central Africa called Lake N'yassi. (Indeed, in the 1830s he even organised an expedition to prove his theory, though unfortunately it failed abysmally for reasons that remain rather obscure.)

Aligned against Cooley were opponents such as the geographer **Charles Beke**, who preferred the idea that the Nile had its source in a mountain range in the interior – possibly, as Encisco (p142) had stated in the 16th century, the legendary Mountains of the Moon – and looked upon the discovery of snow on an East African mountain as evidence to back up their theories. Indeed, when Rebmann and Krapf's accounts first reached Britain, Beke was only too keen to accept their every word as gospel and even went so far as to suggest that Kilimanjaro was now the most likely source of the Nile.

And that, for the next decade or so, was that: Rebmann and Krapf continued to visit Kilimanjaro and continued to see snow, while Cooley and the gang back in England continued to refute their every utterance and enjoy the majority of public opinion.

Then in 1862, **Baron Carl von der Decken** made his second and more successful attempt on Kilimanjaro (see p150), this time with his friend Dr Otto Kersten who had replaced Thornton for this second expedition. In reaching a reported 14,200ft (4328m) von der Decken and Kersten came as close to the snow as any European ever had, and the brave baron's subsequent account of the expedition exploded Cooley's theories once and for all:

During the night it snowed heavily and next morning the ground lay white all around us. Surely the obstinate Cooley will be satisfied now.

(cont'd from p145) An extract from the next edition continues the theme:

The cold temperature of the higher regions constituted a limit beyond which they dared not venture. This natural disinclination, existing most strongly in the case of the great mountain, on account of its intenser cold, and the popular traditions respecting the fate of the only expedition which had ever attempted to ascend its heights, had of course prevented them from exploring it, and left them in utter ignorance of such a thing as 'snow', although not in ignorance of that which they so greatly dreaded, 'coldness'.

There was now a third eyewitness claiming to have seen snow on Kilimanjaro, and a baron at that; Cooley's position as a result began to look increasingly untenable, and his support began to ebb quietly away.

If the baron really believed his testimony alone would persuade Cooley, however, he was much mistaken:

So the Baron says it snowed during the night...In December with the sun standing vertically overhead! The Baron is to be congratulated on the opportuneness of the storm. But it is easier to believe in the misrepresentations of man than in such an unheard-of eccentricity on the part of nature. This description of a snowstorm at the equator during the hottest season of the year, and at an elevation of only 13,000 feet, is too obviously a 'traveller's tale', invented to support Krapf's marvellous story of a mountain 12,500 feet high covered with perpetual snow.

But the redoubtable Cooley was fighting a lonely battle now. The Royal Geographical Society withdrew their backing, with Sir Roderick Murchison – presumably between mouthfuls of humble pie – finally admitting that Rebmann and Krapf were probably right after all. As if to add insult to Cooley's injured pride, the Society even awarded their Gold Medal in 1863 to von der Decken for his contributions to the sum of geographical knowledge of Africa. (Incidentally, in addition to his account of Kilimanjaro, von der Decken was also the first European to see and describe Mount Meru.)

Fourteen years after Rebmann had first announced that there was snow on the equator, the world was finally listening to him. Cooley meanwhile, resolutely refused to believe in the existence of snow on Kilimanjaro, carrying his scepticism with him to the grave and leaving behind a reputation for stubbornness and ignorance that has survived to this day.

In Cooley's defence, one has to remember just how little was known about the continent at that time: few people from Europe had ever visited Africa; fewer still had penetrated beyond the coast; and of those who had, even fewer had survived to tell the tale. So the armchair scholars of Europe were forced to rely upon the sketchy mentions of Kili in historical records for their information; and of those descriptions, none since Ptolemy mentions anything about snow.

As some compensation, perhaps, Cooley at least had the satisfaction of knowing that, while defeated in this particular battle, he had gained a partial victory in the wider war: in 1858 a large body of water in the heart of Africa was discovered and was named **Lake Victoria** after Britain's sovereign. This lake would later be proved to be one of the sources of the Nile. Cooley may have got the name and location of this body of water wrong, but his supposition that the Nile had a lake as its source, and not a mountain, had been proved correct after all.

Still bent on spreading Christianity, and undeterred (indeed ignorant) of the scepticism with which his reports in the *Intelligencer* were about to be met back in Europe (see the box p146), Rebmann returned to Rabai-mpia but continued to visit and write about Kilimanjaro and the Chagga region for a few more years.

His second trip, made in November of the same year, was blessed by favourable weather conditions, providing Rebmann with his clearest view of

Kilimanjaro, and the outside world with the most accurate and comprehensive description of the mountain that had yet been written:

There are two main peaks which arise from a common base measuring some twenty-five miles long by as many broad. They are separated by a saddle-shaped depression, running east and west for a distance of about eight or ten miles. The eastern peak is the lower of the two, and is conical in shape. The western and higher presents the appearance of a magnificent dome, and is covered with snow throughout the year, unlike its eastern neighbour, which loses its snowy mantle during the hot season.

On this second trip Rebmann was also able to correct an error made in his first account of Kilimanjaro: that the local 'Jagga' tribe were indeed familiar with snow and did have a name for it – that name being 'Kibo'!

A third and much more organised expedition in April 1849 – at the same time as the account of his earlier visits to Kilimanjaro was rolling off the presses in Europe – enabled Rebmann, accompanied by a caravan of 30 porters (and, of course, his trusty umbrella), to ascend to such a height that he was later to boast that he had come 'so close to the snow-line that, supposing no impassable abyss to intervene, I could have reached it in three or four hours'.

After Rebmann's pioneering work it was the turn of his friend Krapf, now risen from his sickbed, to see the snowy mountain his friend had described in such detail. In November 1849 he visited the Ukamba district to the north of Kilimanjaro and during a protracted stay in the area Krapf became the first white man to see Mount Kenya. Perhaps more importantly, he was also afforded wonderful views of Kilimanjaro, and was able to back up Rebmann's assertion that the mountain really was adorned with snow (see box pp146-7 for quote).

FIRST ATTEMPTS ON THE SUMMIT

Baron von der Decken and Charles New

After the missionaries came the mountaineers. In August 1861 Baron Carl Claus von der Decken, a Hanoverian naturalist and traveller who had been residing in Zanzibar, accompanied by young English geologist Richard Thornton, himself an explorer of some renown who had accompanied (and been sacked by) Livingstone during the latter's exploration of the Zambezi, made the first serious attempt on Kilimanjaro's summit. Initially, despite an entourage of over fifty porters, a manservant for von der Decken and a personal slave for Thornton, their efforts proved to be rather dismal and they had to turn back after just three days due to bad weather, having reached the rather puny height of just 8200ft (2499m). Proceeding to the west side of the mountain, however, the pioneering baron did at least enjoy an unobstructed view of Kibo peak on the way:

Bathed in a flood of rosy light, the cap that crowns the mountain's noble brow gleamed in the dazzling glory of the setting sun... Beyond appeared the jagged outlines of the eastern peak, which rises abruptly from a gently inclined plain, forming, as it were, a rough, almost horizontal platform. Three thousand feet lower, like the trough between two mighty waves, is the saddle which separates the sister peaks one from the other.

Von der Decken also provided the most accurate estimate yet for the height of both Kibo – which he guessed was between 19,812 and 20,655ft (6038.7m to

6295.6m) – and Mawenzi (17,257 to 17,453ft, or 5259.9 to 5319.7m). Thornton, for his part, correctly surmised that the mountain was volcanic, with Kibo the youngest and Shira the oldest part of the mountain.

The following year von der Decken, now accompanied by Dr Otto Kersten who had replaced Thornton as the baron's travelling and climbing companion, reached a much more respectable 14,200ft (4328m) and furthermore reported being caught up in a snowstorm (see box pp148-9). On his return to Europe, the baron described Kibo as a 'mighty dome, rising to a height of about 20,000 feet, of which the last three thousand are covered in snow'.

Following this second attempt, von der Decken urged **Charles New** (1840-75), a London-born missionary with the United Free Methodist Church in Mombasa, to tackle the mountain, and in 1871 New made a laudable attempt to reach the summit. That attempt failed, as did a second attempt in August of the same year; nevertheless, by choosing on the latter occasion to climb on the south-eastern face of Kibo where the ice cap at that time stretched almost to the base of the cone, New inadvertently wrote himself into the history books as the first European to cross the snow-line at the African Equator:

The gulf was all that now lay between myself and it [the snow line]*, but what an all! The snow was on a level with my eye, but my arm was too short to reach it. My heart sank, but before I had time fairly to scan the position my eyes rested upon snows at my very feet! There it lay upon the rocks below me in shining masses, looking like newly washed and sleeping sheep! Hurrah! I cannot describe the sensations that thrilled my heart at that moment. Hurrah!*

On this second expedition New also discovered the crater lake of Jala (today known as Lake Chala), the mountain's only volcanic lake, on Kili's eastern slopes. (Today's visitors are surprised to find the lake is actually well away from the national park, on the border of Kenya and Tanzania, about 50km east of Moshi.)

New's experiences on Kilimanjaro fanned his passion for the mountain and two years later he was back preparing for another assault on the still-unconquered peak. Unfortunately, the volatile tribes living at the foot of the mountain had other ideas and before New had even reached Kilimanjaro he was forced to turn around and head back towards the coast, having been stripped of all his possessions by the followers of the Chief of 'Moji' (Moshi), a highly unpleasant man by the name of Mandara (see p278 & p280). Broken in both health and spirits, the unfortunate New died soon after the attack.

As rumours of New's demise trickled back to Europe, enthusiasm among explorers for the still unconquered Kilimanjaro understandably waned and for the next dozen years the mountain saw few foreign faces. Those that did visit usually did so on their way to somewhere else; people such as **Dr Gustav A Fischer** in 1883, who stopped in Arusha and visited Mount Meru on his journey to Lake Naivasha and declared Kilimanjaro to be fit for 'European settlement', a statement that would have greater resonance later on in the century. There was also the Scottish geologist, **Joseph Thomson**, who became one of the first to examine properly the northern side of the mountain during an attempt to cross the Maasai territories. He also attempted a climb of Kili, though having allowed himself only one day in which to complete the task his attempt was always doomed to failure; in the end he reached no higher than the tree-line at about 2700m. (Failure though he may have been in this instance, his name lives on as a species of gazelle.)

The first European to venture back to the region with the specific intention of visiting Kilimanjaro arrived in the same year, 1883. In an expedition organised by the Royal Geographical Society, **Harry H Johnston** arrived in East Africa with the aim of discovering and documenting the flora and fauna of Kilimanjaro. Though his work did little to further our understanding of the mountain, Johnston's trip is of anecdotal interest in that he later claimed in his biography that he was actually working undercover for the British Secret Service. No documentary evidence has ever turned up to back this claim (though there is a letter written by him to the Foreign Office in which he asks for 40 men and £5000 for the purpose of colonising Kilimanjaro). Much doubt has been cast, too, upon his boast that he reached almost 5000m during his time on the mountain; while his suggestion that Kilimanjaro was 'a mountain that can be climbed even without the aid of a walking stick' was widely ridiculed when first broadcast later that year.

But, whatever the inaccuracies and falsehoods of Johnston's recollections, his journey did at least assure other would-be Kilimanjaro visitors from Europe that the region was once again safe to visit. His visit also served to bring the mountain to the attention of European powers...

COLONISATION

... a country as large as Switzerland enjoying a singularly fertile soil and healthy climate, ... within a few years it must be either English, French or German ... I am on the spot, the first in the field, and able to make Kilima-njaro as completely English as Ceylon.

HH Johnston *The Kilima-njaro Expedition – A Record of Scientific Exploration in Eastern Equatorial Africa* (1886)

In describing the mountain thus, HH Johnston brought Kilimanjaro to the attention of the world's leading powers. Soon the two great colonisers in East Africa, Germany and Britain, were jockeying for position in the region. British missionaries were accused of putting the temporal interests of their country over the spiritual affairs of their flock, while for their part certain German nationals made no secret of the fact they wished to colonise Kilimanjaro.

In 1884, the **Gesellschaft für Deutsche Kolonisation** (GDK), a political party founded by the 28-year-old **Dr Carl Peters** with the ultimate goal of colonising East Africa, persuaded a dozen local chiefs to throw off the rule of the (British controlled) **Sultan of Zanzibar** and, furthermore, to cede large sections of their territory to the German cause; one of Dr Peters' envoys, Dr Juhlke, even managed to establish a protectorate over Kilimanjaro in 1885. The British fought fire with fire, forcing two dozen chiefs (including some of those who had sided with the Germans) to swear allegiance to the sultan – and therefore indirectly to them.

The situation was becoming dangerously volatile, with war looking increasingly likely. After further bouts of political manoeuvring, in October 1886 the two sides met in London and Berlin to define once and for all the boundary between British- and German-controlled East Africa and head off the possibility of war: the border between British-ruled Kenya and German East Africa was now in place.

The first period of German rule over Kilimanjaro proved to be exceptionally harsh and many Germans soon felt uneasy about the excesses of Dr Peters and his followers. In 1906 an enquiry opened in the Reichstag into the conduct of the doctor and his men, in which an open letter by a Herr Eltz (about whom very little is known) was read out to the court. Its contents give an idea of the hatred that the doctor and his men aroused in the locals:

What have you achieved by perpetual fights, by acts of violence and oppression? You have achieved, Herr Doctor, I have it from your own mouth in the presence of witnesses – that you and the gentlemen of your staff cannot go five minutes' distance from the fort without military escort. My policy enables me to make extensive journeys and shooting trips in Kilimanjaro and the whole surrounding country with never more than four soldiers. You have cut the knot with the sword and achieved that this most beautiful country has become a scene of war. Before God and man you are responsible for the devastation of flourishing districts, you are responsible for the deaths of our comrades Bulow and Wolfram, of our brave soldiers and of hundreds of Wachagga. And now I bring a supreme charge against you: Necessity did not compel you to this. You required deeds only in order that your name might not be forgotten in Europe.

Soon German soldiers were being attacked and killed and, with opposition to their rule growing stronger and more organised, they suffered a massive defeat at Moshi at the hands of the Chagga, led by **Meli**, the son of Mandara (see p278 & p280). Though the Germans soon regained control, it was clear to them that a more benevolent style of government was required if they were to continue ruling

❑ THE BIGGEST PRESENT EVER?

There is a widely believed story that the kink in the border between Kenya and Tanzania near Kilimanjaro was created to satisfy the whim of Queen Victoria, Britain's reigning monarch at the time the border was first defined. According to the story, she magnanimously decided to give Kilimanjaro to her grandson, the future Wilhelm II, as a birthday present, following a complaint from him that while Britain had two snowy mountains in her East African territories (Mounts Kili and Kenya), Germany was left with none. In order to effect the transfer of such a generous gift, the border had to be redrawn so that Kili fell to the south of the boundary, in German territory, which is why the border has a strange kink to the east of the mountain.

Alas, however romantic the story, it is simply not true. The kink is there not because of Victoria's largesse, but as part of the agreement struck between Germany and Britain, and it exists not because of Kili, but Mombasa. Britain's territories in East Africa needed a port: the Germans already had Dar and, if the border between the two was to continue on the same bearing as it had taken to the west of Kilimanjaro, they were going to end up with Mombasa too. So a kink was placed in the border to allow Mombasa to fall in British territory.

over their East African territories. This new 'caring colonialism' paid off and for the last few years of their rule the Germans lived largely at peace with their subjects and even forged a useful alliance with the Chaggas during the Germans' push against rebellious Maasai tribes. The Germans also started the practice of building public huts on Kilimanjaro, establishing one at 8500ft (2591m), called **Bismarck Hut**, and one at 11,500ft (3505m) known as **Peters' Hut**, after Dr Carl.

KILIMANJARO CONQUERED

While all this was going on, attempts to be the first to conquer Kilimanjaro continued apace. In 1887, **Count Samuel Teleki** of the Austro-Hungarian Empire made the most serious assault on Kibo so far, before 'a certain straining of the membrane of the tympanum of the ear' forced him to turn back. Then the American naturalist, **Dr Abbott**, who had come primarily to investigate the fauna and flora of the mountain slopes, made a rather reckless attempt.

Abbott was struck down by illness fairly early on in the climb but his companion, Otto Ehlers of the German East African Company, pushed on, reaching (according to him) 19,680ft (5998.5m). Not for the first time in the history of climbing Kilimanjaro, however, this figure has been sceptically received by others – particularly as it is over 100m above the highest point on the mountain!

❑ MEYER'S ROUTE TO THE TOP COMPARED TO THE MODERN TRAILS

While no modern path precisely retraces Hans Meyer's original route to the summit, some of today's paths do occasionally coincide with the trail he blazed. For instance, Meyer and his climbing partner, Purtscheller, began their assault on Kilimanjaro, on 28 September 1889, from **Marangu** village. From there they headed due north up through the trees, arriving two days later at the very upper limits of the forest, where they made camp.

Trekkers on the Marangu trail follow a similar route today, though their starting point is a good deal higher than Meyer's at Marangu Gate rather than Marangu village – which explains why trekkers today need only one day to reach the upper edge of the forest, while Meyer took two. It is also worth noting that, according to the beautifully drawn maps by Dr Bruno Hassenstein in Meyer's book *Across East African Glaciers*, his camp on this second night lay to the south-west of Kifunika Hill at an altitude of 8710ft (2654.8m), whereas the Mandara Huts lie a couple of hours' walk to the east of Kifunika, at a loftier 8999ft (2743m).

On the third day, Meyer struck a westerly course, crossing the Mdogo (lesser) and Mkuba (greater) streams before making camp at an altitude of 9480ft (2889.5m). This was the all-important **Halfway Camp**, the intermediate station that Meyer would use as his base for tackling Kibo. In the history of climbing Kibo, no single spot on the entire mountain, save Uhuru Peak itself, has played a more prominent role: Harry H Johnston had built some huts nearby during his reconnaissance mission of 1883; Meyer himself had camped here during his first expedition on the mountain, with Baron von Eberstein in 1887, and Abbott and Ehlers had also camped nearby in 1889, just a few months before Meyer and Purtscheller arrived. There's even evidence to suggest Count Teleki had also stopped here in 1887; in his account of their attempt on Kili in *Discovery by Count Teleki of Lakes Rudolf and Stefanie*, Lieutenant

(By way of compensation, however, it was on Kilimanjaro that Abbott first identified and collected the species of duiker that now bears his name.)

In spite of their relative failures, both Teleki and Abbott played a part in the success of the eventual conqueror of Kilimanjaro, **Dr Hans Meyer**: Teleki, by providing information about the ascent to Meyer in a chance encounter during Meyer's first trip to the region in 1887; Abbott, by providing accommodation in Moshi for Meyer and his party during their successful expedition of 1889.

Hans Meyer was a geology professor and the son of a wealthy editor from Leipzig (he himself later joined his father's editorial board and became its director, retiring in 1888, one year before the conquest of Kili, to become professor of Colonial Geography at Leipzig University). In all he made four trips to Kilimanjaro. Following the partial success of his first attempt in 1887, when he managed to reach 18,000ft (5486.4m), Meyer returned the following year for a second assault with experienced African traveller and friend Dr Oscar Baumann. Unfortunately, his timing couldn't have been worse: the **Abushiri War**, an Arab-led revolt against German traders on the East African coast, had just broken out and Meyer and his friend Baumann were captured, clapped into chains and held hostage by Sheikh Abushiri himself, the leader of the insurgency. In the end both escaped with their lives, but only after a ransom of ten thousand rupees was paid.

Ludwig von Höhnel speaks of making camp at 9390ft (2862m) by a brook, near some old huts built originally by HH Johnston.

So where is this spot? There are plenty of clues. It is no coincidence, for example, that all these different parties chose to make camp at this site. Then, as now, campsites would have been chosen largely for their proximity to water and other amenities, so we can guess that a mountain stream or brook must run nearby. We also know that Meyer headed almost due west from his camp of the night before and that the spot lies at around 2862m (9389¾ft), above the tree-line. No modern campsite exactly fits this description – the Horombo Huts, the second night's accommodation on the Marangu trail, are too high up at 3657m/11,998ft. Rau Campsite, however, on the soon to be reopened Kidia Route, seems a more plausible candidate: though this campsite is too high at 3260m/10,695½ft, just below it is a glorious stretch of grassland bordering the forest and near a mountain stream that would appear to fit the description given by Meyer. If the 19th-century explorers really did camp around there, they are to be congratulated on choosing one of the most beautiful places on the mountain.

Leaving most of his porters behind at this site – it would be their duty from now on to ferry supplies up to the camp from Marangu – Meyer struck due north up to the Saddle, past the **Spring in the Snow**, or Schneequell (12,910ft/3935m) and on to **Abbott's Camp** (12,980ft/3956.3m), so-called by Meyer because he found an empty Irish stew tin and a sheet of the Salvation Army newspaper *En Avant* at this spot and guessed that this must have been where his missionary friend Dr Abbott had camped a few months previously.

As to their location, according to the maps in Meyer's book the Schneequell lies almost exactly due south of East Lava Hill, the easternmost of the parasitic cones on the Saddle, and would seem to tie in fairly neatly with the Last Water Point.

(cont'd overleaf)

However, on his third attempt, in 1889, Meyer finally covered himself in glory. Though no doubt a skilful and determined climber, Meyer's success can largely be attributed to his recognition that the biggest obstacle to a successful assault was the lack of food available near the top. Meyer solved this by establishing camps at various points along the route that he had chosen for his attempt, including one at 12,980ft (3956.3m; Abbott's camp); one, Kibo camp,

❑ MEYER'S ROUTE TO THE TOP

(cont'd from p155)

The Last Water Point, the Maua River, lies below Zebra Rocks on the Marangu Route (see p285). Abbott's Camp, meanwhile, lies to the north-north-west of here, at a point between the two Marangu Route paths to the Saddle. From here, Meyer's path and the Marangu Route diverge for good. Where Marangu trekkers head roughly north across the Saddle, keeping Kibo to their left, in 1889 Meyer and his two companions, the alpine expert Purtscheller and Mwini Amani, their guide, set off directly for the summit in a more westerly direction, stopping for the night by a prominent rock at 14,200ft (4328.1m). This is **Viermannstein**, the Rock of Four Men, a place popular with Kili explorers in the 19th century. Unfortunately, because it lies far from any trail today, the site rarely features on modern trekking maps; for an approximate location, draw a line running east from Barafu Campsite, and a second due south from the easternmost Triplet: the rock stands near to where they coincide.

Meyer's aim in 1889 was **Ratzel Glacier**, on the south-eastern rim of Kibo. The glacier has now, alas, disappeared, though we know from maps where it was: if walking up to the summit from Barafu Campsite, it would have been on your right when approaching Stella Point. In Meyer's day the glacier covered the entire south-eastern lip of Kibo; it was into this glacier that Meyer and Purtscheller, on 3 October, carved a series of steps that led all the way to the crater rim and a height of 19,260ft (5870.4m).

On this occasion, considerations of time and weather forced them to withdraw back down to camp, having seen – but not scaled – the highest point on Kibo. After a day's rest and contemplation, however, and having decided to bivouac at **Lava Cave** on the slopes of Kibo at 15,960ft (4864.6m), the duo were ready for another assault on the summit. From there, at 3am on a cold October morning, they set off. At dawn they were at the foot of the glacier where, to their delight, they found the glacial stairway that they'd cut two days previously was still there. By 8am they had reached and crossed a large crevasse, the only serious obstacle on the way to the summit. Just 45 minutes later they were back standing on the crater rim, the limit of their achievements two days previously.

On this occasion, however, both time and weather were on their side. Walking around the southern rim of Kibo, they climbed three small hillocks, the middle of which they found by aneroid to be the highest by some 40ft (12¼m) or more. Thus at 10.30am on 6 October 1889, Meyer and Purtscheller wrote themselves into the history books as the first to make it to the highest point in Africa.

So where exactly did they gain **access to the crater**? According to Dr Hassenstein's maps, the 'Lava Cave' lies at the northern end of the large South-East Valley, due west of the middle of the three Triplets. That puts it somewhere to the north-east of Barafu Campsite, and more than 150m (492ft) higher, on one of the rocky spurs that run south-east down from Kibo. Where it certainly is *not*, though many a guide will tell you otherwise, is Hans Meyer Cave on the Marangu Route, which at 5151m (16,899½ft) is simply too high and too far north. The notch by which they gained access to the crater lay almost exactly north-west of this Lava Cave Camp.

'by a conspicuous rock' at 14,210ft (4331.2m); and, finally, a small encampment by a lava cave and just below the glacier line at 15,260ft (4651.2m). Thanks to these intermediary camps, Meyer was able to conduct a number of attempts on the summit without having to return to the foot of Kili to replenish supplies after each; instead, food was brought to the camps by the porters every few days.

Though again this is largely guesswork, all the evidence does seem to point to the fact that Meyer and Purtscheller on this particular occasion passed into the crater rim from a spot very near to **Stella Point** (5745m/18,848½ft); the difference in height (Meyer estimated the height at this point on the crater to be 5778m/18956¾ft) can possibly be ascribed to the fact that Meyer's estimates tend to be over-estimates (his height for Kaiser Wilhelm Peak, as he christened it, but which we now know as Uhuru Peak, for example, is over 6000m) – perhaps because in Meyer's day there was a lot more ice at the summit, which would have raised the altitudes.

Having christened the summit after their Kaiser and taken the topmost stone from the summit as a souvenir (a stone that Meyer later gave to the Kaiser, who used it as a paperweight), the pair then hurried back to Abbott's camp on the Saddle. The next few days were spent trying to conquer **Mawenzi** but with no success, the mountain peak defeating them wholly on the first occasion on 13 October, and an attack of colic brought on by some over-ripe bananas stalling their second attempt two days later. Before returning to civilisation, however, they spent five more days revisiting Kibo: on 17 October they headed to the crater's northern side. There they reached 5572m before confronting a sheer wall of ice that forced them to retreat; and then finally, on the 18th, they approached the crater from the east.

The path Meyer took up to the crater on this occasion is not too dissimilar to the trail up to Gillman's from the Kibo Huts. Meyer and Purtscheller on this final climb bivouacked at a location they called **Old Fireplace** because, to their considerable surprise, they found the remains of a recent campfire there, along with the bones of an eland and some pieces of banana matting. This camp, according to Meyer, sat at an altitude of 15,390ft (4690.9m). It's just possible, therefore, that the Old Fireplace is in fact the site we now call **Jiwe La Ukoyo**, which many local mountain guides insist was once a popular hunters' campsite. From the Old Fireplace, Meyer and Purtscheller climbed up the snow-clad slopes of Kibo once more, gaining access into the crater via a cleft in the rim that is now known as **Hans Meyer Notch**, and which lies just a few hundred metres to the north of Gillman's Point. Though they failed in their attempts to reach the inner cone of the volcano, they were at least able to confirm that the floor of the crater was made up of a mixture of mud and ashes. They were also startled when, peering into the first cone, they came across the carcass of an antelope (which possibly explains what the leopard, whose frozen body was found up here many years later, was doing at this altitude).

After one more unsuccessful attempt on Mawenzi, Meyer and Purtscheller finally decided to call it a day and, on 22 October, they said goodbye to the Saddle for the last time. According to Meyer, the pair had spent 16 days between 15,000 and 20,000ft (4572-6096m), though we know this last figure is an over-estimate of course as the height of Kili is only 5895m/19,341ft. During this time they had made four ascents of Kibo, reaching the crater three times and the summit once, and three sorties on Mawenzi, reaching the 5049m summit of Purtscheller's Spitze (Point) but failing to reach the very top.

He also had a considerable back-up party with him, including his friend and climbing companion, Herr Ludwig Purtscheller – a gymnastics teacher and alpine expert from Salzburg – two local headmen, nine porters, three other locals who would act as supervisors, one cook and one guide supplied by the local chief, Mareale, whom he had befriended during his first trip to the region. These men would help to carry the equipment and man the camps, with each kept in order by Meyer's strict code of discipline, where minor miscreants received ten lashes and serious wrongdoers twenty.

The size of his entourage, however, shouldn't detract from the magnitude of Meyer's achievement: as well as the usual hardships associated with climbing Kilimanjaro, he also had to contend with deserters from his party, the lack of a clear path, elephant traps (large pits dug by locals and concealed by ferns to trap the unwary pachyderm), as well as the unpleasant, rapacious chief of Moshi, Mandara (see p278 & p280). Furthermore, Meyer did not begin his walk *on* the mountain, as today's visitors do, but in Mombasa, 14 days by foot, according to Meyer, from the town of Taveta (which lies to the south-east of Kilimanjaro, in Kenya, and is still a day's walk from the mountain village of Marangu)!

Then there was the snow and ice, so much more prevalent in the late 1800s on Kili than today. Above 4500m Meyer had to trek upon snow for virtually the whole day, even though his route up Kibo from the Saddle is not too dissimilar to that taken by thousands of trekkers every year – and today there is no permanent snow or ice on the route.

The added difficulties caused by the snow are well described in Meyer's book *Across East African Glaciers*. Rising at 2.30am for their first assault on the summit, Meyer and Purtscheller spent most of the morning carving a stairway out of a sheer ice-cliff, every stair laboriously hewn with an average of 20 blows of the ice axe. (The cliff formed part of the now extinct Ratzel Glacier, named by Meyer after a geography professor in his native Leipzig.) As a result, by the time they reached the crater's eastern lip, the light was fading fast and the approach of inclement weather forced them to return before they could reach the highest point of that lip.

On their second attempt, however, three days later on 6 October 1889, and with the

The conquest of Kilimanjaro

Taking out a small German flag, which I had brought with me for the purpose in my knapsack, I planted it on the weather-beaten lava summit with three ringing cheers, and in virtue of my right as its discoverer christened this hitherto unknown and unnamed mountain peak – the loftiest spot in Africa and the German Empire – Kaiser Wilhelm's Peak [now known as Uhuru Peak]. *Then we gave three cheers more for the Emperor, and shook hands in mutual congratulation.*

Hans Meyer
Across East African Glaciers

stairs in the ice still intact from the first ascent, they were able to gain the eastern side of the rim by mid morning; from there it was but a straightforward march to the three small tumescences situated on the higher, southern lip of the crater, the middle one of which was also the highest point of the mountain.

AFTER MEYER

Mawenzi, Pastor Reusch and a frozen leopard

In the decades following Meyer's successful assault on Kili, few followed in his footsteps. Meyer climbed again in 1898, though this time he got only as far as the crater rim. In 1909 surveyor M Lange climbed all the way to Uhuru Peak, and in doing so became only the third (after Meyer and Purtscheller) to reach the summit of Kilimanjaro – a full 20 years after the first two.

The conquest of the last remaining summit on Kilimanjaro, that of Mawenzi (called, somewhat perversely, Hans Meyer Peak), was achieved by the climbers **Edward Oehler** and **Fritz Klute** on 29 July 1912. Thus, 64 years after the first European had clapped eyes on Kilimanjaro, both of its main summits had been successfully climbed. As an encore, Oehler and Klute made the third successful expedition on Kibo and the first from the western side. In the same year, **Walter Furtwangler** and **Ziegfried Koenig** achieved the fourth successful climb and became the first to use skis to descend. Two more successful assaults occurred before the outbreak of World War One, and **Frau von Ruckteschell** kept up the German's impressive record on Kilimanjaro by becoming **the first woman to reach Gillman's Point and the rim of the crater**.

Fresh attempts on Kilimanjaro were suspended for a while during World War One. The countryside around Kilimanjaro became the scene of some vicious fighting, including Moshi itself, which was attacked by British forces in March 1916. Paul von Lettow Vorbeck, the German commander, went down in military history at this time as the man who led the longest tactical retreat ever. But with the Germans' defeat, Kilimanjaro, along with the rest of German East Africa, reverted to British rule.

After the war, attention turned away from Kibo to the lesser-known Mawenzi. In 1924 **George Londt** of South Africa became, by accident, the first to climb South Peak (he was aiming for Hans Meyer Peak but got lost); the peak (4958m), was named after him. Three years later three English mountaineers climbed Mawenzi, including 22-year-old **Sheila MacDonald**, the first woman to do so; the trio then climbed Kibo, with Ms MacDonald writing her name into the record books again as **the first woman to complete the ascent to Uhuru Peak**. In 1930 two British mountaineers, HW Tilman and Eric Shipton, names more usually associated with Everest, climbed Mawenzi's Nordecke Peak – again, like Londt, by accident.

While all this was happening on Mawenzi, over on Kibo another man was writing himself into the history of Kili: **Pastor Richard Reusch**. Missionary for the Lutheran Church, former officer in the Cossack army and long-time Marangu resident, Reusch is said to have climbed the mountain on no fewer than 65 occasions. During his first assault on the summit in 1926 he found the frozen leopard on the crater rim that would later inspire Hemingway (see p163; Reusch cut off part of an ear as a souvenir), while on another sortie the following year he became the first to gaze down into the inner crater, a crater to which he would later give his name. Later work by mountaineer **HW Tilman** and vulcanologist **JJ Richard** led to confirmation, in 1942, that Kilimanjaro was still active, and while this led to some local panic, in 1957 the Tanganyika Geological Survey and the University of Sheffield were able to allay fears by declaring the volcano to be dormant and almost extinct.

KILIMANJARO TODAY

The 20th century witnessed the inevitable but gradual shift away from exploration towards tourism. The most significant change occurred in 1932 with the building of Kibo Hut; name plates and signs were put up too as the mountain was gradually made more tourist-friendly. With a ready base for summit assaults now established, tourists began to trickle into Tanzania to make their own attempt on Africa's greatest mountain.

In 1959 the mountain became the **focus for nationalist feelings** and a symbol of the Tanganyikans' independence aspirations following Julius Nyerere's speech to the Tanganyika Legislative Assembly (see p113 for quote). Nyerere eventually got his wish and, after independence was granted in 1961, a torch was indeed placed on Kilimanjaro (though it is said that bad weather prevented them from actually reaching the summit itself!). Independence also provided

❑ FOR THE RECORD

- **Fastest ascent of Kilimanjaro** As discussed in the introduction to this book, on 13 August, 2014, Karl Egloff of Switzerland, ran to the 5895m summit in 4 hours 56 minutes, thereby becoming the first (and so far the only) man to get to Uhuru Peak from a park gate (in this instance, Umbwe Gate) in under five hours. His feat eclipsed the four-year-old record of Spanish runner Kilian Jornet, set in September 2010, by almost half an hour.
- **Fastest ascent and descent** That's not the end of the story, however, for Karl then trotted back down to Mweka Gate in a total time of 6 hours 42 minutes, thus also beating Kilian's record for the fastest ascent and descent and becoming the first man to break the seven-hour mark.
- **Fastest ascent and descent – unaided** It's good to see that a local man holds one of these records. On 22 February 2006, Simon Mtuy, born and raised on the slopes of Kilimanjaro near Marangu Gate at Mbahe, climbed from Umbwe Gate to the summit and back to Mweka Gate in 9 hours 19 minutes. In doing so, he achieved the fastest ever unaided ascent and descent (by unaided, they mean that he carried his own food, water and clothing). This he managed despite suffering from a nasty bout of diarrhoea, as well as taking a three-minute break at the top to video himself, plus two further breaks to vomit! According to Simon, to prepare for his record-breaking attempt he spent a total of two weeks on the mountain beforehand – including five days at Barranco, four spent at Arrow Glacier and three days on the Crater itself.
- **Fastest ascent (female)** On February 23, 2018, Danish athlete Kristina Schou Madsen reached the summit of Kilimanjaro via the Mweka Route in a speedy 6 hours,

Tanganyika with the chance to rename many of the features of the mountain; in particular, the very summit, dubbed Kaiser Wilhelm Peak by Hans Meyer, was renamed Uhuru Peak – Uhuru meaning, appropriately, 'Freedom' in Swahili.

Since this mountain's moment of patriotic glory, the story of Kilimanjaro has largely been about **tourism**. The early trickle of tourists of 70 years ago is nowadays more akin to a flood, with visitor numbers increasing exponentially from fewer than 1000 in the late 1950s to 11,000 in the 1990s, to the 50,000-plus we see today. What has been an economic boon to the people of Kilimanjaro, however, has brought little benefit to the mountain itself. With the increase in the number of trekkers comes commensurately greater numbers of pressures and problems. Its soil is being eroded, its vegetation is being burnt or chopped, its wildlife is disappearing and its glaciers are melting. Along with these environmental pressures come challenges to its dignity, as climbers dream up ever more bizarre ways of climbing to the top, whether riding up by motorcycle or walking in fancy dress, as discussed in the introduction to this book.

Then there's the problem of **fire**. Every couple of years there is a blaze somewhere on Kili that causes acres of devastation and burns for several days. Depressingly but unsurprisingly, human activity is believed to have been behind the fires. Some point an accusing finger at local farmers who like to clear their farms by fire before the start of the annual rains. Other possible culprits include honey collectors, who make fires to smoke out the bees; we've even heard accusations that those in charge of the park, KINAPA, start fires in order to extract

52 minutes and 54 seconds. Mweka is normally a descent-only route, but has the advantage of being a very direct path to the top. Which is why, I guess, Kristina took that path.

• **Youngest person to reach the summit** Coaltan Tanner, from Albuquerque, New Mexico, in the US, reached the summit on 22 October 2018 at 11.40am. He was born on September 18th, 2012, meaning he was just six years, one month and a few days when he made it to Uhuru Peak. It was actually Coaltan's second attempt at the summit. The first, in July of that year, was aborted when the local guides, fearing that they would have their licences taken away, refused to take him to the summit.

• **Oldest person to reach the summit**: Perhaps surprisingly, this is the record that has changed hands most frequently.

At the time of writing the holder is Anne Lorimor, a former university instructor from Phoenix, Arizona, who reached the summit in July 2019 after a 9-day trek at the grand old age of 89. Anne's climb eclipsed the feat of the previous record holder for the oldest person to get to the top, Fred Distelhorst, from Vail, Colorado, who on July 20th 2017 climbed to Uhuru Peak at the age of 88. Fred's achievement in turn beat the previous record set by Russian octagenarian Angela Vorobeva on October 29th 2015, who took the popular Machame Route to the top at 86 years 267 days. (Impressive, but it's fair to say that it's not the toughest challenge that Ms Vorobeva has faced, having survived of the Siege of Leningrad in 1944!). And Angela's climb beat the previous climb of Anne Lorimor, who first summited Kili, and set the record for the oldest person, when aged 85.

Waterfall at the foot of Kilimanjaro. Engraving by Alexandre Le Roy from *Au Kilima-Ndjaro (Afrique Orientale)* published in 1893.

more money from TANAPA, the body that oversees the administration of all of the country's reserves and parks – though I think this has more to do with the Tanzanians' love of a good conspiracy theory than any basis in reality.

Yet no matter what indignities are heaped upon it, Kilimanjaro continues to inspire both awe and respect in those who gaze upon it. And while man will continue to visit in droves and in his clumsy way will carry on defacing and demeaning it, setting it ablaze and covering it with litter, the mountain itself remains essentially the same powerful, ineffably beautiful sight it always was; perhaps because, while we throw all that we can at it, the Roof of Africa does what it always has done – and what it does best: it simply rises above it all.

Fauna and flora

Kilimanjaro is often called 'The Island Above the Clouds' because it boasts more unique species than many small countries. Many happy years could be spent studying and writing about this mountain's fascinating flora and fauna. The following, therefore, is but the briefest of introductions to the nature of Kilimanjaro.

FAUNA

The survival of our wildlife is a matter of grave concern to all of us in Africa. These wild creatures amid the wild places they inhabit are not only important as a source of wonder and inspiration but are an integral part of our natural resources and our future livelihood and well being.

In accepting the trusteeship of our wildlife we solemnly declare that we will do everything in our power to make sure that our children's grandchildren will be able to enjoy this rich and precious inheritance.

The conservation of wildlife and wild places calls for specialist knowledge, trained manpower and money. And we look to other nations to cooperate with us in this important task – the success or failure of which not only affects the continent of Africa but the rest of the world as well.

Julius Nyerere, in a speech made soon after he became the country's first president, in September 1961. The quote can be found on a bust of him that stands at the entrance to the Tanzanian National Park Office in Arusha.

In order to see much in the way of fauna, you have to be either very lucky or, it would seem, an author of a book on Kilimanjaro. When Hans Meyer was coming down from the mountain in 1889 he spotted an elephant on the slopes. He also found a frozen antelope in the crater. In 1926 a leopard was found frozen in the summit ice by Pastor Richard Reusch (see pp159-60) near a place we now call Leopard Point – providing Hemingway with the inspiration for *The Snows of Kilimanjaro*.

The mountaineer, HW Tilman, saw 27 eland on the Saddle when he passed this way in 1937, with each, according to him, especially adapted for the freezing conditions with thicker fur. In 1962, renowned travel writer Wilfred

Thesiger and two companions were accompanied to the summit by five wild dogs (aka African hunting dogs). Though the dogs then turned round and disappeared after the three men made the summit, paw-prints in the ice proved that this wasn't the first time they had climbed to the top. More recently, Rick Ridgeway claimed he saw a leopard on his ascent, as did Geoffrey Salisbury while leading his group of blind climbers to the summit; and in 1979 a local guide called David was savaged by a pack of wild dogs above the Mandara Huts and lost a finger.

I mention these stories to demonstrate that the more exotic fauna of East Africa does occasionally venture onto the mountain. It just doesn't happen very often, with most animals preferring to be somewhere where there aren't 50,000-plus trekkers (and their crews) marching around every year.

The decline of fauna on Kilimanjaro is perhaps best illustrated by these random quotes I have drawn from *Tanganyika Notes and Records: Kilimanjaro*, an excellently informative book published in March 1965. It's depressing to realise how much more abundant the wildlife appeared even then, just under 60 years ago.

Baboons in the branches of a Dum palm (from *Across East African Glaciers,* Hans Meyer, 1891)

'Millard considers that the elephant population of Kilimanjaro is of the order of 1,500 and from personal observation this appears to be a very reasonable estimate.'

'Giraffe have been seen by Millard in heavy forest within the montane forest belt.'

'Up to about 1950, Rhinoceros were often encountered in the forest above Marangu...They are still to be found from West Kilimanjaro where their position is fairly good around to Kitenden where their numbers have been considerably reduced.'

'Wild Dogs have been seen in the Mandera [sic] *(Bismark) hut area and in the country to the south of Mawenzi (Forest Division).'*

Just for the record, elephants do still wander up the slopes of Kilimanjaro, particularly from Amboseli and from the West Kilimanjaro corridor, though in nothing like the numbers recorded above; giraffe are seldom if ever recorded on the mountain now, though it's feasible that they too may wander up the northern and western slopes; the total population of rhino in the whole of Tanzania is now less than fifty, with the nearest to Kilimanjaro now over 100km away in Mkomazi National Park, to the south-east; while wild dogs are so rare now in Tanzania that a website has even been set up so that those fortunate enough to spot one can tell the world about it!

So in all probability you'll see virtually nothing during your time on the mountain beyond the occasional monkey or

❑ PROTECTING KILIMANJARO

Kilimanjaro has enjoyed some form of protection since the early years of the 20th century under German rule, when the mountain and surrounding area were designated as a game preserve. In 1921 this status was upgraded to become a forest and game preserve, thereby protecting the precious cloud forest that beards Kili's lower slopes.

Another change in 1957 saw Tanganyika National Parks Authority propose that the mountain become a national park, though this wasn't actually realised until 1973 when **Kilimanjaro National Park (KINAPA)** was formed; a park that, for simplicity's sake, the authorities decided would include all land above 2700m. KINAPA didn't actually officially open until 1977; 12 years later, in 1989, the park was declared a **World Heritage Site** by UNESCO. In 2013 it was also honoured as **one of the Seven Natural Wonders of Africa**, along with its neighbours the Ngorongoro Crater and Serengeti migration. Thus Northern Tanzania plays host to three of the seven natural wonders (the Serengeti migration being shared with Kenya), with the others being the Nile River, Sahara Desert, Red Sea Reef and the Okavango Delta.

mouse. Nevertheless, get up early each morning before the other groups have stirred, keep your mouth shut and your eyes open – and you never know...

Forest and cultivated zones

Animals are more numerous in the forest zone than anywhere else on the mountain; unfortunately, so is the cover provided by trees and bushes, so sightings remain rare. The mountain is reputed to be the home of the world's largest population of **Abbott's duiker**, a small and very endangered forest antelope of which there are supposed to be only 2500 left on the planet. Rare, shy and mainly nocturnal, it's not difficult to see why sightings of this duiker are so uncommon.

As with the four-striped grass mice (see p167) of Horombo, it tends to be those few species for whom the arrival of man has been a boon rather than a curse that are the easiest to spot, including **blue monkeys**, which appear daily near the Mandara Huts and which are not actually blue but grey or black with a white throat. These are the plainer relatives of the beautiful **colobus monkey**, which has the most enviable tail in the animal kingdom; you can see a troop of these at the start of the forest zone on the Lemosho Route, and near the Mandara Huts, where a couple are semi-tame. Strangely, despite their beauty, their name is actually derived from the Greek for 'mutilated' as unlike other primates they don't have a proper opposable thumb but a mere stump. This 'deformity' is even more bizarre when one considers that they are amongst the most arboreal of monkeys; in other words, they very rarely drop down to the ground, preferring instead to spend their time in the trees – where you would have thought a proper opposable thumb would be an advantage for grabbing hold of branches etc. Indeed, so rarely does the colobus drop down to the ground that it would normally be rather difficult to spot were it not for its flamboyant coat and its strange, frog-like croak.

Other creatures that you may see, especially if you're with a talented guide, are the noisy, chipmunk-like **tree hyrax** (see box p166). Though nocturnal, shy, and happiest when living in the dark forest, their sheer numbers mean that they can be spotted by a trained eye. However, they are usually more easily heard than seen, their bark-like call being one of the more distinctive sounds of nocturnal Kilimanjaro. **Bushbabies**, or galagos, are also more audible than visible as they come out at night and jump on the roofs of the huts. Here in the forest, too, is the cat-like, **small-spotted genet** with its distinctive black-and-white tail.

Olive baboons, **civets**, **leopards**, **mongooses** and **servals** are said to live in the mountain's forest as well, though sightings are extremely rare; here, too, lives the **bush pig** with its distinctive white stripe running along its back from head to tail.

Then there's the **honey badger**. Don't be fooled by the rather cute name, for as well as being blessed with a face only its mother could love, these are the most powerful and fearless carnivores for their size in Africa. Even lions give them a wide berth. You should too: not only can they cause a lot of damage to your person but the thought of having to tell your friends that, of all the bloodthirsty creatures that roam the African plains, you got savaged by a badger, is too shaming to contemplate. Of a similar size, the **aardvark** has enormous claws but unlike the honey badger this nocturnal, long-snouted anteater is entirely benign. So fear not: as the old adage goes, aardvark never killed anyone. Both aardvarks and honey badgers are rarely, if ever, seen on the mountain.

❑ *'URGENT MESSAGE:*

Location: *Amboseli Game Park, Kenya*
Human population: *150*
Baboon population: *90,000*
Meteorological conditions: *Severe drought*
Water supplies: *Nil*
Situation: *Mutilated bodies discovered. Baboons have turned into man-eating primates – POSITION DESPERATE!'*

Taken from the back cover of terrible 1980s' horror film ***In the Shadow of Kilimanjaro***, supposedly based on a true story. You may like to consider this when walking past a troop of them on your Meru climb.

❑ THE HYRAX: TUSKER OF THE TREES

It's one of those facts that isn't well-known but, once you've heard it, you won't forget it. The hyrax, that shy fluffy bundle of nervous energy that sits motionless in the lower branches of the trees, watching you as you trudge your way through Kili's cloud forest, is actually the closest living relative of the African elephant. The two shared a common ancestor, the tethytheria, about 50 million years ago. And while the two may look decidedly different today, there are some similarities beyond just their DNA. For example both tree hyraxes and their plains cousin, the rock hyrax, actually have tusks growing from their canines, just like their elly rellies. They also have, like elephants, hoof-like rounded nails on the tips of their toes, rather than claw or hoof. Their gestation period is also quite elephantine, particularly for such a small animal, at 7-8 months.

If you think this is all a bit far-fetched, then just to push your credulity beyond breaking point I should also tell you that its other near-relative is the aquatic manatee, or sea cow.

Nor are **porcupines**, Africa's largest rodents. Though also present in this zone, they are both shy and nocturnal and your best chance of seeing one is as road-kill on the way to Nairobi.

One creature you definitely won't see at any altitude is the rhinoceros. Over-hunting has finally taken its toll of this most majestic of creatures – Count Teleki (see p154), for example, is said to have shot 89 of them during his time in East Africa, including four in one day – and, as I said earlier, there are none on or anywhere near Kilimanjaro today.

Heath, moorland and above

Just as plant-life struggles to survive much above 2800m (9186ft), so animals too find it difficult to live on the barren upper slopes. Yet though you may see little, there are a few creatures living above the treeline on Kilimanjaro. The prime example is the **four-striped grass mouse**, which clearly doesn't find it a problem eking (or should that be eeking?) out an existence at high altitude; indeed, if you're staying in the Horombo Huts on the Marangu Route, one is probably running under your table while you read this, and if you stand outside for more than a few seconds at any campsite you should see them scurrying from rock to rock. Other rodents present at this level include the **harsh-furred** and **climbing mouse** and the **mole rat**, though all are far more difficult to spot. (Your best chance of seeing the harsh-furred mouse is probably on Shira Plateau, particularly amongst the heather by the toilets near the caves at Machame's Shira Caves Campsite and, less often, at Shira 1 Campsite on the Lemosho Route.)

For anything bigger than a mouse, your best chance above 2800m is either on the Shira Plateau, where **buffalos and other grazers** roam occasionally, or on the northern side of the mountain on the Northern Circuit and Rongai Route. Kenya's Amboseli National Park lies at the foot of the mountain on this side and many animals, particularly **elephants**, amble up the slopes from time to time in the search for minerals that they can extract from the rocks. **Grey** and **red duikers**, **elands** and **bushbucks** are perhaps the most commonly seen animals at this altitude, though sightings are still extremely rare.

None of these larger creatures lives above the tree-line of Kilimanjaro permanently, however, and as with the **leopards** that occasionally make their way up the slopes, they are, like us, probably no more than day-trippers.

On Kibo itself the entomologist George Salt found a species of **spider** that was living in the **alpine zone** at altitudes of up to 5500m. What exactly these high-altitude arachnids live on up there is unknown – though Salt reckoned it was probably the flies that blew in on the wind, of which he found a few, and which appeared to be unwilling or unable to fly. What is known is that the spiders live underground, better to escape the rigours of the weather. I've also seen a white butterfly on the way up to Mawenzi Tarn Huts at 4122m; once again, I can only assume that it has been blown up the slopes from the moorland or forest zone.

AVIFAUNA

Kilimanjaro is great for birdlife. The cultivated fields on the lower slopes provide plenty of food, the forest zone provides shelter and plenty of nesting sites, while the barren upper slopes are ideal hunting grounds for raptors.

In the **forest**, one of the easier birds to spot is the dark green **Hartlaub's turaco**, partly because of its noisy, monkey-like call, and partly because when it flies, viewers are treated to flashes of bright red under-wings. If you're lucky you may also come across black and white **tropical boubous** (bell shrikes) and **silvery-cheeked hornbills**, though to be honest you're more likely to see hornbills on Meru, and even in Arusha near The Outpost Lodge, than on Kilimanjaro.

Hartlaub's turaco

Montane white-eyes – small green birds with distinctive white circles around their eyes – can be found around Machame Huts and occasionally elsewhere on the mountain; another habitué of the Machame Huts is the **common stonechat**, a relative of the more common alpine chat (see below) but slightly more striking in appearance, with a white stripe on its black wings and a chestnut patch on its breast.

Other small birds said to live in the forest include the **speckled mousebird** that hangs around the fruit trees, and the **trogon** which, despite a red belly, is difficult to see because it remains so motionless in the branches. Smaller birds include the **Ruppell's robin chat** (black and white head, grey top, orange lower half) and the **common bulbul**, with a black crest atop its head and yellow beneath the tail.

Further up the slopes, the noisy, scavenging, garrulous **white-necked raven** is a constant presence on the mountain during the day, eternally hovering on the breeze around the huts and lunch-stops on the lookout for any scraps. Smaller but just as ubiquitous is the **alpine chat**, a small brown bird with white side feathers in its tail, and the **streaky seed-eater**, another brown bird (this time with streaks on its back) that often hangs around the huts. For some reason, over the past few years the campsites have been invaded by **dusky turtle doves**, bronze of feather and brazen in character. The **alpine swift** also enjoys these misty, cold conditions. The prize for the most beautiful bird on the mountain, however, goes to the dazzling **scarlet-tufted malachite sunbird**. Metallic-green save for a small scarlet patch on either side of its chest, this delightful bird can often be seen hovering above the grass, hooking its long beak in to reach the flies sheltering in the lobelias and proteas.

Climbing further, you reach raptor territory. You'll rarely see these birds up close as they spend most of the day gliding on the currents looking for prey. **Augur buzzards** are very occasionally spotted hovering in the breeze; these are impressive birds in themselves – especially if you're lucky enough to see one up close – though not as large as the **crowned eagle** and the rare **lammergeyer**, a giant vulture with long wings, a wedge tail and a tufty beard beneath the beak.

White-necked raven

Dusky turtle dove

Four-striped grass mouse

Streaky seed eater

Malachite sunbird

Colobus monkey

Blue monkey

Skink or grey lizard

Eastern tree hyrax

Vervet monkeys (Meru)

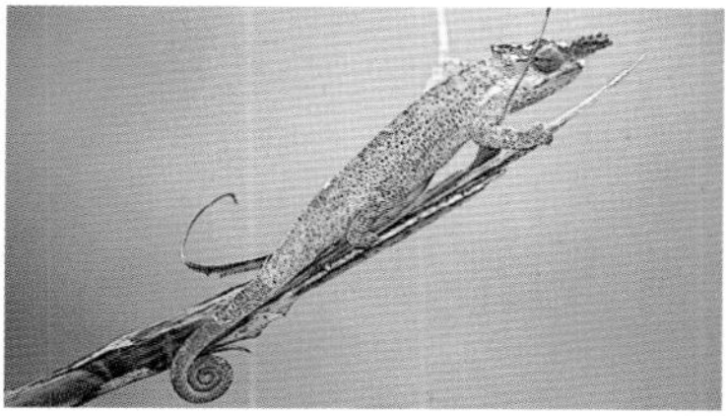

Two-horned chameleon

Lammergeyer

FLORA

It is said that to climb up Kilimanjaro is to walk through **four seasons in less than a week**. It is true, of course, and nowhere is this phenomenon more apparent than in its flora. The variety of flora found on Kilimanjaro can be ascribed in part to the mountain's tremendous height and in part to its proximity to both the equator and the Indian Ocean. Add to this the variations in climate, solar radiation and temperature from the top of the mountain to the bottom (temperatures are estimated to drop by 1°C for every 150m gain in altitude), and you end up with the ideal conditions for highly differentiated and distinctive vegetation zones. In all, **Kilimanjaro is said to have between four and six distinctive zones**, or 'seasons', depending on whom you read.

Cultivated zone and forest (800m-2800m)

The forest zone, along with the cultivated zone that lies below it, together receive the most rainfall – about 2300mm per year – of any part of the mountain. The forest also houses the greatest variety of both fauna (see p163) and flora.

For the layman, it may be difficult at first to identify the individual species of **tree**, though some do stand out. On the Marangu Route the first trees you'll possibly notice – and Antipodeans should recognise – are actually non-native: the pale-barked **eucalyptus** was planted by the first park warden of Kilimanjaro, though it is now a tree that his successors are trying to eradicate as it takes so much water from the land. Enormous **camphor trees** (*Ocotea usambarensis*) also flourish at this altitude, as do **fig** trees, **avocado** and *talamontana*, or **wild mango**. On the Umbwe Route in particular you'll also find, in the lower reaches of the forest, **coffee** growing in abundance. Further up the slopes towards the upper limit of the zone, the smooth grey **African holly** (*Ilex mitis*), with its characteristic red and yellow fruit, becomes the dominant tree. **African redwood** (*Hagenia abyssinica*), though nothing like as common, is perhaps more recognisable with its enormous, blousy, pink-flowered panicles – it's quite the campest tree on the mountain.

Seradoxus
Fireball lily

Trifolium usambarensis

Podocarpus (left) and *juniper* (right)

Another instantly recognisable species is the giant fern, also known as a **tree fern** (*Cyathea sp*), which clearly enjoys the damp conditions, as does **old man's beard** (*Usnea sp*), which lies draped over most of the branches at the upper limit of the forest zone. At about the same altitude is the **podocarpus**, with its slender-finger leaves, and the **juniper** whose leaves, at least when gazing up at the canopy, look similar; put examples of each side by side, however, and you can clearly see the difference between them (see photo, p170). With the drier climate the trees of the northern slopes are slightly different, with **olive trees** now abundant and one species, ***Olea kilimandscharica***, indigenous to the mountain.

Incidentally, a report in late 2016 in the *New Scientist* magazine announced that a group of scientists from the University of Bayreuth in Germany have discovered that Africa's tallest indigenous tree is on Kili! Measuring a whopping 81.5 metres, the tree is of the species ***Entandrophragma excelsum***, a member of the mahogany family, and a stand of them was found thriving in the mountain's cloud forest, with each tree in the stand estimated to be around 500-600 years old. While it may seem a surprising coincidence that the continent's highest mountain should also be the home of Africa's tallest tree, upon reflection it does make sense. The combination of lush, moist conditions and nutrient-rich volcanic soil is quite rare on the continent.

Impatiens kilimanjari

Impatiens pseudoviola

Begonia meyeri-johannis

Impatiens digitata

Lobelia gibberoa

Polystachyus (orchid)

What catches the eyes of most trekkers is not these giants, however, but the small splashes of colour that grow in their shade: the **flowers**. The star of the montane forest zone is the beautiful ***Impatiens kilimanjari***, an endemic fleck of dazzling red and yellow in the shape of an inch-long tuba. The guides on Kili have christened them **elephant's trunk flowers**, a nickname that makes a lot of sense when you view the flower from side-on. You'll see them by the edge of the path on the southern side of the mountain. Vying for the prime piece of real estate that exists between the roots of the trees are other, equally elegant flowers including its relatives, *Impatiens pseudoviola* and *Impatiens digitata*, and the beautiful **African violet**, *Viola eminii*. Hanging from the trees is the ***Begonia meyeri johannis***, with sweet-smelling white and pink

Parochaetus communis

Kniphofia thomsonii
Red hot poker

Hypericum revolutum
St John's Wort

Protea kilimandsharica
(with malachite sunbird)

flowers that often litter the path like confetti. There's a **lobelia**, too, with blue or pink, distinctive, three-lobed flowers, that thrives in both the forest and the heath zone above. It's very similar to the ones you'll find in the hanging baskets of Europe (though it bears very little resemblance to the lobelias you will see further up the mountain). For that matter, it also bears little resemblance to *Lobelia gibberoa* (forest lobelia), a giant plant almost 5m tall with a whorl of large leaves at its top and a very tall flower spike; these tend to love water and you'll usually find them on the banks of streams. **Orchids** also enjoy the dark moist conditions of the montane forest, in particular *Polystachyus*, with flowers that always resemble, to me at least, insects in flight.

Perhaps the most unusual aspect of Kilimanjaro's forest zone, however, is not the plants and trees that it *does* have but one that it doesn't. Kili is almost unique in East Africa in not having any bamboo at the upper limit of the forest zone, possibly because it is one of the driest mountains and cannot support bamboo stands the way other African mountains can. As a result, the forest zone ends suddenly, with little warning, throwing us immediately into the less shady trails of the ...

Heath and moorland (2800m-4000m)

These two zones overlap and together occupy the area above the forest from around 2800m to 4000m – known as the **low alpine zone**. Temperatures can drop below 0°C up here and most of the precipitation that does fall comes from the mist that is prevalent at this height.

Immediately above the forest zone is the **alpine heath**. (And when I say immediately above, I mean it: it's almost possible to draw a line in the ground on the footpath to mark where the forest ends and the heath starts.) Rainfall here is around 1300mm per year. Both the **giant heather** *Erica excelsa* and the similar but less bushy *Erica arborea* grow in abundance. The latter also exists in the upper part of the forest zone, where it can grow to 10 metres or more; the higher you go, however, the less impressive the specimens, with many refusing to grow beyond 2.5-3m. **St John's wort**, *Hypericum revolutum*, with its distinctive yellow flowers, also grows at this level and occasionally in the upper reaches of the forest too. Most people will know this flower thanks to its anti-depressant properties. Grasses now dominate the mountain slopes, picked out here and there with some splendid wild flowers including the white- or yellow-flowered *Protea kilimandscharica*, an indigenous rarity that can be seen on the Mweka and Marangu trails and, so we've been told, around Maundi Crater – the best place for botanists to spot wild flowers. A whole raft of *Helichrysum* species make their first appearance here too, though certainly not their last; see box p174.

A plant that most readers will recognise instantly is the back-garden favourite *Kniphofia thomsonii*, better known to most as the **red-hot poker**. Climbing higher you'll begin to come across **sedges** such as *Mariscus kerstenii* with, like most sedges, a triangular stalk. If you're extremely lucky you may also spot an orchid, *Disa stairsii*, a short flower with a spike of small pink flowers. Also growing in the grass here is a pretty, delicate **anemone**, *Anemone thomsonii*, with white flowers; a **scabious**, *Scabiosa columbaria*; and, occasionally, a vivid red **gladiolus** that's simply gorgeous, *Gladiolus watsonides*, which you can also find in the upper reaches of the forest belt.

The shrubs are shrinking now: *Philippia trimera* is the most common, along with the gorse-like *Adenocarpus* beside which it often grows; the prettiest shrub in the upper reaches of the heath zone is the pink-flowered *Blaeria filago*. Growing in abundance in patches at this altitude is **African wormwood** (*Artemisia afra*), a waist-high

Gladiolus watsonides

Anemone thomsonii

Carduus keniensis

Adenocarpus mannii

Disa stairsii (orchid)

Bidens kilimandsharica

Lobelia deckenii

Thunbergia alata

Bearded lichen

plant that is more easily distinguished by its pungent aroma, which perfumes the air for entire sections of the trail, than by its rather dreary grey-green leaves. Known to the Chagga as *kichachayia* (my spelling), the wormwood, when placed in hot water and drunk as tea, is said to have medicinal properties and is

❑ IDENTIFYING HELICHRYSUMS (EVERLASTINGS)

Perhaps the most prolific plants on the mountain, and ones that make their appearance just above the forest and continue up to the foot of Kibo (and even, on occasions, on it), are the helichrysums, also known as everlastings. Everlastings are the dry-looking flowers that resemble living pot pourri and grow in clumps all over the moorland (as well as above and below it).

Members of the daisy family, the identification of individual helichrysums is complicated by three factors: firstly there are many **different subspecies**; secondly they change their appearance the further up the mountain they go in order to adapt to the conditions; and thirdly they all look much the same. So how do you distinguish between different types of helichrysums? Well, the easiest one to recognise is *Helichrysum meyeri-johanis*, named after the first man to climb Kilimanjaro, which has a pinkish tinge to its petals. The others, however, require a little more detective work. *Helichrysum kilimanjari* differs from *H meyeri-johanis* in that its flowers are yellowy/brown and when you crush its leaves they give off a distinctive lemon smell. Those two tend to remain in the moorland zone, but in the high desert other species appear. *Helichrysum cymosum* and *Helichrysum splendidum* both bear tight clusters of small yellow flowers, the former being distinguishable by its leaves that hug the main stem tightly in order to protect it from the cold. *Helichrysum citrispinum* also has leaves that perform this function, though its flowers are larger, white, dry, and don't grow in tight clusters. Also present at this altitude is *Helichrysum newii*, named after Charles New, the first man to reach the snowline on Kilimanjaro. A truly remarkable plant, this was the helichrysum that was found at 5670m near the eastern fumarole in the crater – a record on the mountain. It is believed that the heat from the fumarole allowed this plant to survive the extreme cold.

Helichrysum meyeri-johanis

Helichrysum kilimanjari

Helichrysum citrispinum

Helichrysum splendidum

Helichrysum cymosum

Helichrysum newii

a good cure for a bad stomach.

Climbing ever further you'll soon reach the imperceptible boundary of the moorland zone, which tends to have clearer skies but an even cooler climate. Average per annum precipitation is now down to 525mm. At this altitude, perhaps the weirdest plant on the mountain is the strange *lobelia deckenii*, another endemic species. These curious, phallic- and cabbage-shaped plants take eight years to flower (the purple-blue flowers are hidden inside the leaves to protect them from frost), and enjoy a symbiotic relationship with *Nectarinia johnstoni*, the dazzling green malachite sunbird. It is said that any insects at this altitude are attracted by the flowers of the lobelia and by the warmth and shelter that the velvet leaves supply. This in turn attracts the sunbirds who feed on the flies – and in doing so pollinate the flower. The lobelias are at their best in February and March.

Artemisia afra
African wormwood

Lobelia deckenii
flowers

Scabiosa columbaria

Hebenstretia dentata

Sharing the same cold, bleak environment are the most distinctive plants on the entire mountain: the giant **tree groundsel**, or **dendrosenecio** (until recently called simply 'senecio', a name that you will see crop up in most books and is used by all the guides too). Even without the name change the literature on these plants is most confusing so I am grateful to Mr Eric Knox, director of Indiana University Herbarium and the leading authority on these plants, for his help here. There are two main dendrosenecio species on Kilimanjaro. The first is *Dendrosenecio kilimanjari*, which has two subspecies: *D. kilimanjari ssp cottonii* is found only above 3600m and has dull, mustard-coloured flowers. They

Dendrosenecio kilimanjari (tree groundsel) *ssp kilimanjarii*

Dendrosenecio kilimanjari (tree groundsel) *ssp cottonii*

Leonotis nepetifolia

Dierama pendulum

cleverly protect themselves from the cold by using their dead leaves (which are like felt) to insulate their trunks. These groundsels are slow growers; according to some guides, you can estimate the age of a groundsel by counting the number of 'cabbages' or rosettes, with each 'cabbage' representing about 25 years' growth. They tend to favour the damper, more sheltered parts of the mountain, which is why you'll see them in abundance near Barranco Campsite as well as other, smaller valleys and ravines. The second subspecies, *D. kilimanjari ssp kilimanjarii*, thrives further down the slopes, can grow up to 5m high, and on the rare occasion it flowers the petals themselves are yellow and grow from a one-metre-long spike. Even further down, at a range of between 2750 and 3350 metres at the fringes of the montane forest, we get the second dendrosenecio species, *Dendrosenecio johnstonii*. Your best chance of seeing these giants is along the Machame Route where they form surprisingly big trees.

Ranunculus oreophylus
Yellow star

Haplocarpha rueppellii

Arabis alpina
Alpine rock cress

Alpine desert (4000m-5000m)

At this altitude, only three species of tussock grass and a few extraordinarily rugged flowering plants can withstand the extreme conditions. This is the alpine desert, where plants have to survive in drought conditions (precipitation here is less than 200mm per year), and put up with both inordinate cold and intense sun, usually in the same day. The **everlastings** continue to dominate, though they are shorter and stumpier now, presumably huddling nearer to the ground to protect themselves from the wind. At this altitude flowers need special strategies to cope. The striking **yellow star**, *Ranunculus oreophylus*, and *Haplocarpha rueppellii* both do so by hugging the ground, better to avoid the wind and feed on what little warmth the ground can provide. The other yellow flowers at this altitude are the straggly **senecio species**, usually found surviving, if not exactly thriving, in the lee of the rocks and boulders. The shy white *Arabis alpina* or **Alpine rock cress** also clings on to survival at this chilly altitude by sheltering behind rocks.

Ice cap (5000m-5895m)

On Kibo, almost nothing lives. There is virtually no water. On the rare occasions that precipitation occurs, most of the moisture instantly disappears into the porous rock or is locked away in the glaciers. That said, specimens of *Helichrysum newii* (see p174), an **everlasting** that truly deserves its name, have been found in the crater, and **moss and lichen** are said to exist almost up to the summit. While these mainly orange lichens may not be the most spectacular of plants, it may interest you to know that their growth rate on the upper reaches of Kilimanjaro is estimated to be just 0.5mm in diameter per year; for this reason, scientists have concluded that the larger patches of lichen on Kilimanjaro could be amongst the oldest living things on earth, being hundreds and possibly thousands of years old!

The people who live around Kilimanjaro: the Chagga

With regard to the Chagga people, they are a fine, well-built race. Their full development of bone and muscle being probably due to the exercise they all have to take in moving about on steep hills: they seem intellectually superior to the general run of coast Natives, and despite their objectionable traits (almost always present in the uneducated Native), such as lying, dirty habits, thieving, &c., they are certainly a very nice and attractive race.

Rev A Downes Shaw *To Chagga and Back – An Account of a Journey to Moshi, the Capital of Chagga, Eastern Equatorial Africa* (1924)

Kilimanjaro is the homeland of the **Chagga people**, one of Tanzania's largest ethnic groups. It is fair to say that when you are in Moshi, Marangu or Machame, there is little indication that you are in a 'Chagga town'. Yet in the smaller villages, though waning year by year, traditional Chagga culture remains fairly strong and occasionally a reminder of the past is uncovered by today's tourist, particularly when passing through the settlements on the less-visited eastern side of Kilimanjaro. Such finds make visits to these villages truly fascinating.

Do not, however, come to Kilimanjaro expecting to witness some of the more extreme practices described in this section. This point needs emphasising: the Chaggas' traditional way of life has been eroded by the depredations of Western culture and, as far as I know, is now largely extinct. Indeed, much of the material on which the following account is based is provided by the reports of the 19th- and early 20th-century Europeans who visited the area; in particular, Charles Dundas's comprehensive tome, *Kilimanjaro and its People*, which was first published way back in 1924. (Incidentally, you can see a portrait of Dundas in Moshi's Union Café, where he's celebrated as the first boss of the Kilimanjaro Native Cooperative Union, KNCU; see p235.)

This, of course, begs the question: why have I included in a modern guide to Kilimanjaro descriptions of obsolete Chagga practices and beliefs that were largely wiped out almost 100 years ago? Well, research revealed the relevance of this inclusion since there are still faint echoes of their traditional way of life that have survived into the present day. Reading this admittedly brief account of the Chagga and how they lived and thought a century ago could provide you with a better understanding – and thereby some insight – into the mind, beliefs and behaviour of the people who live in Kilimanjaro's shadow today.

ORIGINS

The Chagga are believed to have arrived between 400 and 250 years ago from the north-east, following local upheaval in that area. Logically, therefore, the eastern side of the mountain would have been the first to have been settled.

Upon their arrival these new immigrants would have found that the mountain was already inhabited. An aboriginal people known as the Wakonyingo, who were possibly pygmies, were already living here, as indeed were the Wangassa, a tribe similar to the Maasai, and the Umbo of the Usambara mountains. All of these groups were either driven out or absorbed by the Chagga.

Initially, these new immigrants were a disparate bunch, with different beliefs, customs and even languages. With no feelings of kinship or loyalty to their neighbour, they instead settled into family groups, or **clans**. According to Dundas, in his day some 732 clans existed on Kilimanjaro; by 1924, however, when his book was published, some of these clans were already down to just a single member.

These family ties were gradually cut and lost over time as people moved away to settle on other parts of the mountain. Thus, in place of these blood ties, people developed new loyalties to the region in which they were living and to the neighbours with whom they shared the land. Out of this emerged 20 or so states or chiefdoms, most of them on a permanent war footing with the other 19. Wars between the tribes and indeed between villages in the same tribe were commonplace, though they usually took the form of organised raids by one village on another rather than actual pitched battles. Slaves would be taken during these raids, cattle rustled and huts burned down, though there was often little bloodshed – the weaker party would merely withdraw at the first sign of approaching hostilities and might even try to negotiate a price for peace.

❑ *DRACAENA AFROMONTANA* – THE CHAGGA'S CONSTANT COMPANION

Known as *masale* by the locals, the inedible and – at least compared to some of the beautiful plants on Kilimanjaro – rather unedifying *Dracaena afromontana* has nevertheless been cultivated and used by the Chagga since time immemorial, to the extent that it's now almost their tribal emblem. Nobody knows why this should be but it's clear that where the outside world sees an unspectacular green plant of little practical use, the Chagga see a shrub whose spiritual qualities and symbolism are far more important than the practical and nutritional value inherent in other plants.

You'll probably first come across the *dracaena* in one of the mountainside villages where it's still commonly used as a boundary marker, with a row of them planted to form a fence to demarcate the extent of a person's property. According to some Chagga guides, this is because *dracaena* is able to ward off evil spirits which, so it is said, are unable to pass through a line of them. The plant was also traditionally a symbol of contrition and an appeal for clemency. If you were in dispute with a neighbour, for example, or had somehow wronged somebody, the best way to ask for forgiveness would be to give them a *dracaena* plant. Do so, and they would need a very strong reason for not pardoning you.

Indeed, in some Chagga villages it is said that the *dracaena* is a Chagga's constant companion, accompanying a person throughout their life from their first breath to their last. There's some truth to this, too, because in some Chagga villages it was customary to give the sap of the plant to newborns before they took their mother's milk for the first time; while when it came to burying a village chief, the corpse would traditionally have been wrapped in *dracaena* leaves before being interred.

❑ CHAGGA/KICHAGGA LANGUAGE – A QUICK INTRODUCTION

The language of the Chagga, Kichagga, is classified as a Niger-Congo language and has various **dialects** including Vunjo, Rombo, Machame, Huru and Old Moshi. The following is a very brief introduction to that dialect spoken in Marangu. As Chagga is rarely written down, compiling this 'phrasebook' wasn't easy; indeed, many of the spellings below are nothing more than phonetic guesswork.

For their help with this box I am indebted to my Chagga chums, Amina Malya and Vincent Munuo; and especially Frank Mtei, who came up with the first draft of the translations below, and Alex Minja for his expert help too.

1	*kimu*	**2**	*shiwi*	**3**	*shiraru*	**4**	*shina*	**5**	*shitanu*
6	*shirandaru*	**7**	*mfungare*	**8**	*nyanya*	**9**	*kenda*	**10**	*ikumi*

Yes / No	*Ye'e / Ote*	I have a headache	*Ngiwawiyo mrue*
Please	*Ngakuterewa*	I feel sick	*Ngiwawiyo*
Thank you	*Aika*	I am very cold	*Ngiichoo mbeo*
How are you?	*Shimbonyi shapfo?*	Will you carry me?	*Ochirima ingiira*
Very well, thank you	*Nashicha kapisa, aika*	I do not like porridge	*Ngikundi msopfo*
How old are you?	*Nuore maka inga?*	I cannot feel my fingers	*Ngiichue shimnue shewaawaa*
I am British	*Inyi nyimwingeresa*	There is an elephant sleeping in my tent	*Kuwore njofu eela itentiny lyako*
I am American	*Inyi nyimwamerikany*	A leopard is biting my leg	*Kuwore rung'we ilya kurende koko*
Don't mind	*Molaswe*	We are together!	*Luilose!*
How far is it to the camp?	*Ngeshika masaa yenga handun gendelaa?*		
How many times have you climbed the mountain?	*Ni mara tsinga ulemro msari?*		

Eventually the number of groups was whittled down to just six tribes, or states, with each named after one of the mountain's rivers. So, for example, there are the Wamoshi Chaggas (after the Moshi River) and the Wamachame Chaggas who settled near Machame River. With all this intermingling going on, a few words inevitably became used by all the people living on the mountain – and from this unlikely start grew a common language, of which each tribe had its own dialect. Similar customs developed between the tribes, though as with the language they differed in the detail. However, it was only when the Germans took control of the region during the latter part of the 19th century and the local people put aside their differences to present a united front in disputes with their colonial overlords that a single ethnic group was identified and named the Chagga. From this evolved a single, collective Chagga consciousness.

Today the Chaggas, despite their diverse origins, are renowned for having a strong sense of identity and pride. They are also amongst the richest and most powerful people in Tanzania, thanks in part to the fertile soils of Kilimanjaro, and in part to the Western education that they have been receiving for longer than almost any other tribe in East Africa, Kilimanjaro being one of the first places to accept missionaries from Europe. Take a tour around Tanzania and you will also find the Chagga people to be one of the most widespread of all the

❑ THE CHAGGA VIEW OF KILIMANJARO

The summit of Kilimanjaro is and always has been as enchanting to the Chagga as it has been to visitors. According to Dundas, the Chagga view the Kibo summit as something beautiful, eternal and strengthening, its snows providing streams that support life, while the clouds that gather on its slopes provide precious rainfall.

By comparison, the plains that lie in the opposite direction are seen as oppressively hot, where famine stalks, drought and malaria are rife and large creatures such as crocodiles and leopards prey on man. Indeed, so venerated is Kilimanjaro that the Chagga dead are traditionally buried facing towards Kibo, and the side of the village facing the summit is known to be the honourable side, where meetings and feasts are held and chiefs are buried. Furthermore, when meeting somebody, he who comes from higher up the slopes of Kilimanjaro should traditionally greet the other first, for it is he who is coming from the lucky side.

Intriguingly, some Chagga myths about Kilimanjaro are remarkably accurate. In particular, the Chagga traditionally believed that the mountain was formed by a volcano – even though the main eruption that formed Kibo occurred around half a million years ago, way before the arrival of man. What's more, there is a story in Chagga folklore concerning the twin peaks of Mawenzi and Kibo, in which Mawenzi's fire burns out first, and the Mawenzi peak is forced to go to Kibo, whose fire was still burning. Parallels between this story and what scientists now believe really happened – with Kibo continuing to erupt long after Mawenzi expired – are remarkable.

Did the Chagga climb to the top of Kilimanjaro before the Europeans?

The answer is: probably not. The quote on p148 by Rebmann in which he talks about '*the popular traditions respecting the fate of the only expedition which had ever attempted to ascend its heights*' suggests that he had information that they had tried only once – and failed. True, they definitely seem to have reached the snowline before the *mzungu* (white man) arrived: their belief that Kibo was covered in a magic silver which melted on the way down suggests as much.

Furthermore, Rebmann's guide refers to the snow on the summit of Kilimanjaro as 'coldness' (see p145), and later on Rebmann discovers the Chagga have a word for snow: Kibo. What's more, Meyer found traces of a hunting expedition on the Saddle. All of which seem to confirm that they had climbed Kilimanjaro and had some experience of snow. But the fact that Charles New's entourage of porters and guides were buck naked when they climbed up to the snow-line suggests that they were, on the whole, unused to the conditions on Kibo; that, and the fact that the name Kilimanjaro, if it is of Chagga origin (about which, see box pp140-1), roughly translates as 'That which is impossible for birds', suggests they thought that it was therefore impossible for man to reach the top.

Charles Dundas is equally sceptical of the notion that the Chagga climbed Kilimanjaro before Meyer:

It is inconceivable that natives can ever have ascended to the crater rim, for apart from cold, altitude and superstitious fears, it is a sheer impossibility that they could have negotiated the ice. Nor is there any tradition among the natives that anyone went up as high... Rebmann tells us that Rengwa, great-grandfather of the present chief of Machame, sent an expedition to investigate the nature of the ice, which descends very low above Machame, but is impossible to scale. Only one of the party survived, his hands and feet frozen and crippled for life; all the rest were destroyed by the cold, or by evil spirits, as the survivor reported.

tribes, seemingly able to settle in even the furthest-flung corners of the land and – thanks to their talent for trade and politics – to thrive and prosper too.

SOCIAL STRUCTURE AND VILLAGE LIFE

Hans Meyer notes in his book that the biggest Chagga settlement when he visited in 1889 was Machame, with 8000 people. 'Moji' (Moshi) had 3000, as did Marangu. Each family unit, according to him, lived in two or three extremely simple thatched huts in the shape of beehives, with a granary and small courtyard attached. There are several examples of these **'beehive' huts** still dotted around Kilimanjaro's slopes. Only the **chief**, the head of village society and its lawmaker, lived in anything more extensive. The chief of every village was often venerated by his subjects and to meet him required going through an elaborate ceremony first. According to his report in the *Church Missionary Intelligencer*, Johannes Rebmann, the first white man to see Kilimanjaro, had to be sprinkled with goat's blood and the juice of a plant and was then left waiting for four days before being granted an audience with Masaki, the chief of Moshi. While modern society has reduced his role to a largely ceremonial one, the chief is still a widely respected person in village life today – though thankfully there is now less ceremony involved when paying him a visit.

There are other similarities between the Chagga society of yesterday and today. The economy was, then as now, largely agricultural, using the environmentally destructive slash-and-burn technique for clearing land. **Bananas** were once the most common crop, and though banana bushes were largely replaced by **coffee** plantations in the early 20th century, both are still grown today, usually side by side.

When it came to trading these bananas and coffee in former times, instead of the Tanzanian shilling people used red and blue glass beads as currency, or lengths of cloth known as *doti*. One hundred beads were equal to one *doti*, with which you could buy, for example, twenty unripe bananas; twelve *doti* would get you a cow.

RELIGION AND CEREMONIES

Unsurprisingly for a people that has been subjected to some pretty relentless missionary work for over a century, most Chagga are today **Christian**. Traditional beliefs are still held by some, though the intensity of the beliefs and the excesses of many of the rituals have largely disappeared. Superstition played a central role in traditional Chagga religion: witchcraft (*wusari* in Chagga) formed a major part, **rainmakers** and rain-preventers were important members of society and dreams were infallible oracles of the future; indeed, many Chagga were said to have dreamt of the coming of the white man to Kilimanjaro.

The traditional faith was based around belief in a god called **Ruwa**. Ruwa was a tolerant deity who, though neither the creator of the universe nor of man, nevertheless set the latter free from some sort of unspecified incarceration. Ruwa had little to do with mankind following this episode, however, so the

Chagga instead **worshipped their ancestors**, whom they believed could influence events on Earth. Chagga mythology has many parallels with stories from the Bible, including one concerning the fall of man (though in the Chagga version, a sweet potato was the forbidden fruit, and it was a stranger rather than a serpent that persuaded the first man to take a bite); there are also stories that bear a resemblance to the tales of Cain and Abel, and the great flood.

The Chagga faith also had its own **concept of sin** and their own version of the Catholic practice of confession. In the Chagga religion, however, it is not the sinner but the person who is sinned against who must be purified, in order that the negative force does not remain with him or her. This purification would be performed by the local medicine man, with the victim bringing along the necessary ingredients for performing the 'cleansing'. These included the skin, dung and stomach contents of a hyrax (the small tree-dwelling mammals that live on Kilimanjaro); the shell and blood of a snail; the rainwater from a hollow tree and, as with all Chagga ceremonies, a large quantity of banana beer for the medicine man. These ingredients would then be put into a hole in the ground lined with banana leaves and with a gate or archway built above, which the victim would then have to pass through. This done, the victim would be painted by the medicine man using the mixture in the hole. This entire ceremony would be performed twice daily over four days.

Chagga warriors
(from *Across East African Glaciers*, **Hans Meyer**, 1891)

Medicine men did more than care for one's spiritual health; they looked after one's physical well-being too. For the price of a goat and, of course, more banana beer, the medicine man would be able to cure any affliction using a whole host of methods – including spitting. If you were suffering from a fever, for instance, you could expect to be spat upon up to 80 times by the medicine man, who would finish off his performance by expectorating up your nostrils and then blowing hard up each to ensure the saliva reached its target. For this particular method, the traditional payment was one pot of honey – and probably some more banana beer.

The Ngasi

The Ngasi was a brutal rite-of-passage ceremony that marked the passing of boys into adulthood. The ceremony was presided over by the so-called King of Ngasi, a man who had the authority to viciously flog any boy taking part in the ceremony who displeased him.

Before the Ngasi started, boys who were to take part were summoned from their houses by the singing of lugubrious songs at the gate of their homes. From there they were taken to the place of ceremony deep in the forest and the proceedings began. **Hunting** formed a large part of the Ngasi; boys were tested on their ability to track down and kill game, the animals caught being smeared with the novices' excrement. Another test they had to undergo was to climb a tree on the riverbank and cross the river by clambering along its branches to where they intertwined with the branches of the trees on the other side. After this, a chicken would be sacrificed and the boys ordered to lick the blood.

The final part of the initial stage was the most horrific, however: orders were secretly given to the boys to slay a crippled or deformed youth amongst their number. Traditionally, the victim was killed in the night. The parents were never actually told what had happened to their son and, as all present at the Ngasi ceremony were sworn to silence, they rarely found out the whole story. The boys then moved to a new camp. They were now called Mbora and were free to collect the old clothes that they had shed at the start of the Ngasi (one set of boy's clothes, of course, was left unclaimed). They then repaired to the chief's house for a feast, from where they headed home.

After the tribulations of the ceremony the boys were allowed a month's holiday before they returned to the chief's house to participate in the sacrificing of a bull. They were then free to head back to their homes, raping any young women they chanced to meet on the way; the poor women had no redress. The Ngasi was now at an end; the boys who successfully completed the ceremony were now men.

Matrimony

Ver hard on Wachaga to get wife, but when he get her she can make do plant corn, she make wash and cook and make do work for him. Ingreza [English] *man very much money to spend. She wife no can wash, no plant corn, herd goats or cook. All money, much merkani (cloth), heap money, big dinner. She eat much posho. She no can cook dinner. She only make 'Safari' and look. Porr, porr Ingreza man.* A local's view of matrimony as recorded in **Peter MacQueen**'s book *In Wildest Africa*, published in 1910.

After the Ngasi, boys were free to marry. **Marriage** was arranged by the parents, though the boy and girl involved were allowed to voice their opinions – and unless the parents were particularly inflexible, these opinions would count for something. Furthermore, in order for the boy to stand a chance with his potential suitor, he had to woo her. The Chaggas' **courtship** process involved, as elsewhere in the world, a lot of gift-giving, though the gifts followed a strict set of rules: spontaneity played little part in this process. The first gift, for example, from the man to the woman, was always a necklace. The Chagga male would be well rewarded for his generosity, for traditionally in return the girl would dance naked all day with bells attached to her legs. Over the following days other gifts were exchanged until the time came when the girl, having visited all her relatives, would be shut away for three months. No work would be done by the girl during this time and she would be given fattening food and kept in a cage. At the end of this period a **dowry** would be paid, the marriage ceremony performed and the bride would be carried on the back of the Mkara (the traditional Chagga equivalent of the best man) to her new husband's house.

KILIMANJARO ECONOMY

Tourism is the biggest earner in the region, though **agriculture** is still very much part of the local economy. The volcanic soil of the mountain slopes, so rich with nutrients, is amongst the most fertile in East Africa. Thanks to the regular and reliable rainfall blown in from the Indian Ocean (see pp136-8) and the proliferation of springs trickling forth from the bare rock, Kilimanjaro is also one of the damper parts of the region, and the south-eastern slopes particularly so, thus increasing still further the agricultural fecundity of the mountain.

On the lower slopes of Kilimanjaro annual staple crops such as beans, maize and millet are grown, while cash-crops such as Arabica coffee are planted in the *kihamba* land further up the mountainside. Bananas are also grown at this altitude, their leaves and stems providing both a nutrient-rich mulch for the coffee trees and fodder for the livestock that are traditionally grazed at this height. In Chagga society it is customary for a farmer's land to be divided between his sons on his death; whilst this may seem a fair way of dividing land, it also means that a farmer's landholdings diminish in size with every generation and many farms are now less than a hectare in size.

The Chagga are also keen bee-keepers, the hives being hollow sections of a tree trunk closed at both ends and left to hang in trees; you may see these hives placed (illegally) in Kilimanjaro's forests or by the side of the Arusha–Marangu road. Once the swarm has taken possession and completed the combs, the bees are smoked out and the honey collected.

The people who work on Kilimanjaro treks: your mountain crew

Though the Chagga make up the bulk of the people who work in the tourist industry on Kili, you'll find that your crew is probably made up of a patchwork of different tribes, with representatives from the Meru, Maasai and Pare tribes – and many others – working as part of your team.

Let us have a look more closely now, at the jobs they do:

PORTERS

My guide was as polite as Lord Chesterfield and kindly as the finest gentleman of the world could be. So I owe much to the bare-footed natives of this country, who patiently for eight cents a day bear the white man's burden. **Peter MacQueen** *In Wildest Africa* (1910)

The wages may have gone up – a porter today could earn almost US$10 per day if the minimum wages were enforced – and all now have footwear of some description. But the opinion expressed back at the beginning of the 20th century by the intrepid MacQueen is much the same as that voiced by thousands of trekkers in the 21st.

These men (and the ones hired by trekkers are nearly always male, though female porters are occasionally seen on the mountain) never fail to draw both gratitude and, with the amount they carry and the minimum of fuss they make about it, admiration from the trekkers who hire them. Ranging in age from about 18 (the minimum legal age, though some look a good deal younger) to 50 (and occasionally beyond this), porters are amongst the hardest workers on Kilimanjaro. To see them traipsing up the mountain, water in one hand, cooker in another, rucksack on the back and picnic table on the head, is staggering to behold. And though they are supposed to carry no more than 20kg (plus 5kg of their own luggage), many, desperate for work in what is an over-supplied market, manage to bypass the weight checks at the gates to carry much more.

And if that isn't enough, while at the end of the day the average trekker spends his or her time at camp moaning about the hardships they are suffering – in between cramming down mouthfuls of popcorn while clasping a steaming hot cup of tea – these hardy individuals are putting up the tents, helping with the preparation of the food, fetching more water and generally making sure that every trekker's whim is, within reason, catered for.

Yet in spite of appearances, porters are not indestructible. Though they rarely climb to the summit themselves, several still die each year on the slopes of Kilimanjaro. The most common cause of death, perhaps unsurprisingly given the ragged clothes many wear, is exposure. For this reason, if you see a porter dozing by the wayside and it's getting a bit late, put aside your concerns about depriving him of some much needed shut-eye and wake him up: many are the tales of porters who have perished on Kilimanjaro because they took forty winks and then couldn't find their way to camp in the dark. It's this kind of horror story that has caused so much concern over recent years and led to the formation of organisations such as the **Kilimanjaro Porters Assistance Project** (see pp60-4).

How many . . .

Of course, you don't need to worry about this question as your agency will determine how many porters each expedition employs. Nevertheless, it's worth examining how they work this out as so many trekkers are surprised (and often horrified) when they discover how many porters are going to be climbing with them. As a general rule, the larger the number of trekkers, the fewer porters per person are required and, if you take the Marangu Route (where no tent is needed), you can probably get away with as few as two per trekker. On other routes, where tents are necessary, around three porters or more per person is the norm.

Sound a lot? Well, remember that in addition to carrying your rucksack, all your food and camping equipment needs to be lugged up the mountainside too, as well as all those items (eg cooking and medical equipment for the group, possibly a portable toilet too) that are not exclusively yours but from which you will doubtless derive some benefit.

Those looking to save every last shilling often ask the agency to cut down on the number of porters. But this is neither easy nor particularly worthwhile, given that the cost of a porter's wages is a relatively minor part of the overall cost. What's more, you're also tempting the agency to overload each porter in order to reduce their total number – leading to the kind of illegal practices described on pp61-2.

So, in general, accept the agency's recommendations as to the number of porters on your expedition and make sure that they're not overloaded. You could always offer to carry your own backpack, of course, but from my observations the people who do this tend to have more trouble acclimatising and thus have a lower chance of reaching the summit. (Nevertheless, there are certain companies that arrange 'minimally supported' style climbs where fitter and more experienced trekkers can, for a lower price than the company's regular treks, carry some of their own luggage; see box pp98-9.)

Finally, if the prospect of having someone else carry your luggage up makes you feel a little less, well, virile, you may like to know that the great Count Teleki – see p154 – took no fewer than 65 porters up the mountain with him!

. . . and how much?

The porters' wages are paid by your agency. All you need to worry about is how much to give them as a **tip** (see pp32-3) at the end of the trek. Given the privations they suffer over the course of an average expedition and the often desultory wages they earn in return, their efforts to extract as much money as possible from the over-privileged *mzungu* (Swahili for 'white person') are entirely forgivable.

One elaborate yet surprisingly common method is for the porters to pretend there are more of them than there actually are; which, given the large numbers of porters running around each campsite and the fact you don't actually walk with them on the trail, is a lot easier to achieve than you may think. It's a technique hinted at by John Reader in his excellent 1982 book *Kilimanjaro*:

I hired four porters for part of my excursion on Kilimanjaro. The fourth man's name was Stephen, or so the other three told me. I never met Stephen himself. Our gear seemed to arrive at each campsite without his assistance and I am not aware that he ever spent a night with us. I was assured that he was engaged elsewhere on tasks essential to the success of my journey, but I occasionally wondered whether Stephen actually existed. I was particularly aggrieved when he failed to collect his pay in person at the end of the trip. The other guides collected it for him. They also collected his tip.

The practice is common enough to have been given a name – *kirunje*, which is Swahili for 'shadow'. This sort of thing shouldn't happen if you're with a reputable company but it's a good idea anyway to **make sure you meet your team at the start of the trail before you set off**. This will help to prevent this sort of scam and it's good manners too. While at the end, to ensure each porter gets his fair share, dish the tips out yourself – *do not* give them to your guide to hand out on your behalf unless you are sure your agency has systems in place to prevent the guide pocketing it all for himself; see pp60-4 for why this is so.

Nevertheless, providing you have paid a reasonable tip (and for guidance over what is the correct amount, see pp32-3), don't fall for the melodramatics but simply thank them warmly for all their endeavours over the course of the trek. Once they realise your conscience remains unpricked it will all be handshakes and smiles and, having pocketed the money, they'll soon trot off happily enough.

GUIDES

If portering is the first step on the career ladder of Kilimanjaro, it is the guides who stand proudly on the top rung. Ornithologist, zoologist, botanist, geologist, tracker, astronomer, butler, manager, doctor, linguist and teacher, a good guide will be all of these professions rolled into one. With luck, over the course of the trek they'll also become your friend.

The metamorphosis from porter to guide is a lengthy one. Having served an apprenticeship by lugging luggage, a few talented and ambitious ones are eventually promoted to the position of **summit porter**. In addition to carrying their fair share of equipment, they are also expected to perform many of the duties of a fully fledged guide. This includes, most painfully of all, escorting trekkers on that final, excruciating push to the summit, as well as carrying the client's day-pack if they are struggling.

From there the next logical step is to become a fully fledged guide. Standing between them and a licence is a period of intensive training conducted by the park authority, KINAPA (Kilimanjaro National Park Authority). The training camp lasts around a month and covers various subjects, including lessons on caring for the mountain environment, customer care, first aid, and, of course, altitude sickness. At the end the trainees are expected to climb to the summit en masse to prove their fitness for the job. At Uhuru Peak, the very highest point in Africa, a warden hands out pieces of paper to each successful summiteer with a code written on it. That code allows the recipient to enter into the final exam; without it, they can't complete the course.

Those who successfully graduate are ranked either as a full route guide or as an assistant guide and are given different licences accordingly. They are now free to tout themselves around the agencies looking for work. A newly qualified guide will probably have to settle for being an **assistant guide** in order to secure work. For this he'll receive a higher wage than a porter (and a summit porter) and a commensurately greater proportion of the tips – though not as much as he would receive if leading the climb himself. Note that I say 'he' as the majority of guides are male, though that situation is, slowly, changing.

5 ARRIVING IN EAST AFRICA: DAR ES SALAAM & NAIROBI

The following chapter is devoted to helping you take your first few steps in East Africa. It contains guides to the two cities you are most likely to fly into if you're not flying straight into Kilimanjaro Airport – namely **Dar es Salaam** (Tanzania) and **Nairobi** (Kenya). The guides to the two cities are deliberately rather brief but they should be adequate for finding your way around and for choosing somewhere to sleep and eat, as well as to experience something of metropolitan East Africa.

I explain, at the end of each description, how to get to Kilimanjaro. **Kilimanjaro International Airport** is, of course, the most convenient airport for the mountain and with more and more airlines flying there (for more details see pp34-7) this chapter is getting less and less relevant and may be surplus to requirements in the future; but for this edition, at least, I've decided to keep it in.

Dar es Salaam

Dar es Salaam (commonly just called Dar) is a city with a bit of an identity crisis: a large metropolis which behaves as if it were a small and sleepy seaside town; a city that was at the forefront of the country's struggle for independence in the 1950s yet still contains the finest collection of dusty old colonial buildings in possibly the whole of East Africa; and a place that everybody thinks is the administrative capital of Tanzania – but isn't.

It *is* the commercial heart of the country, however, and has been almost since its inception in the 1860s by Sultan Sayyid Majid of Zanzibar. Intended as a mainland port for many of the goods and spices being traded on his island, the sultan, clearly a man of poetic bent, named his new city Dar es Salaam (Haven of Peace). And peacefully was how it spent its first few years, as the sultan died soon after founding the city, allowing Bagamoyo, a dhow port to the north, to emerge as the pre-eminent harbour on this particular stretch of the east coast.

Missionaries from Europe added fresh impetus to Dar with their arrival in the 1880s but it was the coming of the Germans in 1891 that really gave this city a fillip, the colonials feeling that the harbour here was more suitable to their steam-powered craft than Bagamoyo.

Having made Dar their seat of power, it remained the capital until 1973 when it was decided to move the legislature to Dodoma, smack in the geometric heart of the country – which probably seemed like a good idea at the time, until somebody pointed out the shortage of water and other basic amenities there. Indeed, the parliament only actually relocated there in 2017 and the presidential offices in May 2023!

So while the capital may be Dodoma, much of the politicking and indeed everything else of importance still takes place here in Dar. It's also a city with ambition, with shiny high-rises sprouting up throughout the centre and the country's first mass transport system, the DART, introduced at the start of 2016. The population, over 5 million according to the national census of 2022, is said to be the fastest growing in sub-Saharan Africa too.

For tourists, there's nothing particularly special to warrant a long stay; but by the same token, don't fret too much if you do have to spend some time in Dar: it's pleasant, it's laid back and, compared to Nairobi, it's a whole lot saner.

WHAT TO SEE AND DO

None of Dar's attractions is going to make your eyes pop out on springs from their sockets but the **walking tour** that I've outlined on the map around the

❑ NATIONAL MUSEUM OF TANZANIA

The National Museum of Tanzania (💻 www.nmt.go.tz; Shaban Robert St; daily 9.30am-6pm; Ts12,000) fares badly when compared to Kenya's version. Nevertheless, the exhibits themselves remain mildly diverting at times and the buildings are a cool escape from the heat of the day. And if you manage to avoid the marauding school parties you may well have the entire complex to yourself, with only the cleaner for occasional company.

Most of the more interesting exhibits can be found in the first couple of rooms, located upstairs from the ticket desk. The **Hall of Human Origins** is absorbing, describing as it does our evolution through the millennia, with the help of some apposite replicas of Leakey's discoveries at **Olduvai Gorge**. Next door, the **History Gallery** maps out in pretty concise and thorough detail the story of Tanzania, including some interesting articles on the early explorers as well as – inevitably – a lengthy discourse on Tanzania's fight for independence. The third room is even more interesting, an exhibition devoted to **African Rock Art** with detailed descriptions and photographs of primitive and prehistoric carvings and paintings from all over the continent, from the Sahara to southern Africa. Take your time wandering around – it's fascinating.

Returning downstairs, a small courtyard plays host to half-a-dozen **historic cars** and a small **memorial garden** dedicated to the 12 victims who perished in the US Embassy bombing in Dar on 7 August 1998. Similar in style to the one in Nairobi (see p196), the **sculpture** here includes twisted metal, a rusting motorbike and a window pane shattered by the blast.

The **original museum building** that stands beyond is now all but empty, though I'm pleased to see that one of the weirdest exhibits to be found in any museum anywhere in the world, namely the country's first ATM, established in 1997 and looking pretty much like any other ATM you see today, is still in situ. It's not plugged in, by the way, so don't try feeding your card into it.

downtown district of Kivukoni, starting and finishing at the old German Boma, is fine for those with a cursory interest in the place. For those in a hurry, the **National Museum** (see box p189) at least is worth seeing, being the most absorbing and, for Kili-bound trekkers, the most relevant attraction in Dar.

The sights mentioned on the map on p193 aren't the only attractions in the city. Many tourists with time to kill take the ferry from by the Slipway Hotel in Msasani (see map opposite) to Bongoyo Island. I also love wandering around the market district of **Kamata** (Ts8000 by bajaj from Msasani). Frenetic and friendly, it's *exactly* what you expect and want an African metropolis to sound, look and smell like. Just leave your valuables at home.

ARRIVAL

By air

Though safer than arriving in Nairobi, it still pays to be on your guard when landing in Dar: like a recently hatched turtle taking to the ocean for the first time, you are at your most vulnerable when you land in a new country – and even in the 'Haven of Peace' there are still plenty of sharks out there.

Julius Nyerere International Airport is about 12km south-west of the city centre. There are a couple of ATMs, several moneychangers and a **taxi counter** which has a set rate of US$50 to take you into the centre. You could try to negotiate a lower rate with the drivers themselves; or you could walk a few hundred metres to the main road, cross over and take a **bus** into town for Ts500, or hail a cab for about Ts46,000.

Overland

If arriving by **bus** from most places in Tanzania you'll fairly certainly be dropped at the new Magufuli Bus Terminal, which is unfortunate, as it's miles from downtown Dar (Ts16,000 by bajaj (tuk tuk), taxi Ts23,000). Fortunately, buses serving Moshi and Arusha tend to use the Shekilango terminal (see map opposite), which is much closer. A taxi to the centre from Shekilango will be around Ts11,000, or Ts8000 by bajaj.

ORIENTATION

Though Dar es Salaam stretches on for miles, the two main areas of interest to visitors stand next to each other on the seafront; the only places that tourists may be interested in that can't be found in these two areas are the bus terminals and the airport. Which of the two places you use as your base should depend, to a large degree, on what you want to do. If you want to take in the city's sights, and spend a few hours browsing its excellent museum, **downtown Dar**, also known as **Kivukoni**, the oldest part of the city, is the place for you.

Navigating your way around downtown here is no easy task. Things are fairly straightforward on the coast, where Kivukoni Rd and Ocean Rd (now called Barack Obama Drive) follow the shore from the old German Boma (see map p193) to Ocean Road Hospital and beyond. But step back from the shore and you find yourself in a labyrinth of small streets, many of which curve imperceptibly but dramatically enough to confuse and disorientate. Keep the map on p193 with you, using it first to help you find your way to the **tourist office** where they sometimes hand out a photocopied map of the city.

If all that sightseeing sounds a bit too energetic and your preference is to lounge on a beach, staying in **Msasani Peninsula/ Masaki** (see map opposite), to the north of downtown, is definitely the way to go. This has the nicest hostel and a much better choice of restaurants and cafés, as well as the better souvenir shops and even the best English-language bookshop in the whole of Tanzania. It's also safer and, indisputably, more laidback. But it does also lack the character of downtown and it's often hard to feel like you're in one of Africa's foremost cities.

Of course, it's not impossible to stay in Msasani and travel to the city centre – the two are, after all, next to each other, divided only by the Selandar and Tanzanite bridges, and given how easy it is to book transport these days, it's not difficult to travel between the two.

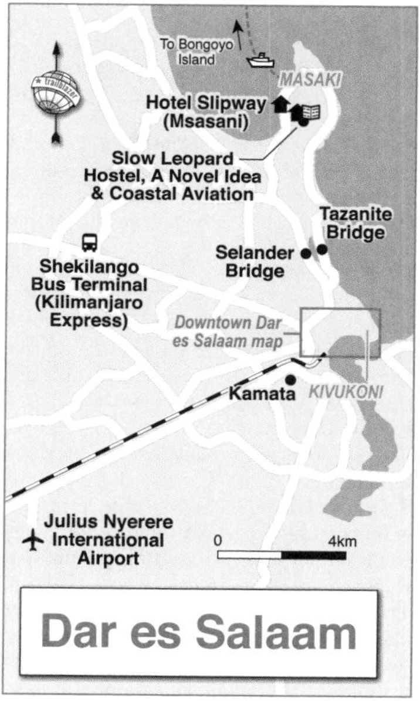

GETTING AROUND DAR

The first thing to do when you get to Dar is to download either the Bolt (the best one for Dar) or Uber **apps** onto your phone. These services have taken off in a big way in the city and you can order bajaj (tuk tuks) as well as regular taxis. I don't think I'm exaggerating when I say that these apps have cut, at a stroke, the hassle of haggling as the price is pretty much agreed before your transport even reaches you. To give you an idea of price, between downtown Dar (Kivukoni) and the Msasani Peninsula it's around Ts5000 by bajaj. Just remember, however, that if you say you want to pay by card, you may find nobody is willing to take the fare.

For public transport there's **Dar Rapid Transit**, or **DART**; fares are just Ts750 and the buses travel along lanes exclusively set aside for them. The most useful route for most people is the one which runs between Magafuli Bus Terminal (via Shekilango, for buses to Moshi and Arusha) and the centre of town. **Regular buses** (Ts500) also ply all the main routes, though finding where they start and stop can be difficult. Ask locals, your hotel, or take a cab. Fortunately, downtown Dar is compact enough to walk around.

SERVICES

There's a **tourist information office** (Mon-Fri 8am-4pm, Sat 8.30am-1pm) in Matasalamat Building on Samora Avenue in Downtown Dar (see map p193). It depends who is working there when you call in but I found the staff to be friendly and patient, if not always particularly knowledgeable.

For money, there are **ATMs** everywhere. To change cash, try the moneychangers on the corner of Samora Avenue and Azikiwe St (see map p193).

The main **post office** (Mon-Fri 8am-4.30pm, Sat 9am-1pm) is on Maktaba/Azikiwe St (see map p193). You won't have any trouble finding a restaurant or hotel with wi-fi in Dar; they are everywhere.

For a **bookshop**, A Novel Idea (open daily 10am-6pm) in the Slipway Hotel complex, Masaki, is by far the best for English-language tomes.

Also in Masaki are a couple of good **supermarkets**, Village Supermarket on Chole Road (daily 8.30am-9pm) and Shoppers Plaza on Haile Selassie Road (daily 8.30am-10pm).

WHERE TO STAY (see map p193)

The following are listed in **price order**, with the **cheapest first**. As is usual, the more expensive places don't tend to publish rack rates anymore, for their prices change constantly according to demand. For details of the abbreviations, see box p192.

• ***YMCA*** (☎ 022-213 5457; Upanga Rd; sgl/dbl Ts25,000/28,000) Clean-ish and safe-ish, the YMCA offers private rooms

Dar's **area code** is ☎ 022; if phoning a landline from outside Tanzania dial ☎ +255-22. **Mobile (cell) phone** numbers start ☎ 07.

for the same price that the Slow Leopard (see below) offers a space in a 10-bed dorm – though in all other aspects the Slow Leopard wins hands-down. Note that rooms aren't self-contained.

• ***Safari Inn*** (☎ 022-213 8101/2; Band St, off Libya St; s/c sgl/dbl Ts42,000/52,000 with fan; Ts72,000 for the suites with television). Still a popular budget choice and all the rooms are en suite, though some are a bit gloomy and lack windows.

• ***Slow Leopard*** (see map p191; ☎ 0744-928481, 🖳 www.theslowleopard.com/dar-es-salaam; Chole Rd; s/c dorm/sgl/dbl Ts36,000/102,000/114,000 including a good breakfast) The No 1 choice for budget travellers, no question. Run by Englishman Henry Jones, whose enthusiasm for the city is infectious, it's a friendly place with some spotlessly clean private rooms and dorms. There are some thoughtful touches too, including mosquito repellent distributed on the tables in the bar and huge mossy nets protecting the dorm beds. The only negative I can see is that at the weekends the bar can get rowdy, and it might be a good idea to avoid the adjacent 10-bed dorm then.

• ***Peacock Hotel*** (☎ 022-211 4071, 🖳 peacock-hotel.com; Bibi Titi Mohamed St; s/c sgl/dbl US$70/100) Refreshingly free of any pretension, this ugly but friendly establishment is seeing more and more tourists. It's perfectly OK, with all the facilities you'd expect from a hotel of this class and it's so nice to be welcomed by receptionists who seem genuinely glad you've dropped in.

• ***Hotel Slipway*** (see map p191; ☎ 022-260 0893, 🖳 hotelslipway.com; Slipway Rd; s/c sgl/dbl US$105-190/125-210) Certainly the most characterful place in Masaki, despite appearances the Slipway is actually only a few decades old. Nevertheless it has plenty of character, largely thanks to the many restaurants, bars and souvenir stalls that have attached themselves to it like barnacles from the adjacent Indian Ocean. I'd heard that the hotel was the place to go in the evenings for a sundowner and at this time at least it's the centre of the social scene in Dar.

• ***Four Points by Sheraton*** (☎ 022-211 7050, 🖳 marriott.com; corner of Azikiwe St & Sokoine Drive; s/c sgl/dbl from approx US$155/175) In a better location than the Serena Hotel (see below), its nearest rival, though not with quite the same level of sophistication, the former New Africa stands on the site of the Germans' original Kaiserhof. Home to one of Dar's oldest casinos as well as a host of bars and restaurants, the Sheraton's rooms have everything you'd expect from a hotel of this calibre, including mini-bar, satellite TV, wi-fi etc.

• ***Dar es Salaam Serena Hotel*** (☎ 022-221 2500, 🖳 www.serenahotels.com/dar-es-salaam; Ohio St; s/c rooms start from sgl/dbl US$221.50/248) This Middle-Eastern/Zanzibari-style place has changed hands a couple of times since the first edition of this book and used to be the top place in the town centre before the arrival

❑ ABBREVIATIONS

Throughout this book I have used the following abbreviations when writing about accommodation: **pp** means per person; **s/c** is short for self-contained, a local term meaning that the room comes with a bathroom (ie the room is en suite or a bathroom is attached); while **sgl/dbl/tpl** means single/double/triple rooms.

So, for example, where I have written 's/c sgl/dbl/tpl US$35/40/45', I mean that a self-contained single room costs from US$35 per night, a self-contained double costs US$40 and a self-contained triple costs US$45.

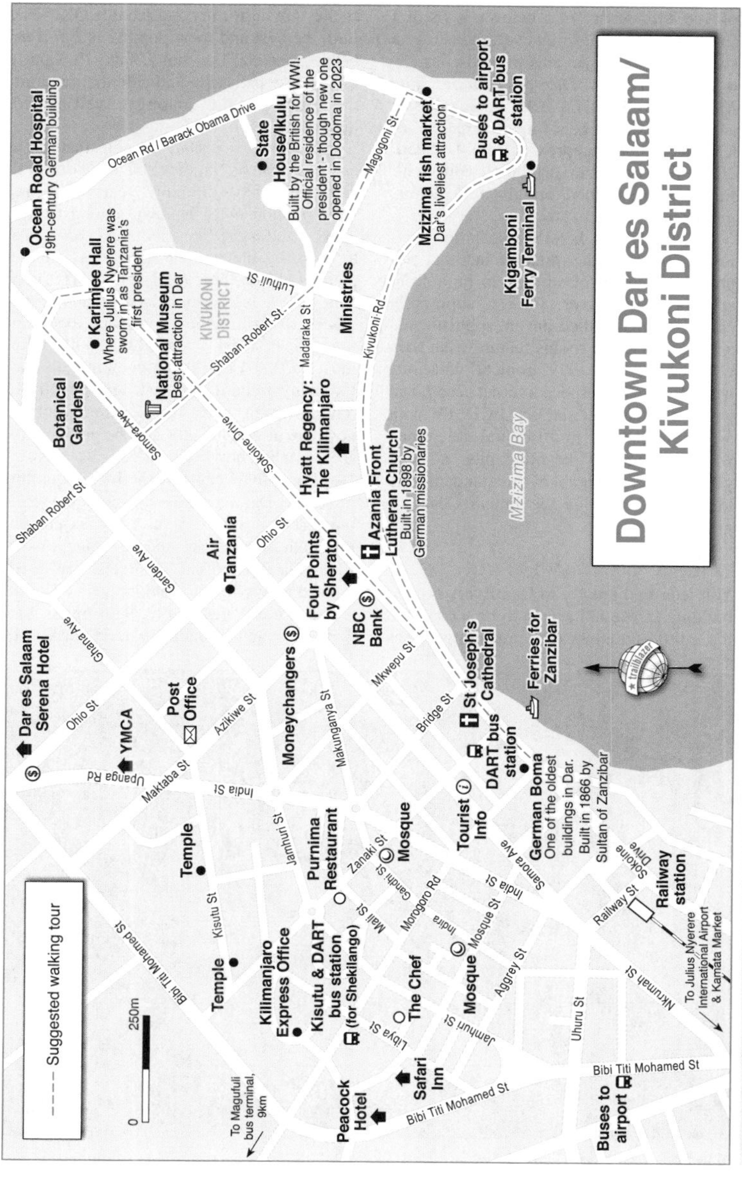
Downtown Dar es Salaam/
Kivukoni District
Suggested walking tour
0
250m
Ocean Road Hospital
19th-century German building
Ocean Rd / Barack Obama Drive
State House/Ikulu
Built by the British for WWI. Official residence of the president - though new one opened in Dodoma in 2023
Karimjee Hall
Where Julius Nyerere was sworn in as Tanzania's first president
National Museum
Best attraction in Dar
KIVUKONI DISTRICT
Luthuli St
Shaban Robert St
Madaraka St
Ministries
Magogoni St
Mzizima fish market
Dar's liveliest attraction
Buses to airport
& DART bus station
Kigamboni Ferry Terminal
Kivukoni Rd
Botanical Gardens
Samora Ave
Sokoine Drive
Hyatt Regency: The Kilimanjaro
Azania Front Lutheran Church
Built in 1898 by German missionaries
Mzizima Bay
Air Tanzania
Ohio St
Garden Ave
Four Points by Sheraton
NBC Bank
Ghana Ave
Dar es Salaam Serena Hotel
Ohio St
YMCA
Post Office
Moneychangers
Azikiwe St
Makunganya St
Mkwepu St
Bridge St
St Joseph's Cathedral
Ferries for Zanzibar
trailblazer
Upanga Rd
Maktaba St
India St
Jamhuri St
DART bus station
Tourist Info
German Boma
One of the oldest buildings in Dar. Built in 1866 by Sultan of Zanzibar
Temple
Purnima Restaurant
Zanaki St
Gandhi St
Mosque
Samora Ave
India St
Sokoine Drive
Railway St
Railway station
Kisutu St
Bibi Titi Mohamed St
Temple
Kilimanjaro Express Office
Kisutu & DART bus station (for Shekilango)
Mali St
Morogoro Rd
India
Mosque St
Mosque
The Chef
Aggrey St
Libya St
Jamhuri St
Uhuru St
Nkrumah St
To Julius Nyerere International Airport & Kamata Market
To Magufuli bus terminal, 9km
Peacock Hotel
Safari Inn
Bibi Titi Mohamed St
Bibi Titi Mohamed St
Buses to airport

of The Kilimanjaro (see below). It's still a fine establishment, however, boasting a swimming pool, gym and all mod-cons.

• ***Hyatt Regency Dar es Salaam: The Kilimanjaro*** (☎ 0764-701234, 🖳 daressalaamkilimanjaro.regency.hyatt.com; Kivukoni Rd; rooms approx sgl/dbl US$250/285) Yet another luxury hotel, you won't find a more refined or, given its name, *appropriate* place to stay.

Actually, the hotel's association with Kili is tenuous, other than the fact that you need a mountain of *shilingi* to be able to stay here. However, it *is* a supremely comfy, fountain-filled haven, sophisticated and shiny and the rooms feature what they describe as 'elegantly tropical' interiors, wood floors, high-speed internet access and wi-fi, international satellite LCD TV with movie channels, multilingual telephone voicemail and all the other bits 'n' bobs you'd expect of a hotel of this standard. The location overlooking the Indian Ocean is great too.

WHERE TO EAT AND DRINK

You won't go hungry in Dar. Every second building in Masaki seems to be a café and it's a little pointless recommending places as they are uniformly and reliably OK. That said, the best and most popular is ***Epi d'or*** (🖳 epidor.co.tz; Tue-Sun 7.30am-10.30pm), a Lebanese patisserie and café that remains the most popular amongst well-heeled locals.

In downtown Dar, do note that most eateries close on Sundays. One that doesn't, and which has for many years been the most popular place in town amongst travellers – and indeed just about everyone else to judge by the frenetic 'busy-ness' of the place – is ***The Chef*** (daily noon-11pm) on Chagga St. It is a popularity that is well deserved: tasty, huge portions of food and fair prices (mains Ts4000-22,000, with most Ts7000-12,000) is a combination that for many is hard to resist, and travellers, having eaten here once, often venture nowhere else in the city. Just be prepared to share a table, however – it gets that busy.

For truly cheap-eats the Indian quarter of central Dar, particularly around the temple-laden Kisutu St (and its extension Pramukh Swami St) and the junction of Indira Gandhi and Zanaki streets, is as good a place as any to start looking.

Purnima (Mon-Fri 9am-6pm, Sat 8am-2pm, Sun 6.30am-2pm), on Zanaki St,

Above: Sorting the catch by the fish market at Mzizima.

is a great little place, reputedly the oldest Indian restaurant in the country (est 1958), where a vegetarian thali will make you poorer by only Ts10,000. There are plenty of other similar places around here – follow your nose to find them.

MOVING ON – TO KILIMANJARO

By bus to Moshi and Arusha

The **Kilimanjaro Express** office is located by the old Kisutu bus station, now a collection of food stalls, in the heart of downtown on Libya St near the DART station. Tickets cost around Ts45,000 to either Moshi or Arusha; the journey is around 10-11 hours to Moshi, 13-14 hours to Arusha. (Don't believe them when they say it takes 6-7 hours. It doesn't.)

Most **buses to Tanzanian destinations (and beyond)** depart from **Magufuli Bus Station** but, thankfully, for Arusha and Moshi, the Kilimanjaro Express buses (and other companies) tend to use the more convenient **Shekilango bus stand** as their base. A taxi from downtown Dar (Kivukoni) or Msasani to Shekilango will set you back about Ts15,000; a bajaj about Ts12,000. Alternatively, catch the DART (see p191) that starts at Mzizima fish market, on the seafront to the west of the Azania Front Lutheran Church, continues through the centre of town (including stops at the DART bus station behind the tourist office and at Kisutu) and on to Shekilango (Ts750); look for any bus heading to Kimara. It's a painless and cheap way of getting there.

By train to Moshi and Arusha

Trains depart the Kamata railway (🖳 www.trc.co.tz) station in Dar for Arusha via Moshi on Mon, Wed and Fri at 2.30pm, arriving the next morning at about 7.30am (supposedly). Yes it's slow, but it's also cheap (3rd class Ts16,500, 2nd Ts23,500, and 2nd sleeper is Ts39,000) and doubtless more memorable than a flight or bus ride. Note that you can't buy tickets for your chosen train until the previous one has left; so, for example, if you wanted to buy a ticket for the Monday service, you would have to wait until Saturday morning (ie after the train had left on Friday) to purchase one. A bajaj from downtown Dar to Kamata is approx Ts5000, or it's Ts8000 from Msasani.

By plane to Kilimanjaro and Arusha airports

The most reliable flights to Arusha or Kilimanjaro Airport are operated by **Precision Air** (🖳 precisionairtz.com), who fly three times daily to Kilimanjaro from Dar and a couple of times a day to Arusha Airport too. The annoying thing is that their flights to Arusha Airport often go via Zanzibar, adding 50 minutes onto the travel time. The good news is that flights to Kilimanjaro Airport start at just US$51. Alternatively, there is **Auric Air** (🖳 www.auricair.com), who operate daily flights to Arusha Airport only, though again are cheap, starting at just US$75 for non-residents.

The national carrier **Air Tanzania** (🖳 www.airtanzania.co.tz) have their main office on Ohio St and operate 3-4 flights daily to Kilimanjaro Airport (2-3 direct, 1 via Zanzibar) and one to Arusha Airport (via Zanzibar).

Of the smaller airlines, **Air Excel** (🖳 airexcelonline.com) have a flight daily to Arusha Airport (at 4.20pm; 2¼hrs flying time as they go via Zanzibar). **Flightlink** (🖳 www.flightlink.co.tz), in the same building as KLM, at the southern end of Chole Rd in Masaki, operate two morning flights daily via Zanzibar to Arusha Airport. **Coastal Aviation** (🖳 coastal.co.tz) have their offices in Slipway Hotel in Masaki and have two daily flights to Arusha, at 8am and 4pm, though they do take 2¼hrs each.

Getting to the airport Look for the bus at the fish market signed Gongo La Mboto (or an abbreviated version of this); it also stops just south of the junction of Mohamed and Uhuru streets (see map p193) – useful for those staying at this side of town. Leave in plenty of time – it can take over an hour depending on traffic and it's a 5-minute walk from the road to the terminal. The bus is Ts500; a taxi is around Ts35,000 for the same journey, or Ts45,000 from Masaki.

Nairobi

As rough as a lion's tongue and as raw as a baboon's backside, East Africa's largest city has come quite a long way since its inception in May 1899 as a humble railway supply depot on the Mombasa to Kampala line. It is a city that has suffered much from plagues, fire and reconstruction – and that was just in its first 10 years – yet it has obstinately continued to prosper and grow, rising from a population of approximately zero in 1898 to around three and a half million today.

Official recognition of the city's increasing importance arrived in 1907 when the British made it the capital of their East African territories; you can still find the occasional colonial relic in the city, from the Indian-influenced architecture of a few downtown buildings (shipped over from the subcontinent, Indians supplied much of the labour force used to build the railway) to some distinctly elegant hotels and orderly public gardens (including one, just to the north of Kenyatta Avenue, which still bears a statue of Queen Victoria).

But if you came with the specific purpose of seeing a faded colonial city you'd be disappointed because as the capital of the Kenyan republic and the UN's fourth official 'World Centre', Nairobi is East Africa's most modern, prosperous and glamorous metropolis. It is also, first and foremost, black Africa at its loudest and proudest.

❑ NAIROBI NATIONAL MUSEUM [off map p199]

If you have time to see only one sight in Nairobi, the **National Museum** (💻 museums.or.ke/nairobi-national-museum; off Museum Hill, near Uhuru Highway; daily 8.30am-5.30pm; Ks1200, Ks1500 including entrance to the Snake Park) is definitely the one to head for, an institution that is not only almost as old as the city itself (having been established way back in 1910) but which effortlessly manages the difficult feat of justifying the rather cheeky entrance fee.

Virtually every gallery holds something of interest for the visitor. True, the first couple of rooms, where many of Kenya's creatures – including every species of Kenya's avifauna – has been stuffed and put on display, may feel a little anachronistic in this day and age; though even here there are some highlights, including the skeleton (and, in the courtyard, a model, faithfully cast in fibreglass) of **the nation's favourite pachyderm**, Ahmed, an elephant so huge its tusks alone weighed an incredible 68kg each. The next couple of galleries are my favourites, however. They study in great detail (but never tediously so) the different theories behind the evolution of man, illustrated by many of the actual skulls and other fossils that helped to shape these theories.

Heading upstairs, more treats await including a room devoted to the history of Kenya and another that studies the cultures, art and festivals of the nation's tribes, with particular focus on how they celebrate the various rites of passage of their members' lives. This floor is also where you'll find rooms that are mainly given over to contemporary photographic and art exhibitions which I find are usually well worth seeing and a pleasant respite from the more serious, educational exhibits elsewhere.

> ❑ **KENYA VISA RULE CHANGE!**
>
> In early 2024 it was announced that Kenya would require travellers to get an eTA (US$30) online in advance, rather than a visa, before arrival in Kenya; see p120.
>
> This is great news as previously citizens of most countries needed a visa and a single-entry visa used to cost US$50, though if you were staying in Kenya for less than 72 hours, you could get a transit visa for US$20.

A WALKING TOUR OF DOWNTOWN NAIROBI

It is still possible, and indeed pleasant, to walk around the **Commercial Business District** (CBD), the political, historical, financial and spiritual centre of the city, and I've marked the route of a potential (sweaty) walking tour that you can take on the map on p199. You can start it wherever you like, though I've arbitrarily chosen the railway station and nearby Railway Museum.

This tour is best done on a Sunday morning, when the hassle from touts is at its lowest and the gospel choirs are out in force on the streets and in the parks. (Note that the number one attraction in central Nairobi is the **National Museum**; this used to be part of this tour too – it's within walking distance – but the construction of new highways has made that particular walk just too dangerous to consider now so maybe catch a cab. But it is still well worth visiting and details of it can be found in the box opposite.)

SECURITY

A few years back some inspired wag dubbed Kenya's capital 'Nairobberi', and less-inspired wags have been retreading that joke ever since. Tired as the gag may be, however, it does still have relevance, for Nairobi's reputation as East Africa's Capital of Crime is well founded.

To be fair, the authorities are trying to improve matters, at least in the centre, blocking off many of the darker back streets. There seem to be fewer beggars and touts populating the centre too. There is also a 'beautification' programme going on, which seems to involve a lot of tree-planting.

Nevertheless, the need to be wary when out on the streets of Nairobi remains paramount. The **most notorious hotspot** is the area immediately to the east of Moi Avenue, including River Rd and the bus stations. During the day violent robbery is rare simply because it's so packed with people; pickpocketing, on the other hand, is rife at this time, probably for the same reason. At night, both techniques are common.

To avoid becoming another victim, **be vigilant**, leave valuables at your hotel (having first checked their security procedures) and make sure they give you a receipt for any goods deposited. Furthermore, tuck moneybelts under your clothing and don't walk around at night but take a taxi, even if it's for just a few hundred metres.

It can only be to your advantage if you are over-cautious for your first couple of days in the capital. After that, if you're still staying here, you can begin to appreciate Nairobi's charms – which do exist, and are not entirely inconsiderable – and can begin to moan, like the rest of the travellers here, about how unfair guidebook writers are about Kenya's capital.

ARRIVAL

By air

Jomo Kenyatta Airport (also known as Nairobi International Airport) is 18km from the centre of Nairobi. If you're just transferring to another flight here signs should point the direction you need to go.

If you're staying in Kenya, however, make your way to passport control.

Having passed through immigration (and shown several people your Covid vaccine certificate, if that is still necessary by the time you read this) you should then collect your luggage. Depending on which terminal you arrived at the Arrivals Hall may be free of facilities, though wander around the airport and you'll find moneychangers and ATMs, the latter being your best bet for a fair rate at the airport, or you could pay for your cab in dollars and wait to change money in town.

You have a number of choices in tackling the journey from the airport to the centre of Nairobi. 'Official' **airport taxis** cost about Ks3000 (US$20-25), **Ubers** start at around Ks1000-1400 (US$7-10), but you may need to leave the airport to get one. The exact amount depends on the time of day and your bargaining skills. Before 8pm you can take the **No 34 bus** that runs down River Rd with a stop on Moi Avenue (Ks100). Remember to be careful of pickpockets on this route.

By bus

Arrive in Nairobi by **shuttle bus** from Arusha/Moshi and, if they don't drop you off at your hotel, you'll be dropped off by Jevanjee Gardens right in the heart of the action. Arrive by **'ordinary' bus**, on the other hand, and you could well be dropped off near the infamous River Rd, home to a significant minority of ne'er-do-wells – take care!

ORIENTATION & GETTING AROUND

Despite decades of unplanned growth, a mass of sprawling suburbs and a wholesale aversion to street numbers, central Nairobi is actually very easy to navigate, with nearly everything of interest to the traveller within walking distance of Kenyatta Avenue.

A couple of obvious landmarks are the enormous tower of the **Kenyatta International Convention Centre**, to the south of City Hall, and the even more enormous **Nation Centre**, a red Meccano-type structure nestling between two giant cylindrical towers just off the eastern end of Kenyatta Avenue. Central Nairobi is fairly compact and the fit will be able to walk everywhere. Buses and *matatus* (Kenyan minibuses) run from early morning to late at night, though **I strongly advise you to take taxis after dark**. During the day things are much safer, though keep your wits about you.

❑ SEVEN USEFUL THINGS TO KNOW ABOUT KENYA

- The official **language** is Swahili. For a quick guide to Swahili, see p374. In addition, many Kenyans speak both their own tribal language and English, which is widely spoken everywhere.
- As with Tanzania, Kenya is **three hours ahead of GMT**. Note that, in addition to standard time, many locals use **Swahili time**, which runs from dawn to dusk (or 6am to 6pm to be precise). See pp124-5 for details on how to convert between East African time and Swahili time.
- The Kenyan **currency** is the shilling (Ks). At the time of writing, €1=Ks161, US$1=Ks151, UK£1=Ks186. Don't change money on the street.
- As with Tanzania, Kenya's **electricity supply** uses the British-style three-pin plugs on 220-240V.
- The **international dialling code** is ☎ 254; the Nairobi code is 020 and numbers starting with 07 are for mobiles.
- The **emergency telephone number** is ☎ 999.
- **Opening hours** are typically 8am to 5 or 6pm with some establishments shutting on Sundays. Banks, post offices etc have their own hours, see p200.

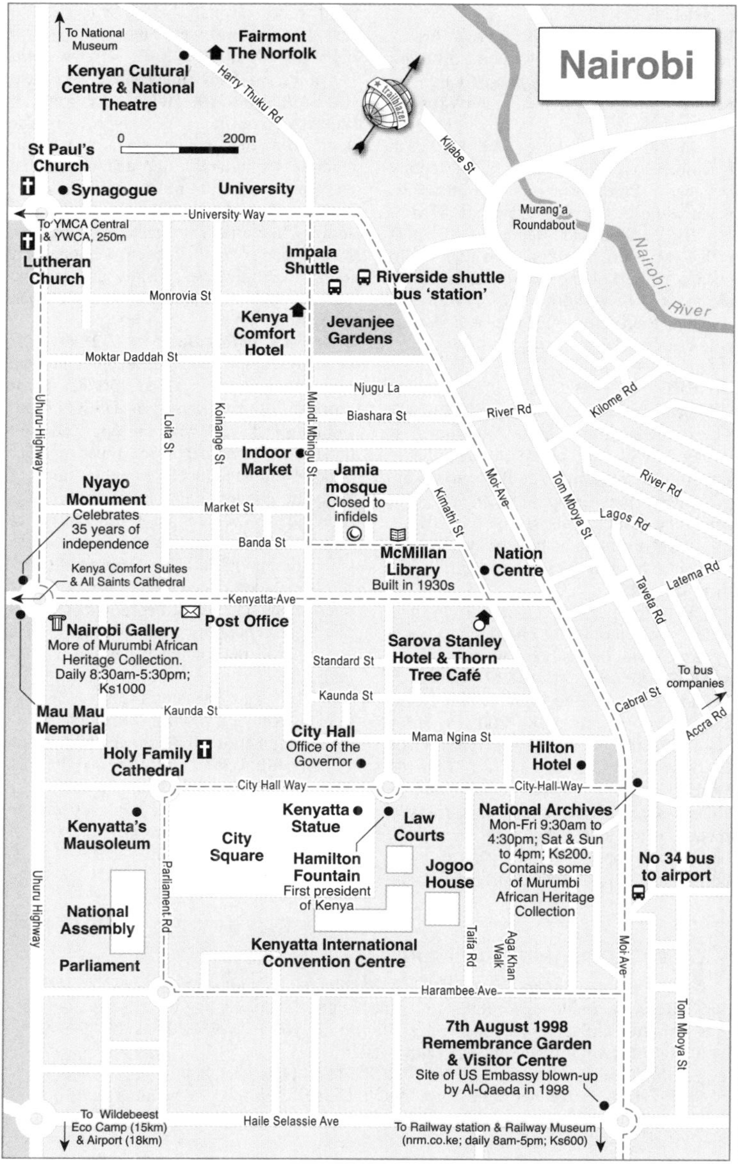
Nairobi
To National Museum
Fairmont The Norfolk
Kenyan Cultural Centre & National Theatre
Harry Thuku Rd
Kijabe St
0 200m
St Paul's Church
Synagogue
University
University Way
To YMCA Central & YWCA, 250m
Lutheran Church
Impala Shuttle
Riverside shuttle bus 'station'
Murang'a Roundabout
Nairobi River
Monrovia St
Kenya Comfort Hotel
Jevanjee Gardens
Moktar Daddah St
Njugu La
Biashara St
River Rd
Kilome Rd
Uhuru Highway
Loita St
Koinange St
Mundi Mbingu St
Indoor Market
Jamia mosque
Closed to infidels
Moi Ave
Tom Mboya St
River Rd
Kimathi St
Lagos Rd
Nyayo Monument
Celebrates 35 years of independence
Market St
Banda St
McMillan Library
Built in 1930s
Nation Centre
Latema Rd
Taveta Rd
Kenya Comfort Suites & All Saints Cathedral
Kenyatta Ave
Nairobi Gallery
More of Murumbi African Heritage Collection.
Daily 8:30am-5:30pm; Ks1000
Post Office
Sarova Stanley Hotel & Thorn Tree Café
Standard St
Kaunda St
To bus companies
Cabral St
Accra Rd
Mau Mau Memorial
Kaunda St
City Hall
Office of the Governor
Mama Ngina St
Hilton Hotel
Holy Family Cathedral
City Hall Way
City Hall Way
Kenyatta's Mausoleum
City Square
Kenyatta Statue
Law Courts
National Archives
Mon-Fri 9:30am to 4:30pm; Sat & Sun to 4pm; Ks200.
Contains some of Murumbi African Heritage Collection
Hamilton Fountain
First president of Kenya
Jogoo House
No 34 bus to airport
Uhuru Highway
Parliament Rd
National Assembly
Parliament
Kenyatta International Convention Centre
Taifa Rd
Aga Khan Walk
Moi Ave
Harambee Ave
7th August 1998 Remembrance Garden & Visitor Centre
Site of US Embassy blown-up by Al-Qaeda in 1998
Tom Mboya St
To Wildebeest Eco Camp (15km) & Airport (18km)
Haile Selassie Ave
To Railway station & Railway Museum (nrm.co.ke; daily 8am-5pm; Ks600)

SERVICES

Banks are usually open Monday to Friday 9am-3pm, Saturday 9-11am. Foreign exchange bureaux open later, though on Saturday they, too, often close early (usually noon).

Many banks have **ATMs** (cash machines) as well, with most accepting Visa cards. Be on your guard for onlookers when withdrawing money from an ATM.

Big, bright and gleaming, the **post office** (Mon-Fri 8am-6pm, Sat 9am-noon) occupies a fairly large slice of valuable real estate at the western end of Kenyatta Avenue. Registered, recorded and normal deliveries can be made here.

WHERE TO STAY

(For details of abbreviations see box p192.) The following list of hostels and hotels is arranged with the cheapest first. Those intending to **camp** should check out Wildebeest Eco Camp (US$20, US$35 if using one of their tents), listed on p201.

River Rd remains the cheapest area in the centre but few Westerners seem to stay there these days.

In Nairobi, safety is a concern in some of the hotels, though the ones I have chosen to recommend in this book are fine.

• ***YMCA Central*** (☎ 020-272 4066/4116, 🖳 hostels.ymcakenya.org/#; State House Rd; non s/c sgl/dbl 1500/2800; s/c dorm/sgl/dbl Ks2000/3200; add Ks600 per person for half-board, Ks1000-1100 full-board). Despite the name, women, atheists and the elderly are all welcome at this friendly, secure hostel, a fair choice for those on a budget who don't fancy their chances in the hurly-burly of the River Rd area but still want to be reasonably close to town. The real clincher, however, is the pool.

• ***YWCA*** (☎ 020-802 2613, 🖳 www.ywcakenya.org/parkview-suites.php; State House Rd; sgl/dbl Ks3500/5000) As with its brother above, the YWCA is not just for young Christian women – it's open to all regardless of gender, age and faith. This one gets better online reviews than the YMCA, possibly because the rooms are actually like little apartments, with en suite shower and a small kitchen. Personally, I found it a little less friendly and lacking atmosphere but I could have just called in at the wrong time.

• ***Kenya Comfort Hotel*** (☎ 0722-608865, 🖳 kenyacomfort.com; Jevanjee Gardens; rack rates start at US$15/50/60/70 for dorm/sgl/dbl/tpl rising to US$60/70/80 sgl/dbl/tpl if you want air-con and TV; breakfast is another US$10 per person) Superbly situated just five minutes north of Kenyatta Avenue – and, more importantly, right next to where the shuttle buses to Arusha and Moshi pull in and depart, which is handy. Though it looks fairly petite, features include a sauna and steam room, internet and 95 en suite bedrooms. All in all this represents pretty good value for central Nairobi and one of the better lower mid-range choices.

Note that the hotel has a second branch, ***Kenya Comfort Suites*** (☎ 0734-608866; junction of Milimani and Ralph Bunche Rd; US$65/80/90 for sgl/dbl/tpl), with slightly bigger and better rooms and a swimming pool, though it's a 20-minute walk from the city centre in the district of Milimani. Don't get the two confused when booking online.

❑ HOTELS NEAR NAIROBI AIRPORT

Over the past few years several hotels have sprouted up within a mile or two of Jomo Kenyatta International Airport – so if you're put off from visiting the city because of its (slightly unfair) reputation for being dangerous, you'll be pleased to know that you no longer have to travel into the capital itself.

Many of the international hotel chains have places, including Four Points by Sheraton (🖳 www.marriott.com), Hilton Garden Inn (🖳 www.hilton.com) and Crown Plaza (🖳 www.ihg.com).

● ***Wildebeest Eco Camp*** (☎ 0734 770733, 💻 wildebeestecocamp.com; 151 Mokoyeti Road West, Langata; rates are US$45 in a dorm, US$110/150 sgl/dbl in cottage; tents US$70/110 sgl/dbl with shared facilities, luxury tents US$180/220/260 sgl/dbl/tpl) Simply put, this is a wonderful place. The private rooms are clean and pleasant but it's the fragrant, bird-filled tropical grounds and frog-filled pond that truly steal the show, bordered as they are by deluxe en suite safari tents that provide some of the most appealing accommodation in the capital, with cotton sheets and full electricity. There are also dorms, a campsite and a restaurant with wi-fi too. All in all it's worth both the (admittedly high) prices and the very lengthy trip out of town (it lies about 15km from the centre, or about an hour given the usual traffic).

● ***Sarova Stanley*** (☎ 0719 048000, 💻 www.sarovahotels.com/stanley-nairobi; corner of Kenyatta Avenue and Kimathi St; US$190 for s/c sgl/dbl, room only, though significant discounts are available online and the prices vary according to demand). A luxury hotel with a bit of character, the Stanley first opened its doors to the very well-heeled in 1902 – making it just a few years younger than the city itself. Edward, then Prince of Wales, Ernest Hemingway, and Hollywood's finest from Ava Gardner to Clark Gable have all rested their eminent heads on the Stanley's sumptuously stuffed pillows. Edwardian elegance still abounds, though the demands of the modern client have led to the introduction of a shopping arcade, swimming pool and gymnasium. The hotel also plays host to **Thorn Tree Café** (see column opposite).

● ***Fairmont The Norfolk*** (☎ 020-226 5000, 💻 www.fairmont.com/norfolk-hotel-nairobi; Harry Thuku Rd; room-only prices start at sgl/dbl US$240 though cheaper rates are available online) Nairobi's *other* historic hotel, and younger by two years, the Norfolk has been oozing class from its premises since it first opened its doors on Christmas Day 1904. Boasts the same facilities as the Stanley plus a fine collection of rickshaws and old tractors in the central courtyard and a more peaceful, out-of-town feel.

WHERE TO EAT AND DRINK

Kenya's cuisine is virtually indistinguishable from Tanzania's, being hearty, meaty and with an emphasis firmly on quantity rather than quality.

For cheaper and more mundane fare, there are any number of **fast-food places** around River Rd and Tom Mboya St, though be warned, 'kebab' is usually a battered sausage containing meat of unknown origin, and not the kind of kebab you'd enjoy on a Friday night after the pubs have closed back in your home country. (For that, you need to ask for a *shwarma*.)

More upmarket fast-food restaurants include ***Chicken Inn*** and ***Creamy Inn***, branches of which can be found throughout the city. None of them particularly stands out – just choose one that looks busy and friendly and you'll be fine.

Thorn Tree Café (see Sarova Stanley column opposite) is something of a Mecca for travellers. Indeed, Lonely Planet even named its online forum after this very café.

Now on its third acacia, the original idea behind planting a tree in the middle of the courtyard was so that travellers could leave messages for other travellers on its thorns. Unfortunately, trees being trees, the roots of the previous two eventually started to undermine the building itself and had to be destroyed. Furthermore, Health & Safety has intervened and the tree is now encircled by noticeboards where you pin your messages – which reduces both the romance and indeed the *raison d'être* of the tree somewhat. And when I looked, few of the messages were by travellers, for travellers, but were mainly announcements of people's birthdays and even reviews of the restaurant itself. The fact that they were all laminated too, suggests that the hotel has strict control over what goes up there these days. All most disappointing. Anyway, enough moaning: the food here is great, particularly for a post-climb breakfast feed-up, though be prepared to pay through the nose for the privilege.

MOVING ON – TO KILIMANJARO

By air

Precision Air (🖳 precisionairtz.com) fly at least twice daily each way directly between Nairobi and Kilimanjaro International; they are pretty much the only reliable operator between the two airports at this time. **To get to Nairobi International Airport**, take a City Hoppa No 34 bus which leaves from virtually opposite the Hilton Hotel. Leave plenty of time as this service frequently gets snarled in heavy traffic. Alternatively, a taxi will cost you about US$30-40.

By coach or shuttle bus

Though there are **coach** operators willing to take you to Arusha, few can be recommended without hesitation. Far more convenient for most people are the **shuttle buses**. There are two main companies operating shuttles to Arusha (and several smaller, newer ones). **Riverside** (☎ 0725-999121, 🖳 www.riverside-shuttle.com), on the first floor of Lagos House, Monrovia St, right on Jevanjee Gardens, is the most established. Nearly next door is **Impala Shuttle** (☎ 0727-377771, 🖳 www.impala shuttles.com). At the time of writing both were advertising just one service a day, at 8am (which continues on to Moshi); the 2pm service has yet to be revived since Covid, though as it used to arrive in Arusha after dark, it was never the best option. The fare for non-residents is US$25 to Arusha, US$35 to Moshi.

Crossing the border between Kenya and Tanzania

The drive between Nairobi and Arusha is fascinating, not least because you may find yourself sharing the road with camels, zebras, impalas, giraffes and Maasai tribesmen on bikes. Despite the chaos of hawkers, warriors and travellers that surrounds the **Namanga crossing**, the border formalities are straightforward. Laborious, but straightforward. They've recently built what they call a one-stop border point. The idea is that you enter into the building on one side, and by the time you emerge the other side you have done all the bureaucracy necessary to cross between the two countries. Which sounds great in theory but in practice, at the time of research, was incredibly slow, and a process that used to take as little as ten minutes now takes two hours.

The process within this one-stop border point is as follows. The first thing to do is unload all your luggage from your vehicle and take into the building with you. Having passed through the X-ray machine at the entrance, visit the first window on your right to show your yellow fever certificate (and Covid certificate if that is still necessary) and pick up a **health declaration form**. Fill this in while you wait for an interminably long time in the queue at the next window, where you get your **Kenyan exit stamp**. That done, shuffle to the next set of windows where you can show your health declaration form and pick up your **Tanzanian visa** (US$50 cash only) and entry stamp.

After all that, you're ready to rejoin your vehicle and head to Arusha. There's an **ATM** just after passport control (although it charges for withdrawals) and a money-changer in a shack just beyond that, its signboard displaying the kind of lousy rates that you find only at borders. Don't change anything if you don't have to, for even those who have to catch one of the **dalla dallas to Arusha** from here may be able to pay in Kenyan shillings (the Tanzanian shilling price is Ts7000).

If traffic is on your side, roadworks are few and the border process runs smoothly, the whole journey from Nairobi to Arusha will take six hours. So count on it taking eight. And add a couple of hours on top if you're heading to Moshi.

ARUSHA, MOSHI & MARANGU

6

Kilimanjaro International Airport

Is Kilimanjaro the only mountain to have its own international airport? The airport is situated roughly equidistant between Moshi (43km away) and Arusha (50km away), just under 6km to the south of the main road running between the two.

ARRIVAL AND DEPARTURE

Arriving

Arriving is straightforward. The terminal is small and you'll instantly be ushered into Immigration and Passport Control where you fill out a blue arrival form. If you arrived from a country where yellow fever is prevalent – even if you were only changing planes there – you will probably have your **yellow fever certificate** (see p120) checked too. Fail to have it and you may have to pay something in the region of US$20-50 and you could be given the jab there; or you could, in theory, be refused entry into the country altogether (though I've never heard of that actually happening).

The immigration formalities are usually easily negotiated, especially as Kilimanjaro is also one of only four places in the country where you can pick up a visa on arrival (see pp119-20). Once you've made your way through passport control and having collected your baggage, the only thing now separating you from Tanzania is customs from which, safely negotiated, you emerge into the outside world. There is an ATM in its own separate booth to your right outside the hall though they charge for withdrawals. Again, if you can wait until you get into town there are ATMs that don't charge a fee (see p122).

To get to Moshi or Arusha, about 40 or 50 minutes away respectively, costs US$50 in a taxi (locals pay around US$35 but I've not heard of a tourist paying this price) or you may be lucky enough to get a shuttle bus depending on which airline you flew in with: Precision Air/Kenya Airways operate their own shuttle service (Ts10,000) for internal flights, as do Air Tanzania for their services between Kilimanjaro Airport and Zanzibar, Dar es Salaam, Entebbe and Mwanza. Fly in with any other airline, however, such as KLM, Ethiopian, Qatar or Turkish, and if you don't already have a transfer arranged, you'll have to take a taxi, there being no public transport to and from the airport.

Departing

Leaving Tanzania, things are laborious but simple. Before you're even allowed in the terminal building you have to pass your bags, belts and shoes through an X-ray machine. Successfully negotiate that and you'll be faced by a bank of check-in desks but before you can even think of approaching them you'll be guided to a makeshift security desk where your passport will be scrutinised by some friendly official. While waiting in the queue for this it's probably worth picking up one of the **exit forms** dotted around the hall – it will save you time later on.

Boarding passes collected and bags checked in, from there you turn right to Passport Control where you hand over the white form. You may be asked to use the fingerprint scan again, presumably to make sure you're leaving with exactly the same fingers that you arrived with.

Don't be in too much of a hurry to get through to your flight's departure lounge for there's even less to do there. Instead, peruse the small string of souvenir shops, have a coffee from the café and check your email using the airport's free wi-fi.

❑ ARUSHA VERSUS MOSHI – WHERE SHOULD YOU BASE YOURSELF?

For most people, this question is moot, as you'll quite rightly choose your trekking company first before anything else and they, in turn, will decide where you're going to stay (which is nearly always in the same town as their offices).

And it's true that, of the two, Moshi is the more pleasant option and if you are in Tanzania just for Kilimanjaro it's no contest.

But if you're going on safari afterwards around the parks of the Northern Circuit (in particular Manyara, Tarangire, Ngorongoro and Serengeti), there's a strong case to be made that Arusha is actually the superior base. Why? Well, Arusha is two hours nearer to those parks than Moshi. Which means that you get two hours more looking at the wildlife on your first day in one of those parks than if you were based in Moshi. And yes, it's true that those who are based in Moshi have, by the same reasoning, more time to spend on Kili. But the fact is that you'll still do the same amount of walking on the first day wherever you're based and whatever time you start your mountain hike, so it doesn't really matter if you're closer to the mountain.

So if you can't decide between two companies, but one is based in Moshi and one in Arusha, maybe that can be the deciding factor: choose the Arusha-based company if you're going on safari, but Moshi if you're not.

Arusha

Arusha may only be Tanzania's third largest city (after Dar and Mwanza) but it is, nevertheless, one of considerable consequence. During the days of British rule, Arusha was considered the *symbolic* halfway point between Cairo and Cape Town – the two termini of the old British Empire in Africa. (It should be noted, by the way, that the *actual* midpoint between Cape Town and Cairo lies not here but somewhere in central Congo.) It was also in Arusha that Britain officially gave Tanzania its independence – and it maintains a central role in African affairs today. It is, for example, the home of the brand-new Headquarters of the East African Community – a union between Tanzania, Kenya, Rwanda, Burundi and Uganda that was originally forged in the '70s and has been revived. It is also the venue for sorting out issues from all over Africa – including the Tanzanian-brokered peace talks on Burundi and, most famously, the Rwanda War Crimes Tribunal in Arusha International Conference Centre (AICC), which finished in 2015.

And there's no sign of Arusha's momentum ending any time soon as an enormous amount of investment, much of it from China, floods the city, leading to the construction of several spanking-new high rises and some much-needed road-improvement schemes. This has led to an atmosphere of excitement – and a real sense that this is a city that's going places. Arusha can also boast some of the best tourist amenities in the country, a chaotic and occasionally fascinating central market and several pretty quarters filled with jacaranda and bougainvillea blossoms (not to mention the occasional wooded grove where vervet monkeys and silver-cheeked hornbills can still be spotted crashing and calling through the branches). However, despite these attractions, with the call of the wild from Kilimanjaro, Ngorongoro and the Serengeti beckoning, it's a rare tourist who stays long enough to savour them.

Arusha Monument

WHAT TO SEE AND DO

Very little is the short answer. There are a couple of museums. By **Arusha Monument** there's **Arusha Declaration Museum** (daily 9am-5pm; Ts12,000) that could conceivably be worth visiting – but only if you're absolutely sure you've finished preparing for your trek, have written all your postcards, bought all your souvenirs, sent all your emails, cut all your toenails and done all your laundry. Consisting in the main of a few photos and a number of traditional tools and weapons, I suppose some might find this place provides a useful though patchy précis of Tanzanian history from palaeolithic times to the death of Tanzania's first president, Julius Nyerere, and the authorities are to be commended for trying. Overall it's worthy, if not exactly worthwhile.

The **Natural History Museum** (Mon-Fri 9am-6pm, Sat & Sun 9.30am-6pm) is better, thanks in large part to the photos of local wildlife by Swedish ex-pat Dick Persson. The photos are, in general, very good and tend to concentrate on the more 'unsung' creatures of Tanzania – the frogs, otters, lizards and hyraxes – and the less-visited parts of the country. Add to this a detailed run-down of the history of the Boma and overall this museum provides a fairly diverting way to spend an hour or so, though the entrance fee of Ts12,000 (or US$6) is a bit steep.

The **African Cultural Heritage Complex** (Mon-Sat 9.30am-5pm, Sun 9.30am-2pm; free) lies to the west of town on the way to Arusha Airport. The most interesting thing about the first, smaller building is the roof, which has been designed to resemble the Kibo summit. Inside, however, you'll find little more than a market for woodcarvings and while there's no denying the artistry that's gone into the sculptures on sale, the designs themselves may be a bit too elaborate to appeal to Western tastes. Behind it are more units selling fine quality souvenirs and gifts, though at US$100 for a cushion cover this is definitely stuff that you'd buy only for people you actually care about.

This place, however, has been rather overshadowed by the huge construction next-door, the design of which has been based on those potent African symbols: the spear, the shield and the drum. The reason for these architectural inspirations can be found inside, where a spiral ramp leads you through gallery after gallery of African art, including some fantastic antique bronze sculptures from Benin and wooden totems from all over West Africa on the lower ground floor. Most of the other galleries contain more modern exhibits, largely paintings and photos of various African scenes.

As all the exhibits (including the antiques) are for sale, this giant art gallery – said to be the largest in Africa – could be seen as little more than an upmarket version of the souvenir shop next door. But I think a gentle meander around is a great way of whiling away an hour or so; some of the art is great; and you don't, of course, get any hassle from vendors.

With such a dearth of formal attractions in town, perhaps the most educational and entertaining thing you can do in Arusha is visit a **football game** at the **stadium** to the north of the bus station; it will teach you more about Tanzanians (or at least the male half of the population) and what makes them tick than any papier-maché diorama or reconstructed Maasai dwelling. Some of the games are rather low-key but attend a big league match and you're in for a treat.

ARRIVAL

By air

Arusha Airport (or 'the little airport' as it's commonly called locally to distinguish it from Kilimanjaro International) lies to the west of the city and serves internal flights only. Currently under renovation, there aren't many facilities here and much of the official stuff – the checking-in etc – is done under temporary awnings.

A taxi into town will set you back about Ts20,000 (though they'll ask for Ts30,000), or you can walk or catch a *boda boda* (motorbike taxi; Ts500-1000) to the main junction (about one hot, dusty kilometre) and wait for a dalla-dalla to pass by (Ts600); you shouldn't have to wait more than a minute or two.

Not to be confused with Arusha Airport, **Kilimanjaro International Airport** (for details, see p203) lies to the other (eastern) side of town, 44km along and 6km to the south of the road to Moshi. A taxi (US$50; 1hr) is the only realistic way of getting from the airport to Arusha, unless you're lucky enough to arrive with an airline that arranges a shuttle; or, if you're daft enough, hitch to the main Arusha–Moshi road and catch a Coaster bus (Ts2000).

For details on **getting to the airports** see the box p222.

By bus

Arriving in Arusha by **public bus**, expect to be dumped (sometimes literally) at the bus station at the southern end of Colonel Middleton Rd.

If you reach Arusha by **shuttle bus**, on the other hand, tell the driver where you wish to jump out in the town centre and he should drop you there; if not, the chances are you'll be dropped off at the terminal on Simeon Rd just south of the Gran Meliá Hotel, or a little further south if you took the Impala shuttle. From here you'll have to catch a cab or walk to your destination.

ORIENTATION & GETTING AROUND

Arusha is bisected by the **Goliondoi River Valley**, a narrow and shallow dip in the town's topography. The division is more than just geographical: to the west is downtown, the busier, noisier and more fun part of Arusha, where most of the cheap lodgings can be found. To the east of the valley lies the tourist centre, where most hotels, safari companies and better restaurants are located. This eastern section is further divided by a second river, the **Themi**, that runs along the back of such major landmarks as Arusha Hotel and the AICC.

Arusha is not a big place, most things are within walking distance of each other and **getting around** is not a major hassle, though to get from one half of town to the other it's a good idea to take a **dalla-dalla**; they charge Ts500 for short trips around town or Ts600-700 for destinations further afield. **Taxis** are distinguishable by their white number plates (other vehicles have yellow ones); they charge around Ts5000 for a trip within the town centre.

Thanks to a flood of cheap motorbikes from Asia there's a two-wheeled alternative to the taxi. **Boda boda**, or **Toyo** (also very commonly called '**piki piki**'), is the local term for these motorbike taxis; there's no arguing that they are both cheap (Ts10,000 will get you from Arusha all the way to Usa River) and the best form of transport for slicing through the traffic. Before hopping eagerly onto one, however, bear in mind that there's already a special wing at Meru Hospital devoted just to victims of Toyo accidents – drivers, passengers and bystanders – with passengers by far and away the largest contingent, probably because few if any boda boda drivers supply their customers with a crash helmet. As with taxis, the drivers will come and find you, though they can usually be found at the main road junctions.

SERVICES

Tourist information

The tourist information office (Mon-Fri 8am-4pm, Sat 8.30am-1pm) is on Boma Rd. Full of brochures, the office is not wonderful but it is the best unbiased source of information on the city and the safari circuit. They keep a list of licensed tour agencies in both Moshi and Arusha (now numbering over 1100!), have a list of local markets that you can visit and even have a rundown of bus, train and boat services from Tanzania to East African destinations. They don't have much useful info on Kilimanjaro but, in spite of this, it's still the best tourist office in East Africa.

Banks and changing money

There are **ATMs** all over the city, particularly towards the eastern end of Sokoine, down from the Clock Tower, and in the TFA Complex, where you'll find most banks represented. For the banks that aren't charging commission for withdrawals from their ATMs, the only one I could find was Ecobank, who have an ATM in the parking lot at the TFA, as well as in Mafao House next to Air Tanzania near the Clock Tower.

As for changing money, the **money changers** are far more efficient than the banks. The most established are Kadoo, with branches at the TFA and on Sokoine south of the Clock Tower.

Communications

The **post office** (PO; Mon-Fri 8am-4.30pm, Sat 9am-noon) is by the Clock Tower, hidden away behind the electronic advertising board. There's a second branch, Meru Post Office (Mon-Fri 8am-1pm & 2-4.30pm, Sat 9am-noon), at the western end of Sokoine near the backpacker hotels.

If you've brought your mobile (cell) **phone** it should work though it'll be expensive to make a call or send a message. See my advice about buying a local SIM card (p125) and remember you can always use Skype/WhatsApp/Zoom and other free internet-based communication services.

Most hotels offer free **wi-fi** to their guests. Of the wi-fi services provided by the cafés and restaurants, ***Fifi's*** (see p218) and, at the other end of town, ***Msumbi Coffee*** in the TFA (see opposite), seem to be the most reliable and popular.

Airline offices

Several airlines have closed their offices in Arusha over the past few years, including

❑ DANGERS AND ANNOYANCES IN ARUSHA

The hassle from **flycatchers** (ie touts who approach you in the streets trying to sell treks and safaris) seems to be growing again. They have a job to do and a need to earn money like the rest of us, but there's no doubting how tiring it is dealing with them on such a frequent basis, and many are the tourists who scuttle back to the safety of their hotel sooner than they anticipated. If – or rather, *when* – you are hassled just be polite but firm, don't stop walking and they soon get the message. I always find that a friendly smile goes a long way too.

Pickpocketing is rare but does happen, particularly in those busy places such as the bus station and central market. Keep any valuables out of sight and safely tucked away, preferably in the safe back at the hotel. If you have to bring them with you use a money-belt and keep a close eye on everything. This is particularly true if someone does something unusual – tugs at your arm or even spits at you – as this maybe a distraction technique while his partner steals from you.

As for potential dangers, well **it's always hazardous stepping out in Arusha after dark**. Between 7 and 9pm, while the streets are still fairly busy, you should be OK, as long as you stick to the main streets where people are still milling about – and assuming those streets are well lit. But don't even think about going out after dusk east of the Themi River (ie east of Arusha Hotel). Dark, quiet, and full of hotels where Westerners are staying, if I were a mugger this is where I would hang out. To be safe, the golden rule you should follow is that once the sun disappears, take a cab. The extra expense is something you'll quickly forget; get attacked, however, and that is something that will stay with you forever.

Qatar Airways, Turkish Airlines and KLM. Instead they are represented by **Voyage** (☎ 0682-666006; Mon-Fri 9am-5pm, Sat to 1pm), on the ground floor of Ngorongoro Tourism Center.

• **Air Excel** Arusha Airport (☎ 0739-102546, 🖳 airexcelonline.com; Mon-Fri 8.30am-1pm & 2-5pm, Sat 8.30am-1pm). The offices sit in the big blue-roofed building at the far end of the parking lot.

• **Air Tanzania** NSSSF Mafao House, Old Moshi Rd (☎ 027-252 0177, 🖳 www.airtanzania.co.tz; Mon-Fri 8am-1pm & 2-5pm; Sat & Sun 9am-1pm) Air Tanzania operate just one flight from Arusha Airport, to Zanzibar via Dar, a service that operates six times per week (daily except Fri). Their timetable from Kilimanjaro Airport is more extensive, with flights to Dar, Zanzibar, Mwanza and Entebbe. They also operate a shuttle service to take passengers to and from Kili airport.

• **Auric Air** Arusha Airport (🖳 auricair.com; Mon-Fri 8.30am-5pm, Sat to 1pm) One of several companies flying small planes to mainly tourist destinations, in this case from Arusha Airport to Serengeti, Dar, Zanzibar and Dodoma, as well as Kigali (Rwanda) and Entebbe (Uganda).

• **Ethiopian Air** Boma Rd (🖳 ethiopianairlines.com; Mon-Fri 8.30am-1pm & 2–5pm, Sat 8.30am-1pm).

• **Flightlink** Arusha Airport (☎ 0689 141356, 🖳 www.flightlink.co.tz; Mon-Fri 8-5pm, Sat 8am-5pm).

• **Kenya Airways** 1st floor, Ngorongoro Tourist Center, Ngorongoro Roundabout (🖳 www.kenya-airways.com; Mon-Fri 8am-5pm, Sat 9am-1pm).

• **Precision Air** 1st floor, Ngorongoro Tourist Center, Ngorongoro Roundabout (☎ 0784 402026, 🖳 precisionairtz.com; Mon-Fri 8am-5pm, Sat 9am-1pm).

• **Regional Air** Sable Square Shopping Village, beyond Arusha Airport (🖳 regionaltanzania.com). Tanzanian affiliate of AirKenya and, as with Auric (see above) and Coastal (🖳 coastal.co.tz), a useful company to contact if you want to fly to one of the parks on the Northern Circuit, as well as Dar and Zanzibar.

• **RwandAir** On the first floor of the NIC building on Boma Rd, opposite Africafé (🖳 rwandair.com; Mon-Fri 8am-5pm, Sat 9am-1pm).

Shopping

You can get most things in Arusha; it's just a question of knowing where to look. Some of the shops seem to have been deliberately set up with tourists and ex-pats in mind, particularly those at the **TFA complex** at the western end of Sokoine, where you'll find **TSM Outdoor Adventure**, a well-stocked camping/trekking shop, and one of the better English-language bookshops in the city (see below); and even a **massage** parlour, **Ai Care** (☎ 0629 141981; Ts100,000 for an hour's Swedish deep tissue and Ts126,000 for a hot-stone massage). These arcades may lack charm and feel a little sterile; but that's probably the point of them, and if you're missing home these places are unrivalled in Arusha.

• **Books** The two branches of chaotic **Kase Bookshop** (Mon-Fri 9am-5.30pm, Sat 8am-2pm), on Boma Rd and to the west of the Clock Tower, are long established and convenient. At the TFA, **A Novel Idea** (Mon-Sat 9am-5.30pm), an offshoot of the one in Dar, has perhaps the best selection.

• **Electrical goods/cameras Benson & Co**, now occupying almost an entire block on Sokoine, should be your first port of call for electrical goods, camera batteries, repairs and so forth. Note, however, that they're not cheap! Across the road is their technical department where they can unlock phones – again, for a hefty fee.

• **Pharmacy Moona's** (Mon-Fri 8.45am-5.30pm, Sat 8.45am-2pm) lies near the eastern end of Sokoine, a few hundred metres down from the Clock Tower. The staff speak good English. Towards the western end of Sokoine there's **Belleview Pharmacy** (Mon-Fri 8.30am-5pm, Sat 9am-2pm, Sun 10.30am-12.30pm) which, unusually, is open for a couple of hours on Sunday.

• **Souvenirs** You won't have any trouble finding souvenirs in Arusha – indeed, often they come and find you. *(cont'd on p212)*

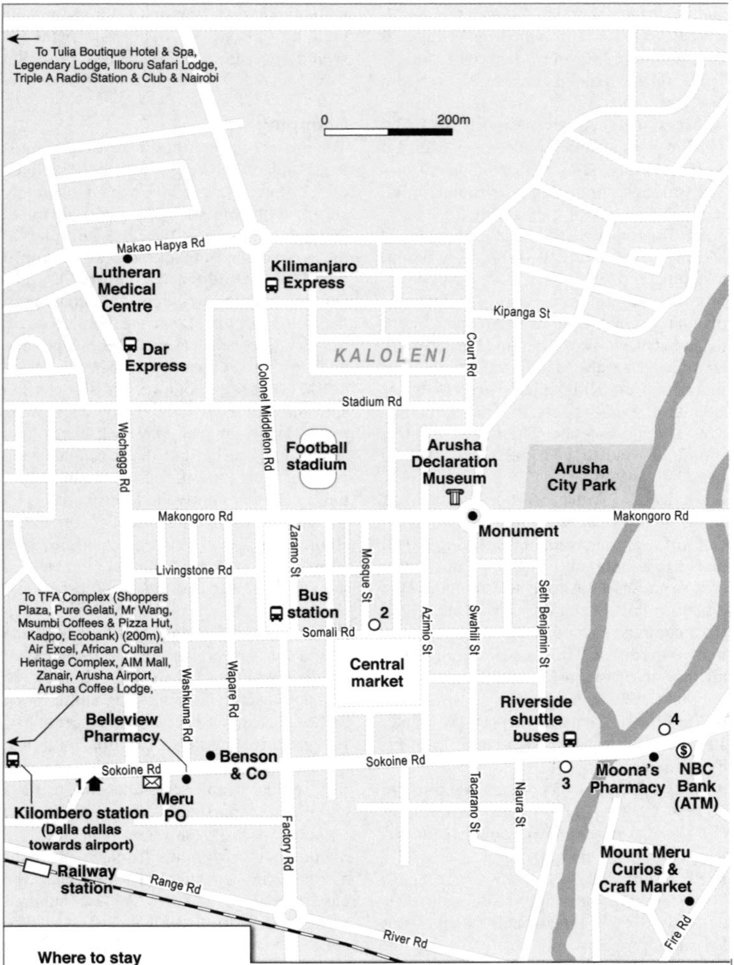

Where to stay

1 Arusha Backpackers
7 Four Points by Sheraton Arusha, The Arusha Hotel
12 Palace Hotel Arusha
13 New Safari Hotel
14 Mount Meru Hotel
17 Tulia Retreat Hotel & Spa
19 Kibo Palace
20 The African Tulip

Where to eat and drink

2 Khan's
3 Green Hut House of Burgers
4 Serengeti Coffee House
5 Fifi's
6 Raptor Coffee Bar
8 Themi Living Garden
9 Coffee Culture
10 Kitamu Coffee
11 Africafé
15 George's Tavern
16 Spices & Herbs
18 Flame Tree
21 Amber
22 Picasso Café

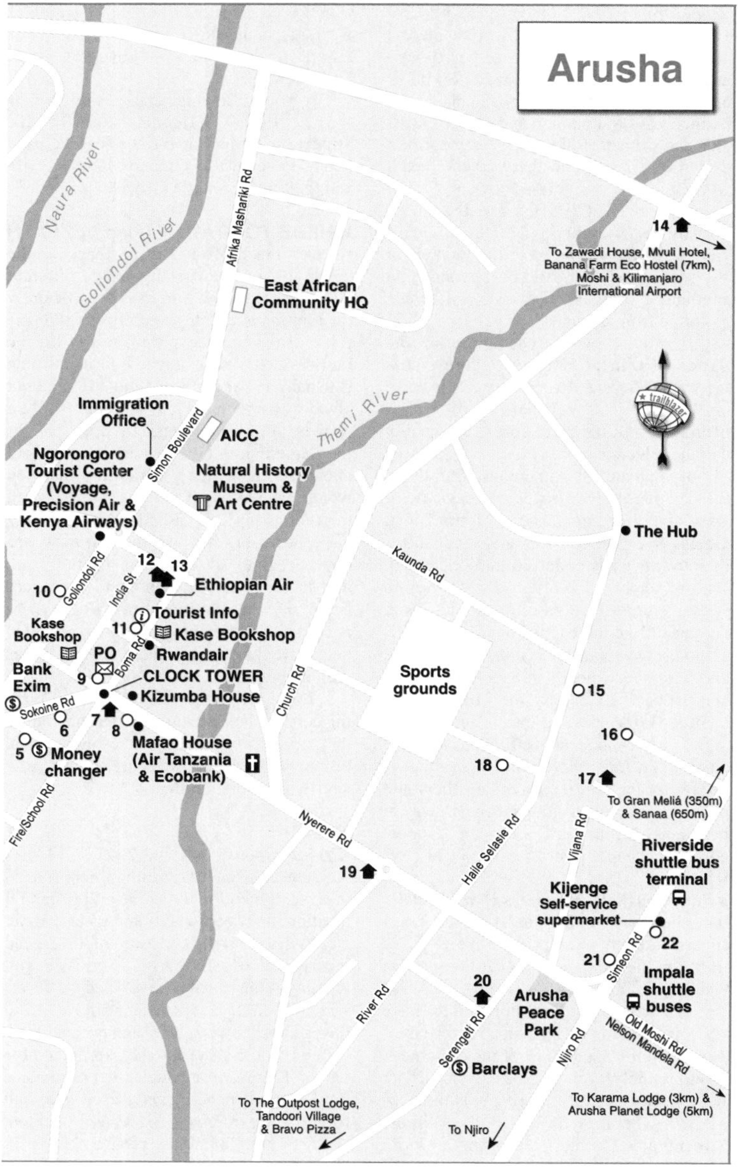
Arusha
Naura River
Goliondoi River
Afrika Mashariki Rd
East African Community HQ
14
To Zawadi House, Mvuli Hotel, Banana Farm Eco Hostel (7km), Moshi & Kilimanjaro International Airport
Themi River
Immigration Office
Simon Boulevard
AICC
Natural History Museum & Art Centre
Ngorongoro Tourist Center (Voyage, Precision Air & Kenya Airways)
The Hub
Kaunda Rd
12
13
Ethiopian Air
10
Goliondoi Rd
India St
Tourist Info
Kase Bookshop
11
Kase Bookshop
Rwandair
PO
Boma Rd
Bank Exim
9
CLOCK TOWER
Sports grounds
15
Sokoine Rd
Kizumba House
Church Rd
6
7
8
16
5
Money changer
Mafao House (Air Tanzania & Ecobank)
18
17
To Gran Meliá (350m) & Sanaa (650m)
Fire/School Rd
Nyerere Rd
Haile Selasie Rd
Vijana Rd
Riverside shuttle bus terminal
19
Kijenge Self-service supermarket
22
21
Simeon Rd
Impala shuttle buses
20
Arusha Peace Park
River Rd
Serengeti Rd
Njiro Rd
Old Moshi Rd/ Nelson Mandela Rd
Barclays
To The Outpost Lodge, Tandoori Village & Bravo Pizza
To Njiro
To Karama Lodge (3km) & Arusha Planet Lodge (5km)

(cont'd from p209) Some of the stuff is of a poor quality, however. The first place I advise you to go – in fact urge you to go – is **Sanaa** (🖳 www.sanaa.co.tz), a few doors up from Gran Meliá Hotel. Sanaa is the brainchild of Mama Sam and all the craftsmen and women at Sanaa have some sort of disability. There are leatherworkers, metalworkers, weavers, glass-blowers, seamstresses – the list goes on and the stuff's actually really rather good. So do make your way here if you're in the market for any sort of souvenir. And if you can't find anything, treat yourself to a consoling cup of coffee from the café (see p219).

It is also worth checking out the **African Cultural Heritage Complex** (on the way to Arusha Airport. Yes it's incredibly 'touristy', and yes some of it is *waaay* overpriced but the pieces are good quality and the selection is vast.

If you can't be bothered to head there, the best place *in town* for an overview of what's on offer can be had at **Mount Meru Curios & Crafts Market**, a vast collection of souvenir stalls collected into one handy site on School Rd (aka Fire Rd, as the fire station is at the bottom of the street) about 300m south of the Clock Tower.

Manage to make it out of here alive and with some money still in your pocket and perhaps you can try the **Museum Art Centre** (Fri-Wed 9am-6pm, Thur to midnight), adjacent to and affiliated with the Natural History Museum. Here about a dozen painters, dressmakers, jewellers and other craftsmen and women beaver away in little huts. All the stuff is for sale, supposedly at a cheaper price than if bought elsewhere.

• **Supermarkets Shoppers Plaza** (usually just shortened to Shoppers) is the latest supermarket to attempt to make a go of things in the TFA Complex, at the western end of Sokoine.

As with previous stores that have occupied this space, it's not the cheapest grocery in town and most of the customers, unsurprisingly, are ex-pats. Even further west, next to Cultural Heritage, is the AIM Mall, where you'll find **Village Supermarket** (daily 7.30am-7.30pm), which is not dissimilar but feels even more Western, and you'll find a lot of US/European food brands here that you won't find elsewhere.

If you're staying at the other end of town, little **Kijenge Self-Service Supermarket** on Simeon Rd is at the back of the lot that also contains Picasso Café and the Impala Shuttle Office.

WHERE TO STAY [map pp210-11]

As with much of the rest of Tanzania, the hotels in Arusha officially charge different rates for locals and foreigners, particularly for mid-range and high-end hotels. For the prices listed below, I have opted to list the **non-residents' rate** only; the residents' rate is usually lower by 5% or more though not always; sometimes it's just the shilling equivalent of the non-resident price.

Note that in previous editions I talked about the 'rack rate', ie the rate that you would have to pay if you just turned up on their doorstep and asked to stay. These days, however, they assume that everyone books online, so for many of the more upmarket hotels you won't find any prices listed anywhere at reception. Where there isn't a rack rate the prices I have listed below are the ones I found online. All rates include breakfast.

Do check online sites such as 🖳 booking.com, 🖳 hotels.com or 🖳 airbnb.com as they may advertise lower rates and special offers. I have divided the hotels into approximate price order.

Hostels

Kizumba House (☎ 0767 264373, 🖳 sites.google.com/view/kizumbahouse/home) deserves a mention for its incredibly central location, its cheerful staff and its casual but clean style. Set in a cluster of tin-roofed rondavels overlooking Themi River, Kizumba consists of 4- and 5-bed s/c dorms with mosquito nets, towels, pillow, (thin) duvets, hot showers, wi-fi and even slippers (!), and at just US$10pp they are incredible value. There are a couple of twin rooms (US$30-40 depending on season; s/c) and triple/family rooms (US$52-54; s/c) too. An enormous breakfast is also thrown in (not literally) at their excellent bar-restaurant, ***Cap-ellas***. All in all, it's really great value and my current favourite in this price bracket.

Curiously, the most popular budget option for Arusha is not actually within the city centre but a few miles east of it. Set amongst banana groves in the foothills of Mount Meru is a proper travellers' place, the colourfully decorated ***Banana Farm Eco Hostel*** (☎ 0753-583958, 💻 bananafarm.eco). The hostel offers free tours around the banana farms as well as hikes to local waterfalls, though most residents seem to prefer lazing the day away on one of the hostel's many hammocks and swings. The rooms are charming but basic and don't come with nets, but there is wi-fi in the central courtyard. Emphasising its green credentials, the hostel also keeps half a dozen cows for their milk and bio-gas. Prices are sgl/dbl/tpl US$11/18-25/25-30. The place is beloved by volunteers, who tend to have a proprietorial attitude towards the place (ie, they act like they own it), so book ahead as it's very popular.

Back in town, the long-standing ***Arusha Backpackers*** (can book through online agencies such as 💻 booking.com) is still, well, standing, in its less-than-ideal location by a petrol station forecourt on Sokoine. (Invest in some heavy-duty earplugs for your best chance of sleeping beyond dawn.) It's not a bad place, with rooms (none self-contained) meticulously cleaned daily and the showers spotless, and there's hot water in the taps too. There's also wi-fi, though the connection is patchy at best and confined to the restaurant.

They also throw in a reasonable buffet breakfast in their charming rooftop café, where you can feast on muesli, toast and fruit while your eyes feast on great views over the city towards Meru. It remains good value with rates for B&B beginning at just US$9pp for a spot in a 4-bed dorm or US$8-12/18-22/27-36 sgl/dbl/tpl (the higher prices are for the rooms with windows; note that a small single is cheaper than a bed in a dorm).

Lower price hotels: US$70-120 for a double (high season price)

My favourite in this section is ***The Outpost Lodge*** (☎ 0754-318 523, 💻 outpost-lodge.com; off map p212 to the south-east) which lies down Serengeti Rd, a lane so exclusive that Arusha's usual noise of traffic and touts is replaced by the soothing sound of people brushing the dust from the street. Popular with tour groups. The Outpost has its own wi-fi (communal areas only) and laundry service and a lovely lounge area kitted out, as with the rooms, in simple but relaxed, comfy style. Hidden among the lush overgrown garden are 28 self-contained rooms, each with TV, nets and fans, and there's a small pool and attractive bar/restaurant area. B&B here costs US$50/70/87 s/c sgl/db/tpl; very good value and a reliably great hotel.

Tulia Boutique Hotel & Spa (☎ 0755-700001, 💻 tuliahotelandspa.com), north of town on the way to Nairobi, is popular with a couple of trekking and safari companies. Style-wise, the 23 comfortable rooms with wi-fi, fan (but no mosquito net) are definitely designed to appeal to well-heeled Tanzanians rather than *mzungu*, but despite this the place is often buzzing with tourists too. Price-wise, their rack rates are sgl/dbl/tpl US$95/110/140.

❑ ABBREVIATIONS

Throughout this book I have used the following abbreviations when writing about accommodation: **pp** means per person; **s/c** is short for self-contained, a local term meaning that the room comes with a bathroom (ie the room is en suite or a bathroom is attached); while **sgl/dbl/tpl** means single/double/triple rooms.

So, for example, where I have written 's/c sgl/dbl/tpl US$35/40/45', I mean that a self-contained single room costs US$35 per night, a self-contained double costs US$40 and a self-contained triple costs US$45.

The hotel has now spawned a smaller, prettier sister. ***The Tulia Retreat Hotel and Spa*** (☎ 0753-700001, 🖳 tulia-retreat-hotel-spa.business.site) on the other side of town among the African embassies on Vijana Lane. More suited to Western tastes, there's a nice pool and dining area but do try to avoid the rooms adjacent to them, as they can get particularly noisy. Rates-wise, they're fair at US$100/120/150 for sgl/dbl/tpl.

Mvuli Hotel (☎ 0757-848633, 🖳 mvulihotels.co.tz; sgl/dbl/tpl US$58/73/106) and ***Zawadi House*** (☎ 0767-500852, 🖳 zawadihouse.com; sgl/dbl/tpl US$90/110/130) are two places set in lush gardens to the north-east of Arusha, but within the city boundaries, that surprise you with the quality of their accommodation given the reasonable rates they charge. Both can be very quiet, but what they sometimes lack in atmosphere they more than make up for in the comfort of their high-spec rooms – and it does mean you get the pool to yourself.

Mid-range hotels: US$120-160 for a double (high season price)

In the dusty suburbs north of town stand some lovely brick and thatch rondavels built round a huge pool (the most impressive in the Arusha region, in my opinion). ***Ilboru Safari Lodge*** (☎ 0784-270357, 🖳 ilborusafarilodge.com; off map to the north-west) is a great place. Each rondavel is divided into two rooms that each come with fan and nets; there is wi-fi by the pool and in reception, while the upstairs restaurant has a large menu. All in all, very impressive, my only slight concern being that at the time of research rumours were circulating that the Dutch manager, who has done so much to make this place so appealing, was due to move on. Prices are sgl/dbl/tpl US$78.50-114.50/113-156/162-210 depending on season.

Karama Lodge (☎ 0754-475188, 🖳 karama-lodge.com) lies 3km south-east of town along Old Moshi Rd/Nelson Mandela Rd. An unusual lodge, the Karama is tucked quietly on a hillside facing away from Arusha; it boasts 22 stylish en suite rooms housed in log cabins on stilts, with views of Meru from many. A sauna, pool, massage and yoga room complete the facilities. Rates start as low as sgl/dbl/tpl US$83/122/152 in low season, rising to US$111/149/215 in the high season. While the place undoubtedly has its charms, I do have a couple of concerns: firstly, the neighbourhood dogs are notoriously loud and frequently spoil what is otherwise a very tranquil location with their all-night barking; and secondly, this place does seem to change management on a fairly regular basis, which leads to an inconsistent quality of service – so it's a good idea to check online first before booking to see what the latest reviews say.

A couple of kilometres further along Old Moshi Rd/Nelson Mandela Rd is ***Arusha Planet Lodge*** (☎ 0686-141670, 🖳 planet-lodges.com/arusha-planet-lodge/) which is maturing nicely. I still think the concrete 'bandas' look a little plain but readers really like this place and besides, any shortfall in the exterior's appearance is more than offset both by the comfort of the interior, for each have air-con, television, phone and the hottest showers in town (which are just lovely after a Kili trek). The service, too, is faultless, and the pool inviting. Rates are sgl/dbl/tpl US$70-111/96-135/126-195 depending on the season.

Expensive hotels: US$160 and above for a double (high season price)

There are few more potent symbols of the upturns in Arusha's fortunes – and the massive investment pouring in from China – than that bloody great erection known as ***Palace Hotel Arusha*** (☎ 027-554 5800, 🖳 palacehotelarusha.com), a giant glass-and-steel monolith that reaches skywards, dazzling in the African sunlight. I hardly need tell you that the rooms within are all self-contained and have every sort of modern convenience, from wi-fi to air-con, satellite TV and safe deposit box. Price-wise it's not as eye-watering as one might expect, with sgl/dbl US$145-250/155-260 per room, rising to US$400/420 for the suites.

Across the golf course, ***Mount Meru Hotel*** (☎ 027-297 0256, 🖳 mountmeru hotel.co.tz) used to be the Holiday Inn

❑ ACCOMMODATION AROUND ARUSHA

Whilst I have spent pages describing the accommodation in Arusha, the fact of the matter is that most of you will have booked your trek before you arrive and your agency in turn will have arranged your hotel; and it's more than likely that this accommodation won't even be in Arusha but outside it, where several swish, smart and salubrious lodges are situated, surviving on the patronage of foreign travel companies and their local agents. It's hard to criticise these places except that they do tend to be in the middle of nowhere.

Arusha Coffee Lodge (☎ 254-730-127000, 💻 elewanacollection.com/arusha-coffee-lodge/at-a-glance) consists of 30 luxury chalets (or 'plantation houses') that are just gorgeous. Unlike the other hotels in this section, the Lodge lies towards the local airport. The private chalets on the plantation are served by a pool and they also offer a massage service. Another thing in its favour is its lovely café, just by reception. Owned by the Elewana chain, prices start at s/c sgl/dbl US$370/410 in the low season, high season sgl/dbl US$479/628.

Legendary Lodge (☎ 0743-647344, 💻 classic-portfolio.com/home/members/legendary-expeditions) is a completely charming, luxurious property, incorporating 12 huge cottages (including two with two bedrooms), each with their own lounge and fireplace. The cottages are set around the colonial home of a former coffee farmer in lush gardens 5km north-west of the city on the way to Nairobi, with good views of Meru. Rates, including transfers to and from Arusha Airport, are US$335pp per night for half board. Note that, despite the eye-watering prices, there is no pool on the premises; for that you have to go to a nearby member's club. It's the only place I've found that has its own helipad, which shows you the sort of clientele they are aiming at and, unsurprisingly, it is often used by Abercrombie & Kent and Nature Discovery (pp100-1) for their clients.

Firmly in the luxury bracket, ***Onsea House*** (see map below; ☎ 0679-933207, 💻 onseahouse.com) is a delight. Everything, from the locally made furniture to the outdoor pool with views across to Meru, the friendly and conscientious staff and the tranquil setting on Namasi Hill, 7km east of Arusha, is spot on. And I haven't yet mentioned the food, overseen by Axel, who was working in Michelin-starred restaurants at the age of 16 and now passes his knowledge onto his talented chefs. The rates – s/c sgl/dbl US$180-260/225-325 – are not cheap even by Arusha's standards but they are very fair value. It remains one of my favourites.

(cont'd on p216)

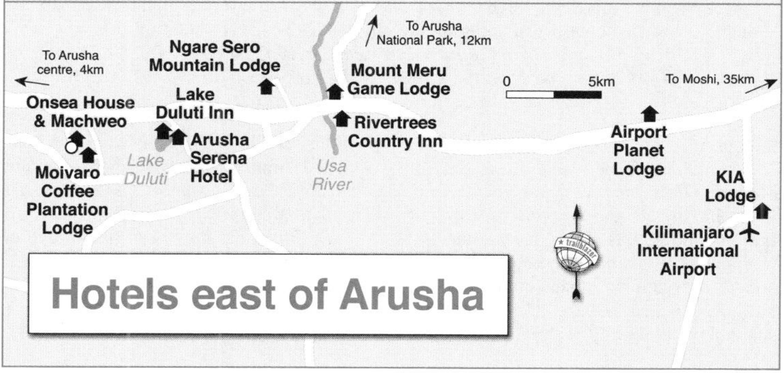

ACCOMMODATION AROUND ARUSHA

(cont'd from p215) Once upon a time the only problem with Onsea was one of availability, its four double rooms (plus two in the separate cottage by the pool) frequently booked up well in advance. They have alleviated that problem, however, by building a nine-room establishment next door. Linked by a bridge and with the same sense of understated style, ***Machweo Wellness Retreat & Fine Dining*** (for contact details see Onsea House box p215) is nevertheless also quite a different entity to its elder sister. For where Onsea House is more homely, cosy and intimate, Machweo, while still exquisitely tasteful, is slightly more 'showy', with rooms boasting satellite TVs and even bathtubs in the Honeymoon suites; there's also a spa here. Rack rates are sgl/dbl/tpl US$165-220/195-270/260-390.

Not too far away at the end of a bumpy dirt track about 7km east of Arusha, 2km south of the road to Moshi, is ***Moivaro Coffee Plantation Lodge*** (☎ 0754-324193, 💻 moivaro.co.tz), consisting of 40 cottages, each hidden away amongst the lush vegetation of the verdant grounds. Each room is en suite and has a veranda, as well as a fan, fireplace and mosquito net; though wi-fi is available in the main building only, perhaps unsurprising given that the cottages are so spread out. The lodge also boasts a swimming pool and bar. A massage service is available, too, which will enable you to while away the hours when you're not on the mountain. Rates: s/c sgl/dbl/tpl US$173-230/ 227-315/296-415 for B&B.

Arusha Serena Hotel (see map p215; ☎ 0682-310007, 💻 serenahotels.com/arusha) is one of many Serena properties in Tanzania and yet another lodge that is situated on a coffee plantation, though this time at Tengeru and with the added attraction of Lake Duluti behind. This gorgeous location and the grand, almost baronial reception/restaurant area aren't quite matched by the 42 rooms in concrete bungalows but nevertheless some have full sunken baths and lake views and all have wi-fi. Rates are s/c sgl/dbl US$75/151 low season, up to US$201/290 in peak season.

A little further along, ***Ngare Sero Mountain Lodge*** (see map p215; ☎ 0764-305 435, 💻 ngare-sero-lodge.co.tz) is one of my favourites. A really lovely choice, it's reachable only by crossing a small footbridge over a tranquil pond where cormorants sunbathe and colobus monkeys peer through the branches. The lodge started life as a colonial farmhouse back in 1905 though the original building (which has now been divided into two rooms) has been added to, with tasteful self-contained chalets (with walk-in wardrobes) spread around the perimeter of the lawned grounds. Those who have booked with Summits Africa (see pp103-4), Nature Discovery (see pp100-1) or one of the other more expensive trekking outfitters may end up here – and there's nothing to complain about if you do. Rates (sgl/dbl US$272-315/344-400) are seasonal.

The delightful ***Rivertrees Country Inn*** (see map p215; ☎ 0743-600160, 💻 rivertrees.com) sits on the banks of the Usa River, 22km east of Arusha. It's a stylishly

though it's since been fully renovated, restored and reopened by the president of Tanzania after years of being mothballed. It's a bit impersonal, as you may expect from a building this size (it has around 180 rooms), but it is still extremely well maintained, everything is manicured to within an inch of its life and the rooms are supremely comfy and feature all the usual facilities including air-con, wi-fi, satellite TV and mini-bar. Rates start at sgl/dbl US$225/255 and go up to US$560 for the Presidential Suite.

Even that has now been superseded in the swanky stakes by the ***Gran Meliá Arusha*** (☎ 0746 982400, 💻 www.melia.com/en/hotels/tanzania/arusha/gran-melia-arusha). Part of a multinational chain, rustic inn, the cosy, slightly 'shabby chic' reception and lounge making good use of old reclaimed wood, while the 31 self-contained guestrooms, two cottages and large thatched River House – which contains two double rooms – are similarly understated and tasteful. But it's the grounds that, for this author at least, are the biggest draw, the Inn's many great old trees offering both welcome shade for residents and a perfect habitat for birds; indeed, the whole place comes alive with magnificent birdsong throughout the morning.

With wi-fi in every room, a kitchen that bakes its own bread and an attentive, conscientious staff, you have the ideal option for those looking for a little luxury out of town. Both Roman Abramovic and King Charles III have stayed here, and if it's good enough for them, it'll probably be good enough for you. High-season rates for their standard rooms are s/c sgl/dbl/tpl US$232/307/406 B&B, or it's US$827 for the River House, which can accommodate up to six guests, and US$1230 for the exclusive use of the Farm House, accommodating up to ten guests.

Opposite is another establishment that's full of character. ***Mount Meru Game Lodge & Sanctuary*** (see map p215; ☎ 0689-706760, 💻 mtmerugamelodge.co.tz) was established back in 1959 (the founder's son is now in charge) although its colonial style harks back to an earlier era. The 23 large, en suite rooms (with wi-fi) in wooden bungalows are comfortable and the restaurant is renowned among ex-pats who flee Arusha to dine here at weekends; alas, the **animal sanctuary** that used to set this lodge apart is now much reduced, though you'll still find monkeys and storks roaming the grounds. Rates are s/c sgl/dbl from US$157/274 for B&B.

Moving further east, the next hotel of note is ***Airport Planet Lodge*** (see map p215; ☎ 0623-816485, 💻 planet-lodges.com/airport-planet-lodge/), sister of the highly regarded Arusha Planet Lodge (see p214). As with that hotel, Airport Planet's main draws are its facility-filled and very large en suite rooms, stuffed with features such as TV, safe, mosquito net and air-con. The Executive rooms are even bigger and include fridge, couch and bath too. A great pool, restaurant/bar and free shuttle bus to the airport complete the picture. Not cheap – sgl/dbl/tpl US$136-185/188-232/205-304 – but a lovely place to start, or finish, your Tanzanian odyssey.

KIA Lodge (see map p215; ☎ 0754-780125, 💻 kialodge.co.tz) is another link in the Moivaro chain (see opposite) and is the original 'airport hotel' for Kilimanjaro International Airport which sits just 1.5km – and a free shuttle ride – away. It's decorated in a smorgasbord of Tanzanian styles, from the Zanzibar-style reception, the Tinga-Tinga paintings in the restaurant and the Makonde woodcarvings in the rooms. Their hilltop location also allows you unequalled views of both Kili and Meru, as well as distant glimpses of the Pare Mountains and Maasai plains. Lovely. Rates are s/c sgl/dbl/tpl US$158-215/196-284/259-374 for B&B.

this 171-roomed behemoth is as luxurious as you'd expect. I could rave on about the feature-heavy rooms but, for me, the two things that set it apart are the lovely rooftop restaurant, which is the nearest you'll come to staring eyeball to eyeball with Meru; and the lovely bird-filled gardens complete with infinity pool and even a waterfall. Rates-wise, it's US$279-334/290-345 for sgl/dbl; add US$45-53 for a room facing Meru. Suite prices are US$666-2328 depending on the season and specification.

No review of Arusha's hotels would be complete without mention of the oldest of the lot; the Arusha Hotel which is actually fairly anonymous despite its location in the very heart of the action by the Clock Tower. Formerly known as the New Arusha, the name change was only sensible considering it opened in 1894 (though the current building dates 'only' from 1927). It's since changed its name again, thanks to a change in ownership, and is now known by the rather ridiculous title of ***Four Points By Sheraton Arusha, The Arusha Hotel*** (☎ 027-297 7777, 🖳 www.marriott.com). Despite all the changes, it remains amongst the most swish and plus of all the town-centre hotels. The restaurant is very good, the swimming pool delightful and the rooms sumptuous and kitted out with television, wi-fi and, of course, a bathroom. Prices are sgl/dbl from US$260/290.

Many people are now migrating a few hundred metres east along Nyerere Rd to ***Kibo Palace Hotel*** (☎ 0753-036444, 🖳 kibopalacehotel.com/kibo-palace-hotel-arusha/), with rooms from sgl/dbl US$200/230 rising to US$480/520 for the suites. With every room en suite and boasting wi-fi, a TV, telephone and safe, this is a great addition to the hotel scene in Arusha, particularly as the service is consistently praised by guests. There's even a small gym and pool for that last-minute Kili workout.

Still further east, ***The African Tulip*** (☎ 027-290717, 🖳 theafricantulip.co.tz) is yet another fine establishment in this neck of the forest. It's named after the bright orange flowers that grow on the trees along this lane. Rooms are huge and kitted out with every possible modern convenience including flat-screen TVs, remote-controlled aircon, phone and the fastest wi-fi in Arusha. Aside from all this high-tech gadgetry, it's worth mentioning that it's also a very comfortable hotel in a shiny, glamorous sort of way, and the buffet breakfast spread is the largest in the city, with both Marmite and Vegemite available! Rates are sgl/dbl US$140/210, rising to US$380 for the 2-bedroom suites.

WHERE TO EAT AND DRINK

[see map pp210-11]

Arusha is a good place for foodies, with African, Oriental and Indian eateries abounding. Some also advertise 'Continental food', which basically means any dish that doesn't fit into one of the categories above.

Cafés and breakfast spots

Note that pretty much all the eateries listed in this section also serve lunch and dinner, and pretty good at it they are too. But they have been listed in this category because they advertise themselves as coffee houses and it is coffee for which they are primarily known. Do peruse the menus, however, or you'll be missing out on some real treats.

If it's pastries you're after for breakfast, then actually the cafés in the two big supermarkets – ***Shoppers*** (daily 8am-10pm) in the TFA Complex and ***Village Supermarket*** (daily 7.30am-7.30pm) in the AIM Mall – are hard to beat. They are probably the two best bakers in town though, of the two, I prefer the latter – if only because Shoppers makes the cardinal sin of selling their pastries in the café at one price, but then sells exactly the same item more cheaply just 20 yards away in the shop! That aside, they're both great – expect to pay Ts2000-5000 per pastry.

As for independent cafés, my current favourite is ***Kitamu*** ('delicious'; daily 10am-11pm) on Goliondoi Rd. It has a decent line-up of coffees and a good selection of breakfasts including a tasty Mt Kili (toasted sandwich with bacon, cheese and fried eggs served with tomatoes, mayo and sweet chilli sauce). I also like ***Fifi's*** (Mon-Fri 7.30am-9pm, Sat & Sun 8.30am-9pm) on Themi Rd, just off Sokoine, for its huge coffee, milkshake and smoothie selection, its menu of Western favourites (sandwiches, burgers and salads etc) and its super-quick **wi-fi**. There's also ***Africafé*** (Mon-Fri 7.30am-9pm, Sat & Sun 8am-9pm), on Boma Rd by the tourist office, a comfy place serving great platefuls of very tasty – though expensive – grub; best value, I think, is the Afri omelette (sausage, onions, tomatoes and chilli) for Ts13,000. Be warned, however, that when they say 'large coffee' on the menu, they mean it; my latte came in a beer mug!

Just round the corner on the roundabout is ***Coffee Culture*** (daily 8am-9pm), which is small and frequently stuffed to the rafters with *mzungu*, who flock here to enjoy the laid-back vibe and better-value food; try their Spanish omelette (Ts10,000).

Moving down Sokoine, ***Raptor Coffee Bar*** doesn't look or feel too dissimilar to the two outlets just mentioned but the seats are comfy, the music's played at just the right volume, and you have to love a place that offers both a Nutella sandwich (Ts7000) and fish fingers & chips (Ts10,000) on its menu. Not far away on the opposite side of the road, ***Serengeti Coffee House*** (daily 8am-10pm) serves good coffee, but its main draw is its balcony from where you can watch the chaos of Sokoine Rd below and be thankful you are not, for that moment at least, part of it.

Inside **Sanaa** (see p212; daily 9am-7pm) there's a lovely if expensive ***café*** where you can sit and look over the grounds of the Gran Meliá Hotel, while its residents presumably look down (in every sense) on you.

Finally, in the TFA Complex, of the two cafés standing opposite each other across the parking lot I prefer ***Msumbi Coffees*** (Mon-Sat 7.30am-8pm, Sun 8am-4pm) as it has better coffee (just), comfier seats, strong wi-fi and delicious cake (Ts5000-6000).

Lunches and snacks

As with the category above, the definition here is rather loose: most of the places below also serve dinner; furthermore, most of the eateries in the categories above and below also serve snacks and lunches, of course. Nevertheless, in my experience the following tend to be more popular during the day and for this reason I've put them here.

Starting at the **TFA complex**, the first is ***Pure Gelati*** (daily 8am-10pm), ostensibly an ice-cream parlour but one that also serves some of the biggest and tastiest salads in Arusha. On Sokoine, ***Green Hut House of Burgers*** is a bit of a misnomer, for burgers feature but seldom on the menu. This is a great little place for lunchtimes, however, with cheap, simple but filling local fare the order of the day including *maandazi* (a sort of fried bread; Ts700), *mishkaki* (meat – usually lamb/goat – skewers; Ts2000), *kitumbua* (a sort of rice cake or pattie; Ts700) and several dishes featuring that tasteless Tanzanian staple, *ugali* (a stodgy cornmeal or cassava mush). Note that both locals and tourists have found out about this place so you may find yourself sharing a table with strangers – come before 12.30pm if you'd rather not. Note, too, that this place is shut in the evenings.

On Nyerere Rd, ***Themi Living Garden*** (12.30-2.30pm) is a lovely lunchtime-only organic vegetarian eatery that's part of an important social project that aims to empower Tanzanian women through business and social inclusion. It also provides a healthy alternative to much of the restaurant fare on offer in Arusha. The food is both delicious and cheap (I was charged Ts6000 for a meal of rice, lentils, yams, cabbage and vegetable stew) and the setting, by a part of the river that's been cleaned up and given over to growing many of the restaurant's ingredients, is lovely. Moving still further east, over on Simeon Rd, there's ***Picasso Café*** (Mon-Sat 10am-10.30pm, Sun 10am-10pm), yet another smart café and one with a good pizza/burger menu. Relaxed and unpretentious, I like it here.

Dinner

This isn't a comprehensive guide to dining in Arusha but it does include most of the most popular eateries – at least amongst climbers – in the city.

Asian food, local barbecues ... and an Ethiopian A favourite with locals and ex-pats alike, ***Khan's*** has been specialising in Tanzania's hearty, cheap and simple brand of spicy local and Indian cuisine for well over 30 years. A garage by day, at around 5pm it transforms itself into a barbecue to serve up a fantastic mixed grill of halal mutton, chicken and beef kebabs (Ts18,000), with chips & naan bread and a serve-yourself table full of salads and spicy sauces all included. It's just to the north of the Central Market on Mosque St so be careful around here after dark – take a cab.

Speaking of spicy cuisine, on Simeon Rd is another Indian but the polar opposite to the unpretentious Khan's. ***Amber*** (Wed-Mon noon-11pm, Tue from 4pm) is a swish, chic and classy new addition to the restaurant scene and the first place I've been to in

Tanzania – indeed, anywhere – where there's no *physical* menu to peruse, just a QR code to scan to bring up the dishes on your phone. If that feels a bit gimmicky, there is at least substance behind the style with some lovely dishes (mains Ts20,000-30,000; their mutton rogan josh, Ts23,000, is delicious) in some very swanky surroundings.

A third Indian place, ***Tandoori Village*** (Tue-Sun 11am-11pm), on Serengeti Rd, also demands my recommendation with its delicious subcontinental food (mains Ts15,000-20,000). There are plenty of veggie options, as you would expect, and while I haven't eaten everything from the huge menu – that would take a month or two – the Banasari chilly chicken masala (boneless chicken cooked in fresh chilli and spring onion paste and hot spices; Ts15,000) is a delight.

Also east of Themi River, hidden amongst the jacaranda trees on Kenyatta Rd, is ***Flame Tree*** (daily 10am-10pm). Now under Chinese management, this is an enormous Asian restaurant with a fittingly large menu including such very familiar and tempting dishes as Cantonese grilled pork (Ts20,000) or crispy stir-fried duck (Ts29,000). The food is good and the drinks menu is one of the biggest in the city. The most popular Chinese place in town, however, is ***Mr Wangs*** in the TFA. Dishes are expensive (mains Ts16,000-30,000, rising to Ts75,000 for the seafood platter), but they serve the kind of ridiculously oversized portions I usually make for myself if I'm home alone for the evening.

For something a little different, a trip to that longstanding Ethiopian favourite ***Spices & Herbs*** could be in order. With vegetarian dishes for Ts13,500-16,000 as well as meat dishes (around the Ts18,500 mark), this place has been garnering praise from hungry travellers for years. Try the *yebeg tibs* – lamb cooked in Ethiopian butter with onions, green peppers and rosemary (Ts18,500) – and you'll see why.

Western food On Haile Selassie Rd, ***George's Tavern*** (☎ 0782 943690; Tue-Sun 11am-11pm) is a great place for a post-trek feed-up with a large and lovely **Greek menu** (George himself is Cypriot) including an entire page in the menu devoted to kebabs from around the world. There's another page devoted to vegetarian food, plus, of course, moussaka. Pizzas cost from Ts18,000 up to Ts30,000 for the 'Fully Loaded'; it ain't cheap by Arusha standards, but how many other chances are you going to get to celebrate climbing Africa's highest mountain!

For pizzas, my favourite is ***Bravo*** (daily noon-10pm), on Jandu Rd, where the menu is very Western (pizzas for Ts12,000-22,000) but the setting is very Tanzanian, with dining tables dotted around a large garden. For something entirely more familiar, there's a ***Pizza Hut*** (☎ 0746 982 660, 💻 www.pizzahut.co.tz; daily 10am-11pm; pizzas Ts9000-38,000) at the TFA complex with both eat-in and takeaway available.

Finally, the best food in town (or, rather, just outside it) is at ***Onsea*** (see p215), where the manager used to work in Michelin-starred restaurants in London. It's food with finesse – they describe it as Belgian and French brasserie-style with an African touch – and usually exquisite, with the menu changing daily. Count on spending about US$70 per head for three courses including wine, US$20 less for residents.

❑ THE TOP FIVE PLACES TO CELEBRATE IN OR AROUND ARUSHA

In no particular order (for details see above unless specified):

- **Spices & Herbs** Classy Ethiopian food, good for sharing.
- **Onsea** Posh nosh for the smarter summiteer.
- **George's Tavern** An extensive bar and a menu to please everyone, and you can always stroll up to The Hub nightclub if you want to extend the night.
- **Flame Tree** Good food, extensive drinks menu, pool table – lots of fun.
- **Amber** (see p219) Swish, sophisticated and, luckily, delicious too.

NIGHTLIFE

Nightclubs Arusha is the **nightclub** and **live music** capital of northern Tanzania, attracting rastas and ravers from far and wide. Unfortunately, as with any large city, the scene changes rapidly and what's recommended here may well be out of date by the time you arrive.

One place that's almost certain to remain, however, is ***Triple A*** (just northwest off the map on p210), a radio station and also one of Arusha's most popular nightspots. Open Fridays and Saturdays (Ts10,000), the action begins at about 8pm and carries on 'til dawn. Its star has been somewhat eclipsed by the arrival of ***The Hub Sports Bar & Lounge*** on Haile Selassie Rd which is busy most nights and feels more tourist-friendly than Triple A.

Cinema AIM Mall hosts the city's best **cinema**, Regalz. The seldom-visited mall out at Njiro also still has one.

Drinking and playing pool Twiga describes itself as **Tanzania's first craft ale brewery**. Their location, within the shiny AIM mall, feels a bit incongruous but to my surprise their 25-minute brewery tours (free) are proving popular with tourists. Indeed, some Kili climbers even focus their post-trek celebrations on the A-Mall, combining a session in ***Twiga Brew Pub*** (Tue-Sun 11am-10pm) with a trip to one of the neighbouring restaurants. I find the sudden switch from mountain to mall rather jarring, but overcome that gear change and it's an OK place and they show English football on the telly (a feature they share with ***Picasso Café*** on Simeon Rd).

On the other side of town, ***Flame Tree*** (see Where to eat) has a large alcoholic menu and a pool table to while away the evening.

MOVING ON

By bus, shuttle, train or plane

To Moshi Those heading towards Kili will find the **local 'Coaster' buses** are the most convenient way to travel the 81km to Moshi. They run throughout the day from the main bus station, with the last one around 5pm (Ts3000). Always an intimidating place to go, negotiating the bus station is actually fairly straightforward and there'll usually be a tout on hand to point you to the right bus as soon as they see you. Once you're aboard sellers will come to your window with sunglasses and sunhats, papers and perfumes, cake and Coke; everything, in fact, to keep you cool, comfortable, fed and fragrant for the journey.

True, using a Coaster bus is not a particularly comfortable way to travel but other options are thin on the ground, with Moshi ill-served by the **shuttle bus** companies. **Riverside** (☎ 0757 091120, 💻 riverside-shuttle.com), in ACU Building near a pharmacy on Sokoine Rd, have one bus per day at 2pm (US$10). **Impala Shuttle** (☎ 0743 666663, 💻 www.impalashuttles.com) operate a daily bus to Moshi (US$10) that calls in at Arusha at around 2pm on its way from Nairobi to Moshi. The services for both companies depart from the parking lot on Simeon Rd, though if you book in advance you might get picked up from your hotel – depending on the state of the traffic.

To Nairobi Of the **bus** companies, **Dar Express** (daily 3pm; Ts25,000), in offices on Wachagga Rd, offer a good and safe service to Nairobi.

As for the **shuttles**, both **Riverside and Impala** (see above) run a daily service to Nairobi, at 8am (arrive 2-3pm). They charge US$25 for foreign tourists. As with all shuttles, they *should* pick you up from your hotel, though these days many of the shuttles pick up passengers only if they are staying at hotels near the shuttle bus car park on Simeon Rd.

To Dar es Salaam There are several bus companies plying this route, the most experienced and reliable being **Kilimanjaro Express** (5/day at 5.50am, 6am, 6.10am, 6.45am & 7.30am; Ts37,000-40,000). Second choice is **Dar Express** (see above; 2/day at 6am for Ts35,000 and 8.30am for Ts45,000).

Kilimanjaro Express's office is in Kaloleni, while Dar Express are a few hundred metres to the west (a plot they share with several other operators); see map pp210-11.

Trains run three times a week to Dar via Moshi from the railway station on Station Rd, south of Arusha Backpackers. The trains leave on Tuesday, Thursday and Saturday at 2.30pm, arriving in Dar early in the morning (second class sleeper is Ts44,400).

If flying, remember that Arusha effectively has two airports: **Arusha Airport** is only about 20 minutes from the centre of the city and **Kilimanjaro International Airport** (see pp203-4) is less than an hour away.

See pp208-9 for details of the airline offices in Arusha.

❑ GETTING TO KILIMANJARO AND ARUSHA AIRPORTS

To Kilimanjaro International

Precision Air (🖳 precisionairtz.com) and **Kenya Airways** (🖳 kenya-airways.com) also offer a shuttle service to and from KIA for their flights for a very reasonable Ts10,000. The shuttle leaves 2½ hours before their flights. You pay onboard, with the shuttle bus leaving from the parking lot behind New Safari Hotel. **Air Tanzania** offer a similar service and for the same price for their passengers, though their services leave 3 hours prior to the flight's departure. Remember with all shuttles to phone or call in at the airline office beforehand to see if you need to book your place, and to confirm from where you should catch the shuttle.

A **taxi** to the airport officially costs US$50, though with bargaining this can be reduced slightly.

To Arusha Airport

With no airlines laying on a shuttle service, you have to rely on taxis or public transport. Virtually opposite the TFA complex is Kilombero bus station, a muddy and chaotic patch of land from where dalla-dallas head west towards Arusha Airport (listen out for the touts shouting 'Kisongo'), dropping passengers off by the junction a kilometre from the terminal for Ts1000; from there you can walk, or catch a *boda boda* (see p207) for Ts1000. If you're carrying all your luggage, you've got to be seriously tightfisted to opt for this rather than take a taxi from town (Ts15,000 minimum, though Ts20,000-30,000 is more normal).

Moshi

Cheaper, quieter, nearer and prettier, Moshi sits in the shadow of Kilimanjaro and, for climbing the mountain, is perhaps a superior base to neighbouring Arusha, 81km to the west. As the unofficial capital of the Chagga world, most visitors find Moshi a little more interesting too. The missionaries who followed in the wake of Rebmann gave the Chaggas the advantage of a Western education and this, combined with the agricultural fecundity of Kilimanjaro's southern slopes, has enabled the Chaggas to become one of the wealthiest, most influential and most securely self-aware groups in the country. Moshi has reaped the benefits too, prospering to the point where it is now one of the smartest towns in Tanzania (though grim poverty is still not difficult to find, as anybody who has walked around Moshi at night, stepping over the sleeping bodies of the dispossessed lying on the pavements as they do so, can testify).

Though the Chaggas are the dominant force in town, Moshi is a cosmopolitan place, with a large ex-pat community (as well as a huge number of short-term teenage volunteers) and a highly visible Indian minority; this colourful ethnic mixture is reflected in the architecture, with a huge Hindu temple abutting an equally striking mosque and with dozens of small churches and chapels scattered in the streets thereabouts. There also seems to be more civic pride in Moshi than in other parts of the country. Indeed, the only dark cloud for tourists here is the inordinate amount of hassle they suffer from trekking agency touts, 'artists' and the like. Look beyond this, however, and you're sure to find Moshi charming, friendly and a lovely place for a stroll. Take an amble any afternoon and you'll pass sewing machinists stitching shirts on sun-baked sidewalks, blade sharpeners spraying sparks from their cycle-powered grinders and smiling school kids shouting salutations to the sweaty *mzungu*. It can also boast enough facilities to enable you to organise a trek – and enjoy some long nights of celebration at the end.

ARRIVAL

The (sometimes unreliable) Precision Air shuttle is *usually* there to pick up passengers from **Kilimanjaro Airport** and take them to Moshi for Ts10,000. Air Tanzania also operate a shuttle for the same price.

However, if you arrive on KLM (which has a shuttle to Arusha but not Moshi) or any other airline, both domestic and international, you'll have to catch a cab to Moshi (US$50).

Flights to **Moshi Airport** are so seldom that hopefully you'll already have your transport from there sorted; you'll be lucky to find a taxi waiting at the airport. Coastal Air, the main airline serving this airport, no longer have an office in Moshi.

Arrive **by bus** and you'll be dropped off at the terminal on Mawenzi Rd, 200m south of the Clock Tower and within walking distance of many hotels.

As for the **train**, the station is within easy walking distance of the town centre, about a five-minute stroll from the Clock Tower roundabout.

ORIENTATION

According to Harry Johnston (see p152), Moshi could simply mean 'town' or 'settlement', though as with everything Johnston wrote, this could well be wrong. Indeed, Moshi also translates as 'smoke' – a reference, perhaps, to its situation at the foot of a volcano? What is certain is that Moshi is compact but expanding fast, and where once upon a time almost everything of interest to the holidaying visitor lay on or near the main thoroughfare, **Mawenzi Rd** (aka Nyerere Rd, which is also more commonly known as Double Rd), these days there's no real focal point to the town and the best restaurants, hotels and other tourist amenities are scattered around all four corners of Moshi. However, it still helps to think of Mawenzi Rd, and its northern extension, **Kibo Rd** (the two names borrowed from the two main peaks of Kilimanjaro), as the main spine of the town, for together they run all the way from the market at Moshi's southern end to the

❑ AMANI

Like many other street children in Tanzania, Peter was driven to the streets because of extreme poverty and neglect. Born to alcoholic parents who struggled to keep a roof over the family's head and food on the table, Peter was malnourished and sick from an early age. Although Peter was nine when he came to Amani, his physical size alone made him look years younger. With the help of Amani's dedicated team, Peter is healthy and growing fast. He is doing well in school and is looking forward to a positive and happy future.

Despite the Chaggas' reputation among Tanzanians for prosperity and power, the region is not immune to the problems afflicting the rest of the country and that includes the malaise of street children. And while the stories of each child are unique, the general themes of neglect, poverty and desperation are a common theme with all of them.

Whatever the reason is for ending up on the streets, the door is always open to them at Amani Children's Home. Founded in 2001 by dedicated Tanzanians, from its original base in Moshi, Amani has expanded its operations and now has centres in Arusha and Singida regions, caring for hundreds of children ranging from age 5 to 17 at any given time.

Most children come to the centre with the social workers who are employed full time by Amani to meet and rescue children living and working on the streets. Some of the kids are orphans who've lost both their parents, in many cases to AIDS, while others have run away from home because of the physical, mental or sexual abuse they faced there. Once on the streets it's a precarious existence. Boys can try to graft a living by collecting scrap metal, begging or stealing; for girls, a life on the streets is even more dangerous, with many ending up as prostitutes or working as domestic slaves from a young age.

Life in Amani

Once in the Amani Centre, they are washed, fed and given new clothes. Social workers interview the children to learn about their backgrounds, hear how they ended up on the street and assess what their chances are of potential reunification with immediate family or relatives. At the centre children quickly adapt to the daily routine of making beds and cleaning the dormitory and communal areas. They have responsibilities such as washing their clothes and, after each meal, their own dishes.

After breakfast most attend school either externally or in Amani's on-site primary education programme, which ranges from the Starters class for those who have never been to school or are deemed too old to join the first grade, to Classes A, B and C which are accelerated programs to get children to the educational level they should roundabout on the main road to Arusha at its northern end adorned with the statue of a soldier marching north towards Kilimanjaro. Separating Mawenzi Rd from Kibo Rd is a second roundabout adorned with a **Clock Tower** (or should that be 'Coke tower', given the soft-drink sponsorship of the roundabout), which if Moshi has to have one is, I suppose, the best candidate for the spiritual centre of town. There is a second road running parallel to Double Rd, officially christened **Market St** though known by most people as Single Rd, which terminates at the Clock Tower.

To the north lies the suburb of **Shanty Town** (see map p228), home to some great restaurants, a few fine hotels and some massive houses.

GETTING AROUND

Dalla-dallas drive up and down the main Mawenzi and Market streets for Ts500, though it doesn't take long to walk anywhere. The one exception to this rule is

be attaining at their age. School ends mid afternoon and then it is free-time for art, games, practising acrobatics, playing with a skipping rope etc; but for many children, the highlight of the day is the afternoon football match.

Despite the security and relative normality provided by the home – at least compared to their life on the streets – the aim is to eventually reunify the children with their parents or extended family, having first evaluated that such a move would be appropriate. Indeed, at Amani they create a place for healing with the Upendo Programme (*upendo* is Swahili for 'love'), where each staff member serves as a 'parent' to several children, supervising them and listening to their problems.

In 2007 Amani made the move from the family house in which it began to a purpose-built centre. At one time in the old house 65 children shared a bedroom but in the new facility each child has his or her own bunk bed. Then in 2013 Amani launched the Safe House and Drop-in Center in the Arusha region, with the goal of helping more young girls and boys. The growth of Amani is due to the dedication of the staff and careful management of funds. As an essentially secular organisation (respecting the children's beliefs and values of Christian and Muslim faiths) the centre is not supported by any one institution or organisation but instead relies on donations – the majority of Amani's support comes from individuals and families who visited the centre or heard about its good work and wanted to help.

Visiting Amani

Amani welcomes new volunteers and needs those who either have a good working knowledge of Swahili or are willing to learn. Volunteers must be willing to commit to stay for three months or more (by which time Amani reckons your Swahili will be of an acceptable level). But if you can't commit that kind of time, don't despair. There is an option for short-term volunteers (Amani Ambassadors) who commit to raising funds to support Amani's work/projects, to spend 4-5 days with the kids to witness the work that Amani does.

It is also both possible and worthwhile to **visit the centre** and spend some time with the kids (prearranged visits only). Many tourists find that turning up to join in the afternoon football (soccer) game (daily around 3pm) is a good idea, being an easy way to mix and bond with the kids without the need for a common language, as long as it's booked in advance.

Whether you want to arrange a visit, make a donation or merely find out about their work, have a look at their website (💻 amanikids.org).

Trust me, if you've got a day to spare in Moshi, there's no more rewarding a way to spend it.

Shanty Town: a **taxi** to KCMC (the hospital on the far edge of Shanty Town) will cost Ts6000 from the town centre; **motorbikes** (also called boda boda, Toyo or piki piki) cost around Ts2000 and rickshaws (bajaj) – which are very popular here – T2500.

A new bus terminal is in the pipeline – and has been for more than half a decade now – but all inter-city buses seem to still use the terminal in the town centre.

SERVICES

Banks & ATMs

There are **ATMs** everywhere but the only one I found in Moshi that doesn't charge commission is KCB on Boma Rd.

Communications

The **post office** (PO; Mon-Fri 8am-4.30pm, Sat 9am-noon) is by the Clock Tower at the junction with Boma Rd. There's also a **DHL office** (Mon-Fri 8am-5pm, Sat 9am-noon) opposite the YWCA on Boma Rd. **Wi-fi** is commonplace in Moshi with even some of the cheapest hotels offering it as well as many cafés, restaurants and bars.

Airline offices

Precision Air (☎ 0272-753495, 🖳 precisionairtz.com; Mon-Fri 8am-5pm, Sat 8am-2pm) is in KNCU Building. **Air Tanzania** (🖳 www.airtanzania.co.tz; Mon-Sat 8am-5pm, Sun 9am-1pm) is now in Kibo Tower by Nyumbani Hotel.

Laundry

Your hotel will probably have some sort of laundry service or you can visit **iSmart** (Mon-Fri 7.30am-6pm, Sat to 5pm) on Boma Rd.

Swimming pools

The YMCA and Salinero Kilimanjaro, Ameg and other hotels charge to use their pools (Ts7000 at YMCA, though others typically charge Ts20,000); in all these places hotel guests can use the facilities for free.

Massage

Lala Salama (☎ 0754-030071, 🖳 lalasalamaspa.strikingly.com), which translates as 'Sweet Dreams', is a small, NGO-sponsored spa in Kibo Tower on Boma Rd offering a one-hour massage service for Ts45,000 and a foot massage for Ts30,000. Most of the big hotels also offer some sort of massage service.

Shopping

• **Trekking equipment** Finally, Moshi can boast a decent trekking equipment supplier. Indeed, they've now got two! **AT Gear** (☎ 0763-586729, 🖳 www.atgeartz.com; daily 8.30am-5.30pm; sample prices: trekking poles US$10, sleeping bags US$25-50, waterproof trousers US$10, all for a 5- to 7-day trip), are on New St, near Zebra Hotel.

There's an even newer place, **Gilman's Outdoor Store** (🖳 www.gilmansoutdoor.com; Mon-Sat 8.30am-5pm) on Boma Rd, with most of the equipment sourced from Europe. Sleeping bags here are US$35 per trek to rent, regardless of the duration. Just one word of caution: while these places are indubitably a godsend, do remember that your agency should be able to supply you with most major bits of equipment that you might have forgotten to bring and they may be included in the price too.

Other items you may well have overlooked but will find extremely useful include: chapsticks (along with mosquito repellent and most other pharmaceutical needs), which can be bought from the **Third Millennium pharmacy** on Mawenzi Rd.

• **Maps and books** about Kili can be bought from **iCurio** on Guinea St near Kindoroko Hotel or **Blue Zebra** (daily 5.30am-6pm) on the ground floor of Kibo Tower. See also Souvenir shops opposite.

• **Supermarkets and other possibly useful stores** Up the hill to the west of the Clock Tower on Boma Rd is **Abbas Ali's Hot Bread Shop** (Mon-Fri 8.30am-5/6pm, Sat to 3/4pm), a very pleasant place with great fresh bread and pastries. Opposite is **Aleem's** (Mon-Fri 8.45am-1pm & 2-5pm, Sat to 4pm only), which seems to have been going forever and has a loyal ex-pat following. There are branches of **Rafiki Supermarket** all over the city including in the NSSF building, on Mawenzi (Double)

Rd, near the junction of Market St and Aga Khan Rd as well as by Moshi Leopard Hotel.

The **central market** does, of course, also sell food including some great fresh veg, and you'll probably be eating some of it on your trek. Out in Shanty Town (see map p228), **Woodland Shoppers** is a pretty central option on Lema Rd.

• **Souvenir shops** There are plenty of souvenirs to buy in Moshi and many places willing to flog them to you.

Two in particular deserve special mention: **Shah Industries** is a leather workshop housed in what used to be a rice mill. It's a strange combination but a beautiful place and a worthy one too: over a third of the workers at Shah Industries have some sort of disability. Definitely worth looking around, it lies to the south-east of town across the train tracks on the way to Springlands Hotel. Up to the west of the Clock Tower, on Boma Rd, in the YWCA, is **Moshi Mama's Craft Cooperative** – again, excellent stuff and a worthy cause behind it.

Of the 'regular' souvenir shops, the best in terms of choice and quality is **iCurio**, just round the corner from Kindoroko Hotel, with a decent array of stock including a fine line in Kilimanjaro Beer T-shirts.

At the northern end of town on the ground floor of Kibo Tower, **Blue Zebra** (daily 5.30am-6pm) sells pretty much the same stuff you've seen everywhere else, just lots more of it. Below, in the basement, is their gallery, again with a vast amount of stock stacked leaning against each other on the floor. See also Maps and books opposite.

WHERE TO STAY [see map p228-9]

The following is not an exhaustive list but whilst there are some cheaper places at the southern end of town, many refuse to accept Westerners. Manage to persuade one to let you stay and you can expect to pay around Ts10,000 per night, though the chances are it'll be assumed you want bed and broad rather than bed and board.

See the box on p231 for volunteers' accommodation and box on pp232-3 for accommodation out of Moshi.

Those looking to **camp** are advised to head out of town to ***Weru Weru River Lodge*** (🖳 www.weruweruriverlodge.com; US$20 per night, or US$40 if using their tents; see p234) or ***Rafiki Backpackers*** (see p231) US$10 per night, or US$9 with your own tent). Or you can go to Marangu, where virtually every hotel allows camping in their grounds.

As with Arusha, you may be able to get a cheaper rate for your accommodation by booking online through 🖳 booking.com or 🖳 airbnb.com.

As for hotels that definitely do welcome tourists, they are as follows:

Hostels and cheap hotels (less than US$20 per double)

There are two places in Moshi that capture the lion's share of the backpacking trade. The first, in the centre of town on Mawenzi Rd, is ***We Travel Hostel*** (☎ 0715-820280, 🖳 wetravelhostel.com) which has two self-contained doubles (US$25 for single, US$30 for two people) with air-con, two triples (US$20-30 not self-con) and several spick-and-span dorms (usually divided between the sexes; US$7-8) with enormous bunk-beds, each with mosquito net, fan, wi-fi, and lots of charging sockets. There's also a pleasant restaurant roof terrace and prices include a decent breakfast. The door is always locked so ring the bell to your right.

The other popular option is ***Mountain Bikes House*** (☎ 0625-691407). The name is appropriate, for the boss is Muksin Mushi, the first Tanzanian to cycle to the top of Kili unsupported. It took him 43 hours to do so, reaching the summit on April 7th 2017 – the same year, incidentally, that he started to hand-build with his friends this charmingly ramshackle hostel on Shanty Town's Kibong'oto Rd.

Much of the building material has been taken and repurposed from elsewhere, including bicycle tyres for handrails on the stairs and some century-old windows given new life in the main building.

(cont'd on p230)

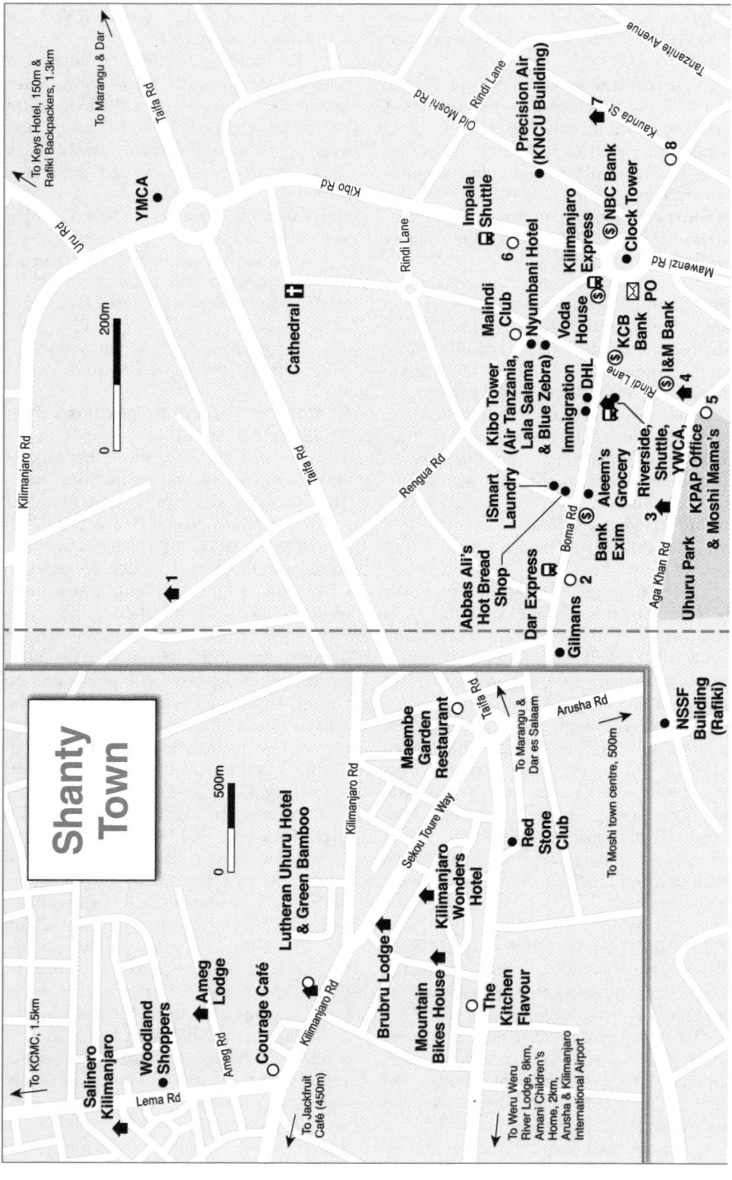
Shanty Town
0
500m
0
200m
To Keys Hotel, 150m & Rafiki Backpackers, 1.3km
To Marangu & Dar
Taifa Rd
Uru Rd
YMCA
Kilimanjaro Rd
Kibo Rd
Old Moshi Rd
Rindi Lane
Tanzanite Avenue
Precision Air (KNCU Building)
Kaunda St
7
8
Impala Shuttle
6
Malindi Club
Nyumbani Hotel
Kilimanjaro Express
NBC Bank
Clock Tower
Mawenzi Rd
PO
Cathedral
Voda House
KCB Bank
I&M Bank
4
5
Kibo Tower (Air Tanzania, Lala Salama & Blue Zebra)
Immigration
DHL
Riverside, Shuttle, YWCA, KPAP Office & Moshi Mama's
Rengua Rd
iSmart Laundry
Aleem's Grocery
Bank Exim
Boma Rd
3
Aga Khan Rd
Uhuru Park
Abbas Ali's Hot Bread Shop
Dar Express
2
Gilmans
1
NSSF Building (Rafiki)
Maembe Garden Restaurant
Taifa Rd
To Marangu & Dar es Salaam
Arusha Rd
To Moshi town centre, 500m
Red Stone Club
Kilimanjaro Rd
Sekou Toure Way
Lutheran Uhuru Hotel & Green Bamboo
Kilimanjaro Wonders Hotel
Brubru Lodge
Mountain Bikes House
The Kitchen Flavour
Ameg Lodge
Courage Café
Kilimanjaro Rd
Ameg Rd
Woodland Shoppers
Salinero Kilimanjaro
Lema Rd
To KCMC, 1.5km
To Jackfruit Café (450m)
To Weru Weru River Lodge, 8km, Amani Children's Home, 2km, Arusha & Kilimanjaro International Airport

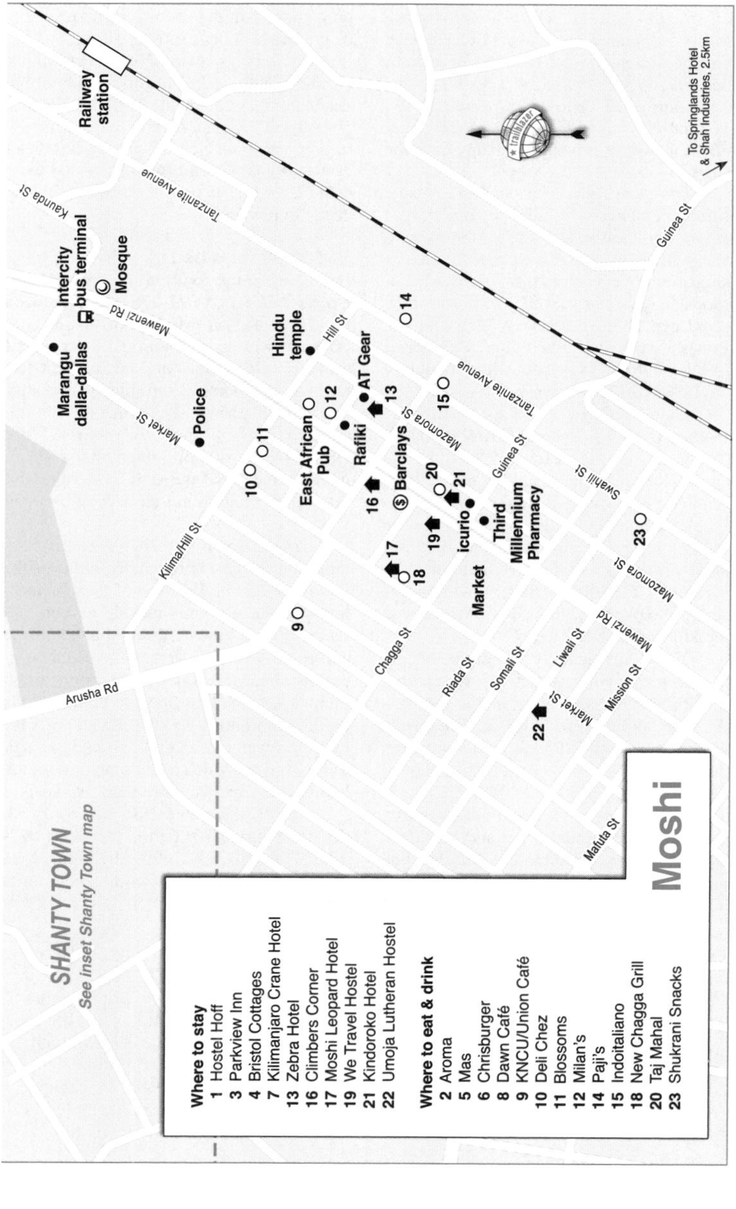
Moshi
SHANTY TOWN
See inset Shanty Town map
Railway station
Intercity bus terminal
Mosque
Marangu dalla-dallas
Police
Hindu temple
East African Pub
Rafiki
AT Gear
Barclays
icurio
Third Millennium Pharmacy
Market
To Springlands Hotel & Shah Industries, 2.5km
Kaunda St
Tanzanite Avenue
Mawenzi Rd
Market St
Hill St
Kilima/Hill St
Mazomora St
Guinea St
Swahili St
Chagga St
Riada St
Somali St
Liwali St
Mission St
Mafuta St
Arusha Rd
trailblazer
Where to stay
1 Hostel Hoff
3 Parkview Inn
4 Bristol Cottages
7 Kilimanjaro Crane Hotel
13 Zebra Hotel
16 Climbers Corner
17 Moshi Leopard Hotel
19 We Travel Hostel
21 Kindoroko Hotel
22 Umoja Lutheran Hostel
Where to eat & drink
2 Aroma
5 Mas
6 Chrisburger
8 Dawn Café
9 KNCU/Union Café
10 Deli Chez
11 Blossoms
12 Milan's
14 Paji's
15 Indoitaliano
18 New Chagga Grill
20 Taj Mahal
23 Shukrani Snacks

(cont'd from p227) There are also some lovely suspended rattan seats outside each cottage. Rates are just US$6-8 for a dorm bed, US$25 for a double. If it wasn't for the 20-minute walk into town, and the dirt floors that cover everything, including residents, in dust, this would probably have the edge.

Trying to muscle in on this duopoly, ***Climbers Corner*** (☐ climberscornermoshi.com; commonly known as the former Haria Hotel) is almost a carbon copy of its neighbour, We Travel Hostel, with similar rooms, layout, and even location – they stand next to each other on Mawenzi Rd. Prices are not dissimilar either, with dorms (4-8 beds) for US$8 a bed, while s/c dbl/tpl are US$22/24 respectively.

There's another option just south of the market. ***Umoja Lutheran Hostel*** (☎ 0769-239860, ☐ umojahostel.org; look for the sign 'KKKT Umoja Hostel') is clean, well-run and the al-fresco eating area is certainly pleasant and popular with locals. The rates, too, are decent, at Ts15,000/25,000 sgl/dbl for rooms with shared bathrooms, or s/c sgl/dbl Ts30,000/40,000, all with breakfast. Inexplicably, however, Westerners tend to ignore this place.

There are actually a couple of old hotels where you can get a private room that's cheaper than a dorm bed in a hostel. At first sight, everything at ***Kindoroko Hotel*** (☎ 0753-377795, ☐ kindoroko.com; Mawenzi Rd) looks great, with rates of sgl/dbl/tpl Ts23,000/34,500/46,000 for a self-contained private room with hot water, towel/soap, fan, mozzie net and breakfast. It also has a great rooftop bar. But then you actually stay there, and you realise that the TV isn't working, and there are no working plug sockets in the room – just some very dangerous-looking exposed wiring.

Not too far away, ***Hotel Buffalo*** (☎ 0756-508501, ☐ buffalocompanyltd@yahoo.com; sgl/dbl/triple Ts30,000/35,000/50,000, all s/c and fans or air-con in the triple rooms), on New St, at least has clean bright rooms with mosquito nets and even cable TV – but there is a general feeling of decay to this place.

US$20-80 for a bed

Beginning in the south of the town, ***Moshi Leopard Hotel*** (☎ 027-275 0884, ☐ leopardhotel.com), on Market St, is an old favourite with tour groups and independent travellers alike. Boasting an excellent terrace bar, the rooms are en suite, very comfy and include a fridge, TV, wardrobe, air-con and balcony. Rates for tourists are US$50/60 s/c sgl/dbl, which is fair value; it's a shame about the staff, however, who often can't seem to muster a smile between them.

Zebra Hotel (☎ 0766-998648) is a large but fairly commonplace hotel in the middle of Moshi. Features of their facility-heavy en suite rooms include air-con and fan, satellite TV, wi-fi, direct-dial telephone and room service. I've heard several complaints about the water pressure once you climb above the first floor, so do check this before committing to stay. Rates are very fair, however, at US$30/35-40/45 s/c sgl/dbl/tpl (prices which at the time of research hadn't increased for more than five years).

Across the other side of the Clock Tower, ***Kilimanjaro Crane Hotel*** (☎ 027-275 1114, ☎ 0733-176999, ☐ kilimanjarocranehotel.co.tz) seems to be more of a local businessmen's hotel. It's a decent-

❑ ABBREVIATIONS

Throughout this book I have used the following abbreviations when writing about accommodation: **pp** means per person; **s/c** is short for self-contained, a local term meaning that the room comes with a bathroom (ie the room is en suite or a bathroom is attached); while **sgl/dbl/tpl** means single/double/triple rooms.

So, for example, where I have written 's/c sgl/dbl/tpl US$35/40/45', I mean that a self-contained single room costs US$35 per night, a self-contained double costs US$40 and a self-contained triple costs US$45.

❑ ACCOMMODATION FOR VOLUNTEERS & LONG-TERM RESIDENTS

It seems a little ironic, perhaps, that what is traditionally one of the wealthiest and most developed parts of Tanzania is also the one area that receives more interest from NGOs, charities and the like. As a consequence, Moshi is flooded with volunteers working on any number of projects in the town and surrounding area. This has led in turn to the establishment of a couple of hostels designed specifically to cater for these longer-term residents.

First up, and run by the friendly Simbo, the 28-guest capacity ***Hostel Hoff*** (☎ 0787-225908, 🖳 hostelhoff.com) houses only long-term guests (ie those staying a minimum of one month) unless there is availability in the low (rainy) seasons. Hugely popular with volunteers, accommodation is largely in gender-divided **dorms** (with mosquito nets and lockable drawers) though there are a couple of double/twin **rooms**, all of which are clean and *usually* tidy (though the possessions of long-term residents inevitably tend to sprawl out over time onto every available surface). There are even two **safari tents** in the garden though these are very popular and tend to be taken by those residents who are staying the longest. Rates are very reasonable at US$19-21pp per day including buffet breakfast, dinner and laundry. They also run the successful trekking agency, African Scenic Safaris (see p86). All in all, a nice place run by nice people.

Rafiki Backpackers (☎ 0714-422500, 🖳 rafikibackpackers.com) is located out in peaceful Rao, 20 minutes' walk north of town and east of Shanty Town. This hard-to-find hostel (ask for Uhuru Museum – which most locals know, and which is actually a bar – as it's by there) is clean and cheap at US$10 for a dorm bed or US$20/30/45 for sgl/dbl/tpl with breakfast, wi-fi and use of the kitchen and a fridge; camping is US$10, or US$9 if you have your own tent. Overall, it's a nice, safe and friendly option – albeit a fair distance from town.

enough place, however, with 30 smart rooms, sauna and even a very small pool. Singles, which have showers, TV and telephone, are US$60; doubles and triples have both bathtubs and showers and go for US$80/100 respectively.

Lutheran Uhuru Hotel (☎ 0753-037216, 🖳 uhuruhotel.org) sits in fairly vast grounds in leafy **Shanty Town** (see map p228; don't get this hotel confused with Lutheran Umoja Hostel in central Moshi). It's a quiet, relaxed place, the only activity coming from the team of gardeners maintaining their carefully manicured gardens. The rooms are very pleasant – particularly those in the new Kibo or Kilimanjaro wings – and all are self-contained with mosquito nets and wi-fi. The tariff is *slightly* high at US$60/80 s/c sgl/dbl in the Mawenzi Wing (where there's air-con and TV), US$55/75 in the Kilimanjaro and Kibo wings (with TV and fan); nevertheless, it maintains a healthy trickle of customers. So if you don't mind catching some form of transport or walking a fair distance to get to Moshi – or are happy doing nothing all day except watch gardeners water the grass – it's fine.

US$80 and above per double

Bristol Cottages (☎ 027-275 5083, 🖳 bristolcottages.com), on Rindi Lane, describe themselves as 'The countryside hotel in the middle of town', though the noise from the buses revving up the hill outside rather shatters that boast. I didn't find it perfect: my mozzie net was too small for the bed; the boast that there's wi-fi in every room is true only if no-one else is using it when you want to; and the toilet was in danger of toppling over every time someone sat on it. Rates-wise, the smart cottages, all with large TV and mosquito net, go for US$95/115/145 s/c sgl/dbl/tpl; the new wing, a little noisier due to its proximity to the road, is consequently slightly cheaper at US$85/105 s/c sgl/dbl, while there are some suites with a mountain view that will set you back US$105/125/155 s/c sgl/dbl/tpl. All overpriced but just about OK.

Just a few metres up the hill on Aga Khan Rd is another smart place. ***Parkview Inn*** (☎ 0754-052000, 🖳 pvim.com) was once a bijou B&B boasting just 12 rooms or so but these days it's a fairly enormous monolith with 49 rooms of elegant (if monotonous) uniformity and the facilities – TV, telephone, wi-fi, air-con and bath or shower – of a large chain hotel. Thankfully, however, it still retains its friendly informality. Rates are US$75/90/120 for s/c sgl/dbl/suite.

For the top places in Moshi you have to go to the north of the Arusha–Moshi road to **Shanty Town** – a smart and peaceful area of jacaranda-lined avenues. The first, the huge ***Kilimanjaro Wonders Hotel*** (☎ 027-275 1984, 🖳 kiliwonders.com), is gargantuan, its sheer size a bit incongruous in the normally discreet, understated Shanty Town. The 44 rooms (with satellite TV, wi-fi, air-con and safe) are sumptuous, as is its gardens, spa and pool, and rates reasonable, starting at just US$130/150 sgl/dbl. Best of all, however, is the rooftop bar from where you can eyeball Kili.

If you head north-west on Lema Rd then east off that onto Ameg Rd you come to something of a curiosity. Maybe it's the high concrete walls surrounding the place,

❑ ACCOMMODATION NEAR MOSHI AND AROUND KILIMANJARO

The foothills, lower slopes and surrounding plains of Kilimanjaro are dotted here and there with some very pleasant accommodation; it is unlikely you will stay at any of them *unless* your trekking agency puts you up in one as part of your Kilimanjaro package. And if you do then congratulations – I think that on the whole they offer some of the most pleasant and interesting accommodation in the region. Note that I haven't included all hotels or lodges, of course; almost every village has some sort of accommodation so I have narrowed my survey down to just those that market themselves to tourists. Note, too, that I have not included the hotels in Marangu; you can find these on pp240-1.

The following hotels are ordered from west of Moshi round to the east.

House of West Kili (☎ 0784-872668, 🖳 houseofwestkili.com) Located in **Lawate, Sanya Juu**, this place is probably the most suitable candidate if you're looking to cut the travelling time to the start of the Shira or Lemosho routes. Sixteen huge rooms sit about 20 minutes' drive from Boma N'Gombe on the Arusha–Moshi road. Very comfy, there are no TVs but instead the owner hopes you'll participate in a couple of local activities, including bird-watching at the nearby swamp or visiting a local sacred Maasai hill. Rates start at about US$108 per room.

Ndarakwai Ranch (☎ 0742-021233, 🖳 ndarakwai.co.tz) Set in 11,000 acres in the **Siha District**, on the lower western slopes of Kilimanjaro; unlike the others in this section – with the exception of Simba Farm Lodge, below – this ranch is less a stopover on the way to the mountain than a destination in itself: nine en suite, wi-fi-connected tents on raised wooden platforms, each on land that teems with 70 species of mammal and 300 species of birds. Beautiful, if above the budget of most trekkers at around sgl/dbl/tpl US$474/338/294 per person high season, with game drives extra.

Simba Farm Lodge (☎ 0784-687335, 🖳 simbafarmlodge.co.tz) Originally owned by Swiss-German settlers, and with one of its buildings dating back to 1910, the 5000-acre Simba Farm is certainly one of the more venerable lodges in the area and one of the more charming too. Nine rooms, all individually decorated, are dotted amongst the flower beds, with a children's play area and pool. It's a lovely relaxed maybe it's the uniform whitewashed, green-roofed chalets, or maybe the popular pool where everybody seems to congregate – whatever it is, there's something about ***Ameg Lodge*** (☎ 0754-058268, 🖳 ameg lodge.com) that's reminiscent of a 1950s' British seaside holiday camp. Thankfully, the bland exteriors belie some quite stylish rooms, each with shower, satellite TV, air-con, wi-fi, veranda and phone. Prices (all rooms are doubles) start at sgl/dbl US$85-130/135-165. In addition to the pool, guests are also entitled to use the hotel gym.

Back on Lema Rd, another vast, gleaming monolith, ***Panama Garden Resort*** (☎ 027-275 2566, 🖳 panamagar denresort.co.tz) boasts 45 shiny rooms with balconies as well as 25 cottages with all the facilities you'd expect (air-con, TV etc) plus such surprises as a coffee maker in each room. The grounds include a lovely pool with a bar and BBQ area. Once more, the prices are perhaps not as wince-making as you might expect at US$70/90/150 sgl/dbl/tpl for B&B.

Salinero Kilimanjaro (☎ 0677-100010, 🖳 www.salsalinerohotel.com/kili manjaro.html) is a conglomeration of 27 rooms hidden behind high hedges to the west of Lema Rd. All accommodation comes with air-con, TV and fridge, with the executive rooms boasting bathtubs and hairdryers too. Guests seem to enjoy the place, with the cottages getting the best reviews. The inviting sun-kissed pool is my favourite in Moshi. With the high-season

place, the closest to the start of Kili's Shira and Lemosho routes, and pretty fair value at sgl/dbl US$65-80/90-120, with lunch and dinner US$15 extra each. They also offer camping at just US$10 per night. Well worth it, I think!

Millie Lodge (☎ 0677-100010, 🖳 www.salsalinerohotel.com/millie.html), just 500m down from Machame Gate, is the sister lodge of one of Moshi's smartest addresses, Salinero Kilimanjaro (above). As you'd expect, Millie maintains the standards of its sibling, with 22 very smart self-contained rooms, some with balconies and views of Kibo. Rates are US$140/200/250 for B&B, but given the paucity of eateries around here you'll probably want the full-board option at sgl/dbl/tpl US$180/280/320.

Hotel Aishi Machame (☎ 0786-221788, 🖳 aishi-machame.com) lies in the village several kilometres down from Kili's Machame gate. Boasting 30 en suite rooms with wi-fi and telly in each, it's a nice if slightly odd-looking place with a pool and some very precisely manicured grounds; but like many in this section it survives mainly – indeed, almost exclusively – from the business of tour groups; as a result, if you aren't part of a group you may feel a little isolated and lonely. Rates are sgl/dbl US$90/110 B&B; add US$15 per person per meal for half- and full-board.

Stella Maris Lodge (☎ 0686-663244, 🖳 stellamarislodge.com) Located on the outskirts of Moshi just south of the road to the airport, in a village that goes by the name of **Mailisita**, blancmange-coloured Stella Maris is a not-for-profit hotel stuffed with facilities (wi-fi, air-con, satellite TV, conference facilities, balconies on all the rooms) where all profit goes to paying the teachers at the attached primary school and buying food for the children under the auspices of Mailisita Foundation (🖳 mailisita .org), a US initiative. Prices are US$75/85/100 for sgl/dbl/tpl for B&B.

Nearby, ***Lindrin Lodge*** (☎ 0673-273123, 🖳 lindrinlodge.com) is a comparatively new place a little to south of Stella Maris. Neat little chalets set into some manicured grounds with a small pool; the rooms are not as 'luxurious' as their website emphasises but they're pleasant enough, with wi-fi and mosquito net, and there's a spa and massage service too – which could be handy after the trek. Rates are US$100/150/200 for B&B; add on US$20 per person for every meal.

prices at sgl/dbl/tpl US$140/200/250 and suites US$300, this may be one of the more expensive places in town but it's also one of the smartest.

Accommodation connected with the trekking companies

Several tour companies in Moshi have decided to sink some of their hard-earned profits into property and, in particular, hotels. It makes perfect sense, of course, enabling the companies to fulfil their clients' requirements from the moment they arrive in Tanzania to the moment they leave – and to make a profit at every step too.

It's worth noting here that even if you aren't a client of the trekking company you can still stay with them, though you'll have to pay the prices given below; whereas those who have booked a trek with them will find their accommodation is included in the package.

On Uru Rd, ***Keys Hotel*** (☎ 0755-486377, 🖳 www.keyshotelstz.com) is a traditional-looking family-run hotel and one of the smartest addresses in Moshi. In the main building it's doubles only, all coming with TV, telephone, toilet, shower with hot/cold running water and air-con. There are also 15 small thatch-and-cement cottages in the grounds which are quite fun. All rates (sgl/dbl/tpl US$100/115/135 in the cottages, or US$110/125/145 in the main building) include continental breakfast. See p95 for Keys Hotel Tours.

Up in Shanty Town, ***Brubru Lodge*** (☎ 0767-655994, 🖳 brubru-lodge.com) is owned by one of the more popular trekking agencies on the mountain, Altezza, but is no longer named after them, instead taking its moniker from a small black-and-white bush shrike. The air-conditioned rooms are supremely comfy and the pool's a beauty too; it's also reasonable value at sgl/dbl US$90/100. The hotel is open to anyone, but thanks to Altezza's popularity, it's usually their clients who fill the place. See p88 for Altezza Tours.

Chanya Lodge (☎ 0675-7722247, 🖳 chanyalodge.co.tz) lies 6km east of town, a 32-room establishment owned and run by Shah Tours (see p102 for contact details). A buffet breakfast is included; a good pool, wi-fi, sauna and a pretty garden are just some of the attractions here. The staff are nice too. Prices are around US$100 for a double though you may be able to find cheaper if booked online.

Zara-run (see p107) ***Springlands Hotel*** (🖳 springlandshotel.com-tanzania.com/en), 2km to the south of Moshi, provides shuttle buses throughout the day to and from the town centre. As Zara's popularity as a trekking company continues to dwindle, so the hotel gets less and less busy, to the point where they now allow anyone to stay, not just their clients. Still, most people who stay here are happy with what they find, the pool being the main attraction.

Snowcap Cottages (☎ 0759-114527, 🖳 snowcap.co.tz) Homely little chalets in a pleasant spot near old Rongai Gate, simple but cosy, but it's the main building with its open fire, TV lounge and a well-stocked bar that's the real draw. Prices are US$80 a double half-board. A lovely spot. Book through Snowcap, see p103.

Weru Weru River Lodge (☎ 0747-463659, 🖳 weruweruriverlodge.com) Also in **Mailisita** and owned by successful Moshi trekking agent Ahsante (see p86), this is their latest venture; a huge, semi-luxury, facility-filled place with 32 air-conditioned veranda-fronted rooms, bar, coffee lounge, swimming pool, wi-fi and two conference halls.

The charming wooden fittings and stone floors more than compensate for the slightly plain nature of the buildings but all in all it's very impressive and rates are fair at US$140/190/250 for sgl/dbl/tpl B&B; add US$15-20 per person for half-board, and another US$20 per person on top of that for full board. The bar, by the way, is large, well stocked and a terrific place to celebrate reaching Uhuru.

WHERE TO EAT AND DRINK

[see map pp228-9]

Cafés to consider

As befits a town that grew wealthy on the back of the bean with the caffeine, Moshi has some rather decent little coffee houses.

KNCU Café (🖳 kncutanzania.com/the-union-cafe; Kilimanjaro Native Coffee Union, better known as ***Union Café***; daily 7am-8.30pm) is named after and run by Africa's oldest surviving cooperative, an organisation that represents some 60,000 farmers who grow coffee on Kili's lower slopes. It's a history that it is clearly proud of, with the walls adorned with portraits of previous chairmen of the co-op and there's even a working coffee roaster. The coffee (Ts4000 for a double espresso) is, of course, both organic and fantastic, there's a lengthy list of teas too (all Tanzanian) and the menu is Western and covers salads, sandwiches, quesadillas and the inevitable pizzas. The veranda is a lovely place to watch the world go by and enjoy that caffeine buzz. Its faults? Well, it's very *mzungu* heavy so if you want to get away from your fellow tourists this is not the place to come; oh, and they served my latte in a glass, which is, of course, an abomination. Other than that crime, this place is great.

Some fierce competition is provided in Shanty Town (see map p228) by the relatively new but rather brilliant ***Courage Café*** (daily 8am-8pm). Founded by an NGO concerned with eradicating sex trafficking and rescuing women caught up in the trade (🖳 courageworldwide.org), the café has some lovely sofas on which to lounge and enjoy the super-fast wi-fi and excellent food. If you're in Shanty Town, don't miss it. Nearby, ***JackFruit Café*** (off map p228; daily 11am-10pm) is pretty much the most Western place in Moshi and wouldn't look out of place in Sacramento or Sussex. The large grounds may be typical of Shanty Town, but inside the café there's very little evidence that you're in Tanzania at all. As such, it's perfect for those who just want to escape Africa for a while and sip on a flat white (only the second place I found that offered this). To get here, where Lema Rd bends sharp right you should continue straight on, taking a right at the fork a few metres later.

If, instead, you want to mingle with the locals, but still want to enjoy a coffee in salubrious surroundings, your best bet is ***Aroma*** (daily 6am-8pm). They serve little except drinks and the odd snack, and cater mainly to locals, but is a great choice for those who find themselves at this end of town. Also at the northern, Clock Tower end of town, ***Dawn Café*** (🖳 cafe.dawntanzania.com; daily 7.15am-8.30pm) has much to admire. For starters, it has the fastest wi-fi I could find in town and it's also the only other place that serves a flat white (and it's good, too; Ts5000). So I was ready to rave about this place, until I made the mistake of ordering food which, unbeknownst to me, seems to suffer the same gestation period as your average elephant. My advice: order food only if you've got a *lot* of time on your hands, but do come for the coffee.

Finally, the former Coffee Shop that served ex-pats, volunteers and climbers for decades has sadly gone, to be replaced by ***Blossoms*** (🖳 blossomscafe.co.tz; daily 7am-10pm) a rather shiny wine bar. While the interior looks a bit soulless, and those plastic seats are unpleasantly adhesive on a hot day, thankfully they've kept the lovely garden at the back which is where you should head. The food menu is extensive and Western but unimaginative.

Lunch and dinner

• **Local food** On the northern end of Uhuru Park, with the entrance on Aga Khan Rd, is a bar, ***Mas'***, that serves some decent *nyama choma* (grilled meat) at fair prices (Ts10,000 including a beer).

At the southern end of town, on Swahili St opposite East Point Hotel, is one steadfastly African joint: ***Shukrani Snacks*** (noon-8pm) is a Somali-run establishment that's popular and cheap – Ts5000 should be more than enough to fill your stomach and slake your thirst. The place is *mzungu* friendly and won't rip you off.

For more homegrown East African cooking there are several choices. The most popular amongst travellers, and not just for its location, ***Taj Mahal*** (daily 7am-10pm) sits right by Kindoroko Hotel and despite the Indian name is actually a great place for local fare such as meat skewers (Ts500 each) and Zanzibar pizza (a sort of omelette filled with mince, onions and an egg and a great way to fill up for just Ts1000). A couple of blocks away, ***New Chagga Grill*** (daily 8am-10pm) near Moshi Leopard Hotel has a small menu but it includes a huge mountain of *mchemsho kuku* (boiled chicken, vegetables and bananas) for just Ts6500 for a quarter of a chicken.

• **Indian food** The ageless ***Indoitaliano*** (daily 11am-9.30pm) continues to pack 'em in night after night. The name may conjure up all sorts of unappealing fusions but really it's just a straightforward Indian restaurant that happens to make some delightful pizzas too (Ts8000-20,000).

A block or two away, ***Paji*** (Mon-Fri 11am-3pm & 6-10pm, Sat & Sun 10am-3pm & 6-10pm) provides welcome sanctuary, a lovely peaceful spot with a small but delicious Indian menu (veggie mains Ts7000, others Ts8000-12,500) and views across a hockey pitch (with games at Mon, Wed & Fri at 6pm) to the hills beyond. Even though there was a Moshi-wide power-cut when I visited they still managed to rustle up a fantastic kauai chicken (Ts9000) and for subcontinental sustenance their food is as good as anything else in town; their bar is very well stocked too. Just one word of warning: the streets around here are particularly dark and it's best not to wander around alone at night.

Nearby is perhaps my favourite place in Moshi. Half of ***Milan's*** (daily 11am-9.30pm) is taken up with a typically scruffy snack café of the kind you find all over the country. The other half, however, is rather different: a cute little eatery with hand-stitched place mats that boasts an extensive menu of cheap and delicious Indian vegetarian food, including dosas, samosas, bhajis and thalis. Fair value and their masala dosas (Ts13,000) and thalis (Ts15,000) provide proof that God loves us and wants us to be happy.

• **Burgers & barbecues** Just north of the Clock Tower roundabout, ***Chrisburger*** claims to stay open 24 hours and offers very good-value dishes; if you can get a seat on its leafy veranda it's a good place to hide away and watch the world go by. Once again it's great value, with nothing over Ts10,000 (for simple meals such as steak & chips) and their hamburgers, reputedly the best in town, just Ts3000-5000.

Green Bamboo (see Shanty Town map p228) is a massive place, open all day (8am to late) and specialising in set menus, including a meat-heavy version (including lamb, steak, spare ribs, chicken wings, beef sausages etc) for Ts27,000, and a less indigestion-inducing vegetarian version for Ts15,000. The main attraction, however, is the lovely (and huge) garden where you can feast on flesh while listening to the strains of 'Bringing in the Sheep' on the Hammond organ being piped through the speakers – the restaurant is, after all, located in Shanty Town's Lutheran Hotel.

• **Chinese** ***The Kitchen Flavour*** (💻 thekitchenflavourrestaurant.co.tz; Mon-Sat 8.30am-9.30pm) is a lovely retreat from the heat with some of the best Chinese food I've had in Africa (mains Ts12,500-18,000); their beef cashew (Ts18,000), in particular, was delicious and served with a surprising (and welcome) degree of spicy heat. Indian, local and continental dishes are also available – but it's Chinese that is their forte, and what I heartily recommend.

• **Restaurants with big menus (including local dishes)** Some people may be put off by the appearance of ***Deli Chez*** (💻 www.delichez.co.uk; Wed-Mon 9.30am-9.30pm), which from the outside looks like a fast-food café, though the ground floor décor owes more to the aesthetics of a wedding reception. But upstairs you'll find a very pleasant shaded terrace where the food is fine and fair value, with a huge menu encompassing good-value Chinese (Ts12,000 for mains), curries (Ts10,000 for mains) and Swahili food (Ts4000-7000). Note, however, that alcohol is not allowed on the premises.

Maembe Garden (see map p228; Mon-Sat 8am-10pm, Sun 10am-10pm) boasts spacious open grounds with a kids' play area, a leather shop, occasional live music and, best of all, an imaginative menu of sandwiches, Swahili food and other dishes rarely seen in this part of the world (eg fish & chips, Ts20,000, or grilled pork chop served with roast potatoes and banana for the same price).

NIGHTLIFE

On the main Moshi–Arusha road, ***Red Stone Club*** (entrance Ts5000-10,000) is a proper, purpose-built nightclub with plenty of outdoor seating and a large indoor dance-floor. On a good night you'll get a good mix of locals and ex-pats/tourists here.

A few metres west of Nyumbani Hotel, the entrance of ***Malindi Club*** is through a set of concrete elephant legs, while inside you'll find a cavernous, friendly place serving food and beer, occasionally hosting karaoke nights and showing **premier league football** on the telly; it can, however, get a little too raucous at times.

A similar experience, though this time nearer most of the hotels, is provided by ***East African Pub***, a real rowdy locals' hangout that lovers of English football will adore, with live premiership matches the main entertainment. They also serve a decent plate of *nyama choma* (grilled meat).

For live sport (and, indeed, televised sport), the best option is ***Paji Restaurant*** (see opposite) where, every Monday, Wednesday and Friday at 6pm you can watch the hockey from their veranda.

For those who prefer a less frenetic end to their trip there are few activities more pleasant than sitting at a **rooftop bar**, sipping a cold beer, staring at Kibo, and thanking God you're not up there. Kilimanjaro Crane Hotel, Kindoroko and, best of the lot, Kilimanjaro Wonders Hotel in Shanty Town, can all help here (and you don't need to be staying at any of them to enjoy the privilege).

MOVING ON

By bus

Arusha, Marangu and Tarakea

Heading to **Arusha**, 'Coaster' buses (the small 30-seat minibuses; Ts3000) leave regularly throughout the day from the bus terminal on Mawenzi Rd. Big buses are usually a little cheaper at Ts2500. For **Marangu** catch one of the dalla-dallas from the adjacent terminal (Ts2000) labelled to 'Mwika' or 'Kilema'. If you've arrived early in the morning and nothing seems to be leaving from here, try round the corner on Mawenzi (Double) Rd – they often wait here too.

The **shuttles** – Impala (☎ 0754-293119, 💻 www.impalashuttles.com) and Riverside (☎ 0756-963654 and ☎ 0755-996453, 💻 www.riverside-shuttle.com) – both charge US$10 for the 2-hour journey to Arusha, their buses leaving at 6am from their respective offices; Riverside are in the YWCA building on Boma Rd, while Impala are next to Chrisburger. If you're staying in the town centre they should offer to pick you up from your hotel, though do emphasise this when buying your ticket.

Nairobi **Shuttle buses** to Nairobi leave from outside their respective offices (see above). Both Riverside and Impala have cut their service to just one per day from Moshi, with both leaving at 6am and costing US$35. Cheaper are the big **buses**, though for travel to Nairobi they're not recommended due to lack of comfort and the fact that they arrive at the bus terminal there after dark.

Dar es Salaam There are plenty of **bus** companies plying the route to Dar. The total journey time from Moshi is something like 9-10 hours. **Kilimanjaro Express** are the most reliable carrier and have the best buses. Services to Dar leave at 6.15am, 7.30am, 8.30am, 9.30am and 3.30pm (Ts37,000-45,000, the more expensive tickets for those buses with toilet and air-con); their big new office-cum-waiting-room-cum-bar-cum-hotel can be found opposite the Clock Tower.

Dar Express, on Boma Rd, are their nearest rivals, with buses at 7.15am, 8.15am and 10am (Ts45,000, or Ts35,000 for the non-VIP 10am bus).

By air

For details of flights (in and) out of **Kilimanjaro International**, see pp34-7.

Getting to Kilimanjaro Airport takes about 40-45 minutes from Moshi. There is no public transport and while you can take an Arusha-bound bus from Moshi and jump off at the junction, that still means you have to hitch or get a boda boda (Ts5000) for the final 6km to the airport itself.

Precision Air run a shuttle service (Ts10,000, or Ts15,000 for their international flights) to coincide with their domestic flights; the bus leaves from outside their offices 2-3hrs prior to departure (though do check first). A **taxi** costs US$50; bargaining can reduce this but you'll struggle to get much of a discount at night.

Moshi does actually have its own airport and Coastal (🖳 coastal.co.tz) do occasionally call in to connect with most of their extensive East African network, as well as a couple of other, smaller airlines – but only if there's demand.

By train

Trains run three times a week to Dar, on Tuesday, Thursday and Saturday at 6.30pm, supposedly arriving in Dar at 9.30am (second class sleeper is Ts44,400).

Marangu

According to legend, Marangu got its name when the first settlers in this part of Kilimanjaro, astonished by the lush vegetation, well-watered soils and the countless waterfalls they found here, cried out in delight 'Mora ngu! Mora ngu!' ('Much water! Much water!'). It remains a verdant and extremely attractive place, at least once you move away from the small huddle of shops and hustlers by the bus stop (situated in a part of the town called **Marangu Mtoni**, which literally translates as 'Marangu in the River') and start to climb up the hill towards Marangu Gate.

The town, 14km along the Himo–Taveta highway, is extremely elongated but is in reality little more than two roads running up the mountain, with a filigree of dusty paths branching off both.

WHAT TO SEE AND DO

Always one of the prettiest villages on Kili's slopes, for some reason over the past couple of years Marangu has become the unofficial centre of Chagga culture – and it's really fascinating.

You can try to find many of the attractions yourself – they're all pretty well signed – but it's much nicer and easier to hire one of the local kids who'll doubtless come up to you to offer themselves as guides (give them around Ts5000 per day). And while none of these 'Chagga' sights is going to have you rushing to your phone in order to tell your nearest and dearest back home of the wonders you have seen, nevertheless it's good to see some sort of revival of a fascinating culture that would otherwise be confined largely to the history books. What's more, though your interest in Chagga culture may be slight, the chance to walk around one of the prettiest, homeliest parts of Tanzania should not be passed up; it's a lovely way to spend a day.

In previous editions I've faithfully pointed out the various caves, waterfalls, museums and coffee tours available. But for this edition I've come to the conclusion that there's really no point. The museums and coffee tours in particular seem to come and go with each new edition, and new caves, too, seem to be discovered (dug?) with every passing year; which makes my review of them out-of-date almost before it's printed. So the following are just the more established sights of Marangu.

The first port of call is usually **Kinukamori Falls** (daily 8am-5pm; US$5), just 10 minutes' walk up from the bridge. As lovely as these are, I feel that this is one sight that maybe should have been left as it was, for the addition of a **Hall of Chagga Culture** – an open-air series of statues or dioramas lining the eastern path down to the falls, each depicting some aspect of Chagga culture or history – seems unnecessary and adds nothing to the beauty of the place. Indeed, with

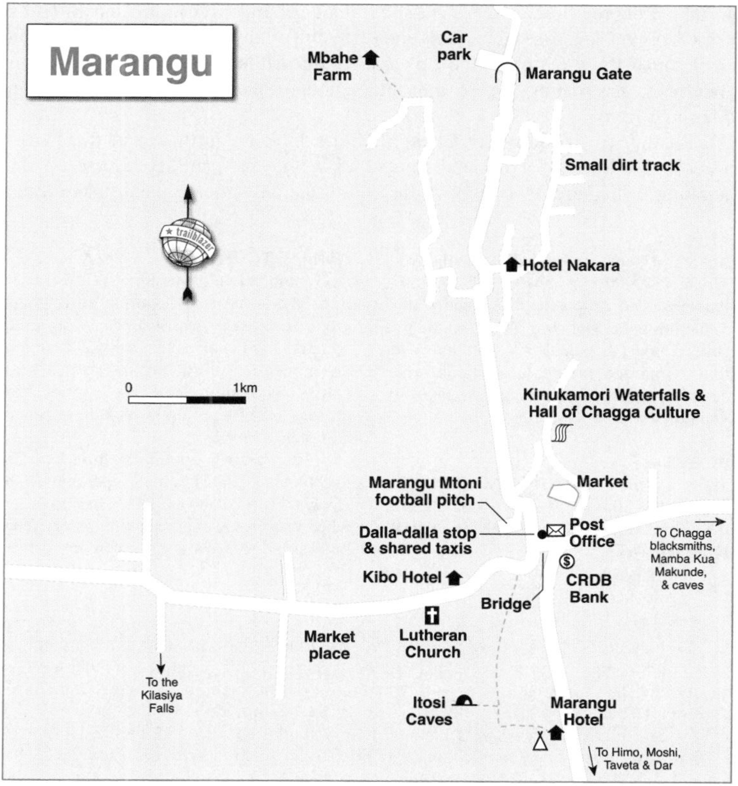

that god-awful statue of a woman about to plunge to her death that's now been installed at the top of the falls, this is one 'enhancement' that is anything but.

Sticking with the falls, many people's favourite sight in Marangu is the delightful **Kilasiya Falls**. The waterfalls are just part of the attraction, for it's the local flora that really catches the eye and many of the plants have been labelled. Reached via a steep muddy path, the falls are exquisite; there are even a couple of natural swimming pools in the gorge for those who fancy a cold dip. It's a great place to have lunch. Like most waterfalls there's a negotiable entrance fee.

Those who've really got a taste for all this Chagga culture may also like to venture east to the village of **Mamba Kua Makunde**. Walking up the hill from the main road you'll soon hear the sound of the **Chagga blacksmiths**, making anything from weapons to farm implements, often with little children working the bellows to keep the fires hot. It's free, though they'll sting you if you want to take a photo. Nearby, there are some underground **caves** once inhabited by the Chagga. Claustrophobic, dark and difficult for anyone bigger than a hobbit to negotiate, they're not the most pleasant of attractions though they are, in their own way, fascinating. There are some other caves, **Itosi**, signposted from Marangu Hotel.

Finally, for modern-day Chagga culture look no further than the twice-weekly **markets** (Monday and Thursday) in the main village square by the junction, which are lively and, by the end of the day, often quite drunken too.

ARRIVAL

Marangu is reached by **dalla-dalla** from Moshi (Ts2000) in about 60-90 minutes. Passengers are dropped by the junction next to the bridge in Marangu Mtoni. A ride in a **shared taxi** (six people on seats made for four) from the bridge to Marangu Gate costs Ts1000-1500 – make sure you specify you don't want a private hire.

SERVICES

There's a **post office** (PO; Mon-Fri 8am-1pm & 2-4.30pm, Sat 9am-noon) close to the bridge. Across the main road is a CRDB **bank** with **ATM**.

WHERE TO STAY

Accommodation in Marangu is fairly luxurious and survives by catering to the tour-group trade. As such, it tends to be quite upmarket and expensive. One way to avoid the high price of staying in a hotel is to **camp**: ***Marangu Hotel*** (see opposite) charges US$10 per night including use of all hotel amenities.

The cheapest option for those with an aversion to canvas is the venerable ***Kibo Hotel*** (☎ 0754-038747) which has no peers when it comes to character and history. The hotel still displays a sign welcoming former

❑ ABBREVIATIONS

Throughout this book I have used the following abbreviations when writing about accommodation: **pp** means per person; **s/c** is short for self-contained, a local term meaning that the room comes with a bathroom (ie the room is en suite or a bathroom is attached); while **sgl/dbl/tpl** means single/double/triple rooms.

So, for example, where I have written 's/c sgl/dbl/tpl US$35/40/45', I mean that a self-contained single room costs US$35 per night, a self-contained double costs US$40 and a self-contained triple costs US$45.

US president Jimmy Carter above the entrance. It's a perfect symbol of the faded yet fascinating grandeur of the place and of the time-warp it appears to be living in now. Miss Havisham would feel right at home here, as the place has changed little since I first visited in 2001, with antique German maps and other paraphernalia from the last two centuries adorning reception. If you want to stay, try to get a room in the main building as those in the garden are starting to look very faded. Don't expect wi-fi, but do note that some of the rooms have baths. Rooms are overpriced at sgl/dbl/tpl US$25/30/45 but I think it's worth it just to wallow in this much nostalgia, for it remains an absorbing place to wander around even if you don't intend staying. Take the bar, for example, with its antique till, or the framed descriptions of various climbing expeditions around Africa and beyond – none of which date from after 1991. It's been struggling for a while now, and to be honest I'm amazed it's still going. But a little piece of me will die when it does finally close its doors.

On the road back to Moshi there's another old favourite – and, once again, I mean *old*. ***Marangu Hotel*** (☎ 0754-886 092, 💻 maranguhotel.com) was once a farmhouse dating back to the early 1900s, and has been providing accommodation for climbers and travellers since the 1930s. The hotel is a couple of kilometres south of town (about a 10-minute walk) on the way to Himo and it stands in 9 acres of gardens (with pool and weaver birds chattering away in the trees). The food is great too; rates are sgl/dbl/tpl US$105/190/285 in the low season, US$140/240/335 in the high. Their main claim to fame, however, is not the hotel, as venerable and delightful though it may be, but their treks – about which, see pp69-70.

For something built this century, try the friendly ***Nakara Hotel*** (☎ 0754-277300, 💻 www.nakarahotels.co.tz). Formerly Hotel Nyumbani – and, before that, the Nakara once more – the friendly informality of this place is immensely likeable. Rooms, all self-contained, include hot water; they also promise a wi-fi connection everywhere, including in the restaurant (which has a grand fireplace) and out in the well-maintained garden. Presumably it's hoping to rely on tour groups to fill its 17 rooms. Rack rates are sgl/dbl US$50/100 B&B; add US$10pp for half board, and another US$10pp for full board.

Mbahe Farm (☎ 0787-740282, 💻 mbahefarm.com) is set in 13 acres in the Marangu 'suburb' of the same name, a couple of kilometres west of Marangu Gate. Owned by one of the top trekking companies on the mountain, SENE (see p103), and used by them (though not exclusively) to house their clients either side of their trek, Mbahe Farm consists of eight lovely rustic rooms plonked amidst the vegetable patches on this busy little farm. Coffee is amongst the myriad of crops grown here and Simon, the boss of SENE, provides demonstrations of the process of making coffee from bean to cup and sells the stuff too. Bicycle tours and day hikes are also available. Costs for those who aren't climbing with SENE is US$150/250 sgl/dbl full board including a guided Mbahe village walking tour – well worth it.

MOVING ON

Dalla-dallas back to Moshi (Ts2000) leave when full from the main junction at Marangu Mtoni; don't worry about finding one – they'll find you.

7 SAFE & MINIMUM IMPACT TREKKING

Safe trekking

Came to cave. Men cold. Passed two corpses of young men who died of exposure, a short time ago. The vultures had pecked out their eyes, the leopards had taken a leg from each.

From the diary of **Peter MacQueen** as recorded in his book *In Wildest Africa* (1910)

Because of the number of trekkers who scale Kilimanjaro each year, and the odd ways in which some choose to do so, many people are under the mistaken impression that Africa's highest mountain is also a safe mountain. Unfortunately, as any mountaineer will tell you, there's no such thing as a safe mountain, particularly one nearly 6000m tall with extremes of climate near the summit and ferociously carnivorous animals roaming the lower slopes. Your biggest enemy on Kilimanjaro, however, is likely to be neither the weather nor the wildlife. KINAPA are shy about revealing how many trekkers die on Kili each year, though I reckon it's somewhere between three (a good year) and eight (a bad one; see pp244-5). The main culprit behind these fatalities is nearly always the same: the altitude.

The authorities do try to minimise the number of deaths: guides are given some training in what to do if one of their group is showing signs of acute mountain sickness (AMS) and trekkers are required to register each night upon arrival at the campsite and have to pay a US$20 (plus VAT) 'rescue fee' as part of their park fees (though what this actually gets you is unclear). But you, too, can do your bit by avoiding AMS in the first place. The following pages discuss in detail what AMS actually is, how it is caused, the symptoms and, finally, how to avoid it. Read this section carefully: it may well save your life. Following this, on pp252-5 you'll find details of other ailments commonly suffered by trekkers on Kilimanjaro.

(Incidentally, for those climbing Meru the above introduction and the following advice are all relevant. Of course, given Meru's lower altitude, the risks of AMS are consequently lower; though this is offset by the slightly higher risk of plunging to your death on a vertiginous, ice-covered slope – or of being killed by the native wildlife!)

WHAT IS AMS?

AMS, or **acute mountain sickness** (also known as **altitude sickness**), is what happens when the body fails to adapt in time to the lack of available oxygen at altitude. As you climb, the atmospheric pressure drops by about one-tenth for every 1000m of altitude you gain. Thus the air pressure at the top of Kilimanjaro is approximately 40% of that found at sea level. As a result, every time you breathe on Kibo you take in only about half as much air, and thus oxygen, as you would if you took the same breath in Dar es Salaam. This can, of course, be seriously detrimental to your health; oxygen is, after all, pretty essential to your physical well-being. All your vital organs need it, as do your muscles. Your lungs load your red blood cells with oxygen and then your heart pumps them round your body delivering oxygen to your muscles and organs as they go.

Fortunately, your body is an adaptable piece of machinery and can adjust to the lower levels of oxygen that you breathe in at altitude. Unconsciously you will start to breathe deeper and faster, your blood will thicken as your body produces more red blood cells and your heart will beat faster. As a result, your essential organs will receive the same amount of oxygen as they always did. This process is known as **acclimatisation**. But your body needs time before it can effect all these changes. Though the deeper, faster breathing and heart-quickening happen almost as soon as your body realises there is less oxygen, it takes a few days for your blood to thicken. With Kilimanjaro, of course, a few days is usually all you have on the mountain, and the changes may simply not happen in time. The result is AMS.

There are **three levels of AMS**: mild, moderate and severe. On Kilimanjaro, it's fair to say that most people will get some symptoms and will fall into the mild-to-moderate categories. Having symptoms of **mild AMS** is not *necessarily* a sign that the sufferer should give up climbing Kili and descend immediately. Indeed, most or all of the symptoms suffered by those with **mild AMS** will disappear if the person rests and ascends no further that day; assuming they make a full recovery while resting, ascent to the summit can continue.

The same goes for **moderate AMS**, though here the poor individual and his or her symptoms should be monitored far more closely to ensure they are not getting any worse and developing into **severe AMS**. This is a lot more serious and sufferers with severe AMS should always descend immediately, even if it means going down by torchlight in the middle of the night.

The following describes the symptoms of the various levels of AMS.

What are the symptoms?

The symptoms of **mild AMS** are not dissimilar to the symptoms of a particularly vicious hangover, namely a thumping headache, nausea and a general feeling of lousiness.

An AMS headache is generally agreed to be one of the most dreadful headaches you can get, a blinding pain that thuds continuously at ever-decreasing intervals; only those who have bungee-jumped with an elasticated rope that's just a bit too long will know the intense, repetitive pain of AMS. Thankfully, the usual headache remedies should prove effective against a mild AMS headache though do be careful as they can also mask any worsening of symptoms; and do tell your guide as he needs to know your symptoms and what you have taken to ease them in order to judge how well you're faring. As with a hangover, mild AMS sufferers often have trouble sleeping and, when they do, that sleep can be light and intermittent. (**NB: do not take sleeping tablets** to counter this as they suppress breathing and thus will worsen your condition.) Sufferers can also experience a lack of appetite. Given the energy you've expended getting to altitude in the first place, both symptoms can seem surprising if you're not aware of AMS.

Moderate AMS is more serious and requires careful monitoring of the sufferer to ensure that it does not progress to severe AMS. With moderate AMS, the sufferer's nausea will lead to vomiting and the headache will not go away even after pain-relief remedies; in addition the sufferer will appear to be permanently out of breath, even when doing nothing. With moderate AMS, it is possible to continue to the summit **but only after a prolonged period of relaxation** that will enable the sufferer to make a complete recovery. Unfortunately,

❑ DEATHS AND INJURIES ON KILIMANJARO

It is almost impossible to ascertain with any degree of accuracy the number of people who die on Kilimanjaro each year. The one organisation that knows the exact body count, KINAPA, the park authority, doesn't want to release them, for fear that it would impact negatively on the number of people who climb the mountain each year, resulting in a loss of revenue. Similarly, the companies are understandably reluctant to advertise when a client dies on one of their climbs.

Luckily, a couple of decades ago a study by Markus Hauser addressed precisely this topic. In the paper, *Deaths due to High Altitude Illness among Tourists Climbing Mount Kilimanjaro*, Hauser studied autopsies from 1996 to 2003 and found that over those eight years only 25 people died. Ranging in age from 29 to 74, with 17 male and 8 female, the reports tell us that 14 of the deceased were victims of High Altitude Illness (HAI), of which five had HAPO and one HACO (see p246 for both), while eight had symptoms of both. Causes of death amongst the other 11 victims include two who died of pneumonia, three of trauma (ie a fall) and one from appendicitis.

Extrapolating from these figures, given that there are over twice as many people who climb the mountain each year now, **I estimate the number of people who die on Kili each year to be about six or seven**.

It should be noted that the study does not include the death of porters, for whom a post-mortem is not compulsory and thus the number of fatalities they suffer is more difficult to quantify with any degree of accuracy. Remember that more porters climb Kili than tourists, at a ratio of about three to one on every trek – so you would think perhaps there would be three times as many deaths amongst them. They also put their bodies under extra stress because of the heavy loads they are carrying, and the fact that the food they eat and the conditions in which they sleep are far inferior. Many of them also still turn up on Kili with insufficiently warm clothing. But of course they seldom climb up Kibo to the summit unless the trek includes a night at Crater Camp, so the highest altitude they reach is usually about 4600m. So given all these factors, **the best educated guess I have is that about the same number of porters and other mountain crew die on the mountain each year too**.

treks run to tight schedules and cannot usually change their itineraries mid hike. Whether you, as a victim of moderate AMS, will be given time to recover will depend largely upon how fortunate you are and whether the onset of your illness happens to coincide with a scheduled rest day or not.

With **severe AMS**, on the other hand, there should be no debate about whether or not to continue: if anybody is showing symptoms of severe AMS it is imperative they **descend immediately**. These symptoms include a lack of coordination and balance, a symptom known as **ataxia**. A quick and easy way to check for ataxia is to draw a 10m line in the ground and ask the person to walk along it. If they clearly struggle to complete this simple test, suspect ataxia and descend. (Note, however, that this lack of coordination can also be caused by hypothermia or extreme fatigue, so ensure the sufferer is suitably dressed in warm clothing and has eaten well before ascertaining whether or not he or she is suffering from ataxia.)

Other symptoms of severe AMS include mental confusion, slurred or incoherent speech, and an inability to stay awake. There may also be a gurgling, liquid sound in the lungs combined with a persistent watery cough which may

The conclusion that can be drawn from all these statistics is that climbing Kilimanjaro, as with any ascent of a seriously big mountain, is inherently a risky undertaking; one that is made all the more dangerous by the rapidity with which climbers are expected to reach the summit (as I mention elsewhere in the book, if the standard guidelines for ascending a mountain were followed on Kilimanjaro, people would take 12 days to reach the summit from 12,000ft (3658m), not the usual 24 hours that is taken on Kili!).

Further investigation suggests that KCMC, the hospital at the foot of Kilimanjaro, sees a trekker every two to three weeks – and more in the rainy season when hypothermia, an injury from slipping and altitude sickness are all, according to the statistics, more likely.

Perhaps even more disconcerting than the deaths, however, are the cases of those who survived their climb but were never quite the same again: of the ship's captain who climbed Kilimanjaro, got into trouble, came down unconscious and, though he pulled through, was not able to continue working due to the permanent effect climbing the mountain had had on his cognitive powers. Or the people who end up blind in one or even both eyes following a Kili climb (it is estimated that 1-2% of people who climb Kili will get some sort of bleeding at the back of the eye). As I've already written, deaths on Kilimanjaro are seldom publicised; but those who suffer some sort of permanent injury or disability following their climb never receive *any* attention, and it is concerning to think how many of them there may be…

I never want to put anyone off climbing Kili. I have seen how happy people are after a successful climb, and I've received many letters and emails from people over the years saying how it has completely changed their life, giving them a confidence and self-assurance that was previously lacking. Getting to the top of Africa's highest mountain is a wonderful experience. But in order to climb safely, you need to be fully aware of the risks and do everything you can to make sure you minimise them as much as possible; because the last thing I want is for you to end up as just another statistic.

produce a clear liquid, a pinky phlegm or possibly even blood. There may also be a marked blueness around the face and lips, and a heartbeat that, even at rest, may be over 130 beats per minute.

These are the symptoms of either HACO and HAPO, as outlined below, while ways to treat somebody suffering from AMS are given on pp249-52.

HACO AND HAPO

Poor Mapandi, a carrier whom I had noticed shivering with fever for the last day or two, stiffened, grew cold and died beside me in the mud.

Peter MacQueen *In Wildest Africa* (1910)

HACO (High Altitude Cerebral Oedema) is a build-up of fluid around the brain. It's as serious as it sounds. It is HACO that is causing the persistent headache, vomiting, ataxia and the lack of consciousness. If not treated, death could follow in as little as 24 hours, and less if the victim continues ascending.

Just as serious, **HAPO (High Altitude Pulmonary Oedema)** is the accumulation of fluid around the lungs. It's this condition that causes the persistent cough and pinkish phlegm. Again, the only option is to descend as fast as possible. In addition, one of the treatments outlined on pp249-52 should also be considered.

GO *POLE POLE* IF YOU DON'T WANT TO FEEL POORLY POORLY – HOW TO AVOID AMS

Haraka haraka haina baraka 'Great haste has no blessing' – a common Swahili saying.

'Pole pole' is a phrase you'll probably hear more than any other on Kili. It's Swahili for 'slowly slowly' and is usually uttered by guides to dissuade their charges from ascending too fast.

AMS can be avoided, but the only surefire way to do so is to **take your time**. Opting to save money by climbing the mountain as quickly as possible is a false economy: the chances are you will have to turn back because of AMS and all your efforts (and money) will be wasted. According to one respected agency, their average success rates based on the number of days their clients' took in getting to the top are as follows:

6 days: 75% of clients made it to the top
7 days: just over 80%
8 days: 90%
9 days or more: over 98%.

As you can see, the longer you take the greater your chance of getting to the top.

According to the Expedition Advisory Committee at the Royal Geographical Society, the recommended acclimatisation period for any altitude greater than 2500m is to sleep no more than 300m higher than your previous night's camp, and to spend an extra night at every third camp. But if you were to follow this on Kilimanjaro's Marangu Route, for example, from Mandara Huts you would have to take a further *eight* nights in order to adjust safely to the Kibo Huts' altitude of 4713m – whereas most trekkers take just two days to walk between the two. The EAC realise that the short distances and high *per diem* cost of climbing Kilimanjaro make this lengthy itinerary impractical, so instead they recommend a pre-trek acclimatisation walk up Mount Meru (4566m at the summit) or Mount Kenya (4895m to Point Lenana, the third highest peak on the mountain and the highest point that non-climbing 'trekkers' can reach). This is an excellent idea if you have the time and money and are feeling fit; providing you do one of these walks *immediately* before you climb Kili, these treks can be beneficial – and the views towards Kilimanjaro from Meru are delightful too (see pp257-69 for a description of this route).

But what if you don't have the time or money to do other climbs? The answer is to plan your walk on Kilimanjaro as carefully as possible. If you've enough money for a 'rest day' or two, take them. These 'rest days' are not actually days of rest at all – on the Marangu trail, for example, guides usually lead their trekkers up from Horombo to the Mawenzi Hut at over 4500m before returning that same afternoon. But they do provide trekkers with the chance to experience a higher altitude before returning down the slopes, thereby obeying the mountaineers' old maxim about the need to **'climb high, sleep low'** to avoid mountain sickness.

The route you take is also important. Some of the routes – the Machame, Lemosho and Shira trails via the Barafu Huts, for example – automatically enable you to 'climb high, sleep low' on the third or fourth days, when the trail climbs above 4500m (around Lava Tower) before plunging down to an altitude of 3986m at Barranco Huts where you spend the night. Some of the shorter trails, however, do not: for example, it is possible for a trekker walking at an average pace on the Marangu, Umbwe or the shorter of the Rongai trails to reach Kibo in three days and attempt an assault on the summit for that third night. This sort of schedule is far too rapid, allowing insufficient time for trekkers to adapt to the new conditions prevalent at the higher altitude. This is why a higher proportion of people fail on these trails and it is also the reason

❑ IF YOU'RE FARTING WELL, YOU'RE FARING WELL – OTHER EFFECTS OF ALTITUDE AND ACCLIMATISATION ON THE HUMAN BODY

In addition to AMS, there are other symptoms suffered by people at high altitude that are not in themselves usually cause for any concern.

The first is the phenomenon of **periodic breathing** (aka sleep apnoea). What happens is that, during sleep, the breathing of a person becomes less and less deep until it appears that he or she has stopped breathing altogether – to the obvious consternation of those sharing the person's tent. The person will then breathe or snore deeply a couple of times to recover, causing relief all round.

Another phenomenon is that of **swollen hands and feet**, more common amongst women than men. Once again, this is no cause for concern unless the swelling is particularly severe. Another one that is, once again, far more common among women than men, is **irregular periods**. The need to **urinate** and **break wind** frequently are also typical of high-altitude living and, far from being something to be concerned about, are actually positive indications that your body is adapting well to the conditions. As is written on an ancient tombstone in Dorset:

Let your wind go free, where e'er you be,
For holding it in, was the death of me.

why, particularly on these shorter trails, **it is imperative that you take a 'rest' day on the way up**, to give your body more time to acclimatise.

How you approach the walk is important too. Statistically, men are more likely to suffer from AMS than women, with young men the most vulnerable. The reason is perhaps obvious. The competitive streak in most young men causes them to walk faster than the group; that, and the erroneous belief that greater fitness and strength (which most men, mistakenly or otherwise, believe they have) will protect them against AMS. But AMS is no respecter of fitness or health. Indeed, many experienced mountaineers believe the reverse is true: the less fit you are, the slower you will want to walk and thus the greater chance you have of acclimatising properly. The best advice, then, is to **go as slowly as possible**. Let your guide be the pacemaker: do not be tempted to hare off ahead of him but stick with him. That way you can keep a sensible pace and, what's more, get to know him better and ask him any questions about the mountain and Tanzania that occur to you along the way.

There are other things you can do that many say will reduce your chances of getting AMS. One is to **eat well**: fatigue is said to be a major contributor to AMS, so try to keep energy levels up by eating as much as you can.

❑ DIAMOX

Acetazolamide (traded under the brand name Diamox) is the wonder drug that fights AMS and the first treatment doctors give to somebody suffering from mountain sickness. It works because it is a **carbonic anhydrase inhibitor**. This means that the kidneys are forced to expel bicarbonate, thus re-acidifying the blood, which stimulates breathing, thereby allowing a greater amount of oxygen to enter into the bloodstream.

A lot of climbers were initially a bit sceptical about Diamox, worrying whether it actually helped to fight AMS or merely masked the symptoms. Indeed, I've spoken to an expert in the field of altitude sickness who is still not convinced by Diamox. It was, after all, developed as a treatment for the eye disease 'glaucoma' and its beneficial effects on AMS sufferers were noticed only much later. These dissenting voices are fewer in number now and it seems widely accepted that it really is a most effective drug against altitude sickness. That's not to say that it works for everyone, however; for some reason, some people just don't seem to derive any benefit from the drug at all.

It's worth noting that while Diamox is widely regarded as a boon, there are still many questions to be answered about it. It's not unusual for climbers to be given different prescriptions by their doctors: **the majority will have 125mg tablets, for example, and will be expected to take them twice a day**; others will have 250mg tablets and will be told to take them either once or, more often, twice per day; while still others will be issued with a single 500 or even 750mg tablet and told to take it only if they are feeling ill.

That last prescription leads us onto the second major question about Diamox: Should the drug be used as a cure for when someone starts developing symptoms of mountain sickness? Or should it be used prophylactically, taking it daily from the start of the walk to prevent AMS occurring in the first place? The disadvantage with doing this, according to one doctor serving on the Annapurna Circuit in Nepal, is that by using Diamox prophylactically, you are using up one possible cure. That is to say, should you begin to suffer from AMS even though you've been taking Diamox, doctors are going to have to look for another form of treatment to ensure your survival.

Dehydration can exacerbate AMS too, so it is vital that you **drink every few minutes** when walking; for this reason, one of the platypus-style water bags (Camelbaks), which allow you to drink hands-free without breaking stride, is invaluable (see pp43-5).

Wearing warm clothes is important too, allowing you to conserve energy that would otherwise be spent on maintaining a reasonable body temperature. Although there hasn't been a serious study on this subject, many people swear that carrying your own rucksack increases your chance of succumbing to AMS. **Hire a porter to carry your baggage** (the agencies will assume you want to unless you specify otherwise).

HOW TO TREAT AMS

Sat down beside P.D. in the mud. Gave him one bottle of champagne. Revived him greatly.
Peter MacQueen *In Wildest Africa* (1910)

It is possible that on your trek you will see at least one poor so-and-so being wheeled down Kilimanjaro, surrounded by porters and strapped to the strange unicycle-cum-stretcher device that KINAPA uses for evacuating the sick and

At the moment the jury is still out as to what is the best dose and prescription for Diamox, though for what it's worth around 80% of our climbers who decide to take them do so prophylactically, either at the very start of the trek or on day three when they are at an altitude of around 3500m or so; 125mg twice a day is the usual regime prescribed from here.

However you decide to take it, there are a couple of **rules you should always follow**: consult your doctor before taking Diamox to discuss the risks and benefits; and secondly, if you do take it, remember to try it out first at home to check for any allergic reaction, as Diamox is a sulfa derivative and some people do suffer from side effects, particularly a strange tingling sensation in their hands and feet.

Oh, and because Diamox is a diuretic, I would take it once in the morning and once you arrive at camp in the afternoon. That way you'll avoid getting up several times overnight to pee.

Are there any other drugs that are as effective as Diamox?

I am grateful to reader Erasmus Schneider for pointing me in the direction of two studies that both suggested that the humble Ibuprofen could also be an effective weapon against altitude illness – and with fewer side effects. The first study, published in 2012 in *National Center for Biotechnology Information* (💻 ncbi.nlm.nih.gov) concluded that 'Compared with placebo, Ibuprofen was effective in reducing the incidence of acute mountain sickness.' A second study published in the same journal concluded that 'Ibuprofen and acetazolamide were similarly effective in preventing high altitude headache. Ibuprofen was similar to acetazolamide in preventing symptoms of AMS [my underlining], an interesting finding that implies a potentially new approach to prevention of cerebral forms of acute altitude illness.' For the moment I would still recommend Diamox over Ibuprofen all the time – as the second study says, it is effective against the symptoms but not necessarily against the cause of altitude sickness – but it will be interesting to hear what other studies have to say in the future.

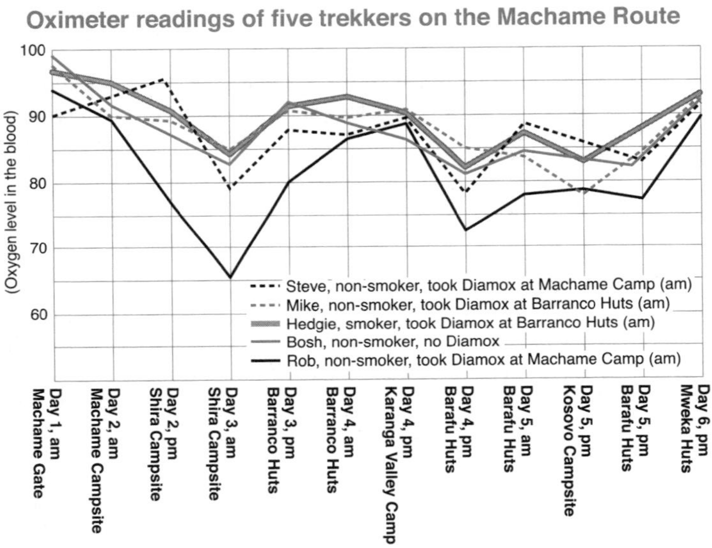

This table shows the oximeter readings of five trekkers on the Machame Route. You can see how the amount of oxygen in the blood decreases as they ascend the mountain. Perhaps the most interesting feature of the graph, however, is the way that everybody's oxygen saturation declines and climbs at the same places.

Despite the differences in each individual's readings, it may interest you to know that all of the climbers made it to the top.

suffering from the mountain. **Descent** is the most effective cure for AMS but in some severe cases it is not enough.

Diamox (see box pp248-9) is also usually given, though again, if the victim has been suffering for a while, or Diamox is not available, some other treatment may be used. Such other treatments include:

Dexamethasone is useful for treating severe AMS and, in conjunction with other treatments, in treating HACO. Two 4mg tablets should be given to the HACO sufferer, followed by one tablet every 6 hours until the victim has recovered. Some doctors are horrified at the thought of giving a person a steroid on the mountain (which is what Dexamethasone is), but many mountaineers are convinced of the benefits it can bring.

Nifedipine is useful in treating HAPO though is hard to source in Africa and thus is seldom seen on the mountain. To administer the drug, prick a 10mg capsule many times with a pin before giving to the sufferer who should then chew it thoroughly before swallowing. If the victim then shows signs of breathing more easily, this should be repeated 15 minutes later. The drug has the side-effect of lowering blood pressure but can be most effective in helping treat victims of HAPO; some people even continue to ascend if they respond well to the drug – though I don't recommend this.

Gamow hyperbaric bag This is a man-sized bag into which the victim is enclosed. The bag is then zipped up and inflated. As it is inflated, the pressure felt by the sufferer inside the bag is increased, thus mimicking the atmospheric conditions present at a lower altitude. The disadvantage with this method is one of inconvenience. The cumbersome bag has to be taken up the mountain and, worst of all, in order to work effectively once the patient is inside, the bag must be kept at a constant pressure. This means that somebody must pump up the bag every two or three minutes. This is tricky when at least two other people are trying to manoeuvre the bag (with the patient inside it) down the slopes. Some of the upmarket trek operators carry one with them and KINAPA are trying to make this compulsory for all groups on the Western Breach, where descent – should it be necessary – is very difficult. If you are going to spend some time on the summit or in the crater, or if you know that helicopter rescue is available

❑ THE LAKE LOUISE ACUTE MOUNTAIN SICKNESS TEST

What is the Lake Louise Scale?

The Lake Louise test was developed in the early 1990s to both diagnose Acute Mountain Sickness (AMS) and to judge its severity. The test takes the form of a simple questionnaire that is given to the climber. On it the climber is asked if he or she is suffering from any of the following four symptoms:

Headache
Gastrointestinal Upset
Fatigue/Weakness
Dizziness/Light-Headedness

The climber is asked to 'grade' each symptom from 0 to 3. For example, if the climber does not have a headache he or she would give that a score of zero. If the headache was mild, a score of 1 would be given, 2 if the headache is moderate, and 3 means the climber has a severe, pounding headache.

How do you interpret the results?

The scores for each symptom are then totted up and **if the climber fulfils the following criteria, it is assumed that he or she has AMS:**

1) The climber has reported having some sort of headache (ie he or she gave their headache a score of at least 1);
2) He or she also has at least one other symptom on the above list;
3) The *total* score is three or more.

If the climber has just a severe headache, (ie, he gives his headache a score of 3), but no other symptom, that is also be categorised as AMS.

To give you an example, a climber has indicated that she has a mild headache (for which she is given 1 point), moderate nausea (2 points), mild fatigue (1 point), but no dizziness or light-headedness (0 points for each). Her total would be four, which would indicate that she is suffering from AMS.

Though the test may seem rather too simplistic, many guides on Kili do say that it provides a useful, systematic tool for diagnosing AMS and to help judge its severity.

(so you can wait inside the bag for the helicopter to arrive), a Gamow bag could prove invaluable; otherwise, a rapid descent should be possible and still the best solution.

Oxygen Giving the victim extra oxygen from a bottle or canister does not immediately reverse all the symptoms, though in conjunction with rapid descent it can be most effective. A (very) few companies are now supplying their clients (for a fee) with an **ALTOX** system, where oxygen is fed to the client through cannulas inserted in their nose while they are ascending. It sounds uncomfortable but for those who are very worried about altitude, or who *know* they are susceptible, this could be the difference between success and failure.

OTHER POTENTIAL HEALTH PROBLEMS

But Mike is far more ill today. The five paying hikers know this because it has become the habit of all to monitor the health of everyone else. The question "How are you?" on this mountain is not rhetorical. The words, in each case, from each hiker, give way to a distinct and complicated answer, involving the appearance or avoidance of blisters, of burgeoning headaches, of sore ankles and quads, shoulders that still, even with the straps adjusted, feel pinched. Mike's stomach feels, he is telling everyone, like there is actually a large tapeworm inside him. Its movements are trackable, relentless, he claims, and he's given it a name: Ashley, after an ex-girlfriend. He looks desperate for a moment of contentment; he looks like a sick child, lying on the bathroom floor, bent around the toilet, exhausted and defeated, who's forgotten what it was to feel strong.

David Eggers, from his short story *Up the Mountain Coming Down Slowly*

Coughs and colds

These are common on Kilimanjaro. Aspirin can help alleviate some of the symptoms. Lozenges containing anaesthetic are useful for a sore throat, as is gargling with warm salty water. Drinking plenty helps too. A **cough** that produces mucus has one of a number of causes; most likely are the common cold or irritation of the bronchi by cold air which produces symptoms that are similar to flu. It could, however, point to AMS. A cough that produces thick green and yellow mucus could indicate bronchitis. If there is also **chest pain** (most severe when the patient breathes out), a high fever and blood-stained mucus, any of these could indicate **pneumonia**, requiring a course of antibiotics. Consult a doctor.

Exposure

Also known as **hypothermia**, this is caused by a combination of exhaustion, high altitude, dehydration, lack of food and not wearing enough warm clothes against the cold. Note that it does not need to be very cold for exposure to occur. Make sure everyone is properly equipped, *including* your porters.

Symptoms of exposure include a low body temperature (below 34.5ºC or 94ºF), poor coordination, exhaustion and shivering. As their condition deteriorates the shivering ceases, coördination gets worse making walking difficult and the patient may start hallucinating. The pulse then slows and unconsciousness and death follow shortly. Treatment involves thoroughly warming the patient quickly. Find shelter as soon as possible. Put the patient, without their clothes, into a sleeping-bag with hot water bottles (use your water bottles filled with hot water and wrapped in something to prevent burning the victim); someone else should take their clothes off, too, and get into the sleeping bag with the patient: there's nothing like bodily warmth to hasten recovery (and who knows, it could be the start of something beautiful).

Frostbite

The severe form of frostbite that leads to the loss of fingers and toes rarely happens to trekkers on Kilimanjaro (though I do know one guide to whom this has happened). You could, however, be affected if you get stuck or lost in particularly inclement weather. Ensure that all members of your party are properly kitted out with warm socks, boots, gloves and woolly hats.

The first stage of frostbite is known as 'frostnip'. The fingers or toes first become cold and painful, then numb and white. Heat them up on a warm part of the body (eg an armpit) until the colour comes back. In cases of severe frostbite the affected part of the body becomes frozen. Don't try to warm it up until you reach a lodge/camp. Immersion in warm (not hot!) water (40°C or 100°F) is the treatment. Medical help should then be sought.

Gynaecological problems

If you have had a vaginal infection in the past it would be a good idea to bring a course of treatment in case it recurs.

Haemorrhoids

If you've suffered from these in the past bring the required medication with you since haemorrhoids can flare up on a trek, particularly if you get constipated.

Snowblindness

Though the snows of Kilimanjaro are fast disappearing, you are still strongly advised to wear **sunglasses** when walking on the summit – particularly if you plan on spending more than just a few minutes up there – to prevent this uncomfortable, though temporary, condition. Ensure everyone in your group, including porters, has **eye protection**. If you lose your sunglasses a piece of cardboard with two narrow slits (just wide enough to see through) will protect your eyes. The cure for snow-blindness is to keep your eyes closed and lie down in a dark room. Eye-drops and aspirin can be helpful.

Sunburn

Protect against sunburn by wearing a hat, sunglasses and a shirt with a collar that can be turned up. At altitude you'll also need high-factor sunscreen for your face and some zinc cream or similar for your lips.

Care of feet, ankles and knees

A twisted ankle, swollen knee or a septic blister on your foot could ruin your trek so it's very important you take care to avoid these. Choose comfortable boots with good ankle support (see pp39-40). Don't carry too heavy a load. Wash your feet and change your socks regularly. During lunch stops take off your boots and socks and let them dry in the sun. Attend to any blister as soon as you feel it developing.

❑ TOILET ETIQUETTE

The toilets at the various camps come in for a lot of stick from trekkers. And rightly so, too, because for the most part they're bloody awful. KINAPA do try to maintain and improve the facilities, but the sheer number of trekkers who use them – and the fact that some of these trekkers were patently never schooled in even the basic skill of cleaning up after themselves – mean that these toilets are in the same parlous physical state as their old wooden forebears, and smell just as bad too.

But whatever their state and no matter how unpleasant they may be, you still have an obligation to use them (unless you've paid for having a private toilet dragged up the mountain for your use). There are few sights on Kilimanjaro more depressing than the clods and streamers of used toilet roll hiding behind rocks and hanging from bushes surrounding each campsite. It's hard to understand why some people think it's OK to sleep in a campsite surrounded by their own turds, rather than spending two minutes inside one of the public loos, no matter how disgusting the latter. But if you happen to be one of them, the following tips may help you overcome your terror of the toilet:

- If you're worried about being disturbed by a fellow trekker, on hearing someone approach try coughing, whistling, screaming or otherwise alerting them to your presence *before* they have a chance to invade your space.
- Conversely, when approaching the toilet, give any occupants inside fair warning of your presence by approaching noisily and knocking before entering. It's only polite.
- If it's the smell that worries you, a bandanna round your nose and mouth can help.
- Visiting the toilet in the early morning – when the stuff inside is frozen solid and the stench is reduced – is also a good plan.
- While inside the toilets you have a responsibility to keep things tidy. It can be difficult to maintain balance and aim but if you do miss, do the decent thing and tidy up.

Going outside

If you really, really, really can't wait to reach one of the toilets, the least you can do is deliberate before you defecate. Firstly, make sure you're at least 20m away from both the path and any streams – the mountain is still the main source of water for many villages and they would prefer it if you didn't crap in their H_2O. Secondly, having done your business, dispose of your toilet paper properly. I recommend just wrapping it in unused toilet paper, tucking it in a corner of your bag away from anything else, and disposing of it at the next toilet you come to. See also below.

If we all follow these rules maybe, just maybe, Kilimanjaro will remain Earth's most beautiful mountain – rather than resembling one huge, 5895m-high pile of human faecal matter.

Modern innovations

Over the past couple of years a couple of companies have introduced some modern innovations in an effort to tackle the disappointingly large amount of toilet paper that litters trails both on Kili and indeed in many other hiking hot-spots. I'm indebted to one of our climbers, Emily Winks, for both bringing my attention to, and then reviewing, one potential solution: a '**kula cloth**' (see box p44).

Another climber, Kelly Flinn, pointed me in the direction of **PACT Outdoors** (💻 pactoutdoors.com) and their range of al-fresco 'Bathroom Kits', which include an ergonomic, lightweight shovel; some decomposable wipes; and, best of all, some tablets that are made from mycelium from fungi, which naturally break down poo (and the wipes) faster, as well as killing bacteria that threaten waterways, wildlife and public health.

Blisters There are several ways to treat blisters but prevention is far better than cure. Stop immediately you feel a 'hot spot' forming and cover it with a piece of moleskin or Second Skin/Compeed. If a blister does form you can either burst it with a needle (sterilised in a flame) then apply a dressing or build a moleskin dressing around the unburst blister to protect it.

Sprains You can reduce the risk of a sprained ankle by wearing boots which offer good support. Watch where you walk, too. If you do sprain an ankle, cool it in a stream and keep it bandaged. If it's very painful you'll probably have to abandon your trek. Aspirin is helpful for reducing pain and swelling.

Knee problems These are most common after long stretches of walking downhill and particularly so amongst more senior trekkers. It's not helped by the state of the Mweka Trail, which is pretty treacherous in places. It's important not to take long strides as you descend; small steps will lessen the jarring on your knee. It may be helpful to wear knee supports and use walking poles for long descents, especially if you've had problems with your knees before.

Minimum impact trekking

'Manya ulanyc upangenyi cha ipfuve' – 'Do not foul the cave where you have slept' (A Chagga proverb that refers to the habits of the baboon who are said to 'foul their caves' until there comes a point where the stench compels them to find alternative accommodation.)

KINAPA (see box p165) does try to keep Kilimanjaro clean. At all huts and campsites, trekking groups have their rubbish weighed by the ranger; if there's any evidence that some rubbish has been dumped (ie if the rubbish carried weighs less at one campsite than at the previous camp) the guide could have his licence temporarily revoked and/or have to pay a heavy fine. It's a system that would appear to have loopholes but until recently Kili *was* a very clean mountain, and though it can be frustrating to have to wait for your guide every morning while the rubbish is weighed, it's a small price to pay for a pristine peak. Sadly, from time to time standards slip, to the extent that a few of them actually organise clean-up treks on the mountain.

While it's easy to blame the authorities for the sorry state of Kili, trekkers are just as culpable. After all, pretty much all of it is our rubbish. But you can help Kilimanjaro become beautiful once more by following these simple rules that apply to almost every mountain anywhere in the world.

Some guidelines

• **Dispose of litter properly** In theory, all you should have to do is give your litter to your crew: given the stiff punishments they receive for leaving rubbish behind (see above), this should ensure all waste is taken off the mountain. Unfortunately, despite all the cleaning crews and the weighing stations at each campsite, the system clearly isn't perfect. Whatever you decide to do, don't give

used batteries to porters; keep them with you and take them back to the West where they have the facilities to dispose of them properly (the batteries that is, not the porters).

• **Don't start fires** There's absolutely no need for fires on Kilimanjaro: for cooking, your crew should use kerosene stoves, while for heat, put another layer of clothes on or cuddle up to somebody who doesn't mind being cuddled up to.

• **Use the purpose-built latrines** True, some of them could do with emptying (especially the toilet at the Barranco campsite, which is now so full that the pile of human waste is in danger of developing a snowy summit all of its own), but this is still better than having piles of poo behind all the bushes on the trail and toilet paper hanging from every bough.

Ladies, if you really, really have to go en route to the next campsite, there is a thing called a kula cloth (see p44) as an alternative to toilet paper. And if it's a number two that you want to do, check out the PACT Outdoors Bathroom Kit (see box p254).

• **Leave the flora and fauna alone** Kili is home to some beautiful flowers and fascinating wildlife but the giant groundsels rarely thrive in the soils of Europe and the wild buffalo, though they may look docile when splashing about in the streams of Kili, have an awful temper that makes them quite unsuitable as pets. It's illegal to take flora and fauna out of the park, so leave it all alone. That way, other trekkers can enjoy them too.

• **Boil, filter or purify your drinking water** This will help to reduce the number of non-returnable, non-reusable, non-biodegradable and very environmentally unfriendly plastic mineral water bottles that are thankfully now banned on Kili.

• **Stay on the main trail** The continued use of shortcuts, particularly steep ones, erodes the slopes. This is particularly true on Kibo: having reached the summit, it's very tempting on your return to slide down on the shale like a skier and you'll see many people, especially guides, doing just that.

There's no doubt that it's a fast, fun and furious way to get to the bottom, but with thousands of trekkers doing likewise every year, the slopes of Kibo are gradually being eroded as all the scree gets pushed further down the mountain. Laborious as it sounds, stick to the same snaking path that you used to ascend.

• **Wash away from streams and rivers** You wouldn't like to bathe in somebody else's bathwater; nor, probably, would you like to cook with it, do your laundry in it, nor indeed drink it. And neither would the villagers on Kili's lower slopes, so don't pollute their water by washing your hair, body or clothes in the mountain streams, no matter how romantic an idea this sounds.

If your company is halfway decent your guide will bring some hot water in a bowl at the end of the day's walk with which you can wash. Dispose of it at least 20m away from any streams or rivers.

MOUNT MERU

8

INTRODUCTION

Mount Meru, which overlooks Arusha from the north, is used by many trekkers as a **warm-up trek** – an *hors d'oeuvre* to the main course of Kili if you like. And a perfect starter it is too: though smaller, it's also quite similar in that to reach its volcanic summit you have first to climb through a number of vegetation zones before embarking on the final night-time march to the highest point on the crater rim and thus the summit itself. What's more, at 4566m (14,980ft), it provides the trekker with the perfect opportunity to acclimatise to Kilimanjaro's rarified atmosphere. In other words, the mountain offers a taste of the challenges that lie ahead on Kilimanjaro, whilst also whetting the appetite for the thrills and beauty of that mountain.

However, Meru is worth doing as much for the differences as for the similarities it shares with its neighbour. In particular, there's the greater abundance of **wildlife**. Lying at the heart of Arusha National Park, a reserve that's teeming with animals, it's an odd trekker who doesn't finish the trek with his or her camera filled with pictures of buffalo, giraffe, elephant, bushbuck, dik dik, suni, colobus, blue monkey and warthog. Luckier ones may also see leopard and hyaena, while twitchers will be more than content with the number of birds on offer, from the noisy Hartlaub's turaco to the silver-cheeked hornbill and black-and-white bulbul.

Leopard track (Mt Meru)

If all this sounds like your idea of a perfect holiday – a safari-and-trek all rolled into one – you're probably right, though there is one point that needs to be emphasised: **do not underestimate Meru**. Though it may be more than a thousand metres lower than Kili, it's still well above the height necessary to bring about **altitude sickness** and with almost everybody taking just over two days before reaching the summit, the risks are not small.

There is also **more night-time scrambling** to be undertaken on the smaller sibling. Indeed, without a shadow of a doubt my most nerve-racking ascent was several years ago on Meru and not Kili. True, this had much to do with the fact that there had been heavy rain the evening before the night-time walk to the summit, a downpour which quickly froze and caused the entire trail from Saddle to summit to become covered with a layer of ice. Inconvenient on the first part of that nocturnal ascent, on the second half it became positively dangerous, causing us to scribble hurriedly a last will and testament in my notebook. Indeed, it was thanks only to the hard work of the guides, who dug out footsteps in the ice with a piece of rock or the back of their heels – footsteps in which, taking my lead from King Wenceslas, I then trod – that I gained the summit at all. And it was only by inching my way back down, bottom pressed into the ice, limbs looking for any piece of rock or other non-slippery material to put my weight on, that I made it back down to write this guide.

So though Meru may not carry the cachet, prestige or the sheer scale of Kili it's no pushover – and maybe it's no coincidence that the first successful recorded ascent, though still in dispute (being credited to either Carl Uhlig in 1901 or Fritz Jaeger in 1904), occurred at least a dozen years *after* the conquest of Kilimanjaro. Meru remains an awfully big mountain – the 10th highest peak in Africa in fact – and as such it should be treated with respect.

PRACTICALITIES

The route

There is only one *main* route up Meru. It begins at Momela Gate, around 15km from the main Ngongongare entrance to the park where you pay your park fees. Having paid up and driven those 15km, past the plain known as Little Serengeti (Serengeti Ndogo) because of its similarity to Tanzania's most famous park, you arrive at **Momela Gate** (altitude 1597m/5240ft) where you pick up your ranger and possibly hire your porters.

The route from Momela Gate to the summit is punctuated by **two sets of accommodation huts**: the first are the **Miriakamba Huts** (2503m/8212ft), a day's walk from Momela Gate; and the second are the **Saddle Huts** (3560m/11,680ft), lying a short day's walk from there. From the Saddle Huts it's a further day's walk – or rather, a night's walk – to the summit.

Which path to take Though I just stated above that there's only one path to the summit of Meru, that's not entirely true for, in fact, on this first day there are **two possible paths**, the split between the two occurring just five minutes along the trail. There are also a couple of variations to this main trail invented by rangers, which tend to cross from one path to the other. Most trekkers, of course, will want to take both paths, one on the way up and the other on the way down. The question is, therefore, which path to take first?

Regarding these two trails, **the first** is a longer and more circuitous route that follows a 4WD dirt track as it swerves drunkenly and only very approximately along the course of the Ngare Nanyuki (the river you cross on a bridge right at the beginning of the trek) and Jekukumia rivers through the forest before turning north to cross the Crater Plain to the huts. As for the **second option**, this is a much more direct path and, on first sight at least, would appear to be the more tempting. It includes a crossing of the Meru Plain that's alive with Africa's tallest mammal (the giraffe) and its most bad-tempered (the buffalo), and could also take in a diversion to the beautiful Tululusia Falls (if you haven't already visited them on the way up, of course, which is where I describe them on p261). Weirdly, there's very little forest on this route, the path sticking to the top of a grassy, largely tree-less ridge.

Unless you specify otherwise the chances are your ranger/guide will take you on this shorter, steeper path; and it is indeed a wonderful walk. However, I advise you to leave this option until the end and instead **choose the longer trail for your ascent**. Why? Simply because, in my experience, most trekkers are too tired on the last day of their trek to attempt the longer trail on the way down, whatever their intentions when they began their trek. (Indeed, if you're on a three-day trek you may well not even have time to do the longer trail on the last day.) In other words, if you don't take the longer path now, for the ascent, the chances are you'll miss out on it altogether. There's also the matter of acclimatisation to consider, for taking over four hours to climb the 906m to Miriakamba Huts is more sensible than taking just two or so, as you would on the shorter trail. So don't be too eager to get amongst the animals on the plain at the foot of Meru but instead choose the longer trail for your ascent and save the shorter trail for the way down; and this is how I've described the trek in the route description beginning on p261.

The cost

Trips up Meru are usually offered by the agencies in both Arusha (the best place to organise such a trek) and Moshi, and are for either three or four days. **Don't be misled into thinking that if you book a four-day trek you are more likely to reach the summit because of the extra day's acclimatisation**; that extra day is actually spent on the *way down*, not up. So, while I like to have the extra day to descend – it's a bit too much of a rush otherwise to go from the summit to Momela Gate in one day and I was grateful to spend a second night at Miriakamba – if you're on a tight budget you'll save around US$112 in **park fees** by taking a day less. These park fees tend to be a little cheaper than the equivalent charges on Kili and are as follows (all prices from 2023):

- Conservation fee (formerly known as Park Entrance fee): US$50 per day. Unusually, between mid March and mid May there's a low season discount of US$45 per day. There's also a 50% discount for under 16s.
- Hut fee: US$30 per night; US$10 for under 16s
- Rescue fee: US$20 per trip
- Guide/ranger fee: US$15 per day

Once again there is **18% VAT** to pay on top of each of these fees.

Thus for a 4-day/3-night trip you're looking at a total figure of US$370 plus VAT. On top of this you'll probably need to pay the equivalent **porters/guide fees** to enable them to enter and stay in the park. All these fees will be factored into the total amount the trekking agency charges for your trek so needn't concern you too much here. However, do note that you will in fact be accompanied by at least two guides on your trek: one (at least) supplied by the agency and one by the park (whom I have called a ranger/guide to avoid confusion).

The **ranger/guide** supplied by the park **is compulsory**, for it is he who carries the gun that could, should any of the local fauna take an unhealthy interest in your party, come in very handy. However, these rangers in my experience are often better guides, with good English and a greater knowledge of the park, mainly because they spend most of their time in it. Indeed, on one of my previous treks I didn't even see the guide who had been supplied by the trekking agency until I got to the Miriakamba Huts at the end of the first day!

Trekking with an operator

The trekking operators in Arusha usually charge US$700-1100pp for four days, depending on group size and the specifications of the trek. You may want to factor into this fee a night or two at one of the lodges near the park. This will enable you to make an early start in the morning (though treks are officially not allowed to start until 10am anyway, so as not to disrupt the animals' dawn hunt).

The top choice is the eccentric ***Hatari Lodge*** (🖳 hatari.travel), which has real history and character. The lodge is named after the John Wayne film that was shot on the farm. Indeed, one of Wayne's co-stars, a German actor called Hardy Krüger, actually ended up giving up Hollywood for Arusha, and bought the farm on which the lodge is set soon after the film was completed. With a small library, long bar, breakfast terrace and great views of both Kili and Meru, this is a refreshingly different safari lodge with décor and location that are best described as quirky. Prices start at around US$345 per person full board in a twin/double even in the very low season, in addition to the park fees. If you

❑ PRESSURE FROM GUIDES FOR A BIG TIP

One of the uglier aspects of many Meru climbs is the pressure exerted by guide and ranger in tandem on the poor trekker to pay a sizeable tip. Sit in the Miriakamba or Saddle Huts and you'll see them sidle up to their clients, innocently ask them how their dinner was, make a light bit of chit chat – and then launch into a speech about how much they are expecting to receive in gratuities. I have heard tales of people paying fortunes after being subjected to such pressure and of other trekkers being left in tears after being forced to hand over far more than they were initially expecting. Suffice to say, I think it's well within your rights to tell these gentlemen in no uncertain terms to get lost. Furthermore, you could also tell them that if they are to get a tip (which, of course, they are entitled to if they have carried out their job professionally) **it is entirely up to you how much you'll pay**, and that if they don't leave you alone the tip will be reduced in size accordingly. If they continue, report them to both the park authority and the agency with which you climbed. See pp32-3 for tips on tipping on Kili; on Meru the daily rate should be pretty much the same for porters, cooks and guides, though you'll also have to factor in tips for the ranger who should get the same amount as the guide.

I am a great supporter and admirer of the guides and rangers and the work they do – but this is a deeply unpleasant practice and needs to stop.

have the time, come here for a drink even if you're not staying. There are cheaper places to stay near the Ngongongare entrance gate.

STAGE 1: MOMELA GATE TO MIRIAKAMBA HUTS (VIA THE LONGER ROUTE) [MAP A, p263]

Distance: 13.8km (8½ miles); altitude gained: 906m (2972ft)
Though this longer route avoids the fauna-filled Meru Plain, there's still an abundance of wildlife to be seen. In addition to the beasts of the savannah that can still be espied behind the screen of acacias, within the first five minutes – no, make that three – of starting one trek up Meru I also encountered dik dik and suni standing motionless in the scrub lining the path, while a little further on a troop of baboons greeted my approach by turning their backs to us to display their red-raw fundaments.

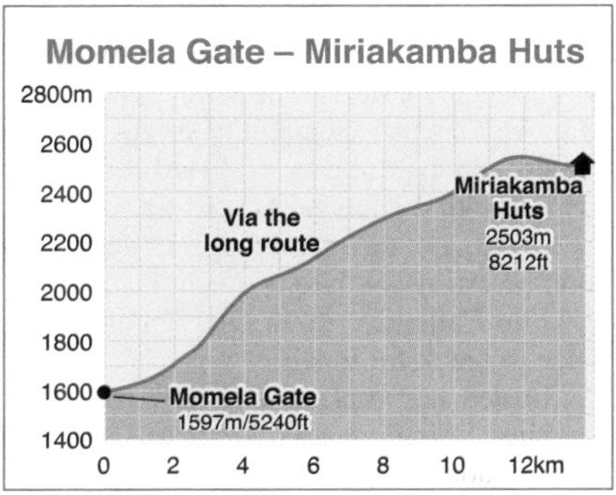

It's a hot and dusty start to the trek but a distinctly memorable one; even on this longer route I guarantee you'll see more animals within the first half-hour of your expedition than you would in a month on Kili. If your guide is amenable, you can also take the path off right to visit the impressive **Tululusia Falls**.

The scenery changes slightly as you reach the junction with the path to Campsite 3 and the path bends right (west), with both the gradient and the size of the trees increasing. (These campsites, incidentally, are not for the use of trekkers.) The first junipers, bearded with lichen, appear and the whole trail now takes on a lusher, greener aspect. Continuing up the hill, your guide, bored with the repetitive twists and turns of the official trail, may take you on a well-known short-cut, emerging back onto the trail just before a stream with a marshy patch of grassland to the left – nicknamed **Meru's Garden** by the guides and often populated by bushbuck and blue monkey – and the summit beyond. A good opportunity for a photo, methinks. A second photo opportunity occurs just a minute later with the first of several signposted **Kilimanjaro viewpoints**.

Regardless of whether you take photos at these places or not, one sight which I can almost guarantee will have you reaching for your Rolleiflex is the **arched fig tree**, a magnificent strangler fig (*Ficus thonningii*) which has now completely enveloped its host and arches across the track. It is reminiscent of

For details about the features shown on the trail maps in this guide, please see p270.

The famous arched fig tree

those pictures you see of giant redwoods in California which have cars driving through them – though in this instance it is said to have been elephants who have passed through the tunnel formed by the tree, widening the gap as they do so.

The path, illuminated by popcorn cassia (*Cassia didymobotrya*; incorrectly called candle bushes by many guides) in season, heads north soon after to cross an open area with a good view of the summit and possible sightings of buffalo on the **Itikoni Plain** to the south of the trail. (Not far after this, just past Itikoni Campsite, there's a path that heads off to the north that more and more trekkers are taking for their ascent; I've marked the path on Map A. It's a path that boldly strikes out in a northerly direction to meet with a stream, which it follows westwards before crossing the water to head north again to meet with the Lenganassa River and the 'other' trail from Miriakamba Huts.)

Sticking to the main track, the northerly direction is but temporary, the path soon reverting south to acquaint itself with the sweet-water **Jekukumia River** at **Maio Falls**, at 2157m (7077ft) altitude a picturesque spot and a delightful place to break for lunch.

Rested and replete, you now return to the main track as it continues its weaving, wriggling way westwards up the slope. It's a pleasant stroll, the gradient seldom steep and the stands of juniper and podocarpus providing essential shade. The forest is still alive with animals, too, even though they may be more difficult to see.

Your ranger/guide, however, should be able to point out the tracks of hyaena, snake, leopard, giraffe or buffalo and your walk will, more than likely, be accompanied by the bark of the bushbuck, call of the colobus monkey (which sounds curiously like a frog) and the broken-klaxon honk of Hartlaub's turaco (which, just to confuse matters, sounds curiously like a monkey). If you're lucky, a crash in the undergrowth or in the branches will give away the precise location of these shy creatures, or indeed of giraffe or buffalo.

The scenery is just as pleasant as before lunch, but by now tiredness and a desire for change will probably have set in, along with a wish that the track, for a few metres at least, would follow a straight line.

Thankfully, about an hour after leaving the falls the **first red hot pokers** (*Kniphofia thomsonii*; Map B) appear, a flower that heralds the imminent arrival of **Kitoto Viewpoint**, with views east-north-east over the Momela Lakes and east-south-east over the fauna-filled Ngurdoto Crater, the original centre and raison d'être of Arusha National Park before it merged with Meru to create the park you find today.

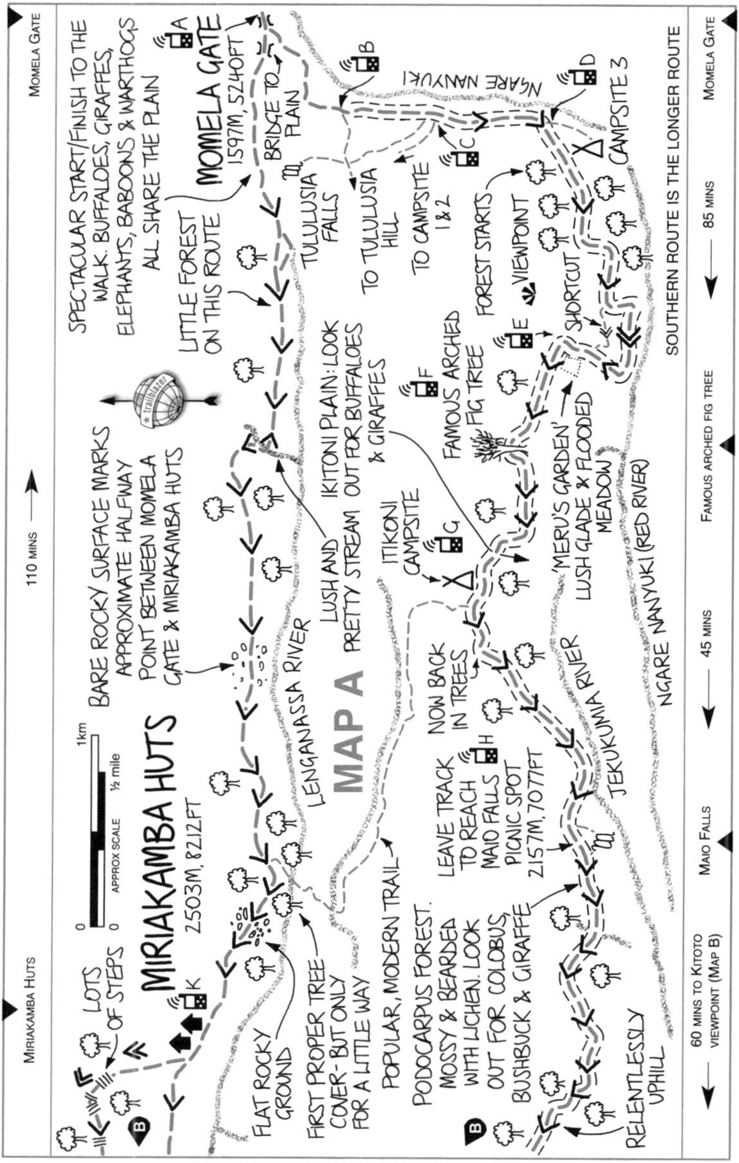
MIRIAKAMBA HUTS
110 MINS
MOMELA GATE
SPECTACULAR START/FINISH TO THE WALK. BUFFALOES, GIRAFFES, ELEPHANTS, BABOONS & WARTHOGS ALL SHARE THE PLAIN
MOMELA GATE
1597M, 5240FT
BRIDGE TO PLAIN
TULULUSIA FALLS
TO TULULUSIA HILL
TO CAMPSITE 1 & 2
NGARE NANYUKI
CAMPSITE 3
LITTLE FOREST ON THIS ROUTE
FOREST STARTS
VIEWPOINT
SHORTCUT
BARE ROCKY SURFACE MARKS APPROXIMATE HALFWAY POINT BETWEEN MOMELA GATE & MIRIAKAMBA HUTS
LUSH AND PRETTY STREAM
IKITONI PLAIN: LOOK OUT FOR BUFFALOES & GIRAFFES
FAMOUS ARCHED FIG TREE
ITIKONI CAMPSITE
'MERU'S GARDEN' LUSH GLADE & FLOODED MEADOW
NGARE NANYUKI (RED RIVER)
LENGANASSA RIVER
MAP A
NOW BACK IN TREES
LEAVE TRACK TO REACH MAIO FALLS PICNIC SPOT 2157M, 7077FT
JEKUKUMIA RIVER
APPROX SCALE
0 1km
0 ½ mile
MIRIAKAMBA HUTS
2503M, 8212FT
LOTS OF STEPS
FLAT ROCKY GROUND
FIRST PROPER TREE COVER - BUT ONLY FOR A LITTLE WAY
POPULAR, MODERN TRAIL
PODOCARPUS FOREST. MOSSY & BEARDED WITH LICHEN. LOOK OUT FOR COLOBUS, BUSHBUCK & GIRAFFE
RELENTLESSLY UPHILL
SOUTHERN ROUTE IS THE LONGER ROUTE
85 MINS
FAMOUS ARCHED FIG TREE
45 MINS
MAIO FALLS
60 MINS TO KITOTO VIEWPOINT (MAP B)
MOMELA GATE

From now until the end of this first stage the path feels more alpine. It's still upwards, at least until you reach a clearing with unrestricted views of the petrified lava flow that runs down from the ash cone to the plateau on which you stand – the so-called **Crater Plain**. This plain, though more than 2600m (8530ft) above sea level, still attracts an abundance of game including giraffe, hyaena, leopard, elephant and buffalo.

On the northern edge of this mini plain is the dry, rocky river-bed of the upper reaches of the **Lenganassa River**, which you follow downhill to your first night's destination.

Miriakamba Huts (Map A) are a smart pair of accommodation huts and accompanying buildings at an altitude of 2503m/8212ft. The huts are divided into rooms for four people in two bunk beds and are popular not only with tourists but also, if the amount of dung is anything to go by, buffalo and elephant too; for this reason, I advise you to take care when nipping out to the loo at night.

There are also good views across to Kilimanjaro from the toilets and the viewing platforms at the back of the dining hut.

STAGE 2: MIRIAKAMBA HUTS TO SADDLE HUTS [MAP A, p263; MAP B, p267]

Distance: 6.1km (3¾ miles); altitude gained: 1057m (3468ft)

Everybody has their favourite section of the Meru trek and the walk from the Miriakamba Huts to the lunch stop at Mgongo Wa Tembo is mine.

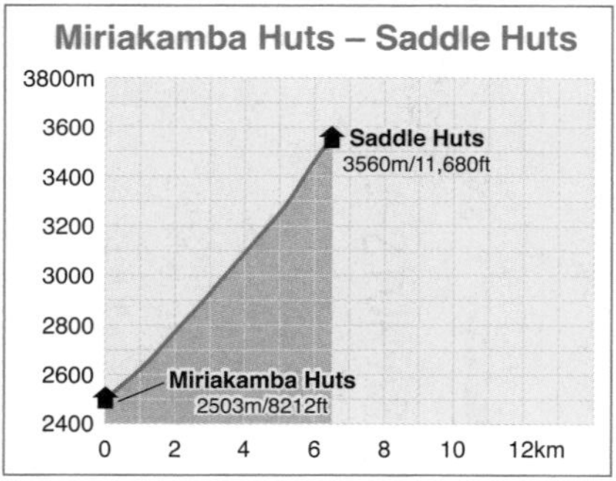

There's something gentle and gorgeously pastoral about the grassy slopes that puts one in mind of the rolling hills of England for some reason – the exotic flora and piles of elephant crap notwithstanding. Indeed, it's the unusual flora – the *Hagenia abyssinica* with its heavy pink/brown blossom, for example, or a species of lobelia (see pp171-2) which resembles in no way the lobelias you'll find in your hanging baskets back home – and the continuing presence of the park's larger fauna that add so much to the day. Even the path is impressive, a wooden staircase leading west up the slopes of the ridge towards the Saddle. Then, of course, there are the views over your shoulder of Kilimanjaro glowering at its little brother, its white summit glistening in the sun. It's a great morning's walk. Nor does the interest for trekkers wane much after lunch as the path enters the alpine zone. The trees diminish in size before disappearing altogether, to be replaced by the heathers that flourish at this altitude.

The only problem with the latter half of this second day is that it can become slightly monotonous after a while and impatience and ennui can set in. But don't be in too much of a hurry: from the moment you set off it's vital you take it *pole pole* because of the altitude.

So, from Miriakamba adopt a funereal speed from the word *Twende* ('Go!'). After a few minutes traversing the ridge, the trail heads off up the steps of the mountain's eastern flanks. The path zig-zags for much of the morning, with juniper and hagenia lining the way together with the occasional stand of *Lobelia gibberoa*, whose younger plants display an impressive phallic brush growing out of their tops. Elephants can occasionally be seen along this stretch, so do make sure you stick close to the man with the gun.

The path soon bends in a more northerly direction, with great views of Kili to your right framed by the local vegetation. There are some venerable old fallen trees here with some vivid red mountain gladioli growing from the trunks. Following the zig-zags, **Mgongo Wa Tembo** ('Elephant's Back'; about 3086m/10,124ft) is reached, the usual lunch-stop on this second stage with views south over the Crater Plain.

The path continues to climb after the break, soon leaving the forest for something altogether more alpine with *Philippia excelsa* and *Erica arborea* now proliferating. If you're lucky, you may also come across chameleons that, despite being cold-blooded creatures, somehow thrive in this region.

It's a bit of a relentless, monotonous trek but it's not long before the **Saddle Huts** (3560m/11,680ft) are reached. As with Miriakamba, these are smart huts that almost put those on Kilimanjaro to shame. Yet despite the altitude the huts still get the occasional interloper from Africa's animal kingdom, including elephant and buffalo passing through on their way to the grasslands further west.

There's little to do up here, allowing you to spend the rest of the afternoon climbing the nearby 3805m (12,484ft) **Little Meru**, a simple 45-minute trudge that the guides will often allow you to do by yourself; it's a climb that takes you to an altitude not far short of Rhino Point which you'll be visiting tonight – so remember to climb *pole pole* even though there maybe no-one to regulate your speed. That done, you can relax and prepare yourself for the exertions of the night to come ...

STAGE 3: SADDLE HUTS TO THE SUMMIT (AND BACK TO MIRIAKAMBA HUTS) [MAP B, p267]

Distance: 5.5km (3½ miles); altitude gained: 1006m (3301ft)

The ascent – Saddle Huts to the Summit

And so to the final ascent, and if the height of Meru is invaluable for acclimatising, so this night-time march is wonderful preparation for that final push to Kili's Uhuru Peak. True, this walk is shorter and, unlike the relentless zig-zags taking you up Kibo's slopes, more varied and direct. But the experience of waking up at some godforsaken hour to undertake a chilly high-altitude trek up a very big African volcano, before contouring around the crater rim to reach the

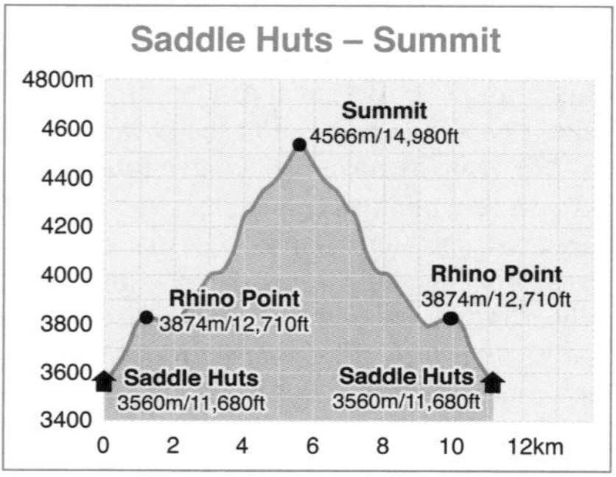

highest point as the sun rises to the east, is useful training indeed.

The stage begins with a crossing of the Saddle before bending south to the start of the climb. It's a walk that sees you leave behind the larger vegetation – the ericas and philippias – on a winding path that eventually joins the crest of a ridge that brings you out at **Rhino Point** (3874m/12,710ft), the climb's first landmark.

Thereafter the route traverses a rockface, with chains to help you complete this section, then bends west and, having descended to cross another **rockface** at the head of a lush (by the standards of this altitude) depression, climbs to follow the lip of the Meru Crater. For the next couple of hours the path follows the course of the crater rim. Being night, of course, you'll have to wait until the morning for views of the crater itself, though beyond it you should be able to see, in the distance, the lights of various settlements as well as Kilimanjaro International Airport and even, in the far distance, the Mererani tanzanite mine, working away through the night.

Mount Meru – Route to the Summit

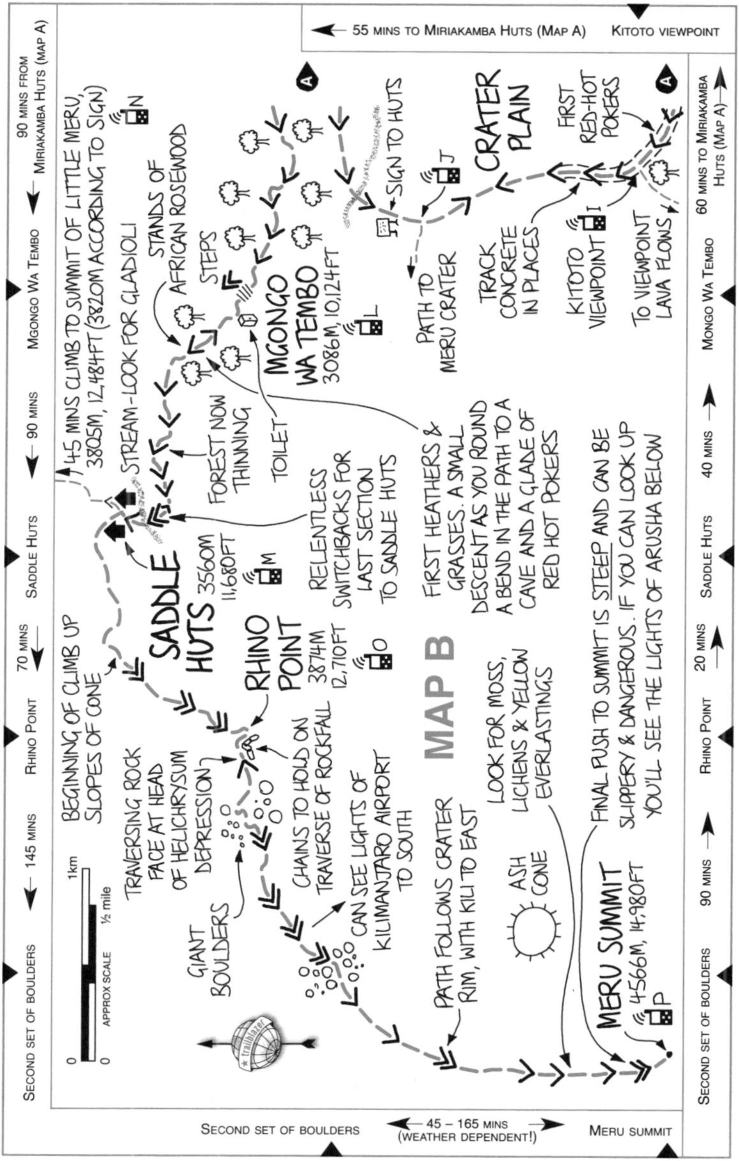
90 MINS FROM MIRIAKAMBA HUTS (MAP A)
MGONGO WA TEMBO
90 MINS
SADDLE HUTS
70 MINS
RHINO POINT
145 MINS
SECOND SET OF BOULDERS
55 MINS TO MIRIAKAMBA HUTS (MAP A)
KITOTO VIEWPOINT
60 MINS TO MIRIAKAMBA HUTS (MAP A)
MONGO WA TEMBO
40 MINS
SADDLE HUTS
20 MINS
RHINO POINT
90 MINS
SECOND SET OF BOULDERS
45 – 165 MINS (WEATHER DEPENDENT!)
MERU SUMMIT
45 MINS CLIMB TO SUMMIT OF LITTLE MERU, 3805M, 12,484FT (3820M ACCORDING TO SIGN)
N
STREAM - LOOK FOR GLADIOLI
STANDS OF AFRICAN ROSEWOOD
STEPS
SIGN TO HUTS
J
CRATER PLAIN
FIRST RED-HOT POKERS
FOREST NOW THINNING
TOILET
MGONGO WA TEMBO
3086M, 10,124FT
L
PATH TO MERU CRATER
TRACK CONCRETE IN PLACES
KITOTO VIEWPOINT
I
TO VIEWPOINT LAVA FLOWS
SADDLE HUTS
3560M 11,680FT
M
RELENTLESS SWITCHBACKS FOR LAST SECTION TO SADDLE HUTS
FIRST HEATHERS & GRASSES. A SMALL DESCENT AS YOU ROUND A BEND IN THE PATH TO A CAVE AND A GLADE OF RED HOT POKERS
BEGINNING OF CLIMB UP SLOPES OF CONE
RHINO POINT
3874M 12,710FT
O
MAP B
TRAVERSING ROCK FACE AT HEAD OF HELICHRYSUM DEPRESSION
CHAINS TO HOLD ON TRAVERSE OF ROCKFALL
LOOK FOR MOSS, LICHENS & YELLOW EVERLASTINGS
FINAL PUSH TO SUMMIT IS STEEP AND CAN BE SLIPPERY & DANGEROUS. IF YOU CAN LOOK UP YOU'LL SEE THE LIGHTS OF ARUSHA BELOW
GIANT BOULDERS
CAN SEE LIGHTS OF KILIMANJARO AIRPORT TO SOUTH
PATH FOLLOWS CRATER RIM, WITH KILI TO EAST
ASH CONE
MERU SUMMIT
4566M, 14,980FT
P
0 1km
0 ½ mile
APPROX SCALE
trailblazer

Eventually, about 3½ hours after setting off, the crater rim begins to bend noticeably south. As it does, hopefully at the same time the eastern horizon will start to turn pink and orange with the onset of the new day, and the silhouette of Kili can clearly be discerned, with both Kibo and Mawenzi summits visible.

On the summit of Mount Meru

The summit seems tangibly closer, too, so it's disheartening to discover that it's still a minimum of an hour away – or nearer three if it's been snowing and your guides have to create a path in the ice using nothing but the heels of their boots as spades and bits of rocks as shovels! It can be a little terrifying, too, with one false step sending you plummeting down the icy slopes. Take care!

At the **summit** (4566m/14,980ft) – which used to be called Socialist Peak, though they've since taken away the sign – there's little save a flag, a sign and a box containing a book where you can sign your name. There are also, of course, great views over Arusha to the west and Kili to the east, with Meru's perfect ash cone below you.

The descent – the Summit to Miriakamba Huts

Photos taken and hands shaken, it's time for the descent – and isn't it wonderful to be able to walk at a speed of your choosing again! It's also interesting to see how different in daylight the path looks. Look back from **Rhino Point**, for example, to the climb up to the crater rim – was it really that steep? Notice, too, while renegotiating the descent from the summit, all the mini bumps and craters to the north and west of Meru which were hidden on the way up.

The ash cone below the summit of Mount Meru

The descent back to the Saddle, though wearying, shouldn't take more than 2½-3 hours. Those who've opted to spend four days on the mountain will take an hour or so back at the **Saddle Huts**, packing their bags, eating some well-earned food and maybe getting a little shut-eye, before the 2-hour return stroll down to Miriakamba where they'll be spending the night.

Those on the 3-day trip will also have an hour to recover at the Saddle Huts, though for them the walk down is, of course, that much longer. If you're reading this at the Saddle Huts after your ascent to the summit, you'll probably appreciate now why I suggested taking the long route on the first stage and saving the shorter route for now.

STAGE 4: MIRIAKAMBA HUTS TO MOMELA GATE (VIA THE SHORTER ROUTE) [MAP A, p263]

Distance: 6.5km (4 miles); altitude lost: 906m (2972ft)

It may be downhill all the way, but this last day is most definitely *not* an anti-climax.

The descent from Miriakamba is hard on your knees, of course, but by way of compensation there's some unusual flora (check out the pink *Impatiens* growing right on the path and the hardy Sodom's apple trees, *Solanum sodomaeum*, growing by the side of it), a charming little river to cross and, of course, a crossing of the buffalo- and warthog-filled Meru Plain at the very end, with Kili as an awe-inspiring backdrop.

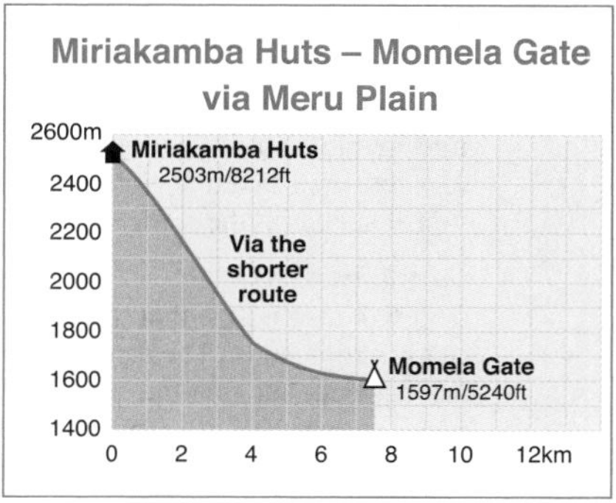

If you haven't already seen them this walk could also include a brief diversion to the impressive **Tululusia Falls**, just a few minutes off the path to the south before the plain. Isn't it curious, by the way, how there's so little forest on this route compared to the dense, dark cloud forest on the first day – even though they both cover the same altitude?

Even with the diversion you should find yourself back at Momela Gate just two hours or so after setting off. There'll just be time to distribute tips, collect your certificates (one for Mount Meru, possibly one for Little Meru too) and say your farewells to your companions. It's been a wonderful walk, hasn't it? You've seen some beautiful birds, flowers and animals, taken in some breath-taking views and through sheer bloodymindedness climbed to the very summit of Tanzania's second highest mountain.

Now it's time for the highest…

9 TRAIL GUIDE & MAPS

Using this guide

ABOUT THE MAPS IN THIS GUIDE

Scale

Most of the **trekking maps** in this guide are drawn to the same scale, namely 26mm to 1km (1⅔ inches to the mile). The exceptions are the maps which depict the final ascent to the top, ie the trails up to Uhuru Peak on Kibo (Map Nos 6, 13, 18 & 33), a trek which is usually made at night. On these maps the scale has been doubled (ie 52mm to 1km or 3⅓ inches to the mile) to allow for more detail to be drawn on them.

Walking times

The times indicated on the maps should be used only as an approximate guide. **They refer to walking times only and do not include any time for breaks and/or food**. Overall you may find you need to **add around 30-50%** to my times depending on your walking speed and the time taken for rest breaks to get an idea of the total time you'll spend on the trail.

Gradient arrows

You will also notice that there are '**gradient arrows**' on the trekking maps in this book. The arrows point uphill: two arrows mean that the hill is steep, one that the gradient is reasonably gradual. If, for example, you are walking from A (at 80m) to B (at 200m) and the trail between the two is short and steep, it would be shown thus: A – – – – >>– – – – B.

For route overviews see pp67-72.

Note: In the following descriptions, the treks have been divided into stages, with each stage roughly corresponding to a day's trekking. For this reason, throughout the text the words 'stage' and 'day' have been used interchangeably.

❑ WHAT'S IT LIKE ON THE MOUNTAIN?

Fun. It really is. Sure, the last push to the summit is hard, as some of the quotes used later in this book clearly indicate, but don't let that put you off. Kilimanjaro is a delightful mountain to climb:

But we had much to compensate us for all we had to give up. The charm of the mountain scenery, the clear, crisp atmosphere, the tonic of 'a labour we delight in' and the consciousness now and again of success achieved, all went far to make our fortnight's arduous toil a happy sequence of red-letter days.

Hans Meyer *Across East African Glaciers*

The days are spent walking through spectacular landscapes which change every day as you pass through different vegetation zones. The pace is never exhausting, as you have to walk slowly in order to give yourself a chance to acclimatise. What's more, at the end of the day, while the guides are cooking your dinner, you are free to wander around the campsite and, as you bump into the same people time and again over the course of the trek, a sense of community soon develops. Then as night falls and you tuck into the huge plates of food cooked by your crew, the stars come out, stunning everyone into silence. This is the favourite time of day for most people: rested, replete with food and with a day of satisfactory walking behind and a good night's sleep ahead, it's natural to feel a sense of comfort and contentment, with the thought of wild animals possibly lying nearby serving to add a pleasing frisson of excitement.

Bed? It's too early. I feel too good. Aaah, I wonder if there'll ever be another time as good as this. **Gregory Peck**, in the film version of *The Snows of Kilimanjaro*

Of course, walking up from less than 2000m or thereabouts to 5895m does, as you can probably imagine, take a lot of effort and the night walk to the summit is unarguably tough. But short of actually carrying you up, your crew will do everything in their power to make your entire experience as comfortable as possible. In fact, they'll spoil you: not only do they carry your bag, but at the end of the day's walk you'll turn up at camp to find your tent has already been erected, with a bowl of hot water lying nearby for you to wash away the grime of the day. A few minutes later and a large plate of popcorn and biscuits will be served with a mug of steaming hot tea or coffee.

Accommodation on the trail

I got back in time to see P.D. lying on sloping ground, slipping off the stretcher, and in great pain. Small fire had been made under the root of a great tree. Rain soon came on and wiped out the fire ... tent was not put up and we were all in great misery. Men with tent lost in the darkness. Thought if the rain stopped we could go on in the moonlight. Rain did not stop. **Peter MacQueen** *In Wildest Africa* (1910)

Unless you are on the Marangu Route, accommodation on the mountain will be in tents brought up by your porters. (Do not be tempted to sleep in any of the caves as that is against park regulations.) On the Marangu Route, camping is forbidden; instead people have to sleep in huts along the route. (You will see people camping on this route but they are trekkers who took the Rongai Route to ascend and are now descending on Marangu.) The sleeping arrangements in these huts are usually dormitory-style, with anything from four to twenty beds per room.

Confusingly, away from the Marangu Route **many of the campsites are actually called 'huts' but don't be fooled**: they are called huts because of the green shacks you'll find at these campsites which are usually inhabited by the park rangers. Trekkers used to be allowed to sleep in these huts too, many, many years ago but no longer – except in emergencies such as high winds etc. *(cont'd overleaf)*

❑ WHAT'S IT LIKE ON THE MOUNTAIN?

(cont'd from p271) The only other buildings you will possibly see along the trail are the **toilets**. Most are of the same design, namely a little wooden hut with a hole in the floor, though several are being upgraded and some now even have seats. Some are in better condition than others; all I will say is that some people are terrible shots, while other latrines are in desperate need of emptying before the contents become Kilimanjaro's fourth peak. The problem with them is not one of design but durability – they all look great when they're built, but after a couple of years the doors are often half off, the smell of ammonia is overpowering and there's crap everywhere. So, just like your first kiss, you'll never forget your first toilet on Kilimanjaro.

Food on the trail

Remember to tell your operator if you have any special dietary requirements – because meat, nuts, gluten and dairy form a substantial part of the menu on Kilimanjaro.

A typical **breakfast** will involve eggs (boiled or fried), porridge, a saveloy (possibly with some tomatoes too), a piece of fruit such as a banana or orange, some bread with jam, honey or peanut butter and a mug of tea, hot chocolate or coffee.

Lunch is sometimes prepared at breakfast and carried by the trekker in a daypack, though most companies these days set up tables at the lunch stop and cook food on site. If you are obliged to carry a packed lunch, expect it to contain a boiled egg, sandwiches, a banana or orange, all washed down with some tea that's been kept warm in a flask and carried by your guide.

At the end of the day's walking, **afternoon tea** is served with biscuits, peanuts and, best of all, salted popcorn.

The final and biggest meal of the day, **dinner** usually begins with soup, followed by a main course including chicken or meat, a vegetable sauce, some cabbage or other vegetable, and rice or pasta. It used to be the case that potatoes would be amongst the first items to be eaten because they are so heavy, but as most companies now organise a resupply halfway through the trek this isn't always the case anymore.

Drink on the trail

Porters will collect **water** from the rivers and streams along the trail. Some of this they will boil and maybe purify for you at the start of the day to carry in your water bottles. Of course as you climb ever higher water becomes more scarce. On the Machame trail, for example, the last water point is at Karanga Valley, the lunch-stop/campsite before Barafu. On Marangu, it's just before the Saddle. While for those heading on the Rongai Route, the last water point is a place called Mbogo, which translates as 'buffalo' because of the number of them that make a pilgrimage there to slake their thirst. For this reason it is essential you carry enough bottles or containers for *at least* three litres.

In camp, **coffee** and **tea** are served and maybe **hot chocolate** or **Milo** (chocolate with malt) too – all usually made with powdered milk. Remember that caffeine, present in coffee and tea, is dehydrating, which can be bad for acclimatisation. Caffeine is a diuretic too (ie you will want to urinate frequently – something you should already be doing a lot as you adapt to the higher conditions).

By the way KINAPA, the park authority, is looking to increase the supply of water higher up the mountain. It's a long-term project – the complications involved in installing pumps to send water all the way to Barafu, Kibo or School Huts without ruining the look of the mountain mean there is no quick fix.

See also the Trekkers' experiences box on pp274-5.

The Marangu Route

Because this trail is popularly called the '**Tourist Trail**' or '**Coca Cola Trail**', some trekkers are misled into thinking this 5- or 6-day climb to the summit and back is simply a walk in the (national) park. But remember that a greater proportion of people fail on this route than on any other. True, this may have something to do with the fact that Marangu's reputation for being 'easy' attracts the more inexperienced, out-of-condition trekkers who don't realise that they are embarking on a **36.55km (22¾ miles) uphill walk**, followed immediately by a 36.55km knee-jarring descent. But it shouldn't take much to realise that Marangu is not much easier than any other trail: with the Machame Route, for example, you start at 1811m (5942ft) and aim for the summit at 5895m (19,341ft). On Marangu, you start just a little higher at 1905m (6250ft) and have the same goal, so simple logic should tell you that it can't be that much easier. Indeed, the fact that this route is often completed in 5-6 days as opposed to the 6-7 days it takes to complete Machame would suggest that this route is actually more arduous – and gives you some idea of why **more people fail on this trail** than on the so-called 'Whiskey Route'.

The main reason why people say that Marangu is somehow easier or 'softer' is because it is the only route where you **sleep in huts** rather than under canvas. The accommodation in these huts should be booked in advance by your tour company, who have to pay a deposit per person per night to KINAPA in order to secure it. To cover this, the tour agencies will probably ask you to pay them some money in advance too. This deposit is refundable or can be moved to secure huts on other dates, providing you give KINAPA (and your operator) at least seven days' notice.

Kilimanjaro seen from Lake Jipé
(from *The Kilima-njaro Expedition – A Record of Scientific Exploration in Eastern Equatorial Africa* **HH Johnston**, 1886)

The fact that you do sleep in huts makes little difference to what you need to pack for the trek, for sleeping bags are still required (the huts have pillows and mattresses but that's all) though **you can dispense with a ground mat for this route**. Regarding the sleeping situation, it does help if you can get to the huts early each day to grab the better beds. This doesn't mean you should deliberately hurry to the huts, which will reduce your enjoyment of the trek and increase the possibility of AMS. But do try to **start early each morning**: that way you can avoid the crowds, beat them to the better beds, and possibly improve your chances of seeing some of Kili's wildlife too.

❑ TREKKERS' EXPERIENCES

Of course, everybody's experience of climbing Kili is different. The majority of correspondence I get is of the 'had the time of my life' variety, which is particularly lovely to receive, especially as it's great to know other people enjoyed the experience as much as I always do:

What a fab trip! And yes, we all made it to the top (one of us with a humungous, vice-like headache, but our good guide carried her pack on the last leg)!! And best of all, we all came back friends! Anneliese Dibetta (Canada)

A few letters also contain some useful advice:

If I can make any strong recommendations it is the truth and value of 'pole pole'... I redefined the phrase pole pole and from the first step to the last I went the pace I needed to do to keep my heart rate even and not get out of breath. More often than not I was way behind the group, always had one of the guides or assistant guides with me and not once did I feel pressured to go faster. It was the key to my success.
Clare Wickens (US)

I found the trail up the Western Breach to be tough but not necessarily dangerous. I think the 'toughness' came from being at the altitude we were at – which raised both the level of exertion needed to climb and the fatigue I was experiencing from the trip so far – more than the trail itself. As I watched the porters trot by with large loads (five dozen eggs on one guy or our dining table and chairs) I realised how easy the trail really was even though at the time I was feeling taxed by it. Patti Wickham (US)

One general observation would be that although everyone said how much it was to do with altitude, I didn't realise the extent of it. I thought I'd tire easily and be breathless, but didn't understand how half the people would have headaches, and people would be running out of the dining hall to vomit. I was mentally prepared for something physically demanding, but not for feeling ill and having a headache for days on end...

As you come up to Kibo, a few people said they start to get excited and want to get it over with quickly. I'd say it's worth advising them to make sure they keep going slowly, and warn them that a lot of people suddenly feel really tired during the last 5-10 minutes of the walk. Richard Evans (UK)

One or two of them were quite encouraging too:

Two of us were not really in good enough shape to complete Kili by any route, no scrambling experience, and no strong expectation of summiting, but by taking seven

In terms of **duration**, the Marangu Route is one of the shorter trails; indeed, it's the only trail where you can buy a permit for just five days. Many people, however, opt to take an extra day to acclimatise at Horombo Huts, using that day to visit the Mawenzi Hut at 4535m/14,879ft. From a safety point of view this is entirely sensible and aesthetically such a plan cannot be argued with either, for the views from the path to the huts across the Saddle to Kibo truly take your breath away – assuming you have some left to be taken away after all that climbing.

One aspect of the Marangu Route that could be seen by some as a drawback is that it is the only hike where you **ascend and descend via the same path**.

days and by doing the scramble in the daylight, all made it to the summit, and back down to Mweka Gate, happy, safe and sound. John Wickham (US)

And pretty much everyone expresses a mix of gratitude and awe about their mountain crew and, in particular, their guides:

....I started my summit push after not sleeping the previous night. I managed the first few hours but then the fatigue kicked in and I was ready to give up. I sat helplessly on a stone and started to fall asleep. My body was shutting down. I had exhausted all my energy reserves by then. It is only because of Robert and his care that I managed to summit. He worked so hard on me. He helped me physically to go up, supporting me by my elbow but also mentally, constantly reminding me that I can do it and talking to me all the way up to keep me from falling asleep. He went far and beyond to help me and it's not an overstatement to say that my summit was way more of his success than my own.

....on my way down the mountain, something got in my eye and scratched my cornea..I was in a lot of pain, the eye was tearing. I tried to keep going but it was getting worse. I finally stopped on the side and started crying from pain and helplessness because I couldn't continue. And again, Robert turned out to be my guardian angel. He put a patch over my eye, and holding my arm tightly, he brought me down to the point where park rangers came for me in their car. 10km on slippery stones with only half of my vision. Robert saved me hundred of times from slipping and falling, sometimes slipping himself and risking a fall just to save me. The debt of gratitude I have towards him is tremendous. Not only is he so knowledgeable and experienced but it was his patience, care and keeping calm when I panicked that kept me going. Magdalena Tarnowska (Canada), who made it to the top in 2023.

That's not to suggest, of course, that everyone has a pleasant time...

I've had a lovely few days but now I have a headache and feel like shit. Please leave me alone. Thank you.

Overheard at Barafu Camp and shouted by an anonymous German hiding inside his tent while his group readied themselves for the final climb.

For a couple of days I thought you must have a great job: travel around the world and write about it. I now know better. I feel sorry for you. I thought climbing Kilimanjaro was hell. I would ask for a big raise in your salary if I were you...

Fellow trekker Mark Burgmans (Holland), advising me via email.

❑ PHONE RECEPTION ON THE MARANGU ROUTE

One big advantage with this trail is that, at the time of writing, it was the only one where wi-fi had been installed at the campsites and, so I am told, on the trail. It's free for 30 minutes per day but you have to pay after that. Regarding general phone reception, it depends which network you're with but Vodacom and Airtel users get reception around Mandara Huts, and from there I reckon there's coverage for around 50 per cent of the trail. Horombo Huts has good reception. After that, reception at Kibo Huts was pretty much non-existent but you only have to wait to **William's Point** and from there you should have contact with the outside world again for the rest of your ascent almost up to Uhuru Peak.

However, there are a couple of arguments to counter this perception: firstly, between Horombo and Kibo Huts there are two paths and it shouldn't take too much to persuade your guide to use one trail on the ascent and a different one on the way down (see p285).

Secondly, I think that the walk back down the Marangu Route is one of the most pleasurable parts of the entire trek, with the gradients more gentle than on other descents and splendid views over your shoulder. Furthermore, it offers you the chance to greet the crowds of sweating, red-faced unfortunates heading the other way with the smug expression of one for whom physical pain is now a thing of the past and whose immediate future is filled with warm showers and cold beers.

STAGE 1: MARANGU GATE TO MANDARA HUTS

[MAP 1, p279; MAP 2, p281]

Distance: 8.3km (5¼ miles); altitude gained: 818m (2684ft)

The woods are lovely, dark and deep,
But I have promises to keep,
And miles to go before I sleep,
And miles to go before I sleep.

From the poem *Stopping by Woods on a Snowy Evening*, by **Robert Frost,** as seen on a sign-writer's wall in Moshi

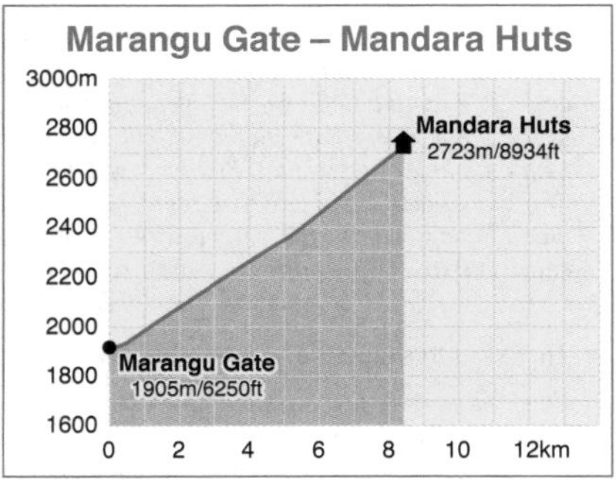

As the headquarters of **KINAPA** (Kilimanjaro National Park), you might expect Marangu Gate (altitude 1905m/6250ft) to have the best facilities of all the gates and it doesn't disappoint.

Not only does the gate have the usual **registration office** but there's also a sheltered picnic area, a smart toilet block and a **shop** (daily 8am-6pm) that has a good collection of books and souvenirs. There's also a scale model of the mountain above the car park, presumably put there so any dads who are climbing can joke to their family about how the mountain looks so much smaller in real life. You can ignore him by turning your back on the model to browse the small booth run by Kilimanjaro Guides Cooperative, by the entrance to the car park, where you can **hire any equipment** you may have forgotten to bring, from essentials such as hats and fleeces, coats, trekking poles and water bottles to camping stuff that you almost certainly won't need on the trail such as stoves and so forth, which should be provided by your operator.

Having gone through the laborious business of **registering** (a process that usually takes at least an hour, though it can be quicker if you manage to get here before the large tour groups arrive), you begin your trek by following the trekkers' path which heads left off the road (which is now used solely by porters). You may still find the odd eucalyptus tree around the gate, one of the few non-native plants on the mountain. They were introduced, according to the version I've heard, by the first chief park warden of Kilimanjaro, a man who married a relative of Idi Amin – the former despot of Uganda later shooting him in an argument, so the story goes. As an 'alien' species and one that consumes a lot of water, the eucalyptus trees are slowly being eradicated by the authorities from the national park itself. (It has to be a gradual process, however: look through the trees to your right just after you start out and you'll see a big open area – the ugly result of eradicating the trees too quickly.)

This first day's walk is a very pleasant one of just over 8km and though the route is uphill for virtually the entire time, there are enough distractions in the forest to take your mind off the exertion, from the occasional troop of **blue monkeys** to the vivid red *Impatiens kilimanjari*, a small flower that has become the emblem of Kilimanjaro.

The path soon veers towards and then follows the course of a **mountain stream**; sometimes through the increasingly impenetrable vegetation to your right you can glimpse the occasional small **waterfall**. Ask your guide to point out any tree hyraxes too. Almost impossible for the untrained *mzungu* to spot, a *really* good guide will be able to show you several without much effort.

After about 1¼ hours a wooden bridge leads off the trail over this stream to the picnic tables at **Kisamboni** (2281m/7484ft) and a brief encounter with the 4WD porters' trail. This is the halfway point of the first stage and in all probability it is here that you will be served lunch.

... ferns and heaths were plentiful, the last-named preponderating as we got higher up. At a height of 6,300 feet, however, all these were merged in the primaeval forest, in which old patriarchs with knotted stunted forms stood closely together, many of them worsted in the perpetual struggle with the encroachments of the parasitical growths of almost fabulous strength and size, which enfolded trunks and branches alike in their fatal embrace, cripp-

Note: In all the route descriptions, do remember that the times quoted are approximations and, more importantly, refer to **walking times only** with no time spent resting, taking photos etc.

Add on 30-50% to get an estimate of the total time spent on the trail.

ling the giants themselves and squeezing to death the mosses, lichens, and ferns which had clothed their nakedness. Everything living seemed doomed to fall prey to them, but they in their turn bore their own heavy burden of parasites; creepers, from a yard to two yards long, hanging down in garlands and festoons, or forming one thick veil shrouding whole clumps of trees. Wherever a little space had been left amongst the many fallen and decaying trunks, the ground was covered with a luxurious vegetation, including many varieties of herbaceous plants with bright coloured flowers, orchids, and the modest violet peeping out amongst them, whilst more numerous than all were different lycopods and sword-shaped ferns.

Lieutenant Ludwig von Höhnel
Discovery by Count Teleki of Lakes Rudolf and Stefanie (1894); see pp380-1

Returning to the trail and turning right, you continue climbing north for 30 minutes to another bridge, again leading off to the right of the trail; your path, however, heads off to the left, directly away from the bridge. The trail is a little steeper now as you wind your way through the forest. It is a very pretty part of the walk, with varieties of *Impatiens* edging the path and, draped amongst the trees, the white-flowered *Begonia meyeri-johannis*; though by now you may be feeling a little too tired to enjoy it to its fullest.

Press on, and 15 minutes later yet another bridge appears which you *do* take (see Map 2). Like some sort of botanical border post, the bridge heralds the first appearance of the **giant heathers** (*Erica excelsa*) on the trail, with masses of **bearded lichen** liberally draped over them; though the forest reappears intermittently up to and beyond Maundi Crater it's the spindly heathers and stumpy shrubs of the second vegetation zone, the alpine heath and moorland, that now dominate.

It was a relief to enter the rain forest, and it is a relief to leave it in early afternoon, emerging into an open meadow of grass six feet high. However, by now I am very tired – astonishingly tired – and the path up the meadow is steep. I am wondering how much farther I must go. There are no signposts to tell me how I am doing, how far before we reach the huts. Unable to plan, unable to pace myself, I find my fatigue feels extreme. Do I have an hour still to go? Two hours? Then I see, on a ridge above the high grass, the brown geometric A-frames of the Mandara huts. They are very close. It is only four o'clock in the afternoon. I am not really so tired after all.

Michael Crichton, taken from his collection of essays, *Travels* (1988)

From this bridge, the first night's accommodation, **Mandara Huts** (2723m/8934ft), lies just 35 minutes away. If you have the energy, a quick 15-minute saunter to the parasitic cone known as **Maundi Crater** is worthwhile both for its views east over Kenya and north-west to Mawenzi and for the wild flowers and grasses growing on its slopes. On the way to the crater, look in the trees for the bands of semi-tame monkeys, both blue and colobus, that live here and are particularly active at dusk.

Incidentally, Mandara Huts, together with Horombo Huts (see pp284-5), are the only huts on the mountain to be named after people rather than a places. The people in question were both local Chagga chiefs. Mandara was the chief when the huts were first built, in 1942. He is also the descendant of the most famous Chagga chief of all, who was also known as Mandara (1845-91). This Mandara was the fearsome leader of the Moshi tribe, a warrior whose skill and bravery

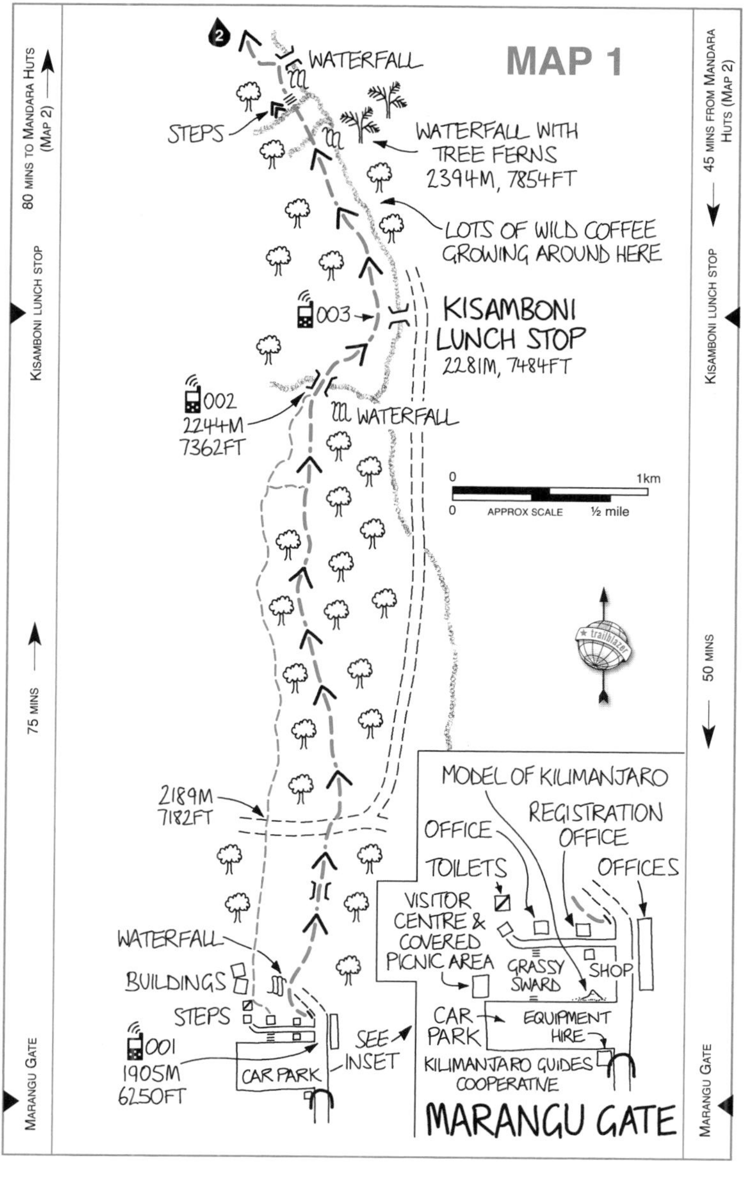
MAP 1
80 MINS TO MANDARA HUTS (MAP 2)
45 MINS FROM MANDARA HUTS (MAP 2)
KISAMBONI LUNCH STOP
KISAMBONI LUNCH STOP
75 MINS
50 MINS
MARANGU GATE
MARANGU GATE
WATERFALL
STEPS
WATERFALL WITH TREE FERNS 2394M, 7854FT
LOTS OF WILD COFFEE GROWING AROUND HERE
003
KISAMBONI LUNCH STOP 2281M, 7484FT
002 2244M 7362FT
WATERFALL
0 1km 0 APPROX SCALE ½ mile
trailblazer
2189M 7182FT
MODEL OF KILIMANJARO
REGISTRATION OFFICE
OFFICE
TOILETS
OFFICES
VISITOR CENTRE & COVERED PICNIC AREA
GRASSY SWARD
SHOP
WATERFALL
BUILDINGS
STEPS
001 1905M 6250FT
SEE INSET
CAR PARK
CAR PARK
EQUIPMENT HIRE
KILIMANJARO GUIDES COOPERATIVE
MARANGU GATE

on the battlefield was matched only by his stunning cupidity off it. Mandara once boasted that he had met every white man to visit Kilimanjaro, from Johannes Rebmann (the first European to see Kili) to Hans Meyer (the first man to successfully climb it), and it's a fair bet that all of them would have been required to present the chief with a huge array of presents brought from their own country. Failure to do so was not an option, for those who, in Mandara's eye (he had only one, having lost the other in battle), were insufficiently generous in their gift-giving, put their lives in peril. The attack that led to the death of Charles New (see p151), for example, was said to have been orchestrated by Mandara after New had 'insulted' him by refusing to give the chief the watch from his waistcoat. Read any of the 19th-century accounts of Kilimanjaro and you'll usually find plenty of pages devoted to this fascinating character – with few casting him in a favourable light.

The huts themselves have been restored and replaced in recent years and while the large 20-bed dormitories above the dining hall still exist, it's largely the preserve of group bookings these days. Everybody else sleeps in the smart and cosy 4-bed dorms which really are an upgrade on the previous accommodation. And for an upgrade on the upgrade, KINAPA have also installed **'luxury' two-bed 'VIP' accommodation**, which has its own en suite shower, hot water and central heating (though even the park authority itself says that the last two features aren't working very well).

At the time of writing these VIP huts are being let out and lucky guests aren't being charged any extra for them; though this will change when Kibo Huts also get some, thus ensuring that they're available all along the Marangu Route.

STAGE 2: MANDARA HUTS TO HOROMBO HUTS

[MAP 2 opposite; MAP 3, p283]

Distance: 12.5km (7¾ miles); altitude gained: 998m (3274ft)

On this stage, in which you gain almost a kilometre in altitude, you say a final goodbye to the forest and spend the greater part of the day walking through the bleaker landscape of Kilimanjaro's moorland.

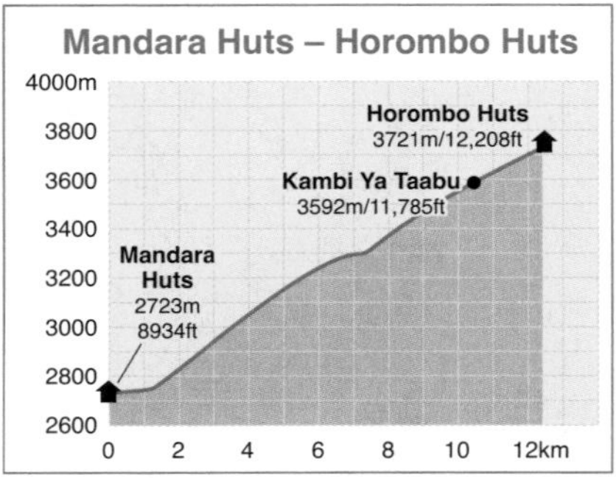

If the weather's clear you will get your first really good look at the twin peaks of Kili, namely spiky Mawenzi and snow-capped Kibo; they will continue to loom large and will doubtless appear in just about every photo you take from now to the summit. The proteas, giant groundsels (*Dendrosenecio kilimanjari*) and phallic lobelias (*Lobelia deckenii*) also make

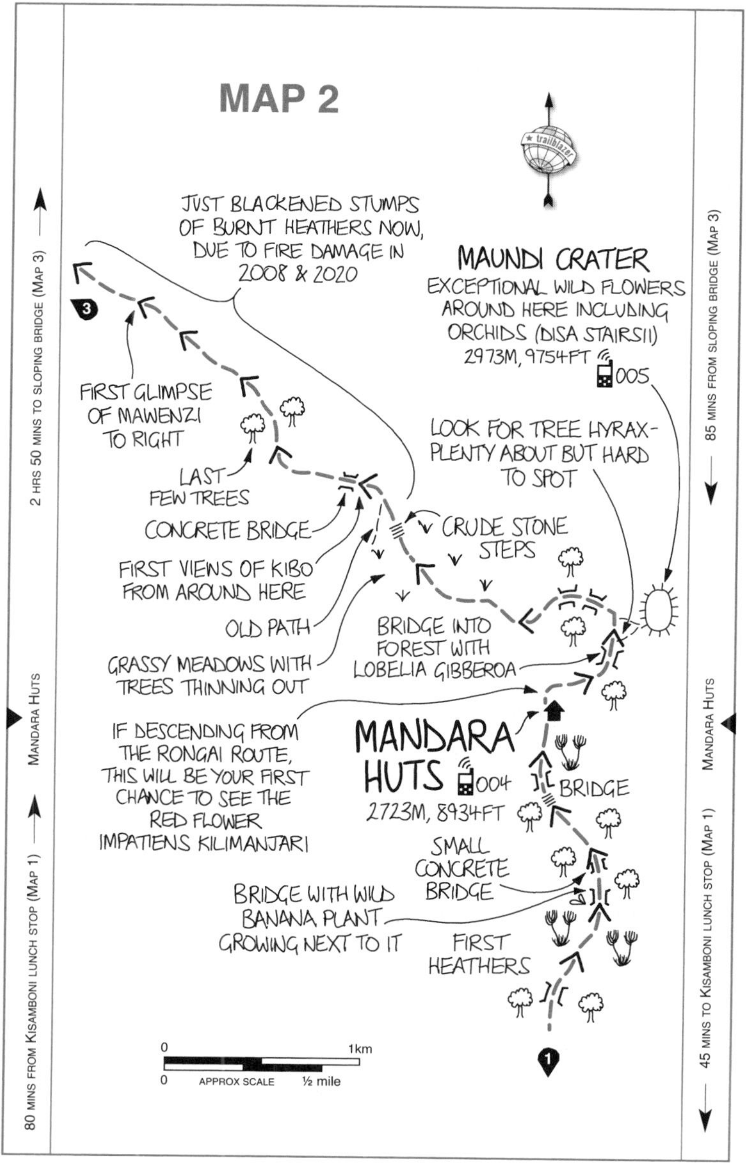
MAP 2
trailblazer
JUST BLACKENED STUMPS OF BURNT HEATHERS NOW, DUE TO FIRE DAMAGE IN 2008 & 2020
MAUNDI CRATER
EXCEPTIONAL WILD FLOWERS AROUND HERE INCLUDING ORCHIDS (DISA STAIRSII)
2973M, 9754FT
005
3
FIRST GLIMPSE OF MAWENZI TO RIGHT
LAST FEW TREES
LOOK FOR TREE HYRAX- PLENTY ABOUT BUT HARD TO SPOT
CONCRETE BRIDGE
CRUDE STONE STEPS
FIRST VIEWS OF KIBO FROM AROUND HERE
OLD PATH
BRIDGE INTO FOREST WITH LOBELIA GIBBEROA
GRASSY MEADOWS WITH TREES THINNING OUT
IF DESCENDING FROM THE RONGAI ROUTE, THIS WILL BE YOUR FIRST CHANCE TO SEE THE RED FLOWER IMPATIENS KILIMANJARI
MANDARA HUTS
004
2723M, 8934FT
BRIDGE
SMALL CONCRETE BRIDGE
BRIDGE WITH WILD BANANA PLANT GROWING NEXT TO IT
FIRST HEATHERS
1
0 1km
0 APPROX SCALE ½ mile
2 HRS 50 MINS TO SLOPING BRIDGE (MAP 3)
MANDARA HUTS
80 MINS FROM KISAMBONI LUNCH STOP (MAP 1)
85 MINS FROM SLOPING BRIDGE (MAP 3)
MANDARA HUTS
45 MINS TO KISAMBONI LUNCH STOP (MAP 1)

their first appearance, with the groundsels growing in some abundance towards the latter part of the walk and especially around Horombo Huts.

The whole landscape as far as the eye could reach was a medley of dull grey lava slabs, dotted with the red-leafed protea shrub (Protea Kilimandscharica) and stunted heaths, which became smaller and smaller as we rose higher. Not a sound disturbed the silence of this uninhabited mountain mystery; not a sign of life broke the stillness save a little ashy-brown bird that hopped about the boulders, flipping its tail up and down. And to add to the impression created by the eerie scene, huge senecios lifted to a height of 20ft their black stems and greyish-yellow crowns and stood spreading out their arms in the deep moist gullies, like ghostly sentinels of the untrodden wilds.

Eva Stuart Watt *Africa's Dome of Mystery* (1930)

The day begins with a stroll through the monkey forest towards Maundi Crater. After 15 minutes you cross a small bridge and, leaving the last significant expanse of forest behind, enter a land of tall grasses and giant heathers. **Wild flowers** rarely seen elsewhere, such as the pinkish *Dierama pendulum*, abound in this little bumpy corner of the mountain. Crossing bridges over (often dry) water courses, on a clear day you may be able to make out, atop one of the many undulations, some **picnic tables** and toilets amongst the heather; this will be

❑ THE FIRE OF WHONA 2020

In October 2020 I was awoken early in the morning by the arrival of several WhatsApp messages on my phone. A couple of them were accompanied by photos, taken by guides who were on Kibo at the time, of an orange glow on the side of the mountain near Horombo Huts. The cause of this light was, of course, a giant fire that had begun on the Marangu Route, destroying over 70 sq km of vegetation in the heath and moorland zone. The blaze spread quickly thanks to a combination of dry vegetation and strong winds, and was only finally extinguished a week later thanks to the efforts of 600 locals, a helicopter from Kenya that dropped buckets of water on the blaze, as well as some welcome rains a few days later.

In addition to the devastation it caused to the natural landscape, nine of the older huts at Horombo were also destroyed.

According to KINAPA, the fire was started by a porter who was warming some food for his climbers and accidentally set the surrounding grass on fire. That poor man was eventually taken to court but no judgement was ever brought, with KINAPA deciding against pressing for a conviction. The damage was already done, they concluded, so what was the point in pursuing a penniless porter in this way?

Of course, fires on Kili are nothing new; I've been writing about them since the first edition of the guide. And while someone – usually a porter, though occasionally it's honey collectors who light fires to smoke out the bees from their hive – is nearly always to blame, the fire itself can also be seen as part of a natural process. After all, there's no doubt that almost as soon as the blaze dies out, the regeneration process begins and from seemingly immolated stumps burst new green shoots. And in a strange way, the fire can be a blessing for climbers. On my own inspection of the devastation caused by this latest conflagration, I saw a herd of over 20 eland ambling up the slopes of Mawenzi – a herd that, if the vegetation hadn't been largely burned to the ground, would doubtless have remained hidden!

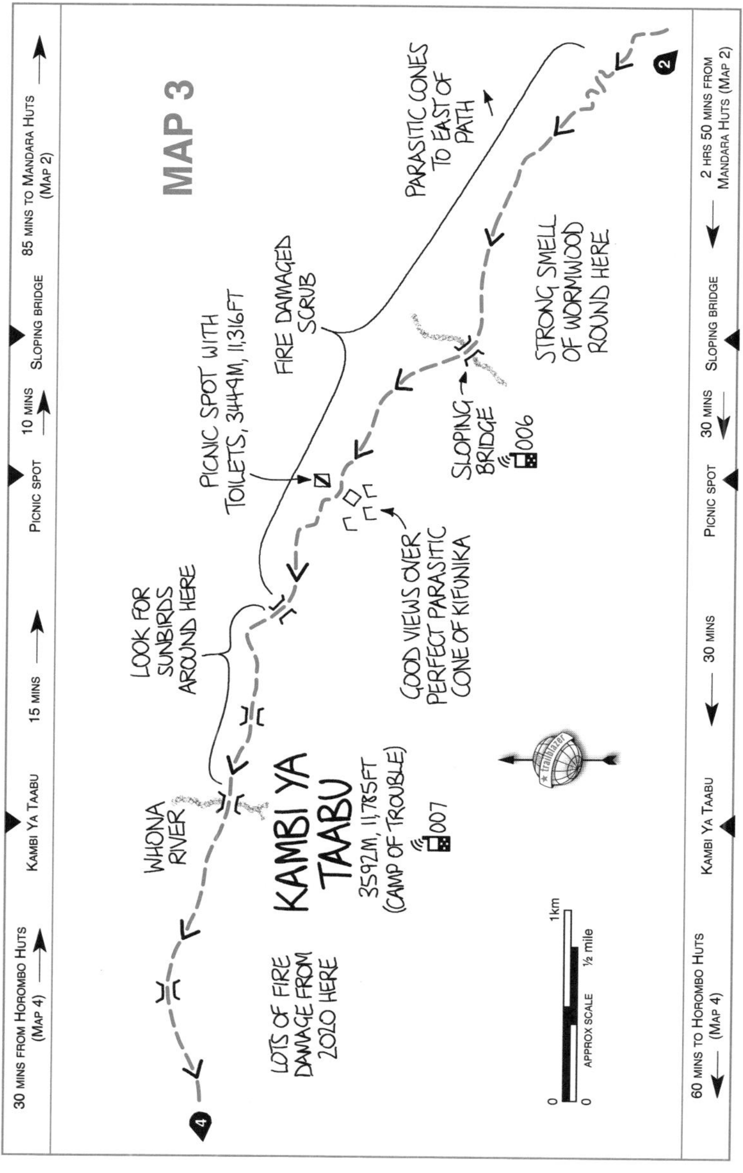
MAP 3
85 MINS TO MANDARA HUTS (MAP 2)
SLOPING BRIDGE
10 MINS
PICNIC SPOT
15 MINS
KAMBI YA TAABU
30 MINS FROM HOROMBO HUTS (MAP 4)
2 HRS 50 MINS FROM MANDARA HUTS (MAP 2)
SLOPING BRIDGE
30 MINS
PICNIC SPOT
30 MINS
KAMBI YA TAABU
60 MINS TO HOROMBO HUTS (MAP 4)
PARASITIC CONES TO EAST OF PATH
FIRE DAMAGED SCRUB
STRONG SMELL OF WORMWOOD ROUND HERE
PICNIC SPOT WITH TOILETS, 3449M, 11,316FT
SLOPING BRIDGE
006
GOOD VIEWS OVER PERFECT PARASITIC CONE OF KIFUNIKA
LOOK FOR SUNBIRDS AROUND HERE
WHONA RIVER
KAMBI YA TAABU
3592M, 11,785FT (CAMP OF TROUBLE)
007
LOTS OF FIRE DAMAGE FROM 2020 HERE
APPROX SCALE
0
1km
0
½ mile

your lunch stop, reached after a fairly trying 30-minute climb from the **sloping bridge** (Map 3). The guides typically call this the halfway point in the day but they're being unnecessarily pessimistic: Horombo Huts lie just 90 minutes away, the path tracing a generally westward course across a number of (dry) stream beds including the head of the Whona River that runs through a valley known as **Kambi Ya Taabu**, which translates, rather melodramatically, as the 'Camp of Trouble'.

Horombo Huts (3721m/12,208ft) are generally regarded as the most pleasant of those on the route: small A-frame shelters partitioned down the middle, with each side holding beds for four people. They cater for a transient population of around 160 trekkers plus porters and guides as well as a more permanent population of four-striped grass mice whose numbers are now almost at plague proportions; indeed, some of them have now forsaken their grassy homeland to

❑ MAWENZI

Though less than 8km of nothingness (namely the Saddle) separates the foot of one from the foot of the other, the twin peaks of Kibo and Mawenzi could scarcely be more different. Where Kibo is all gentle slopes and a perfectly circular crater, Mawenzi is spiky, steep, and rises to a series of peaks like the back of a stegosaurus. Furthermore, where the former is at least partially covered in glaciers, the other stands naked, or at least wears no permanent raiment of ice, its sides too steep to allow the glaciers a secure-enough footing. And while Kibo is easily accessible to walkers, any assault on Mawenzi involves some serious preparation, specialist equipment and no small amount of technical skill.

Indeed, the only similarity between the two peaks is their enormity: Mawenzi's **Hans Meyer Peak**, at 5149m, is the third highest in Africa (after Kibo and Mount Kenya, the latter being just 50m taller). Its smaller size when compared to Kibo can be ascribed to the fact that the Mawenzi volcano died out first, while the forces that formed Kibo continued to rage for a few thousand years after Mawenzi had become extinct, pushing Kibo above the height of its older brother. Erosion then caused the collapse of Mawenzi's entire north-east wall, releasing the waters of a lake that had formed in its crater down into the valley below.

The jagged appearance of its summit is due to the formation of **dykes**. This is where lava, pushed into gaps in the crater rim, solidified over time and, being harder than the original rock, remained while the softer rock eroded. Today, this hardened lava is also rather shattered, which, combined with its steep gradients, makes Mawenzi extremely dangerous to climb. John Reader, in his book *Kilimanjaro*, tells of two Austrian climbers who perished on their descent from the summit of Mawenzi, with the body of one of them found dangling by a rope snagged to the rocks. Such is the difficulty associated with any climb of Mawenzi that, rather than risk clambering up the peak to recover the corpse, the park authority decided instead to hire a marksman to shoot at the rope with a rifle.

For years the peak was closed to mountaineers but that changed in 2017 when a new (and hopefully safe) route up Kili's second summit opened up to climbers. Before you can tackle it, however, you'll need to prove to the park authority that you have the necessary climbing qualifications and you'll also need to pay an extra US$750 on top of the regular park fees, presumably to cover the cost of the marksman's bullets in case you, too, should end up dangling.

scavenge in the main dining hall. The huts are also the busiest on the route, catering not just for those ascending the mountain but those coming back down too, as well as those who spend the day here acclimatising.

Speaking of which, if you have opted for an **acclimatisation day** the chances are you'll be led by your guide on the northern route (aka Mawenzi Route, see box p361) past the **Zebra Rocks** (a collection of rockfaces stained by water that resemble the flanks of a zebra) and up to **Mawenzi Hut** at 4535m/ 14,879ft (see Map 4, p286). Not only will this afford you magnificent views of your ultimate destination across the Saddle but it is also, of course, wonderful exercise to help you to cope with the thin air of Kibo later on.

The benefits of taking this extra day may not be immediately apparent but will hopefully manifest themselves later on as you saunter up Kibo with at most a minor headache, while littering the trail around you are the weeping, retching bodies of the AMS-sufferers who opted not to take the extra day. Oh, and the huts are also near enough to allow you to return to Horombo for a late lunch.

STAGE 3: HOROMBO HUTS TO KIBO HUTS

[MAP 4 p286; MAP 5, p287]

Distance: 9.5km (6 miles; 10.3km/6½ miles on the Mawenzi alternative); altitude gained: 993m (3258ft)

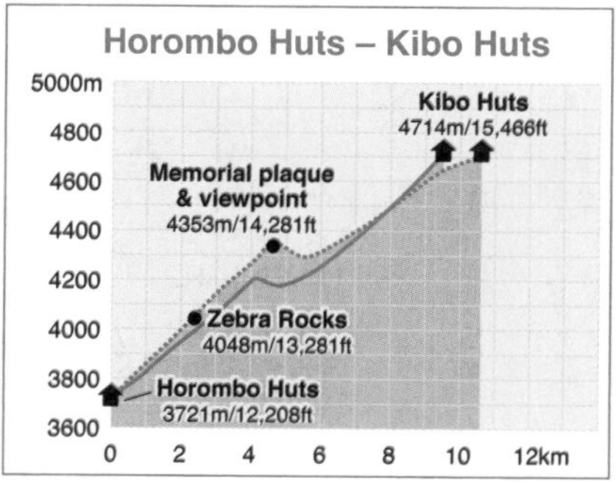

The path to Kibo from Horombo divides; almost invariably you will be led along the southern (left-hand) route, which I describe now.

If your guide is amenable, however, you may like to ask him on the return from Kibo to use the more northerly route, particularly if you did not take a day to acclimatise at Horombo (those who did will be familiar with much of this northerly path, which I have called the Mawenzi Route and describe, starting at Kibo Huts, on p361).

The 9.5km **southern path** seems rather steep at first as it bends left (north-west) and up through the thinning vegetation of the moorland. Looping north, just under 30 minutes after leaving Horombo you come to the tiny mountain stream known as **Maua River** (3914m/12,841ft). If you haven't been given any

Note: In all the route descriptions, do remember that the times quoted are approximations and, more importantly, refer to **walking times only** with no time spent resting, taking photos etc.

Add on 30-50% to get an estimate of the total time spent on the trail.

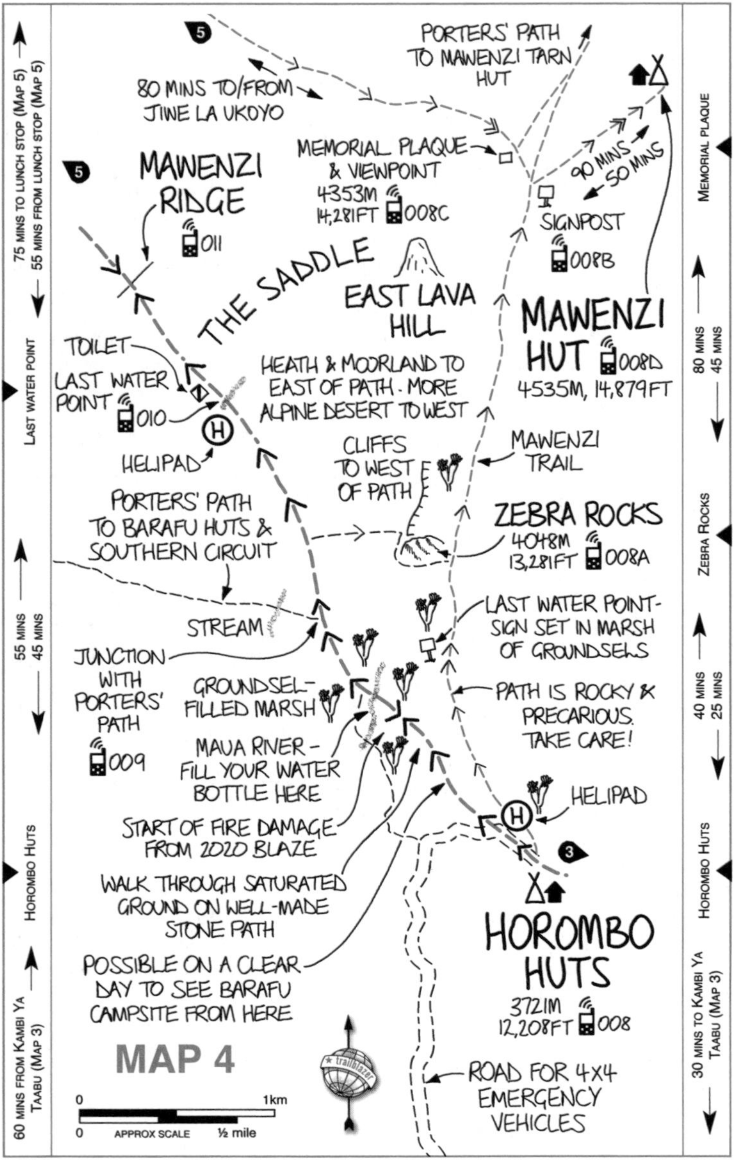

75 MINS TO LUNCH STOP (MAP 5)
55 MINS FROM LUNCH STOP (MAP 5)
LAST WATER POINT
55 MINS
45 MINS
HOROMBO HUTS
60 MINS FROM KAMBI YA TAABU (MAP 3)
MEMORIAL PLAQUE
80 MINS
45 MINS
ZEBRA ROCKS
40 MINS
25 MINS
HOROMBO HUTS
30 MINS TO KAMBI YA TAABU (MAP 3)
PORTERS' PATH TO MAWENZI TARN HUT
80 MINS TO/FROM JIWE LA UKOYO
MEMORIAL PLAQUE & VIEWPOINT
4353M 14,281FT 008C
90 MINS
50 MINS
SIGNPOST
008B
MAWENZI RIDGE
011
THE SADDLE
EAST LAVA HILL
MAWENZI HUT
008D
4535M, 14,879FT
TOILET
LAST WATER POINT
010
HELIPAD
HEATH & MOORLAND TO EAST OF PATH. MORE ALPINE DESERT TO WEST
CLIFFS TO WEST OF PATH
MAWENZI TRAIL
PORTERS' PATH TO BARAFU HUTS & SOUTHERN CIRCUIT
ZEBRA ROCKS
4048M 13,281FT 008A
STREAM
LAST WATER POINT- SIGN SET IN MARSH OF GROUNDSELS
JUNCTION WITH PORTERS' PATH
009
GROUNDSEL-FILLED MARSH
PATH IS ROCKY & PRECARIOUS. TAKE CARE!
MAUA RIVER - FILL YOUR WATER BOTTLE HERE
HELIPAD
START OF FIRE DAMAGE FROM 2020 BLAZE
WALK THROUGH SATURATED GROUND ON WELL-MADE STONE PATH
HOROMBO HUTS
POSSIBLE ON A CLEAR DAY TO SEE BARAFU CAMPSITE FROM HERE
3721M 12,208FT 008
MAP 4
trailblazer
ROAD FOR 4X4 EMERGENCY VEHICLES
0
1km
0
APPROX SCALE
½ mile
5
5
3

or enough water by your crew this is where you should fill up your water bottles, for the water from this point on is rather brackish. The terrain climbs steadily but not steeply after Maua.

Some of Kili's many parasitic cones soon move into view for the first time. The **Last Water Point**, well signposted and rather incongruously furnished with picnic tables, marks the beginning of the uphill approach to **Mawenzi Ridge**, beyond which lies **The Saddle**, the dry, barren terrain separating Kilimanjaro's two major peaks. With **Middle Red Hill** (Map 5), a large parasitic cone, ahead of you to the right, you find yourself descending into a rather flat, extremely windswept and dramatic landscape, the only decoration provided by a few tufts of grass, some hardier floral species such as the aptly named everlastings, and a number of boulders and smaller stones, some of which have been arranged into messages by previous trekkers. It is for these kinds of views that you brought your camera, for the light at this altitude is frequently superb, and while many of your photos may never be printed it's a fair bet that a few will be destined for the mantlepiece.

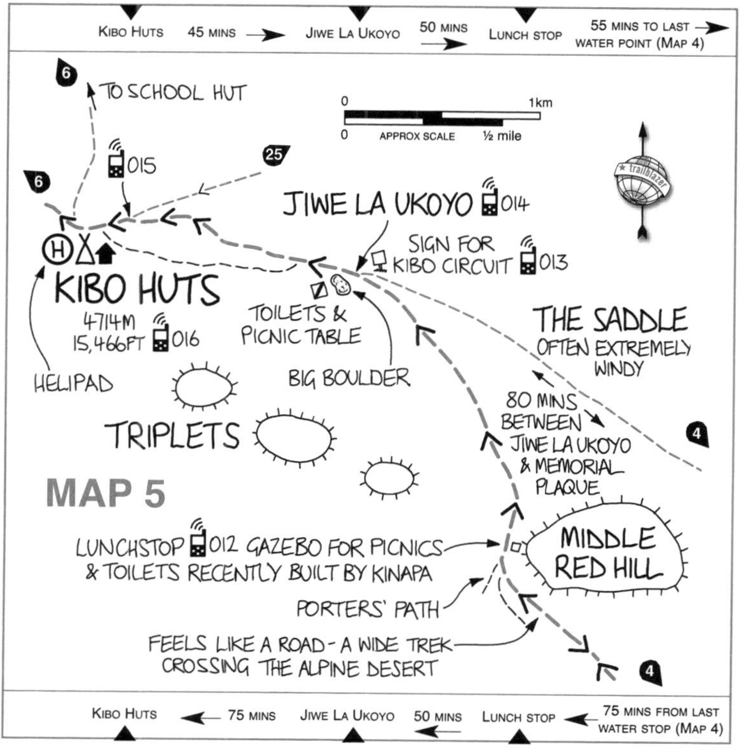

The path heads almost due north between the Kibo summit on your left and the Middle Red on your right, whose western slopes shelter trekkers from the often howling wind and more often than not provide the venue for **lunch**. A rather smart picnic shelter has been built here. Opposite the shelter is the **junction** with the porters' path, this section being largely used by porters as a short-cut to Barafu.

Your path for the afternoon continues northwards across the Saddle. It's a bit of a weary trudge on a steadily inclining path to **Jiwe La Ukoyo**, a former campsite with some toilet huts, picnic tables and a huge boulder (*jiwe* means 'rock' in Swahili). It is also the meeting point between the two main paths from Horombo. Thereafter the path turns sharply westwards towards the **Kibo Huts**, which nestle snugly on the lowest slopes of the summit after which they were named. Though the huts look close, you still have around 1¼ hours' walking from Jiwe La Ukoyo; it's a tough walk too, a gradual but relentless uphill slog to round off what has already been a fairly wearying day.

The accommodations at Kibo Hut are reminiscent of a Siberian prison camp. Triple-decker bunks line all four tin walls; in the middle of the room, a central pit for eating. The wind whines through the cracks in the walls; nobody removes any clothing indoors. We have dinner at 5:00 p.m., porridge and tea. Nobody can eat much. We are all thinking about the ascent. We must reach the top before ten in the morning, because after that the weather is likely to sock in, closing off the views and making the summit dangerous. If we climb too slowly, we risk being turned back from the summit because of the weather.

Michael Crichton, taken from his collection of essays, *Travels* (1988)

Thankfully, the accommodation at Kibo Huts has improved since Crichton's day (he climbed way back in 1975). The draughty stone huts are still there but, as elsewhere on the Marangu Route, some smart wooden chalets have also been built which are much more pleasant. If your company's any good, a member of your crew will have scampered ahead to secure a spot in one of them for you. A sign on the door of the main hut tells you that you are now at 4750m (15,584ft; though I think it's a little bit lower than this at 4714m/15,466ft); a second sign warns you that Gillman's Point is still five hours away...

STAGE 4: KIBO HUTS TO GILLMAN'S POINT AND UHURU PEAK [MAP 6, p291; MAP 33, p371]

Distance: 6.25km (4 miles); altitude gained: 1181m (3875ft)

And so you come to the testing part of the walk. No matter how tough you have found the trekking so far, it was but a leisurely promenade compared to what lies ahead for you tonight.

The path to Gillman's Point on the crater rim has been in your sights since the previous afternoon when you crossed the Saddle and saw it rearing up at an angle of 16° (John Reader's estimate) behind the Kibo Huts. I think that one of the reasons why this route has a higher failure rate than any of the others is down to the difficulty of this last stretch, which seems steeper and the ground less solid than on other routes. The stretch between Gillman's and Uhuru Peak also sees a high percentage of people giving up, presumably because of the greater distance, even though the gradient is less steep and the hard stuff is, in theory at least, largely behind them. All of which means that the chances of failure on this route are comparatively high – and of making it, but throwing up or passing out along the way, are even higher.

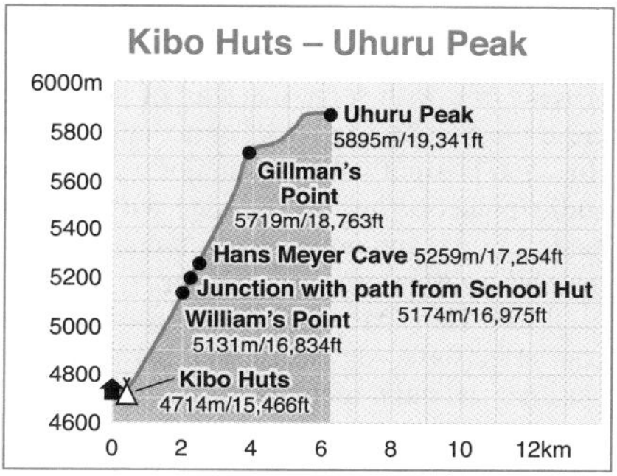

Just remember the golden rule: when it comes to climbing Kibo, there is no such thing as too slow. The mountain was formed around 500,000 years ago and has remained much the same ever since, so I think it's reasonable to assume it will still be there in the morning, no matter what time you arrive at the top.

I find a rhythm and try to lose my thoughts to it but feel the first pain of a stomach cramp and then another, and I feel the nausea starting and the headache that I recognise all too well ... The pain is sharp in my head and my cramping is still with me; if I feel this way how is Danny doing with no sleep and nothing in his stomach from the vomiting after dinner?
Rick Ridgeway, *The Shadow of Kilimanjaro – On Foot Across East Africa*

What you can't see from Kibo Huts, and yet what is rather good about this path, is that there are a number of landmarks on the way, the main ones being

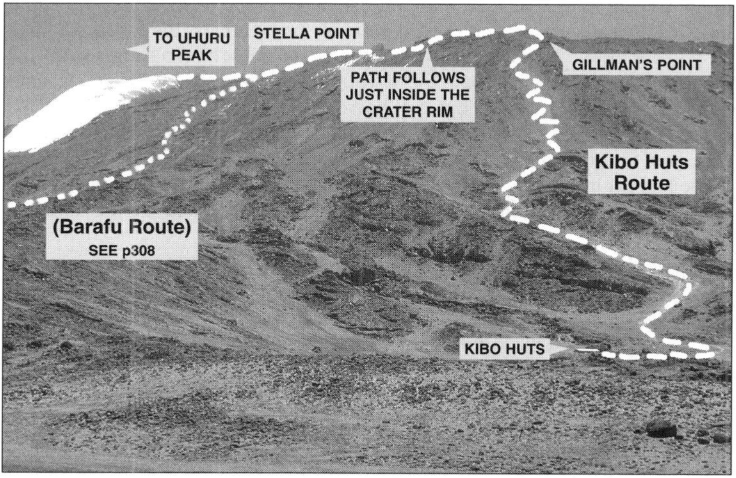

Kibo Huts Route

William's Point at 5131m (16,834ft) and Hans Meyer Cave at 5259m (17,254ft), that act as milestones, helping both to break up the journey and to provide you with some measure of your progress. **William's Point** – or rather, the large east-facing rock immediately beneath it – lies 1¾ hours from Kibo Huts and is usually the first major resting point. **Hans Meyer Cave**, a small and undistinguished hollow adorned with a plaque commemorating the Hungarian hunter, Count and *bon viveur* Samuel Teleki, who is believed to have rested here in 1887, is 30 minutes further on.

From Hans Meyer Cave it's a case of following the scree **switchbacks**; if you've mastered the art of walking in a zombie-like trance, now is the time to put that particular technique into action.

By some transcendental process I seemed to take on the characteristics of a Shire [horse], *my head lowered, resolute, I just plunked one foot in front of t'other, mentally munching nothingness.*

Sebastian Snow *The Rucksack Man,* writing about his attempt to walk from Tierra del Fuego to Alaska across the Americas. It's a good example to follow for your walk to Gillman's Point

This part, as you pinball back and forth on a stretch of fine scree bounded by two boulder-strewn slopes, is extremely exposed and if there's any wind about, you will almost certainly feel it here. If you bought one in Moshi, now is the time to put on your balaclava: your friends will be too concerned with their own situation to laugh at you. By the way, look behind you and you'll see a line of torches snaking up the slope in a scene that feels almost Biblical; while ahead of you, other torches far ahead on the trail are virtually indistinguishable from the stars.

Gradually the zig-zags begin to reduce in size like the audiograph of an echo. You are now entering the final phase of the climb to Gillman's, though it takes an hour to complete and you'll probably be breathless the whole way. It's easy to get lost in the dark on this final stretch, so don't be too surprised to find other trekkers to the left and right of you on a different path. Assuming your guide is at least halfway competent, however, you should find yourself at the crater's edge at **Gillman's Point** (5719m/18,763ft); if, upon arrival at the crater rim, you find no signpost welcoming you to Gillman's, the chances are the guide has got his bearings slightly wrong and has led you to the slightly lower point of **Johannes Notch**. No matter: Gillman's is just a three-minute scramble up to your left.

Gillman's Point is 960m above Kibo Hut [I actually make it 1005m], *that is almost the equivalent of three Empire State Buildings standing one on top of another. The horizontal distance between Kibo Hut and Gillman's Point is roughly 3000 metres, so the gradient averages about 1:3.3 and the distance covered on the way up is about 3300m – the equivalent of nine Empire State Buildings laid end to end up the incline.*

John Reader *Kilimanjaro*

If the wind is not too high, Gillman's is a good spot to sit for a few minutes, get your head together, contemplate the star-spangled sky with the silhouette of Mawenzi to the east, and congratulate yourself on having earned a nice certificate for making it to the crater rim, having completed the hardest part of the

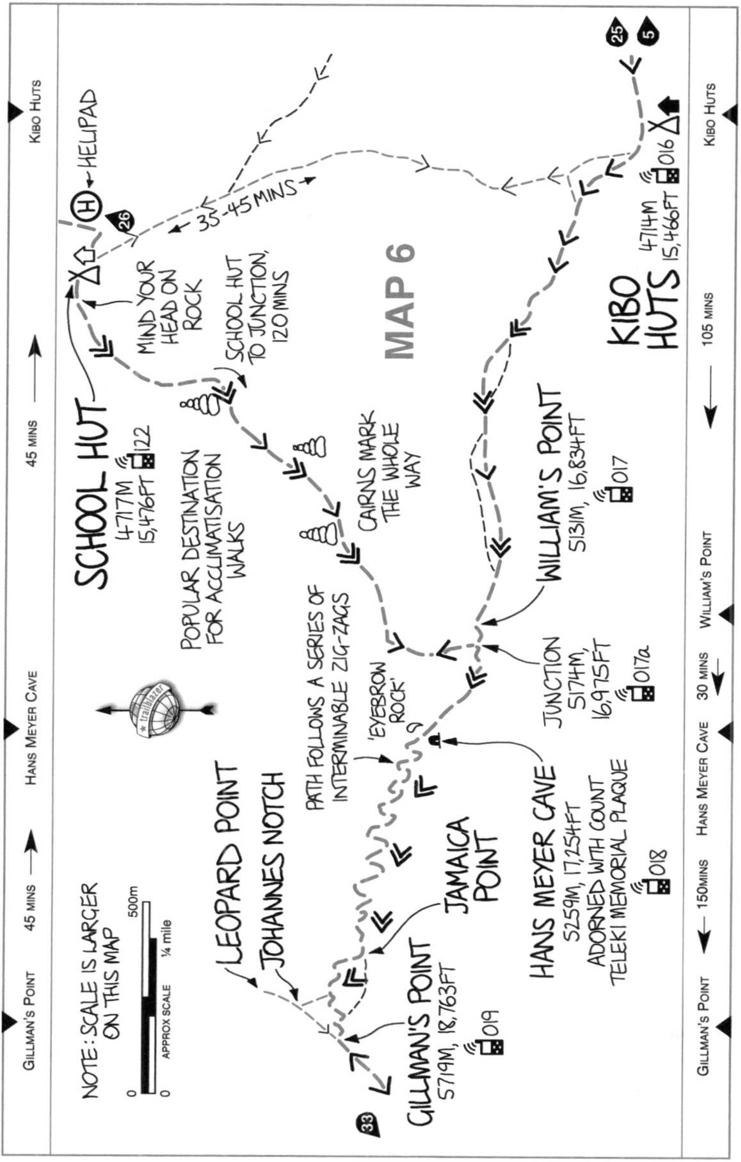
MAP 6
Gillman's Point
45 mins
Hans Meyer Cave
45 mins
Kibo Huts
Helipad
26
35-45 mins
School Hut
4717m
15,476ft
122
Mind your head on rock
School hut to junction, 120 mins
Popular destination for acclimatisation walks
Cairns mark the whole way
25
5
Kibo Huts
4714m
15,466ft
016
William's Point
5131m, 16,834ft
017
Junction
5174m,
16,975ft
017a
Path follows a series of interminable zig-zags
'Eyebrow Rock'
Hans Meyer Cave
5259m, 17,254ft
Adorned with Count Teleki memorial plaque
018
Leopard Point
Johannes Notch
Jamaica Point
Gillman's Point
5719m, 18,763ft
019
33
Note: scale is larger on this map
0
500m
0
¼ mile
Approx scale
trailblazer
Gillman's Point
150mins
Hans Meyer Cave
30 mins
William's Point
105 mins
Kibo Huts

trek. At least, it's the hardest part physically; the hardest part from a psychological point of view now awaits as you try to muster up the energy and enthusiasm to tackle the walk to **Uhuru**. Because if Kilimanjaro is the Roof of Africa, all you've done so far is make it to the eaves.

Though the time varies slightly throughout the year, as a rough guide you need to be at Gillman's at around 4.45am in order to have a chance of seeing the sunrise at Uhuru at around 6am. If you've no chance of making it by then, consider seeing the sunrise from somewhere along the way: from Stella Point, for example, or overlooking Rebmann Glacier, or from one of the lesser peaks before Uhuru. To be honest, who really cares? You've made it this far, you're still going, so where you first glimpse the sun is of little to no consequence.

See Map 33 on p371 for details of the summit and the walk around the crater rim. The first part of this walk is undulating as you ride the rim's peaks and troughs; if the sun has yet to rise, you may well need your head torch as you walk in the moon-shadow. From **Stella Point**, 30-45 minutes to the south of Gillman's, the path begins to climb more steadily. Though nothing like as steep as that which has gone before, at this stage any incline is a major challenge. Don't be too disheartened by the many false summits you will encounter along the last part; instead, distract your mind from the pain and exhaustion by looking at the huge and beautiful icefields to your left and the sheer, desolate enormity of the crater on your right. A gorgeous dawn at the summit, and a certificate back at Marangu Gate, are the prizes that await...

For details of what you can actually see at the summit, turn to pp369-73, while for a description of the designated descent path, turn to the **Marangu Route descent** on pp360-2.

The Machame Route

Then they began to climb and they were going to the East it seemed, and then it darkened and they were in a storm, the rain so thick it seemed like flying through a waterfall, and they were out and Compie turned his head and grinned and pointed and there, ahead, all he could see, as wide as all the world, great, high, and unbelievably white in the sun, was the top of Kilimanjaro. And then he knew that there was where he was going.

Ernest Hemingway, *The Snows of Kilimanjaro*

For most of the last decade, if you were to ask any guide or tour agent which was their favourite walk on Kilimanjaro, often they would choose this, the Machame-Mweka Route (usually just shortened to the Machame Route, a convention I have adopted here). While today its sheer popularity has led many to reconsider their choice and look at other routes more favourably, it is still not difficult to see why this route remains so in vogue: beginning on the south-western side of the mountain, the path passes through some of the mountain's finest features, including the **cloud forest** of Kili's southern slopes, the dry and dusty **Shira Plateau** and the delightful groundsel-clad **Barranco Campsite**.

> *Is it so small a thing*
> *To have enjoy'd the sun,*
> *To have lived light in the spring,*
> *To have loved, to have thought,*
> *to have done;*
> *To have advanc'd true friends,*
> *and beat down baffling foes?*
> **Matthew Arnold**
> *Empedocles on Etna* (1852)

Furthermore, you have a choice of ascent routes to the summit with thrill-seekers opting for the daunting **Western Breach Route** (if open), while the majority head for the lengthy, long-winded climb up the **Barafu Trail**, with Rebmann Glacier edging into your field of vision on your left as dawn breaks behind Mawenzi on your right. In addition, unlike the Marangu Route, on Machame you don't use the same path to descend but instead you come down via the Mweka Route, a steep but pretty trail encompassing inhospitably dry mountain desert and lush lowland forest in a matter of a few hours.

For all these reasons, Machame is now the busiest trail on the mountain. Another reason could be that while the Machame Route is widely reckoned to be that much harder than the Marangu Route (and is thus nicknamed the Whiskey Route, in opposition to Marangu's softer soubriquet of the 'Coca Cola trail'), the proportion of trekkers who reach the top using this route is marginally but significantly higher. This could be down to a number of factors: the Machame Route allows people to acclimatise better because it's longer (**40.41km/25 miles to the summit via Barafu** as opposed to 36.55km/22¾ miles on Marangu); when it comes to climbing the slopes of Kibo, the Barafu Route is more straightforward than the route from Kibo Huts to Gillman's, as it is largely conducted on the firm terrain of a ridge rather than sliding, shifting shale; or maybe the Machame's higher success rate is merely an indication that more experienced, hardened trekkers – ie the very people who are presumably most likely to reach the summit – are more inclined to choose this route.

The following description assumes you will be taking the Barafu Route to the summit. This walk via Barafu traditionally lasts for six days and five nights, though it is now more common for trekkers to opt for an extra night during the

❑ PHONE RECEPTION ON THE MACHAME ROUTE

It depends which network you're with, of course, but mobile (cell phone) reception on the Machame Route seems to be OK by the standards of Kilimanjaro. There's reasonable reception at **Machame Huts**, and at **Shira Caves** I was told that reception is OK if the weather's good. Often you'll see the porters climb up the rocks surrounding the camp to use their phones here so you may want to follow them; the traditional afternoon 'acclimatisation' walk offers more opportunities to get a connection.

At **Lava Tower** there is fair reception, and while you have to wander around the camp to get anything at both **Barranco** (you may well have to wait until you reach the top of the Barranco/Breakfast Wall to get reception here) and **Karanga**, it is good at **Barafu**, intermittent at **Stella Point** and fine near **Uhuru Peak**.

The **Millennium Camp**, on the descent, also has good mobile reception. If you are taking the Western Breach Route, please see the box on p315 for a summary of your mobile reception from Lava Tower.

ascent, usually at Karanga Camp, halfway between Barranco and Barafu camps. Not only does the extra day aid acclimatisation but it also reduces from almost six to three the number of hours walked on the day that precedes the exhausting midnight ascent to the summit, thereby allowing trekkers more time to recover their faculties, relax and prepare themselves for the final push to the top.

Incidentally, those daredevils wishing to try their hand at the Arrow Glacier/ Western Breach Route will leave the regular Machame Route on the third day; the map on p301 and the box on p304 indicate where. You can then find a description of that path to the summit on pp325-9.

STAGE 1: MACHAME GATE TO MACHAME HUTS

[MAP 7, opposite; MAP 8, p297]

Distance: 10.75km (6¾ miles); altitude gained: 1210m (3970ft)

Coming from Moshi, the drive to Machame Gate, sitting at an altitude of 1811m (5942ft), takes just under an hour. Passing through Machame village you'll soon arrive at the gate itself, a small collection of buildings huddled around a 4WD car park. **Register** in the office and make sure you use the **toilet facilities** on site – you may not think much of them now but, believe me, compared to some of the latrines on the trail these are heavenly.

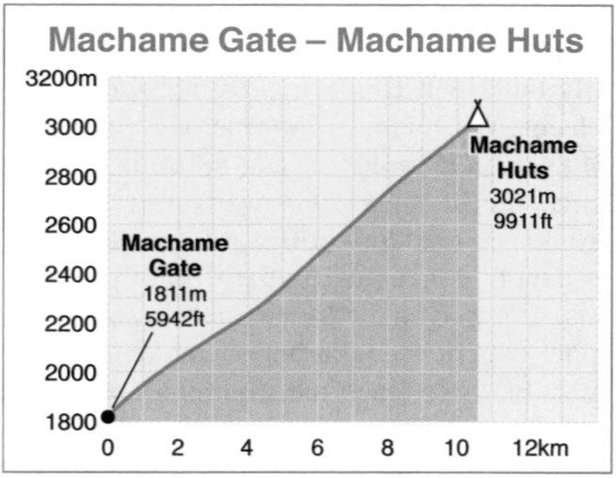

Back at the car park, porters are busy haggling over who is going to take what, guides are reporting to KINAPA reception to wrestle with the red tape, while the trekkers are packing away their lunchboxes and quietly steeling themselves for the rigours ahead. To one side of this chaos is the beginning of the trail...

This 10+ kilometre first day is a long and sweaty one. It starts with a 3km (2 mile) amble up a 4WD track, a wide snaking trail that cuts through the kind of deep, dark enchanted forest that Hansel and Gretel would be familiar with. Green moss hangs thickly from the branches that creak and groan in the wind; it's a magical start to a wonderful adventure. After 45 minutes the 4WD road comes to an end, the gentle curves and steady incline giving way to a narrower, steeper but now beautifully maintained pedestrian-only path that continues all the way to Machame Huts. Looking to the side of the path you'll notice that the vegetation

Note: In the descriptions, the treks have been divided into stages, with each stage roughly corresponding to a day's trekking. For this reason, throughout the text the words 'stage' and 'day' have been used interchangeably.

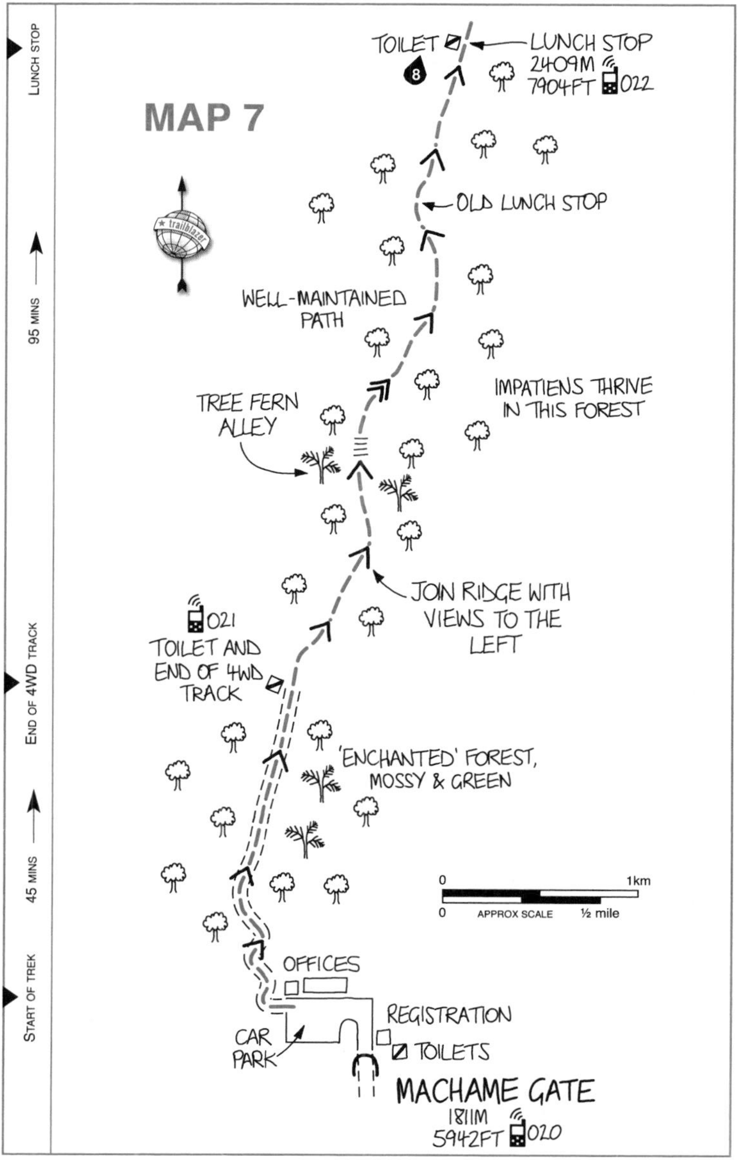
MAP 7
LUNCH STOP
95 MINS
END OF 4WD TRACK
45 MINS
START OF TREK
TOILET
8
LUNCH STOP
2409M
7904FT 022
OLD LUNCH STOP
WELL-MAINTAINED PATH
TREE FERN ALLEY
IMPATIENS THRIVE IN THIS FOREST
JOIN RIDGE WITH VIEWS TO THE LEFT
021
TOILET AND END OF 4WD TRACK
'ENCHANTED' FOREST, MOSSY & GREEN
0
1km
0
APPROX SCALE
½ mile
OFFICES
REGISTRATION
TOILETS
CAR PARK
MACHAME GATE
1811M
5942FT 020
trailblazer

is already changing as you progress deeper into the **cloud forest**, the scarlet and yellow *Impatiens kilimanjari* and pink *Impatiens pseudoviola* now flourishing between the roots of the 30-metre tall trees; tree ferns also proliferate here.

About a hundred minutes beyond the end of the 4WD track, the path widens momentarily to form several small **clearings**, one of which has en suite toilet facilities, that make for popular lunch stops. Those who've already drunk their water bottles dry can replenish their supplies from the stream down in the valley to the west. Listen out for the primate-like call of the black (actually very dark green) and red turaco which nests around here, and watch your lunch too: it's not uncommon for the forest rodents to sneak into lunchboxes and drag off a samosa or two.

The post-prandial path varies little from that which has gone before, though the gradient increases slightly the higher you climb. As the forest gradually begins to thin out you'll notice that you are actually walking on a narrow forested spine between two shallow valleys, with a stream – more audible than visible – bubbling to the right of the trail.

Around two hours after lunch a **signpost** appears, warning against the careless discarding of cigarette butts; as well as dispensing some sound advice, this sign also marks the border between the cloud forest and the heath, where long grasses dominate and the robust trees of the forest give way to the spindly, tree-like giant heathers. *Kniphofia thomsonii* (known to you and me as red hot pokers) make their first appearance at this altitude at certain times of year, as do several other wild flowers and shrubs such as the bushy *Philippia excelsa*. With the forest thinning, Kibo peak looms into view for the first time to the east.

Machame village in the late nineteenth century. Engraving by **Alexandre Le Roy** from *Au Kilima-Ndjaro* published in 1893.

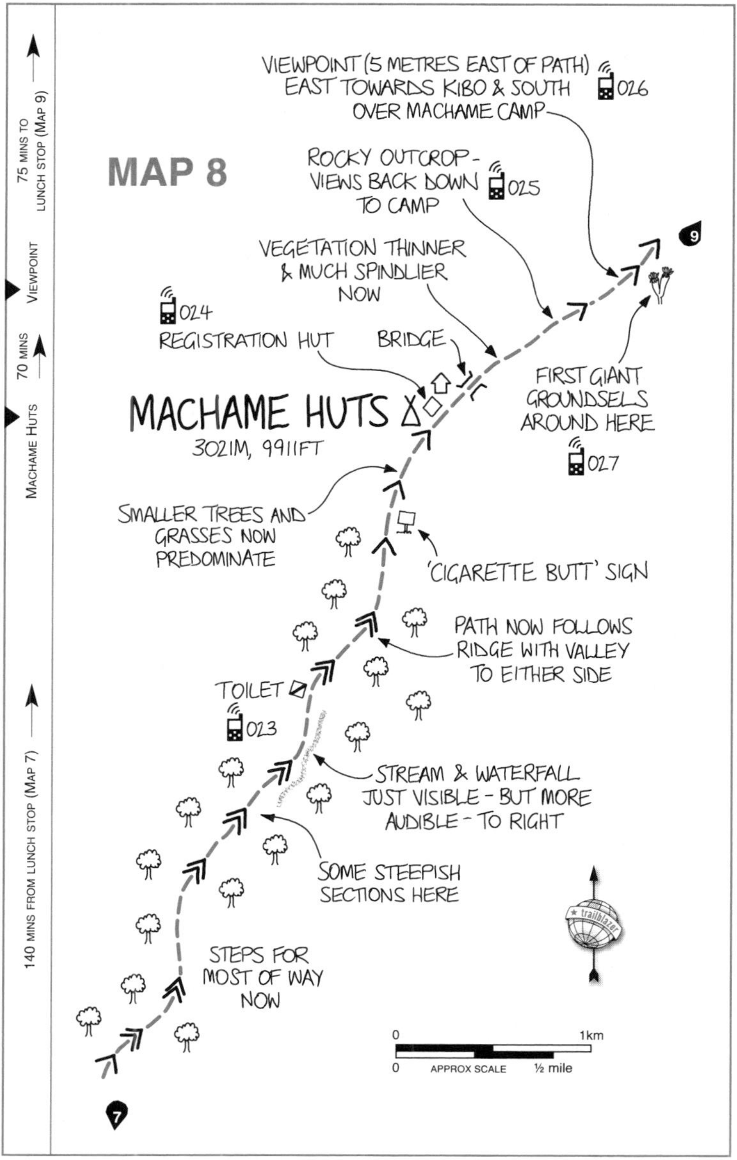
MAP 8
75 MINS TO LUNCH STOP (MAP 9)
VIEWPOINT
70 MINS
MACHAME HUTS
140 MINS FROM LUNCH STOP (MAP 7)
VIEWPOINT (5 METRES EAST OF PATH) EAST TOWARDS KIBO & SOUTH OVER MACHAME CAMP
026
ROCKY OUTCROP - VIEWS BACK DOWN TO CAMP
025
VEGETATION THINNER & MUCH SPINDLIER NOW
024
REGISTRATION HUT
BRIDGE
MACHAME HUTS
3021M, 9911FT
FIRST GIANT GROUNDSELS AROUND HERE
027
SMALLER TREES AND GRASSES NOW PREDOMINATE
'CIGARETTE BUTT' SIGN
PATH NOW FOLLOWS RIDGE WITH VALLEY TO EITHER SIDE
TOILET
023
STREAM & WATERFALL JUST VISIBLE - BUT MORE AUDIBLE - TO RIGHT
SOME STEEPISH SECTIONS HERE
STEPS FOR MOST OF WAY NOW
trailblazer
0
1km
0
APPROX SCALE
½ mile
9
7

It is only 20 minutes from the forest edge to **Machame Huts** (3021m/9911ft), a series of level pitches cut into the grass, each with its own toilet. Make sure you sign your name in the **registration book** and aim to pitch your tent as high as possible for the best views: by the green hut is a good spot, affording views to the east up to Kibo and south-west towards Mount Meru. Look out for the birdlife too, which is abundant round here, with olive thrush, common stonechats and flocks of montane white-eye all resident, in addition to the usual seedeaters, alpine chats and white-necked ravens that are ubiquitous on the mountain.

By the way, having climbed to 3021m you are now higher than the top of Mawson Peak, at 2745m (9006ft) the highest point in Australia.

STAGE 2: MACHAME HUTS TO SHIRA CAVES

[MAP 8, p297; MAP 9, opposite]

Distance: 5.3km (3¼ miles); altitude gained: 818m (2684ft)

Everyone is waking up. She hears the pouring of water, the rattle of pots, the thrufting of tents. Rita is so tired and so awake she comes close to crying. She wants to be in this sleeping bag, not awake but still sleeping, for two and a half hours more. In two and a half hours she could regather her strength, all of it. She would have a running start to this day, and could then leap past anyone. **David Eggers**, from his short story about a Kilimanjaro climb *Up the Mountain Coming Down Slowly.*

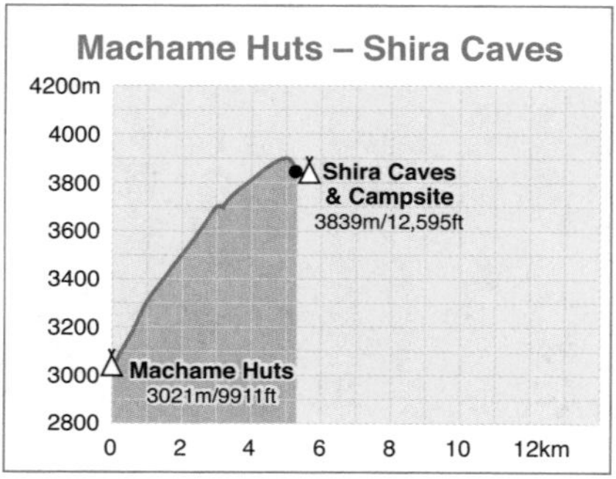

This leg of the trek is short but a little strenuous as you ascend from 3021m/9911ft up to the Shira Plateau, finally coming to a halt at the Shira Caves at 3839m/12,595ft. Parts of this walk are a bit steep and the skinny, naked heathers at this altitude provide little shade from the heat; what's more, the path is extremely dusty, particularly towards the end of the dry season, so if you have gaiters you'll probably be thankful for the protection they provide (and remember to keep your camera bag tightly closed too to prevent dust inveigling into any valuable equipment). In spite of all this, by taking it slowly, resting frequently and enjoying the en route views that encompass Kibo, Meru and all points in between, this day needn't be too taxing and if you're on a 6-day schedule, this may prove to be the easiest day of them all. Indeed, many guides now try to have the walk finished by one or two o'clock, in the hope of beating the afternoon rains that regularly douse this part of the mountain.

The walk starts as it goes on for much of the morning, with a steepish climb north up through forests of stunted, twisted heather bushes; while ahead of you

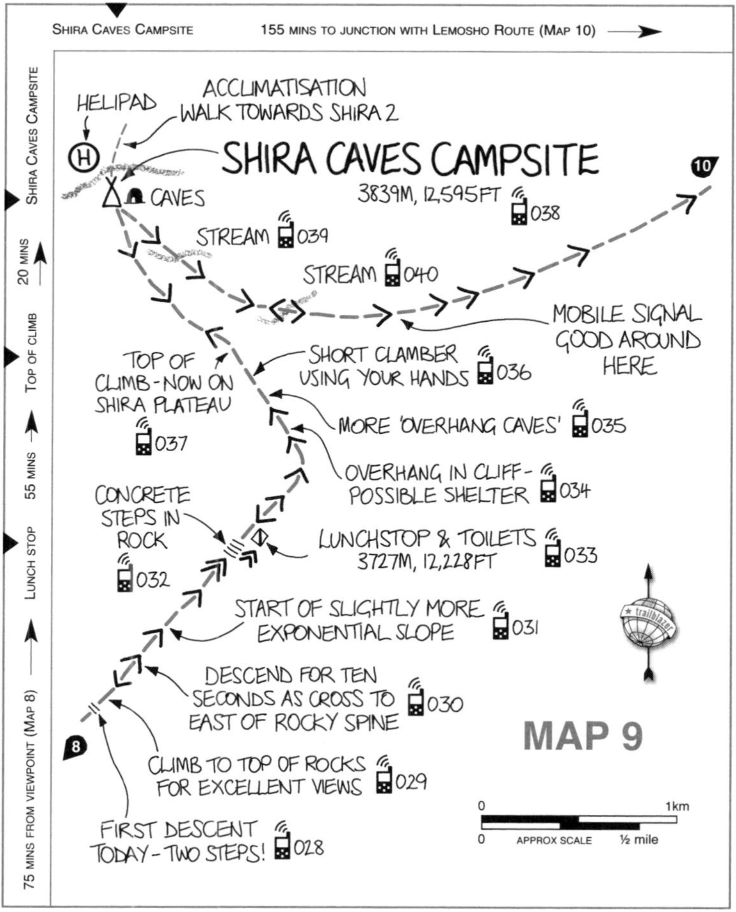

in the distance is the lip of Shira Plateau. The path winds its way up to the top of a ridge formed by a petrified lava flow, occasionally allowing trekkers some splendid **views** over Machame Huts and the village below as well as the flat Tanzanian plains beyond. Giant groundsels (*Dendrosenecio kilimanjari ssp cottonii*), the squat, chunky trees with the green-leaf crown, begin to dot the path and Kilimanjaro's desiccated **helichrysums**, ubiquitous above 3000m, appear here for the first time, like living pot pourri. Note, too, how most of the vegetation not only diminishes in size as you climb higher but the taller plants seem to bend as one towards the plateau, as if pointing the way.

After passing a number of **viewpoints** and clambering from one side of the ridge to the other, the gradient of the trail increases exponentially towards the **lunch stop**, hidden from view behind a rocky outcrop. The effort expended in reaching here is worth it, for while munching on chicken legs and boiled eggs you can savour yet more views of Kibo as well as all points south.

You'll also be able to observe the line of porters and trekkers on the path ahead and from them you can pick out the afternoon's trail, which initially continues north and up, before bending fairly sharply to the north-west, cutting a near horizontal line beneath the rim of the plateau. But though the worst of the day's climbing is behind you, don't be fooled into thinking this is an easy section, for the path on this north-westerly trail undulates considerably as it climbs over rocks and boulders and it can be tiring in the searing afternoon heat. As a distraction, the first of Kilimanjaro's celebrated moorland **lobelias** (*Lobelia deckenii*), both phallic and cabbage-shaped and growing to a height of around two metres, appear by the trail.

Just under an hour after lunch the plateau is gained and the path continues northwards. Look out for Shira Plateau's distinctive, shiny black **obsidian** rock (see p130). Your camp for the night is **Shira Caves Campsite** (3839m/12,595ft).

Looking west from the campsite, ask your guide to point out **Shira Cathedral** and **East Shira Hill** which line the southern boundary of Shira Plateau, and, behind them to the far west, **Johnsell Point** and **Klute Peak**, the highest points of the Shira Ridge, the western rim of the oldest of Kili's three craters. Mount Meru, too, is still visible to the west on the horizon. For an afternoon stroll, your guide will probably take you via the helipad and the caves themselves on the path leading towards Shira 2 Campsite, a stroll of less than half an hour in total.

Incidentally, by reaching Shira Caves you are now at a higher altitude than Mafadi (3450m/11,319ft), the highest peak in South Africa.

STAGE 3: SHIRA CAVES CAMPSITE TO BARRANCO HUTS

[MAP 9, p299; MAP 10, opposite; MAP 11, p303]

Distance: 10.3km/6½ miles via Lava Tower (7.1km/4½ miles to Lava Tower, 3.2km/2 miles from there to Barranco); altitude gained: 147m/482ft (788m/2585ft up to Lava Tower, then 641m/2103ft descent to Barranco)

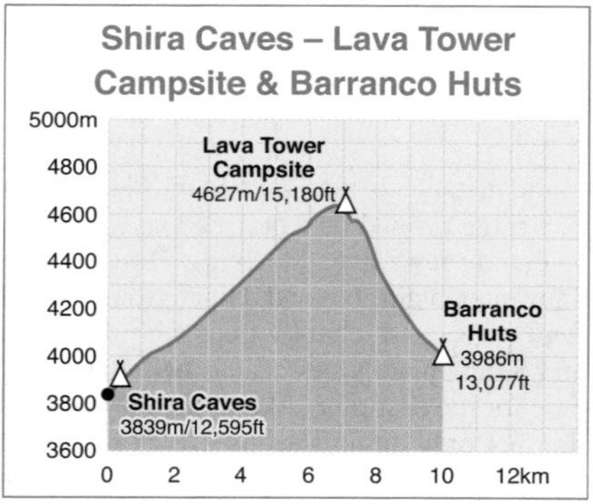

Rita wakes up strong. She doesn't know why but now she feels, with her eyes opening quickly and her body rested, that she belongs on this mountain. She is ready to attack.

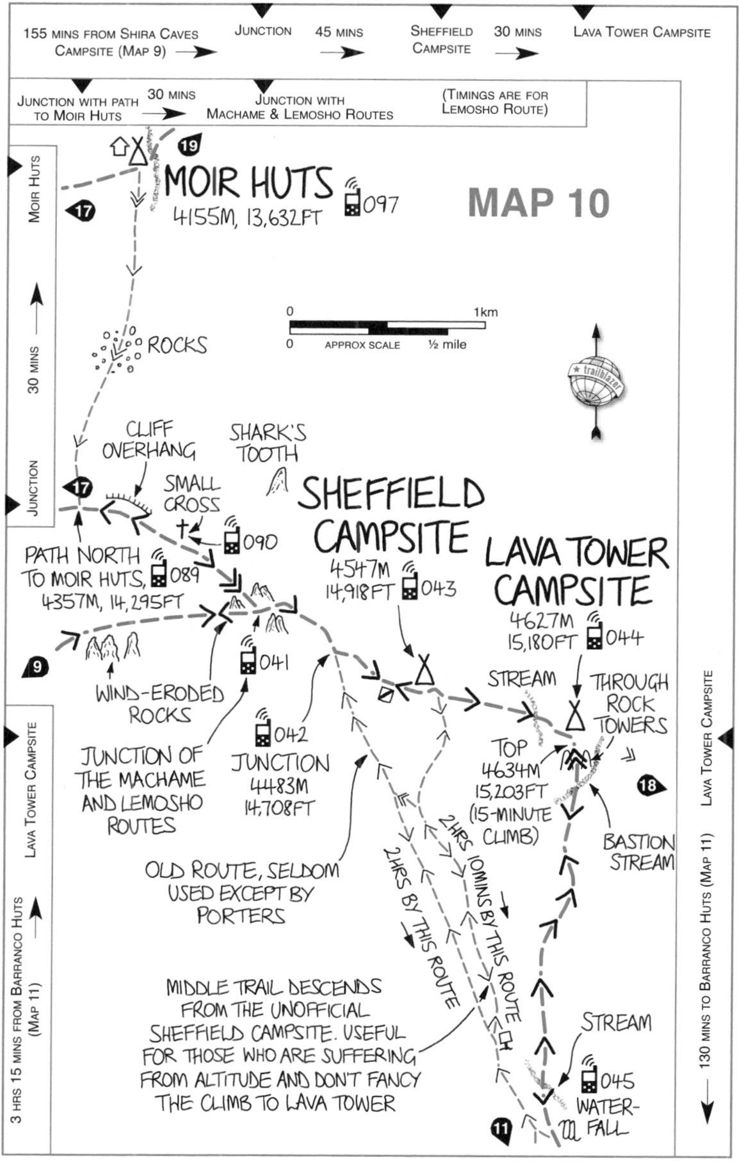
155 MINS FROM SHIRA CAVES CAMPSITE (MAP 9)
JUNCTION
45 MINS
SHEFFIELD CAMPSITE
30 MINS
LAVA TOWER CAMPSITE
JUNCTION WITH PATH TO MOIR HUTS
30 MINS
JUNCTION WITH MACHAME & LEMOSHO ROUTES
(TIMINGS ARE FOR LEMOSHO ROUTE)
MAP 10
MOIR HUTS
4155M, 13,632FT
097
MOIR HUTS
30 MINS
JUNCTION
0
1km
0
APPROX SCALE
½ mile
trailblazer
ROCKS
CLIFF OVERHANG
SHARK'S TOOTH
SMALL CROSS
090
SHEFFIELD CAMPSITE
4547M
14,918FT
043
LAVA TOWER CAMPSITE
4627M
15,180FT
044
PATH NORTH TO MOIR HUTS,
089
4357M, 14,295FT
041
WIND-ERODED ROCKS
JUNCTION OF THE MACHAME AND LEMOSHO ROUTES
042
JUNCTION
4483M
14,708FT
STREAM
THROUGH ROCK TOWERS
TOP
4634M
15,203FT
(15-MINUTE CLIMB)
BASTION STREAM
OLD ROUTE, SELDOM USED EXCEPT BY PORTERS
2HRS BY THIS ROUTE
2HRS 10MINS BY THIS ROUTE
MIDDLE TRAIL DESCENDS FROM THE UNOFFICIAL SHEFFIELD CAMPSITE. USEFUL FOR THOSE WHO ARE SUFFERING FROM ALTITUDE AND DON'T FANCY THE CLIMB TO LAVA TOWER
STREAM
045
WATER-FALL
LAVA TOWER CAMPSITE
3 HRS 15 MINS FROM BARRANCO HUTS (MAP 11)
LAVA TOWER CAMPSITE
130 MINS TO BARRANCO HUTS (MAP 11)

She will run up the path today, barefoot. She will carry her own duffel. She will carry Shelly on her back. She has slept twice on this mountain but it seems like months. She feels sure that if she were left here alone, she would survive, would blend in like the hardiest of plants – her skin would turn ice green and her feet would grow sturdy and gnarled, hard and crafty like roots. **David Eggers**, *Up the Mountain Coming Down Slowly.*

During this section you cover over 10km (6½ miles) as you move from the western to the southern slopes of Kibo; by the end of it you may feel slightly disappointed to learn that, for all your efforts, you will have gained just 147m/482ft in height, from Shira Caves at 3839m/12,595ft to Barranco, situated at an altitude of 3986m/13,077ft. Nevertheless, this third stage is vital for acclimatisation purposes, for during the day you will climb to a respectable **4627m/15,180ft** if taking the path via Lava Tower. (There's another path which breaks off from this path before the little-used and unofficial **Sheffield Campsite**, 4547m/14,918ft, which is great for those who can't quite manage the climb up to Lava Tower; and a third and older trail which is lower still.) Don't be surprised, therefore, if by the end of it you have a crashing headache: this is normal and is only cause for concern if it is accompanied by other symptoms of mountain sickness, or if the pain hasn't disappeared by the morning.

The day begins with a steady, gentle ascent through the dry, boulder-strewn terrain of Shira Plateau towards the western slopes of Kibo, which appears from here so white and so *huge* that it looks vaguely unreal, as if it's the painted backdrop of a stage. Some trekkers also insist that the summit of Kibo, from this angle, resembles the profile of a Native American Indian chief at rest. (No, I can't really see it either.) At first the path meanders somewhat, rising and falling regularly as it negotiates the gentle folds of the plateau before finally settling on a roughly easterly direction, with a steady, shallow incline for most of the next 6km (3¾ miles). Notice how the vegetation has declined until only a few everlastings and lichen manage to cling to life. Ahead, facing you down, is the brilliant white smear of Penck Glacier.

Soon after the **junction with the Lemosho Route** the path loops to the south-east and divides. Once upon a time it was only those people who opted to tackle the summit on the more difficult Western Breach Route who headed east towards **Lava Tower**; these days, however, most guides recognise the acclimatisation benefits of taking this climb and also opt for this route, before then diverting off down to Barranco Huts. As for the

'...an extraordinary arborescent plant, since named *Senecio Johnstonii*... Its trunk was so superficially rooted and so rotten that, in spite of its height and girth, I could pull it down with one hand. (from *The Kilima-njaro Expedition*, **HH Johnston**, 1886; note that the tree he is talking about and depicting is no longer called *Senecio johnstonii* but *Dendrosenecio kilimanjarii ssp cottonii*).

more southerly route, this is now largely the preserve of porters and those trekkers who aren't doing so well and need to descend quickly to Barranco. (This more gentle, southerly trail bends round to the right before the unofficial Sheffield Campsite, reaches a high point of 4530m/14,862ft, then descends quickly via a series of zigzags into a gully. It then bends south-east once more, following the contours of Kibo's lower reaches as it crosses two more streams. Less than an hour later the trail meets a proliferation of signposts, from where it's downhill all the way to Barranco.)

Back at Lava Tower the more popular, higher route splits again. The route up to Arrow Glacier soars above, while the path to Barranco drops steeply south to a stream, and rises and falls a couple of times before plummeting, finally and fabulously, into the delightful **Barranco Valley**, rich in groundsel and lobelia. A huge gouge in the southern face of Kibo to the south-west of Uhuru Peak, the valley is in places 300m (almost 1000ft) deep and was formed when a huge

❑ KIBO ASCENT VIA THE WESTERN BREACH/ARROW GLACIER ROUTE

The Western Breach Route (when open) is a harder, shorter, more dangerous and less popular alternative trail than the standard Machame Route to the summit that travels via Barafu Huts. But it's also a great walk that delivers you directly to Kibo's crater floor, allowing you to explore its features – the Furtwangler Glacier, Reusch Crater and Ash Pit, to name but three – as well as affording supreme views of the Shira Plateau, Barranco Valley and the summit of Mount Meru.

The route starts at Lava Tower Campsite. You can find a full description of the Arrow Glacier/Western Breach Route starting on p325-9.

landslide swept southwards down from the summit about 100,000 years ago. From **Barranco Huts Campsite** (3986m/13,077ft) and its environs you'll have spectacular views of Kibo's southern face, the Western Breach and the mighty Heim Glacier, with glacial moraine tumbling southwards towards the camp. Few are the trekkers who do not rank this campsite as their favourite on this trail. Indeed, so beautiful is it that it's tempting to linger outside one's tent after dark and savour the sights and scenery of this most spectacular site – though in reality, the cold soon chases most people into their sleeping bags. Unfortunately, there has been a spate of thefts from tents on the mountain and Barranco has experienced more than its fair share of them. Do be careful, make sure your tent is zipped up when you're not in it and keep your valuables on you.

By the way, though you have gained only 147m/482ft since this morning, by climbing to Lava Tower Campsite (4627m/15,180ft) you have reached an altitude that's just 7m (23ft) shy of the highest mountain in Switzerland, the Dufourspitze; bother to climb up Lava Tower itself, which takes about 15 minutes or so, and you'll have climbed 57m (187ft) higher.

STAGE 4: BARRANCO HUTS TO BARAFU HUTS

[MAP 11, p303; MAP 12, opposite]

Distance: 9.2km (5¾ miles); altitude gained: 676m (2218ft)

At this altitude this is a long stage; so long that many trekkers prefer to tackle it over two days, camping for the night above Karanga Valley, the last place to get water on the Machame Route. As you walk along the path the great glaciers of Kili's Southern Icefields – Heim, Kersten and Decken – will appear on your left one

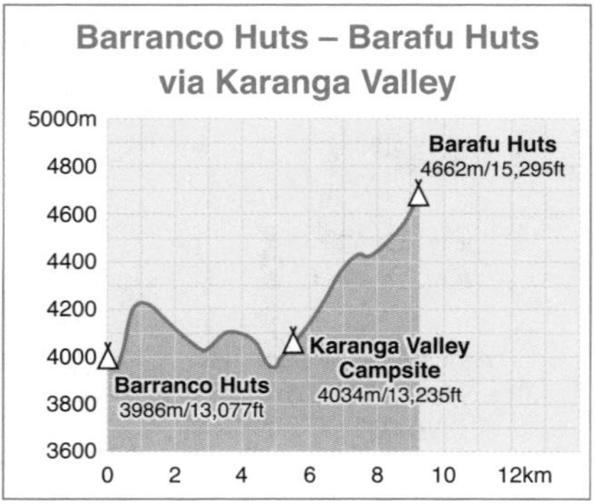

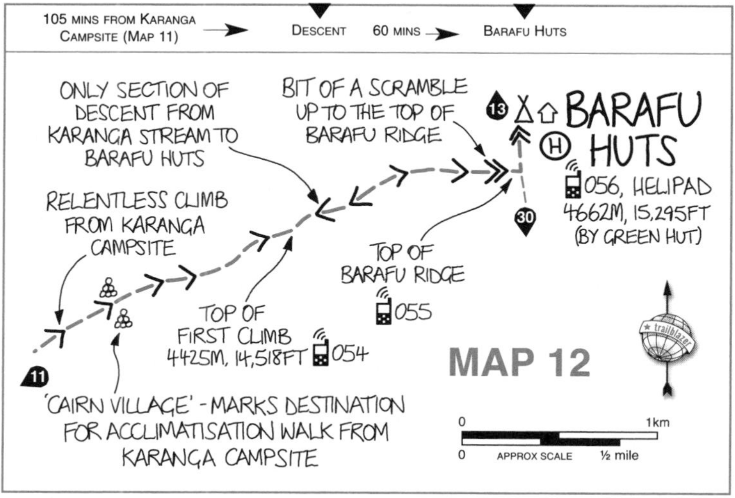

after the other. Curiously, although this stage sets you up nicely for the final push to the summit, by the end of the day you will actually be further from Uhuru Peak (as the lammergeyer flies) than you were at the start of the day at Barranco.

The hardest part of the day occurs right at the beginning, with a near vertical scramble to the east of the campsite up **The Barranco Wall** or **Breach Wall** (now more commonly called the **Breakfast Wall**, as it is usually tackled after breakfast). In my experience most trekkers actually get a real kick out of this climb, probably because it provides such a welcome change from the relentless *pole pole* trudge of the previous stages. You'll have to stash your walking poles away for this first section, because at times you'll need to use both hands to haul yourself up the groundsel-dressed slopes.

People talk in hushed, fearful tones about the Wall's main feature, the so-called '**Kissing Rock**', and how it forces you to tiptoe on the very edge of the path, with an almighty fall awaiting those who lose their footing. But in reality it's all rather straightforward and no trekker, as far as I know, has ever plunged to their demise on this section.

False summits along the way shouldn't discourage you as you progress up the Wall for after about 80 minutes you'll reach its true summit; here you can

Note: In all the route descriptions, do remember that the times quoted are approximations and, more importantly, refer to **walking times only** with no time spent resting, taking photos etc.

Add on 30-50% to get an estimate of the total time spent on the trail.

sit on the bare rock and enjoy the views west over Mount Meru and on a clear day south-east towards the Pare Mountains, with the great Heim Glacier over your shoulder to the north, and relish the prospect of the relatively gentle descent into the next gully below.

At the bottom of this pretty little gully, and having crossed the small stream that flows through it, you come to a **flat gravel area**, possibly once a camping spot and, by the amount of loo roll hanging from the bushes, a popular pit stop too. Your guide will lead you along an undulating trail cutting south before ascending to surmount the eastern edge of a sheer-sided valley. The path quickly veers away east from the precipice, however, to traverse a **desert slope** where the silence and stillness are positively deafening, before finally descending down the western, lusher slopes of the **Karanga Valley**. Lobelia, heather and other greenery reappear for a while as you descend along the rock-and-mud path, a path that you share in places with a mountain stream.

Karanga Valley is, in the words of John Reader, 'narrow, steep and exquisite' and is a small oasis of green, albeit a cold and windswept one. Beautiful shimmering green **malachite sunbirds** nest around here; you may spot them feeding on the lobelias.

Those who plan to cover this leg in two days rather than one will camp at the top of the next climb, a very steep 20-minute ascent on a switchback path. This is the somewhat misnamed **Karanga Valley Campsite** (4034m/15,235ft); I say misnamed because, of course, it's above the valley and not in it; also, *karanga* is Swahili for 'peanut' – yet I doubt nuts have ever grown up here. It's an unlovely place, windswept and ramshackle, with something of the atmosphere of a refugee camp about it. At this altitude it's often hemmed in by clouds which unfortunately obscure its best feature, namely the lovely views it affords of Kibo's southern face. By the way, for those who are staying here the distance from Barranco to Karanga is **5.5km** (3½ miles) and despite all your efforts this morning you will now be just **48m** (157ft) higher than when you set off from Barranco.

At the campsite the trail takes a leftward turn, heading in a north-easterly direction on a steady, relentless incline, with the Kersten and Decken glaciers a permanent presence to your left. The scenery now becomes even more barren as you make your way between the boulders and over the shattered rocks and stones of this misty mountain slope. Even the trail is faint. Only the collection of cairns that mark the destination for those on an acclimatisation walk from Karanga give any indication that man has passed this way before. If George Lucas is looking for somewhere wild, inhospitable and unearthly as a location for his next Star Wars film, he could do a lot worse.

At the top the path bends more to the east and descends into a shallow valley that, if anything, is even drier and more blighted than the previous section. Once again, the Southern Icefields loom ominously to your left, with Rebmann Glacier appearing for the first time.

Barafu Huts (4662m/15,295ft), your destination for this leg, lies at the end of this valley, reached after a short scramble up a cliff-face and a 15- to 25-minute walk almost due north. Barafu means 'Ice' in Swahili and the camp is probably called this because of its proximity to Rebmann Glacier, away to the north-west. It's a chilly, charmless spot. By the way, at 4662m (15,295ft) you are now higher than Mount Elbert, at 4401m (14,439ft) the highest mountain in the Rocky Mountains.

Try to get some food and rest as soon as possible and sort out your preparations for the next stage before it gets dark: you've got a long night ahead. But don't stress if you don't manage to sleep tonight: in all honesty, few people do.

STAGE 5: BARAFU HUTS TO STELLA POINT AND UHURU PEAK [MAP 13, p309; MAP 33, p371]

Distance: 4.86km (3 miles); altitude gained: 1233m (4045ft)

But now, apparently, the mountain was inhabited by fiery beings who baffled man's adventurous foot: the mountain receded as the traveller advanced, the summit rose as he ascended; blood burst from the nostrils, fingers bent backwards... even the most adventurous were forced back. **Richard Burton** in *Progress of Expedition to East Africa*, reporting the rumours he had heard about Kilimanjaro while residing in Tanga (circa 1857).

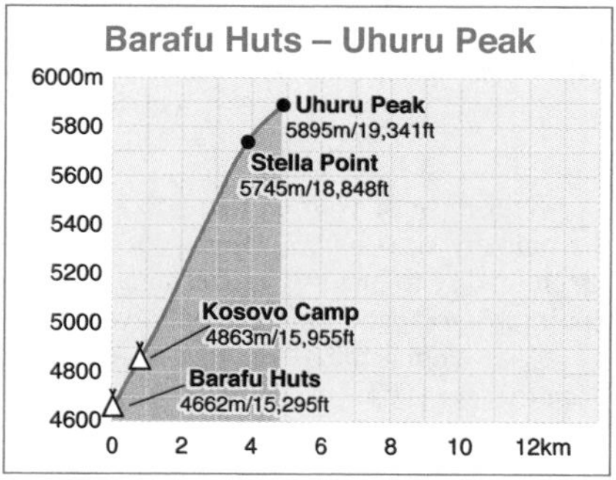

And so you come to the final ascent. For the past five days or so you've enjoyed some wonderful walking and miles of smiles; but now it's time to do the hard yards.

The climb itself is a vigorous push to Stella Point and the crater rim, followed by a 45-minute trudge up to Uhuru Peak, the highest point in Africa. It's tough, no doubt about it, but if you manage to avoid sickness or injury there's no reason why you shouldn't be clutching a certificate come tomorrow evening.

This final stage usually begins at around midnight; this not only allows trekkers the chance to see sunrise from the summit but also leaves enough daylight to allow for the long descent to the next night's campsite, with an hour's recuperation back at Barafu on the way. As such, you can leave most of your **luggage** at Barafu while you tackle the ascent, though you should take any valuables with you (there have been a few robberies from tents left unguarded), as well as your **camera**, spare memory cards/film and batteries and all your **water**, which should be kept in **insulated bottles** or it'll freeze up and be useless on the ascent.

Cameras, particularly digitals and feature-heavy SLRs, have been known to freeze in these conditions as well so keep them (or at the very least their batteries) insulated, preferably by putting them in an inside pocket or wrapped in clothing in your daypack.

Barafu Route

Wear most of your **clothes** too – you can always take a layer or two off in the unlikely situation you find yourself getting too hot – and have your **head-torch** readily to hand (with fresh batteries installed) when you wake up so you don't have to spend time and energy looking around for it before you go.

Carry your sunhat, sunglasses and suncream as well – you'll need them once the sun is up.

Good luck!

At 4am by the light of a hurricane lamp, and wrapped in everything that could give warmth, I started with Mawala, the headman, and Jonathan, our guide, on the long uphill pull of 4000ft over loose scree and fissured rocks. The cold was intense, and Mawala got two of his toes frost-bitten ... our breathing had become so difficult that we could barely drag ourselves along and had to sit down every few yards to recover breath, now and again sucking icicles and nibbling Cadbury's Milk Chocolate. Yet the steep ascent was mostly over projecting ridges of lava slabs and presented no real obstacle beyond the extreme altitude. Here and there, however, we struck a bed of loose shingle, which mockingly carried us backwards at every footstep almost the whole distance of our tread.

Eva Stuart Watt *Africa's Dome of Mystery* (1930)

The way to the summit starts, as you've probably already observed from Barafu, by scrambling over the **small cliffs** at the northern end of the camp in what is the steepest part of the trek save for the final push to Stella Point.

About 1¾ hours into the trek, you pass through **Kosovo Camp** (4863m/15,955ft). Go on the internet and you'll find people stirred to paroxysms of joy and enthusiasm about this spot that verge on the spiritual. To be

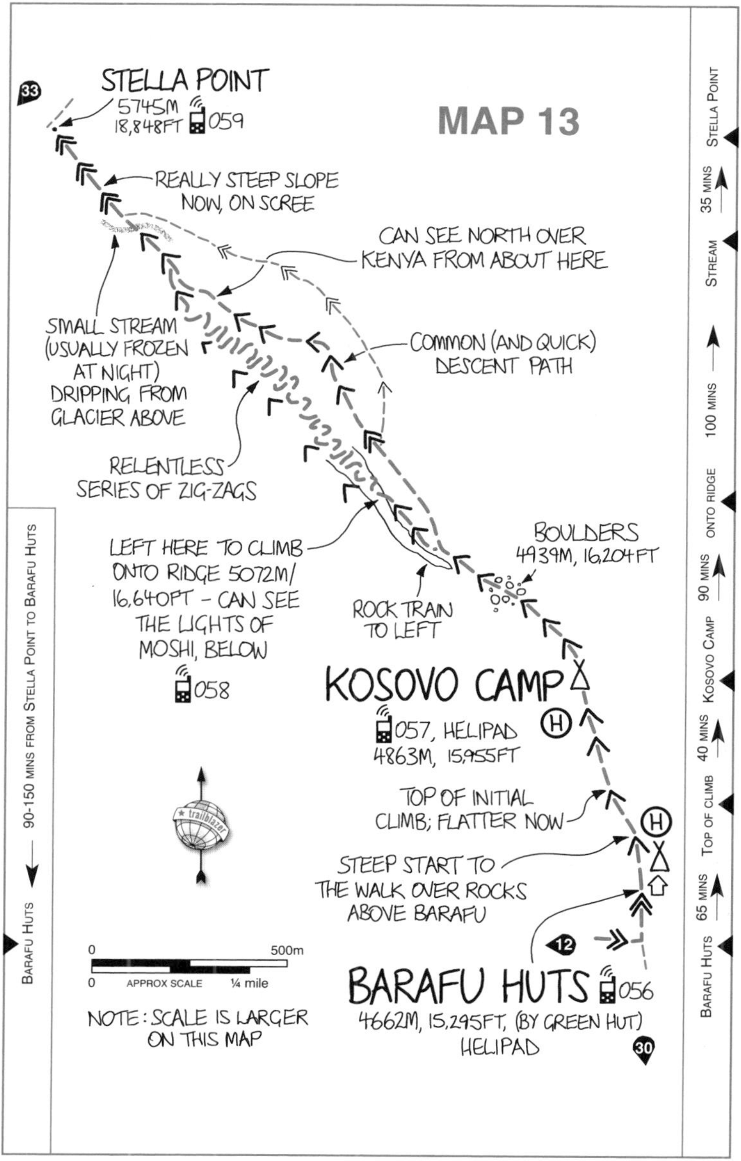
MAP 13
STELLA POINT
5745M
18,848FT 059
REALLY STEEP SLOPE NOW, ON SCREE
CAN SEE NORTH OVER KENYA FROM ABOUT HERE
SMALL STREAM (USUALLY FROZEN AT NIGHT) DRIPPING FROM GLACIER ABOVE
COMMON (AND QUICK) DESCENT PATH
RELENTLESS SERIES OF ZIG-ZAGS
LEFT HERE TO CLIMB ONTO RIDGE 5072M/ 16,640FT – CAN SEE THE LIGHTS OF MOSHI, BELOW
058
BOULDERS 4939M, 16,204FT
ROCK TRAIN TO LEFT
KOSOVO CAMP
057, HELIPAD
4863M, 15,955FT
TOP OF INITIAL CLIMB; FLATTER NOW
STEEP START TO THE WALK OVER ROCKS ABOVE BARAFU
BARAFU HUTS 056
4662M, 15,295FT, (BY GREEN HUT) HELIPAD
0 500m
0 APPROX SCALE ¼ mile
NOTE: SCALE IS LARGER ON THIS MAP
trailblazer
Barafu Huts
90-150 mins from Stella Point to Barafu Huts
Stella Point
35 mins
Stream
100 mins
Onto Ridge
90 mins
Kosovo Camp
40 mins
Top of Climb
65 mins
Barafu Huts
33
12
30

honest, it's a chilly, godforsaken spot and, as such, is no different to any other campsite around here – and you (or your trekking company) have to spend an extra US$100 per person to stay here. But it *is* quieter than Barafu, and, of course, 1¾ hours closer to the summit too – which I guess accounts for all the praise lavished on it. Plus you may be pleased to know that you are higher than Mont Blanc, the highest mountain in Western Europe (4807m/15,771ft).

Climbing still further, the path now ascends to a rocky ridge, in the shadow of which you initially walk before taking a sharp left to surmount it and walk along its spine. You are now heading directly for the summit and Stella Point, a direction you will maintain for nearly the entire night.

The **switchback path** begins in earnest once you leave the ridge and continues for most of the next two hours or more. It is pointless describing the scenery on this section, for the chances are you won't be able to see much beyond the radius of your torch-beam and you probably won't be keen on surveying the landscape now anyway.

If it's a clear night, however, you may be able to see **Rebmann Glacier** ahead of you to your left, with the ice-free **Stella Point** a little to its right in the distance. Picking your way through the trail of knackered trekkers and exhausted assistants, ignore the sound of people retching and sobbing and remember to keep your pace constant and very slow, even if you feel fine: you've come this far and now is not a good time to get altitude sickness. This is when you need to take yourself off to your happy place and perhaps, for a little while, forget where you really are.

In the end, what seemed to work is to think of a nice warm swimming pool in California. Or the nice beer and curry dinner I will have when I get back to civilization. Hawaiian palm trees and surf. Scuba diving. Something far from my present surroundings. A pleasant fantasy or daydream.

Michael Crichton, describing the tactics he employed during his 1975 climb up Kili, as recorded in his collection of travel essays entitled *Travels*.

Though you probably won't notice it, the path actually drifts slightly to the north over these three hours, before crossing a **stream** that is usually frozen at night. You are now just 35 minutes from **Stella Point** (5745m/18,848ft), but it's a painful, tear-inducing half-hour on sheer scree. The gradient up to now has been steep, but this last scree slope takes the biscuit; in fact, it takes the entire tin. In just about everybody's opinion this is the hardest part of the climb, when the cold insinuates itself between the layers of your clothes, penetrating your skin, chilling your bones and numbing the marrow until finally, inevitably, it seems to freeze your very soul.

The situation seems desperate at this hour and you can do nothing; nothing except keep going. It's one thing to fail to reach the summit because of altitude sickness; quite another to fail from *attitude* sickness.

The situation was appalling, there was a grandeur and a magnificence about the surroundings which were almost too much for me; instead of exhilarating, they were oppressive.
Charles New, the first person to reach the snowline on Kilimanjaro, in his book *Life, Wanderings, and Labours in Eastern Africa* (1873)

The ground underfoot is just one more obstacle at this stage, the distinctive **shale and gravel slopes** of Kibo causing you to slip back with every step. Everybody has their own way of tackling this, with some trekkers stabbing their poles hard into the ground to aid their balance, while others walk with a Chaplin-esque gait, their feet splayed outwards to stem the slide back. Whatever way you choose, you'll find it hard work.

Lift one foot and then the other, just enough to place it higher; don't use any more energy than you need to and breathe deeply between each move. Rhythm is everything, rhythm and pacing, and when you are in it your thoughts go and it is dreamlike, but you are still here in the moment, the cone beam of light coming from your forehead tying you through the blackness to the lava slope of this mountain that in your mind you see rising to a rare glacial height above the acacia-studded plain of Africa.
Rick Ridgeway *The Shadow of Kilimanjaro – on Foot across East Africa* (1999)

Make it to Stella and you can afford to relax a little. To give you an idea of your achievement, you are now higher than the summit of Russia's Mount Elbrus, at 5642m/18,511ft the highest peak in Europe.

If you really, absolutely, positively, definitely can't do any more, take comfort from the fact that you have already matched the feat of respected climber HW Tilman, for whom Stella Point was the highest point reached on his first attempt on the summit; and you can always use his excuse – he thought that this *was* the highest point – too. (Mind you, as if to prove that it was ignorance and not a lack of fortitude that prevented him from reaching Uhuru, he then went on to conquer the much-harder Mawenzi Peak a few days later.) Take comfort, too, from the fact that you have also earned yourself a certificate; a certificate, moreover, that's identical – save for a couple of words – to the one they give you if you reach the summit. But for most trekkers, those two words – 'UHURU PEAK' – are everything. Words that are worth all the money, time and energy one has spent in getting to this point; and which are certainly worth the extra 45 minutes it takes to stagger around the crater rim (see Map 33, p371), passing minor pinnacles such as **Elveda** and **Hans Meyer** points before finally arriving, just as Hans Meyer himself did well over a century ago, at **Uhuru Peak**: the true summit of the mountain and the highest point on the whole continent. You are now enjoying an unrivalled view of Africa – nobody on this chaotic, crazy, charismatic continent is currently gazing down from as lofty a vantage-point as you.

When you finally manage to tear yourself away from the summit, you have, like all trekkers who have taken the Machame Route, to take the **Mweka Route** back down; and this you'll find described on pp362-8.

The Lemosho, Shira Plateau & Northern Circuit routes – an introduction

Without doubt Kibo is most imposing as seen from the west. Here it rises in solemn majesty, and the eye is not distracted by the sister peak of Mawenzi, of which nothing is to be seen but a single jutting pinnacle. The effect is enhanced by the magnificent flowing sweep of the outline, the dazzling extent of the ice-cap, the vast stretch of the forest, the massive breadth of the base, and the jagged crest of the Shira spur as it branches away towards the west.

Hans Meyer *Across East African Glaciers* (1891)

These treks (see map opposite) have been put together simply because they have a lot of features in common, the main one being that both involve a crossing of the expansive Shira Plateau which stretches out for around 13km to the west of Kibo. This plateau is actually a **caldera**, a collapsed volcanic crater: when you are walking on the plateau, you are actually walking on the remains of the first of Kilimanjaro's three volcanoes to expire, over 500,000 years ago; it was then filled by the lava and debris from the later Kibo eruption.

The plateau also has a reputation for its **fauna**, largely thanks to its proximity to both Amboseli National Park in Kenya and the West Kilimanjaro Wildlife Corridor, from where herds of elephant, eland, buffalo, and big cats such as lion and leopard have been known to wander. Indeed, when I was writing the first and second editions of this guide, trekkers on these routes had to be accompanied by

❑ HOW I HAVE ORDERED THIS SECTION

The difficulty with writing a description of the trails that cross the Shira Plateau is that there is no one official Lemosho Route and no one official Shira Plateau Route either. With the Northern Circuit variation only adding to the confusion, this is not the most straightforward section to write about, or presumably comprehend.

So, for simplicity's sake, I have assumed in the following descriptions that from Shira 1 Campsite the **Lemosho Route** will head towards Shira 2/Shira Huts (either straight there or via the Cathedral) and from there to Lava Tower. This is the route most people follow when they book a Lemosho trek. From Lava Tower it's more common to go round the southern side of Kibo and head to Barranco Campsite and Barafu Huts, a route you can read about on pp300-7. But the **Lemosho Route is also the most common trail taken by those who are looking to climb via the Western Breach**, and this is the route I take in the following description.

For the **Shira Route**, I have assumed that from Shira 1 people will head to Moir Huts and from there round the northern side of Kibo on the **Northern Circuit**.

Bear in mind that the various stages of these routes are interchangeable; it is just as feasible for you to start off on the Shira Plateau Route, for example, and head round to Barranco Campsite, or begin on the Lemosho Route and go to Moir Huts and the Northern Circuit – or indeed to ignore both options and head up the Western Breach! There are **several paths** and a number of possible campsites too. For these reasons, the descriptions of these routes may not tally exactly with your own experience; so look at the itinerary your company has provided so you can see which parts are relevant to you.

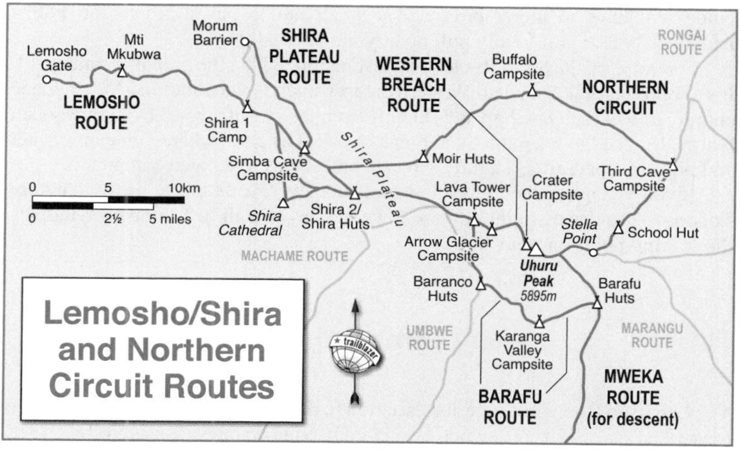

an armed ranger to protect them. That said, you will be very, *very* lucky to see any evidence of visiting wildlife on the plateau, save for the odd hoof-print and the occasional sun-dried lumps of scat and spoor. So, while the proximity of Africa's finest wild beasts adds a certain frisson of excitement to the walk, don't choose either of these trails purely on the strength of their reputation for spotting game: it's an awful long way to come just to see some desiccated elephant shit.

The journey to Lemosho/Shira

Getting to the start of the Lemosho/Shira Routes is a bit of a bind; before you can even contemplate any actual hiking you first have to suffer a two-hour 'African massage' (the local euphemism for any sort of vehicular ride on a typically rutted African track). As a result of the extra effort and petrol required to get here, these two trails often cost a little more than the more accessible Marangu, Umbwe and Machame trails.

Thus, for much of the first day you won't be walking anywhere but will be strapped into the back of a jeep as it glides along the Arusha–Moshi highway before turning off at **Boma Ng'ombe** ('Cattle Corral'; 26km from Moshi). From there it bounces along for another hour and a half past **Sanya Juu** (22km/13½ miles from the turn-off and virtually the last place to get supplies), **Ngarenairobi** and **Simba Farm** (a huge estate to the left of the road). Your

❑ ROUTE NAME CONFUSION

Just to confuse matters, just **occasionally the Lemosho Route is called the Shira Plateau Route** (or just Shira Route), particularly by foreign agencies keen to promote the fact that you'll be walking across the Shira Plateau. Ask your operator to indicate *exactly* which of the two routes you will be taking. If your first night's accommodation is Big Tree Campsite (Mti Mkubwa in Swahili), it's the Lemosho Route that you'll be following, regardless of what your trekking operator calls it.

guide will have to alight briefly at a small hut to pay a fee to the Forest Authority before you finally pull up at your destination.

For those on the Shira Route, that destination will be the **gate of Londorossi**. It's a weird place, a Spaghetti Western outpost stuck in the middle of Africa, made entirely of wood, divided up and shut off from the outside world by high wooden fences designed to keep the local fauna at bay. The gate, where you can register and pick up a **permit**, is slightly separate and stands in its own compound.

If you've chosen the Lemosho Route, however, you turn off the road before Londorossi to drive straight up the lower slopes of Kili to **Lemosho Glades** – the starting point for your trek...

The Lemosho Route

The Lemosho Route is a superior variation to the traditional Shira Plateau Route (described on pp329-37), which is seldom used nowadays. It used to be one of the quietest on the mountain. Once upon a time only the Umbwe Route, which has a reputation for being the most difficult trail, and the Shira Route, which largely follows a road for its first couple of days, were less popular. However, its popularity has grown fast and it's now the third busiest, behind only the Marangu and Machame routes and there are many guides who reckon it's overtaken the Marangu trail now and could soon be challenging Machame for the top spot. This is not surprising, for this 7- to 8-day yomp (though some companies take as many as 10 days) takes you through the remote and pristine cloud forest of West Kilimanjaro and across the Shira Plateau to the highest point in Africa and back down again. As mentioned before, the assault on the summit is conducted via either the tricky **Western Breach Route** (if open; see pp325-9) or via Barranco, Karanga Valley and Barafu to Stella Point on the **Barafu Route** (a description of which begins on p307). A few companies also offer a route that utilises the Northern Circuit (see p334), and an ascent to the summit via School Huts and Gillman's Point (see p350). Whatever ascent route you take, the usual **descent route is the Mweka trail** (see pp362-8).

It's the first day or so, when you are walking through the forests on Kilimanjaro's western slopes, that is the real reason why this trail has overtaken the old Shira Plateau Route as the main path attacking Kilimanjaro from the west. With the latter you are often driven all the way up to the plateau, missing out on some fine forest, which you experience only through a car window. But by starting in the forest, taking the Cathedral diversion (see opposite) and using the Barafu Route to get to the summit you'll be on the **longest official ascent route on Kilimanjaro at 46.96km/29 miles** (though it can be just 33km/20½ miles if taking the direct route to Shira Huts and then the Western Breach).

Other advantages with this route? Well from personal experience I think the birdlife is the most diverse and interesting of any on the mountain. Though I admit I can't actually back this up with any statistical proof, the fecundity of the

❑ **PHONE RECEPTION ON THE LEMOSHO ROUTE**

Trekkers with mobile (cell) phones will find little opportunity to use them on the first half of the Lemosho Route. The first place I have ever managed to get reception was after leaving the forest on the second morning, though this happened only once; the first place where it's just about certain you'll get reception is by the **Cathedral** on the third morning. That said, others have managed to get reception near **Shira Ridge**, the highest point on the second day. **Shira Huts** has reception if you're prepared to search for it on the boulders around the campsite, and reception is OK at **Lava Tower**. Thereafter it depends on which route you're taking. For the Western Breach, reception is fair at **Arrow Glacier**, you can sometimes get it at **Crater Camp** too and, so it is said, near the **summit**.

If you're taking the Barafu Route to the top, see the box on p293 for a summary of mobile reception on this section of the route.

forest means many species are able to thrive under its canopy. The Lemosho Route allows for more variations and diversions from the main route than any other trail, including diversions to the **Shira Cathedral**, on the southern side of the plateau, or to Moir Huts, on the north-western side of the mountain. Indeed, one of the joys of the Lemosho Route is the variety of trails one can take and itineraries one can build – there is no one standard 'Lemosho Route'.

Though it's a great route, Lemosho is not without its **drawbacks**. For one thing, I reckon it to be the **wettest route** though meteorology doesn't back me up; in my experience it always seems to rain on this side of the mountain more than anywhere else.

Though it varies from month to month, the amount of **rubbish** on the trail and especially at the campsites can be distressing too. How anyone could be stupid enough to drop sweet wrappers, batteries, used toilet roll and all manner of litter in somewhere as lovely as the western forest is beyond me.

STAGE 1: LEMOSHO GLADES ENTRANCE GATE TO MTI MKUBWA/ BIG TREE CAMP [MAP 14, p317]

Distance: 4.8km (3 miles); altitude gained: 396m (1299ft)

After four hours or more sat in the bus, it is with no small relief that you alight, grab your daypack, and have some lunch (probably) at the new gate at **Lemosho Glades** (2389m/ 7838ft).

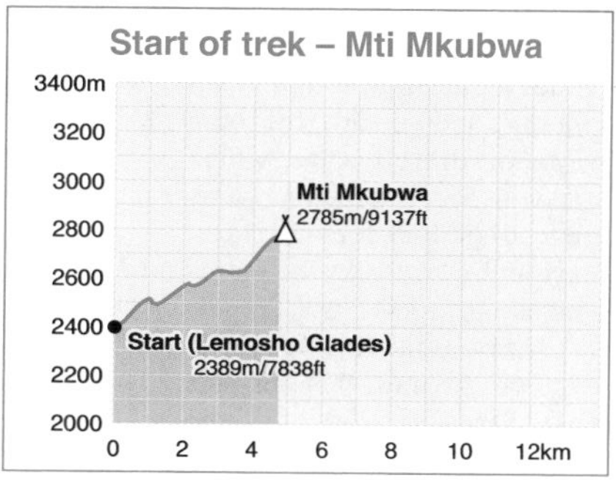

It may already be late in the day by the time you start walking, although the first night's camp lies only around two hours from the end of the road. There are enough steep gradients in these two hours to check all your equipment is comfortable and your limbs are in full working order. The conditions are often misty and cool on this first stage through the forest; ideal weather for walking, if not for taking photos.

As you can tell from the map opposite, landmarks in the forest are few; nevertheless, it's still a splendid start to your trek. At times there is an almost Jurassic quality to the trail, a feeling that you've stumbled into some Lost World – a sense that I can ascribe only to the untamed nature of the forest on this side of the mountain and the complete lack of any evidence that humanity has passed this way. It's just wonderful. It helps too, of course, that throughout today you'll be sharing the forest with colobus and blue monkey and the rarely encountered buffalo, elephant, lion and leopard.

In addition to the fauna, you'll be sharing the path with many of the celebrities of Kilimanjaro's floral kingdom, including the two most prominent *Impatiens* species, *kilimanjaro* and *pseudoviola*, as well as millions of soldier ants; while watching over the whole shebang are those giants without which there would be no forest, in particular the camphor, podocarpus and hagenia trees. Look out, too, for the *Lobelia gibberoa* and ask your guide to point out the *Dracaena afromontana*, locally known as the *masale*, which though seemingly unimpressive is held in high esteem by the Chagga (see box p178).

Your destination for this first stage is the campsite known officially (ie by nobody) as the **Forest Camp**, and unofficially (ie by everybody) as **Mti Mkubwa**, or **Big Tree Camp** (2785m/9137ft), for obvious reasons. Lying at the top of a ridge in the shade of a wonderful spreading podocarpus, as with all the campsites on Kili there's little to it other than a piece of flat ground, a couple of long-drop toilets and a ranger's hut. But it's still many people's favourite stopping point on the trail, with the noise of the turaco, hyrax and colobus in the trees at both dusk and dawn making for a quintessential African night.

STAGE 2: MTI MKUBWA/BIG TREE CAMP TO SHIRA 1 CAMPSITE

[MAP 14, opposite; MAP 15, p319]

Distance: 7.9km (5 miles); altitude gained: 719m (2359ft)

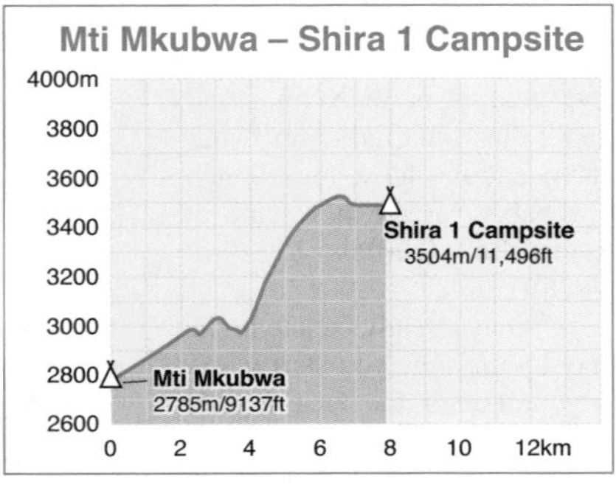

You've spent a whole day travelling, registering, walking and sweating and you are still some way short of the plateau, which you will finally reach towards the end of this second stage, leaving the forest for the moorland as you do so.

Many trekkers' favourite stage on the trail, this 4hr-plus walk (though with all the

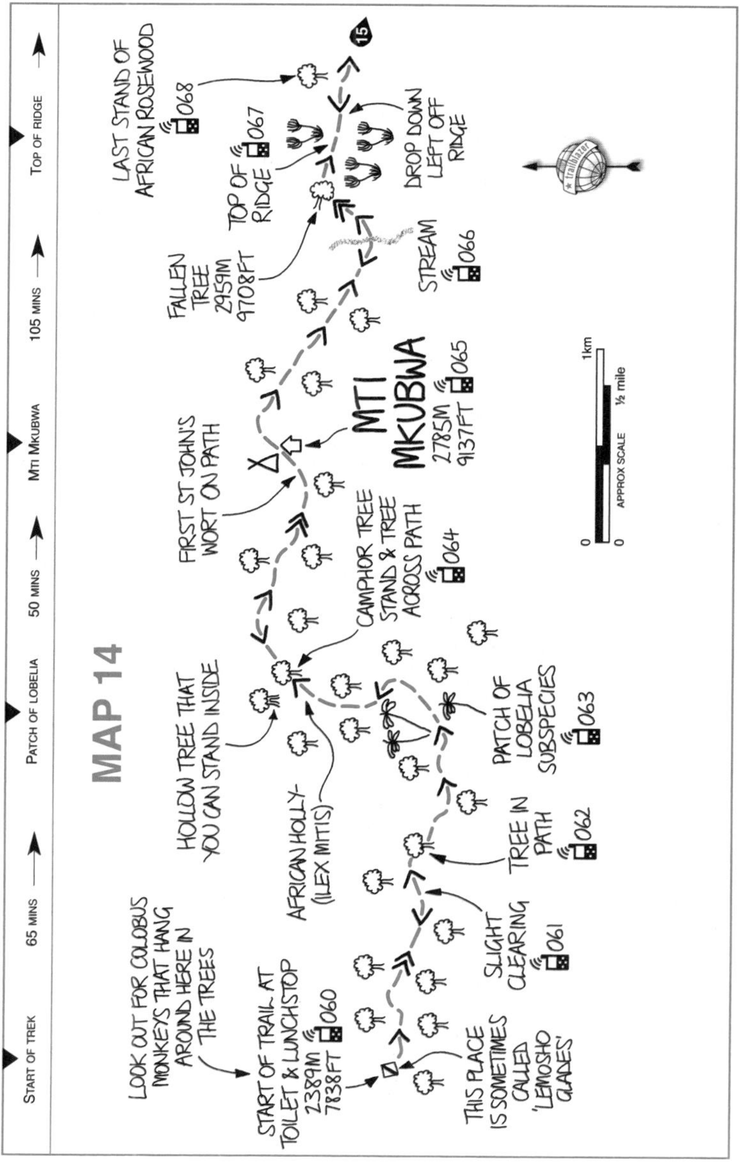
MAP 14
START OF TREK
65 MINS
PATCH OF LOBELIA
50 MINS
MTI MKUBWA
105 MINS
TOP OF RIDGE
LOOK OUT FOR COLOBUS MONKEYS THAT HANG AROUND HERE IN THE TREES
START OF TRAIL AT TOILET & LUNCHSTOP 2389M 7838FT
060
THIS PLACE IS SOMETIMES CALLED 'LEMOSHO GLADES'
SLIGHT CLEARING
061
TREE IN PATH
062
AFRICAN HOLLY (ILEX MITIS)
HOLLOW TREE THAT YOU CAN STAND INSIDE
PATCH OF LOBELIA SUBSPECIES
063
CAMPHOR TREE STAND & TREE ACROSS PATH
064
FIRST ST JOHN'S WORT ON PATH
MTI MKUBWA
2785M 9137FT
065
APPROX SCALE
0
1km
0
½ mile
FALLEN TREE 2959M 9708FT
STREAM
066
TOP OF RIDGE
067
DROP DOWN LEFT OFF RIDGE
LAST STAND OF AFRICAN ROSEWOOD
068
15

breaks you'll need it will take a full day) is something of a red-letter day too. For not only do you forsake forest for moorland and get your first proper views of the Shira Plateau and its accompanying ridges and peaks but it is on this stage that, finally and fabulously, you get your first views of Kibo.

These rewards are not gained without effort, however; during today you'll be climbing over 700m, taking you above 3500m and into the realm of dastardly HACO and its equally evil twin, HAPO (see p246). So do make sure you go *pole pole* – or you may end up feeling poorly poorly.

The day begins just as the last one left off, as you head in a general easterly direction and generally upwards too, though with plenty of minor variations as you negotiate the folds and creases of Kili's forested slopes. Eventually you find yourself heading north-east to climb to the top of a ridge, the point where you actually gain the top being marked by a large **fallen tree**. As with many of the larger trees in this neck of the woods, this giant used to show signs of having been scorched around the trunk – the unmistakable handiwork of honey-seekers who burn the hollow inside the tree in order to smoke out the bees, making it easier to gain access to their produce.

Heading east and up along the ridge, it's not long before the trees start to diminish in size and number to be replaced by their hardier cousins in the heather and stoebe families. These soon begin to crowd you in on both sides but not enough to obscure your view north over the valley. It's a valley you eventually join, too, as you continue your eastward and upward progress, contouring gently to the valley floor to reacquaint yourselves with the decorative **African rosewood**, *Hagenia abyssinica*, here making one last stand.

The relentless uphill is finally interrupted by a short descent to what was once a popular lunchstop (Map 15) – popular, that is, until the litter left behind drove guides and their trekkers to find another dining-room to frequent and, in time no doubt, to despoil too. This better **lunch-spot** lies at the top of the next ridge; while there's no water up here (whereas there is in the original picnic site down below) the views are better, particularly to the north over the river known as Ngare Nairobi and the 4x4 road of the Shira Plateau Route beyond.

From this new location the path once again points east then bends south, following the ridge, before heading east once more to contour around the slope of what is – though you may not realise it just yet – the northern extremity of the **Shira Ridge**.

The path's gradient, steep since lunch, flattens out as you contour along this northern slope and drops at the **first sight of Shira Plateau**. This is the moment you've been waiting for all day: standing at 3536m/11601ft above sea level, the Shira Ridge to your right, snow-capped Kibo ahead and the plateau unfurled at your feet with your next two days' trekking mapped out for you upon its face. More immediately, beneath you lies the green uniport of **Shira 1 Campsite** (3504m/11,496ft), a spot that's popular with four-striped grass mice, streaky seed-eaters and white-necked ravens as well as the usual foreign itinerants in lurid Gore-Tex.

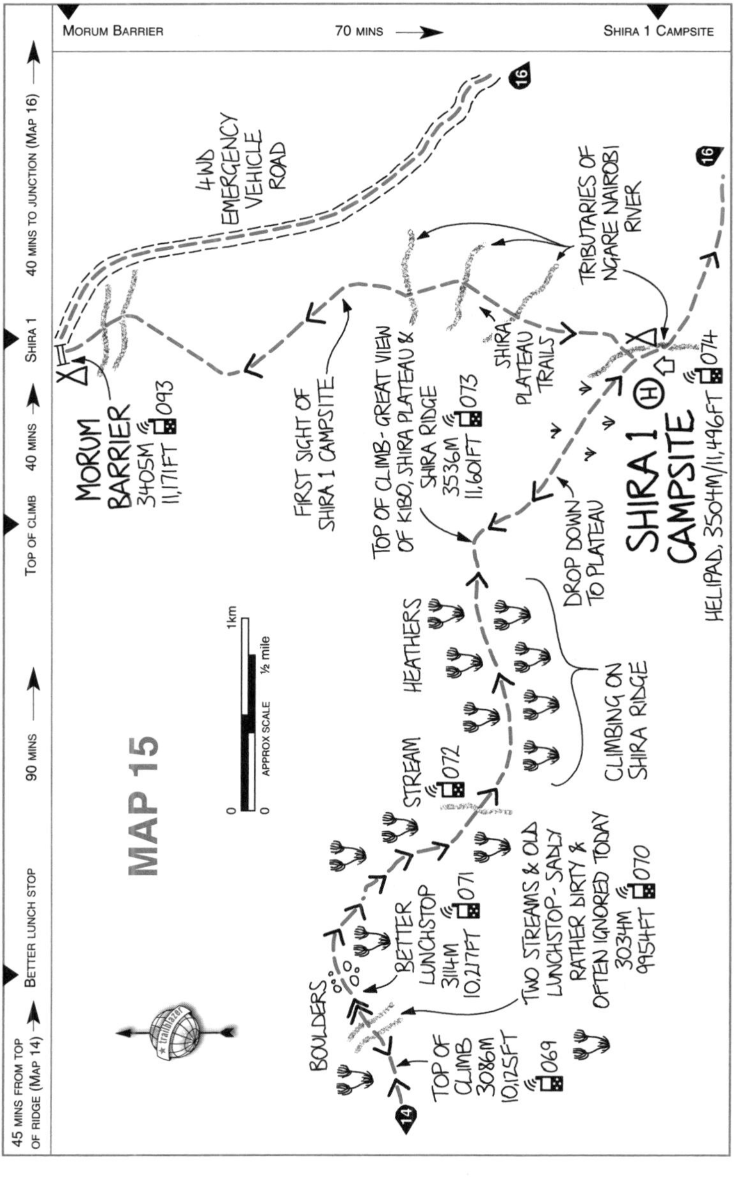
45 MINS FROM TOP OF RIDGE (MAP 14) →
BETTER LUNCH STOP
90 MINS →
TOP OF CLIMB
40 MINS →
SHIRA 1
40 MINS TO JUNCTION (MAP 16) →
MORUM BARRIER
70 MINS →
SHIRA 1 CAMPSITE
MAP 15
APPROX SCALE
0
1km
0
½ mile
BOULDERS
TOP OF CLIMB 3086M 10,125FT 069
BETTER LUNCHSTOP 3114M 10,217FT 071
TWO STREAMS & OLD LUNCHSTOP - SADLY RATHER DIRTY & OFTEN IGNORED TODAY 3034M 9954FT 070
STREAM 072
HEATHERS
CLIMBING ON SHIRA RIDGE
TOP OF CLIMB - GREAT VIEW OF KIBO, SHIRA PLATEAU & SHIRA RIDGE 3536M 11,601FT 073
DROP DOWN TO PLATEAU
FIRST SIGHT OF SHIRA 1 CAMPSITE
MORUM BARRIER 3405M 11,171FT 093
4WD EMERGENCY VEHICLE ROAD
SHIRA PLATEAU TRAILS
TRIBUTARIES OF NGARE NAIROBI RIVER
SHIRA 1 CAMPSITE
HELIPAD, 3504M/11,496FT 074
14
16
16

STAGE 3: SHIRA 1 CAMPSITE TO SHIRA 2/SHIRA HUTS

[MAP 15, p319; MAP 16, opposite; MAP 17, p323]

Distance: 6.9km (4¼ miles, though it's 10.1km/6¼ miles – via the Cathedral); altitude gained: 391m (1282ft)

As mentioned in the introduction, one of the advantages of the Lemosho Route is the number of variations one can take. And this third stage is perhaps the one with the greatest range of options, for not only are there are several destinations, there are also different ways of reaching them.

In order to introduce some sort of clarity and simplicity, I've chosen as my destination for this third stage the Shira Huts (also known as Shira 2), simply because it's to there that most people head. But it is not unheard of for some companies to head on to Moir Huts, on the north-western side of Kibo, before dropping back south to Barranco, or even to carry on round the Northern Circuit, as discussed on p329.

There are **two main ways of getting to Shira Huts** from Shira 1: the regular direct trail slicing north-west to south-east across the plateau; or the popular detour via Shira Cathedral on the plateau's southern rim. Though it's not too strenuous, this latter option does provide some useful if marginal acclimatisation as you climb to 3862m (12,671ft) before briefly dropping again. Furthermore, as if the lack of a blinding AMS headache later on wasn't reward enough, there are also the views from the top of the Cathedral across the plateau and towards Kibo; as it takes no more time than the regular route, I recommend you select this option if given the choice. Though if you do choose this variation try to set off early as the clouds often roll in by mid morning, obscuring any decent views. As it is the alternative route to the main trail, however, I have described the route via the Cathedral second, beginning on p322.

Shira 1 Campsite to Shira 2/Shira Huts: the regular route

This 'original' trail may seem less attractive than its younger alternative but that's not to dismiss it altogether. After all, no stroll across the Shira Plateau could ever be described as dull. Shira Huts is the main campsite on the plateau, equipped with a rangers' office, some smart toilets and a particularly prominent suggestion box, as if to invite criticism from trekkers – given the often filthy state of the campsite, it's probably going to get it.

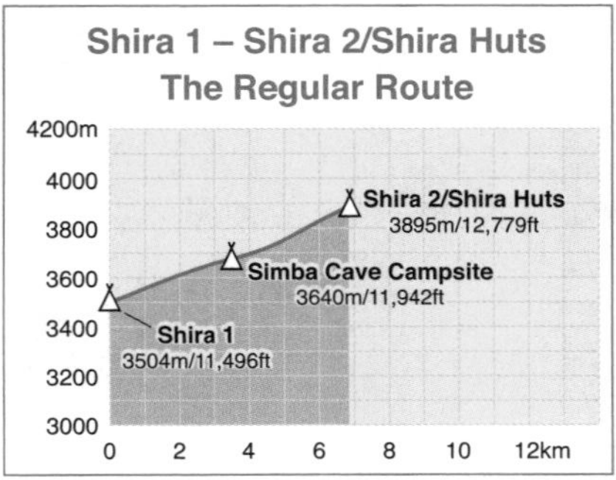

To get to Shira Huts involves just under three hours of steady uphill walking. From Shira 1 you head south-east through the heath and moorland of the plateau; watch out for buffalo tracks and those of other animals – klipspringer, dik dik – that cross the plateau

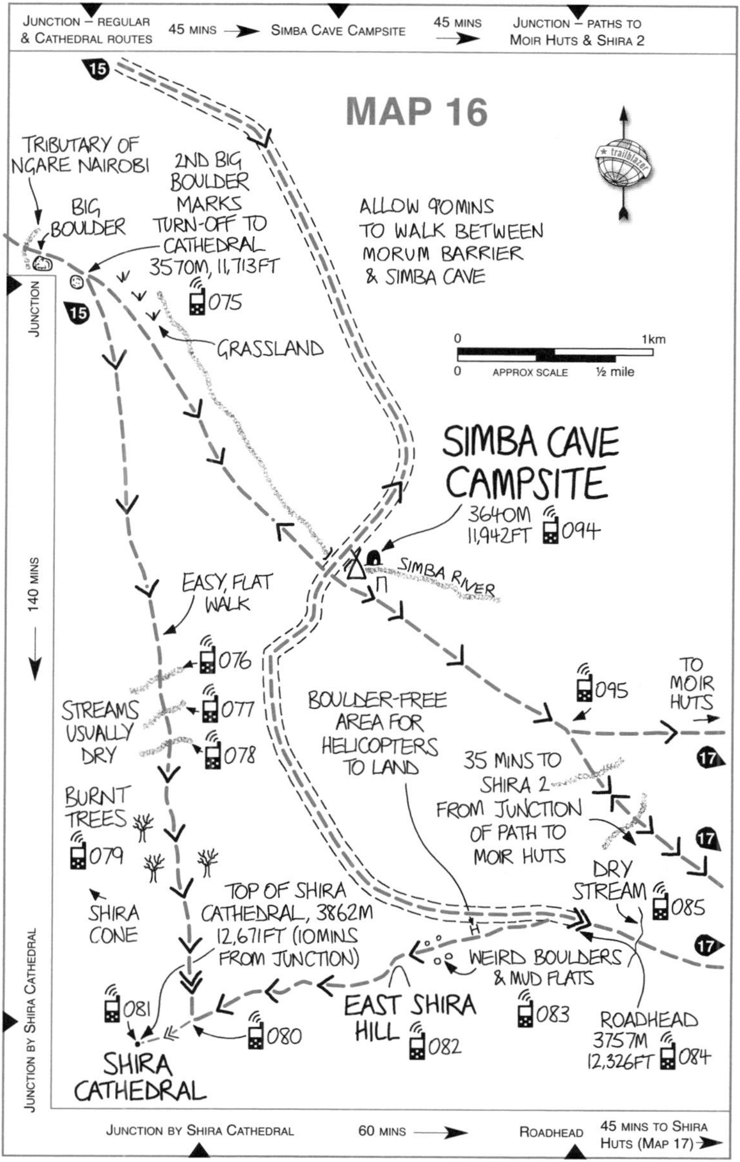

JUNCTION – REGULAR & CATHEDRAL ROUTES
45 MINS
SIMBA CAVE CAMPSITE
45 MINS
JUNCTION – PATHS TO MOIR HUTS & SHIRA 2
MAP 16
15
TRIBUTARY OF NGARE NAIROBI
BIG BOULDER
2ND BIG BOULDER MARKS TURN-OFF TO CATHEDRAL 3570M, 11,713FT
075
ALLOW 90 MINS TO WALK BETWEEN MORUM BARRIER & SIMBA CAVE
trailblazer
JUNCTION
GRASSLAND
0 1km
0 APPROX SCALE ½ mile
SIMBA CAVE CAMPSITE
3640M 11,942FT 094
SIMBA RIVER
140 MINS
EASY, FLAT WALK
076
077
078
STREAMS USUALLY DRY
BOULDER-FREE AREA FOR HELICOPTERS TO LAND
095
TO MOIR HUTS
17
35 MINS TO SHIRA 2 FROM JUNCTION OF PATH TO MOIR HUTS
BURNT TREES
079
SHIRA CONE
TOP OF SHIRA CATHEDRAL, 3862M 12,671FT (10MINS FROM JUNCTION)
DRY STREAM
085
WEIRD BOULDERS & MUD FLATS
081
EAST SHIRA HILL
082
080
083
ROADHEAD 3757M 12,326FT 084
SHIRA CATHEDRAL
JUNCTION BY SHIRA CATHEDRAL
60 MINS
ROADHEAD
45 MINS TO SHIRA HUTS (MAP 17)

in search of salt and fresh grazing. Come to think of it, watch out for the buffalo themselves – encountering one can seriously ruin your holiday.

Cross the unimpressive trickle of the waterway that will, further down the slopes, become the torrent of the Ngare Nairobi, and about 85 minutes from breaking camp you reach the plateau's crossroads.

It is here that the Lemosho Route meets the 4x4 track of the Shira Plateau Route; here too that you meet the deep-ish creek of the Simba River. Shame, then, that such an important landmark should be marked only by a couple of toilets belonging to **Simba Cave Campsite** (3640m/11,942ft), used largely by those on the (old) Shira Route (see p324). The **cave** itself is a rather forlorn effort lying north-east of the junction.

From here it's another 40-45 minutes of marching, past the junction with the path to Moir Huts and on to the top of a ridge, from where you can see the green roof of your destination, **Shira 2/Shira Huts** (3895m/12,779ft). It's a fairly direct 35-minute path from the junction that takes you there, crossing a couple of shallow ridges and a stream along the way.

By the way, on arriving at Shira Huts you will be higher than the top of Großglockner, at 3798m (12,461ft) the biggest mountain in Austria.

Shira 1 to Shira 2/Shira Huts: alternative route via Shira Cathedral

This route begins by following the regular trail as it heads south-east across the southern half of the plateau, turning off south by a big and distinctive boulder just after crossing the Ngare Nairobi (Map 16).

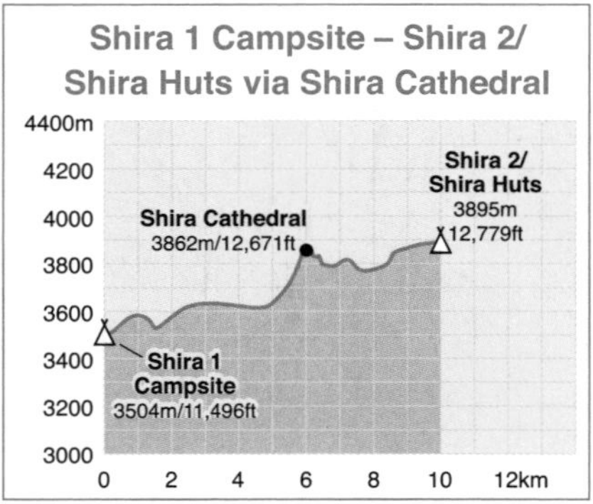

Note that from this boulder you can already see your final destination on this stage, the Shira Huts, in the far distance. It's a long trek across to the foot of the Cathedral, with **Shira Cone** (aka Cone Place) the only major landmark nearby, but it's not a trek that's lacking in interest. In all probability you should see the first *lobelia deckenii* of your trek, standing sentinel-straight as they peer above the grass to check on your progress. You may also see many animal tracks on the trail, including klipspringer, eland and dik dik, hoofprints that betray this path's origins as a trail used by animals in search of salt, minerals and fresh grazing.

Crossing many (usually dry) **stream-beds**, all of which, when filled with water, feed into the Ngare Nairobi, you start to climb through heather trees to the foot of the rounded hump known as **Shira Cathedral** (3862m/12,671ft). The summit is gained soon after, the whole expedition from Shira 1 taking just under three hours.

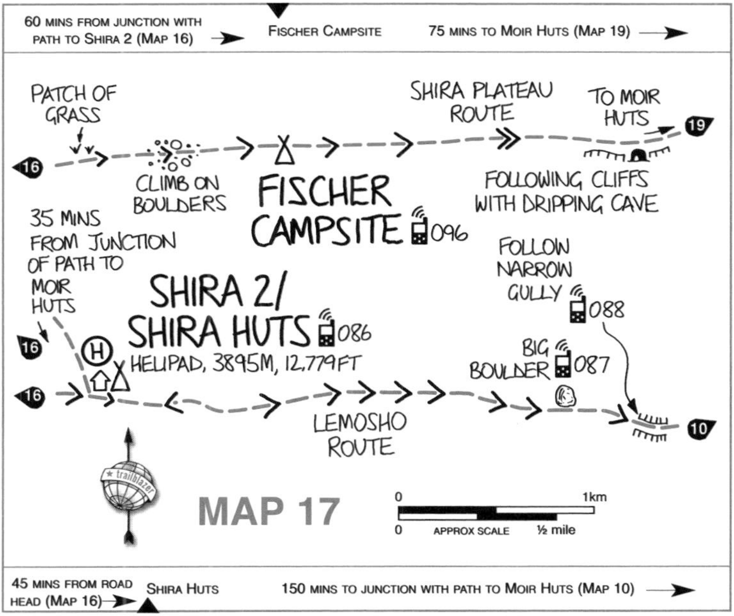

Panorama-wise, not only are there the delights of the plateau ahead, including Moir Huts to the north-east and Kibo to your right, but behind and to the east of the Cathedral your guide should be able to point out the faint traces of the Machame Route etched into the slopes. This is also the most reliable place on the plateau to get **phone reception**.

From the summit you make your way north-east across **East Shira Hill** and the other undulations of the plateau edge, eventually arriving at a strange muddy area sprinkled with boulders, the lack of vegetation being due to poor drainage according to one guide.

The eastern end of this area has been converted into a makeshift **helipad**. Just a couple of minutes later you come to the **roadhead** – the final termination of the 'rescue road' that emergency vehicles use when ferrying people from the mountain (and the continuation of the road that those on the old Shira Route take to gain access to the plateau, though they alight at Morum Barrier – see pp330-1). It may be the end of the road, but you still have a further 45 minutes up to **Shira 2/Shira Huts** (Map 17; 3895m/12,779ft) and the day's end.

Note: Do remember that the times quoted are approximations and, more importantly, refer to **walking times only** with no time spent resting, taking photos etc.

Add on 30-50% to get an estimate of the total time spent on the trail.

STAGE 4: SHIRA 2/SHIRA HUTS TO LAVA TOWER CAMP/ BARRANCO HUTS [MAP 17, p323; MAP 10, p301]

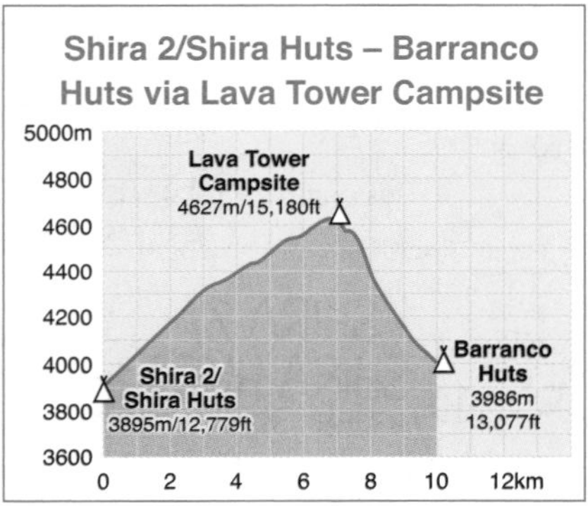

Distance: 10.1km (6¼ miles) to Barranco Huts (6.9km/4¼ miles to Lava Tower); altitude gained: 91m/299ft (732m/2402ft to Lava Tower Campsite, then 641m/2103ft descent to Barranco Huts)
If, over the past three days, you've found the crowds on the Lemosho Route rather disappointing, I'm afraid today it's only going to get a whole lot worse. For it's on this stage that your path merges with the even more popular Machame Route. Nor is it just any hope of solitude that you'll be bidding farewell to on this stage: the Shira Plateau also takes a final bow. As a result of all that relentless ascending you've been doing, you'll also be leaving the World of Heather for the Land of Lichen. True, those opting for the trek round the southern side of Kibo will reacquaint themselves with heathers, stoebes, lobelias and senecios at the magical Barranco Valley. But from now until the summit, the Barranco and other valleys excepted, it is the alpine desert that prevails.

As mentioned on p314, there are two alternative routes to the summit – and it's on this stage that the two paths diverge. You can read about both of them from p300 onwards (regular route via Barranco Valley and the Barafu Route) and opposite (Western Breach Route).

But before the Lemosho and Machame Routes unite, you first have about three hours of uphill walking. As you probably expect, it's an easterly climb up the fairly gentle slope of the Shira Plateau, gradually forsaking the heather and moorland for something altogether more barren, where lichen-covered boulders predominate. Look out on the ground for small shards of shiny black obsidian (see pp130-1), not forgetting to look up occasionally to see Meru in the distance over your right shoulder. There are few steep passages to this stage, save for a brief clamber up a narrow gully that precedes the **junction with the little-used path to Moir Huts campsite** (Map 10, p301), which lies about 30 minutes away (see p332). There's also a path from here to the foot of **Shark's Tooth** (25 mins), the pointy little peak sitting to Kibo's west. Further on, the junction with the main Machame Route, that has been contouring that ridge from the Shira Caves, is marked by some weird mushroom-rock formations.

Soon after, the path loops to the south-east and divides, with most people heading off east on a deceptively lengthy and fairly steep trail towards the Lava Tower, passing through the unofficial **Sheffield Campsite** (from where there is a further trail heading south to Barranco). The **Lava Tower Campsite** (4627m/15,180ft) is squeezed between Kibo and the tower itself. Though not the most direct path to Barranco, this route is useful in order to gain some much-needed altitude that could be vital in the battle against mountain sickness.

If you are taking the longer route to the summit via Barranco, Karanga and Barafu campsites, turn to p302 for a description of your trek; while if you're continuing on the Western Breach, read on.

THE WESTERN BREACH ROUTE TO UHURU PEAK [MAP 33, p371]

[Note: As we go to press the Western Breach Route is currently closed] Over the years the Western Breach Route has acquired a certain aura and a reputation as the hardest of the summit routes. Nor is this reputation entirely undeserved. Though it's the shortest, time-wise, it's also the steepest (with the mean gradient of the route said to be 26°) and there's a bit of non-technical and very basic scrambling involved. What's more, and most worryingly, this trail is subject to occasional rockfalls and there are a couple of places where your guide should stop and listen out for any heading in your direction. The park authority actually closed the route for a while in 2006, following the deaths of three American climbers in a rockslide near Arrow Glacier; though it was subsequently reopened, agencies now issue protective helmets to all trekkers during their climb on this route, and KINAPA will ask you to sign a waiver form too. They also insist that everybody is away from Arrow Glacier Campsite before 5am, so that nobody is walking in 'the danger zone', where the risk of rockfall is at its greatest – after the sun has risen.

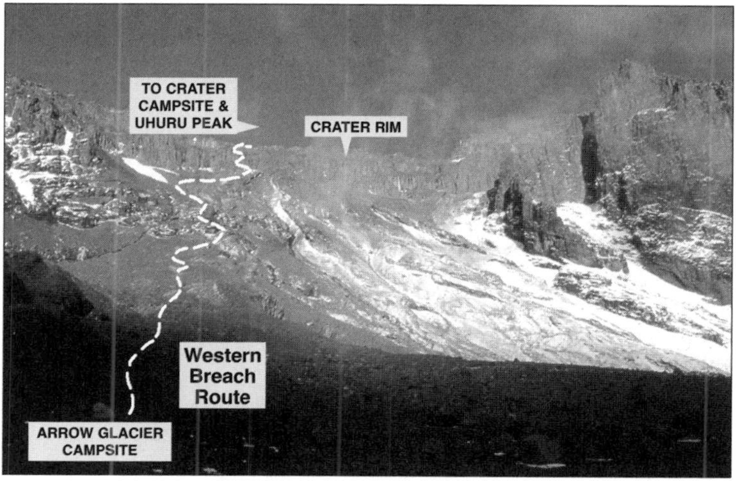

Western Breach Route

The general consensus amongst Kili connoisseurs is that these measures are a good thing for it's much easier to tackle 'The Breach' at night, when the scree, shale and rocks are frozen and thus less likely to move when you step on them. Furthermore, after dark the occasionally vertiginous drops are invisible, which makes climbing for vertigo sufferers much easier. But in spite of all these measures, there is still the occasional death from falling rocks on the Western Breach, with the most high-profile being that of entrepreneur Scott Dinsmore in 2015.

That said, to hear some people talk about the Western Breach you'd think you'd need the climbing capabilities of your average housefly in order to make it to the top. Suffice to say: you don't. Yes, this route is a little trickier in parts. And yes, after snowfall the route up can be icy and an ice axe may be required in extreme conditions. And yes, there are stretches that are more exposed and where, almost uniquely on the mountain, a head for heights is required. But as with all the routes in this book no technical climbing know-how is necessary; just the ability to haul yourself up with your hands on occasion when required.

So what are the benefits of doing this route? Well, firstly, the Western Breach is the only one that enters directly into the crater. As such, this is the most convenient route to take if you want to explore the Ash Pit, Reusch Crater, Furtwangler Glacier and the other features of the summit. (Though it's possible to visit these features even though you climbed to the summit on other routes, not many trekkers actually do so.) And the other main benefit of climbing via the Western Breach is, of course, the kudos that comes with having conquered the hardest non-technical route Kilimanjaro has to offer.

Do note, finally, that this route, though the shortest way to the top, is often the most expensive if you intend to camp at the summit because it is usual for porters to receive a premium to climb up Kibo. This is understandable; on all other routes they don't go above around 4700m/15,420ft (ie the altitude of the last campsite/huts), whereas here they have to go to the crater (above 5700m/18,700ft) and carry all their load up the trickiest route too. There's also a US$100 park fee to camp in the crater.

STAGE 5: LAVA TOWER CAMPSITE TO ARROW GLACIER CAMPSITE

[Map 18, opposite]

Distance: 2.5km (1½ miles); altitude gained: 244m (801ft)

By my reckoning this particular leg, even if taken *pole pole*, lasts little longer than 75 minutes, yet it's not unusual for trekking operators to set aside an entire day for it. In one respect this seems a little over-cautious and does lead to a situation where,

Lava Tower Campsite – Uhuru Peak

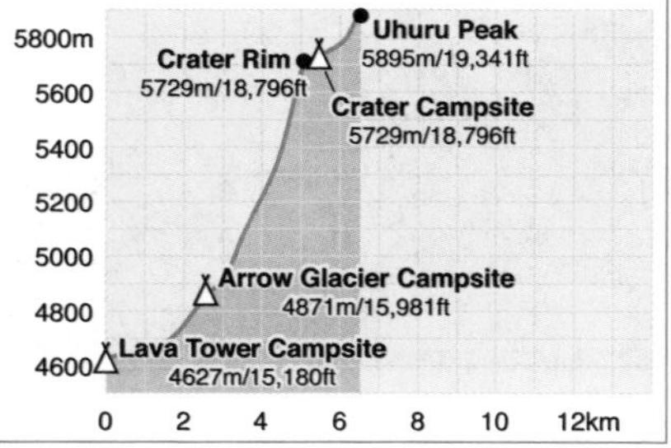

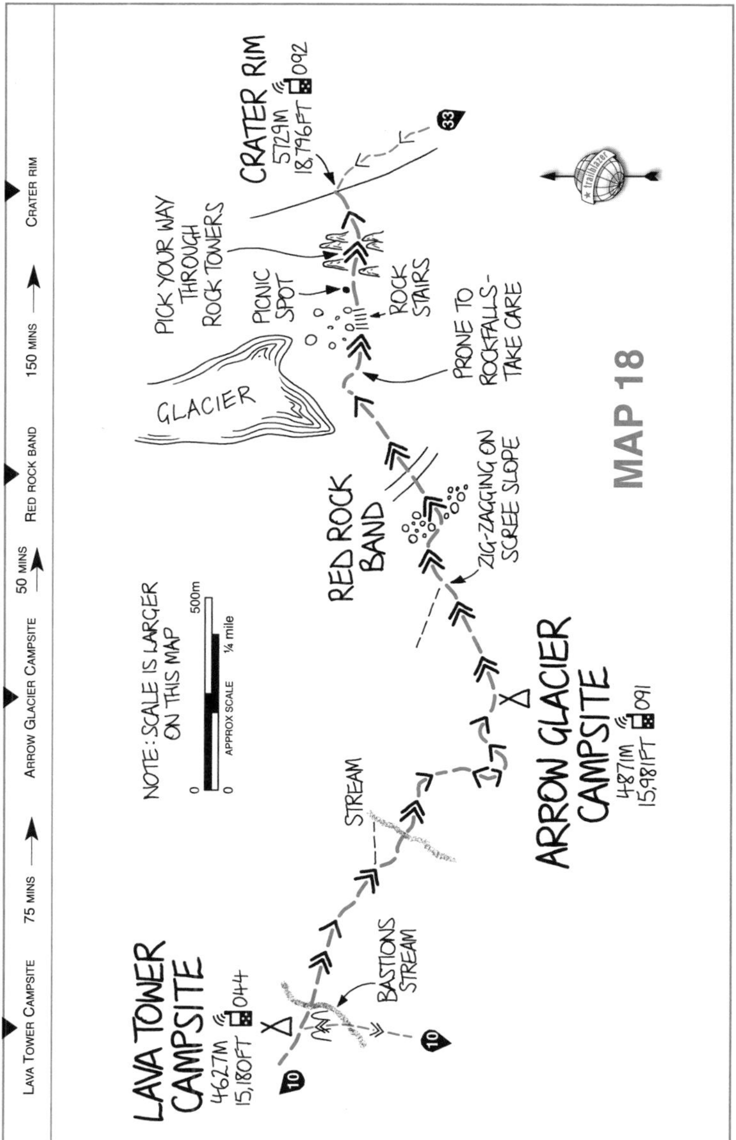
LAVA TOWER CAMPSITE
75 MINS
ARROW GLACIER CAMPSITE
50 MINS
RED ROCK BAND
150 MINS
CRATER RIM
LAVA TOWER CAMPSITE
4627M
15,180FT
0144
10
10
BASTIONS STREAM
STREAM
NOTE: SCALE IS LARGER ON THIS MAP
0
500m
0
APPROX SCALE
¼ mile
ARROW GLACIER CAMPSITE
4871M
15,981FT
091
ZIG-ZAGGING ON SCREE SLOPE
RED ROCK BAND
GLACIER
PRONE TO ROCKFALLS- TAKE CARE
ROCK STAIRS
PICNIC SPOT
PICK YOUR WAY THROUGH ROCK TOWERS
CRATER RIM
5729M
18,796FT
092
33
trailblazer
MAP 18

those 75 minutes aside, you'll be spending the rest of your day freezing your butt off inside your tent. On the other hand, it's a good idea to take your time at this altitude. After all, save for the Crater Camp this is the highest place where you can pitch your tent on the mountain (the altitude of Arrow Glacier Campsite being 4871m/15,981ft); and that kind of altitude should always be taken seriously.

Furthermore, the walk, though only brief, is still quite exhausting, it being uphill all the way. You begin by crossing a stream or two (one of which, **Bastions Stream**, runs below Lava Tower) before climbing steeply in a south-easterly direction to the top of a ridge. Near the top of the climb you pass an old trail running directly from Lava Tower to the Western Breach Route that bypasses Arrow Glacier Campsite altogether; it's a path that's seldom used these days and unless your guide points it out to you, it's easily missed.

Descending for a few seconds to a stream and then climbing to a second ridge, by following the direction of *that* ridge eastwards you soon come to **Arrow Glacier Campsite**. Engulfed by avalanches and often subject to the vagaries of the extreme conditions up here, this place has always been a bit of a mess and little has changed. Whilst the rubbish is depressing, it's the toilets that are the most revolting spectacle, with the ones that haven't been destroyed now home to an entirely new geological form: neither stalactite nor stalagmite, but stalacshite. Console yourself with the thought that if you're not spending a night on the summit, you probably won't be spending a full night here but should be away by 2am; and anyway, KINAPA want everyone to have left by 5am. Happy Camping!

Incidentally, at Arrow Glacier Campsite you are now just 6m/20ft lower than the summit of the Vinson Massif – at 4877m/16,001ft, the highest point in Antarctica.

STAGE 6: ARROW GLACIER CAMPSITE TO UHURU PEAK

[Map 18, p327; Map 33, p371]

Distance 4km (2½ miles); altitude gained: 1024m (3360ft; see profile p326)

Mungu akipenda, tutafika – If God wants it, we shall arrive

Though I've talked as if there is one set path from campsite to crater rim, this isn't actually the case; the path changes as snow and rockfalls dictate. Every guide has his own way of tackling the ascent, too. As such, Map 18 (p327) and the description that follows may differ from the exact route you end up taking. But whatever route you take, rest assured it will be steep and it will be exhausting.

Having said that each path up the Western Breach is unique, your guide will doubtless aim for the rocky ridge that you can see from Arrow Glacier Campsite which runs from the rock towers near the crater down towards the camp (and is often called the 'Stone Train'). It will take around 1¾ hours before you properly join this ridge (soon after crossing a second stream), a walk that includes the most dangerous part of the ascent, where **rockfalls** are frequent. Furthermore, this area is often also covered in snow and many a guide has lost the path here.

Successfully gain the ridge and about 15 minutes later you'll find yourself at the foot of the so-called **Rock Stairs** – natural steps that, after the shifting scree and rocks of the previous 1¾ hours, come as something of a relief. These stairs are also viewed as a 'Point of No Return' by the porters who, once they see that you've reached here, consider there's no turning back and thus break camp and march off to Mweka (unless you're planning to sleep at Crater Camp, of course, in which case they'll be right behind you).

The stairs take about 40 minutes to tackle, at the end of which you find yourself on a small, flat space that's often used as a **picnic spot** by those tackling the Western Breach during the day. Dirty and chilly, a more inhospitable picnic spot it would be hard to find, though you do get great views down to Barranco Campsite. Beyond the picnic site the stairs are replaced by a path that's just as steep, though you have to tackle this section without the benefit of any steps. The trail picks its way between the **rocky towers** guarding the crater. Persevere for another 40 minutes and you'll find yourself finally gaining the **crater rim** (5729m/18,796ft), with the much diminshed remnants of **Furtwangler Glacier** on your left the first of many sights up here. Walking on level ground for a change, it takes around 10 minutes to reach **Crater Campsite** (also 5729m), set amongst boulders at the foot of the climb up to Uhuru.

The path up to **Reusch Crater** and the **Ash Pit Viewpoint** (40 mins) bends north round and behind Furtwangler Glacier. For more on what's up here, see p373.

The **stiff switchback climb** up to **Uhuru Peak**, 50 minutes away, lies to the south of the campsite, clearly etched into the crater wall. It's a hard climb and you'll be cursing every zigzag and switchback on the way. But keep going: the sense of achievement at the top is beyond compare. And it's a feeling that will stay with you all the way down, and all the way back to your home country. Because if you get to the summit, you'll believe you can do anything.

Oh, to be able to bottle that feeling...

The Shira Plateau Route including the Northern Circuit

This is the older of the two trails that cross the Shira Plateau and, in my opinion, definitely the inferior. That said, a few companies insist this is the better route, for reasons I shall come to in a moment.

My problems with this route are twofold. Firstly, and in my opinion most importantly, you miss out on the forest zone on the way up, for it's usual for trekkers on the first day of the Shira Route to be driven to the Morum Barrier, which lies above the forest at the start of the Shira Plateau. And it's not just any old forest either, for the jungle on this western side of Kili is the best on the mountain. That, I think, is little short of unforgivable.

The second problem I have is that the Official Shira Route is actually a 4WD track used by emergency vehicles. In other words, you'll be walking on a track that's been designed with vehicles in mind – which can never be as fun as walking on a trail made for pedestrians. Though to be fair to the companies that do offer this route, most of them these days seem to turn off the 'road' as soon as they can in favour of one of the many other paths that criss-cross the plateau – in effect ending up on one of the Lemosho Route variants – and some don't actually walk on the road at all.

All of which begs the question: why do the companies who patronise this route think it's better than Lemosho? Well from what I can gather, it's simply because they reckon that if you are going to have a 7- or 8-day trek, spending those days at a higher altitude (Morum Barrier, where you start walking, is at 3405m), will enable you to acclimatise better and thus have a better chance of reaching the top than if you'd spent one or two of those days at a lower altitude trudging up Kilimanjaro's western slopes. All of which may be true – though to my mind this still doesn't compensate for missing out on the forest of the western slopes, which you now see only through a car window. And besides, isn't being driven halfway up the mountain sort of, well, cheating?

So I guess it comes down to a matter of opinion and taste: if your sole reason for setting foot on the mountain is to get to the summit, the Shira Plateau Route *may* be a better route for you. But if you have any interest in the more complete experience, one that includes both ascending and descending via *all* the various vegetation zones, Lemosho wins hands down.

PREPARATION

The journey to Morum Barrier

A journey of a thousand miles begins with a single step, said the inscrutable 6th-century BC philosopher Lao-tzu. Thankfully, for those of you who have chosen this route, your own journey will be a lot shorter than 1000 miles and your first step will be onto a bus that will convey you to **Londorossi Gate**. It is a rare trekker who begins his or her walk here, however, so – ramblers registered and permits purchased – you'll rejoin the bus as it conveys you up the slopes, through pine plantations, forest and moorland, with the occasional monkey or baboon crossing your path and the waters of the Ngare Nairobi a capricious companion to your right.

Eventually the twisting track bifurcates in the shadow of Morum Hill. A few metres on from this divide are the remnants of what was clearly some sort of concrete gatepost – the remnants of the old **Morum Barrier** (3405m/11,171ft). Several information boards stand nearby and there's a toilet here too. It's a lonely place: the landscape windswept, the flora dry and scrubby, the fauna virtually non-existent. Indeed, it almost feels as if humanity has abandoned this corner of the mountain and coming across the remains of the barrier always puts me in mind of that moment when Charlton Heston comes across the Statue of Liberty at the end of *Planet of the Apes*. Rather than sink to your knees and bewail the demise of Homo sapiens, however, as Charlton did, I advise you to keep your spirits up and get walking. Incidentally, by driving to 3405m you are only 2m short of the *combined* altitudes of the highest points of Scotland, Wales and England – namely Ben Nevis (1344m/4409ft), Snowdon (1085m/3560ft) and Scafell Pike (978m/3209ft) respectively – and you haven't even started walking yet!

STAGE 1: MORUM BARRIER TO SHIRA 1 OR SIMBA CAVE CAMPSITE [MAP 15, p319; MAP 16, p321]

Morum Barrier to Shira 1: Distance: 3.75km (2¼ miles); altitude gained: 99m (325ft)

Morum Barrier to Simba Cave Campsite: 6.5km (4 miles); altitude gained: 215m (705ft)

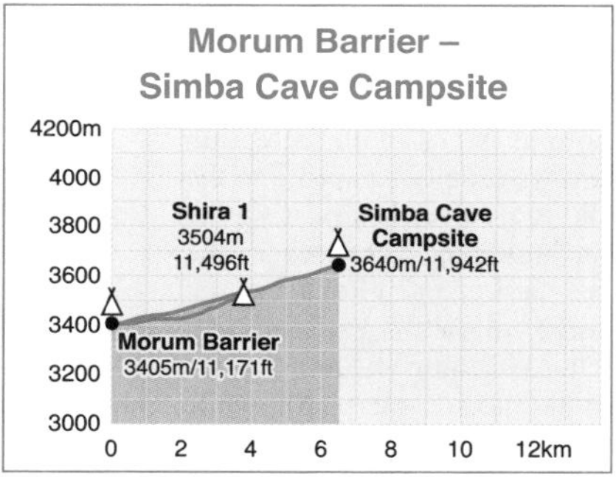

Morum Barrier marks the start of the Shira Plateau, where you'll be spending the next couple of days. Occasionally, groups turning up late are forced to **camp** here though if everything has gone smoothly thus far it's more usual to walk to one of the campsites on the plateau, with Shira 1 or Simba Cave Campsite being the only realistic choices.

Shira 1 (3504m/11,496ft) is reached via a narrow trail that heads south from the information boards. The trail crosses several streams but the whole walk takes only 70 minutes or so; from Shira 1 you continue along the Lemosho Route to Shira 2 (possibly via Shira Cathedral, as described on p322) and Lava Tower (see pp324-5); or your trekking company may have opted to head towards Moir Huts and possibly continue from there round the Northern Circuit, which I describe on p334.

Those who instead opted to stay at **Simba Cave Campsite** (3640m/ 11,942ft), reached by walking along the road for about 90 minutes, have essentially the same

❑ PHONE RECEPTION ON THE SHIRA PLATEAU ROUTE

Phone reception on the Shira Route is best described as patchy at best. You can get some sort of reception, sometimes, in a few isolated places on the Plateau, particularly near the campsites. You may be lucky enough to get something on the **ridge above Moir Huts** which the guides say is reliable – though I have failed to get reception on more than one occasion and even when I do it's not great.

You can sometimes have success at **Pofu Camp** on the Northern Circuit but there is little reception at Third Cave so, after that, the next time you'll be able to use your mobile phone will be at **Gillman's** (doubtful), **Stella** (probably) or **Uhuru Peak** (maybe).

options. The campsite, adorned with several weatherbeaten old wooden toilets as well as the cave itself, marks the main junction between the road and the Lemosho Route. (Incidentally, I don't know of any company that still uses the 'road' after Simba Cave, with more easterly footpaths, described as part of the Lemosho Route on p322, being superior alternatives.)

STAGE 2: SIMBA CAVE CAMPSITE TO MOIR HUTS

[MAP 16, p321; MAP 17, p323; MAP 19, opposite]

Distance: 6km (3¾ miles); altitude gained: 515m (1690ft)

Around 45 minutes from Simba Cave lies a **junction** marked with little more than a simple sign, with direction arrows usually scraped into the dirt too. Nevertheless, it's quite an important place, where the regular Lemosho Route and the route to Moir Huts divide. Those heading to Shira 2/Shira Huts should see p320; while those heading towards Moir Huts and the Northern Circuit should read on.

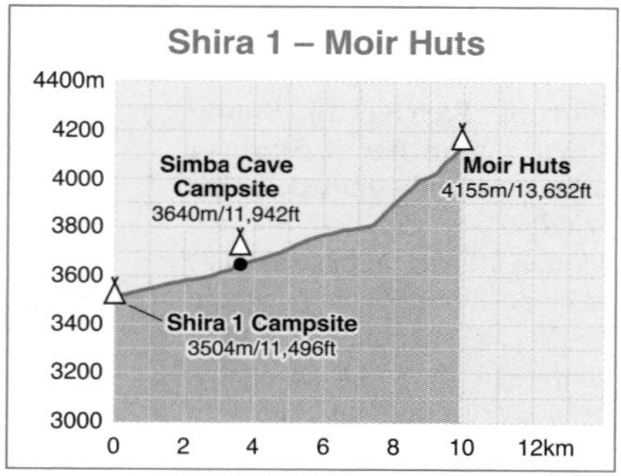

From the junction with the main trail a 135-minute path picks its way between boulders, around or over petrified lava flows, and through grassy swards. The main 'landmark' is the **disused Fischer Campsite**, named after Scott Fischer who did much to pioneer this route with his company Mountain Madness and who perished on the slopes of Everest. Hunt around for (or ask your guide to show you) the small plaque that commemorates him and admire the resplendent giant groundsels that thrive in this chilly location.

Just over an hour's schlep afterwards the path curves in the shadow of some **low cliffs** past an impressive **dripping cave** just before the **Moir Huts** (4155m/13,632ft). Set in a lovely sheer-sided valley that sees few visitors, the campsite is more peaceful than almost any other on the mountain; alas, it also means the cleaning crews seldom drop by, so there's often plenty of rubbish around. Furthermore, apart from the three toilets, the only other building is a ruined pyramid-shaped hut, built as a sleeping shelter but now sadly vandalised. As a result, the whole camp does feel a bit cold and bleak. Even the white-necked ravens don't bother scavenging around here, the pickings presumably being too slim, and the silence as a result can be positively deafening. A rare touch of warmth and pleasure, however, is provided by the seedeaters which, lacking the social graces of their brethren at lower altitudes, happily hop into your tent in search of crumbs. There's also a great deal of pleasure to be had in views that take in both the Shira Ridge – where you have just come from – and snow-laden Kibo where, all being well, you'll be going...

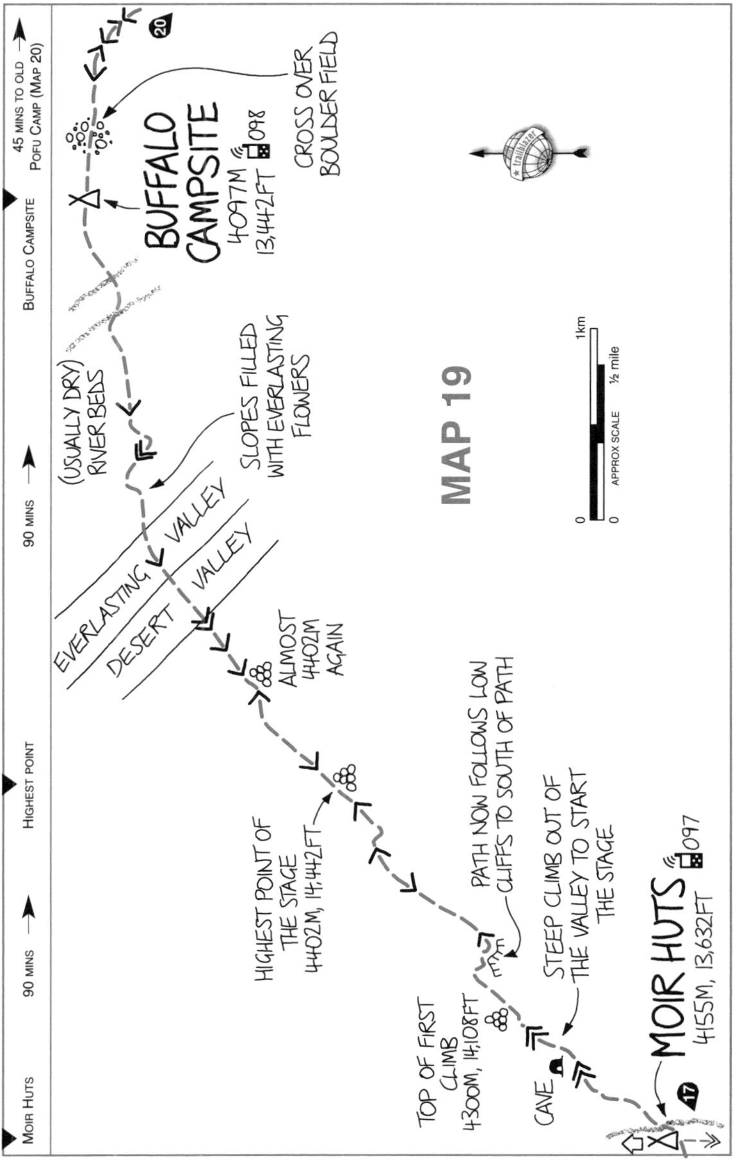
Moir Huts
90 mins
Highest Point
90 mins
Buffalo Campsite
45 mins to old Pofu Camp (Map 20)
MAP 19
MOIR HUTS
4155M, 13,632FT
097
CAVE
TOP OF FIRST CLIMB
4300M, 14,108FT
STEEP CLIMB OUT OF THE VALLEY TO START THE STAGE
PATH NOW FOLLOWS LOW CLIFFS TO SOUTH OF PATH
HIGHEST POINT OF THE STAGE
4402M, 14,442FT
ALMOST 4402M AGAIN
DESERT VALLEY
EVERLASTING VALLEY
SLOPES FILLED WITH EVERLASTING FLOWERS
(USUALLY DRY) RIVER BEDS
BUFFALO CAMPSITE
4097M
13,442FT
098
CROSS OVER BOULDER FIELD
17
20
trailblazer
APPROX SCALE
0
1km
0
½ mile

STAGES 3 & 4: THE NORTHERN CIRCUIT (MOIR HUTS TO THIRD CAVE CAMPSITE)

[MAP 19, p333; MAP 20, opposite]

At first sight, the Northern Circuit, which drapes around the northern face of Kibo, appears to offer little to the Kili climber, especially when compared to its counterpart the Southern Circuit. For one thing, the northern trail lacks such attractions as the lovely Barranco Valley and its photogenic campsite, the charm of the sunbird-flitted Karanga Valley, the busy excitement of Barafu Campsite and the scrambling challenge of the Barranco/Breakfast Wall.

Furthermore, the Southern Circuit is nearer to civilisation, with Moshi and the neighbouring villages both visible, on occasion, and less than a day's walk away, which may prove vital if you run into difficulty and need to descend quickly. In contrast, there is no such descent available on the Northern Circuit; if you need to evacuate from this side of Kibo you'll have to walk to the Shira Plateau or the Saddle and work out how to get back down from there.

So far, so unattractive. But there is one quality the Northern Circuit has that its southern neighbour lacks: **solitude**. For while the Southern Circuit resounds to the footfall of just about every trekker who opted for the Machame, Umbwe, Lemosho and Shira routes – not to mention their crews – the Northern Circuit sees very few people. True, visit in the high season and you may bump into trekkers who have signed up to one of the 'alternative' routes offered by the big companies such as Team Kilimanjaro, Nature Discovery/Thomson and Kilimanjaro Experts plus those companies who, lacking imagination, merely copy them; but even then there's a slight possibility you will have the whole path to yourself. For the Northern Circuit is not part of any of the 'official' routes but instead exists to offer those who want to avoid the crowds the chance to do so.

The path around the northern side of Kibo can be completed in one day – though it is more normally divided into two stages, with a night spent at Pofu Camp or one of the smaller, scruffier neighbouring campsites. Altitude-wise, and assuming you are going from west to east ie from Moir Huts to Third Cave Campsite, you actually lose a little in altitude – from 4155m to 3936m. This, however, fails to convey the sometimes quite large and sweaty climbs and descents you have to make on your way round and you will in fact climb to 4402m/14,442ft at one point; as such, this route is pretty good for acclimatisation.

Though I have written this from west to east, this is one of those paths which sees walkers heading in both directions. I do apologise but those few of you walking from east to west (having come, perhaps, from the Rongai Route) will have to read this description backwards, as it were...

> **Note**: Do remember that the times quoted are approximations and, more importantly, refer to **walking times only** with no time spent resting, taking photos etc.
> Add on 30-50% to get an estimate of the total time spent on the trail.

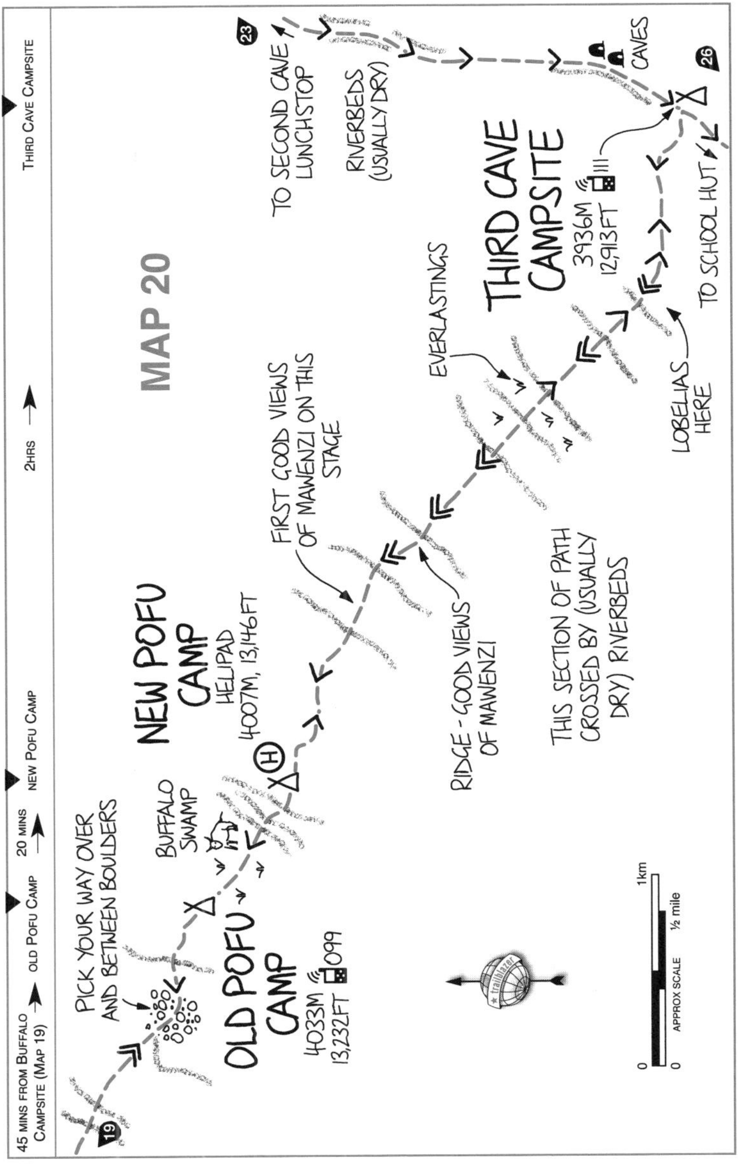
MAP 20
45 MINS FROM BUFFALO CAMPSITE (MAP 19)
OLD POFU CAMP
20 MINS
NEW POFU CAMP
2HRS
THIRD CAVE CAMPSITE
PICK YOUR WAY OVER AND BETWEEN BOULDERS
OLD POFU CAMP
4033M 13,232FT
BUFFALO SWAMP
NEW POFU CAMP
HELIPAD
4007M, 13,146FT
FIRST GOOD VIEWS OF MAWENZI ON THIS STAGE
RIDGE - GOOD VIEWS OF MAWENZI
THIS SECTION OF PATH CROSSED BY (USUALLY DRY) RIVERBEDS
EVERLASTINGS
LOBELIAS HERE
THIRD CAVE CAMPSITE
3936M 12,913FT
TO SECOND CAVE LUNCHSTOP
RIVERBEDS (USUALLY DRY)
CAVES
TO SCHOOL HUT
19
23
26
0
1km
0
½ mile
APPROX SCALE
trailblazer

TRAIL GUIDE & MAPS

Moir Huts to Old Pofu Campsite [Map 19, p333; Map 20, p335]

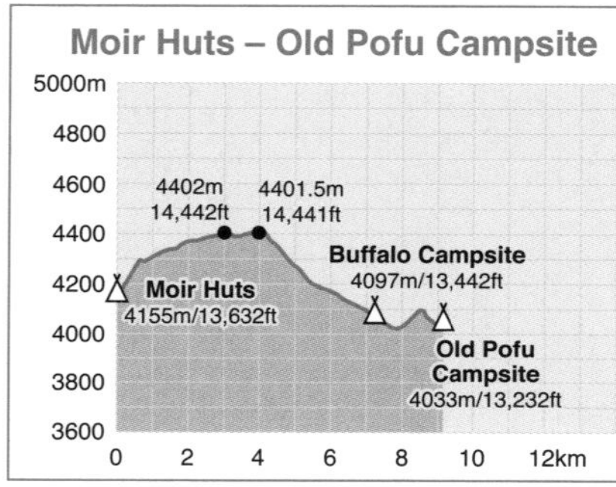

Distance: 9.2km (5¾ miles); altitude *lost*: 122m (400ft) (247m/810ft up to the high point then 369m/1211ft descent to Pofu)

As mentioned, peace and solitude are the main characteristics of this path. In terms of acclimatisation, you actually achieve the lofty altitude of 4402m/14,442ft today before falling to Old Pofu Camp at 4033m/13,232ft. It won't be unusual, therefore, for people to feel some symptoms of altitude sickness (often a headache) by the time they arrive at one of the campsites. So do try to go *pole pole* and to drink lots to avoid this. Furthermore, don't set off from Moir Huts if you're feeling any effects of the altitude. Moir might feel remote – but it's only going to get even more remote …

The walk begins with perhaps the steepest climb of the day, a relentless slog up a barren slope to exactly 4300m (14,108ft). Cairns both mark the top of the ascent and the way forward, as you spend your day making your way around Kibo's northern face, dropping down into the many north–south valleys before clambering back out of them. Though this can get a little monotonous, note how the character of each valley is different from its neighbours, with some decorated with everlastings, others blanketed in heathers, and still others virtually pure, lifeless desert. Eventually, after three hours, you'll come to the first of the campsites on this side of Kibo, known as **Buffalo Campsite**, followed in short order by some **boulders** that you need to scramble over to reach the second (45 mins) and only official campsite (and the only one with proper toilets), known as **Old Pofu**.

It has to be said that all these camps are all fairly uncharismatic places, perched on chilly ridges between the valleys. It will probably come as no surprise to you that I think cleaning crews should visit this side of Kibo more often; though the number of trekkers passing this way is small, over time the mess they and their crews leave builds up considerably. Unfortunately, there's not much to distract you from the mess except to sit and watch the mist roll in and, on occasion, clear again, giving you the chance to spot the eland that are said to hang about in these parts and after which the campsite is named. If the skies are clear enough you should get a full frontal view of Kibo, while Mawenzi peers coyly over your shoulder and the lights of Kenya twinkle in the far distance below.

Old Pofu Campsite to Third Cave Campsite [Map 20, p335]

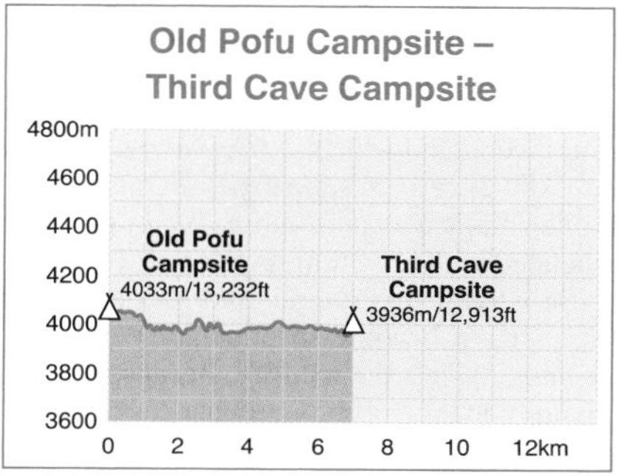

Distance: 6.8km (4¼ miles); altitude *lost*: 97m (318ft)
Unsurprisingly this stage continues in pretty much the same vein as the previous one as the path continues on its merry traverse around the northern slopes. Once again the trekker is asked to negotiate numerous valleys, mostly dry, one or two slightly more fecund, and one at the very start of the day that is, so it is said, favoured by buffaloes in search of water and minerals. The gradients aren't quite as dramatic on this stage and the day slightly shorter though you'll still find yourself pretty puffed out by the time you reach **Third Cave Campsite** (3936m/12,913ft). The reason for this is clear when you look at the gradient profile and see how much ascending and descending you have to do on this stage. The views, however, provide ample compensation, with Kibo to your right and Mawenzi gradually looming larger and larger ahead of you, though you won't see much of the glorious Saddle that separates them until the next stage.

For details of Third Cave Campsite, please see p348, while for details of your trail from here you'll need to consult this book in conjunction with the itinerary your operator has provided – with School Hut, Kibo Huts and even Mawenzi Tarn just three of the possible destinations.

The Rongai Route

Please convey to the seven blind climbers who reached the summit of Kilimanjaro my warm congratulations on their splendid achievement.

Queen Elizabeth II in a telegram to Geoffrey Salisbury who, with his team of seven young, blind African trekkers and four sighted companions, used the Rongai Route in 1969 for their attempt on the mountain. The trek was covered on the front pages of African newspapers and all the trekkers received a hero's welcome. Indeed, three pairs of boots worn by the trekkers were put on display in Uganda's National Museum!

Probably due to the improvement in the road heading from Marangu to the Kenyan border that leads to the start of this trek, the Rongai Route has become increasingly popular over the past couple of years. It's still only the fourth-most popular trail (after Machame, Lemosho and Marangu), but where once you had a 50:50 chance of having the trail to yourself, these days you'll be lucky indeed to avoid your fellow hikers.

While many will see Rongai's new-found popularity as a drawback, it can't be denied that it is deserved – even though, at first glance, this trail seems decidedly unattractive. The lower slopes on these north-eastern slopes have been denuded by farmers. The 'proper' native forest that you eventually walk through is not that spectacular, being little more than a narrow band of (albeit pretty) woodland which soon gives way to some rather hot and shadeless heathland. And then there's the expense: the cost of a Rongai trek can be higher than all other trails except Lemosho/Shira Plateau due to the higher transport costs associated with travelling to the start of the trek.

So why, if this route is more expensive, far-flung and barren than all the others, has it become so popular? Well for one thing, there's the **wildlife**. Because of its proximity to Amboseli, your chances of seeing the local fauna here are greater than on any other route bar those starting in the far west below Shira Plateau.

Colobus monkey
(from *The Kilima-njaro Expedition,* **HH Johnston**, 1886)

During the research for the first edition of this book I encountered a troop of colobus monkeys, while later that same day I came across an elephant skull, with elephant droppings and footprints nearby; and at night my little party was kept awake by something snuffling around the tents (a civet cat, according to my guide, though presumably one wearing heavy hobnail boots to judge by the amount of noise it was making).

Buffalo and eland also frequent the few mountain streams on these northern slopes (though, as previously mentioned, these streams, never very deep, are almost always dry except in the rainy season and consequently the buffalo choose to bathe elsewhere for most of the year;

❑ PHONE RECEPTION ON THE RONGAI ROUTE

Mobile reception on the Rongai Route is not great, though it's better if you are taking the Mawenzi Tarn variation. As always, reception depends a lot on which network you are with. Guides say you can get reception by the **Hut at Simba Camp** – though I have to say I've never managed it.

One place where I do always get reception, however, is at the popular resting place on the large flat rock during the second morning. **Second Caves** also has reasonable reception. Thereafter, however, on the regular Rongai Route the chances to use your phone are limited.

Those taking the trail via Mawenzi Tarn will find reception at **Kikelelwa** comes and goes; while at **Mawenzi Tarn** it is also intermittent, though more reliable by the toilets. Crossing the Saddle there is usually no reception, so the next time you'll be able to use your mobile phone will be at **Gillman's** (possibly) or **Stella Point**.

though occasionally they head up the slopes in search of minerals that they lick off the rocks).

The **flora** is different here too, with its juniper and olive trees. Even the drive to the start is interesting: from Moshi the road passes through a rural Chagga heartland, so giving you the chance to see village life Chagga-style (see below), which I heartily recommend. Furthermore, if you manage to find other trekkers to join you and split the cost, the transport should not be too expensive.

And if, at the end of the **23.8km/15 miles** (or 33.65km/21¾ miles if taking the Mawenzi Tarn diversion to Kibo Huts) ascent to Uhuru Peak, you do feel you've somehow missed out on some of the classic features of Kili – such as an extensive stretch of deep, dark forest, or giant groundsels – fear not, as both can be found in abundance on the 36.55km-long (22¾-mile) Marangu Route, **the designated descent** for those coming from Rongai.

Before I describe the route in detail, I should point out that when I say I love the Rongai Route, what I really mean is that I love the version of the Rongai Route that takes you via the **Mawenzi Tarn Hut Campsite**. This trail not only allows you to savour some gobsmacking views across to Kibo from the top of the ridge above the tarn but also gives you the chance the following day to walk across the Saddle, many people's favourite part of the mountain.

The problem with the regular Rongai Route is that, thanks to a change in the park regulations, you *have to* take six days to complete it; where, really, it was designed as a five-day trail and it does only take five days to walk up and down it even if you're going *pole pole*. As a result, those on the regular route are forced to take a 'rest day', usually at Third Cave Campsite from where, in all probability, they'll be marched up to the Saddle and back to aid acclimatisation. It's not ideal and for this reason more and more people are taking the Mawenzi Tarn Hut Route – which is entirely the better route anyway.

PREPARATION

The journey to Loitokitok and New Rongai Gate

What was once one of the more arduous aspects of trekking on the Rongai Route – getting to the start – has since become much easier thanks to the improvement of the road from a muddy, dusty track to a fully fledged tarmac highway. A journey that used to take half a day or more can now be completed in just a couple of hours. But though the journey may be a lot easier it still retains some interest, mainly because it takes you through several Chagga villages.

Your journey to the start of the trek will, in all probability, take you via **Marangu Mtoni** (see p238) and on round the dry, eastern side of the mountain, through the villages of **Mwika** and **Mrere** in the heart of the Rombo District. After them, in order, the villages of **Shauritanga**, **Olele**, **Usseru**, **Mashima** and **Kibaoni** emerge in fairly rapid succession before, eventually, you arrive at **Tarakea**, the largest settlement. There is also a border post with Kenya in Tarakea; presumably your driver will know *not* to take the road leading to it but instead to keep on following the road which now heads north-west.

The wooden settlement of **Loitokitok** lies a few minutes on from Tarakea, where a track on the left branches up to the park gate, situated at around 2379m (7805ft). From the old Rongai gate you can see the smart and lovely ***Snowcap Cottages*** (see p234 for details), which resemble (from this distance at least) Swiss-style chalets.

STAGE 1: NEW RONGAI GATE TO SIMBA CAMPSITE

[MAP 21, opposite; MAP 22, p342]

Distance: 4km (2½ miles); altitude gained: 256m (840ft)

It's a short but lovely first day to your adventure. To compensate for the relative lack of forest on this dry northern side, the path takes a deliberately meandering route through the trees to give you a bit more time amongst them.

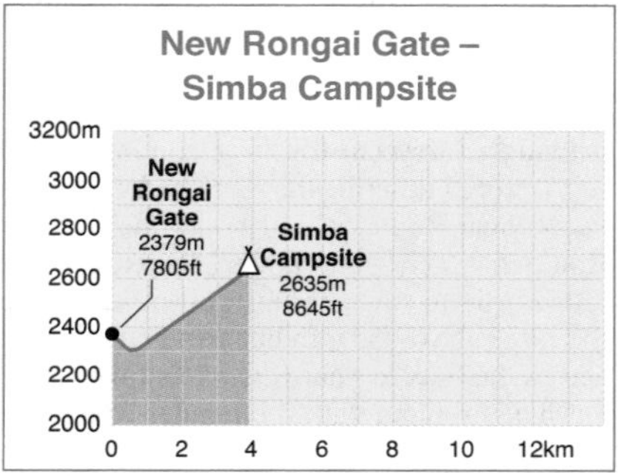

The forest is teeming with wildlife, in particular **colobus monkeys**, so it comes as something of a disappointment to find just how quickly the tall trees of the montane forest give way to the more stunted vegetation of the **heathland**, such as giant heathers and St John's wort.

Leaving the forest on a trail that slowly steepens, about 50 minutes afterwards you cross a stream and a few minutes later reach the first campsite on this route, known as **Simba Campsite**, at an altitude of 2635m/8645ft. It's always good to get to a campsite, and this one in particular is pleasant: surrounded by heathers, with creatures snuffling about the tent at night and birdsong to wake you in the morning, this spot has a pleasingly wild, isolated ambience.

STAGE 2: SIMBA CAMPSITE TO THIRD CAVE CAMPSITE

[MAP 22, p342; MAP 23, p343]

Distance: 5.8km (3½ miles) to Second Cave Campsite/lunchstop; 3.3km (2 miles) to Third Cave Campsite (9.1km/5¾ miles in total); altitude gained: 852m (2795ft) to Second Cave; Second Cave to Third Cave 449m(1473ft); 1301m (4268ft) in total

Camp-life on Kilimanjaro is a capital school for the practice of self-denial.

Hans Meyer *Across East African Glaciers*

This day perhaps lacks the variety of others on the trail. For most of the day you will be walking up slopes flanked with heather with the twin peaks of Kilimanjaro keeping a watchful eye as you progress. During this stage you will bid farewell to those lucky trekkers who opted to take the extra day and visit the

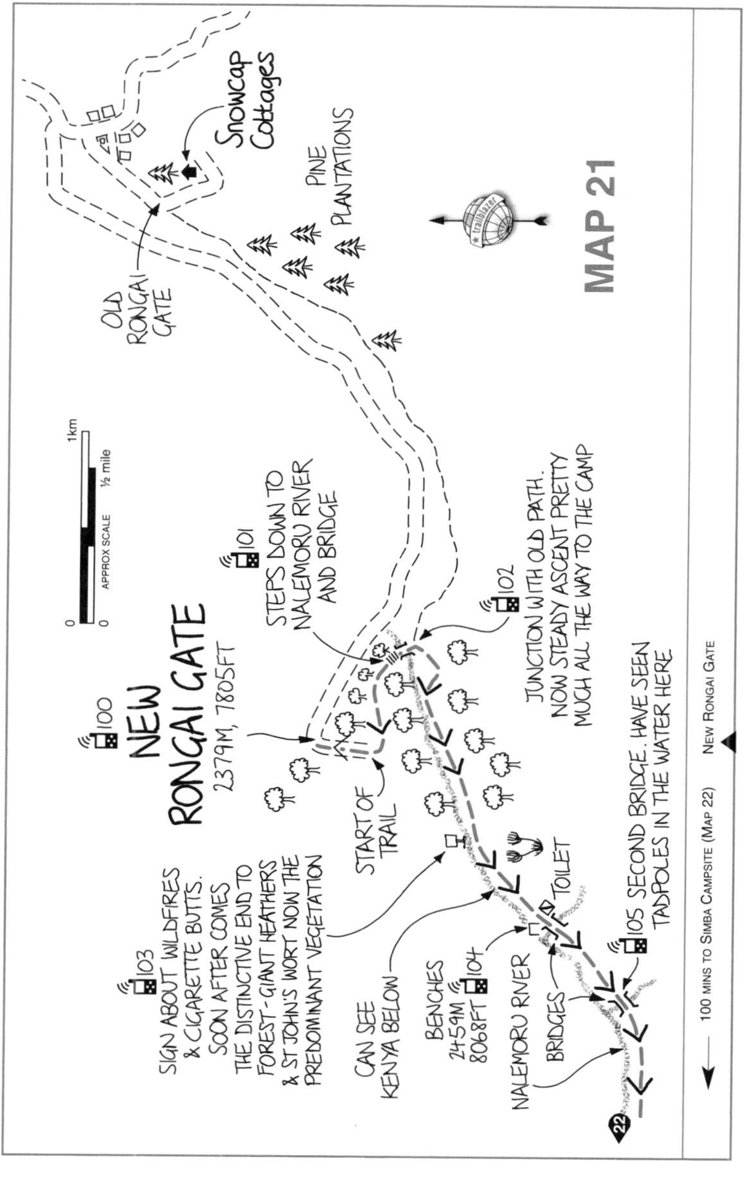
MAP 21
Snowcap Cottages
PINE PLANTATIONS
OLD RONGAI GATE
APPROX SCALE
0
1km
0
½ mile
100
NEW RONGAI GATE
2379M, 7805FT
101
STEPS DOWN TO NALEMORU RIVER AND BRIDGE
102
JUNCTION WITH OLD PATH. NOW STEADY ASCENT PRETTY MUCH ALL THE WAY TO THE CAMP
START OF TRAIL
103
SIGN ABOUT WILDFIRES & CIGARETTE BUTTS. SOON AFTER COMES THE DISTINCTIVE END TO FOREST-GIANT HEATHERS & ST JOHN'S WORT NOW THE PREDOMINANT VEGETATION
CAN SEE KENYA BELOW
TOILET
BENCHES
104
2459M 8068FT
NALEMORU RIVER
BRIDGES
105 SECOND BRIDGE. HAVE SEEN TADPOLES IN THE WATER HERE
22
100 MINS TO SIMBA CAMPSITE (MAP 22)
NEW RONGAI GATE

Mawenzi Tarn via Kikelelwa Campsite; they will go their own way after lunch (on a route described on pp344-5.) Taking the more direct path, by the end of today you will have ascended more than 1300m. But there's no gain without pain and today is long, involving almost 4½ hours of steady walking on a steep, dusty path. Take comfort from the fact that tomorrow is much easier, and that you have already ascended almost 2000m from the gate and are now well over halfway to the summit.

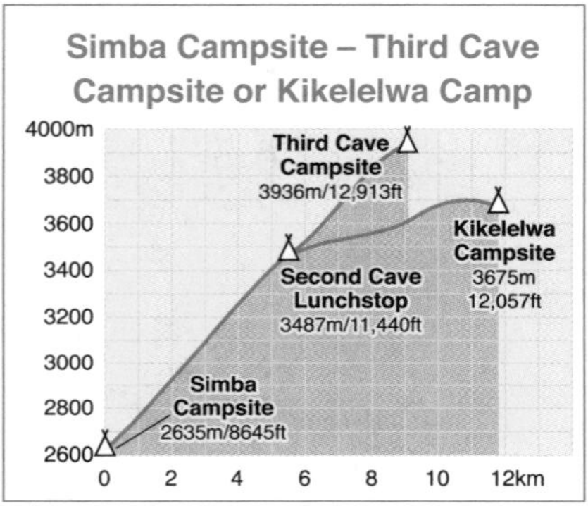

If you haven't already been doing so, this is also the time to take things deliberately *pole pole* ('slowly slowly' in Swahili) – you're reaching some serious altitudes now and mountain sickness stalks the unwary.

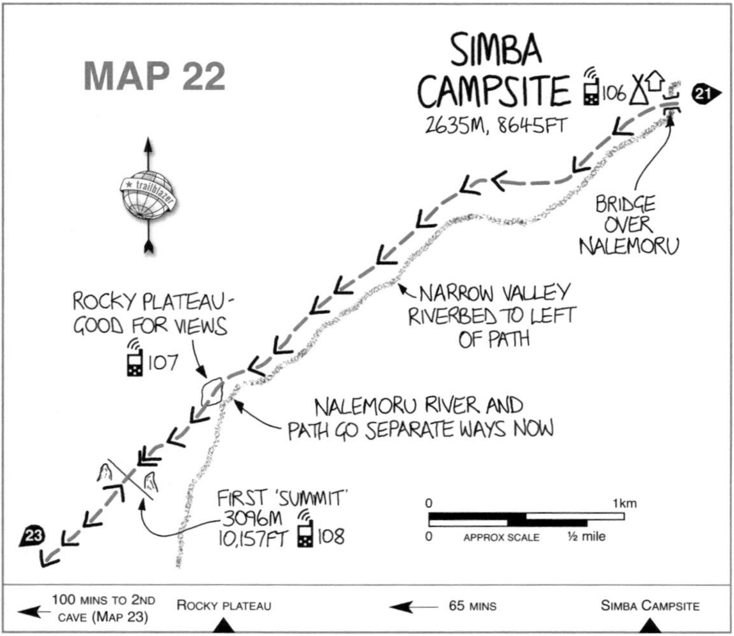

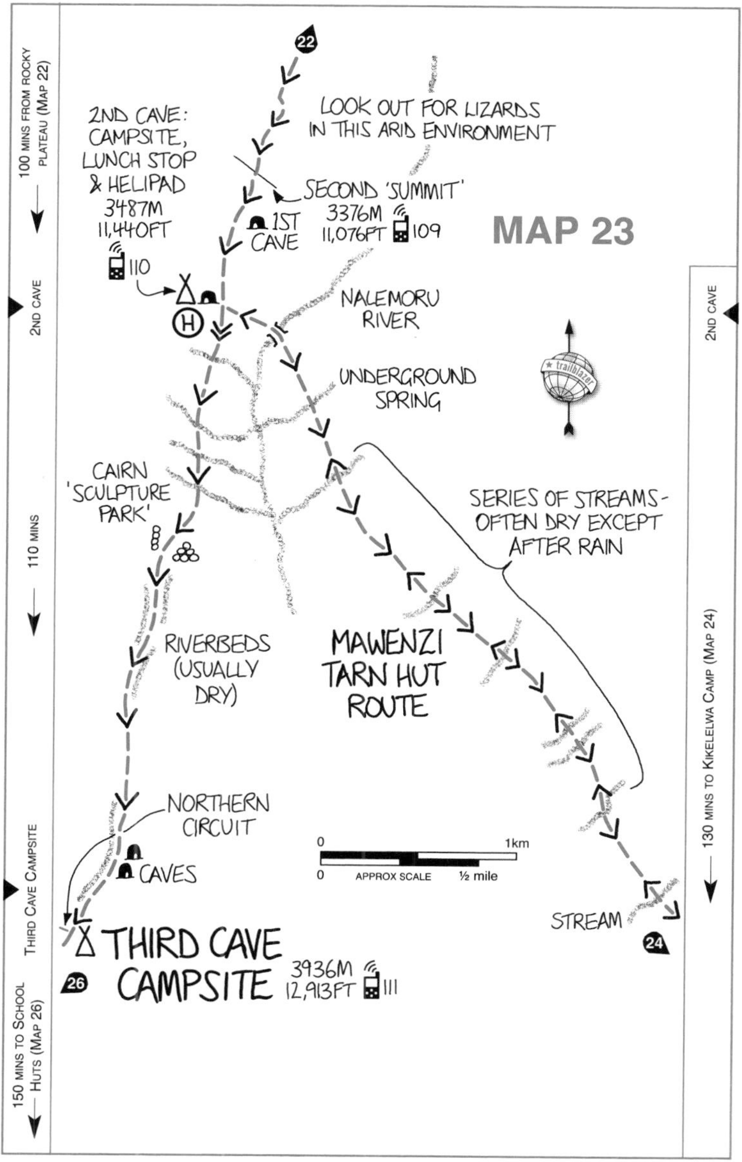
100 MINS FROM ROCKY PLATEAU (MAP 22)
2ND CAVE
110 MINS
THIRD CAVE CAMPSITE
150 MINS TO SCHOOL HUTS (MAP 26)
22
LOOK OUT FOR LIZARDS IN THIS ARID ENVIRONMENT
2ND CAVE: CAMPSITE, LUNCH STOP & HELIPAD 3487M 11,440FT
110
SECOND 'SUMMIT' 3376M 11,076FT
109
1ST CAVE
MAP 23
H
NALEMORU RIVER
UNDERGROUND SPRING
trailblazer
CAIRN 'SCULPTURE PARK'
SERIES OF STREAMS - OFTEN DRY EXCEPT AFTER RAIN
RIVERBEDS (USUALLY DRY)
MAWENZI TARN HUT ROUTE
NORTHERN CIRCUIT
CAVES
0
1km
0
APPROX SCALE
½ mile
STREAM
24
THIRD CAVE CAMPSITE
3936M 12,913FT
111
26
2ND CAVE
130 MINS TO KIKELELWA CAMP (MAP 24)

The path at the start of this stage is, perhaps surprisingly, a westward one, its goal seeming to be the northern slopes of Kibo rather than the eastern slopes you will eventually climb. The heathers are gradually shrinking in size now too and while some trees still cling on at this altitude, they are few in number and scattered. For these reasons, the first part of this stage is rather shadeless and very hot.

After 45 minutes a **river bed** (dry for the best part of the year) joins you from the left and the path follows its course for most of the next hour. Look

❑ THE MAWENZI TARN HUT ROUTE

[MAP 23, p343; MAP 24, p346; MAP 25, p347]

Though I am treating this path as an 'alternative' to the main trail, because you have to spend a minimum of six days on the Rongai Route (where previously you could do it in five), I think the majority of people are now taking the trek to the Tarn. **If you happen to be one of them then good for you**: it is wonderful. Great views, lovely scenery and it's a useful way to acclimatise too. If you are offered this version of the Rongai Route, don't hesitate.

From Second Cave to Kikelelwa Campsite

Distance: 5.95km (3¾ miles); altitude gained: 188m (617ft)

From Second Cave, the usual lunchstop on the second day, the path takes an abrupt south-easterly turn directly towards the jagged peak of Mawenzi. Traversing open moorland the path meanders and undulates; assuming you've already walked from Simba Camp this morning, you will feel rather drained by the time you stumble into **Kikelelwa Camp** (3675m/12,057ft), situated near a couple of caves by Kikelelwa River, with giant groundsels and lobelias flourishing nearby. (Incidentally, I don't know why this should be so but whenever I have walked this stretch of the path – which must be a good half-dozen times now – it has always been either raining or very misty. That said, it has always brightened up in the evening to reveal Kibo's snowy summit peaking over the ridge that separates the campsite from the Saddle.)

Compared to the morning where you gained over 850m, this afternoon's walk increases your altitude by less than 200m, though the distances of the two parts are about the same and, given the amount of up- and downhills, this latter walk is just as exhausting.

Kikelelwa Camp to Mawenzi Tarn Hut Campsite

Distance: 3.75km (2⅓ miles); altitude gained: 627m (2057ft)

Though this stage to Mawenzi Tarn is relatively short at less than 4km and is usually completed in a morning (allowing time for a brief acclimatisation trek in the afternoon for those who feel up to it), it's also steep as you

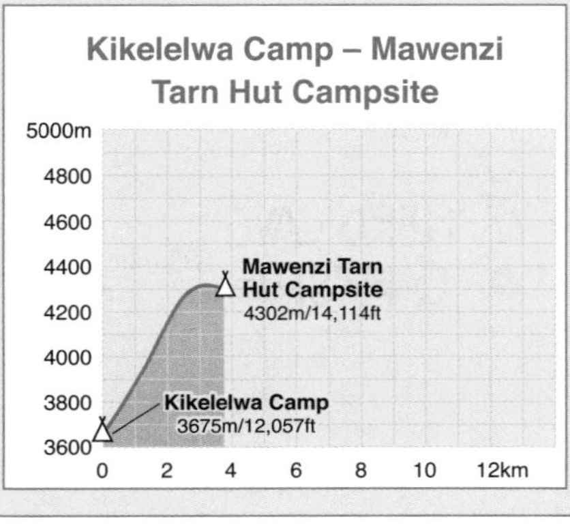

back occasionally and, weather permitting, you should be able to see a number of villages on the Kenyan side of the border, the sunlight glinting off the metal roofs. Continuing upwards, the path steepens slightly and begins to turn more to the south. The terrain up here is rather rocky and bumpy.

The path continues south-south-west, rounding a few minor cliffs and hills and crossing a number of false summits, before eventually flattening out and arriving at a small, waterless cave. As inviting as the cave and the shade it offers now appear, this is not your lunch stop. *(cont'd on p348)*

gain more than 600m/1969ft, the path shedding the moorland vegetation as it climbs steadily.

Mawenzi Tarn Hut Campsite (4302m/14,114ft) is situated in one of the most spectacular settings, in a cirque beneath the jagged teeth of Mawenzi. There's a small ranger's hut here and a toilet block.

Assuming the walk here was trouble-free you will have most of the afternoon to go on an acclimatisation climb up the ridge to the west; if you're lucky, the sky will be clear, affording you fantastic views of Kibo, though in all probability you'll merely catch the odd glimpse through the clouds that usually roll in across the Saddle in the afternoon. But no matter, for you'll get the same views tomorrow morning when the skies should be clearer and the sun will be behind you too. The views back down to the Tarn – which, to be honest, is little more than a puddle with delusions of grandeur – are great too.

Mawenzi Tarn Hut Campsite to Kibo Huts

Distance: 8.9km (5½ miles); altitude gained: 412m (1352ft)

This lovely day begins with a slight retracing of your steps before you strike out westwards, crossing the ridge and dropping down the slope to tiptoe along the beautifully barren Saddle's northern edge. With views like screensavers to east and west, it's a rare trekker indeed who doesn't rate this day as their favourite on the mountain. The flora is sparse but do look out for eland which are said to stroll up here.

You have three destinations at the end of this third day: if you're on a 6-day trek you'll probably be heading to Kibo Huts, on the lower slopes of Kibo. If you've booked a 7-day trek, however, the chances are you'll be marched down to Third Cave Campsite and a reunion with the regular Rongai Route.

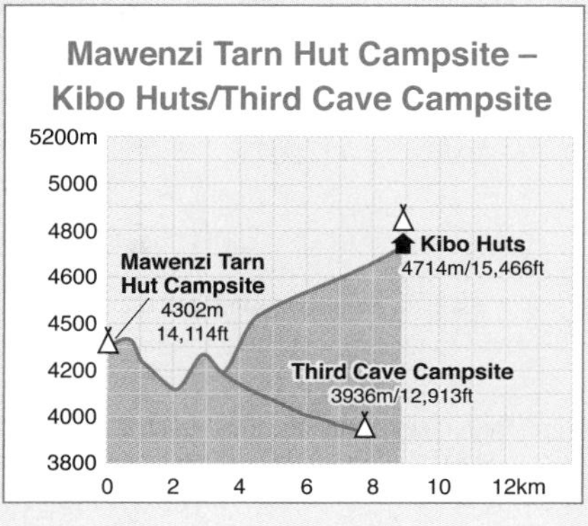

Depending on which hut you end up at, see p350 for the continuation of your walk up to Gillman's from Kibo Huts.

While if you ended up at Third Cave Campsite, read on (p348)...

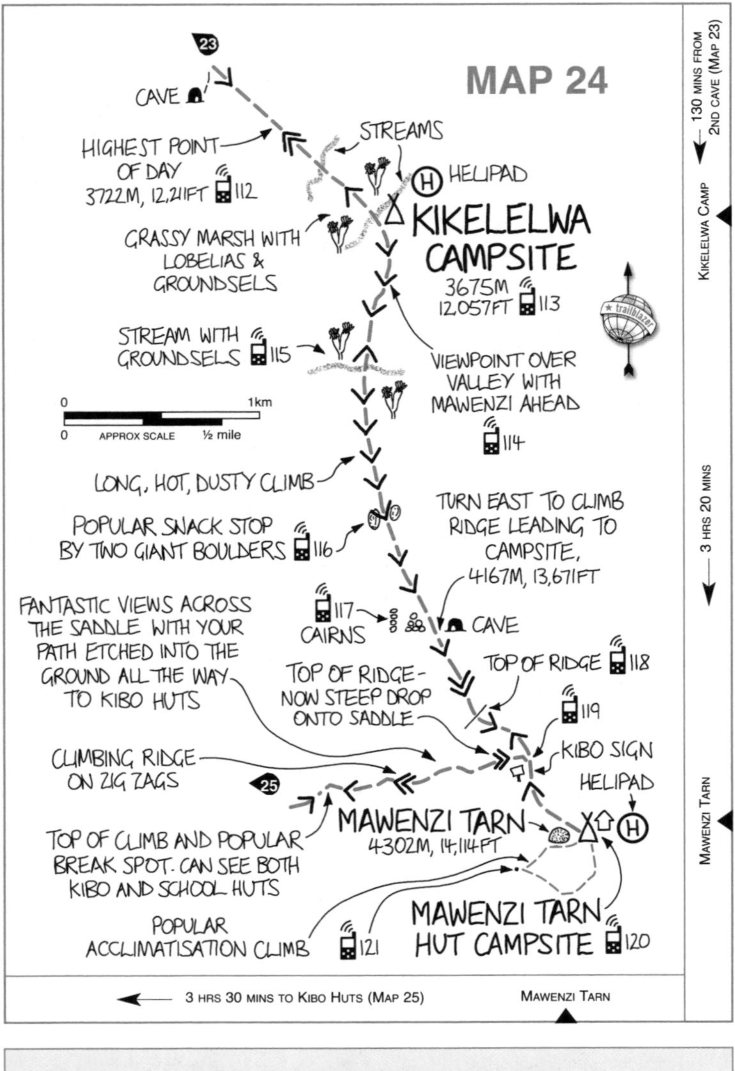

Note: Do remember that the times quoted are approximations and, more importantly, refer to **walking times only** with no time spent resting, taking photos etc.

Add on 30-50% to get an estimate of the total time spent on the trail.

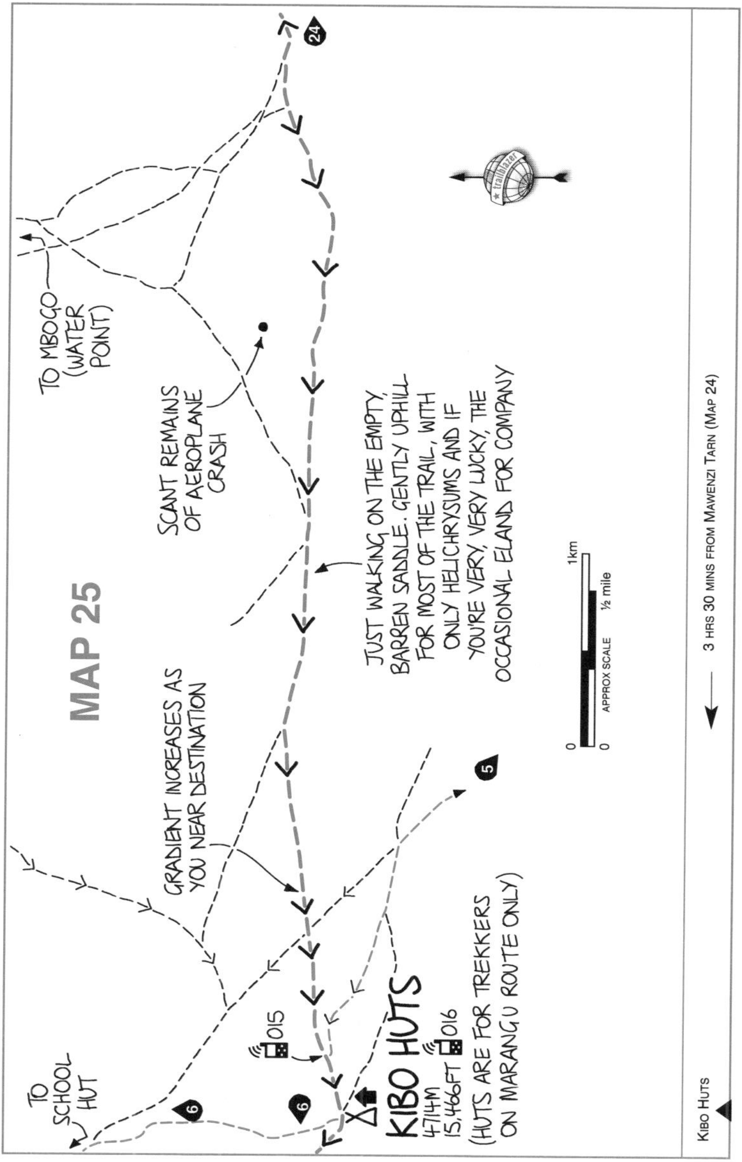

TRAIL GUIDE & MAPS

(cont'd from p345) That lies 20 minutes further on through lizard country of bare rocks and long grasses and is known as the **Second Cave** (3487m/11,440ft).

Before setting off in the afternoon, make sure you are on the correct trail, for the path to the Mawenzi Tarn Hut branches off at this point (see box p344): if your destination is the Third Cave Campsite but you find yourself heading south-east, reconsider. The path to the Third Cave begins behind and above the caves. Crossing a wide and usually dry riverbed, which in the rainy season is sometimes used as a playground by buffalos, the path continues drifting southwards across increasingly arid terrain, the 'dry flower' helichrysum now interspersed amongst the heathers.

While the walk between Second and Third Caves is, by Kilimanjaro standards, unremarkable, just before the halfway point there is, surreally, a '**cairn sculpture park**'. Here the more creative trekkers and porters have left dozens of elegantly arranged rocks and stones artfully balanced into pillars, peaks and other forms; a good place to take a break, methinks.

As huge rocks begin to appear to left and right, temporarily obscuring Mawenzi and Kibo, the unmistakable outline of toilet huts appear ahead on the trail, a sure sign that the campsite is nearing, this time to your left across another **broad and usually dry riverbed**. This is the **Third Cave Campsite** (3936m/12,913ft) where, in all probability, you'll be spending two nights and taking an acclimatisation day in between. During that day it's typical to head to the Saddle for an acclimatisation walk.

STAGE 3: THIRD CAVE CAMPSITE TO SCHOOL HUT [MAP 23, p343; MAP 26, opposite]

Distance: 4.8km (3 miles); altitude gained: 781m (2562ft)

This stage is little more than an *hors d'oeuvre* for the main course, which will be served at around midnight tonight. Yet it may surprise you to find out that over the course of this stage you climb 781m/2562ft. By the end of it you'll be on the eastern slopes of Kibo, with splendid views across the Saddle to Mawenzi.

Looking south-west from the Third Cave Campsite, you should be able to see much of today's path snaking over the undulations of Kibo.

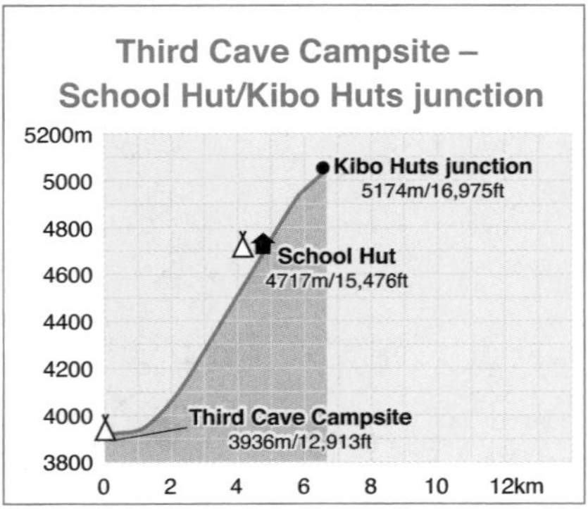

The path begins by retracing the last few steps of yesterday back to the **river bed**, which forks just a few minutes south of the campsite into two distinct tributaries. The path, too, divides at this junction and is signposted, with your trail heading off to the right (west), crossing the western tributary and continuing on towards the foot of Kibo. It's a slow slog southwards up the hill. Even the heathers struggle to survive up here, disappearing for the last time less than an hour outside camp; only the everlastings and the occasional yellow petalled senecio continue to thrive, providing a welcome relief from the relentless greys and browns of the rocky soil.

After about 75 minutes a summit of sorts is reached, whereafter the path now heads more to the west, directly towards Kibo. A porters' path bisects the trail around here, a path so seldom used that the junction is easily missed. No matter, for your path is clear as it bends more to the south, traversing **Kibo's eastern slopes** with the western face of Mawenzi now in full view to your left. Soon after, your guide may take you off the trail and down the hill a little to see the main sight of the day: a **buffalo carcass**, more than a decade old now but preserved by the dry conditions, mounted on top of a boulder. Originally the body was found wedged between some nearby rocks and one can only assume that the buffalo was up here looking for minerals, which they lick off the bare stone, but became trapped between the rocks and couldn't get out again.

The last bit of the walk is steep and the difficulty in getting oxygen into your lungs will leave you feeling quite exhausted. But after just over an hour

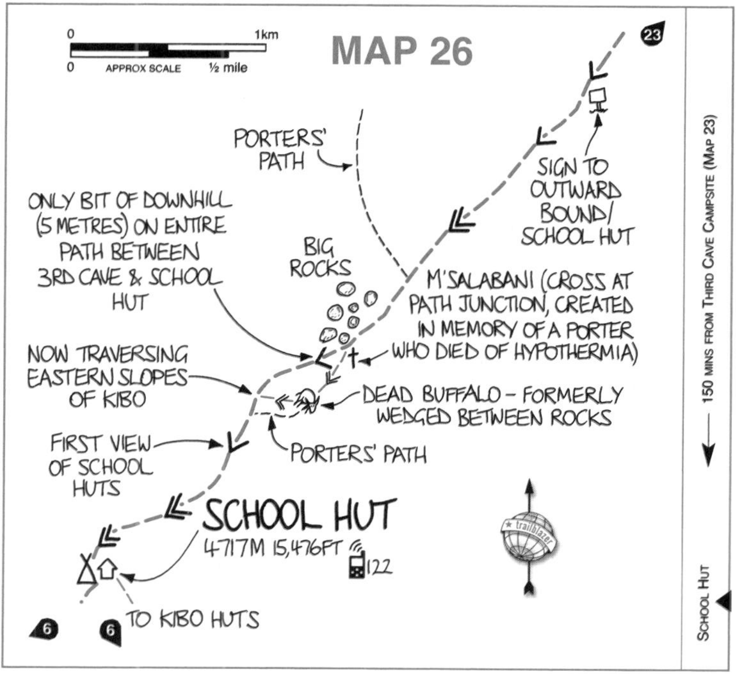

from the western bend in the path you finally reach the **School Hut** (marked as the Outward Bound Hut on some maps, its former name and one that KINAPA would prefer you didn't use), sitting in the shadow of some rather daunting cliffs. The hut sits at an altitude of about 4717m/15,476ft. This, incidentally, is virtually the same height as the Kibo Huts, which are larger, permanently manned by park staff, and the first place to head if you need emergency help. They lie around 45 minutes to the south, the path beginning by the southernmost toilet hut.

STAGE 4: SCHOOL HUT TO UHURU PEAK VIA JUNCTION WITH KIBO HUTS ROUTE [MAP 6, p291]

Distance: 1.9km (1¼ miles) to Kibo Huts route, plus 4km (2½ miles) to Uhuru Peak (5.9km/3¾ miles in total); altitude gained: 457m (1499ft) to Kibo Huts route, plus 721m (2365ft) to Uhuru Peak, 1178m (3865ft) total (see p289 for the Kibo Huts to Uhuru Peak profile)

The higher we climbed the rarer grew the atmosphere and the more brilliant the light of the stars. Never in my life have I seen anything to equal the steady lustre of this tropical starlight. The planets seemed to grow with a still splendour which was more than earthly, ... Assuredly, the nights of lower earth know nothing of this silver radiance.

Hans Meyer *Across East African Glaciers* (1891)

There is no direct trekking route from the School Hut to the crater rim. Instead, the path heads south from the huts to join up with the 'Tourist trail' running from Kibo Huts towards Gillman's Point – the trail I have dubbed the Kibo Huts Route. Your trail joins it between William's Point (5131m/16,834ft) and Hans Meyer Cave (5259m/17,254ft). In my experience, it takes slightly – though only slightly – less time from School Hut to this junction than it does from Kibo Huts, so you may wish to start this stage a little later than you would if walking from Kibo Huts – say at 12.15-12.30am rather than midnight.

Finding the start of the path from the School Hut can be a little tricky in the dark so I recommend you or your guide conduct a little reconnaissance while it's still light to ensure he knows where you're supposed to go. Once you're on the path, which starts with a scramble up the rocks behind the School Hut, the trail becomes fairly clear, being marked with cairns the whole way.

A repetitive pattern emerges during the walk: generally you are walking in a south-south-westerly direction over scree, but every so often the path turns more westerly and climbs more steeply over solid rock – these being petrified lava flows. At the end, a short descent brings you into the Kibo Huts 'valley' and a union with the path up to Gillman's.

After the isolation of the previous two hours, the number of trekkers on this path comes as something of a shock. Hans Meyer Cave lies just 20 minutes above you along a series of switchbacks.

For details of the path up to Gillman's Point from Hans Meyer Cave, turn to p290. For the descent you'll be using the Marangu Route, details of which can be found on pp360-2.

The Umbwe Route

If Marangu is the 'Coca Cola Route' and Machame has the nickname 'The Whiskey Route', what does that make Umbwe, (in)famous as the shortest **(24.7km/15 1/3 miles)** *, steepest and hardest of the trails on Kili? Sure, Machame is *fairly* steep here and there. But on Umbwe, the gradient is such that in a couple of places on the first two days you can stand on the trail and kiss it at the same time. What's more, it's only on the Umbwe Route that you'll be trekking on tree roots for parts of the second day. So while Machame is still popularly called 'The Whiskey Route', since it was remodelled a couple of decades ago that 'whiskey' has been rather watered down; and when compared to the unadulterated Umbwe Route, Machame starts to seem like pretty small beer.

That said, the Umbwe Route is still **a non-technical climb**. Taxing, but not technical. All you need are an iron will and legs of steel; this is truly a trek to test your mettle. The difficulty is that it's so damn relentlessly uphill. Indeed, looking back on the first couple of days I can think of very few places where you actually descend, the longest being the few minutes or so at the end of the second stage when you walk down to Barranco Campsite.

As far as rewards go, while your calves and thighs will curse the day God paired them with somebody who would want to undertake such a climb, your heart and lungs will be thankful for the workout. Your eyes, too, will be grateful you chose Umbwe as they feast upon the scenery, particularly on the second morning as you leave the forest and find yourself walking on a narrow ridge between spindly heathers. The gobsmacking views on either side of the trail here are amongst the most dramatic the mountain has to offer, save for those on the summit itself. Your ears, too, will be glad they're stuck to the side of your head rather than anyone else's for they'll enjoy the break, this being the quietest trail of them all – at least until the end of the second day when you find yourself joining the hordes at Barranco Camp, possibly the busiest on the mountain.

Once at Barranco, you can either follow the majority round to Barafu (for a total of **29.06km/18 miles** from gate to summit, thereby making it longer than the standard Rongai Route) and access the summit via Stella Point; or, if you hanker after the quieter, more dramatic option once again, you can join the path up to Lava Tower and continue to the summit via the Western Breach (see pp325-9). This latter option is the connoisseur's choice, no doubt, though be warned that it's an extremely risky strategy unless you take at least one – and

* It should be mentioned that if you don't visit Barranco Camp but head straight from the Umbwe Route to Arrow Glacier – as some speed ascent climbers do – the distance is even shorter at about 21.2km (13¼ miles).

preferably two – acclimatisation days en route to Arrow Glacier Campsite (see pp328-9 for more details). Otherwise, the trip from Moshi up to Arrow Glacier Campsite, an increase in altitude of almost 4000m/13,123ft, will have taken you just three days which is far too rapid. Do this and you can kiss your summit certificate – and possibly a lot more – goodbye.

So that's Umbwe: dramatic views, blessed solitude and some terrific, invigorating walking – and all without the clutter and chatter of other trekkers. Those who know the mountain consider it Kili's best-kept secret. It's hard to argue with that.

STAGE 1: UMBWE GATE TO UMBWE CAVE CAMPSITE

[MAP 27, p354; MAP 28, p356]

Distance: 9.9km (6¼ miles); altitude gained: 1293m (4242ft)

As the closest gate to Moshi, getting to the start of the Umbwe Route should be uncomplicated as long as the road is intact. Turning off the Moshi–Arusha road just 10 minutes after leaving the former, you bid farewell to the joys of tarmac by heading north on a mud track to Umbwe. Passing banana and coffee plantations you soon reach the gate, where there's little save for some toilets and a couple of friendly and under-worked rangers.

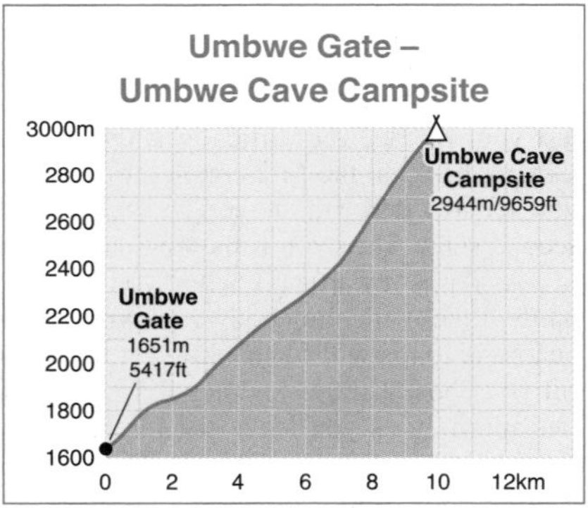

After the usual faffing around at the gate (1651m/5417ft), you eventually begin your walk by setting off on a 4WD road. With monkeys (blue and colobus) crashing in the trees, turacos gliding above them, chameleons stalking amongst the shrubbery and some of Kilimanjaro's more celebrated flora putting in an appearance, including a profusion of *Impatiens pseudoviola* and, further

❑ PHONE RECEPTION ON THE UMBWE ROUTE

Mobile reception on the Umbwe Route is good, though as always it depends a lot on which network you are with. I've sometimes managed to get a signal in the forest on this route, and on the second morning after struggling through the giant heathers I do often get reception. At Barranco reception is not good, though on the ridge before entering the camp it's OK. Then you have two options, of course: if you're taking the Western Breach, up to **Lava Tower** and **Arrow Glacier** it is fine, even up to **Crater Camp** and, so I've been told, almost to the summit.

As for those heading to the summit via Barafu, while it's not great at Karanga I've always got pretty good reception at **Barafu**; while at **Stella**, if you walk around enough, you can get it there too.

❑ ACCLIMATISING ON THE UMBWE ROUTE

Having trekked on the Umbwe Route on several occasions now, I have to confess I have properly fallen in love with the tranquillity and beauty of this trail. It's a joy. And I want other people to love it too. But there is one problem that has to be acknowledged: the route is simply too short and too steep to allow many people to acclimatise properly. As a result, the success rate for getting people to the summit is not as high as it is for the nearby Machame Route; and the risk of death is subsequently higher too.

However, there are a couple of simple remedies for this. Firstly, on the third day, having reached Barranco Camp the previous evening, you should then **take an acclimatisation day**. If you use that day to climb to Lava Tower before returning to camp, the altitude profile you have followed for the first three days almost exactly mimics that of the Machame Route: that is to say, on the first day you climb to around 3000m/9843ft (3021m/9911ft on Machame, 2944m/9659ft on Umbwe), on the second day you make it above 3800m/12,467ft (3839m/12,595ft at Shira Cave Campsite on Machame, 3986m/13,077ft at Barranco on Umbwe), while on the third day on both routes you reach 4627m/15,180ft at Lava Tower before sleeping at 3986m/13,077ft. So in theory the success rate should be pretty much identical too. What's more, there are several paths linking Barranco Campsite with Lava Tower – so you can take a different one for the descent than you did for the ascent.

The alternative to taking an acclimatisation day is to **climb Mount Meru first**, before tackling Umbwe over six days immediately afterwards. By tackling Meru, Kili's little brother, first, you will have already reached 4566m/14,980ft – excellent preparation for Umbwe. True, this itinerary will take more time (assuming you have a day off between the two climbs you're looking at around 11 days in total) and cost more money. But in terms of your overall experience of mountain conquering in Northern Tanzania, this is pretty much the best you can get. If I had 10 days and a few thousand dollars spare, this would be my choice without a doubt.

on, its more glamorous, beautiful, and rarer cousin, *Impatiens kilimanjari*, it's a fine start. Look out, too, for the forest lobelia, *Lobelia gibberoa*, with its strange phallic brush growing out of the top of the plant. This route is one of the few places where you can find them on the mountain, though they appear in greater abundance on Mount Meru. If it's the weekend, you'll also share the path with locals collecting fodder or firewood from the forest.

No matter how interesting this initial walk is, after almost two hours it comes as something of a relief when the road finally ends and the Umbwe Route 'proper' begins. It's a path that continues the north/north-north-east trend of the road, though in my opinion it's considerably more charming.

Almost 1½ hours after leaving the road you reach **Sarumba**, formerly an emergency campsite for those who set off from the gate very late but now used largely as a lunch stop. Soon after you bend right to **join a ridge**, and a spectacular one at that, with the great forested ravine of the Umbwe River on one side and the more modest dip of the Lonzo Stream on the other. No doubt you've also noticed that the trail is getting increasingly steeper. Indeed, this ridge is one of the steepest parts of the first day and in one or two places you'll

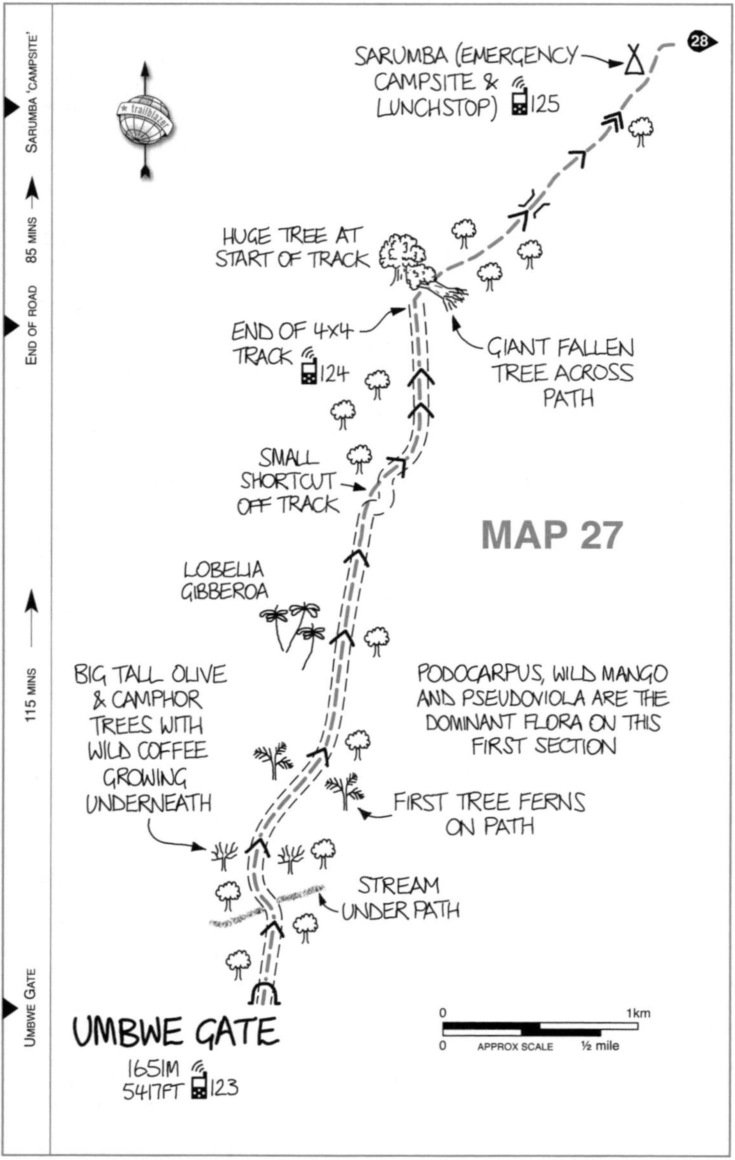
SARUMBA 'CAMPSITE'
85 MINS
END OF ROAD
115 MINS
UMBWE GATE
SARUMBA (EMERGENCY CAMPSITE & LUNCHSTOP) 125
28
HUGE TREE AT START OF TRACK
END OF 4X4 TRACK 124
GIANT FALLEN TREE ACROSS PATH
SMALL SHORTCUT OFF TRACK
MAP 27
LOBELIA GIBBEROA
BIG TALL OLIVE & CAMPHOR TREES WITH WILD COFFEE GROWING UNDERNEATH
PODOCARPUS, WILD MANGO AND PSEUDOVIOLA ARE THE DOMINANT FLORA ON THIS FIRST SECTION
FIRST TREE FERNS ON PATH
STREAM UNDER PATH
UMBWE GATE
1651M 5417FT 123
0 1km
0 APPROX SCALE ½ mile

be using the tree roots to haul yourself up with your hands. Luckily, there are plenty of tree roots around. The forest around here is rich and dark, the forest canopy minimising the amount of light that filters through to the path. Distract yourself from the muffled screaming coming from your calf muscles by admiring the beauty of the forest here, the trees all knobbled, gnarled and heavy with moss. In between breaths, check out the beautiful red *Impatiens kilimanjari*, too, growing between those same tree roots that are helping you progress along the route.

The gradient relents not a jot as you continue along the ridge and across three bridges, the last of which immediately precedes **Umbwe Cave Campsite** (2944m/9659ft). More a glorified overhang than a proper cave, the adjacent campsite dribbles up the ridge and is a charming spot; a quiet place hidden in the upper reaches of the forest.

STAGE 2: UMBWE CAVE CAMPSITE TO BARRANCO HUTS

[MAP 28, p356; MAP 29, p357]

Distance: 5.1km (3¼ miles); altitude gain: 1042m (3419ft)

This second stage of the Umbwe Route is a showcase for the weird and wonderful. It's the stage where you move from the forest, past a magical stretch of giant heathers and on to the moorland zone where giant groundsels – surely the strangest plants on Kilimanjaro – grow in abundance.

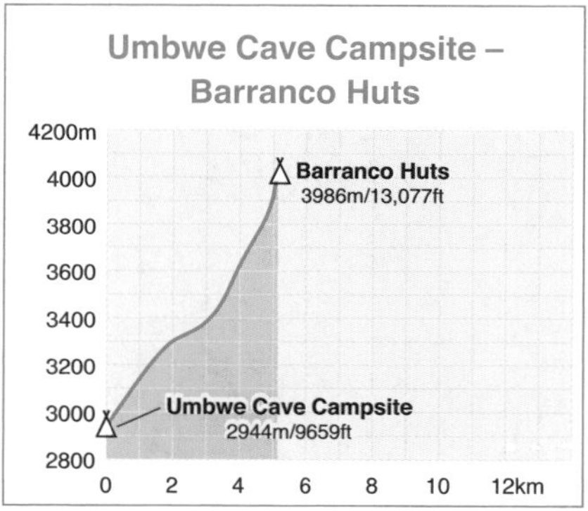

The walking, as with yesterday's stage, is pretty much uphill all the way, and for much of it you'll again be relying on the nearby heathers for handholds as you haul yourself up the trail. It's hard work but again it's tiring rather than technical and thus nothing to fear. By the end you will have reached Barranco Huts, a wonderful spot serving a number of routes and on the border of the alpine desert. Note that Machame Route trekkers will have taken three days to get to this camp, and those on the Lemosho Route four; but it's taken you just two. It should remind you, if you didn't know before, of the importance of building in rest days on the Umbwe Route and of taking it *pole pole* from now on. (See p246 for advice on this.)

The stage starts with a tramp through one of the prettiest sections – no, make that *the* prettiest section – of heathland on the entire mountain, the sunlight penetrating through the giant heathers to dapple the carpet of soft mossy grass. I've never seen heather forest so thick, so uniform, so laden with bearded lichen nor so gorgeous. Though normally lumped together with the moorland above it, here, as with the Mweka Route that you'll be tackling on the way down, the heather zone is so very distinct from it.

As the path veers to the left you notice you're overlooking the vertiginous valley of the Lonzo Stream (a tributary of the Weru Weru) while veer right and you find yourself staring down the giddying ravine of the Umbwe – and you suddenly realise you're balanced on a knife-edge ridge. Vertigo sufferers should perhaps concentrate instead on Kibo which, if the weather's on your side, glistens magnificently ahead.

Around 40 minutes after breaking camp you reach **Jiwe Kamba**, or 'Rope Rock', the name providing a clue as to how trekkers used to tackle this section. The rope's gone now and the park authority has built two paths either side of the rock, so there's no need to clamber *over* it at all any more. Even without this

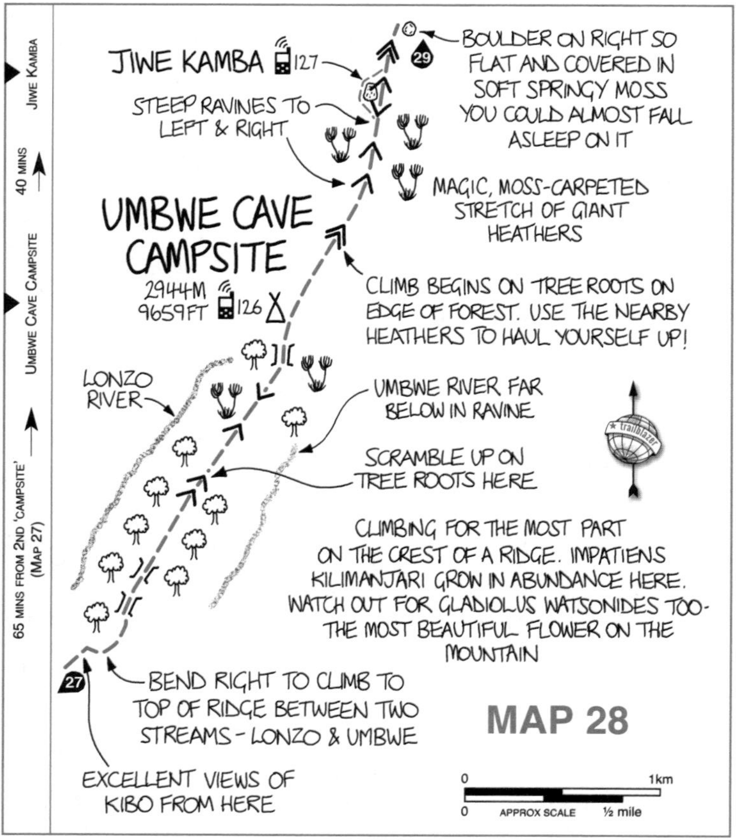

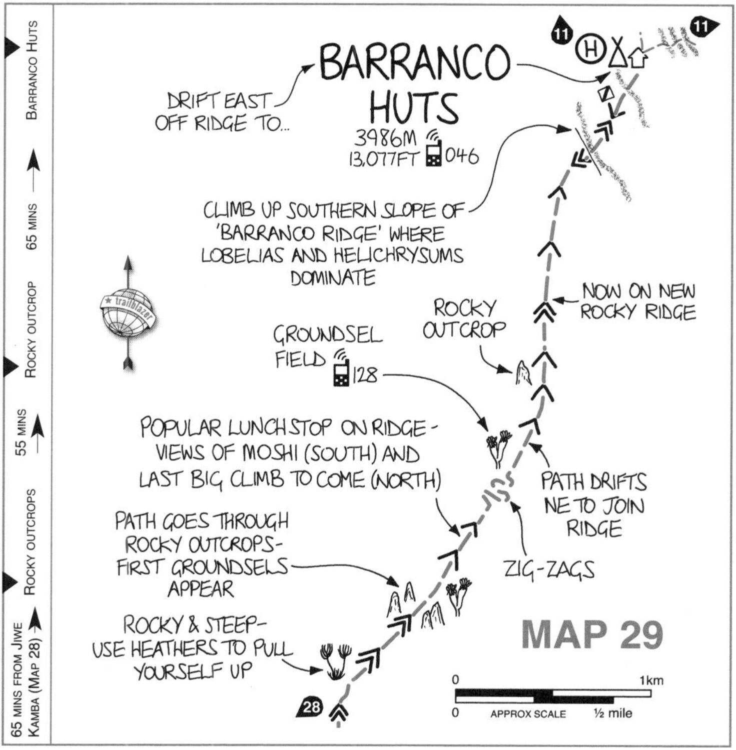

obstacle, however, this is still a testing stretch, as the giant heathers that line the path testify, their trunks burnished like the feet of some sacred icon by the hands of trekkers who have struggled up here before you, grasping onto the nearby vegetation in order to heave themselves up the slope.

As you progress further north the first helichrysums appear, their paper texture and white colour contrasting with the scarlet mountain gladioli, *Gladiolus watsonides*, which survives in both the forest and heathland zones and surely rivals the impatiens and orchids as the most beautiful flower on the mountain. Continue still further and amongst the tussock grass and rocky outcrops the first **groundsels** also put in an appearance, a plant that will dominate the surrounding scenery for the next hour or so.

The ridge which you've been following eventually merges with a new one which you also climb and then follow, still heading north and with Mount Meru now a spectator in the distance to the west. Climbing to yet another rocky ridge, you continue your progress north towards what I will call Barranco Ridge, which you start to climb before turning off right and down to **Barranco Huts** campsite (3986m/13,077ft). For a description, please turn to p304.

It is at Barranco that you have a choice to make: left, north-west and up for Lava Tower Campsite, Arrow Glacier Campsite and the path via the Western Breach to the summit. Or right and east to Karanga, Barafu and the trail up to Uhuru Peak via Stella Point. You will, of course, have already decided one way or the other before you even set foot on the mountain. Whatever route you've opted for, I hope that you factored into your itinerary an acclimatisation day at Barranco. If so, the next stage will be relevant to you too even if you'll be heading in the opposite direction, to Karanga and Barafu, the next day – you can read about this trail on p304. Whereas if you're gunning for the Western Breach, just read on...

STAGE 3: BARRANCO HUTS TO LAVA TOWER CAMPSITE [MAP 11, p303; MAP 10, p301]

Distance: 3.2km (2 miles); altitude gained: 641m (2103ft)

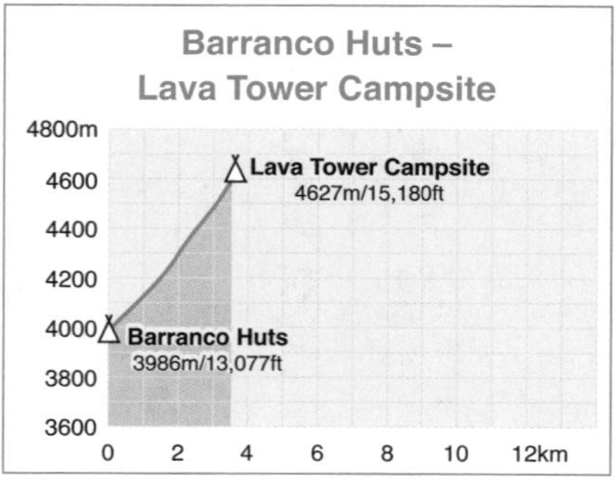

Many of the trails on Kili started as porters' routes. That is to say, the porters established them before the guides and their clients adopted them and, eventually, the authorities too. Furthermore, it is of course the nature of porters to find the quickest route from A to B, with little thought given as to whether it's a pretty or attractive – or even safe! – route.

So it is with today's trail from Barranco up to Lava Tower, from where you start your climb up to the Western Breach. It's a short-cut that was established by porters hurrying down from Arrow Glacier or Lava Tower round to the Mweka Route, in order to meet their clients arriving down from the summit. This trail has become so established as to render the previous route just about obsolete. (That previous route, by the way, continued along the crest of the ridge to the west of Barranco Campsite to the signposted junction at the head of the Barranco Valley and is still marked on most maps though it's a rare guide – indeed, anyone – who'll follow it these days.)

The only problem with this new route is that, as mentioned, it *is* a short-cut, and one moreover used by porters to *descend* from the mountain. As such, as an ascent route many people find it entirely too short and will have succumbed to the pain of altitude sickness by the stage's end. I therefore recommend you take this into consideration and, as discussed several times already, maybe factor two nights at Barranco into your itinerary, with the rest day spent sauntering up to the head of the valley to help you get used to the rarified atmosphere.

The stage begins with a walk up the Barranco Valley. Come here later in the day and you'll find yourself hiking against a tide of trekkers on the Machame, Lemosho and Shira routes all coming the other way down the same path. But assuming you've started walking in the morning it will probably be just you and your crew, allowing you to enjoy undisturbed views of Kibo through the stands of **groundsels**.

About 25 minutes after setting off you leave the main path by a **waterfall** as you continue north, eventually crossing the **stream** you've been following since the day's beginning (and, indeed, as further down it turns into the Umbwe River, since the start of the whole trek). Recrossing it further upstream, you'll find yourself on a slightly gentler trail which continues straight ahead over two streams and on, steeply, up to **Lava Tower**. The entire walking, without breaks, would have taken you just 3¼ hours and you'll probably be at Lava Tower by lunch, allowing you plenty of time to savour this grim campsite's uniquely chilly, godforsaken 'charm'.

For details of the rest of the walk from Lava Tower to the summit, see p326.

❑ **NEW ASCENT ROUTES**

For details of the new ascent routes (Kidia and Irkasswa) see pp387-8.

The descent routes

Do not underestimate the descent!

I'm willing to bet that you've spent a lot of time imagining what it's like to climb Kili – and barely any time wondering what it's like coming down off it again. Which is rather unfortunate, because for many people getting off the mountain after summiting is actually the most difficult part of the whole experience. As one of our climbers, Margaret Brownell, summarised in her post-trek email: *'Going up is only about 40% of the effort on summit day.'*

It's also true that more people injure themselves on the way down than they do on the way up; released from the constraints of *pole pole*, the urge to hurtle down to warmer, more oxygen-rich climes can be impossible to resist. But even if you manage to avoid injury, coming down off the summit is just really hard physically. This is particularly true for older climbers (ie those aged 40 or above), for the impact on your joints, particularly the knees, of all those downhill steps, can be excruciating.

So as you make your way to the top of Kili, do spend a little time thinking about how you're going to get down from it too. Try to **make sure the outer layers you wore to the summit are easy to remove for the way down**, for the mountain warms up quickly once day breaks. Make sure, too, **you've got some**

water left, as it may be a couple of hours before you can get some more. And most importantly of all, unless you're having problems with the altitude and need to descend as quickly as possible, **don't be in too much of a hurry to get back down**; you'll be very tired, you'll probably feel a little lightheaded, and the path from the summit, particularly on the Mweka Route, is one long 13-mile trip hazard. And can you really say you've completed Kili if you were actually carried down on a stretcher for some of the descent?

There are two ways off the mountain. Those who took the Machame, Lemosho, Shira and Umbwe routes to get to the summit take the Mweka descent, which I describe on pp362-8; while those who took the Rongai and Marangu routes on the way up descend by the Marangu Route, which I'll look at now.

MARANGU ROUTE

Stage 1: Uhuru Peak to Gillman's Point to the Horombo Huts [Map 33, p371; Map 6, p291; Map 5, p287; Map 4, p286]

Distance: 15.75km (9¾ miles); (16.55km/10¼ miles – for Mawenzi alternative); altitude lost: 2174m (7133ft)

Few people remain at the summit for long: weariness, the risk of hypothermia and the thought of a steaming mug of Milo at the Kibo Huts are enough to send most people scurrying down. There are **two main ways** of doing this: the **first** is to follow exactly the course from Gillman's to Kibo that you took getting up here, carefully retracing every zig and zag like somebody who has dropped a contact lens on the way up but can't quite remember when or where. It is precisely those people who are in greatest need of getting down fast who usually use this slower method to descend.

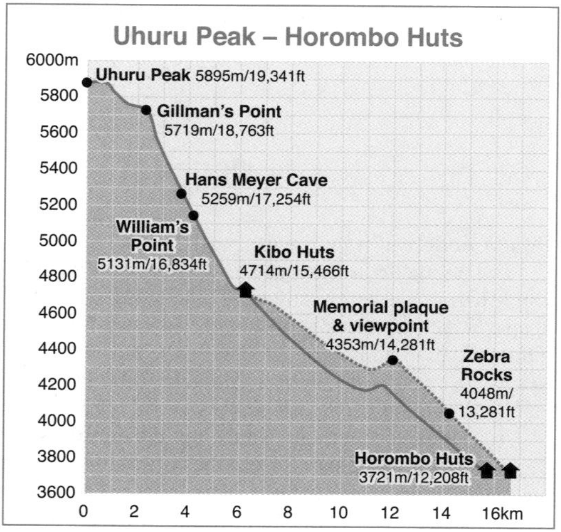

The **second way** is to cut straight through the switchbacks and simply head vertically downwards in a sort of ski-style, using the now defrosted scree to act as a brake on your momentum as you push against it with the soles of your boots, heels first. After the tedium of the previous night's *pole pole*, heel-to-toe exercise, the sheer abandon of this method and the rapid progress made – it takes just over 90 minutes to travel from Gillman's to the huts this way – comes as something of a relief. Take care, however: far more people are injured going down than going up. Furthermore, do remember that every year at least 20,000 pairs of feet tread on this part of the mountain and, at the risk of sounding like a killjoy, pushing down all that scree cannot be doing the mountain any good. Indeed, may I politely request that you use this faster method only if you need to descend rapidly? Otherwise, stick to the switchbacks which will be far less damaging to the mountain – and safer too.

Upon returning to Kibo Huts, your guide should allow you to rest for an hour at least before moving on again to the **Horombo Huts**. If you ascended on the Marangu Route, heed the advice given at the beginning of Stage 3 (see p285) and ask your guide to take you back via a different route to the one on which you ascended. This usually means returning via the Saddle on the Mawenzi Route, a route I describe in the box below. If you return via the southerly, 'usual' route, expect it to take 3¼ hours from Kibo Huts.

If you took the Marangu Route up the mountain, you'll be sleeping in the huts again; while those who took the Rongai Route, which also uses this path to descend, will be camping outside them.

Stage 2: Horombo Huts to Marangu Gate [Map 4, p286; Map 3, p283; Map 2, p281; Map 1, p279]

Distance: 20km (12½ miles); altitude lost: 1816m (5958ft)

Don't be in too much of a hurry to finish your trekking, for today holds lots of

❑ RETURNING VIA THE MAWENZI ROUTE [MAP 5, p287; MAP 4, p286]

This is the more interesting path between Kibo and Horombo Huts, encompassing entire groves of giant groundsels (*Senecio kilimanjari*), Zebra Rocks (see p285) and perhaps the best panorama of them all on Kili. It is also seldom used.

From Kibo Huts the path descends once more to **Jiwe La Ukoyo** (see p288). Though there appears to be but one path from Jiwe, there is in fact another, much fainter path heading more directly towards Mawenzi across The Saddle. If you cannot make it out at first don't worry, just aim for Mawenzi and you will soon notice a faint but distinct path etched into the earth. Ten minutes after Jiwe a junction with the even-fainter **Northern Circuit** is reached (a signpost is the only evidence that there is a junction here at all), and 35 minutes after that the path begins to rise and fall as it follows the contours of Mawenzi's lower reaches.

After another 35 minutes following this undulating terrain you come to a summit of sorts, from where you can rest by a **memorial plaque** (Map 4) and gaze back over what is, in my humble opinion, the finest **panorama** this mountain has to offer: the alpine desert of The Saddle, with a string of parasitic cones leading from the foreground to the foot of Kibo and with Mawenzi just over your shoulder. Spectacular. From here, the path runs due south through heather, past the path leading up to Mawenzi Hut and on to **Zebra Rocks**, then down between the groundsel gullies until, 70 minutes from the unforgettable panorama and 2½ hours since leaving Jiwe La Ukoyo, the roofs of **Horombo Huts** appear beneath you.

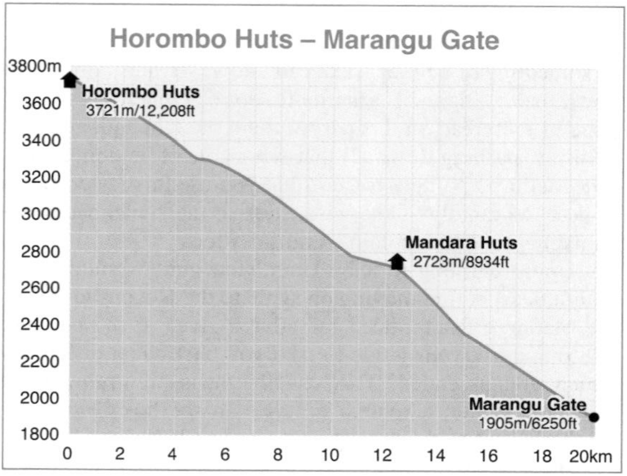

treats for those who take the time to enjoy them. If you have come from the Rongai Route this is the first time you will have seen forest so thick and vast on Kilimanjaro, and it's worth taking the time to appreciate the different flora on this side of the mountain. But even if you ascended by the Marangu Route, it still warrants a second look on the way down. Much of the scenery may be old hat to you by now but remember you've still paid US$70 in park fees alone for the privilege of walking in the forest today, so you may as well make the most of it. And just as Lee Marvin in *Paint Your Wagon* sang that he'd never seen a town 'that didn't look better looking back', so most people will agree that the forest seems so much more welcoming when you're walking *downhill* through it and the views of Kibo are that much more appealing from over the shoulder, knowing you'll never have to climb it again.

It takes about 2 hours 20 minutes to return from Horombo Huts to the **Mandara Huts** which are, typically, the final lunchstop of the trail. From there, it's back into the forest and down to the **gate**, a journey of some 95 minutes. Name registered, tips dispersed and with certificate clutched close to your bosom (you can actually get it laminated at the bookshop at the gate), it's time to return to the land of hot showers and flush toilets. Your adventure is at an end – and civilisation will rarely have felt so good.

After we had taken our baths, and Loren had photographed my heels for posterity, we got dressed and walked to the polished dining room. Paul and Jan were eating silently at one table; other climbers at others. We felt a camaraderie as we sat down to eat. We were very tired, far more tired than hungry, but we were also away in some special world reserved for exhausted athletes, a world in which triumph is muted, the gains countered by the costs.

Michael Crichton, taken from *Travels*, essays about his worldwide wanderings.

THE MWEKA ROUTE

The Mweka Route (21km/13 miles from summit to civilisation) is the designated descent route for the Machame, Lemosho/Shira and Umbwe routes. As such, it is a very busy route. Frequent repair work ensured that the latter section through the forest is once more in good condition, though the same cannot be said of the trail that precedes it, down to Mweka Huts, which has treacherous loose rolling stones, slippery smooth rocks and other hazards en route. It's awful. Good luck!

Stage 1: Uhuru Peak to Barafu Huts and Mweka Huts [Map 33, p371; Map 13, p309; Map 30, p364; Map 31, p366]

Distance: 11.5km (7¼ miles); altitude lost: 2789m (9150ft)

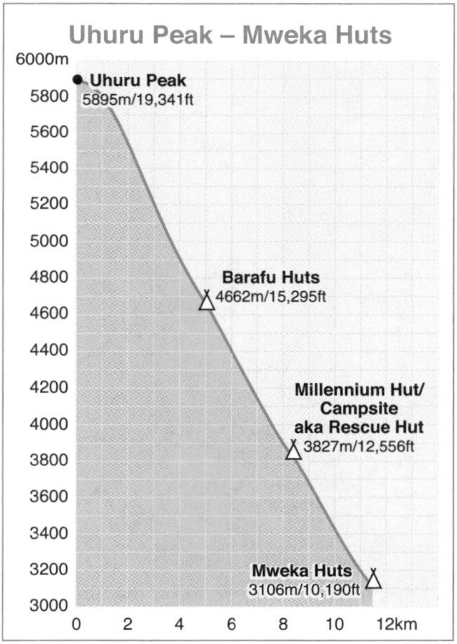

What goes up must come down and that includes you. The path back to Barafu is little more than a retracing of your steps of the previous night (assuming you climbed this way and not the Western Breach Route), though there is a slightly quicker, if more hair-raising approach: descending from Stella Point, after 10 minutes or so you reach a **boulder** which earlier that morning you would have walked around: it's the same boulder that on the ascent marked the very steep last 30 minutes or so to the crater rim.

This boulder also marks the start of a **straight ski-run down** through the gravel that bypasses the zigzags of the regular route. Some people prefer to make it down as quickly as possible so choose this trail; others find it too taxing on both nerves and knees and opt for the **gentler descent**. You will need to decide which is for you, but if possible take the slower option. Note, too, that with the 'faster' descent it's not so easy to find your way back to Barafu: at one point you must turn right to rejoin the main path to camp or you risk ending up being lost in the valley below. A Korean trekker did this in 2008 – and has never been seen again. The entire descent takes about two hours from Stella Point, less if you take the 'fast' route.

You probably feel, on returning to camp, that you have earned the luxury of a brief rest at **Barafu**, and indeed you have. But make sure it *is* brief, for you still have another 150 minutes of knee-knackering downhill before you reach Mweka Huts, your probable home for the night. A pretty monotonous 2½ hours it is, too, as you head off due south and down for the entire 6.64km/4 miles. In its defence, the descent is both large (dropping from 4662m/15,295ft to 3106m/10,190ft) and fairly gradual, which can only be good news for AMS

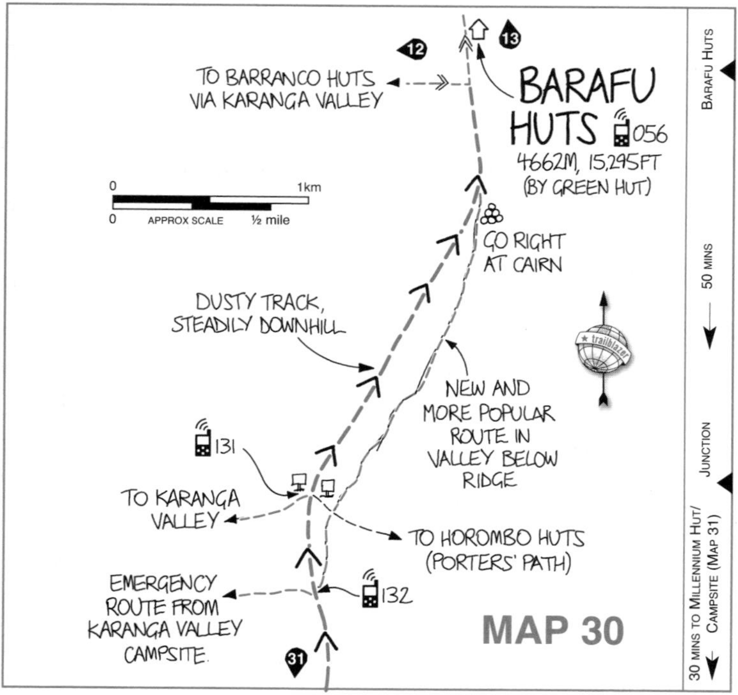

sufferers. There is also some interest to be had in seeing how the vegetation changes along the way: at first, only the incredibly hardy yellow senecios are able to survive at the high altitude, but they are soon joined by their dry-looking cousins in the *helichrysum* family. Not long after that the first heathers appear, to be joined a little later by the proteas. However, it must be said that the **actual path is the worst on the mountain**, full of loose rocks that shift when trodden upon, causing already weary trekkers to stumble, fumble, fall and swear their way down.

Around 50 minutes or so from Barafu you come to a **junction**, marked with a signpost or two, with the little-used Southern Circuit: to your left on the slopes you can see paths from Horombo Huts on the Marangu Route, while to your right are those coming from the Karanga Valley. Another path, an emergency trail from Karanga Campsite for those suffering from altitude, joins the Mweka Route just above the green-roofed hut. This hut was originally established to help out the suffering during the millennium when the mountain was swamped by thousands hoping to see the new era in from the summit. It's remained ever since and, now called the **Rescue Hut** or, more commonly, **Millennium Hut/**

Campsite (though the sign by the warden's hut calls it, rather prosaically, **High Camp**; 3827m/12,556ft), is a campsite for those who prefer something a little quieter than the Mweka Huts; it's also a useful site to use when the Mweka campsite has been flooded by heavy rain. There is also a water source nearby – another advantage over the Mweka Huts and one of the reasons, perhaps, why more and more groups are choosing to stay here.

Immediately afterwards, giant heathers grow for the first time by the dusty path and, further down, the vanilla-coloured **protea** makes its first appearance, and thereafter dominates the pathside vegetation. The protea's presence ensures a healthy population of **malachite sunbirds** live around here too, as well as the little green **montane white-eyes** – so-called because of the distinctive white ring around their eyes. **Chameleons**, surprisingly, also make the heather their home.

You first glimpse **Mweka Huts** (3106m/10,190ft) about 40 minutes before you actually get there as you descend on a ridge between two valleys towards a small heather-clad hill. Rounding this, the path widens and flattens before turning south-west and climbing for a few seconds on the final section to the camp – the only ascent of the entire walk from Barafu. Mweka Huts is unremarkable; the eco-toilets they installed that I raved about in the last edition are now sadly a bit of a blemish on the campsite: malodorous, fly-filled and poo-stained. Nevertheless, Mweka is a happy camp. The porters are happy, for tomorrow is their last day of work and is pregnant with promises of wages and tips. Those climbers who managed to make it to Uhuru Peak are also happy, of course, and often quite jubilant. But even those who didn't make it to the top will find a happiness of sorts in being here, if only because they'll no longer have to walk on that bloody terrible path from Millennium Hut/Campsite again. Even the phone reception is pretty good, which cheers up virtually everyone.

By the way, you may wish to share out your tips at Mweka Huts before you depart on this last leg: as porters all walk at different speeds, this may be the last time the whole group is together.

Stage 2: Mweka Huts to Mweka Gate [Map 31, p366; Map 32, p367]

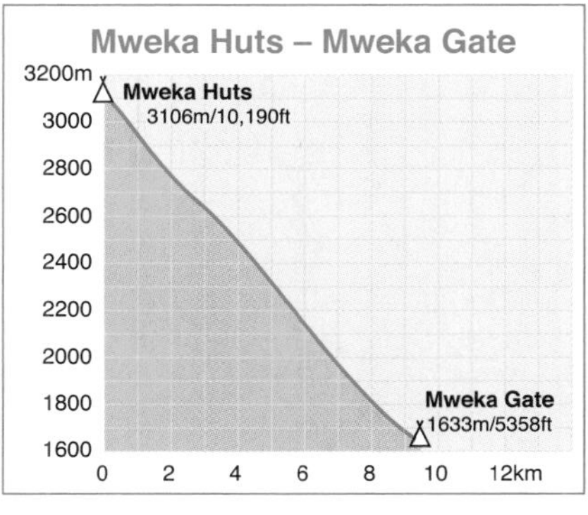

Distance: 9.5km (6 miles); altitude lost: 1473m (4833ft)
By now you'll probably just want to get off the mountain as quickly as possible. But before you think of cashing in on your helicopter rescue insurance and getting a lift down, I should point out that there's still lots of interest to be had before you bid farewell to the mountain. This final section of the path has now thankfully been fully restored following years of over-use. *(cont'd on p368)*

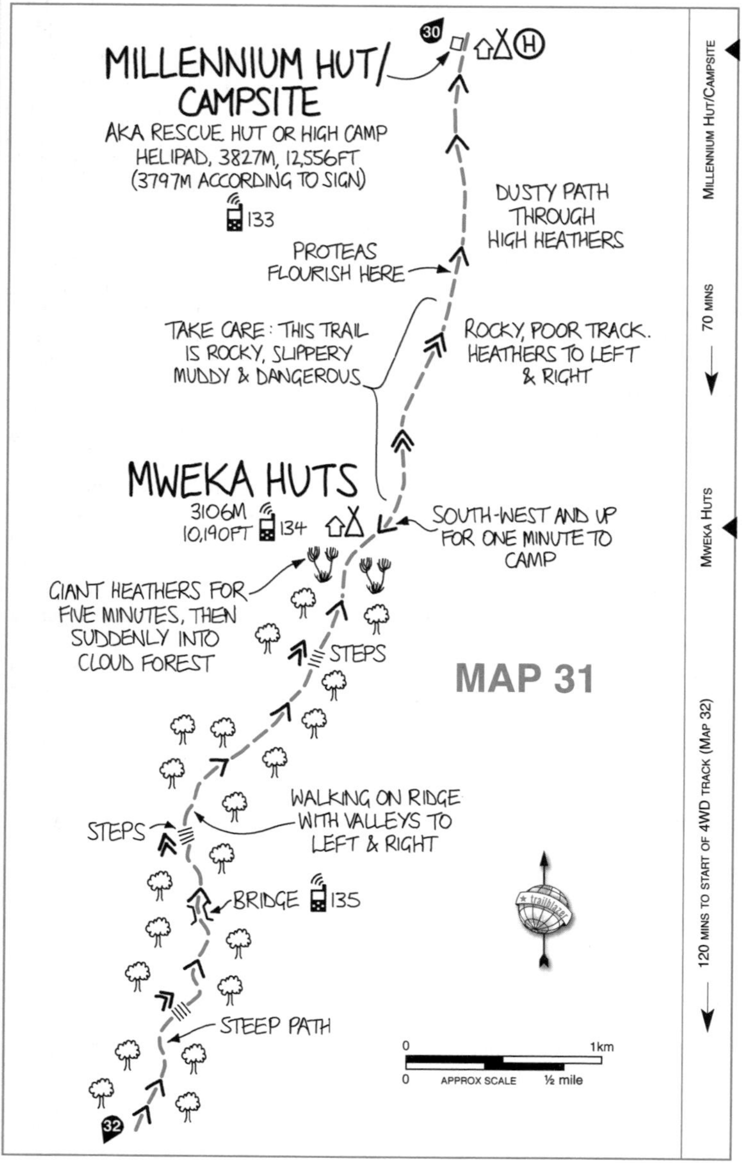
MILLENNIUM HUT/ CAMPSITE
AKA RESCUE HUT OR HIGH CAMP
HELIPAD, 3827M, 12,556FT
(3797M ACCORDING TO SIGN)
133
30
DUSTY PATH THROUGH HIGH HEATHERS
PROTEAS FLOURISH HERE
TAKE CARE: THIS TRAIL IS ROCKY, SLIPPERY MUDDY & DANGEROUS
ROCKY, POOR TRACK. HEATHERS TO LEFT & RIGHT
MWEKA HUTS
3106M 10,190FT
134
SOUTH-WEST AND UP FOR ONE MINUTE TO CAMP
GIANT HEATHERS FOR FIVE MINUTES, THEN SUDDENLY INTO CLOUD FOREST
STEPS
MAP 31
WALKING ON RIDGE WITH VALLEYS TO LEFT & RIGHT
STEPS
BRIDGE
135
STEEP PATH
32
0
1km
0
APPROX SCALE
½ mile
trailblazer
MILLENNIUM HUT/CAMPSITE
70 MINS
MWEKA HUTS
120 MINS TO START OF 4WD TRACK (MAP 32)

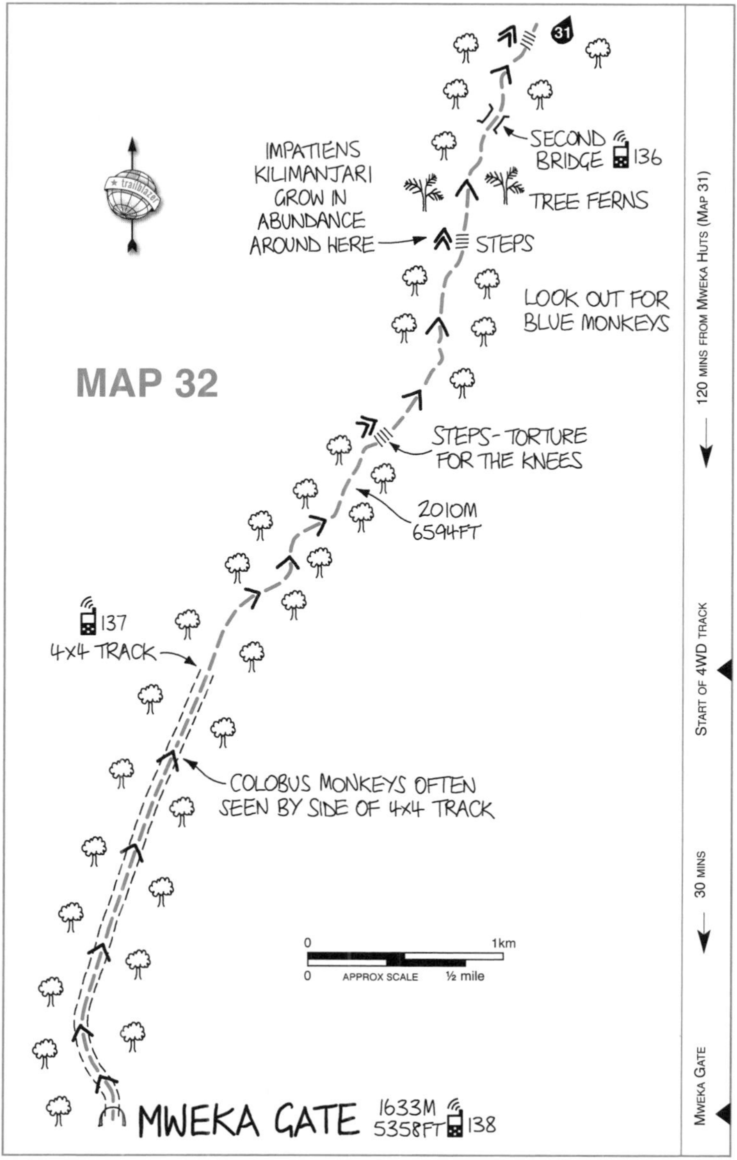
MAP 32
31
IMPATIENS KILIMANJARI GROW IN ABUNDANCE AROUND HERE
SECOND BRIDGE 136
TREE FERNS
STEPS
LOOK OUT FOR BLUE MONKEYS
STEPS- TORTURE FOR THE KNEES
2010M 6594FT
137
4x4 TRACK
COLOBUS MONKEYS OFTEN SEEN BY SIDE OF 4x4 TRACK
0 1km
0 APPROX SCALE ½ mile
MWEKA GATE
1633M 5358FT 138
120 MINS FROM MWEKA HUTS (MAP 31)
START OF 4WD TRACK
30 MINS
MWEKA GATE

(cont'd from p365) The only complaint I have is that the authorities have decided to build steps on the steep parts, which I am sure is good for combatting erosion – but after five days or so of climbing, your knees will be screaming for mercy by the end. This last section follows a very pretty forest trail alive with birdsong and flowers – but whether your mind can concentrate on anything other than the pain in your joints is another matter. Still, if you were having trouble acclimatising to the lack of oxygen available further up the slopes, you'll be delighted by the atmosphere here, which feels so thick and replete with O_2 that you'll wonder why it's not visible.

This stage begins in similar fashion to much of the previous one, by heading south and down. Less than five minutes after you start walking you find yourself in **cloud forest**, the border between this and the giant heather forest so definite and distinct that you could almost draw a line in the ground between the two. Once again walking on a narrow ridge between two valleys, look around and notice how the trees now grow in height and girth, how the moss that grows upon them is thick, green and hearty where before it was stringy and limp, and how flowers such as the *Impatiens kilimanjari* once again make an appearance, and in abundance too. Its cousin *Impatiens pseudoviola* also lines the path, while the occasional, beautiful vivid red mountain gladiolus flourishes here and there, the delicate white flowers of the wild blackberry grow in clusters and the alabaster-white petals of the *Begonia meyeri johannis* litter the trail towards the end.

Around two hours after breaking camp, you'll find yourself walking on the **start of the 4WD track** down to the gate which lies a further 30 minutes away.

At **Mweka Gate** (1633m/5358ft) you can usually buy a souvenir T-shirt to advertise the fact you reached the summit (curiously, there are no equivalent T-shirts for those that did not).

You must also sign the last **registration book** at the nearby park office, from where those who were successful can collect the appropriate certificate. Those who succeeded in reaching Uhuru Peak can usually be seen standing around, their certificates dangling casually yet deliberately from their hands so they are clearly visible to passers-by, in much the same way that Ferrari owners are wont to display their car keys.

Your mountain odyssey is almost at an end: from here, it's a 30-minute drive back to the land of power showers, flush toilets and cold, cold beer. You've earned it – though if you do plan to celebrate in Moshi, please take more care than Hans Meyer did upon his return to town in 1889:

In the evening, to show there was no ill-feeling, I treated the natives to a display of fireworks, in the course of which a spark from a rocket set fire to one of the men's huts.

THE SUMMIT

10

What's at the top?

The crater of Kilimanjaro is a primeval place and decidedly uncomfortable, yet I was drawn to it. The idea of spending some days and nights awoke a compelling mixture of reverential fear and wonder; similar, I suspect, to the compulsion which draws some people unquestioningly to church. And like churches, the crater also invites contemplation of the eternal mysteries.

John Reader *Kilimanjaro* (1982)

It's only when you reach the top of Kibo that you realise the mountain really is a volcano, and all you have done is climb onto the crater rim.

The rim itself is largely featureless, though as the highest point on the mountain it has assumed a pre-eminent role and is the focus of all trekkers. Many of the bumps and tumescences on it have been dignified with the word 'Spitze' or 'Point' as if they were major summits in their own right. Heading clockwise around the rim from **Gillman's**, these features in order are: **Bismark Towers**, **Stella Point** (where those climbing from Barafu first reach the rim), **Elveda** and **Hans Meyer points** and **Uhuru Peak**; while just to the north of Gillman's is **Johannes Notch**, **Leopard Point** and **Hans Meyer Notch**. The distance between Gillman's and Uhuru is a little over 2km, with the crater rim rising 176m (577ft) between the two. The floor of the crater, covered in brown shale and rocks and boulders of all shapes and sizes, lies between 25m/82ft (at Gillman's) and 200m/656ft (at Uhuru Peak) beneath this rim.

Trudging around the rim to Uhuru is achievement enough. There are, however, other diversions to keep you on the summit for longer ...

WALKING ON THE SUMMIT [Map 33, p371]

For most people the conquest of Uhuru Peak and a nice certificate that says as much is reason enough to climb Kilimanjaro. Some trekkers, however, always want to do just that little bit more and if you still have some energy to burn once you've reached the summit you may care to take a quick tour around the crater itself.

Sleeping in the Crater

Most people who tour around the crater will also sleep in the crater – and will have paid extra for the privilege of doing so. There's a US$100 per person fee for this levied by KINAPA, supposedly to pay for maintaining the campsite. Your trekking company might also

ask for more in order to compensate their porters, who would normally climb to just 4662m/15,295ft (Barafu Huts), 4714m/15,466ft (Kibo Huts), 4717m/15,476ft (School Huts) or 4871m/15,981ft (Arrow Glacier), but are now being asked to lug their baggage up to 5729m/18,796ft (the altitude of Crater Camp). Factor in the extra day you should really add to your trek as you'll need to make sure you're properly acclimatised, and you're probably looking at paying around US$250-400 extra to sleep there, though it can be less.

The standard way to reach Crater Camp is to ascend via the Western Breach (see p325). The campsite is, after all, close to the point where climbers on that trail reach the crater. But those who arrived at the crater rim at either Gillman's or Stella Point needn't despair, for there is also a trail from near Stella Point that crosses the crater floor to join up with the path to Reusch.

One of the main problems of spending the night at the summit, in addition to the lack of available oxygen and the biting cold, is how you're going to fill your time up there. Because even if you visit all the sights there – the remains of the Furtwangler Glacier, and the Reusch Crater and Ash Pit (see p373) – that may still leave you with many hours to fill. Hours that may be spent shivering in your tent, and wondering why you paid such a premium for this privilege.

For this reason, it's not unusual for those staying at Crater Camp to actually visit Uhuru Peak *twice* – though, unfortunately, this doesn't mean you get two certificates.

Visiting the crater *without* sleeping there

If you can't afford the time or money to stay at Crater Camp, don't despair: it is still **possible to tour around the crater even if you don't sleep there**. Having hauled your weary carcass to Uhuru Peak, you can then descend from the summit to the crater floor. At the foot of the path that snakes down the side of the crater rim, a trail of sorts heads off to the north round Furtwangler Glacier, away from Uhuru Peak, to the Reusch Crater and Ash Pit. And once you've seen that, you can then continue down the slopes of Kibo to your final camp on the mountain.

Note this will probably add about three hours to what is already a very long and exhausting day. After all, you probably rose about midnight and even without this diversion you probably aren't going to get to your final camp before 4pm. So this diversion to see the sights in the crater could see you reaching your final camp on the mountain after dark (whether that final camp is Millennium Camp, Mweka Camp or Horombo Huts). I should also point out that while we at Kilimanjaro Experts regularly offer this option to our climbers, and many of them, before they set foot on the mountain, express an interest in touring round the crater, once they eventually reach the summit few actually do so. No matter what their intentions on the way up, once they get to the summit the prospect of extending your trekking at this altitude is not, for most people, an appealing one. And you do need to be fully acclimatised – almost preternaturally so. Because if you're struggling with the altitude, spending another 3-4 hours up here to visit the crater is just not sensible.

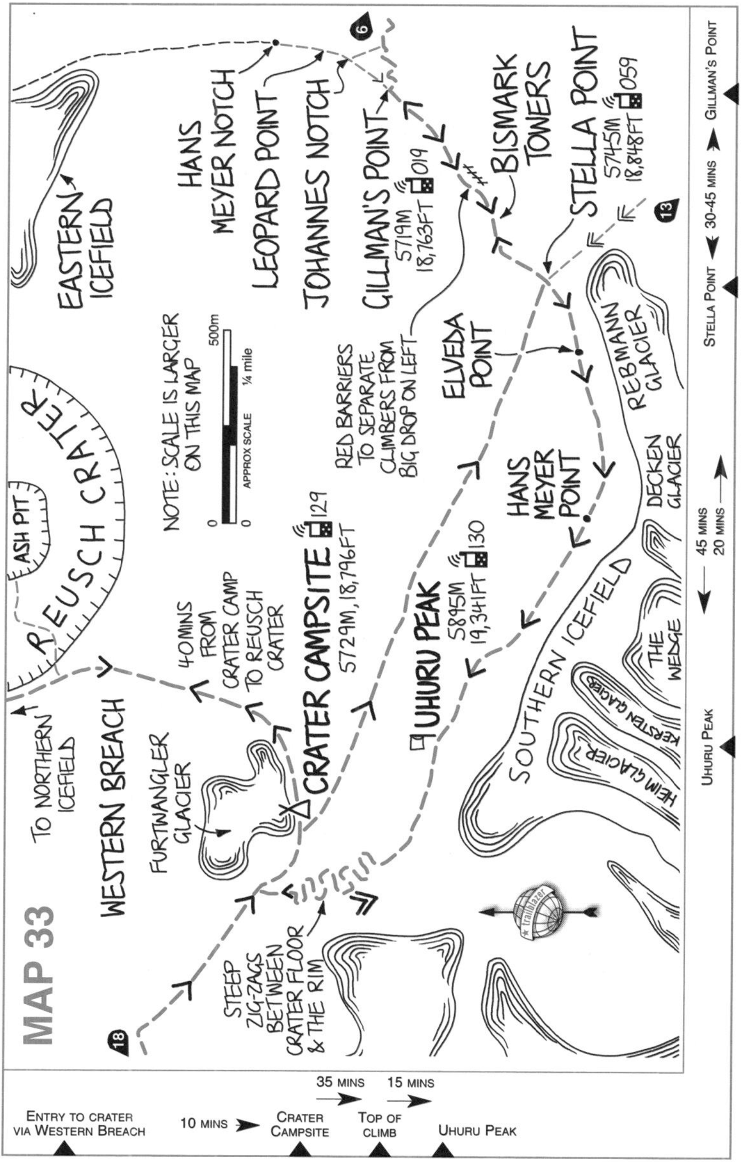
MAP 33
TO NORTHERN ICEFIELD
WESTERN BREACH
FURTWANGLER GLACIER
REUSCH CRATER
ASH PIT
40 MINS FROM CRATER CAMP TO REUSCH CRATER
CRATER CAMPSITE 129
5729M, 18,796FT
NOTE: SCALE IS LARGER ON THIS MAP
APPROX SCALE
0 500m
0 ¼ mile
EASTERN ICEFIELD
HANS MEYER NOTCH
LEOPARD POINT
JOHANNES NOTCH
GILLMAN'S POINT
5719M
18,763FT 019
RED BARRIERS TO SEPARATE CLIMBERS FROM BIG DROP ON LEFT
BISMARK TOWERS
STELLA POINT
5745M
18,848FT 059
6
13
18
ELVEDA POINT
HANS MEYER POINT
UHURU PEAK
5895M
19,341FT 130
REBMANN GLACIER
DECKEN GLACIER
SOUTHERN ICEFIELD
THE WEDGE
KERSTEN GLACIER
HEIM GLACIER
STEEP ZIG-ZAGS BETWEEN CRATER FLOOR & THE RIM
trailblazer
ENTRY TO CRATER VIA WESTERN BREACH
10 MINS
CRATER CAMPSITE
35 MINS
TOP OF CLIMB
15 MINS
UHURU PEAK
UHURU PEAK
45 MINS
20 MINS
STELLA POINT
30-45 MINS
GILLMAN'S POINT

THE SUMMIT

❑ THE FACES BEHIND THE FEATURES

Most Kilimanjaro climbers are aware that Uhuru is Swahili for 'Freedom' and the highest point in Africa was christened this after Tanzania achieved independence in 1961. But do you know after what or whom other features of Kibo are named? Some of them are relatively easy: **Rebmann Glacier** is obviously named after the first European to see Kilimanjaro (see p144), while neighbouring **Decken Glacier** is named after another eminent Victorian, Baron von der Decken, the first man to seriously attempt to climb the mountain. His travel partner, Otto **Kersten**, also has a glacier named after him next to the Baron's.

Meanwhile, **Hans Meyer**– the first man to the summit, of course – has both a Point and a Notch named after him. Another man who *may* have a Notch named after him is the first European to see Kili, Johannes Rebmann (in addition to the glacier I just mentioned). To the south of Johannes Notch, **Bismark Towers** are named in tribute to Otto von Bismark (or Bismarck), German chancellor who united the German states into one country and who was in office when Hans Meyer first conquered Kili.

Most of the other glaciers that haven't already been discussed are named after German and Swiss geologists, geophysicists and earth scientists from the 19th century; in other words, Hans Meyer's friends! Next to Kersten Glacier is **Heim Glacier**, named after Albrecht Heim, world-renowned glacier expert from Switzerland. Hermann **Credner**, Erich von **Drygalski**, Frederich **Ratzel** and Albrecht **Penck** are other German geologists/geographers and other Earth scientists who are celebrated in the names of glaciers on Kili; in Penck's case twice, with both a Great Penck and Little Penck Glacier. There's also **Furtwangler Glacier**, sadly much reduced, which sits on the crater floor and is named after the first man to ski down the side of Kilimanjaro. Herr Furtwangler also has a point on the crater rim named after him, as does the leopard (Leopard Point), which was found frozen in the ice back in the early years of the 20th century.

With most of the features on the summit bagged by the Germans, the Brits who followed them as colonial overlords in Tanganyika were left with little to name.

Two of the most well-known points on the crater rim, **Gillman's** and **Stella Point**, are named after quite obscure figures. The former, for example, was *probably* named after the first man to reach the crater rim after the mountain had come under British protection, one Clement Gillman, who reached this point (but no higher) in 1921. As for Stella Point, there's a nice story behind this. It is named after the wife of Dr Kingsley Latham, a member of the Mountain Club of South Africa, and marks the point that they both reached in 1925. It was at this point that Kingsley, who was suffering terribly from altitude sickness, decided to give up in his attempt to the reach the top. He urged his wife, however, to keep climbing; it was, after all, only another 45 minutes or so to the summit, and if she did so she would become the first woman to the summit of Africa's highest mountain (this being two years before Sheila MacDonald's climb; see p159). Stella, however, clearly a most dutiful wife, refused to go on and demanded to descend with her suffering husband. In tribute, Kingsley forever referred to this point as Point Stella. In subsequent years Kingsley continued to climb (his wife never did) and continued to suffer too. Indeed, he went on to find the frozen leopard mentioned previously, from which Pastor Richard Reusch took an ear as a souvenir (see pp159-60).

Reusch, incidentally, went on to climb the mountain 65 times – a record, I believe, for a non-native – and the inner crater of the Kibo summit was named after him following his 25th ascent of the mountain. His wife is also celebrated on the mountain: **Elveda Point**, which is one of the false summits on the way to Uhuru Peak.

Do note, too, that if you are keen on a tour of the crater after you've reached the summit, **make sure you warn your guide in advance** of your intentions – preferably before you've even started your trek. Some guides will react badly to the idea of spending any longer on the summit than is absolutely necessary; a little gentle cajoling along with a few hints about the size of the tip that awaits them at the end of the trip should do the trick. Make sure, too, that your guide knows his way around up there: you'll probably be a little short of humour as well as breath on the crater rim and following an ignorant guide while he tries in vain to locate the correct path to the Reusch Crater will do little to lighten your mood.

What you can see on the crater

The actual climb up to the rim of **Reusch Crater** is relatively short but surprisingly tiring; if you didn't know you were at altitude before, you will now! This walk can take as little as 30 minutes from Crater Camp, though that's assuming that you are in fairly good shape; and on the summit this is a very big assumption. Having reached Reusch, check out the bright yellow sulphurous deposits, largely on its western side, and the fumaroles that occasionally puff smoke – proof not only that Kili is a volcano, but that it is also an active one. The smell of sulphur is all-pervasive in this crater and the earth is hot to touch. Within Reusch Crater is the 120m-deep (394ft) **Ash Pit** which, though it does not conspicuously contain ash, is said to be one of the most perfect examples of this sort of formation in the world. At 360m (1181ft) across it's also one of the largest. If you reach the Ash Pit, you can truly say you've conquered this mountain.

Map key

Where to stay	Post Office	Mosque
Where to eat	Bank/exchange office	Church/cathedral
Campsite	Tourist Information	Bus station/stop
Hut	Library/bookstore	Rail line & station
Building	Museum/gallery	Other
Public toilet		

Main trail	Steep slope	Tree fern
Other trail	Cliff	Heather
4WD track	Bridge and river	Boulders
Road	Trees	GPS waypoint (008)
Slope	Groundsel	Map continuation (2)

APPENDIX A – A SWAHILI PRIMER

Of the two main languages you will encounter, **Swahili**, the national tongue, is undoubtedly the more useful and the one you will see written on signs and notices. Swahili was originally used by traders on the coast and is thus based on Arabic and various Bantu dialects. Zanzibar is still known as the home of Swahili, where the purest form of the language is spoken. A few words of Swahili will go a long way in Tanzania; although the prefixes and suffixes used can be a little tricky to grasp, any efforts to speak a few words will endear you to the local people. There are plenty of Swahili dictionaries around: street vendors sell little green versions in Arusha or you can pick one up in souvenir stores for about a sixth of the price they charge.

The other language, **Chagga** (sometimes known as **Kichagga**) and its various dialects, is common around Kili but it is unlikely you'll hear it outside the region. You will, however, curry favour with porters and guides on Kilimanjaro by learning a few words; see the box on p179 for a brief introduction. Chagga dictionaries/language books are rare, though you'll find one mentioned on p384.

Swahili – basics

Yes	*Ndiyo*
No	*Hapana*
Good morning	*Jambo*
My name is...	*Jina langu ni...*
How are you?	*Habari gani?*
Please...	*Tafadhali...*
Thanks (very much)	*Ahsante (sana)*
Do you speak English?	*Unasema Kiingereza?*
Help!	*Saidia!*
How much is it?	*Kiasi gani?*
Slowly, slower	*Pole, pole-pole*
Let's go!	*Twendai!*

Food and drink

beans	*maharagwe*
bread	*mkate*
chicken	*kuku*
coffee	*kahawa*
cold	*baridi*
eggs	*mayai*
fish	*samaki*
meat	*nyama*
orange	*chungwa*
pork	*nyama ya nguruwe*
vegetables	*mboga*

Food and drink *(cont'd)*

venison	*nyama ya porini*
water	*maji*

Travel

bus station	*kituo cha mabasi*
airport	*kiwanja cha ndege*
port	*bandari*
railway station	*stesheni*
ticket office	*wanapouza tikiti*
When will we arrive at...?	*Tutafika...jini?*
Is this the direct way to...?	*Hii ni njia fupi kwenda...?*

Places

bank	*banki*
launderette	*kufulia*
post office	*posta*

Days of the week

Monday	*Jumatatu*
Tuesday	*Jumanne*
Wednesday	*Jumatano*
Thursday	*Alhamisi*
Friday	*Ijumaa*
Saturday	*Jumamosi*
Sunday	*Jumapili*

Numbers

1	*moja*	8	*nane*	30	*thelathini*	100	*mia*
2	*mbili*	9	*tisa*	40	*arobaini*	200	*mia mbili*
3	*tatu*	10	*kumi*	50	*hamsini*	1000	*elfu*
4	*nne*	11	*kumi na moja*	60	*sitini*	2000	*elfu mbili*
5	*tano*	12	*kumi na mbili*	70	*sabini*		
6	*sita*	20	*ishirini*	80	*themanini*		
7	*saba*	21	*ishirini na moja*	90	*tisini*		

APPENDIX B – GPS WAYPOINTS

Each GPS waypoint was taken on the route at the reference number marked on the map as below. Note the position format I am using is known as UTM UPS; the map datum is WGS 84 (37 M); you can change both of these on a Garmin GPS by going to Units Setup on the Settings menu, then changing the Position Format and Map datum where necessary.

Note that by some of the waypoints there is a small 'c', which denotes that the waypoint was not found by me and thus I cannot vouch for its accuracy. Any comments on any of the waypoints and their accuracy will be gratefully received. Thanks.

MOUNT MERU

Map	Ref	GPS waypoint	Description
Map A	A	37M 261065 9642331	Momela Gate
Map A	B	37M 260557 9642021	Turn-off to Tululusia Hill
Map A	C	37M 260452 9641613	Turn-off to Campsite 1 & 2
Map A	D	37M 260430 9640906	Turn off to Campsite 3
Map A	E	37M 259270 9640892	Turn-off to viewpoint
Map A	F	37M 258686 9641090	Famous arched fig tree
Map A	G	37M 258127 9641264	Itikoni Campsite
Map A	H	37M 256701 9640742	Maio Falls diversion
Map B	I	37M 254592 9641371	Kitoto Viewpoint
Map B	J	37M 254338 9642470	Turn-off to Meru Crater
Map A	K	37M 255495 9642787	Miriakamba Huts
Map B	L	37M 253925 9643310	Mgongo wa Tembo
Map B	M	37M 252564 9644015	Saddle Huts
Map B	N	37M 252628 9644638	Little Meru
Map B	O	37M 251603 9643468	Rhino Point
Map B	P	37M 249943 9641219	Meru summit

KILIMANJARO – ASCENT ROUTES

The Marangu Route

Map	Ref	GPS waypoint	Description
Map 1	001	37M 335295 9641479	Marangu Gate
Map 1	002	37M 335341 9644784	Bridge
Map 1	003	37M 335676 9645120	Bridge to Kisamboni
Map 2	004	37M 334809 9648242	Mandara Huts
Map 2	005	37M 335400 9648732	Maundi Crater
Map 3	006	37M 330631 9651540	Sloping bridge
Map 3	007	37M 328280 9652715	Kambi ya Taabu
Map 4	008	37M 326490 9652894	Horombo Huts
Map 4	009	37M 325328 9654221	Junction with porters' path
Map 4	010	37M 324892 9655246	Last water point
Map 4	011	37M 324379 9655970	Mawenzi Ridge
Map 5	012	37M 323192 9657409	Lunchstop with toilets
Map 5	013	37M 322614 9658810	Sign for Kibo Circuit
Map 5	014	37M 322447 9658958	Jiwe la Ukoyo
Map 5	015	37M 321300 9659306	Junction with path to Mawenzi Tarn
Map 5 & 6	016	37M 320991 9659232	Kibo Huts
Map 6	017	37M 319713 9659625	William's Point
Map 6	017a	37M 319599 9659653	Junction of paths from School & Kibo Huts
Map 6	018	37M 319400 9659750	Hans Meyer Cave
Map 6 & 33	019	37M 318632 9660028	Gillman's Point
Map 33	130	37M 317075 9659821	Uhuru Peak

The Machame Route (via Barafu Huts and Stella Point)

Map	Ref	GPS waypoint	Description
Map 7	020	37M 304266 9649064	Machame Gate
Map 7	021	37M 304409 9650814	Toilet and end of 4WD track
Map 7	022	37M 305373 9654229	Lunch-stop and toilet
Map 8	023	37M 306531 9656282	Toilet
Map 8	024	37M 307321 9657714	Machame Registration Hut
Map 8	025	37M 307748 9658051	Rocky outcrop
Map 8	026	37M 308080 9658257	Viewpoint
Map 8	027	37M 308137 9658337	First giant groundsels
Map 9	028	37M 308233 9658449	First descent of day
Map 9	029	37M 308315 9658560	Climb to top of rocks for views
Map 9	030	37M 308515 9658753	Ten-second descent
Map 9	031	37M 308807 9659087	Start of steep slope
Map 9	032	37M 309122 9659438	Concrete steps in rock
Map 9	033	37M 309123 9659466	Lunchstop and toilets
Map 9	034	37M 309299 9659975	Overhang in cliff
Map 9	035	37M 309192 9660158	Further overhang caves
Map 9	036	37M 309175 9660179	Short clamber using your hands
Map 9	037	37M 308977 9660464	Top of climb – now on Shira Plateau
Map 9	038	37M 308443 9661064	Shira Caves Campsite
Map 9	039	37M 308730 9660835	Stream
Map 9	040	37M 309299 9660600	Stream
Map 10	041	37M 312517 9661462	Junction of Machame & Lemosho routes
Map 10	042	37M 312859 9661292	Junction
Map 10	043	37M 313415 9661041	Sheffield Campsite
Map 10	044	37M 314131 9660747	Lava Tower Campsite
Map 10	045	37M 313959 9658662	Waterfall
Map 11	046	37M 314325 9657792	Barranco Huts
Map 11	047	37M 315177 9657333	Top of climb ie Barranco/'Breakfast' Wall
Map 11	048	37M 315779 9657062	Stream
Map 11	049	37M 316310 9656600	Climb to top of valley wall
Map 11	050	37M 316315 9656386	Desert slope
Map 11	051	37M 316983 9656046	Valley floor and stream
Map 11	052	37M 316851 9656077	Tortoise Rock
Map 11	053	37M 317089 9655848	Karanga Valley Campsite
Map 12	054	37M 318707 9656657	Top of first climb
Map 12	055	37M 319724 9656918	Top of Barafu Ridge
Map 12, 13 & 30	056	37M 319762 9657263	Barafu Huts
Map 13	057	37M 319592 9658015	Kosovo Campsite
Map 13	058	37M 319249 9658326	Turn left to climb on to the ridge
Map 13 & 33	059	37M 318040 9659630	Stella Point
Map 33	130	37M 317075 9659821	Uhuru Peak

The Lemosho Route (via Western Breach Route)

Map	Ref	GPS waypoint	Description
Map 14	060	37M 294046 9667904	Start of Lemosho Route at Lemosho Glades
Map 14	061	37M 295058 9667784	Slight clearing
Map 14	062	37M 295082 9667762	Tree in path
Map 14	063	37M 295789 9667751	Patch of lobelia
Map 14	064	37M 296078 9668489	Camphor tree stand and tree across path
Map 14	065	37M 297174 9668591	Mti Mkubwa
Map 14	066	37M 298279 9668000	Stream
Map 14	067	37M 299074 9668169	Top of ridge

The Lemosho Route (via Western Breach Route) *(cont'd)*

Map	Ref	GPS waypoint	Description
Map 14	068	37M 299193 9668178	Last stand of African rosewood (left of path)
Map 15	069	37M 299516 9668155	Top of climb
Map 15	070	37M 299765 9668304	Two streams and old lunchstop
Map 15	071	37M 300087 9668487	Better lunchstop
Map 15	072	37M 300897 9667634	Stream
Map 15	073	37M 302211 9667729	Top of climb – first view of Kibo
Map 15	074	37M 303210 9666760	Shira 1 (campsite)
Map 16	075	37M 304514 9665765	Boulder (junction with Shira Cathedral path)
Map 16	076	37M 304809 9663689	First stream
Map 16	077	37M 304843 9663552	Second stream
Map 16	078	37M 304873 9663387	Third stream
Map 16	079	37M 304884 9662988	Burnt trees
Map 16	080	37M 305059 9661945	Junction with path to Shira Cathedral
Map 16	081	37M 304823 9661850	Top of Shira Cathedral
Map 16	082	37M 306091 9662268	East Shira Hill
Map 16	083	37M 306328 9662360	Weird boulders and mud flats
Map 16	084	37M 306876 9662437	Roadhead
Map 16	085	37M 307312 9662331	Dry stream
Map 17	086	37M 308314 9662240	Shira Huts/Shira 2 (campsite)
Map 17	087	37M 310497 9662179	Big boulder
Map 17	088	37M 311028 9662077	Narrow gully
Map 10	089	37M 311568 9661987	Path north to Moir Huts
Map 10	090	37M 312105 9661769	Small cross
Map 10	043	37M 313415 9661041	Sheffield Campsite
Map 10 & 18	044	37M 314131 9660747	Lava Tower Campsite

Western Breach Route to Uhuru Peak

Map	Ref	GPS waypoint	Description
Map 18	091	c 37M 315109 9660256	Arrow Glacier Campsite
Map 18	092	c 37M 316482 9660666	Crater Rim
Map 33	129	37M 316829 9660194	Crater Campsite
Map 33	130	37M 317075 9659821	Uhuru Peak

The Shira Plateau Route

Map	Ref	GPS waypoint	Description
Map 15	093	37M 303371 9669714	Morum Barrier
Map 16	094	37M 306221 9664795	Simba Cave Campsite
Map 16	095	37M 307186 9663697	Junction with path to Moir Huts
Map 17	096	37M 308711 9663477	Fischer Camp

The Northern Circuit

Map	Ref	GPS waypoint	Description
Map 10 & 19	097	37M 311025 9663594	Moir Huts
Map 19	098	37M 316614 9666951	Buffalo Campsite
Map 20	099	37M 317958 9666354	Old Pofu Campsite
Map 20	111	37M 323357 9663335	Third Cave Campsite

The Rongai Route

Map	Ref	GPS waypoint	Description
Map 21	100	37M 329610 9671581	New Rongai Gate
Map 21	101	37M 330242 9671399	Steps down to Nalemoru River
Map 21	102	37M 330248 9671323	Junction with old path
Map 21	103	37M 329351 9670985	Sign about wildfires
Map 21	104	37M 328834 9670717	Benches
Map 21	105	37M 328371 9670227	Second bridge
Map 22	106	37M 327535 9670053	Simba Campsite
Map 22	107	37M 325494 9668733	Rocky plateau

Map	Ref	GPS waypoint	Description
The Rongai Route		*(cont'd from p377)*	
Map 22	108	37M 324934 9668209	First 'summit'
Map 23	109	37M 324279 9667203	Second 'summit'
Map 23	110	37M 324041 9666423	Second Cave (lunch-stop)
Map 23	111	37M 323357 9663335	Third Cave Campsite
The Mawenzi Tarn Hut Route			
Map 23	110	37M 324041 9666423	Second Cave (lunch-stop)
Map 24	112	37M 326938 9662833	Highest point of day
Map 24	113	37M 327477 9662418	Kikelelwa Camp
Map 24	114	37M 327418 9661909	Viewpoint over valley; photo stop
Map 24	115	37M 327332 9661625	Stream with groundsels
Map 24	116	37M 327439 9660935	Popular snack stop by boulders
Map 24	117	37M 327787 9660261	Cairns by cave
Map 24	118	37M 328098 9659970	Top of ridge
Map 24	119	37M 328116 9659841	Junction with path to Kibo Huts
Map 24	120	37M 328485 9659458	Mawenzi Tarn Hut Campsite
Map 24	121	37M 328083 9659117	Top of acclimatisation climb
Map 24	119	37M 328116 9659841	Junction with path to Kibo Huts
Map 25	015	37M 321300 9659306	Junction with path to Horombo Huts
Map 25	016	37M 320991 9659232	Kibo Huts
Map 26 & 6	122	37M 320675 9660736	School Hut
Map 6	017a	37M 319599 9659653	Jctn of paths from School and Kibo Huts
Map 6	018	37M 319400 9659750	Hans Meyer Cave
Map 6 & 33	019	37M 318632 9660028	Gillman's Point
Map 33	059	37M 318040 9659630	Stella Point
Map 33	130	37M 317075 9659821	Uhuru Peak
The Umbwe Route via Western Breach			
(For the route to the summit via Barafu Huts & Stella Point, see waypoints 046-049 & 130)			
Map 27	123	37M 308828 9647282	Umbwe Gate
Map 27	124	37M 309943 9651668	End of 4x4 road & signpost
Map 27	125	37M 311278 9652842	Sarumba Emergency Camp
Map 28	126	37M 312330 9654129	Umbwe Cave Campsite
Map 28	127	37M 312630 9654801	Jiwe Kamba
Map 29	128	37M 313428 9656166	Groundsel field
Map 29 & 11	046	37M 314325 9657792	Barranco Huts
Map 10	045	37M 313959 9658662	Waterfall
Map 10 & 18	044	37M 314131 9660747	Lava Tower Campsite
Map 18	091	c37M 315109 9660256	Arrow Glacier Campsite
Map 18	092	c37M 316482 9660666	Crater Rim
Map 33	129	37M 316829 9660194	Crater Campsite
Map 33	130	37M 317075 9659821	Uhuru Peak

KILIMANJARO – DESCENT ROUTES

The Marangu Route

See p375 for the Marangu Trail waypoints and use them in reverse until Map 4 where you have the option of doing the Mawenzi Route.

The Mawenzi Route

Map	Ref	GPS waypoint	Description
Map 4	008A	37M 325945 9654684	Zebra Rocks
Map 4	008B	37M 326374 9656687	Signpost and junction

Map	Ref	GPS waypoint	Description
The Mawenzi Route *(cont'd)*			
Map 4	008C	37M 326240 9656836	Memorial plaque and viewpoint
Map 4	008D	37M 327617 9657468	Mawenzi Hut
The Mweka Route			
Map 33	130	37M 317075 9659821	Uhuru Peak
Map 33 & 13	059	37M 318040 9659630	Stella Point
Map 12, 13 & 30	056	37M 319762 9657263	Barafu Huts
Map 30	131	37M 319091 9654859	Junction with path to Karanga Valley on one side and a porters' path on the other
Map 30	132	37M 319086 9654264	Emergency route from Karanga Valley
Map 31	133	37M 319144 9653675	Millennium Hut (Rescue Hut) Campsite
Map 31	134	37M 318558 9650985	Mweka Huts
Map 31	135	37M 317765 9649028	Bridge
Map 32	136	37M 317256 9647528	Second bridge
Map 32	137	37M 316526 9645691	Start of 4x4 track
Map 32	138	37M 315727 9644014	Mweka Gate

APPENDIX C – RECOMMENDED BOOKS, MAPS & FILMS

MAPS

Maps of Kilimanjaro are available in Arusha, Moshi and probably your own country. The best one I've found, however, is reliably available only online: ***Kilimanjaro Kibo*** (1:80,000) is written in both English and German and is by some distance the most accurate map available for the mountain.

With profiles of a couple of the routes, GPS points, town plans on Arusha and Moshi, descriptions of the vegetation zones and a review of the retreat of permanent ice, this is also the most informative and useful map. You can order a copy by visiting the publisher's website at 🖳 climbing-map.com.

The most common map I see is the cartoonish ***New Map of the Kilimanjaro National Park***, by Giovanni Tombazzi, which is bright and colourful though in all honesty it's a little inaccurate and the cartoon style means it's of little practical use. Still, it's packed full of information and the flora guide on the reverse is useful. The scale, by the way, is about 1.1cm to 1km (or 1:90,909), with a close-up of the summit on the reverse drawn at a scale of 5.4cm to 1km (about 1:18,518.5). NB **Make sure you get the *New Map*** as the old one really is out of date.

Giovanni also does a map of ***Arusha National Park***, including the route up Mount Meru, that's in a similar style though I think it's inferior to the official map produced by TANAPA called ***Arusha National Park – The Tourist Map***.

Back on Africa's highest mountain, ***Tourist Map of Kilimanjaro*** (1:100,000) by the Ordnance Survey (1989) is the biggest and most beautiful, though once again of little practical use: the routes themselves have been drawn, seemingly, without thought of precision, over the top of what looks an accurate topographical map. It's a little out-of-date, too, and as such it's better in a frame on your wall at home than in your backpack.

Finally, the Canada-based ITM (International Travel Maps) series has produced ***Kilimanjaro & Tanzania North*** (2022), a colourful 1:62,500 map of the mountain, as well as a separate 1:6,250,000 road map of the area.

RECOMMENDED READING

Please note that many of the following are rare and a number are extremely difficult to find. Among those that are readily available are Hemingway's ***The Snows of Kilimanjaro*** (and the 2005 ***Under Kilimanjaro***, the rather long-winded novel-cum-memoir-cum-tribute-to-Africa that recounts Papa Hemingway's time in Kenya); the comprehensive and wonderful book-of-the-IMAX-film ***Kilimanjaro, Mountain at the Crossroads***, by Audrey Salkeld – possibly the most beautiful and absorbing souvenir of your climb that money can buy (the book that is, not Audrey); and John Reader's excellent (though rather bulky) ***Kilimanjaro***.

If you're visiting Zanzibar after Kilimanjaro, you may want to wait and buy your reading material for the mountain there: some of the bookshops in Stonetown have fine selections.

Biography and personal accounts

The original editions of many of the following books, particularly those written during the great days of exploration in the 1800s, are very difficult to find and, short of a miraculous discovery in a secondhand bookstore, the only place you're going to find them is at the British Library or a similar institution abroad. The internet is, of course, another source. For example, I've successfully tracked down online the first edition of the English translation of Hans Meyer's account of his conquest of Kili (see opposite); so now all I've got to do is find the US$9000 the dealers are asking for it. The online auction house eBay is a good place to begin your search. The Canadian-based Voyager Press also have some good stuff on Kili, particularly old reports from the Royal Geographic Society.

Thankfully, publishers such as Forgotten Books and Kessinger now republish several of the most well-known. The printing quality of these books is not brilliant and the maps and drawings – the most beautiful parts of the original tomes – are either rendered very poorly or missing altogether from these reprints. Nevertheless, for most of us it's the only way we'll be able to read and own a copy.

For those books that *are* still in print, your best bet is in Tanzania itself, either in the small souvenir shop by Marangu Gate or in the larger bookshops in Dar and Arusha. Failing that, you could always try online bookshops such as Abebooks and Amazon, on which you will usually be able to track down a copy.

The explorers...

• ***The Church Missionary Intelligencer*** (Seeleys, 1850) Definitely one you'll have to look for in the British Library (or a similar institution elsewhere), this august organ was the first to publish Rebmann's accounts of his three trips to Kilimanjaro as well as Krapf's subsequent visit to the Usambara region (see p178). Volume 1, May 1849, contains most of the relevant texts.

• ***An Essay on the Sources of the Nile in the Mountains of the Moon*** Charles T Beke (Neill and Company, 1848) This short work is of interest not only because it was published at the same time as Rebmann's ground-breaking visit to Kilimanjaro but also because the author still takes as his starting point the work of Ptolemy written 1800 years earlier, thus giving an indication of just how little was known about Africa at that time.

• ***Life, Wanderings, and Labours in Eastern Africa*** Charles New (Cass Library of African Studies, 1971, originally 1873) Charles New set off in 1871 to spread the gospel to Africa's heathen population but it was as an explorer that he is remembered, becoming the first white man to cross the African snow-line during a visit to the Chagga region. This book was written in the months spent in England between his first and second trips, on the latter of which he fell ill and died. Once again, though the account of his time on the slopes of Kili occupies only about a third of the book, it is for the most part fascinating, as much for his description of Chief Mandara and the Chaggas as it is for his climb up the mountain.

• ***Discovery by Count Teleki of Lakes Rudolf and Stefanie*** Lieutenant Ludwig von Höhnel, translated by Nancy Bell (Longmans, Green and Co, 1894) Lengthy, two-volume account of the Hungarian count as he shoots and slaughters his way through East Africa's fauna, written by his companion von Höhnel. Only about a sixth of the book deals specifically with Kili, though that sixth is interesting both for the account of their attempt to climb Kili and their dealings with Chagga chiefs Mandara (whom they try to avoid) and Mareale.

• ***The Kilima-njaro Expedition – A Record of Scientific Exploration in Eastern Equatorial Africa*** HH Johnston (Kegan Paul, Trench and Co, 1886; republished by several publishers including the British Library, 2011) Widely dismissed as exaggeration going on fabrication, this is nevertheless a very entertaining read thanks to Johnston's sense of humour and the scrapes into which he gets. Just possible to find second-hand or pick up the reprint by Kessinger Publishing.

• ***Tracts Relating to Missions*** (Printed by A Lankester, 1878) Yet another work whose habitat is restricted almost entirely to the British Library these days, this collection of missionary accounts includes one by the Rev A Downes Shaw entitled ***To Chagga and Back — An Account of a Journey to Moshi, the Capital of Chagga, Eastern Equatorial Africa***.

• ***James Hannington, First Bishop of Eastern Equatorial Africa – A History of his Life and Work*** EC Dawson (Seeley and Co, 1887) I have to confess I had never heard of this book – nor indeed the bishop – until I came across a copy on eBay (for a tenner!). And fascinating it is too, for though the bishop's own efforts on Kili are fairly paltry, not getting much above the treeline, his diary entries about the Chagga chief Mandara and the region in general are fascinating, and this book is filled with mentions of the great explorers (Johnston, Thomson etc) he encountered during his time in East Africa (before he was finally speared to death in Uganda on the orders of a local king).

• ***Across East African Glaciers – An Account of the First Ascent of Kilimanjaro*** Dr Hans Meyer, translated from the German by EHS Calder (George Philip and Son, 1891) Perhaps the most fascinating book ever written about the mountain, Meyer's beautiful work describes his unprecedented ascent of Kilimanjaro, all illustrated with some lovely sketches by ET Compton. Splendid stuff. Now available in a much less-charming – but much more affordable – reprint by Kessinger Press.

...and those who followed in their wake

With the rise of self-publishing you can now find a slew of memoirs written by those who've conquered Kili, both in traditional paper format and, even more so, as ebooks. I have to say I found most a little dull but that could be because I've climbed the mountain a few times now, whereas those who haven't, or who haven't yet, may find them both useful and fascinating. But there are several other books here that I really enjoyed. In alphabetical order:

• ***Africa's Dome of Mystery*** Eva Stuart Watt FRGS (Marshall, Morgan and Scott Ltd, 1930) Brought up in East Africa, Ms Stuart-Watt describes her life among the Chagga people, including an account of her climb to Kibo's crater rim. Interesting, if only for the fact that there are few accounts of Kibo from this period under British rule.

• ***Another Load of Bull*** David Read (David Read, 2005) Extracted from the author's diaries, this self-published book, the third in the series, is largely about his successful attempt to run Mountainside, a large farm on the lower slopes of Kili. It's very detailed and without a doubt Mr Read led a fascinating life; but with its tales of cattle markets, colonialism and sexual incontinence, I finished this book feeling that I'd just spent several hours trapped in the company of a world-class bore. Shame, because in the hands of a more likeable writer there's probably a decent story here.

• ***Bicycles up Kilimanjaro*** Richard and Nicholas Crane (Oxford Illustrated Press 1985) These two cycled up Kili with Mars Bars taped to their handlebars, to finance the construction of windmills for pumping water in East Africa. The only other person I met who had read this book said he enjoyed it, but I didn't.

• ***Climbing Kilimanjaro at 70*** Richard A Wolfe PhD (Ingalls Publishing 2011) The title pretty much sums up the contents as septuagenarian nuclear engineer Dr Wolfe manages to fulfil an ambition that he first dreamed of when a young projectionist at his local cinema and watched *The Snows of Kilimanjaro* about forty times.

• ***Duel for Kilimanjaro*** Leonard Mosley (Weidenfeld & Nicolson, 1963) Account of the East African campaign during World War I. The fact that I stuck with it to the end, even though my interest in military history is slight, is testament to how well this book is written and what an absorbing story it is. The British, by the way, come across as comically incompetent.

• ***A Girl's Guide to Climbing Kilimanjaro – What you need to know and bring to have a wonderful and comfortable climb*** Rachel Durchslag & Jackie Payne (CreateSpace, 2012) I don't usually review other guidebooks (or indeed read them) but I thought that the standpoint taken by this book was sufficiently different to mine – I am male, after all – that it would be worth seeing what they had to say without fear of being accused of unfairly slating the competition. That said, I couldn't find much that they say in their book that I don't say in this one. So I asked a female friend who's climbed Kili for her unbiased opinion, though she was even more scathing and summed up the book in one simple word: pointless.

• ***Kilimanjaro: Hakuna Matata*** Chris Baker (🖳 lulu.com, 2007) There's nothing unusual about this person's climb, nor about Mr Baker or his writing style. Nevertheless, as a straightforward account of what it's like to climb Kilimanjaro I really think this book is pretty good.

• ***Kilimanjaro – One Man's Quest to go over the Hill*** MG Edwards (CreateSpace, 2012) Man on the verge of a mid-life crisis attempts to climb Kili via the Marangu Route. Maybe I'm biased – he got in touch with me to ask if it was OK to use my maps – but I thought this one of the better accounts written recently.

• ***Kilimanjaro – One Woman's Journey to the Roof of Africa and Beyond*** Deb Denis (Marion Grace Publishing, 2012) Another comprehensive account of one person's climb, covering not only why and when she did it but, most important of all, how she did it. Clearly venturing out of her comfort zone, Deb spent one year preparing for her African adventure, which begins in one of the smallest countries on the continent and ends on its largest mountain. The story of her journey – in both the physical and the personal sense – is an entertaining and thought-provoking one.

• ***Kilimanjaro via the Marangu Route: "Tourist Route" my ass*** Phil Gray (iUniverse Inc, 2006) This book has had some pretty negative reviews on the internet and it is indeed pretty cynical, but it's not as bad as some people will have you believe. Mr Gray seems an amiable fellow, never one to tell it straight when there's the possibility of a gag, and I found the book a readable account of his climb.

• ***Kissing Kibo – Trekking to the Summit of Mount Kilimanjaro via the Lemosho Route*** Sheree Marshall (iUniverse, 2011) Though I found it to be the most error-strewn of the titles here, I have to admit that this book wasn't written for a pedant like me and the middle-aged African-American divorcée author is a lot more engaging than the other author who enjoys making out with mountains, Mr Dorr (see below). The book is also, mercifully, a lot more succinct (Ms Marshall is in Tanzania by page seven, for example, while it takes Mr Dorr 49 pages to reach the same point). Also one of the few accounts of a trek on the Lemosho Route, which makes a change, and includes at the end of the book plenty of practical advice – though given the wealth of mistakes that litter this book, I wouldn't necessarily follow them religiously.

• ***Kissing Kilimanjaro – Leaving it all on top of Africa*** Daniel Dorr (The Mountaineers Books, 2010) Pretty standard account of a pretty standard trek – or rather, treks, for the author returned to climb Rongai having first failed on Machame. Overly thorough and a little too comprehensive, there are too many longeurs to make this an absorbing read. Still, for those seeking a step-by-step account (sometimes literally) of what it's like up there, it's OK – though my goodness the ending is rather melodramatic.

• ***Making the Climb: What a Novice Climber Learned About Life on Mount Kilimanjaro*** John C Bowling (Beacon Hill Press, 2007) Tedious account of a climb by the president of

Olivet Nazarene University (Chicago, USA) that's reminiscent of the dullest of sermons you used to have to sit through as a child – including a liberal sprinkling of prayers throughout the chapters. Read it if you must, but only as a way to build up stamina.

- ***The Road to Kilimanjaro*** Geoffrey Salisbury (Minerva Press, 1997) Though mainly autobiographical, recounting Salisbury's busy life, this book includes a heart-warming, humbling account of an expedition in 1969 by the author to the summit of Kilimanjaro on the Loitokitok (Rongai) Route with a group of eight totally blind African youths, all but one of whom made it to the top.
- ***The Shadow of Kilimanjaro – On Foot Across East Africa*** Rick Ridgeway (Bloomsbury 2006) Well-written account of a walk that begins on the summit of Kilimanjaro and ends at Malindi on the Kenyan coast. Though Kilimanjaro is dealt with in a matter of pages at the front of the book, the narrative style is absorbing and this book is well worth reading.
- ***Snow on the Equator*** HW Tilman (Bell and Son Books, 1937, republished in 2015 by Tilman publishers) Inaccurate account (Kilimanjaro is not an extinct volcano, for example, but a dormant one) by coffee planter, explorer, mountaineer and all-round show-off Harold William Tilman. Nevertheless a very entertaining read and, for all his bluster, Tilman comes across as an entirely likeable fellow.
- ***On Top of Africa – the Climbing of Kilimanjaro and Mount Kenya*** Neville Shulman (Element Books, 1995) Tale of the conquering of these two African giants by the author, with the help of Zen philosophies and his own personal *shin* spirit.
- ***Travels*** Michael Crichton (HardPress Limited, 2011) Travelogue by the author of Jurassic Park that covers everything from swimming with sharks off Tahiti to visiting Mayan Pyramids in the Yucatan. The account of his time on Kilimanjaro is thus just one chapter of many – but despite (or perhaps in part because) of its brevity (just 19 pages in my version), it remains my favourite description of a Kili climb since those of the early explorers – honest, insightful and accurate.
- ***In Wildest Africa*** Peter MacQueen, FRGS (George Bell and Sons, 1910; reprinted by Forgotten Books, 2012) Account of one of the first tourists to visit Kilimanjaro, coming here during the German occupation. Includes a description of their ascent up Kili, during which some of their porters died, and more were frightened by snow and fled (taking the food with them). MacQueen himself only managed to find his way down by following the trail of porters' corpses left behind from an expedition five months previously. He went on to reach a highly credible 19,200ft, the highest, at that time, by an English speaker.
- ***Zombies on Kilimanjaro – A Father/Son Journey above the Clouds*** Tim Ward (Changemakers Books, 2012) I was looking forward to reading this book: the praise on the back cover suggested it was going to be a fun read and, unlike many of the other titles reviewed here, the author has some sort of previous experience when it comes to writing. However, the description of the climb gradually takes a back-seat to the author's turgid analysis of his relationship with his son and his obsession with memes until, by the time I finally reached the last page, I felt more drained than I have ever done climbing the mountain.

Fiction

- ***Bingo Bear was here – A Toy Bear's Climb to the Top of Africa's Highest Mountain*** Gwill York Newman (Sunstone Press 2003) It goes against one's nature to criticise a children's book but when the author implies that Kilimanjaro is in Kenya in the preface, thereby insulting an entire nation, I think the gloves are off. Anyway, this is about the adventures of a stuffed koala from Cleveland, Ohio, as he accompanies the author and her husband to the top of Africa's highest mountain – which *is* in Tanzania. The author lives in New Mexico, by the way, and has since climbed with Bingo in other mountainous places including Kashmir and the American Rockies. Which she probably thinks are in France.
- ***Home on Kilimanjaro*** Margaret Chrislock Gilseth (Askeladd Press, 1998) Novel written by a lady who spent four years teaching in Marangu for the Lutheran Church, written largely from the point of view of her 11-year-old son.

• ***Kilimanjaro Burning*** John B Robinson (Birch Book Press, 1998) Entertaining enough, but other than being set in Tanzania it's not really relevant to the mountain. Nevertheless, good at evoking the country, its sights and smells, for those who know the area.
• ***The Snows of Kilimanjaro*** Ernest Hemingway (Arrow Books, 1994) Short story about a writer plagued by both a gangrenous leg and a rich wife, written by an honorary game warden based in Loitokitok in the early 1950s. Was always regarded as his most autobiographical work until the publication of...
• ***Under Kilimanjaro*** Ernest Hemingway (Kent State University Press, 2005) Hemingway called it fiction but with himself and his wife as the lead characters and the events that are described presumably pretty close to the truth, this book could just as easily have been pigeonholed in the Biography category above. Long and funereally paced, it has its moments but is probably for fans and aficionados only.
• ***Up the Mountain Coming Down Slowly*** David Eggers (from the short-story collection *How We are Hungry*, Penguin 2006) It may be fiction, but it's clearly based on Eggers' own experiences on the mountain. Along with Crichton's (see p383), it's my favourite account of a climb – entertaining, tense and unsettling. Not to be read before a climb, but a great reminder of it – despite the upsetting ending – after a trek.

Chagga language, history & lifestyle

• ***Chagga – A Course in the Vunjo Dialect of the Kichagga Language of Kilimanjaro, Tanzania*** Bernard Leeman and Trilas Lauwo (published in Europe by Languages Information Centre) The best Chagga language book I could find; this tome, written by an Australian who worked as a teacher in the region, deals with the basic structure and grammar and is an ideal introduction to the tongue.
• ***History of the Chagga People of Kilimanjaro*** Kathleen M Stahl (Mouton & Co, 1964) Highly detailed account of the Chaggas, probably more for those with an academic interest in the subject but proof that contrary to popular opinion the Chagga do have an absorbing – and surprisingly lengthy – history.
• ***Hunger and Shame – Child Malnutrition and Poverty on Mount Kilimanjaro*** Mary Howard and Ann Millard (Routledge) Comparatively rich by African standards it may be but, as this book proves, the Kilimanjaro region still suffers from more than its fair share of grinding poverty. With views from family members, health workers and government officials, this book discusses the moral and practical dilemmas of malnourishment.
• ***Kilimanjaro and its People*** The Honourable Charles Dundas OBE (H, F and G Witherby, 1924; reprinted by Routledge, 2014) Probably still the most authoritative account of the Chagga people, this tome is a little dry in places (particularly the rather involved history section) and outdated too (very few of the more extreme Chagga practices, described on pp177-84 of this book, are still conducted today); nevertheless the sections on religion, witchcraft and ritual ceremonies are completely fascinating and offer the most comprehensive insight into how the Chaggas *used to be*, at least, if not how they are today.

Field guides

• ***Birds of East Africa: Kenya, Tanzania, Uganda, Rwanda, Burundi*** Terry Stevenson and John Fanshawe (Helm Field Guides, 2004) Bird guides tend to be amongst the most beautiful books around and this one is no different, with gorgeous drawings by Brian Small, John Gale and Norman Arlott. Reckoned to be *the* authoritative guide.
• ***Birds of Kenya and Northern Tanzania*** Dale A Zimmerman (Helm Field Guides, 2005) Another in the series, just as beautiful – and (slightly) less weighty than the one above.
• ***Kilimanjaro – Animals in a Landscape*** Jonathan Kingdon (BBC Publications 1983) Born in Tanganyika, Kingdon is an artist specialising in the flora and fauna of his homeland. This book, based on a BBC series, contains examples of his work as well as an extended commentary on the creatures that live on the mountain.
• ***Pocket Guide to Mammals of East Africa*** Chris Stuart and Mathilde Stuart (Struik, 2009) Around 160 pages of nice photos of animals.

Field guides to the flora

Strangely, there is no *comprehensive* book on the flora of Kilimanjaro. The boss of trekking company Tusker, Eddie & Amy Frank, did publish one in 2018, ***The Flora of Kilimanjaro***, but to be honest I didn't really find a huge amount in there that wasn't already in this book though it is certainly a more handsome tome than this one. There is ***Field Guide to Common Trees and Shrubs of East Africa*** Najma Dharani (New Holland, 2011) but this, alas, has little relevance to the mountain itself.

Coffee-table books

- ***Kilimanjaro*** John Reader (Elm Tree Books, 1982) Excellent, beautifully written coffee-table book with detailed accounts both of the history and geology of Kili as well as the author's experience of photographing it.
- ***Kilimanjaro: The Great White Mountain*** David Pluth (Camerapix, 2001) Another tome that will have your coffee-table groaning.
- ***Kilimanjaro: To the Roof of Africa*** Audrey Salkeld (National Geographic Books, 2002) The best-looking book on Kilimanjaro, this mighty tome includes detailed sections on history and geology as well as some excellent photographs of the mountain. If you only buy one book about the mountain – other than the one you're holding now, of course! – make it this one.

...AND SEVEN RELEVANT FILMS

- ***Kilimanjaro – to the Roof of Africa*** The 2002 film of the book – or was it the book of the film? Whatever, this IMAX film recounting the experiences of a group of trekkers on the mountain is beautifully shot by film-maker David Breashears. It's the best documentary if you want to know what it's like to climb the mountain, as well as a gorgeous and evocative souvenir for those who have already done so.
- ***Hatari!*** Long on time but short on quality, this 151-minute 1963 epic, starring John Wayne in typical derring-do mode as well as Hardy Krüger (see p260) and the preposterously named Red Buttons, is not great though if you can ignore the paper-thin plot, stilted acting, constipated dialogue and questionable attitude towards the wildlife, women and locals, there's some enjoyment to be had in glimpsing the region as it was in the early '60s. The scenes where they hunt and capture the animals (made, of course, without the benefit of CGI) are also very impressive and the score by Henry Mancini is reliably hummable (particularly the signature tune 'Baby Elephant Walk').

- ***Killers of Kilimanjaro*** With scarcely a swash left unbuckled, this 1959 tale follows the adventures of trouble-shooter Robert Adamson (Robert Taylor) who, arriving in deepest Africa with Jane Carlton (played by the luscious Anne Aubrey) to oversee the completion of a cross-continental railroad, finds he has all manner of continental clichés to contend with, from slave traders (ruthless) to tribes (savage) and, of course, the local fauna (Grrrr!). Will he make it out alive? And complete the railroad too? And get together with Jane? Probably, yes. It's not great but I quite enjoyed it and it has a certain charm. Usually available on eBay, if you're interested.

- ***The Mines of Kilimanjaro*** Italian offering from 1986 that's been dubbed into English. Tobias Hoesl stars as Dr Ed Barkely who travels to East Africa in search of his professor's killers. But as Robert Taylor (see *Killers of Kilimanjaro*, see p385) could have told him, this part of the world is chock-a-block with danger, from savage tribes (in this case, the Gundors), Chinese gangsters (?) and even Nazis (???). And after that, things get *really* weird! And as Robert Taylor could *also* have told him, there are compensations in the form of some lovely scenery and equally comely female company, with Elena Pompei as Eva Kilbrook. All in all, an appalling film but unfortunately not bad enough to be funny – making it possibly the worst couple of hours of cinematic 'entertainment' you will ever experience.

- ***In the Shadow of Kilimanjaro*** It's 1500 men versus 90,000 flesh-eating baboons that have been driven mad by a drought: the odds look bad but if anybody can find a way out of this 1986 dilemma, John Rhys Davis and Timothy Bottoms can. ... Grab some beer and popcorn, settle into your favourite armchair, disengage your brain and enjoy this truly rubbish but succulent serving of '80s ham and corn. Available on eBay.
- ***Snows of Kilimanjaro*** Henry King's 1952 film version of Ernest Hemingway's semi-autobiographical work, with Gregory Peck in the leading role, Susan Hayward as his devoted belle and Ava Gardner as the lost love he pines for – and when you see Ava in this film, you can't blame him. Of course it's the most highbrow film of the seven here and I should like it – but, personally speaking, give me killer baboons any day.

- ***Volcano above the Clouds*** From the Nova PBS stable comes this hour-long documentary from 2003 about a team climbing the Lemosho/Western Breach Route. Ostensibly it's about the team's attempts to discover how much the glaciers' disappearance will affect the water supply and to see whether the volcano is still active, but really it's just a documentary of a climb – and for that it's OK. Contact Nova direct; I found it via Amazon marketplace.

APPENDIX D – NEW ASCENT ROUTES

Ever since the first edition of this guide book, in 2001, the routes *up* Kilimanjaro have remained the same. However, plans are afoot – and indeed construction is well under way – to introduce two new routes to the roster, bringing the total number of ascent paths up to eight.

See map on p398 for the Kidia Route and the Irkasswa Trail

The park authorities, KINAPA, have been slow to release details of the paths, but using a combination of educated guesswork, assumption and experience, I do have some idea of where they'll be and what they'll look like. I've drawn estimates of where both paths will go on the map on p398 and a summary of both routes follows now.

THE KIDIA ROUTE

The first trail, and the one that looks like it will be the first to open, is a trail called the Kidia Route. This trail, which lies between the Mweka and Marangu Routes on Kili's southern slopes, is actually not an entirely new route. In September 2001, the authorities closed the Mweka descent route (see pp362-9) so they could work on restoring it. At the time this was seen as an entirely sensible move, for the Mweka trail was in a parlous state, 'a foot-deep trench where once a path existed' as I wrote back then. Its deterioration was understandable, for where once the number of trekkers on the Machame, Umbwe and Lemosh/Shira Trails had been limited to just 16 per day, those limits were abolished at the end of the 1990s; the resulting increase in footfall had, not unexpectedly, had a deleterious effect on Mweka.

So a new path was born, called, rather unimaginatively, the Alternative Mweka Route by the authorities, but which quickly became known by everyone as the Kidia Route after the village that lies at its end. Having walked down both routes, I expressed a preference for the original Mweka in the first edition of this book:

'As to the relative merits of the two, while both have their attractions I have to say I still prefer the former, if only because the new trail is so exasperatingly long. Where the original sets off like a bullet from a gun towards civilisation and continues unwaveringly in that direction nearly all the way to Mweka Gate, the new path tends to dawdle somewhat; and after spending the entire night walking to the top of a very big mountain, dawdling will probably not be on your list of preferred activities at that moment. This criticism is particularly applicable both to the first day, which goes on for at least one eternity across valley after valley of heather and helichrysum, a repetitive and unvarying landscape that offers little to distract you from the screaming pain in your calf muscles; and of the latter part of the second day, where the path joins a 4WD track that twists, curls, loops and snakes all over the slopes like a python on its stag night.'

If the above descriptions puts you off, I should, for balance, point out three reasons why you shouldn't necessarily dismiss the Kidia Route altogether.

Firstly, I do go on to say that there are certain sections that are just gorgeous. In particular, there is one part that I describe as being 'just divine':

'On the one side, meadows dotted with lobelias between which malachite sunbirds flit in search of nectar and insects; in the other, a slender grove of bearded forest following the course of a bubbling mountain stream, while looking over your shoulder all the while are Kibo and Mawenzi, posing for one last photo before ducking for good behind their lower slopes. If I should ever die on this mountain, I can think of no finer send-off than to have my ashes scattered there.'

Secondly, as you can see from my 'review', the main reason why I criticise the path is because it meanders. But while that is a disadvantage for a descent route, for a trail that you use to climb *up* the mountain it can be seen as an advantage, allowing you to gain altitude more slowly and thus giving your body more time to acclimatise.

The final reason why it's probably best to treat my opinions of 20 years ago with caution is because I can't actually be sure that the new Kidia Route they're building now is the same as the one I took to descend all those years ago. Indeed, while I assume that it's only sensible to follow that original path, and definitely ends in the same place, I know for a fact that it isn't identical to the original trail. Because whereas the original trail ran between Barafu Camp and Kidia village, it is said that the new route avoids Barafu altogether. Indeed, if rumours are to be believed this new Kidia Route blazes its own trail all the way to Stella Point. Having joined everyone else on that final stretch to the summit, I assume, for reasons that I give below, that trekkers will then follow exactly the same path back to Kidia.

But will you be allowed to climb it?

If the idea of climbing an entirely new trail sounds appealing, as it should, then I'm afraid there is probably going to be one enormous obstacle that will prevent you from doing so. The park authority, KINAPA, has designated this trail as a 'VIP Route'. In other words, only a select few people are going to be allowed to use it. Quite how KINAPA is going to decide who is, or isn't a VIP, is unknown at this point, though it's a fair bet that the criteria will be financial; in other words, they'll charge a heavy premium to trekkers on this trail – and if you're willing to pay the extra price for the extra privacy that this route provides, then you're a VIP. (It is for this reason that I assume that trekkers will be taking the same route to get off the mountain; if you are willing to pay extra to keep away from your adoring public on the way up, presumably you will also want to keep away from them on the way down, when you definitely won't be looking your best.)

But if you haven't got the wherewithal to afford the extra price to climb on the Kidia Route, but still love the idea of climbing on a new trail, don't despair: there is another option….

THE IRKASSWA TRAIL

While the Kidia Route is, in reality, just a resurrected old path, the second new path has no forebears. Indeed, I think the only reason that KINAPA have chosen to put this route where they have, is because they looked at a map of Kili and realised that this northern part of the mountain is the most isolated and quietest spot on the mountain – and thus the part that's most ripe for development.

Details of where the Irkasswa Trail will run exactly are, for the moment at least, rather sketchy. I know that it will start at the village that gives the trail its name. Sources in KINAPA have told me that the path then heads pretty much directly for the summit in a south-south-easterly direction, crossing the Northern Circuit somewhere east of Moir Huts. If this is correct then presumably it will then cross the crater of Kibo – a very exciting prospect! – before descending on the Mweka Route (though given the overcrowding that already exists on that route, funnelling Irkasswa trekkers down the Marangu Route instead may be a more sensible idea.) But this is all just educated guesswork and speculation so let's wait and see what KINAPA have to say.

According to those same sources, the path is, like Kidia, due to open in 2024. As the first new trekking route to open on Kilimanjaro for several decades, this is an exciting development and if you're lucky enough to be planning to trek when the path is scheduled to open, it would be worth seeing if you can climb on that path. On the one occasion I visited the village of Irkasswa I found it fascinating and delightfully unspoilt; and the opportunity to climb on a brand-new trail, before the hordes of climbers inevitably frighten away all the wildlife and trash all the campsites, is an exciting one indeed.

ACKNOWLEDGEMENTS

If I were to thank everyone who helped me in researching this sixth edition, well, there wouldn't be any room left in this book for the guide. But there are those trekkers, locals and expats who kindly offered advice and suggestions. So I would like to thank, in no particular order (and Tanzanian unless otherwise stated), the following: Karen Valenti (US), formerly of KPAP, as ever, for all her information and company, and her successor, Kelvin Salla, for his advice and help; Angela Nyaki, Chief Park Warden at KINAPA, and Charles Ngendo (former Warden of Tourism at KINAPA), Vitus Mgaya and Daniel Mweta for giving up their time to talk about their plans for the future of the park; Jo Middleton (UK) for providing me with the article on pulse oximetry; Eric Knox (US) of Indiana State University for his help in identifying the various groundsel species; my colleague Joshua Ruhimbi for his many updates and corrections; Sigi Steven for driving us around the hotels near Arusha for a day; David Concar, UK High Commissioner, for his advice on Dar; Henry Jones (UK/Tan) of Slow Leopard, again for his advice in Dar; Emily Winks (UK) for her research into the kula cloth; Kelly Flinn of PACT Outdoors; and Winnie Kinney. Thanks also to Annie and Nik Robinson and Deanna Redmond for their company on the Rongai Route, and Don Brand, Matt Cser and Jenny Biewer for the laughs on the Full Circuit Umbwe.

Much of the help in writing this edition came from my colleagues at Kilimanjaro Experts. So I would like to thank my fellow directors David Squire, who unflappably puts up with my moods and meltdowns and who helped with updating the Northern Circuit, and Joshua, who makes everything run so smoothly in Tanzania, and seemingly without any effort on his part, and who answered my innumerable questions; and to all our guides, including my learned friend Robert Masha, who taught me more during a Rongai trek last year about the flora and fauna of Kili than I'd learnt on the subject in all my previous treks put together; Ibrahim Mashaka, a great guide who started picking up litter on the trail when I first walked with him, and helped to set the conservation tone for KE; Janeth Jonathan – our first fully fledged female guide, who was so shy when I first met her, but is now a proper boss! Thanks also to top guides Shabani and Kassim Shabani, Kefas Molel and Faraja Mwaijande, all of whom I've yet to trek with, but all of whom have proved reliable, honest, incredibly good at their jobs and essential members of the KE team – and they happen to be good people too; and to all the guides in the KE family including Rajabu Izina, Dickson Kimaro, Mariam Fumbi, Abdalah Msuya, Fakir Msangi, Paul 'Mbongo' Mgoloka, Dickson Festo, Irene & Lightness Laizer, Filomena Alphone, Haruna Mensa, Boniphace, Frednand Kisia, Felix Mwakilema, Hillary Matto, Gideon Meera, Macmilan Nanyaro, Privatus Chitungutu, Filbert Kahigi, George Mbezi, Joseph Phinius, Frank Nnko, Fares Kabaka, driver Sigi Steven and office staffer Scholastica Masolwa.

I hope you all find that, thanks to your input, this sixth edition is even better than the previous five.

I'd also like to thank Zoe and Henry Jr for all the post-research fun on safari and in Zanzibar – happy days!

At Trailblazer I would like to thank Nick Hill for transforming my childlike scribbles into maps of beauty, Anna Jacomb-Hood for editing this edition and for the index, Nicky Slade for proof-reading, and Bryn, as ever, for making the whole thing possible.

INDEX

Abbreviation for Mount Meru: (MM)
Page references in **red** type refer to maps

Abbott Dr 154-5
Abbott's Camp 155, 156
acclimatisation 243, 247
  Umbwe Route 353
accommodation 123-4
  costs 33; on trail (Kili) 271-2, (MM) 258, 260
  see also place name
Acute Mountain Sickness *see* AMS
airlines *see* flights
airports
  Arusha 207, 222
  Dar Es Salaam 190, 195
  Kilimanjaro International 34-5, 188, 203-4
  Moshi 37, 223
  Nairobi 197-8, 202
altitude sickness 129, 243, (MM) 257
  see also AMS
AMS 243-52
apps: GPS 50,
  Dar es Salaam transport 191
arched fig tree 261-2, **263**
Arrow Glacier Campsite 325, **327**, 328
Arrow Glacier Route *see* Western Breach Route
Arusha 204, 205-9, **210-11**, **215**, 212-22
  accommodation 212-18
  climate charts 20
  dangers & annoyances 208
  eating out 218-20
  nightlife 221
  orientation 207
  services 207-9, 212
  sights 205-6
  transport 207, 221-2
ascent routes 67-8, 69-72, 386-8
Ash Pit 131, 133, **371**, 373
ATMs 122
  see also place name
avifauna 168

backpacks 50
banks 121-2
  see also place name
Barafu Huts **305**, 306-7, **309**, **364**
Barafu Route 67, 71, 293, 308, 314
bargaining 128
Barranco 133
Barranco Huts/Campsite 292, **303**, 304, 351, 355, **357**, 358
Barranco Valley **303**
Barranco Wall **303**, 305
bibliography 380-5
Big Tree Camp *see* Mti Mkubwa
birds 168
Bismarck Hut 154
Bismarck, Otto von 372
Bismarck Towers **371**, 372
blisters 255
booking a trek 67-107
  route options 67-72
  through an agent 72-3
  trek package 74-5
  with a Tanzanian operator 76-107
boots 39-40
Breach Wall/Breakfast Wall *see* Barranco Wall
budgeting 28-34, 78-9, 91
Buffalo Campsite **333**, 336
buffalo carcass 349-50
bus services 122-3
  see also place name
business hours 125
  Kenya 198

cable car 111
'cairn' sculpture park **343**, 348
camping equipment 41-3
campsites 47, 155, 271
  see also place name
car hire 123
Carbon Tanazia (CT) 65-6

cash machines *see* ATMs
cellphones *see* mobile phones
Chagga language 140, 178, 384 (books)
Chagga people 45, 119, 126, 127, 140, 141, 154, 177-84, 384 (books)
Chala, Lake 133-4
child discounts 30, 83
climate 16-20
  Kilimanjaro 136-9
  Tanzania 113
climbing: independently in a group 26, 27-8; in a group with friends 25-7
clothing 39-41
cloud forest 296, 314, 368
Coaster buses 122
'Coca Cola' trail 273, 293
Cone Place *see* Shira Cone
Cooley WD 140, 143, 146-9
costs 28-34, 78-9, 91, (MM) 259-60
Covid 54
Crater Campsite 369-70, **371**
Crater Plain (MM) 264, **267**
Crater Rim **327**, 329, 369, 370, 372
credit cards 121
currency: Kenya 198; Tanzania 121
cycling up/around Kilimanjaro 107-10

dalla-dalla minibuses 122-3
Dar Es Salaam 188-92, **191**, **193**, 194-5
day trips 70
daypacks 50-1
deaths on trail 244-5
debit cards 121
Decken, Baron CC von der 148-9, 150-2, 372
Decken Glacier **371**, 372
descent routes 69, 359-68
Diamox 45, 248-9, 250

diarrhoea 129
discounts, child 30, 83
documents 119-20
Dracaena afromontana 178, 316
drinks 127; on trail 272
see also water
driving 123
duffle bags 50
Dundas, Charles 177, 180

East Lava Hill 286
East Shira Hill 321, 323
Eastern Icefield 371
economy 118 (Tanzania), 184 (Kilimanjaro)
Egloff, Karl 7, 160
electricity 124; Kenya 198
elephants 163, 164, 167
Elveda Point 371, 372
equipment, trekking 39-50
eTAs (Kenya) 120, 197
ethical trekking 59-66
companies 90-1
events 110-11
exchange rates 121
exposure *see* hypothermia

fauna 163-8, 256
festivals 124
field guides 384-5
films on Kilimanjaro 385-6
fires 161, 256, 282
first-aid kit 45
Fischer Campsite 323, 332
Fischer, Dr Gustav A 151
fitness 52-4
flights: domestic 37-8, 123; international 34-7, 38
see also airport name
flora 169-76, 256
food 33, 126
on trail 272
foot care 253, 255
footwear 39-40
Forest Camp *see* Mti Mkubwa
frostbite 253
Furtwangler, Walter 8, 159, 372
Furtwangler Glacier 135, 329, 371, 372

gaiters 48-9
Gamow hyperbaric bags 251-2
geographical background 112-13
geology 130-4
Gillman, Clement 372
Gillman's Point 290, 291, 369, 371, 372
glaciers 132, 134-6
GPS waypoints 50, 375-9
Great Rift Valley 130, 131
group trek organising 26
guides 28, 70, 73, 98, 99, 187, (MM) 260

HACO 244, 246, 250
haggling 128
Halfway Camp 154
Hans Meyer Cave 290, 291,
Hans Meyer Notch 157, 371
Hans Meyer Peak 133, 159, 284
Hans Meyer Point 371
HAPO 244, 246, 250
health 129, 252-5
height of Kilimanjaro 132
Heim Glacier 371, 372
helicopter rescue 57
helipads 286, 287, 291, 298, 299, 303, 305, 309, 319, 323, 323, 335, 346, 357, 366
Hemingway, Ernest 163
High Camp 365, 366
high altitude
health 52
masks 54
historical background
Kilimanjaro 139-63
Tanzania 113-18
hitch-hiking 123
Horombo Huts 278, 284-5, 286, 361
huts, accommodation in 271-2, 273, 274, 280 (MM) 258
hypothermia 252-3
hyrax 166

ice-cap/ice retreat 135
independent trekking 25
International Mountain Explorers Connection (IMEC) 60, 64
injuries on trail 244-5
inoculations 54-7
insurance 57-8
internet access 125-6
Irkasswa Trail 387-8
Itikoni Plain (MM) 262, 263

Jagga 145, 150
see also Chagga
Jambo Bwana, tune 61
Jiwe Kamba 356, 356
Jiwe La Ukoyo 157, 287, 288
Johannes Notch 290, 291, 371
Johnsell Point 132, 300
Johnston, Harry H 152, 154, 155

Kaiser Wilhelm Peak 157, 158, 161
Kambi Ya Taabu 283, 284
Karanga Valley/Campsite 303, 306
Kersten Glacier 371, 372
Kersten, Otto 151, 372
Kibo (summit) 130, 131, 132-3, 157, 180, 289, 302, 369-73
Kibo Crater 133
Kibo Huts 287, 288, 291, 347, 350
Kibo Huts Route 68, 289, 350-1
Kichagga *see* Chagga
Kidia Route 155, 386-7
Kikelelwa Campsite 344, 346
Kilimanjaro International Airport (KIA) 34, 35, 188, 203-4
Kilimanjaro Marathon 110
Kilimanjaro National Park (KINAPA) 30, 62, 63, 67, 69, 107, 108, 111, 161, 165, 187, 242, 244, 249, 251, 254, 255, 272, 276, 282, 325, 369, 386, 387, 388

Kilimanjaro Native Cooperative Union (KNCU) 177, 235
Kilimanjaro Porters' Assistance Project (KPAP) 32-3, 60-4, 83, 90-1
Kilimanjaro Trail run 110-11
Kisamboni 277, **279**
Kitoto Viewpoint (MM) 262, **263**
Kosovo camp 308, **309**, 310
Krapf, Dr JL 141, 144-5, 146-7, 148, 149

Lake Louise AMS test 251
Lange, M 159
languages (Kenya) 198
see also Chagga & Swahili
Lava Cave 156
Lava Tower/Campsite **301**, 304, 325, **327**, 359
Leave no Trace (LNT) 59-60
Lemosho Glades 315, **317**
Lemosho Glades Route *see* Lemosho Route
Lemosho Route 70-1, 93, 312-29
Leopard Point 163, **291**, **371**, 372
leopards 163, 164, 167
litter 255-6
Little Meru (MM) 265
Livingstone, David 114, 143, 147, 150
Loitokitok 71, 340
Loitokitok Route 71
see also Rongai Route
Londorossi/Londorossi Gate 313, 330
Londt, George 159

Macdonald, Sheila 159
Machame Gate 294, **295**
Machame Huts **297**, 298
Machame Route 31, 67, 70, 93, 111, 292-311
Maio Falls (MM) 262, **263**
malaria 56
Mandara 151, 153, 278, 280
Mandara Huts 278, **281**, 362
map key 373
map scale 270
maps 379
Marangu 238-41, **239**
Marangu Gate 276-7, **279**
Marangu Route 29, 42, 67, 69-70, 92, 154, 273-92, 360-2
matatu mini buses 123
Maua River 285, **286**
Maundi Crater 278, **281**
Mawenzi (summit) 130, 133-4, 157, 159, 180, 284
Mawenzi Hut 285, **286**
Mawenzi Ridge **286**, 287
Mawenzi Route 285, **286**, 361
Mawenzi Tarn Hut/Campsite 345, **346**
Mawenzi Tarn Hut Route **343**, 344-5
medical kit 45
Meru, Mount 257-61, **263**, 264-6, **267**, 268-9
Meru Plain (MM) 259, 261, 269
Meru's Garden (MM) 261, **263**
Meyer, Dr Hans 135, 155-9, 163, 181, 280, 372
route comparison 154-7
Mgongo Wa Tembo (MM) 265, **267**
Middle Red Hill 133, **287**
Millennium Huts 364-5, **366**
minibus services 128-9
minimum impact trekking 255-6
Miriakamba Huts (MM) 258, **263**, 264
mobile phones 47, 125
mobile phone reception
Lemosho Route 315
Machame Route 293
Marangu Route 276
Rongai Route 338
Shira Plateau Route 331
Umbwe Route 352
Moir Huts **301**, 332, **333**
Momela Gate (MM) 258, **263**, 269
money 121-2
moneychangers 122
monkeys 165
Morum Barrier **319**, 330, 331
Moshi 204, 223-7, **228-9**, 230-8
accommodation 227, 230-4
Amani Children's Home 224-5
eating out 234-6
nightlife 237
orientation 224-5
services 226-7
transport 223, 225-6, 337
Mti Mkubwa 316, **317**
Murchison, Sir Roderick 147, 149
Mweka Gate, **367**, 368
Mweka Huts (Camp) 365, **366**
Mweka Route/trail 69, 362-8

Nairobi 196-8, **199**, 200-2
Nalemuru/moru Route 71
Nalemoru River **341**, **342**, **343**
name, Kilimanjaro 140-1
national holidays 124
New, Charles 39, 150-2, 180, 280
New Pofu Camp **335**
New Rongai Gate 340, **341**
Northern Circuit route 70-1, 92, 312-14, 334-7
Nyerere, Julius 115, 116, 160

obsidian rock 130-1, 300
Oehler, Edward 159
Old Fireplace 157
Old Pofu Camp **335**, 336
online information
climb reviews 77, 80-1
health 56-7
opening hours 125
Kenya 198
overland to Tanzania 38, 202
oximeter readings 250
oxygen 83, 252

parasitic cones/craters 131
park fees 29, 30, (MM) 350
Partner for Responsible Travel scheme 61-2
Penck Glacier 372

people 119 (Tanzania)
see also Chagga people
Peters, Carl/Karl 115, 152-4
Peters' Hut 154
phones *see* telephones
photography 48
planning schedule 21
plastic bag ban 47
Pofu camps **335**, 336
pole pole trekking 246-9
population 118
porters 60-4, 184-7, (MM) 258, 259-60
postal services 126
private treks 26, 27-8
public holidays 124
Purtscheller, L 156, 158, 159
Purtscheller Peak 133

rail services 123
rainfall chart 20
rainy seasons 136-7, 137-8
Ratzel Glacier 156, 372
Rebmann, Johannes 144-5, 146-7, 149, 150, 180, 181, 280
Rebmann Glacier 310, **371**, 372
recordmaking ascents & descents 7-8, 10-11, 159, 160-1
Rescue Hut 364-5, **366**
Reusch, Pastor Richard 159-60, 163, 372
Reusch Crater 131, 133, **371**, 373
Rhino Point (MM) 266, **267**, 268
Richard, JJ 160
Rock Stairs **327**, 329
Rongai Gate (New) 340, **341**
Rongai Route 71, 92, 337-51
routes 67-72, (MM) 257-69
options table 22-3
route maps 270
route specialists 92-3
rucksacks 50-1
Ruckteschell, Frau von 159

Saddle 132-3, **286**, 287, **287**
Saddle Huts (MM) 258, 265, **267**, 268
safe trekking 242-55
safety 128-9
Sarumba 353, **354**
School Hut **291**, **349**, 350
seasons 16-20
Second Cave **343**, 344, 348
security 128-9; Nairobi 197
Shark's Tooth **301**, 324
Sheffield Campsite **301**, 302, 303, 324
Shipton, Eric 159
Shira 1 Campsite 318, **319**, 331
Shira 2/Shira Huts 322, 323, **323**, 331
Shira Cathedral **321**, 322
Shira Caves/Shira Caves Campsite **299**, 300
Shira Cone 322
Shira Peak 132
Shira Plateau 132, 292, 299, 300, 302, 312, 318, 320, 324
Shira Plateau Route 70-1, 92, 312-14, 329-37
Shira Ridge 132, 300, 318, **319**
Shira Route *see* Shira Plateau Route
Shira volcano 130
shopping 127-8
see also place name
shuttle bus services 123
Simba Campsite 340, **342**
Simba Cave Campsite **321**, 322, 331-2
sleeping bags & mats 42
smoking 54
snow on Kilimanjaro 137
debate 146-9
snowfall chart 137
snowblindness 253
Socialist Peak (MM) 268
solo trekking 25, 28
South Peak 133, 159
Southern Circuit 67, 71
Southern Icefields **371**
souvenirs 127-8
star gazing 17
Stella Point 157, 292, **309**, 310, 311, 369, **371**, 372
summit 369-73
statistics 68-9
sunburn 253
sunscreen 46
Swahili language 141, 374
Swahili time 124-5, 198

TANAPA 163
Tarakea 339
Teleki, Count Samuel 154-5, 167, 186, 290
telephones & codes 125, 192
(Kenya) 198
see also mobile phones
temperatures (climate) 20, 138-9
Third Cave Campsite **335**, 337, 339, **343**, 348
Tilman, HW 159, 160, 163, 311
time 124-5; Kenya 198
tipping 32-3, 186, (MM) 260
toilets & facilities 44, 47, 256, 272
topography 131-4
torches 46
Tourist Trail 273, 350
trail runners 40
train services 123
transport 33-4, 122-3
see also place name
tree hyrax 165, 166
trekkers' experiences 271-2, 274-5
trekkers, with disabilities 9, 10
trekking, without porters 98-9
trekking agencies 72-3
trekking operators 73-4, 76-107
budget treks 78-9
ethical companies 90-1
female guides 28, 187
reviews 77, 80-1
route specialists 92-3
see also booking a trek
trekking companions 25-7
trekking costs 28-34
trekking crew 60-4
trekking operator table 81, 84-5, 87
trekking packages 74-5

trekking poles 46
trekking seasons 16-20, 136-9
trekking shoes 40
Triplets, The 133, **287**
Tululusia Falls (MM) 261, **263**, 269

Uhuru Peak 132, 161, 187, 311, 369, **371**
Umbwe Cave Campsite 355, **356**
Umbwe Gate 352, **354**
Umbwe Route 71-2, 92-3, 351-9
UNESCO World Heritage Site 111, 165

vaccinations 54-7, 120
Viermannstein 156
visas 119-20
  see also eTAs
volcanoes 130, 131, 132, 133, 180, 284, 373

wages, staff 30, 32-3 (MM) 259
walking boots 39-40
walking times 270
washbags & washing 44, 256
water 129, 256, 272
  bottles 43-5
  purification 45-6, 256
waypoints 375-9
weather 16-20, 136-9
West Lava Hill 133
Western Breach 131, 133
Western Breach Route 67, 83, 93, 293, 304, 314, 325-9, **371**
Whiskey Route 293
Whona fire 282
Whona River **283**, 284
wi-fi 47, 125-6
Wilderness First Responder (WFR) 73
wildlife *see* fauna
William's Point 290, **291**
World Heritage Site (UNESCO) 111, 165

yellow fever 55, 120, 203

Zebra Rocks 285, **286**, 287, 361

There are plenty of things you can do with Kili other than just walk up it. You can cycle around it (**above**; see p108) or even up it (p107) and there are safaris in the region in the national parks of Kenya and Tanzania. **Below**: Seen through the heat haze, Kilimanjaro looms above Amboseli National Park in Kenya.

Looking over the clouds from Kili to the summit of Mt Meru.